W9-AOR-694

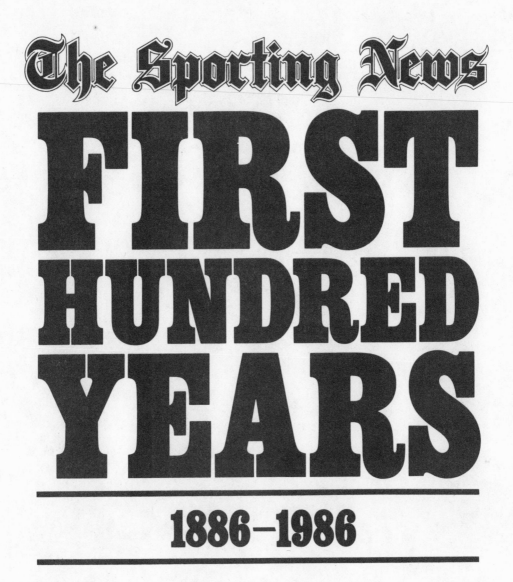

The Sporting News

FIRST HUNDRED YEARS

1886–1986

The Sporting News

FIRST HUNDRED YEARS

1886–1986

Written by

LOWELL REIDENBAUGH

Co-Editors

JOE HOPPEL
MIKE NAHRSTEDT

Design

BILL PERRY

President and Chief Executive Officer

RICHARD WATERS

Editor/The Sporting News

TOM BARNIDGE

Director of Books and Periodicals

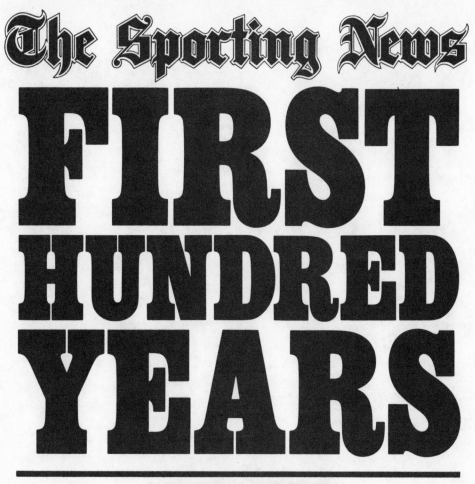

RON SMITH

Published in the United States by The Sporting News Publishing Co., 1212 North Lindbergh Boulevard, St. Louis, Missouri 63132.

A Times Mirror Company

ISBN: 0-89204-204-4
10 9 8 7 6 5 4 3 2

First Edition

CONTENTS

Introduction

History fails to record the circumstances surrounding the birth of The Sporting News.

Was it the consequence of Alfred Henry Spink's desire to capitalize on the baseball frenzy sweeping St. Louis where, a year earlier, the Browns had captured the championship of the American Association, a major league of that era?

Or was it the product of Spink's boundless energies that found him leaping from one enterprise to another in his ceaseless quest for greater stature among the sporting gentry in the burgeoning metropolis on the west bank of the Mississippi River?

Could it have been that the 31-year-old writer-promoter, having noted the success of Sporting Life, vowed to publish a sports journal much superior to that which was produced in Philadelphia?

All of these may have been factors. But, in all likelihood, the seed that germinated into The Sporting News was planted by Joseph Pulitzer. In his last years, Al Spink remembered: "When we were young boys, working for St. Louis dailies for $5 a week, and working the old-time free lunch counters by force of circumstances before the arrival of each pay day, Joe used to say, 'Given a good business manager and an editor who can really write, any newspaper should fast become a good paying institution.' "

Pulitzer applied the formula to the St. Louis Post-Dispatch, which he guided to world renown. Spink used it on The Sporting News with equal success.

Of the conditions that prevailed in March 1886, there is no documentation. But it requires no immoderate imagination to picture the scene at 11 N. 8th St. on that historic day when the first copies of the five-cent paper click-clacked off the press.

All the copy, written in longhand, had been edited. The type had been set by hand and now, in their galluses and celluloid collars, Al Spink and his ink-stained accomplices were gathered around the flat-bed press as the starting switch was thrown.

Chances are that none among them muttered "What hath God wrought!" Nor was any thought given to "This is the start of something big." In all probability, they scanned the first copies for typographical errors, complimented one another on a workmanlike job and then retired to their respective corners to commence work on Volume I, Number 2.

Time has removed the last of those who knew Al Spink in those early days, but from scraps unearthed in the archives of The Sporting News, he is viewed in the late 20th Century as a man worth knowing. He could mingle comfortably in any sort of society. An excellent writer, it is presumed he also was a gifted storyteller, a welcome dinner guest and a prominent figure where the swells of the city gathered, at baseball games, at the racetrack, at ringside or in the downtown saloons.

When Al Spink concentrated his energies on a given project, he never doubted that the venture would succeed. He was instrumental in the organization of the early-day Browns and aided in developing that team into championship caliber. He built a racetrack and equipped it with lights for night horse racing, a startling innovation of the 1890s. When a tornado destroyed the structure, Al erected another at a new location.

He was fiercely loyal and when he came upon two brawlers, one of them a good friend, he interceded unhesitatingly at the risk of great personal injury. When he was wronged by an unprincipled baseball club owner, he exacted justice with his own quick fists; this episode evoked deep personal pride in the young publisher and he informed readers of the fracas in the next issue of The Sporting News.

Al Spink also knew how to market his product. To the modern reader, some of his claims of immense nationwide circulation in the first year of TSN may seem excessive. But he made the country conscious of his paper. Al Spink, suffused with joie de vivre, never hid his candle.

Sports, however, were not Al's only interest. He was a patron of the theater and published a weekly column, "The Stage," in his early issues. Advertisements of attractions in the city, plus sketches of well-rounded leading ladies, attested to Spink's predilection.

If a man could write sports, Al concluded, he also could succeed as a playwright. Spink produced "The Derby Winner," which featured Tod Sloan, later a famous jockey, and amazed audiences with a live horse race on stage.

Encouraged by critical acclaim in St. Louis, Spink took his production on the road, only to discover that dramatic tastes elsewhere did not match those at home. The show bombed. Al dipped into his personal funds to compensate members of the cast and then headed back to St. Louis and The Sporting News.

In his straitened condition, Al accepted a subordinate role in the company he had founded. He was a co-editor under his younger brother, Charles Claude Spink, the type of sound businessman that Joseph Pulitzer had spoken of years before.

Ultimately, the congenial relationship between the brothers started to crumble. Al instituted legal proceedings to regain a financial interest in the firm. He lost, and an ever-widening chasm developed. The brothers were estranged for years, Al in Chicago and Charles in St. Louis. The breach was not healed until April 1914 when they were reunited in a tearful scene as Charles lay dying of a stomach disorder.

Old animosities vanished and injustices, real or fancied, were forgotten. In the issue that reported the death of Charles, Al wrote "An Elder Brother's Tribute," in which he spoke glowingly of the arduous labors and business acumen of his successor.

The new publisher was Charles' son, John George Taylor Spink. In 1925, Taylor wrote to Al, then general manager of the All Star Sports Service in Chicago, requesting his uncle's opinions of The Sporting News. The elder Spink replied in three pages. The paper is, he said, "baseball's one forum and champion. It is, in fact, one of America's great institutions, something to be proud of and (which) gives you a national reputation as a publisher."

Al then commented on the quality of the paper for the past decade. "I feared," he said, "that the one paper I was so proud of would fall from the fine level he (Charles) had established for it. I watched for the outcome carefully. At first the News seemed to lose its grip editorially, then errors in its makeup and proofreading were in evidence. Soon, however, these defects, partly the result of the absence of the old leader, were discovered and the right remedy applied, so that today it is one of the cleanest papers from a typographical and proofreading standpoint that can be found anywhere."

After complimenting Taylor on his excellent staff of correspondents and commenting favorably on his clear vision and conservative attitude in baseball matters, Al offered some fatherly advice: "Take sunshine to your office each day and bring it home with you at night. Make those who work for you love and respect you and bring your children up in the same way. Do these things, dear boy, and many happy days are in store for you." Al signed the letter "Dad."

Al Spink was in his 74th year when he died in May 1928. The graveside eulogy at Woodlawn Cemetery in suburban Chicago was delivered by Kenesaw Mountain Landis, commissioner of baseball and a longtime friend. Landis' tribute consisted, in part, of:

"The last few months of his life were a period of torture and suffering and yet through it all his first consideration was for others lest his condition add to the burden of others around him. Throughout his life his first thought was for others, always stopping to lend a helping hand, and were every man and woman, boy and girl for whom he did a service to lay a single flower on his bier, he would sleep tonight beneath a wilderness of flowers.

"Words are utterly futile to give expression to us at this time, but the highest tribute that man can pay his brother is the silent grief for the stricken man, and so we gather together to console and encourage each other; each the better for his friendship and each, during the days that are to come, the richer by the possession of the sweetness and tenderness of his memory."

To Alfred Henry Spink, whom none of us knew but whose vision and enterprise has provided gainful and pleasant employment for hundreds of sports-loving journalists, this volume is respectfully dedicated.

Four key members of the rough-and-tumble Baltimore Orioles in the late 1890s were (left to right) Willie Keeler, Hugh Jennings, Joe Kelley and John McGraw. The man in the middle is groundskeeper Thomas Murphy.

1886-1900: GROWING PAINS

When the first issue of The Sporting News rolled off the press in mid-March of 1886, major league baseball, represented by the National League and the American Association, was suffering from acute growing pains.

Nicholas E. Young, the fifth president of the 10-year-old National League, issued orders that were blithely ignored. Franchises were moved like pawns on a chessboard. Umpires, frequently recruited from neighborhood saloons for five dollars per game, freely favored the home team to guarantee continued employment. And club executives quarreled endlessly in what was commonly referred to as the "National Pastime."

The dominant team in the National League in the mid-1880s was the Chicago White Stockings, managed by Adrian (Cap) Anson. Its counterpart in the American Association was the St. Louis Browns, piloted by Charles Comiskey, like Anson a first baseman.

In the fall of 1885, the two pennant-winning teams engaged in a seven-game series to determine the foremost club in Organized Baseball. The first game was played in Chicago, the next three in St. Louis, one in Pittsburgh and two in Cincinnati. Each team won three games, while another contest ended in a tie. One Chicago victory was a forfeit, which resulted from Comiskey pulling his team off the field in protest of an umpire's decision.

When the two teams repeated as league champions in 1886, another series—this one better organized and less like a barnstorming tour—was proposed by Chris Von der Ahe, owner of the Browns. In a letter to Albert G. Spalding, owner of the White Stockings, Von der Ahe suggested a series of five, seven or nine games, with the winning team to take all the gate receipts. The challenge was accepted. The seven-game arrangement was agreed upon, with the first three games to be played in Chicago and the remaining games in St. Louis.

The teams split the first four games before the Browns gained an edge in the fifth contest, 10-3. The sixth game matched John Clarkson, Chicago's 35-game winner, against Bob Caruthers, who had won 30 decisions for the Browns. For seven innings, Clarkson hurled magnificently, allowing no runs, but in the eighth, the Browns rallied for three runs to tie the score. A two-run triple by Arlie Latham sent the 8,000 Sportsman's Park spectators into a frenzy.

In the last half of the 10th, with the score still deadlocked, Curt Welch led off and was struck by a pitch. When Anson protested that Welch had stood too close to the plate and made no effort to avoid the pitch, the umpire ordered the center fielder to bat again. Welch promptly singled to center field and advanced to third on an error and a sacrifice. In the hope of picking off Welch, who was taking a big lead, Chicago catcher King Kelly signaled for a pitchout, but the pitch was too high. The ball glanced off Kelly's mitt as Welch stormed across the plate with the winning run. The world championship belonged to the Browns.

"Fans went crazy over the victory," one scribe reported. "Many wept tears of joy, turned somersaults, handsprings, and threw hats, umbrellas and handkerchiefs. Some made runs for the players. As each man was captured in turn he would be carried off the field. Then 3,000 waited outside the dressing room and cheered each player as he reappeared."

After the game, Von der Ahe wrote to Spalding suggesting an exhibition game in Cincinnati. The Chicago official wanted no more of the Browns. He replied: "We must decline with our compliments. We know when we have had enough. P.S.: Anson joins me in the above message."

Next to Anson, Michael Joseph (King) Kelly was the White Stockings' most glittering performer. In that 1886 season, the catcher-outfielder led the league in batting (.388) and contributed 53 stolen bases. Kelly, who had a flair for the theatrical on the basepaths, prompting cries of "Slide, Kelly, slide!" from the crowd, was a free spirit with an ingenious mind. For instance, King Kel is credited by some with devising the hit-and-run play.

In February 1887, Kelly was sold to Boston for $10,000, a shocking figure in a day when most players were receiving $2,000 in annual salary. Kelly agreed to terms with Boston quickly, not because of the $2,000 figure on his contract, but because of the $3,000 that he was offered for "the use of his picture" in team advertising.

King Kelly's superiority on the diamond was

matched by his dominance off the field. An all-night roisterer, Kelly possessed an unquenchable thirst that led Anson to remark, "There's no man living who can drink Kelly under the table."

Although the King batted .394 in 1887, he failed to repeat as batting champion. That failure was due primarily to a new rule used in both leagues that awarded a batter a base hit every time he drew a walk. As a result, 13 players, including Anson, batted over .400.

Kelly remained in the major leagues until 1893, pursuing a baseball-whiskey career in the summer and a vaudeville-whiskey career in the winter. But by the time he was 36, Kelly's once-magnificent talents were badly eroded. In 1894 he managed the Allentown team in the Pennsylvania State League. That November he boarded a boat in New York for Boston, where he was to open an engagement at the Palace Theater. En route, a slight cold developed into pneumonia, and Kelly died on November 8.

When friends began to arrange Kelly's funeral, the player's dress suit could not be found. An investigation revealed that the benevolent King had given the suit to the steamship company as security for a young man who had boarded the boat without paying his fare. When the suit eventually was reclaimed, burial services were conducted.

After the ill-advised, one-year rule that awarded a hit for a base on balls, the major significant change in the code the remainder of the century involved the lengthening of the pitching distance from 50 feet to 60 feet, six inches. At the same time, the pitchers' box, an area roughly five feet by four feet from which the hurler was required to deliver the ball, was eliminated in favor of a pitching rubber.

The most serious upheaval in the major leagues during this period, however, occurred when players, disturbed by deteriorating relations with management, withdrew from the two majors and formed the Players League.

Formation of the outlaw circuit was the culmination of a four-year attempt to win concessions from owners. The movement started in 1885 when John Montgomery Ward, a shortstop for the New York Giants, organized the National Brotherhood of Professional Players, whose objectives were "to protect and benefit its members collectively and individually, to promote a high standard of professional conduct and to advance the interests of the national game." Conceived as a source of relief for players who were severely abused by management, the Brotherhood gradually began to function as a union. Ward, a budding lawyer and president of the Brotherhood, cited the players' major grievance as the reserve clause, which prohibited a player from negotiating with clubs other than the one that held his contract. In 1887, a three-man committee approached the National League about the reserve rule. The owners agreed to listen, then asked the committee, if it could, to offer a more equitable plan. The players could not, and there the matter rested.

In the fall of 1888, A.G. Spalding shepherded two teams on a round-the-world tour. The exhibition games featured many of the league's best players—not to mention some of the top activists in the Brotherhood. When the junket finally wound up in New York City six months later, the tourists were treated as returning conquering heroes and were feted at the famous Delmonico's restaurant. In the midst of the jubilation, however, the players were sobered by the realization that during their absence, the club owners had adopted a salary classification plan in which players were rated from A to E and assigned salaries accordingly, from $2,500 to $1,500.

Too little time remained for the players to make a counterstroke before the 1889 season, but Ward immediately sought the owners' cooperation in getting rid of the classification system, which the players considered even more degrading and unfair than the reserve rule. But the league ignored him. So, Ward devised a new strategy. He summoned members of the Brotherhood to a meeting in July 1889. The players were instructed to seek capital in their respective cities for a new league—a cooperative venture that would favor the players' interests—to begin play in 1890.

The responses were quick and encouraging. Years later, Ward wrote: "Men were found willing to advance the necessary money to start a new league and upon terms most liberal to the players. Many of them were even willing to put in capital without any return whatever out of love for the sport and a desire to see it played on a plane above that upon which it was being operated."

In early November 1889, the Brotherhood announced the formation of a new circuit, the Players League, to rival the National League and the American Association. Most of the big stars of the day joined the majority of players who jumped to the new league, which established clubs in eight cities—Boston, Brooklyn, Buffalo, Chicago, Cleveland, New York, Philadelphia and Pittsburgh.

The National League, though left with few of the top players, fought the rookie circuit vigorously by scheduling and rescheduling games to conflict with Players League games in the same city. And Spalding even offered King Kelly a $10,000 bribe and a three-year contract "at any figure you want to write in" to return to the National League. After mulling the matter over for about 90 minutes, King Kel refused the offer, opting to support the Brotherhood's cause.

Confusion, akin to chaos, prevailed during the 1890 season, and attendance was down everywhere. "The warring parties adopted conflicting schedules," one author wrote, "lied glibly about their attendance, spread false rumors about player demoralization and battles for patronage." There were "court injunctions, contract jumpers, suits for slander. Newspapers chose sides and distorted the situation monstrously. The real estate operators and utility magnates who backed the Brotherhood soon lost the first flush of enthusiasm, but the National League, its attendance riddled, suffered the most."

The Players League eventually was doomed, however, by the inexperience of its club owners. When Spalding suggested that the backers of both leagues get together to discuss the losses all their clubs had suffered, the Players League backers hastily admitted incurring substantial deficits. Spalding, meanwhile, kept mum about his huge losses, thereby maintaining a strong bargaining position. The Players League backers quickly abandoned ship even though they unknowingly had won the battle during the season. The players, losers in their first significant war with management, returned to the National League or the American Association without being penalized for jumping contracts.

War with the Players League crippled the American Association, and the league lasted just one more season. Only a few A.A. franchises had any sort of financial stability, and they were absorbed by the National League, which operated as an eight-team circuit in 1891, then expanded to 12 clubs following the demise of the American Association. Baltimore, Louisville, St. Louis and Washington were added to the eight established N.L. franchises (Boston, Brooklyn, Chicago, Cincinnati, Cleveland, New York, Philadelphia and Pittsburgh) in 1892.

For the first and only time in N.L. history (except for the 1981 strike season), the magnates adopted a split season for 1892, with the first-half champion playing the second-half winner in a postseason series as a means of creating greater fan interest throughout the entire campaign. Boston finished on top in the first-half race and Cleveland in the second half before the Beaneaters captured the league championship in six games, including a tie in the opener.

The admittance of Baltimore into the league signaled the start of one of the brightest chapters in the game's history. Under the leadership of Ned Hanlon, the Orioles won three consecutive flags (1894-96) with such belligerent, boisterous—but brilliant—players as John McGraw, Hugh Jennings, Wilbert Robinson, Willie Keeler and Joe Kelley. With the Orioles, baseball was a win-at-any-price proposition. When conventional methods failed they resorted to fists or freshly sharpened spikes to claw out a victory. From 12th place in 1892, the Orioles climbed to eighth in '93 and then captured the pennant in '94.

Prior to the 1894 season, William C. Temple, a former president of the Pittsburgh club and still a stockholder in the team, offered a handsome cup as a trophy to the winner of a postseason series involving the teams that finished first and second in the regular race. The Orioles were heavy favorites to defeat the New York Giants in the seven-game series, but they showed little stomach for the extra competition after finishing first and being wined and dined by Baltimore hero worshipers. Considering the postseason games little more than exhibitions, the Orioles did not bother staying in shape after clinching the pennant. Hanlon's team lost the series in four games, plunging the Temple Cup donor into deep disgust. He sold his stock in the Pittsburgh club and withdrew from baseball.

After the series it was revealed that a few Baltimore players had entered into side agreements with New York players to split their shares, which amounted to $768 for each winner and $360 for each loser. A split was worth $564. The secret pact was exposed when the Giants refused to honor the agreement, thus adding further stench to the Orioles' defeat.

Baltimore executives urged that the Temple Cup series be discontinued. League officials, however, ruled otherwise, and the series was rescheduled for 1895. Again the Orioles won the pennant, and once more they lost to the second-place team. The Cleveland Spiders, sparked by three victories from the right arm of Denton (Cy) Young, defeated the Orioles four times in five tries.

Baltimore, after being chided for miserable performances in the Temple Cup series the two previous years, finally got serious and gained sweet revenge in 1896. Starting with a first-game thrashing of Young, the Orioles whipped the Spiders four straight times.

In 1897, Baltimore and Boston waged a bitter struggle into the final week of the pennant race. The winner was decided in a hotly contested series that saw Boston defeat the Orioles in two out of three games. Because the fans had spent all their emotions in the final week of the race, attendance was slim at the Temple Cup series, which Baltimore won in five games. The trophy was scuttled after a four-year competition.

One of the umpires in the first two Temple Cup series was Tim Hurst. A product of the hard-coal region of Pennsylvania, Hurst lacked physical size, but he had a quick wit. He is best remembered for his statement about the life of an umpire: "The pay is good, and you can't beat the hours—three to five." And when his wit failed to resolve a dispute, he resorted to his two lightning-quick fists, which he wielded in professional style.

During a game at Cincinnati in 1897, a beer stein sailed out of the stands and struck the umpire in the face. Wheeling, Hurst retrieved the glassware and hurled it back into the stands, where it struck a fireman, knocking him unconscious. Enraged spectators swarmed onto the field, but several policemen arrived first and escorted Hurst to safety, then arrested him on a charge of assault and battery. A local judge fined Tim $100 and court costs.

When occasion demanded, Hurst could be the complete diplomat. In a game at Washington, the arbiter once exchanged angry words with Pink Hawley, Jake Stenzel and Denny Lyons of Pittsburgh. "I'll meet you guys under the grandstand after the game," Hurst snapped, and the fuss ended temporarily.

The players arrived on schedule, as did Hurst, who punched Hawley in the face, back-heeled Stenzel and kicked Lyons in the shins. As the players tried to regroup, Nick Young came upon the scene.

"Timothy, what is all this excitement?" the league president asked.

"Somebody dropped a dollar bill, Uncle Nick, and I said it was mine," came the reply.

"Oh, was that all?" Young said. "I thought it was some kind of riot. Did the dollar really belong to you, Timothy?"

"No, it belonged to Hawley, but Stenzel and Lyons tried to take it away from him, and I wouldn't let them. It was just a pink tea."

"Timothy, you did the right thing," Young said as the two walked away together.

Like every umpire of the period, Hurst skirmished frequently with Andrew Freedman, the fractious owner of the New York Giants. Freedman once barred Hurst from the Polo Grounds, but after a month of dissatisfaction with other arbiters, he invited him to return. "The umpires have got to favor my team," the owner asserted unashamedly at one point, but they never did.

Freedman's most memorable scrape with authority occurred on July 25, 1898, and became known as the "Ducky Holmes case." Holmes, an outfielder with the Giants in 1897, was a member of the Browns and then the Orioles in 1898. In the third inning of a game at the Polo Grounds in New York, Holmes struck out, whereupon a male voice from the stands blistered Ducky's ears. "Oh, Ducky, you're a lobster," a fan said.

"Well, I'm glad I'm not working for a Sheeny anymore," Holmes shouted back.

The outfielder allegedly added a few more choice words before being ordered by umpire Tom Lynch to return to his bench. Holmes did so, but his anti-Semitic remark already had rattled Freedman, who was Jewish. As the teams changed sides, Freedman led a squad of policemen onto the field and tried to remove Holmes from the game. Lynch said he did not hear Holmes' remark and threatened to forfeit the game to Baltimore unless Freedman and the bluecoats left the field. The intruders refused to depart, and Lynch awarded the forfeit.

The club owner then reluctantly reimbursed the spectators who were deprived of a game and demanded that the Baltimore club, which already had been paid its share of the gate receipts, return the check. The visiting team refused and Freedman stopped payment.

The league board of directors later upheld the forfeit, fined the Giants $1,000 for leaving the playing field and suspended Holmes through the end of the season. But as the press, the public and other players rallied behind the outfielder, Holmes, who claimed that he never uttered any obscenities, obtained an injunction permitting him to play. The league directors, fearful of legal action, reconsidered their ruling and reinstated Ducky.

Freedman's unpopularity in New York was matched by that of Frank DeHaas Robison and his brother, M. Stanley Robison, in Cleveland. The owners of the Spiders grew weary of small attendance in Cleveland and purchased the St. Louis franchise, after which they transferred the best Cleveland players to St. Louis. As a result, the Spiders of 1899, playing 113 of their 154 games on the road, compiled the worst record in major league annals. Six times the Spiders lost 11 or more games in a row, including one streak of 24 games. The team's season-high winning streak—two games—was achieved only once. At season's end, Cleveland's record was 20-134 for a minuscule percentage of .130.

At the close of the 1899 season, the National League magnates agreed that the 12-club arrangement, which had been used for eight years, was too unwieldy. If the league were to realize its full potential, it was agreed, a reduction was imperative. Consequently, four franchises—Louisville, Baltimore, Cleveland and Washington—were lopped off. The league then assumed an eight-club figuration—Boston, Brooklyn, Chicago, Cincinnati, New York, Philadelphia, Pittsburgh and St. Louis—that endured for more than 50 years.

This photograph, taken during professional baseball's infancy about 1878, shows the Providence Grays (right) and the Boston Nationals at the Messer Street baseball field in Providence, R.I. This was the period in baseball history when pitchers really did throw from a box and spectators viewed the proceedings from wooden grandstands with limited seating capacity.

A Lucky Day Back in 1886

Al Spink, a man with a vision.

Undoubtedly, Alfred Henry Spink believed in lucky days, perhaps even leprechauns, even though he was of Scottish ancestry.

The first issue of his new sports publication was dated March 17, 1886, and hit the streets of St. Louis on St. Patrick's Day. Ironically, March 17 of that year also was the Lord's Day. With that sort of parlay working in his favor, Al Spink could scarcely fail as the first editor and publisher of The Sporting News.

The initial eight-page journal contained something for virtually everyone with a sporting interest. Baseball was the headline sport with cover stories on "The Game in Gotham," "The White Stockings" and "Harry Wright's Team," in which the Philadelphia manager was quoted as saying that the "Phillies Will Be Among the Leaders This Year."

But there was more. Another page 1 article announced that a "Gentleman's Driving Club" was "Ready for the Road." Cyclists turned to a page 3 column captioned "The Wheel," while other special-interest groups kept abreast of developments through "The Gun," "The Ring" and "The Turf." Reflecting his own passionate interest in the theater, Al Spink also published a column on "The Stage."

Editorially, Al Spink announced, "It is the custom when a new journal of any class is thrust upon an all-confiding and unsuspecting public to launch out into a lengthy editorial as to what the newcomer will do and as to the aims and objects. Now for various reasons The Sporting News intends to ignore this custom and let its readers guess out what its aims and objects are. One thing we must do, however, and that is thank the hundreds of kind friends who have wished us God speed on this new enterprise."

Success came quickly to the infant weekly. Within two months, Spink was able to proclaim: The Sporting News . . . has the largest circulation of any sporting paper published west of Philadelphia."

Spink excepted the Quaker City because it was the home of his major rival, the 3-year-old Sporting Life.

The Sporting News.

Vol. 1, No. 1. ST. LOUIS, MO., MARCH 17, 1886. Single Copies 5 Cents.

[T]HE GAME IN GOTHAM.

[E]sterbrook to Leave New York and Locate in Washington.

[Th]e Coming Base Ball Season to be the Liveliest the Metropolis has ever known—True Inwardness of the Squabble over [illegible].

New York, March 11.—Editor Sporting News:—We have relapsed into the re[l]ase of winter, but await the breaking of [th]ar apathetic spell which the first April [sh]owers will bring. I say we have re[la]psed, and I mean it. Last week the mem[b]ers of the League teams invaded the me[tro]polis, and the patrons of the national [pas]time were awakened to the fact that [illegible] were being made for another [illegible] magnates had [illegible] homes, dia[illegible]

number was taken to manage the Kansas City team. Still I think a better man could have been secured. We were somewhat startled last week by the report that Dan O'Leary had disappeared. The *World* published two anecdotes and quite an obituary of the ex-manager of the Indianapolis club, but Dan is still alive and like Chas. O'Conor and some other eminents has had the pleasure of reading what pleasant things may be said of them. P. Jay.

HARRY WRIGHT'S TEAM.

He Says the Phillies Will Be Among the Leaders This Year.

Philadelphia, March 11.—Editor Sporting News: The players of the Philadelphia Club report here on March 15, and a day later they will leave for Charleston, S. C. They remain there until the 27th, participating and playing games with the local club. We then return home, stopping at Baltimore on our way to play two games. On [April] 1st we open the season at home in a [game] with a college club. On April 5th th[e first] game of a series of seven with the A[thletics] for the local championship w[ill be played]. These seven games will be [played] April 8th, 10th, 14th and [illegible]

THE WHITE STOCKINGS.

Chicago's Great Team Getting Ready for the Trip to Hot Springs.

Gore, Williamson, Pfeffer, Dalrymple, Flint, McCormick, Clarkson, Kelly and all the Champions to [illegible].

Chicago, March 11.—Editor Sporting News:—The White Stockings are dropping in one by one and before this reaches the public they will have all reported ready to start on the Southern trip. Compared with that which attended the last games of last season's schedule, the weather we are now enjoying, to use a Michigan Avenue qualification, is simply lovely. The balmy breezes—but stay, I had better not enter

nies the team south. Columbus is without a regular team but is long on base ball enthusiasm and the inducements Harrington accepted to take his nine there were very liberal, there being no apparent chance of his quitting loser, Elmer Foster, who has signed with the Mets, accompanied the Blues, and will get in his preliminary practice with them.

Anson and his men will leave for Hot Springs, Ark., March 15.

The good time is approaching,
The season is at hand,
When the merry click of the two-base lick
Will be heard throughout the land.
The frost still lingers on the earth, and budless are the trees,
But the merry ring of the voice of spring,
Is borne upon the breeze.

H. E. K.

The Pittsburgs Coming.

Pittsburg, March 12.—Editor Sporting News:—The Pittsburg Club leave here for St. Louis Monday, March 15. Barkley accompanies the nine and will not [illegible] in St. Louis but on the [illegible] He is in good spirits, for [illegible] his suspension, President [illegible] [pro]mised to [illegible]

READY FOR THE ROAD.

The Gentlemen's Driving Club Waiting for the Word.

A Brilliant Season Looked Forward to—The St. Louis Roadsters Preparing for Their Summer Campaign.

The Gentlemen's Driving Club of St. Louis is now entering upon the fifth year of its existence with brilliant prospects of having a most successful season. During the past four years, under the management of President I. R. Trask and his assistant officials the Gentlemen's Driving Club has been steadily growing in popularity and usefulness, until it has become one of the most popular institution of its kind in the West. This season, under the management of President J. W. Teasdale and an admirably selected board of directors, the club will number among its members [illegible]

The first issue of The Sporting News was a mass of gray that featured stories (above) on 'The Game in Gotham' and 'The White Stockings.' Content in Al Spink's creation, however, was not necessarily limited to baseball or even sports. Columns on 'The Stage' and 'The Cue' received as much space in the early issues as sports features on 'The Wheel,' 'The Turf,' and 'The Gun.'

THE STAGE.

ALICE HARRISON.

The Fair Comedienne and her Manager in Real Hot Water.

THE WHEEL

Stillman G. Whittaker.

A Sketch of the Leading Rider of the Western Bicycling World.

Every wheelman who knows or ever has seen

THE OAR.

THE BOSTON BLADES.

The Oarsmen of the Hub Getting Ready for Coming Events.

THE CUE.

The Tournament.

The opening game of the 14-inch balk line [illegible] on Wednesday night,

THE GUN.

ROD AND GUN.

The Time to Kill Game Without Breaking the Law.

Sportsmen and others desiring to inform themselves of the laws governing the killing of

THE TURF.

OUR CRACKS AT MEMPHIS.

The Corrigan, Pate, Lucas, Ashe and other Stables go South.

St. Louis is now well represented at Memphis, whither the [illegible] preceded two of the Corrigan

Success Comes Quickly

Charles C. Spink (left) arrived in 1886 as brother Al trained his editorial guns on Francis Richter (right), editor of the rival Sporting Life.

As the fledgling sports paper gained stature in 1886, Al Spink buckled under the weight of multiple duties. Circulation and advertising responsibilities, in addition to editorial chores, were more than he could handle.

A summons was dispatched to his younger brother, Charles Claude Spink, in the Dakotas. Charles' homesteading dream suddenly vanished in the face of a $50-per-week offer. Shucking his bib overalls and red bandana, Charles caught the first train to St. Louis to rescue his overburdened brother.

In early July 1886, Al Spink published his first "extra." It consisted of a slight makeover on page 1 and was dictated by "A Monster Wager," in which a pair of well known sportsmen, Jack Cassady and William Chambers, bet $10,000 on the outcome of a heavyweight fight between John L. Sullivan and Charles Mitchell. A three-column line sketch of Mitchell accompanied the expose.

With the flush of early success, Al Spink started to flex his editorial muscle. His favorite target became Francis Richter, editor of Sporting Life in Philadelphia. "Who Is F.C. Richter?" asked an October 1886 headline. Readers were then urged to "Read This Racy Letter and Find Out." A third line of the head declared: "Fans and Players Attack the Editor of the Philadelphia Sewer."

The Sporting News' first season as a chronicler of baseball came to a thunderous climax when it reported the victory of the St. Louis Browns over the Chicago White Stockings in the winner-take-all World's Series.

Charles Comiskey's champions of the American Association defeated Cap Anson's National League kingpins, four games to two, with Curt Welch scoring the deciding run on a wild pitch by John Clarkson.

To mark the event, The Sporting News of October 30, 1886, deviated from its basic one-column format and devoted page 1 to individual line sketches of the new world champions. In the journalistic style of the day, deck headlines, the first large and the others successfully smaller, detailed the Series on page 2: "We Gave 'Em the Goose / The St. Louis Browns Clean Out the Chicago White Stockings / The World's Championship Now the Property of This Town / Sketches of the Players, Umpire and Chicago Mascot."

A sketch of a goose helped illustrate the presentation.

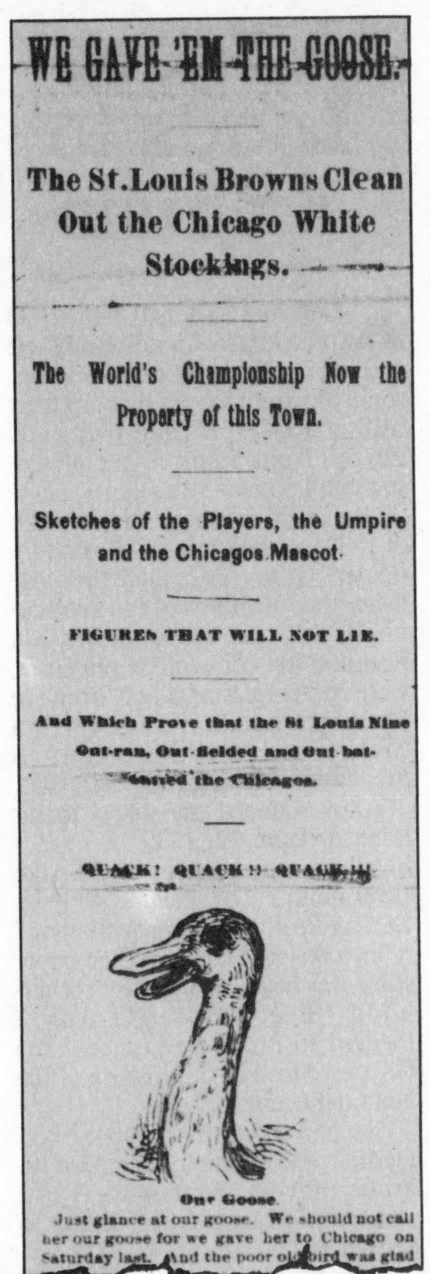

WE GAVE 'EM THE GOOSE.

The St. Louis Browns Clean Out the Chicago White Stockings.

The World's Championship Now the Property of this Town.

Sketches of the Players, the Umpire and the Chicagos Mascot.

FIGURES THAT WILL NOT LIE.

And Which Prove that the St Louis Nine Out-ran, Out-fielded and Out-batted the Chicagos.

QUACK! QUACK!! QUACK!!!

Our Goose.

Just glance at our goose. We should not call her our goose for we gave her to Chicago on Saturday last. And the poor old bird was glad

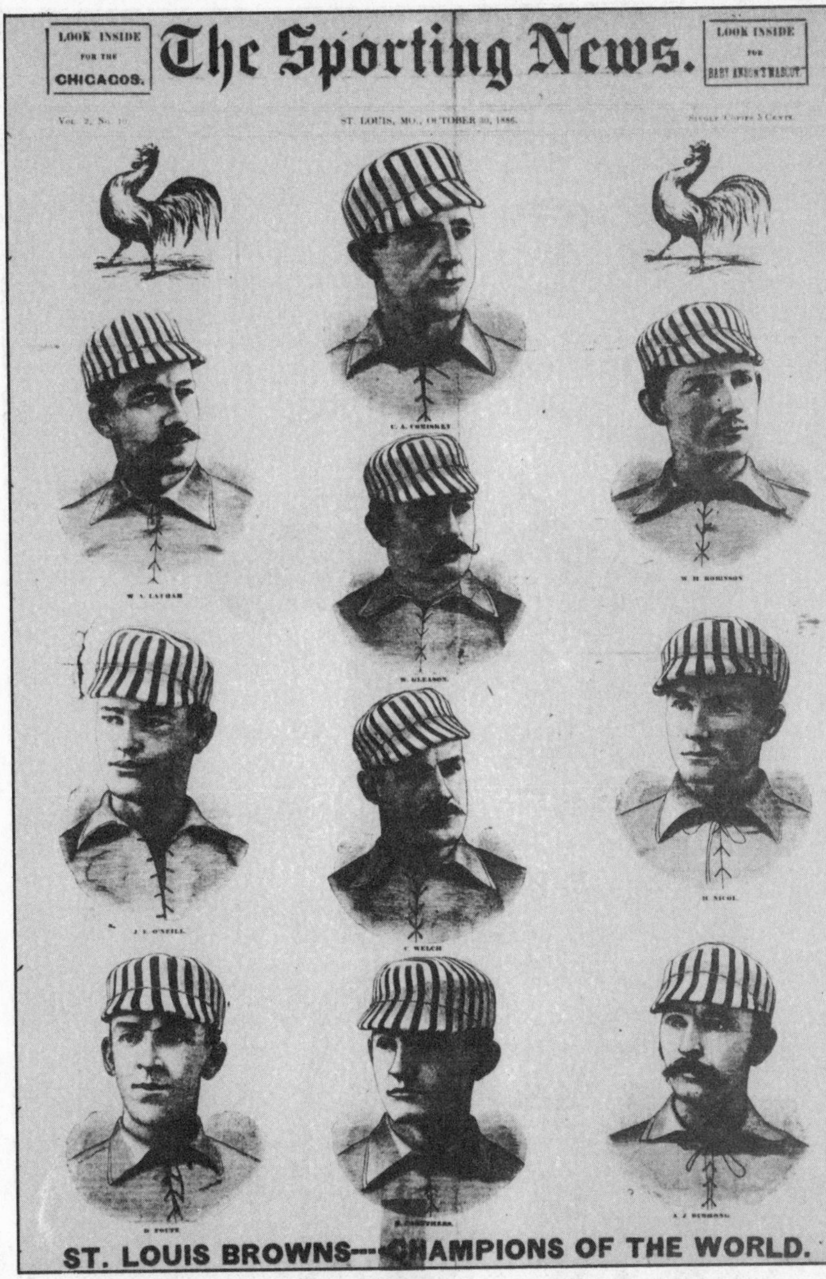

LOOK INSIDE FOR THE CHICAGOS.

The Sporting News.

LOOK INSIDE FOR BABY ANSON'S MASCOT.

ST. LOUIS, MO., OCTOBER 30, 1886.

ST. LOUIS BROWNS---CHAMPIONS OF THE WORLD.

Vol. 1, No. 17. ST. LOUIS, MO., JULY 5, 1886. SINGLE COPIES 5 CENTS.

EXTRA.

A MONSTER WAGER MADE.

John Cassidy Bets $10,000 Sullivan Will Stop Mitchell.

Wm. Chambers Wagers a Like Amount on the Opposite Proposition.

CHARLES MITCHELL.

When the St. Louis Browns defeated the Chicago White Stockings in the 1886 World's Series, The Sporting News reported, with a touch of local braggadocio, 'We Gave 'Em the Goose.' The report, appropriately, was accompanied by an illustration of a goose (above left). Page 1 of the October 30, 1886, issue was devoted to line sketches of the new world champions (above right). The publication's first 'Extra' was occasioned in July 1886 by a 'monster wager' on a prize fight.

A Scoop Leads to A Crisis

A congenial and hail fellow, Al Spink made friends easily. He was the confidant of many players, some of whom would pick up their mail at TSN offices and frequently get tips from Spink about off-season employment.

One such visitor in the summer of 1889 was Joe Quinn, a Boston infielder. Quinn informed the publisher that members of the Brotherhood, a 5-year-old organization founded for benevolent purposes, were contemplating a bolt from the National League to form their own circuit, which would be known as the Players League.

Spink scooped the world in his issue of June 22, 1889. A page 1 headline announced: "Big Strike Imminent / The League Players Getting Ready for a Big Walk Out."

Two weeks later, another cover story was headlined: "The Brotherhood / Every Man But Anson Pledged to Jump the League / The Greatest Move in the History of the National Game."

The players' major grievance was against the owners' decision to grade players from A to E and structure salaries from $1,500 to $2,500.

John Montgomery Ward, president of the Brotherhood, explained: "There remained nothing else for the players to do but to begin organizing on a new basis. The course was decided on at a meeting of representatives of various Brotherhood chapters held at the Fifth Avenue Hotel, New York, July 14, 1889."

While The Sporting News continued to receive news breaks from the Brotherhood, its support of the Players League was nearly fatal. A.G. Spalding and Brothers transferred advertisements from The

A tip from Boston infielder Joe Quinn in 1889 helped TSN scoop the world on news of a budding baseball rebellion.

John Montgomery Ward was president of the Brotherhood, the player organization whose strike plans were hailed in TSN's 1889 scoop.

Sporting News to Sporting Life and The Sporting Times, a new journal funded by the National League. Al Spink christened his rivals "Sporting Death" and "The Spitting Times."

The eight-club Players League operated in 1890. It featured many of the big names of the National League and functioned in conflict with the N.L. schedule.

When the World's Series was played between the champions of the National League and American Association, Spink refused to cover the event because Boston, winner of the Players League pennant, was not included.

Circulation of TSN, which had approached 100,000 in July 1889 when readers hungered for Al Spink's details of the heavyweight bout between John L. Sullivan and Jake Kilrain in New Orleans, plunged alarmingly. A strict austerity program shrouded the sports weekly.

Belatedly, TSN withdrew its support from the Brotherhood, explaining in its editorial columns: "We have gone back on the Brotherhood because that organization allowed itself to be controlled by a lot of capitalists . . . who took the first opportunity to throw the players down. As soon as the players allowed these ducks to run them, they lost their identity and forfeited our support."

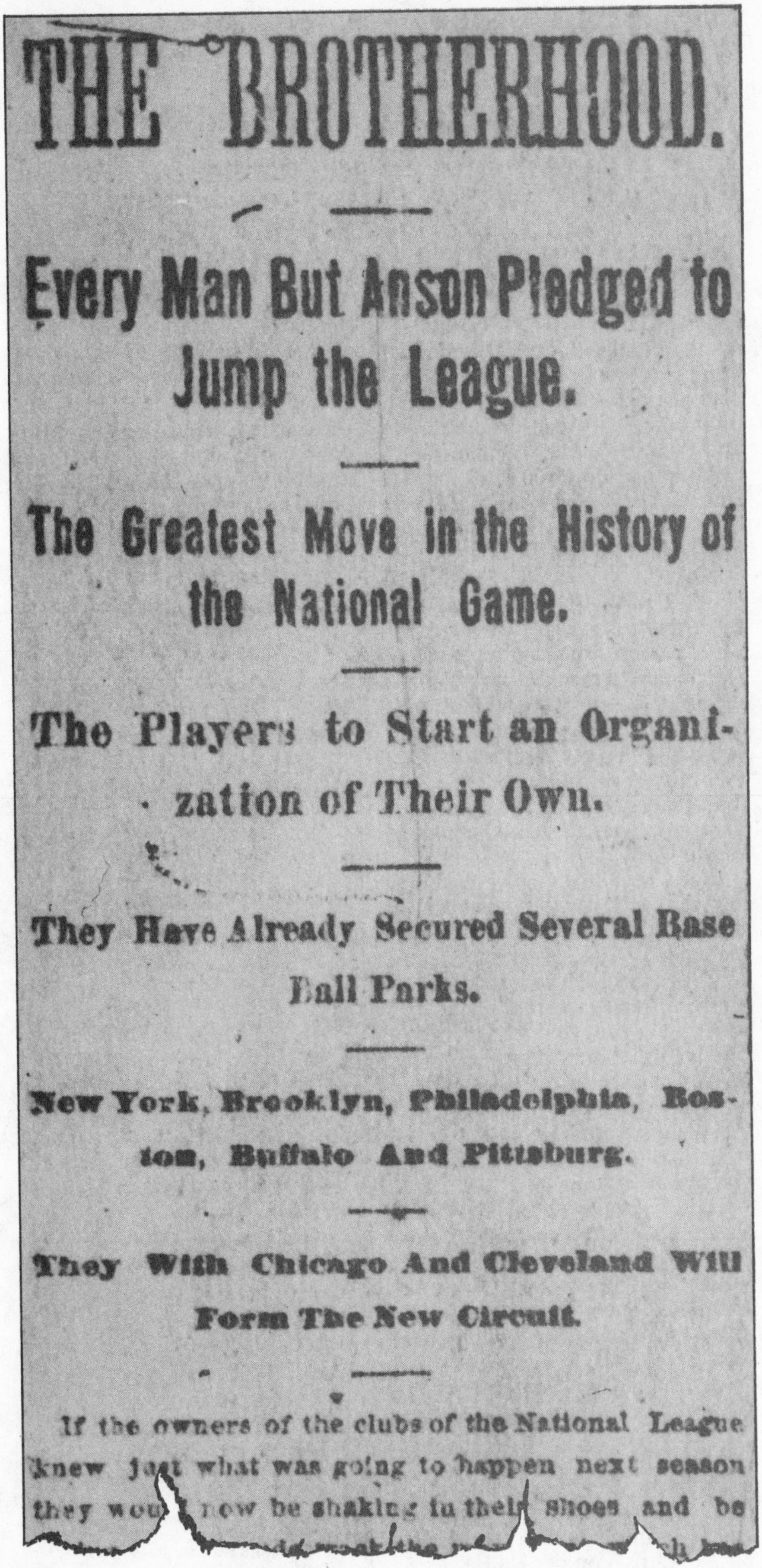

THE BROTHERHOOD.

Every Man But Anson Pledged to Jump the League.

The Greatest Move in the History of the National Game.

The Players to Start an Organization of Their Own.

They Have Already Secured Several Base Ball Parks.

New York, Brooklyn, Philadelphia, Boston, Buffalo And Pittsburg.

They With Chicago And Cleveland Will Form The New Circuit.

If the owners of the clubs of the National League knew just what was going to happen next season they would now be shaking in their shoes and be

Editorial Guns Find A Target

The war between the National and Players leagues ceased after one season. The October 11, 1890, issue of The Sporting News heralded cessation with these headlines: "The Cruel War Ends / The Warring Base Ball Clubs Come Together at Last / An Armistice Declared and Peace Is Certain to Follow."

Al Spink's editorial guns fell silent, but only temporarily. Before long, hostilities erupted on the home front against an old confederate.

In the 1870s, Chris Von der Ahe, a prosperous saloon keeper who was known locally as the "Lucky Dutchman," helped Spink organize the Sportsman's Park and Club Association. Chris was president and Al secretary. They founded the St. Louis Browns, who in 1885-88 won four pennants in the American Association, then considered a major league.

In the early 1890s, however, Von der Ahe's luck ran dry. Attendance dwindled. Charles A. Comiskey, manager of the four-time champion Browns, defected to Cincinnati. Star players were sold and attendance plunged even further. The huge revenues that once were delivered daily to Chris' saloon—and kept a bevy of blondes at his elbow—were no more.

To make his product more attractive to the masses, "der Poss Bresident" converted his ball park into "The Coney Island of the West." Fans could shoot the chutes, watch Wild West shows, listen to an all-girl Silver Cornet Band, bet a bob or two at a three-eighth-mile race track or swill beer at the "Grandstand Club," forerunner of the swank Stadium Clubs of the 20th Century.

Al Spink deplored his old buddy's self-righteous airs and dubbed him "J. Christ Von der Ahe." A four-column cartoon depicted "Chris Von der Ha Ha" as a top-hatted master of ceremonies at a three-ring circus.

When Chris announced that he would start to sell betting pools at games, Spink double-shotted his guns.

A page 1 headline early in 1896 read: "The League Defied / Von der Ahe Will Sell Pools on His Base Ball Grounds / Despite All the League Laws to the Contrary / Will the Old League Masters Laugh at His Action? / A New Syndicate Ready to Take Hold of the Game Here / It is Composed of Gentlemen of Means Who Love the Game / Not for the Money, But for the Pleasure That Is in It."

League officials did not blink away Chris' antics. He was forced out of the game. Climaxing the Dutchman's fall from grace, the Browns were sold at public auction on the courthouse steps.

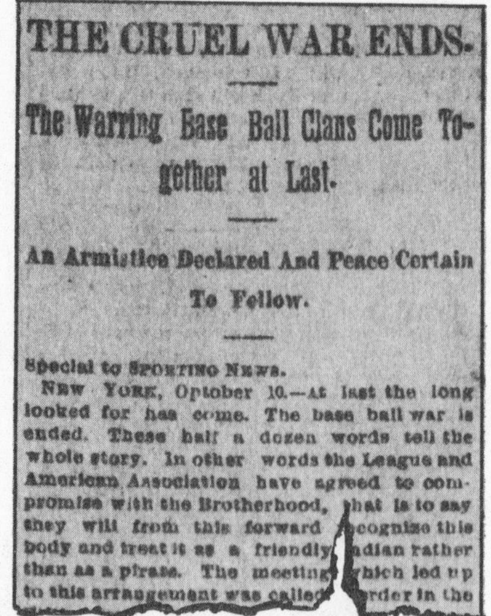

THE CRUEL WAR ENDS.

The Warring Base Ball Clans Come Together at Last.

An Armistice Declared And Peace Certain To Follow.

Special to SPORTING NEWS.

NEW YORK, October 10.—At last the long looked for has come. The base ball war is ended. These half a dozen words tell the whole story. In other words the League and American Association have agreed to compromise with the Brotherhood, hat is to say they will from this forward ecognize this body and treat it as a friendly ndian rather than as a pirate. The meeting hich led up to this arrangement was calle rder in the

The October 1890 headline (above) signaled the end to the one-year player rebellion.

CHRIS VON DER HA! HA'S! PAST, PRESENT AND FUTURE.

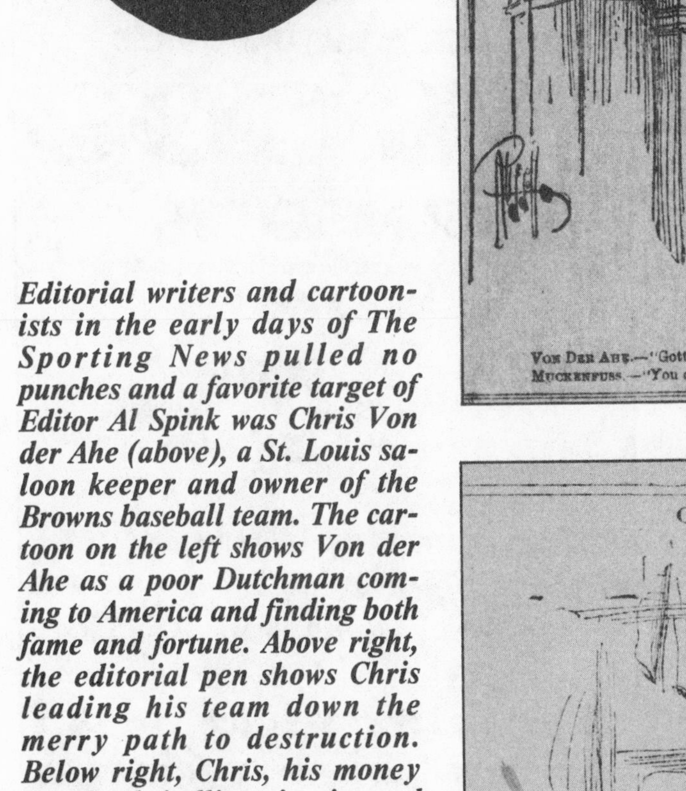

Editorial writers and cartoonists in the early days of The Sporting News pulled no punches and a favorite target of Editor Al Spink was Chris Von der Ahe (above), a St. Louis saloon keeper and owner of the Browns baseball team. The cartoon on the left shows Von der Ahe as a poor Dutchman coming to America and finding both fame and fortune. Above right, the editorial pen shows Chris leading his team down the merry path to destruction. Below right, Chris, his money supply dwindling, is pictured holding a player auction.

VON DER AHE.—"Gott in Himmel! 'Muck,' vos ist los mit der brake? Schtop us, or we aind in it."
MUCKENFUSS.—"You ought to have thought of that last winter, Chris. It's too late now."

CHRIS' SACRIFICE SALE.

VON DER AHE: "Der Public be Damned. I Neetet der Money for der Pooks."

The Sporting News.

PUBLISHED WEEKLY AT
NO. 11 NORTH EIGHTH STREET,
ST. LOUIS, MO.
BY THE
SPORTING NEWS PUBLISHING COMPANY,

To whose order all Checks, Drafts, Money Orders, and Remittances must be made payable.

TERMS:

Subscription, per annum(postage paid)...			$2.00
Six months................	"	"	...$1.00
Three months............	"	"	... 60
Single copies..............	"	"	... 5

INVARIABLY IN ADVANCE.

ADVERTISING RATES:

First insertion..............20c per line, agate.				
Each subsequent insertion.................15c	"	"	"	
Reading Notices............50c	"	"	"	

ST. LOUIS, MO.. MAY 10, 1886.

SPECIAL NOTICE.

CORRESPONDENCE on sporting topics, from any section of the city, State or country, solicited.

COMMUNICATIONS—Manuscript intended for publication should be written on one side of the paper only, and must be accompanied by the writer's name and address (not necessarily for publication, but as a private guarantee of good faith), and all communications, upon any subject, or for any department, must be addressed to THE SPORTING NEWS Publishing Company.

TO THE TRADE.

The trade is supplied at liberal rates by all the leading news companies.

THE SPORTING NEWS is for Sale by All Newsdealers in the United States and Canada.

WE ARE
BOOMING.

THE SPORTING NEWS
TO-DAY
Has the Largest Circulation of any SPORTING PAPER published west of PHILADELPHIA. It is on sale weekly at every NEWS STAND from New Orleans to St. Paul, and west to San Francisco, and is handled by

180

Beware, the Poison Pen

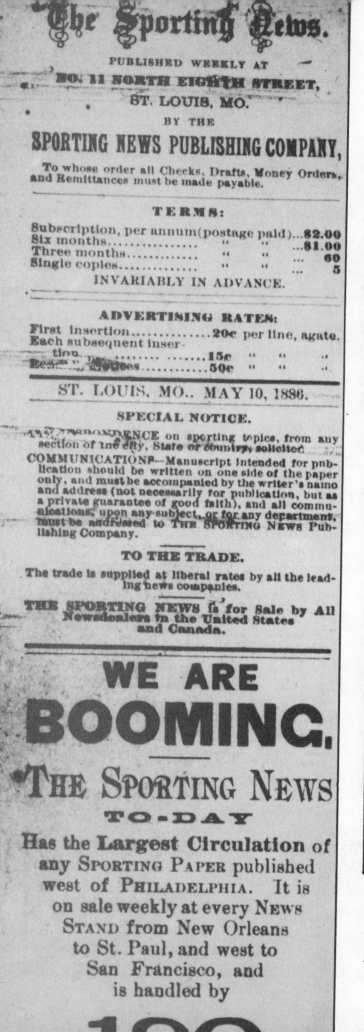

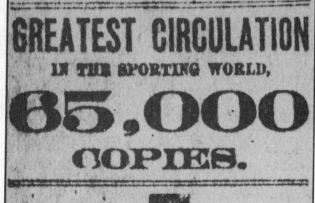

Where complete files can be found, extra copies obtained and subscriptions and advertisements received. A. FRANK RICHARDSON, General Agent for Newspapers of Known Circulation.

THE SPORTING NEWS will not guarantee advertisers any position. Prices are for the run of the paper irrespective of page or location.

GREATEST CIRCULATION
IN THE SPORTING WORLD,
65,000
COPIES.

The Sporting News credentials for 1892 will be out on Saturday, January 30. Correspondents wishing to continue in the service of this paper will confer a favor by sending in their old credentials at once and filing applications for the new.

COLUMBUS joins the Western League.

TOLEDO will likely join the Western

The editorial-page masthead (left) in the early issues of The Sporting News carried subscription and advertising rates as well as special notices to would-be contributors. Editors often made room for progress reports (left) and any necessary instructions to correspondents (above).

Editorials in the early issues of The Sporting News often were simple declarative sentences that relied heavily on the readers' knowledge of sports to identify the subjects under discussion.

One example of the short-but-sweet editorial style of the day is the simple exclamation, "Shine out fair sun."

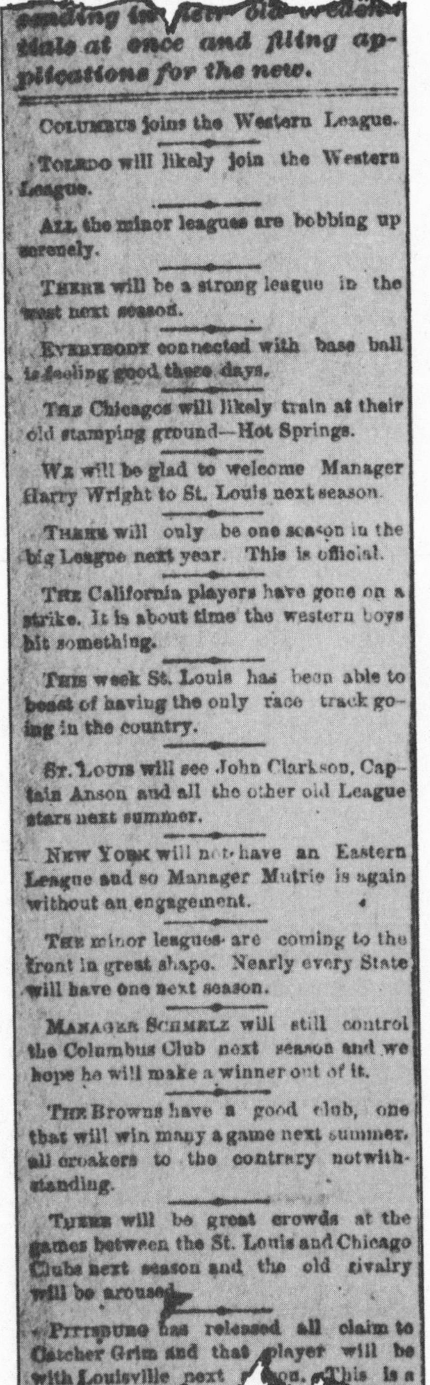

...tials at once and filing applications for the new.

COLUMBUS joins the Western League.

TOLEDO will likely join the Western League.

ALL the minor leagues are bobbing up serenely.

THERE will be a strong league in the west next season.

EVERYBODY connected with base ball is feeling good these days.

THE Chicagos will likely train at their old stamping ground—Hot Springs.

WE will be glad to welcome Manager Harry Wright to St. Louis next season.

THERE will only be one season in the big League next year. This is official.

THE California players have gone on a strike. It is about time the western boys hit something.

THIS week St. Louis has been able to boast of having the only race track going in the country.

ST. LOUIS will see John Clarkson, Captain Anson and all the other old League stars next summer.

NEW YORK will not have an Eastern League and so Manager Mutrie is again without an engagement.

THE minor leagues are coming to the front in great shape. Nearly every State will have one next season.

MANAGER SCHMELZ will still control the Columbus Club next season and we hope he will make a winner out of it.

THE Browns have a good club, one that will win many a game next summer, all croakers to the contrary notwithstanding.

THERE will be great crowds at the games between the St. Louis and Chicago Clubs next season and the old rivalry will be aroused.

PITTSBURG has released all claim to Catcher Grim and that player will be with Louisville next season. This is a

Editorials often were simple sentences that assumed reader familiarity with subject matter.

An editorial column might start off with a statement like that, then descend down one column, each one getting longer. One editorial page featured the following one-paragraph lines:

"It's Professor Boyle now."

— — — ◆ — — —

"Denver's battery is Meinke and Sutcliff."

— — — ◆ — — —

"Howard of the Maroons is quite an athlete."

— — — ◆ — — —

"Ted Sullivan is at work organizing the St. Paul club."

— — — ◆ — — —

"Will White has been recommended to Kansas City."

— — — ◆ — — —

"Bob Hogan will hold down bag No. 1 for the Drummonds."

These short editorials were not always sports-related and sometimes carried a poignant message for an unsuspecting victim. "An actress in New York recently slapped Sarah Bernhardt's face," one 1891 editorial began. "Sarah should be arrested for stabbing the actress with her cheekbone."

In the summer of 1889, the editorial columns of The Sporting News advised readers, "We do not often go into pugilism. But when we do tackle that subject, we do it well."

In a second editorial, readers were told: "This week the editor of The Sporting News is away to the great prize fight (the Sullivan-Kilrain bout in a lumber camp near New Orleans). The local staff are celebrating the Fourth of July and the compositors have not yet got over their Independence Day celebration. So if The Sporting News is not as broad and as live and as good as usual, there is the best of reasons for it, and our kind readers will please bear with us accordingly."

The heavyweight bout was previewed in a six-column story and Al Spink covered Sullivan's victory with a lengthy account. Curiously, however, the paper came out shortly thereafter in opposition to prize fighting.

When Alfred Spink's wrath was aroused, he was merciless in his retaliation against those who opposed his views. Albert G. Spalding, the sporting goods manufacturer and head of the Chicago club, felt the sting of Spink's pen in 1889 when he fought the establishment of the Players League, which was endorsed by TSN.

Ruthlessly, the publisher assailed Spalding, and not only in his opposition to the new circuit. Spink alleged that Spalding's firm had delivered "rotten baseballs" to a number of minor leagues. Another time, Spink wrote, "In his frantic endeavors to get even, Spalding is hiring newspapers to banquet him and buying up others to boom his cause and knock out his hated rivals."

Chris Von der Ahe, the St. Louis Browns owner, was another favorite target. Spink referred to Von der Ahe's team as the Boozers and once wrote: "Our advice to the St. Louis Boozers, who are now in Louisville: Do not come home and all will be forgiven."

A second editorial chortled: "Von der Ahe has started a boycott on The Sporting News. Ever since he commenced the boycott, the circulation has increased wonderfully. This would lead us to believe that our good friends love us for the enemies we have made." The circulation, blazened in large type on the editorial page, was listed at 60,000 copies weekly.

In April 1890, Spink declared optimistically, but not too accurately: "The Sporting News is the greatest sporting paper in America and its price always will remain right at five cents."

Of all the editorials to come from Spink's fertile pen during the formative years, none was more vindictive than that which appeared at midseason in 1890. It read:

"Four dirty, drunken, lousy printers grind out each week a paper called the Printer's Journal. Its main object is blackguarding and blackmailing decent people. It would starve to death but for the fact that funds are furnished its proprietors by their poor daughters, miserable creatures, who exist by selling their bodies to men as low as the scabs responsible for their birth. Some day we shall publish sketches of these harpies, but just now life is too short and our columns are too crowded with news and advertising matter."

Ves-Tong Manufacturing Company's Specialties

VES-TONG AUTOMATIC SHELL VESTS AND JACKETS

These vests are guaranteed to be more complete and to fill the requirements of the shooter more perfectly than anything of the kind on the market today. The material used is the best to be had and the workmanship, style and fit can't be beat.

Ves-Tong Vests and Jackets permit the wearer to carry forty shells without feeling any inconvenience whatever. The weight of the shells is evenly distributed and is all put on the shoulders. As shown in cuts, the shells are always ready for instant use. When one shell is pulled out, another automatically takes its place.

Automatic Shell Vests range in price from $16.50 to $52.80 per dozen
" " Jackets " " " " $26.40 to $66.00 "

12, 16 and 20 Gauge

WRITE FOR CATALOG

Patented June 13, 1911

Patented June 13, 1911

VES-TONG MANUFACTURING COMPANY **WENONA, ILLINOIS**

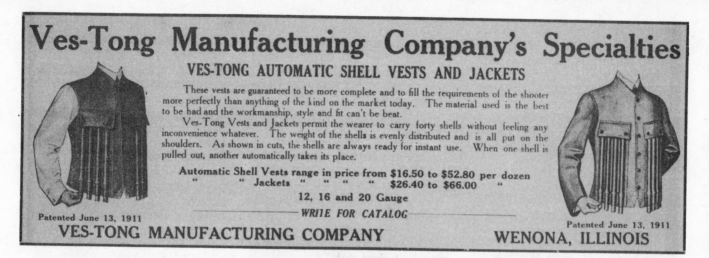

A New Publication

The Sporting News was 13 years old when, in 1899, Charles C. Spink visited a St. Louis sporting goods company in search of advertising.

While there, he was informed that the sporting goods industry urgently needed a trade publication.

"I'll publish one," he promised.

Later, Spink paid a call to the old Meacham Arms Company, where he was shown a trade publication from the East.

"Why couldn't I get out a magazine like this—and do a better job?" he wondered.

Assured that he could without any problem, he asked, "How can I get the advertising?"

Two buyers for the arms company volunteered to write to manufacturers, urging them to advertise in the new publication. The response was nearly 100 percent.

Volume 1, Number 1 of The Sporting Goods Dealer was dated October 1899. It consisted of 32 pages, bound in brown paper and printed in black ink.

"The first issue was so superior to anything else that it caught on immediately," recalled one of the Meacham buyers years later.

Despite the high praise, Spink had some reservations about his product. Nervously, as he prepared for a second issue, he remarked," "It's got to go over, I've got $3,500 tied up in it."

MISSION OF "THE SPORTING GOODS DEALER."

The inaugural issue contained this promise to its readers: "The publishers will spare neither effort nor expense to make The Sporting Goods Dealer indispensable to those to whom it caters."

Also, in the statement of policy was the assurance that "the readers of the Dealer will be kept in touch with the times."

The first issue was heavy with advertising from railroad lines that were attempting to help populate the West.

One ad read: "Nothing more attractive anywhere than an outing along the beautiful Ozark Mountain streams reached via Frisco."

Another announced: "The KATY Flyer! Best Train to the Indian Territory."

The first issue also contained a full-page photograph of A.J. Reach and an article on "How Base Balls Are Made."

There also was news from Pennsylvania, Texas, Indiana, Florida, Montreal, Washington, D.C., the Pacific Coast and elsewhere, as well as a page devoted to information on open season for game in various states.

The shell-jacket ad (above) and the early illustration (left) captured the spirit of what The Sporting Goods Dealer was all about.

After the first three issues, Charles felt confident of his new product. The cover of the January 1900 issue was printed in four colors; the magazine had grown to 68 pages. By the time The Dealer observed its first anniversary in October, it boasted 58 advertisers.

By 1901, the automobile was making its impact upon the American public and The Dealer. A correspondent, writing in "Care of the Automobile," cautioned: "It is obvious that the automobile must be operated cautiously if good results are to be obtained. . . . The novice should be content with a few miles the first day, increasing the distance slightly each day. Trying to make too much speed is very dangerous."

The January 1901 issue demonstrated the progress made by The Dealer in a relatively short time. Ninety manufacturers were represented in its 82 pages.

Early in the century, the publishing company introduced "Toys and Novelties" and "The Toy Buyer's Guide," both of which were sold to a Chicago publisher for $3,500 prior to Charles Spink's death in 1914 so that the Spinks could concentrate on their other publications.

The cover of a 1900 issue of The Sporting Goods Dealer caught the flavor of the era.

Early Advertisements Cover Wide Spectrum

Advertisements in The Sporting News during its first 15 years covered a wide spectrum, ranging from saddle and harness manufacturers to surgical and dental services to all-night saloons to Mrs. Bertha Wupper, the "acknowledged best business medium and fortune teller in the city" on South 13th Street.

Generally, page 8 was devoted exclusively to advertisements of all descriptions. Here Anheuser-Busch might be wedged between a desk company ad and one singing the praises of Kentucky-Bred Trotting Stallions.

The Spalding sporting goods company's ad might be sandwiched between Sprague's Delicatessen and Dairy Lunch and Gianelli, the photographer who guaranteed the best pictures in St. Louis.

Readers also might be advised that the Chicago Opera Company was performing "The Mikado" and "Pinafore" and that Tony Faust's, "the most popular restaurant in the city at the corner of Elm and Broadway," had a ladies' entrance on Elm Street.

To celebrate the Fourth of July, there was a gigantic fireworks display at the Union Grounds featuring a realistic reenactment of "The Battle of Lookout Mountain." Admission 25 cents.

A horse-furnishings ad topped a three-column display by the A.J. Reach Sporting Goods Company, while below a grocery store ad extolled its oatmeal and graham wafers and "original German zwieback."

The Rawlings Brothers, forerunners of the Rawlings Sporting Goods Company, bought space regularly, as did Ben Miller, Fashionable Hatter, All the New and Nobby Styles, Silk and Stiff Hats.

Dr. Owen's Electro-Galvanic Body Belt was a regular advertiser, as was Trask's Selected Shore Mackerel (sometimes oysters) and Julius Winkelmeyer's Brewing Associates.

C.L. Webert advertised "Dress, Ball and Wedding Shoes Made to Order," while Ed. Butler & Son promoted the "Goodenough" horseshoe.

In September 1887, The Sporting News printed its first full-page ad. It was purchased by the manufacturers of Merrell's Penetrating Oil and was illustrated by sketches of Manager Charles Comiskey and eight members of the St. Louis Browns.

Later, the Richardson-Taylor Medicine Company ran several full-page ads directed toward sufferers of chills, fever, dyspepsia and other assorted ailments. The Taylor member of the firm was Charles C. Spink's father-in-law.

When The Sporting News moved its headquarters to a "new and elegant building, 907 Market Street," Al Spink advised his patrons with a large, full-width announcement on page 2.

In the summer of 1888, readers were urged to "Smoke The Sporting News Cigar / Quality Unexcelled." Endorsers included Chris Von Der Ahe, owner of the Browns, Comiskey and Arlie Latham, a prominent member of the team. Also included in the ad was a list of the "agents" who sold the stogie in Missouri, Illinois, Indiana, Kentucky, Tennessee and Arkansas.

On several occasions, Al Spink published special Christmas editions to supplement the regular 52 yearly issues. These usually were loaded with store ads, such as the St. Bernard Dollar Store which carried "The only complete stock of toys, dolls, novelties and Christmas presents in the city and cannot be duplicated in the United States."

One Christmas issue contained ads in 43 of its 56 columns.

Once, in the late 1890s, Al Spink found it necessary to publish an editorial apologizing for the great amount of advertising.

"Our readers will forgive us this week," it read, "for publishing so much advertising matter. Advertising comes only at certain seasons, and when it comes we must make the most of it. The splendid showing of advertising in The Sporting News of today is royal testimony and eloquent tribute to the immense circulation of this paper. It proves better than words that The Sporting News has a larger circulation than any other sporting paper in America. It also proves that we carry more advertising than all other papers of this class combined."

The Sporting News offered an attractive advertising medium when Buffalo Bill's Wild West show came to St. Louis in May 1886.

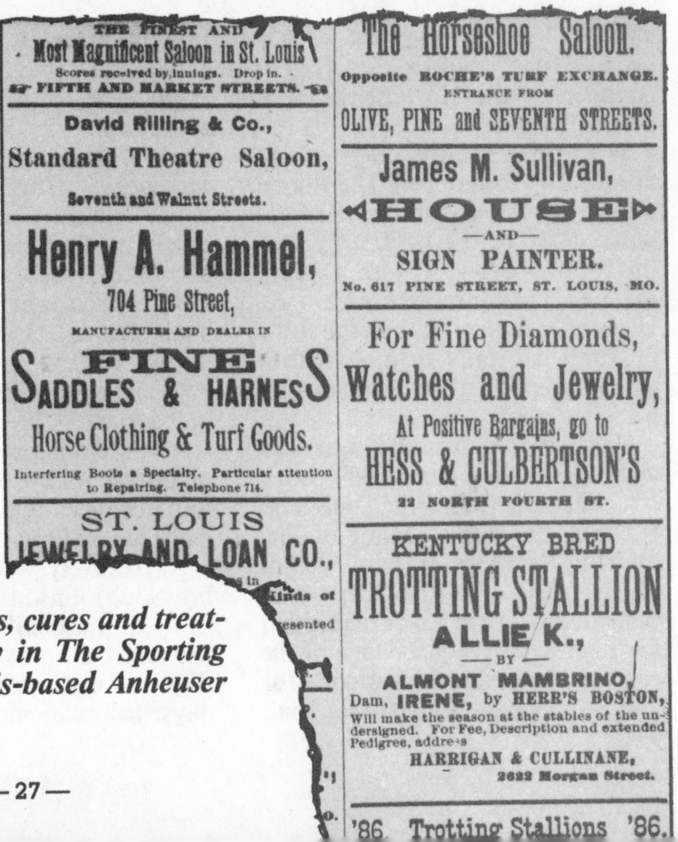

IT WILL PAY YOU TO GET OUR PRICES BEFORE PLACING YOUR ORDER.

[RA]WLINGS BROTHERS, 817 PINE STREET. ST. LOUIS, MO.

"NEVER KNOWN TO FAIL" Tarrant's Extract of Cubebs and Copaiba.

SOLD BY ALL DRUGGISTS.

WEAK MEN & WOMEN

Address Dr. D. H. LOWE, Winsted, Ct.

"FOOTINE" DESTROYS THE ODOR OF THE FEET AND ARM-PITS And Cures the Disease.

BEAUTIFUL WOMEN

FREE REMEDY

SELF-ABUSE

I CURE FITS!

H. G. ROOT, M. C., 183 Pearl St., N. Y.

WEAK MEN CURED.

NO STOMACH DRUGGING

FOR MEN ONLY!

A POSITIVE CURE

ONLY DIRECTORY ON EARTH

MONEY RETURNED IN CASE OF FAILURE.

YOUNG MEN!

MALYDOR INJECTION THE GENTLEMAN'S FRIEND.

MALYDOR MANUF'G CO., Lancaster, O.

OH, MY!

MAN,

THE EVANS MEDICINE CO., Cleveland, Ohio

OPIUM.

$1,000 REWARD for any case of Opium or Morphine Habit I can not cure

LADIES

TO WEAK MEN

Prof. F. C. FOWLER, Moodus, Conn.

DR. A. OWEN'S Electro-Galvanic Body Belt

CURES DISEASES WITHOUT MEDICINES.

ELECTRICITY is LIFE.

Patented August 16, 1887. Improved July 29, 1890.

Incorporated June 10, 1887.

Gents' Belt with Spinal Appliance Knee, Ankle and Arm Bands Attached.

Ladies' Belt with Spinal Appliance Knee, Ankle and Arm Bands Attached.

No. 4 Gents' Belt.

No. 4 Ladies' Belt.

Suspensory.

Back View.

Front View.

The Owen Belt is not a Chain, Wire or VOLTAIC Belt, or a PAD, of any description. It will cure all complaints CURABLE by Electricity or a Galvanic Battery.

Do not waste your money on Belts patented years ago. We have private consultation rooms for ladies as well as gents, and all who call or write us can rest assured they will receive an honest opinion, and if the Belt is not adapted to their case they will be so advised. Open at all times—days, nights and Sundays. Call or write to the doctor. Consultation at the office or by mail free. How to obtain Belts on thirty days' trial see 136 page book. MENTION THIS PAPER.

306 N. Broadway, St. Louis, Mo. THE OWEN ELECTRIC BELT AND APPLIANCE CO.

MALE ORGANS ENLARGED.

HILL'S MANUAL THE GREAT FORM BOOK.

A DIME sent to Jacob C. ..., Boston Herald, will secure a portrait group of the Boston, Cleveland or Brooklyn Base Ball Clubs of the Players' League, or the three will be sent for 25 cents.

POKER NEW HOLDOUT

ADVANTAGE DICE

$525

FREE TO MEN

THE SELF-RESTORER FREE

STAMP COLLECTORS

AGENTS GOODS

TANSYPILLS!

LADIES

MANHOOD Restored.

OUR GIRLS

POKER

BOOK

M-W

LOADED DICE

By 1891, medicine ads (above), offering remedies, cures and treatments for anything and everything, ran weekly in The Sporting News. Otherwise, advertisers, including St. Louis-based Anheuser Busch, carried a local flavor.

THE FINEST AND Most Magnificent Saloon in St. Louis
Scores received by innings. Drop in.
FIFTH AND MARKET STREETS.

David Rilling & Co.,
Standard Theatre Saloon,
Seventh and Walnut Streets.

Henry A. Hammel,
704 Pine Street,
MANUFACTURER AND DEALER IN
FINE SADDLES & HARNESS
Horse Clothing & Turf Goods.
Interfering Boots a Specialty. Particular attention to Repairing. Telephone 714.

ST. LOUIS
JEWELRY AND LOAN CO.,

The Horseshoe Saloon.
Opposite ROCHE'S TURF EXCHANGE.
ENTRANCE FROM
OLIVE, PINE and SEVENTH STREETS.

James M. Sullivan,
HOUSE
—AND—
SIGN PAINTER.
No. 617 PINE STREET, ST. LOUIS, MO.

For Fine Diamonds,
Watches and Jewelry,
At Positive Bargains, go to
HESS & CULBERTSON'S
22 NORTH FOURTH ST.

KENTUCKY BRED
TROTTING STALLION
ALLIE K.,
—BY—
ALMONT MAMBRINO,
Dam, IRENE, by HERR'S BOSTON,
Will make the season at the stables of the undersigned. For Fee, Description and extended Pedigree, address
HARRIGAN & CULLINANE,
2622 Morgan Street.

'86. Trotting Stallions '86.

The Times, They Are Changing

Pictured above is the original building from which TSN was prepared in 1886, when the type was set by hand and papers were printed on a slow flatbed press.

The 13-year-old sports weekly had undergone significant changes by the close of the 19th Century.

Wanderlust had claimed Al Spink. The founder of The Sporting News took a year's leave of absence early in the decade to promote his play, "The Derby Winner." Encouraged by rave reviews in St. Louis, Al took the show on the road, only to meet with a chilly reception that wiped out all his resources.

He tried homesteading in the Dakotas. But when that didn't work out, he returned to St. Louis and resumed his role as editor of The Sporting News as an employee of his brother. He also built and operated a horse track equipped for night racing. By the turn of the century, however, Al was gone for good—to pursue journalistic goals in other areas.

Gone, too, were some of the early features of the paper. Columns on "The Stage" and "The Gun" were replaced by more baseball news. "The Turf" and "The Ring" columns remained, but the patent medicine ads of earlier years also disappeared.

The occupant of the editor's chair was A.J. (Joe) Flanner, a lawyer by profession.

Changes were imminent in baseball as well. A former sports editor from Cincinnati was creating waves of unrest in the Western League. Ban Johnson was about to challenge the National League.

Aggressively, and with a tinge of bravado, Johnson elbowed his way into the baseball picture. He befriended the Spink family, a friendship that endured until Ban's final days. Johnson made certain that The Sporting News was fully informed of his moves and his plans.

One of his major steps, reported in the October 14, 1899, issue, announced: "American League / New Name Adopted by the Western League / National League Will Be Asked to Double Drafting Price and Allow Two Years Service."

A December headline read: "Charges Bad Faith / Johnson's Allegation Against Magnate Hart / American League Can Not Afford to Engage in a War With Present Organization."

A correspondent's dispatch reported that "President Hart of the Chicago Club does not appear to be worried over the proposed location of the American League club in his city under the management of Charles Comiskey."

Ban Johnson and the American League were lurking in the wings.

THE SPORTING NEWS PRESS.

OUR NEW HOME.

THE GROWING CIRCULATION OF THIS PAPER

Foster Perfecting Press Which Prints The Sporting News.

This is an age of advancement and The Sporting News happens to be right in the swim. We can honestly say without hesitation and with the satisfactory complacency that a realization of ambition is always accompanied with, that The Sporting News has outgrown its present home, and seeks a more spacious and commodious one. It is with a feeling akin to pride and at the same time taking a hearty grasp of each good fellow's hand who has devoted a few spare moments in perusing The Sporting News from pole to pole, that we announce a most wonderful increase in our circulation during the base ball season just finished. Never before in our existence has this circulation brought such a [illegible] demand upon us to meet its emergencies. During the last two months of the last Universal championship season it necessitated the hiring of extra help to attend to mailing and shipping, in response to immediate calls for more papers from every section of the country. The cities of the Western League, the Western Association, the South and the Far West have kept us more than [illegible] to supply their wants. Let the good work go on—we are up to the times and before the coming base ball season dawns upon the land we all love The Sporting News will be in a new home and sailing on with the added prosperity which all indications and the present outlook for a wonderful revival and universal interest in the national game assures.

It has taken months and years of untiring effort to settle this sporting paper on the solid foundation that we now find it. We are approaching our tenth birthday and during the years that we have devoted to the propagation of the national game, it must be admitted that we have buoyed ourselves over many vicissitudes and have experienced all the ups and downs that all who look to baseball as a business are bound to experience. When the national game was booming we glided along on the sea of prosperity and when the game came to a temporary decline we were compelled to get a hustle on us and push with all our might. It is indeed ample consolation to say to our dear patrons that we thank them for the high appreciation they have taken of our persevering efforts, crowning them with more than expected prosperity and landing The Sporting News high and dry, not on a shoal of despair, but in the land of promise and with the brightest of bright futures before us.

The new home where the business end of this paper will be conducted is situated in the very center of the commercial portion of St. Louis. Hereafter all the good fellows who were in the habit of giving us a call will find us located in the Insurance Building, at the southeast corner of Broadway and Olive Streets.

Besides moving to better quarters, we have another surprise in store for those who wish us well. It was not so long ago that we purchased one of Walter Scott & Co.'s finest perfecting presses at an enormous expense. This press has a capacity of printing [illegible] copies of The Sporting News every hour. On account of our increasing circulation and [illegible] it [illegible] the interests of [illegible] so that each and every one of them shall receive their papers at the proper time, we are commencing to realize that with even this magnificent press our issuing facilities are inadequate to meet the demand, and we are now making arrangements for the purchase of a Foster angle bar perfecting press.

We realize that next year will be the banner year of base ball. The right feeling has been instilled into the people of this country by the brilliant work of the boys on the diamond during the past season. Every mother's son of them have entered into the spirit of the contest with such a will that the enthusiasm has aroused public sentiment in favor of the national game to such a degree that base ball victories and defeats are not the talk of a few "cranks," as some call them, but are social and household topics. Slow indeed and behind the age must be that small business man who does not wish to know how the Temple Cup games are progressing.

The magnificent race put up by the Western Association and the brilliant work of the great players that have contested in the Western League have had much to do with bringing this renewed interest in the West. Truly the work of both of these model organizations are worthy of more than usual praise, and if any prospective league intends launching itself on the base ball world, it will do well to take either one of these organizations as a pattern.

As we write about our own prosperity, we become so enthused over the work of the boys who make the national game so popular, that we cannot help mentioning facts and giving credit where it is due.

There is another and most important fact that we desire to mention right here. As fast as The Sporting News are printed, The St. Louis News Company, who handle all our papers to newsdealers, have their wagons at our press rooms and as the papers are counted and wrapped they are [illegible]. The Sporting News should be delivered at the time noted. If they are not, our readers in these towns will please notify us of this fact. We will be only too happy to see that any errors of delivery are corrected:

Boston	Saturday, P.M.
Chicago	Friday, A.M.
Columbus	" "
Cincinnati	" "
Detroit	" M.
Cleveland	" "
Toledo	" "
Grand Rapids	" "
Indianapolis	" A.M.
Louisville, Ky.	" "
Lexington, Ky.	" "
Kansas City	" "
St. Joseph, Mo.	" "
Lincoln, Neb.	" P.M.
Sioux City	" "
Omaha	" "
St. Paul	Saturday, A.M.
Minneapolis	" "
New York	" "
Philadelphia	" "
New Orleans	Saturday, A.M.
Denver	" "
Rock Island	Friday, A.M.
Peoria, Ill.	" "
Jacksonville, Ill.	" "
Quincy, Ill.	" "
Des Moines	" "
Burlington	" "
Mobile	Saturday, P.M.
Savannah	" "
Galveston and all points in Texas	" A.M.
Washington, D.C.	" "
San Francisco	Monday, A.M.
Portland, Ore.	" "

This is just to give our readers the time on which they can rely, receiving this paper. If it does not come to hand by the time specified please notify us and we will see where the mistake is made and have it corrected.

In registering complaints, if newsdealers will please state exactly how they have ordered The Sporting News, it will greatly facilitate matters.

EDITOR SPINK

WITH THE WESTERN LEAGUE CHAMPIONS.

A Short Sketch of Each of Watkins' Happy Corn Huskers.

SIOUX CITY, September 29.—SPECIAL CORRESPONDENCE:—The Derby Winner Company are having a pleasant time at Sioux City. We are here for two nights and the people seem to be crazy over the show. Last night the theater was packed. As I write hundreds are flocking into our matinee. To-night The Derby Winner Company give a medal to the most popular player in the Champion Sioux City Club. Every one purchasing a ticket to the performance has been given the right to vote. Last night Frank Genins, our own St. Louis Frank, had the call and nearly every other vote was cast for him. It looks very much as though Frank had become as great a favorite here as at home. His gentlemanly, quiet ways have made him hundreds of friends in this country and he can have the town for the asking. It looks as though he would win the Derby Winner [illegible] a canter.

When The Sporting News disclosed in 1894 that it would move its headquarters to a bigger building, the change was announced with a big page 2 spread that also included a picture of its new printing press. By the late 1890s, a one-year subscription to TSN had dropped to $1 and Al Spink was writing dispatches from other cities (left) while touring with his play, 'The Derby Winner.'

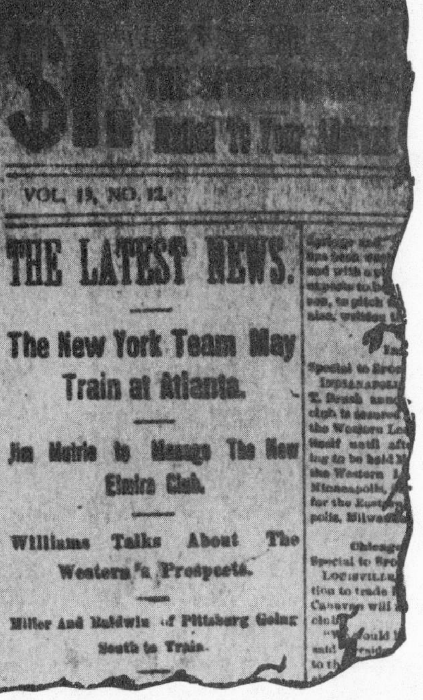

$1.

VOL. 15, NO. 12.

THE LATEST NEWS.

The New York Team May Train at Atlanta.

Jim Mutrie to Manage The New Elmira Club.

Williams Talks About The Western's Prospects.

Miller And Baldwin of Pittsburg Going South to Train.

1901-1913:
BIRTH OF THE A.L.

In the formative years of major league baseball, rowdyism was an accepted adjunct of the game. The player who carried his spikes high and sharp and could deliver a telling blow to opposing players commanded more respect than one who espoused the gentlemanly approach.

Frequently, umpires were as poorly disciplined as the players. Survival often bore a close relationship to an arbiter's pugilistic talents. After an afternoon of warfare at the ball park, an umpire might return to his dimly lit hotel cubicle to discover that the league president had upheld the aggressor and censured the would-be peacemaker.

Andrew Freedman was among the worst of a ruthless element. The New York Giants' owner changed managers almost monthly. He berated players, umpires and writers and once barred from the Polo Grounds a conscientious scribe who correctly quoted him using bad grammar. Around the turn of the century, Freedman and a few sycophants unsuccessfully attempted to convert the National League into a syndicate.

Conditions on the playing field, and often times in the front office, repulsed the gentility who otherwise might have been attracted to the emerging National Pastime. If the game were to prosper, a strong hand would be needed to eliminate the rowdies, give implacable support to the umpires and punish offenders with a firm, judicial authority. Only then could baseball realize its full potential for prosperity and popularity.

Such an individual was Byron Bancroft (Ban) Johnson. During the early 1890s, Johnson was sports editor of the Cincinnati Commercial-Gazette, a position that placed him in contact with Charles A. Comiskey, then manager of the city's National League team, the Reds.

At Comiskey's urging, Johnson accepted the presidency of the Western League, a minor circuit with franchises in Grand Rapids, Sioux City, Minneapolis, Milwaukee, Kansas City, Toledo, Indianapolis and Detroit. Under his dynamic leadership, the loop, which he renamed the American League, prospered impressively and soon was recognized as the foremost minor circuit.

But Johnson sought larger and more fertile pastures. Turning his gaze to the East, he announced in 1901 that he would challenge the 25-year-old National League and operate as a new major loop with franchises in Baltimore, Boston, Chicago, Cleveland, Detroit, Milwaukee, Philadelphia and Washington.

Johnson's bold move presaged the modern major league rivalry. Deadly enemies at first, the two leagues achieved harmony in 1903 through the National Agreement. By its terms, the two leagues submitted to a common authority and operated under a single code. In that same year, New York replaced Baltimore (St. Louis had replaced Milwaukee a year earlier), thereby establishing an alignment that endured for 50 years.

Having wooed and won many topflight stars from the N.L. before peace was declared, the A.L. lost no time in putting down roots. In September of 1903, the Boston Red Sox, winners by 14½ games over the Philadelphia Athletics, felt sufficiently proud and powerful to challenge the Pittsburgh Pirates to a series of games for the championship of the baseball world.

The Pirates had just clinched their third consecutive flag and, while their 6½-game margin did not compare with their 27½-game bulge over Brooklyn the year before, their confidence was high. Managed by swashbuckling Fred Clarke, the Pirates boasted a cast that included Honus Wagner, the league's leading hitter, and a pitching staff led by 20-game winners Deacon Phillippe and Sam Leever. The Bucs accepted the challenge.

Because the National Agreement contained no provisions for a World Series, terms of the Boston-Pittsburgh playoff were arranged by the owners, Henry J. Killilea of Boston and Barney Dreyfuss of Pittsburgh.

Although the playoff had no official stamp, it is regarded as the first modern World Series. It also is unique because the losing players received more money than the winners. The freak circumstances were created by Dreyfuss tossing his club's share of the gate receipts into the players' pool. As a result, each Pittsburgh player in the five-to-three-game defeat received $1,316. Each Boston player was enriched by $1,182.

Boston repeated as American League champion in 1904 and, heartened by its earlier success, challenged the New York Giants to a similar postseason series. The fans clamored for a series and Giants players pleaded for it, mindful that it would mean more than $1,000 for each member. Newspapers editorialized in favor of the series, one going so far as to suggest that the Giants' refusal would "work harm to the club from which it may take years to recover."

But Owner John T. Brush and Manager John McGraw rejected the challenge flatly. Brush had despised Ban Johnson since their days in Cincinnati when Brush owned the Reds and Johnson was a young newspaperman. The McGraw-Johnson bitterness stemmed from the manager's defection as pilot of the Baltimore Orioles in 1902 to accept the Giants' managerial job.

The Brush-McGraw dislike for Johnson was intensified in 1903 when Johnson placed an American League franchise in New York, ignoring the Giants' territorial rights.

"Why should we play the upstarts, or any other American League club?" thundered McGraw. "When we won the National League pennant, we became champions of the only real major league."

Brush was just as hostile. In an open letter, the owner asserted there was no reason why "the dignity of the pennant of the National League" should be "cheapened and jeopardized" by playing a series with the best club of "a minor league."

One year later, conditions were altered greatly. Brush underwent a change of heart and authored a set of rules for the playing of a world championship series. They quickly were adopted by both leagues.

Ironically, the Giants figured in the first World Series played under the sanction of the National Commission, baseball's governing triumvirate. Brush and McGraw could not have written a better Series script. The Giants defeated the A's in five games and each game was a shutout (three by Christy Mathewson and one by Joe McGinnity for the winners, and one by Chief Bender for the losers).

Another phenomenon occurred in 1905. The American League became the battleground for an 18-year-old Georgian who, by sheer will and flaming spirit, emerged as the game's most redoubtable performer over the next 20 years.

Ty Cobb, driven by an unquenchable thirst for success, won the first of his 12 batting titles in 1907, the same year he sparked the Detroit Tigers to the first of three consecutive pennants. Three times the Georgia Peach batted more than .400, but it was a lesser average in 1910 that ignited the frothiest controversy.

Confident that his league-leading mark would secure a fourth successive batting crown, Cobb sat out the final day of the season. He gave little thought to Cleveland's Nap Lajoie, who went on a rampage in a doubleheader at St. Louis. Aided by a curious bit of strategy in which Red Corriden, rookie third baseman of the Browns, played abnormally deep, Lajoie beat out seven bunts and also hit a triple.

There were instant charges and indignation. It was a poorly disguised attempt, said critics, to help the popular Lajoie win a batting title over the unpopular Cobb.

St. Louis management demurred. The Browns insisted that the inexperienced Corriden was instructed to take the irregular position rather than risk decapitation by a line drive off the bat of the powerful right-handed pull hitter.

Ban Johnson settled the issue a week later. After a thorough investigation, the league president announced that Cobb's average was .385, one point above Lajoie.

Cobb was in his third major league season (1907) when he first faced a tall, rawboned righthander whose talents were as remarkable as his own.

Walter Johnson was only 19 years old and fresh out of a semipro league in Idaho when he delivered his first blinding fastball to an American League batter. But the Big Train of the Washington Senators soon was terrorizing opponents with a sidearm delivery that earned him quick recognition as a strikeout king.

Sir Walter was never more brilliant than during a four-day span in 1908. Still shy of his 21st birthday, Johnson shut out the Highlanders three times during a series in New York. Some maintained that Johnson might have done even better if the third day was not a Sabbath, on which no professional sports were permitted in the state.

Johnson's remarkable pitching was not the most memorable event of the 1908 season, however. It was overshadowed by the repercussions of a player's failure to touch second base in a game at New York's Polo Grounds.

Fred Merkle had been signed in 1907 by Brush on the recommendation of a barber when the Giants owner was in Mt. Clemens, Mich., for a health cure. Merkle was the backup first baseman for the Giants on the historic afternoon when he gained everlasting notoriety for doing only what other players had done for years.

The Giants and Cubs, embroiled in a torrid pennant race, were deadlocked 1-1 in the ninth inning of that September 23 game. There were two outs, with New York's Moose McCormick the runner at third base and Merkle at first, when baseball's most controversial play erupted.

On Al Bridwell's single to center field, McCormick raced home with the apparent winning run. However, Merkle, as hundreds had done before him, dashed for the center-field clubhouse rather than fight off the jubilant spectators pouring onto the field.

But, as it turned out, the game was not over. The Giants had not won. At the middle of the diamond, Cubs second baseman Johnny Evers was calling for the baseball. He had detected Merkle's dereliction and, from a source never clearly determined, Evers obtained a ball and stepped on second base. He turned to umpire Hank O'Day. Yes, said the umpire, Merkle was out. By now, the spectators were thronging the field. There was no possibility of continuing play. Confusion reigned for hours, the Giants claiming victory, the Cubs insisting the game was a tie.

Eventually, the league directors decided the game was a tie. If the teams were deadlocked at the end of the 154-game schedule, they ruled, the game would have to be replayed.

The Giants' worst fears were realized. The teams were deadlocked with 98 victories, 55 losses and one tie at the close of the regular season. Once more the teams of John McGraw and Frank Chance squared off. The game was played at the Polo Grounds and attracted so large a crowd that the gates were closed an hour before the first pitch while thousands of other fans watched from bluffs surrounding the park.

The replay went without incident. Christy Mathewson started for the Giants and was staked to a 1-0 lead in the first inning. In the third inning, however, Matty's old nemesis, Joe Tinker, hit a triple to highlight a four-run outburst. That was all the Cubs needed. They went on to win 4-2 behind Mordecai Brown.

In their third World Series, following their stunning upset by the "Hitless Wonder" White Sox in 1906 and their victory over the Detroit Tigers in 1907, the Cubs again whipped the Bengals, four games to one, with Evers, who was chiefly responsible for getting them into the Series, batting .350 and scoring five runs.

For years, Merkle, a highly intelligent player, carried the undeserved stigma of "Bonehead." He was never criticized by McGraw for doing only what others had done before him and remained with the Giants through 1916, after which he played in the majors for another decade.

Repercussions of the Merkle incident did not cease after the close of the season. Rumors that umpire Bill Klem was offered nearly $3,000 to influence the outcome of the playoff game persisted into the off-season. At the National League's annual meeting in December, Klem testified that a physician, Dr. Joseph M. Creamer, had waved a sheaf of bills before his eyes and said, "It's yours if you will give all the close decisions to the Giants and see that they win. You know who's behind me (allegedly the Giant players) and you needn't be afraid. You will have a good job for life."

Dr. Creamer, a well-known figure in New York sporting circles who had a lucrative private practice, asserted that he had never spoken to Klem in his life. President Harry Pulliam and his directors, however, believed Klem. Dr. Creamer was barred from major league parks for life.

The Merkle decision also had a profound effect on Pulliam. Harassed constantly for the anti-Giant verdict and broken in health, he took a leave of absence from the league presidency. He returned to his office after the 1909 season was several weeks old, but on a July night returned to his room at the New York Athletic Club and put a bullet through his brain.

Despite the crushing blow of 1908, the early 1900s belonged to McGraw. In midseason of 1902, the Little Napoleon secured his release as manager of the Baltimore Orioles by paying $7,000 of the club debts from his own pocket. He took charge of the Giants and quickly released 17 of the 29 players on the roster. "I can finish last with 12 players as well as with 29," he explained before proceeding to prove his point.

With players acquired through the liberal funds of new Owner Brush, McGraw won pennants in 1904 and 1905. He did not win another flag until 1911, when the Giants opposed the Philadelphia A's in the World Series. This time the Athletics, humbled by the Giants in 1905, returned the favor, winning in six games as John Franklin Baker batted .375 and earned lasting fame as Home Run Baker by belting two round-trippers, one off Christy Mathewson, McGraw's 26-game winner, and another off Rube Marquard, who had won 24 games.

The Giants repeated as pennant winners in 1912 and were within a few pitches of the world championship when they were struck by another misfortune, second only to the calamity of 1908.

The Giants led the Red Sox, 2-1, in the last of the 10th inning with Mathewson pitching effectively. There appeared no cause for alarm when Clyde Engle led off the last of the 10th with a routine fly to center field. But Fred Snodgrass dropped the ball in what soon became known as "the $30,000 Muff." Snodgrass made a spectacular catch of the next batter's fly, but a walk to Steve Yerkes put a second runner on base with one out. That's when future Hall of Famer Tris Speaker lifted a simple pop foul between home plate and first base as Boston prospects took on an even darker hue. But catcher Chief Meyers and first baseman Merkle let the ball fall untouched.

Reprieved, Speaker singled to drive home the tying run. And when Larry Gardner hit a sacrifice fly to right field, Yerkes pranced home with the decisive run.

McGraw tried to win his second world championship once more in 1913, but again Connie Mack's A's blocked his path. Although Baker did not hit a home run, the third baseman collected nine hits for a .450 average and drove in seven runs as Philadelphia won in five games.

The A's were a dominant factor in the American League for most of the years in the early 1900s and when the N.L. reeled off consecutive world titles from 1907-09, Ban Johnson looked to the A's to restore pride and respectability to his league in 1910. The A's whipped the Cubs in five games and a year later, behind a "$100,000 Infield" that featured Stuffy McInnis, Eddie Collins, Jack Barry and Baker, the A's defeated the Giants in six games.

Mack's most powerful team in the 1910-14 period, he always insisted, was the 1912 aggregation that, lacking incentive after two world championships in a row, finished third. Of the A's 90 victories that year, none could match their winning effort on May 18 at Shibe Park.

Three days earlier in New York, Ty Cobb had vaulted into the stands to pummel a loud-mouthed heckler. Cobb was suspended instantly by Ban Johnson. The next day was an open date. But when the Tigers arrived in Philadelphia, they held a meeting and voted to strike on Saturday if Cobb's suspension were not lifted. A telegram containing the signature of each Detroit player was sent to Chicago informing Johnson of the action.

At the same time, Manager Hugh Jennings advised Owner Frank Navin of developments. Realizing that the Tigers would be liable for a $5,000 fine each day the club did not field a team for a scheduled game, Navin instructed his manager to sign semipros from the Philadelphia area to represent the Tigers on May 18.

Jennings and his coaches scoured the city for talent. The pitcher they selected was Aloysius Travers, a student at St. Joseph's College and later a Jesuit priest. Travers was offered $25 and a like sum if he pitched the entire game. The other players were promised $10 apiece.

Philadelphia's Shibe Park was a fine modern facility when the Athletics

Travers went the distance. He yielded 26 hits, four each by Stuffy McInnis and Amos Strunk and five by Eddie Collins, who also stole five bases. The A's walloped the pseudo-Tigers, 24-2.

As Johnson hopped a Philadelphia-bound train in Chicago, Navin issued a statement in Detroit that revealed, "I am heart and soul in sympathy with the strikers. As a matter of business I had to see to it that there were strike-breakers to take the place of players who walked out or make myself liable for a fine of $5,000 for every day the Tigers failed to appear. I do think that there were wiser ways, however, of settling

and Boston Red Sox played the first game at the stadium in 1909.

the matter than to strike."

Because of the state blue law, there was no Sunday game in Philadelphia and Johnson cancelled the Monday contest. In the interim, he summoned the striking players to his hotel suite where he threatened them with a lifetime suspension from baseball if they persisted in the strike. The threat was not immediately effective. The last resistance did not vanish until Cobb himself urged the players to return to the job.

Each player whose name appeared on the wire to Johnson was fined $100. Cobb was fined $50. His suspension was lifted after 10 days.

Forward March

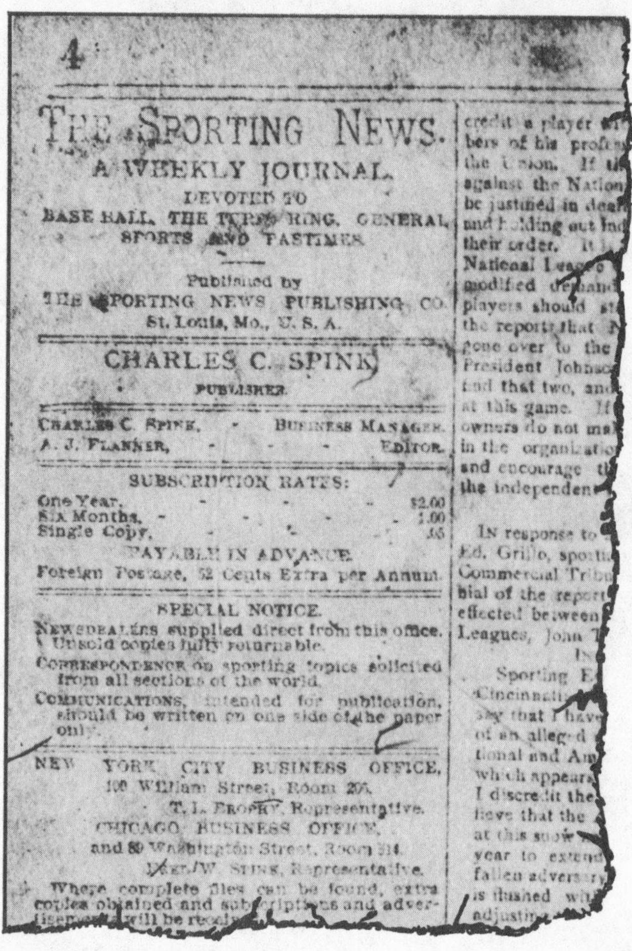

4

THE SPORTING NEWS.

A WEEKLY JOURNAL

DEVOTED TO

BASE BALL, THE TURF, RING, GENERAL SPORTS AND PASTIMES.

Published by

THE SPORTING NEWS PUBLISHING CO.

St. Louis, Mo., U. S. A.

CHARLES C. SPINK

PUBLISHER.

CHARLES C. SPINK, - BUSINESS MANAGER.

A. J. FLANNER, - - - EDITOR.

SUBSCRIPTION RATES:

One Year,	$2.00
Six Months,	1.00
Single Copy,	.05

PAYABLE IN ADVANCE.

Foreign Postage, 52 Cents Extra per Annum.

SPECIAL NOTICE.

NEWSDEALERS supplied direct from this office. Unsold copies fully returnable.

CORRESPONDENCE on sporting topics solicited from all sections of the world.

COMMUNICATIONS, intended for publication, should be written on one side of the paper only.

NEW YORK CITY BUSINESS OFFICE, 100 William Street, Room 205. T. L. BROPHY, Representative.

CHICAGO BUSINESS OFFICE, and 80 Washington Street, Room 314. FRED W. SPINK, Representative.

Where complete files can be found, extra copies obtained and subscriptions and advertisements will be received.

Editorial-page mastheads in the early 1900s were a font of information for correspondents, advertisers and interested readers.

As baseball matured into the national pastime at the start of the 20th Century, The Sporting News strode manfully forward as Charles C. Spink, now in complete command, labored diligently to increase circulation and improve the quality of the paper's contents.

While baseball remained the dominant sport in the five-cent weekly, it was forced to share space with, as the publication's motto noted, "The Turf, Ring and General Pastimes."

The paper solicited "correspondence on sporting topics . . . from all sections of the world," but cautioned would-be contributors that "communications intended for publication should be written on one side of the paper only."

An editorial-page disclaimer advised advertisers that they could not be guaranteed a specific position in the paper and that rates are "for the run of the paper, irrespective of page or location."

In 1901, The Sporting News maintained two business offices outside St. Louis—one in New York and a second in Chicago, where Fred W. Spink, Charles' oldest brother, served as representative.

Charles Spink listed himself as business manager on the editorial-page masthead, while the editor was Joe Flanner, a North Carolinian who had practiced law in the Dakotas before settling in St. Louis, where he had worked earlier as the sports editor of the Post-Dispatch.

Flanner, "quiet, unassuming and enthusiastic," was highly regarded in the baseball fraternity, both for his writing style and for his firm grasp of all aspects of baseball.

Flanner made his most notable contribution to the game and to The Sporting News in 1903. After a truce had been called to end the war between the established National League and the fledgling American League, Flanner and two other nationally recognized writers, B.J. Gaskill of the Cincinnati Post and Frank Patterson of the Baltimore Sun, were directed to draft a national agreement to govern all clubs in professional baseball.

Type for the compact was set in the composing room of The Sporting News, after which the finished product was forwarded to Buffalo, N.Y., where the major league magnates were in conference. The agreement was adopted without change.

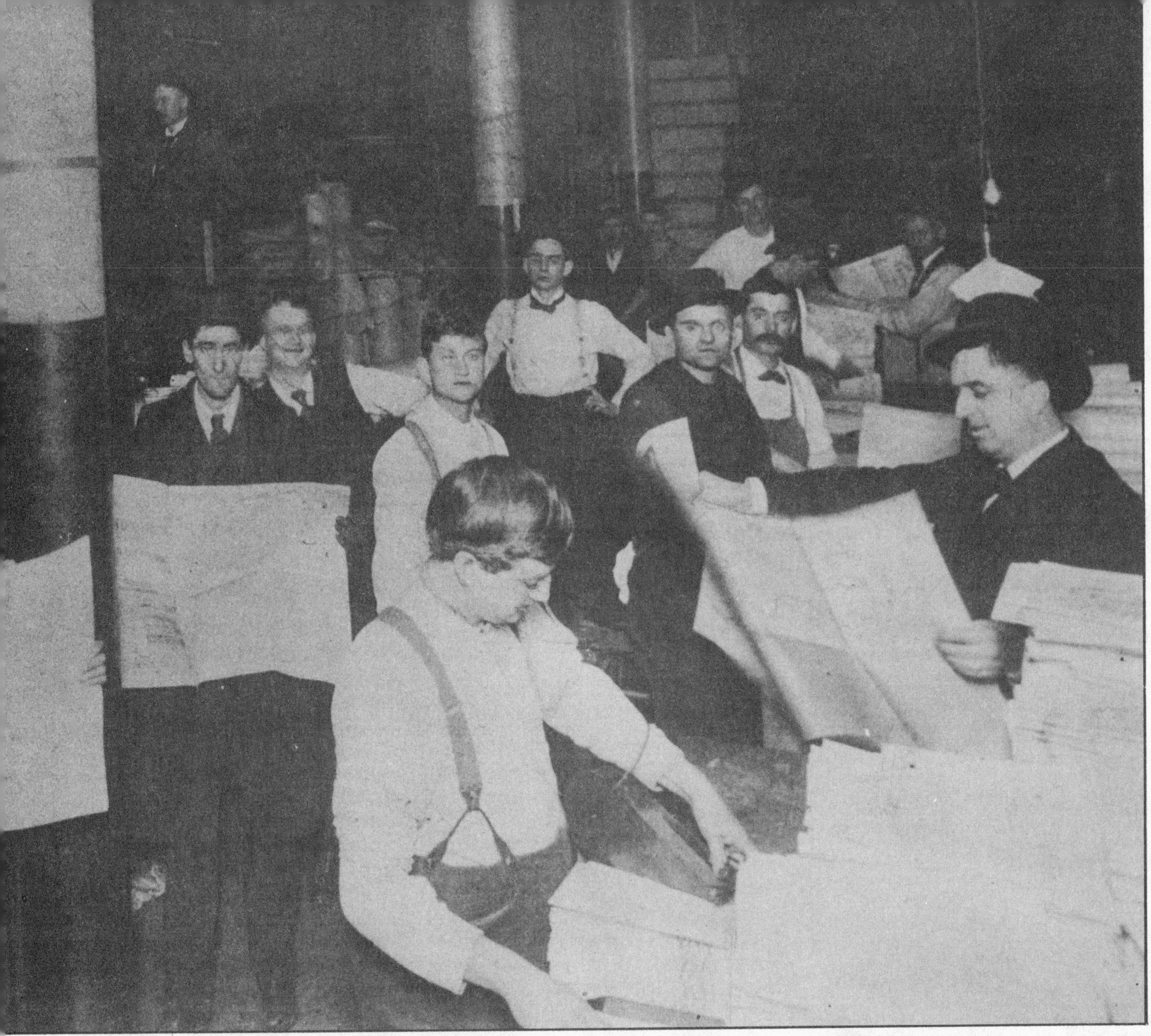

Charles C. Spink (above right), publisher of The Sporting News by the early 1900s, peruses an issue fresh off the press. TSN Editor Joe Flanner (below, second from left) helped draft the 1903 national agreement that governed all clubs in professional baseball.

begin negotiations for the Cincinnati Club, when notified that Brush will entertain a proposition.

Among the many flattering press notices of Reach's American League Guide for 1902 is the following:

"A copy of the American League Guide, published by the A. J. Reach Company, of Philadelphia, has just come to hand, this being the first guide in the field this spring. The book is a revelation in the way of base ball guides, and a credit to the American League. For an official handbook, it is far ahead of anything of the kind yet published, and throughout shows the *literary taste* and *skill* of the editor, Mr. Francis C. Richter, of Sporting Life. The book gives a complete review of the American League's first season as a major league, *exhaustive records* and averages of the American League race and players, portraits and sketches of President Ban Johnson and the various club presidents and group pictures of the various American League teams; in short, everything pertaining to the American League is fully and correctly covered. Much space is given to *chronological reviews* of 1901 *happenings* and to a complete roster for 1902. A review of the National League race and the complete averages of the players of that organization are furnished. As there is nothing omitted or overlooked in the entire base ball field, the Reach American League Guide is necessarily a complete and indispensable handbook of the national game."

The "literary taste and skill" of Editor Richter led him to filch the series of statistical letters written for The Sporting News by Ernest J. Lanigan and incorporate them bodily in the Guide, which the sporting writers have pronounced the best that the A. J. Reach Company ever issued. The chronological review, with the exception of the last two memoranda, was stolen, word for word, from the Philadelphia Record, of December 30, 1901. The matter pirated from the Record starts on page 10 and runs to page 14. The attendance figures of the American and National League clubs, covering five pages, were compiled by Mr. Lanigan. From page 77 to page 113, the Reach Guide is a reproduction of the Lanigan articles in The Sporting News of last winter. The extra-hit records of American League clubs and players, individual batting feats, total hits by teams, big-score games and innings, club batting performances and the pitchers who suffered, noteworthy incidents chronologically recorded, base running of teams and individuals, club and individual sacrifice hit statistics, the most exhaustive analysis of the work of pitchers ever published, shut out statistics, remarkable ninth-inning finishes, games lost and won by a single run, extra-inning games with date, result and pitchers, number of players signed, released and retained, have been appropriated without alteration. The first installment of Mr. Lanigan's review of the National League race, as complete and instructive as his wonderful analysis of the American League contests, as outlined above, covers 21 pages, commencing with page 138 and stopping on page 158. On page 78, there is this reference to the another of the "cribbed" statistics: "The complete long-distance record of the clubs and teams of the American League, as compiled by Mr. Ernest J. Lanigan, is appended." On page 101 is this paragraph: "Following is a review of some of the more important or remarkable incidents of the American League 1901 race, as gleaned from an exhaustive review compiled by Ernest J. Lanigan, the well known Montreal statistician." No credit is given to The Sporting News, for which the articles were specially prepared. Richter's wholesale pilfering is a compliment to The Sporting News and con-

A 'Revelation'

When the 1902 Reach Guide was published and Francis C. Richter, the book's editor, received praise for his effort, TSN loaded its editorial guns (left) and blasted Richter as a dishonorable plagiarist.

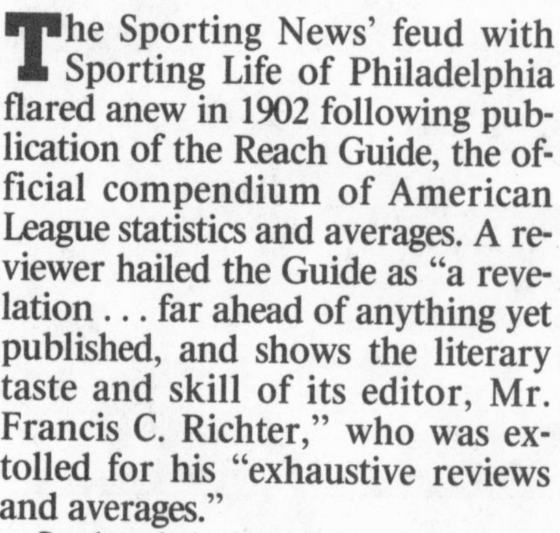

Much of the material contained in the 1902 Reach Guide, TSN claimed, was really the work of Ernest J. Lanigan, one of the all-time great baseball statisticians. Lanigan is pictured (right) near the end of his career.

The Sporting News' feud with Sporting Life of Philadelphia flared anew in 1902 following publication of the Reach Guide, the official compendium of American League statistics and averages. A reviewer hailed the Guide as "a revelation . . . far ahead of anything yet published, and shows the literary taste and skill of its editor, Mr. Francis C. Richter," who was extolled for his "exhaustive reviews and averages."

Such adulation for a rival was more than the Spink-Flanner forces could stomach. Although the Reach Company was a major advertiser in the St. Louis journal, it could not escape censure from the editor's facile pen. Flanner wrote:

"The literary taste and skill of Mr. Richter led him to filch the series of statistical articles written for The Sporting News by Ernest J. Lanigan and incorporate them bodily in the Guide which the sporting writers have pronounced the best that the A.J. Reach Company has ever issued. The chronicled review, with the exception of the last two memoranda, was stolen word for word from the Philadelphia Record of December 30, 1901. The American and National League attendance figures were compiled by Mr. Lanigan. From page 77 to page 113 is a reproduction of the Lanigan articles in The Sporting News last winter. The extra-base hits of American League clubs and players' individual batting feats, total hits by teams, big-score games and innings, club batting performances and the pitchers who suffered, noteworthy incidents chronology, base-running by teams and individuals, etc., etc., etc.

"Richter's wholesale pilfering is a compliment to The Sporting News for which the articles were specially prepared and the specialty of a statistician. The patrons of this paper were not obliged to wait until the start of the season for facts and figures of interest and importance about the 1901 season. Mr. Lanigan presented them in his letter.

The baseball public profited by the injustice done to him (Lanigan) and The Sporting News by the 'fictionalized' matter. The publishers are in no way responsible for the unprofessional and dishonorable practices of the editor with 'literary taste and skill.' He has been paid for the product of Mr. Lanigan's brain and the property of The Sporting News."

To prevent plagiarism in subsequent years, The Sporting News frequently copyrighted articles by Lanigan.

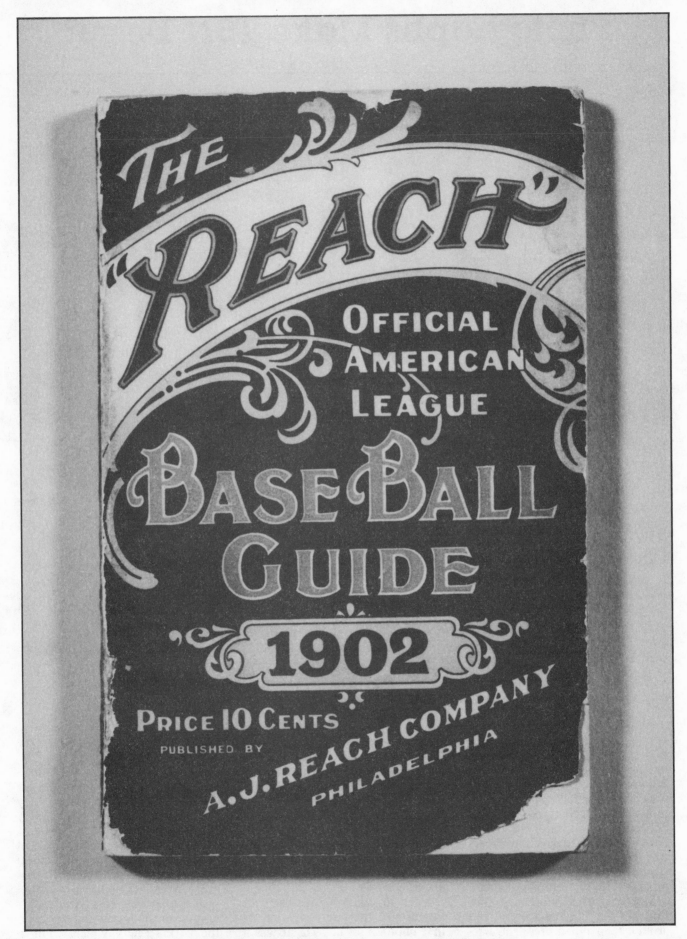

The 1902 Reach Guide carried a price tag of 10 cents.

Photographs Make TSN Debut

This team picture of the American League-champion Philadelphia Athletics appeared in a 1902 supplement to The Sporting News.

In its unrelenting efforts to boost circulation, The Sporting News, in October 1902, offered its readers a bonus in the form of "a handsome, full-page half tone of the famous Pittsburgh team, the 1902 champions of the National League." The likeness of the players was described as so realistic that "those who have seen them several times will know them at a glance."

Moreover, the inducement continued, "The players are grouped around their noted president, Barney Dreyfuss, famed wherever the game is played as a sportsman who takes more pride in the performances of his players than in the enjoyment of the profits which they make for him."

For many years thereafter, photographs of championship teams, prominent executives, managers and players were regular off-season offerings on the pages of The Sporting News.

After 16 years of line-sketch illustrations, the paper printed its first photograph in 1902. It was a picture of Charles Harper, who had signed a Cincinnati contract for 1903.

The next issue contained a four-column picture captioned "Browns' Trio of Bagmen." They were infielders Dick Padden, Barry McCormick and John Anderson.

Pictures became a regular part of the paper thereafter and off-season issues were brightened almost every week with photos of championship teams, from the major leagues to the lowest minors, with the players generally pictured in civilian clothes.

In the early days of The Sporting News, illustrative material appeared as line sketches. That changed in 1902, however, when TSN published its first halftone, a picture of pitcher Charles Harper (above), on its front page. The next issue contained a four-column picture of three Browns players (right) and photographs were used freely from that point on. In October 1902, TSN published a full-page halftone of the Pittsburgh team, with Owner Barney Dreyfuss (above right) as the picture's centerpiece.

The Whipping Boys

Brush's refusal to permit his team to play a World's series with the Champions of the World's team has been condemned in the base ball department of every paper of prominence in the major league circuits and editorially in many of them. As between the major leagues, there is more or less partisans in the representatives of the press, but this question is not one which concerns leagues or individuals, but the base ball public. There is a public demand for a world's series and the owner of one club stands between the game's patrons and their wishes. The thousands who would attend these contests are not more interested than the enthusiasts of the South, the middle West and other sections of the country. The public which supports base ball insists that after the pennant race of each major league has been decided, that the respective winners engage in a series that will determine which is the champion of all champions. The contention that a minor league has a right to recognition is quibbling. Professional base ball is divided into classes—the major and minor leagues and the latter have their classifications. A challenge from Britt or Gans to Jeffries would not affect the latter's title to the championship in pugilism any more than a challenge from the cham-

Two of TSN's favorite editorial whipping boys were New York Giants Owner John T. Brush (left in automobile) and Giants Manager John McGraw (standing). The editorial (above left) takes issue with Brush's refusal to let his National League-champion Giants meet American League-champion Boston in a 1904 World Series. By 1920, McGraw (above) was accustomed to seeing his name dragged disparagingly across the pages of The Sporting News.

6 THE SPORTING NEWS.

"WE ARE CONTENT TO REST ON OUR LAURELS." —JOHN T. BRUSH

CAUGHT ON THE FLY.

CLAIMED BY CLUBS.

MINOR LEAGUE RESERVE LISTS FOR NEXT SEASON.

When John T. Brush refused to let his Giants play Boston in a 1904 World Series, a TSN cartoon showed Boston Manager Jimmy Collins peering over the Polo Grounds fence as Brush attempted to hide.

In the rough-and-tumble days of baseball's infancy, when fear of libel and slander suits was nonexistant, The Sporting News quickly held up to public censure those who strayed from the paths of righteousness.

Two of its favorite whipping boys were John J. McGraw, the brawly manager of the New York Giants, and the club's owner, John T. Brush, sometimes disparaged as "Tooth Brush" or "Dust Brush."

When McGraw resigned as manager of the Baltimore Orioles halfway through the 1902 season to become pilot of the Giants, he was denounced widely as a traitor. A headline in The Sporting News shouted: "In Deep Disgrace / Muggsy McGraw Must Get Out of Baseball."

The headline was designed to provoke unbridled fury in the volatile McGraw. The nickname Muggsy, which he detested, was a holdover from the 1890s when McGraw was the belligerent and brainy third baseman of the old Orioles.

Nor did Spink hesitate to publish a page 1 item in the spring of 1904 that reported McGraw's arrest in Hot Springs, Ark., along with two associates for "pitching silver dollars at a small basket from a distance of 20 feet" in the lobby of a hotel.

"Last week," the article continued, "in the Arlington Hotel ballroom, McGraw, C.T. Buckley and a third party named Duffy won $2,500 from a stranger at the same game, Buckley proving himself almost perfect at the game just introduced here."

Later in 1904, McGraw and Brush fell into public disfavor for their refusal to accept a challenge by the Boston Red Sox for the two pennant winners to meet in a postseason tournament that would determine the world championship. The previous year the Red Sox and Pittsburgh Pirates engaged in a similar tournament that proved popular and resulted in a victory for Boston in the first modern World Series.

The New York officials, however, refused to buckle under public pressure. To them, the American League still was a minor circuit. A cartoon in The Sporting News depicted the Giants' unpopular position. It showed Jimmy Collins, Boston manager, peering over the fence at the Polo Grounds while Brush hid under home plate.

ATTENTION, CORRESPONDENTS.

Early copy is at a premium at all times, but especially at this season. There is a marked revival of interest in the game throughout the country and so many contributions are received each week that some of them are crowded out of the issue for which they are intended. Such a mass of matter comes to this office on Wednesday that it is impossible to use it all, and as every one who has had experience in a weekly paper realizes, it is out of the question to sacrifice letters already in type. Correspondents can greatly aid in preventing this congested condition by sending in copy at least one or two days earlier, instead of mailing it so that it reaches St. Louis on Wednesday.

THE National Agreement provides that the Board of Arbitration may release a player from reservation "when the reserving club has failed to tender to him on or before the first day of March after such reservation, a formal contract." This applies only to minor league players. As there is no such clause in the National League constitution, this formality is not requisite. The National League magnates claim that the option clause enables them to renew contracts with their players by a simple notification of acceptance of their services for another year. Litigation is certain to result over this question.

Editorial-page notices alerted correspondents to any changes in procedure.

Correspondents Had To Be Alert

In the early 1900s, communications between the editor of The Sporting News and his correspondents were conducted through the columns of the editorial page rather than by direct mail.

Whenever changes were in prospect, notice was published on page 4 in the hope that correspondents were sufficiently alert to note the message.

At the close of the 1904 campaign, journalists were advised that "restrictions upon space during the championship season have been removed and from this time until the beginning of the 1905 pennant races the only limit upon the length of articles will be their intrinsic worth."

Pointing out that the absence of box scores would create space for longer newsletters, the notice went on: "Interest in baseball does not die out during the winter months and industrious correspondents never complain of the scarcity of subjects for letters. Reviews of the last race and forecasts of the next, changes in circuits and passing of veteran players and the coming of new candidates for public favor, the best points and weaknesses of individuals and numberless topics make interesting and imaginative reading for the enthusiasts of the game.

"Fidelity and industry during the off-season will be taken into consideration when credentials for the 1905 season are issued."

At the height of the baseball season, it was not uncommon for TSN to publish box scores of as many as 15 leagues, including the majors. In addition to a reduction in the length of newsletters during the summer months, the pages were expanded from seven to eight columns while the size of the paper remained at eight pages.

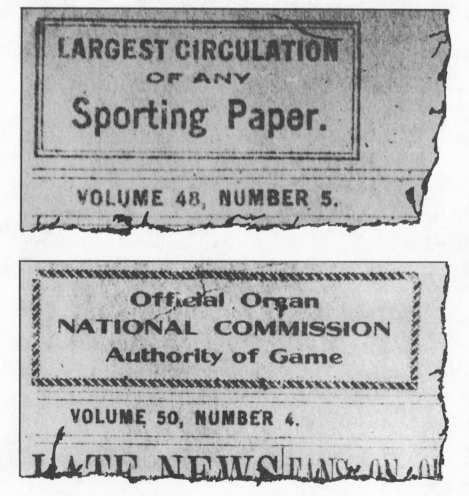

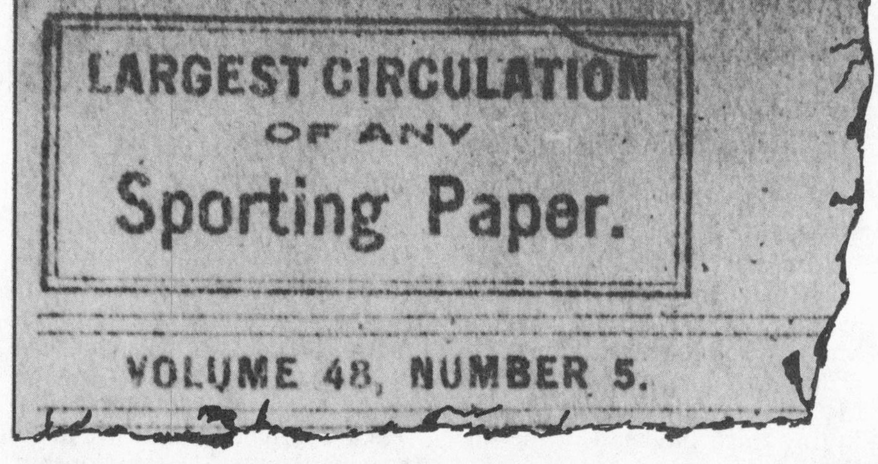

In 1909, The Sporting News bragged in the upper left corner of Page 1 (above left) that it had the 'Largest Circulation of any Sporting Paper.' One year later, however, the publication's emphasis on its role in baseball was evident (below left).

Official Organ
NATIONAL COMMISSION
Authority of Game

VOLUME 50, NUMBER 4.

LATE NEWS

Space for news and feature material was dictated for many years by the presence or absence of baseball box scores (right), depending on the time of the year.

FRAYER-MILLER AUTOMOBILES.

Cooled by Air.
A Forced Draught from Blower.

Distinctively American.
Not a Copy of a Foreign Car.
WE MAUFACTURE PLEASURE and COMMERCIAL CARS.

Frayer-Miller Combination Runabout and Touring Car. Rear Seat Removable.
This is the car which holds the American Records for economy in gasoline and oil, because the cooling is more effective than water cooling. Will be glad to tell you why, if you will write us.

The OSCAR LEAR AUTOMOBILE CO., 1512 Sheridan Ave., Springfield, Ohio.

DIRECTORY OF NATIONAL ASSOCIATION.

EASTERN LEAGUE.

Club.	President.	Manager.
Buffalo	A. E. Foster	Geo. T. Smith
Baltimore	Edw. Hanlon	John Dunn
Jersey City	Ellis Davis	Eugene McCann
Newark	G. T. Stallings	G. T. Stallings
Providence	T. J. Cremlen	Hugh Duffy
Rochester	C. T. Chapin	Edward Kelly
Montreal	Clarence Keith	James Casey
Toronto	J. J. McCaffery	J. J. Kelley

SOUTHERN LEAGUE.

Club.	President.	Manager.
Atlanta	J. W. Heisman	W. A. Smith
Birmingham	R. H. Baugh	Chas. Molesworth
Little Rock	R. C. Hatter	M. J. Finn
Memphis	Frank P. Coleman	Chas. Babb
Mobile	Dr. H. T. Inge	T. C. Fisher
Montgomery	R. J. Chambers	Jas. Ryan
New Orleans	[illegible]	Chas. Frank
Nashville	F. E. Kuhn	Wm. Bernhart

NORTHWESTERN LEAGUE.

Club.	President.	Manager.
Aberdeen	W. H. Macfarlane	R. P. Brown
Butte	R. H. Hall	R. H. Hall
Seattle	D. E. Dugdale	D. E. Dugdale
Spokane	C. H. Wolf	J. E. Quinn
Tacoma	G. M. Shreeder	G. M. Shreeder
Vancouver	A. R. Dickson	A. R. Dickson

I.-I.-I. LEAGUE.

Club.	President.	Manager.
Springfield	R. F. Kinsella	J. McCarthy
Decatur	Dr. W. Chenoweth	G. Reed
Bloomington	C. E. Miller	Wm. Conners
Peoria	C. F. Bartson	Frank Donnelly
Rock Island	W. A. Rosenfield	Louis Cook
Clinton	F. E. Crafts	Chas. Buelow
Cedar Rapids	C. H. Smith	Belden Hill
Dubuque	J. Murphy	Clarence Lowland

TRI-STATE LEAGUE.

Club.	President.	Manager.
Altoona	P. L. Morrison	John S. Farrell
Harrisburg	W. Harry Baker	G. W. Heckert
Johnstown	G. E. Kline	E. O. Arbenbact
Lancaster	Frank H. Trost	Clarence Foster
Reading	J. L. Weitzel	Curt. Weigand
Trenton	Lewis Perrine	Jas. J. Carney
Williamsport	F. C. Dawson	H. S. Wolverton
Wilmington	F. P. Bennett	John A. O'Rourke

AMERICAN ASSOCIATION.

Club.	President.	Manager.
Columbus	E. M. Schoenborn	Wm. J. Clymer
Toledo	W. R. Armour	W. R. Armour
Indianapolis	W. H. Watkins	Chas. C. Carr
Louisville	Thos. A. Parker	Jas. T. Burke
Milwaukee	C. S. Havenor	H. McCormick
Kansas City	George Tebeau	Monte Cross
St. Paul	Geo. E. Lennon	Tim. Flood
Minneapolis	M. E. Cantillon	M. E. Cantillon

PACIFIC COAST LEAGUE.

Club.	President.	Manager.
San Francisco	F. M. Ish	D. W. Long
Oakland	Ed. N. Walter	G. Van Haltren
Los Angeles	W. H. Berry	W. H. Berry
Portland	Judge McCredie	W. H. McCredie

NEW YORK STATE LEAGUE.

Club.	President.	Manager.
Albany	C. Winchester, Jr.	M. Doherty
Troy	W. H. Kabbett	J. J. O'Brien
Utica	H. W. Roberts	C. L. Dooley
Syracuse	Geo. N. Kuntzsch	T. C. Griffin
Binghamton	J. H. Mooney	M. S. Rosen
Scranton	E. J. Coleman	M. Kittredge
Wilkes-Barre	J. S. Monks	Bob Drury
Elmira		Henry Ramsey

SOUTH ATLANTIC LEAGUE.

Club.	President.	Manager.
Augusta	A. H. DeVaughan	Henry Busch
Charleston	J. Alwyn Ball	Pat Meaney
Columbia	W. W. Abbott	Win Clark
Jacksonville	W. C. West	D. J. Mullaney
Macon	W. L. Starr	W. M. Murdoch
Savannah	J. F. Sullivan	Walter Morris

VIRGINIA LEAGUE.

Club.	President.	Manager.
Danville	J. O. Boatright	Robt. Stafford
Lynchburg	Dr. J. A. Anderson	J. A. Westlake
Norfolk	Otto Wells	Robt. Pender
Portsmouth	C. T. Bland	Steve Griffin
Roanoke	Henry Schoen	Chas. Shaffer
Richmond	W. B. Bradley	Perry Lipe

TEXAS STATE LEAGUE.

Club.	President.	Manager.
San Antonio	Morris Block	Geo. C. Leidy
Austin	Del Walker	Wilson Matthews
Waco	W. R. Davidson	D. Cavender
Ft. Worth	W. H. Ward	Doc Curtis
Dallas	J. W. Gardner	J. J. Maloney
Galveston	M. O. Koppen	Frank Welkart
Houston	C. E. Reilly	C. A. McFarland
Shreveport	Capt. W. Crawford	Dale Gear

AMUSEMENTS

Havlin's.

The attraction at Havlin's Theater the week commencing Sunday matinee, September 6, will be one of last season's big successes, "Panhandle Pete," and judging from the advance sale of seats it is quite safe to predict that it will be a record-breaker again this season. The play has been entirely rewritten since its presentation last season and is said to have been improved in many ways. The company is headed by Walter Wilson, the talented and well known comedian, who is supported by a strong company of 15 principals and a chorus of 20.

The next attraction at Havlin's Theater will be one of last year's great hits, the big production of "Shadowed by Three." This play will be presented by a company of 25 players.

Standard.

A trained wolf is one of the novelties of the vaudeville bill at the Standard this week. The animal is exploited by Howard and Linder in a musical comedy sketch.

New Editorial Campaigns

Two of the all-time great managers, Connie Mack (left) and John McGraw (right), posed with Cardinals Manager Gabby Street in 1930. Both were former targets of TSN's blazing editorial guns.

The Sporting News editorial offices in the early 20th Century were vastly different from the sprawling, noisy offices that are associated with the newspapers of today.

The lead editorials during the early weeks of 1905 continued to appear as simple declarative sentences, such as:

"Character and conscience in a club owner are as desirable as capital."

And, "Suppress gambling in its game and you take temptation away from its players."

Before long, however, that style gave way to the conventional system that presented the most timely and important editorial at the top of the column.

Among the strongest editorials of the year was one that appeared during spring training after the Detroit Tigers had played a scoreless tie with a Class C club and the Red Sox were extended to 12 innings by another minor-league club before squeezing out a 1-0 victory.

It was time, said Joe Flanner, for a change in the pitching code. These games were just two of numerous examples, the editorial stressed, "that demonstrates the necessity for legislation against the pitcher. Something must be done to get the game out of the rut in which the spitball has placed it."

TSN relaxed its editorial campaign against player-Manager John McGraw (left) after his Giants had defeated Philadelphia in the 1905 Series. The guns instead were trained on Manager Connie Mack (below) and his A's for their inept Series play.

At the close of the season, The Sporting News relaxed its hostility toward John McGraw and John T. Brush. The Giants owner, reversing his posture of a year earlier in order to regain public esteem, authored a set of rules by which the majors' pennant-winning clubs would meet for the world title. He was rewarded instantly when his New York club defeated Philadelphia in five games, all of them shutouts.

"The Athletics' defeat was so decisive," said the lead editorial, "that their supporters have no excuse to offer. The Giants made the most of their opportunities while (Manager Connie) Mack's men frittered away chances for runs at critical stages. When a sacrifice was needed, a New York batsman made it artistically; when one of Mack's men had an opportunity to advance a runner, he failed miserably. One team played up-to-date ball in every inning of every game; the other resorted to tactics that have been discarded for years."

Brush was recognized in moderation. According to the editorial, he "received congratulations from ally and rival with undisguised pleasure, but nothing was said or done not in the spirit of sportsmanship and comity."

Baseball Reigns Supreme

The World's Sports All Found in the SPORTING NEWS. FIVE CENTS.

The Sporting News.

Largest Circulation OF ANY SPORTING PAPER.

VOLUME 42, NUMBER 6. ST. LOUIS, OCTOBER 20, 1906. SINGLE COPIES, 5 CENTS.

LATE NEWS.

MURPHY TO HAVE CONTROL.

TAFT TO SELL BLOCK OF STOCK.

WAGNER MAY BE PIRATES' MANAGER.

DESERVED TO WIN.

SUCCESS OF COMISKEY'S SOX POPULAR.

CHAMPION OF ALL CHAMPIONS.

COMISKEY'S PEERLESS WHITE SOX.

SOX HUMBLE CUBS.

WON BY BETTER PITCHING AND BATTING.

In October 1906, a five-column photo of Charles Comiskey's champion Chicago White Sox team brightened the cover of The Sporting News.

By 1906, all alien sports were gone from the pages of The Sporting News. All attention was focused on the diamond game in the "Weekly Journal Devoted to the Advancement of the Interests of Organized Baseball."

Eleven major league correspondents—only one in five two-club cities—were permitted to write on any popular topic as long as they devoted some lines to the hometown club, or clubs, at some point in their essays. As a result of such freedom, eight writers featured commentary on the 1906 World Series after the Hitless Wonder White Sox upset the powerful Cubs.

A five-column photo of the new champions brightened the cover while inside Joe Flanner leveled a new attack on gambling in baseball.

"The prominence given to gambling on the World Series is to be regretted," the editor wrote. "A great deal of money was wagered by members of the (Chicago) Board of Trade and by the sporting gentry throughout the country. Gambling on the game is a menace to its integrity and sporting writers should not encourage its practice by featuring wagers of large amounts."

As in the subject of their newsletter, writers were permitted wide latitude in their bylines at the end of the their stories. Some appended their names, such as Abe Yager, who always added "Of the Brooklyn Eagle." Others chose their initials while others chose to mask their identities with pseudonyms. For awhile, the Philadelphia correspondent was identified as "Veteran." In Boston, it was "Hi Hi" and "Rooter" covered baseball occurrences in Cincinnati.

Minor league correspondents were partial to aliases. The Harrisburg (Pa.) journalist signed his copy "Penny." "Bingo" wrote out of Binghamton, N.Y., "Mile High" out of Denver, "Snooty" out of Meridian, Miss., and "Wright Fielding" out of Burlington, Ia.

The above picture shows pressmen, mailers and other TSN employees hard at work in the early 1900s.

Spink and Flanner strutted editorially in 1909 when they announced that T. H. (Tim) Murnane, a famous pitcher-turned-scribe, and Thomas S. Rice had joined the corps of correspondents. The addition of Murnane, a Boston writer, was particularly significant, crowed the editorial, because Tim "has broken his heretofore inviolate rule not to correspond for a weekly journal, a breach which opens The Sporting News for congratulations."

With new talent, the editorial continued, "The Sporting News, for years acknowledgedly the best and brightest of baseball organs, intends to be better and brighter than before."

Rice, one of the more incisive and convincing writers of the period, served briefly as Washington correspondent and for many years as the paper's Brooklyn representative where he was baseball writer for the Eagle.

When The Sporting News added T.H. (Tim) Murnane (right) to its corps of correspondents in 1909, the publication strutted editorially.

Ads Were Varied, If Not Plentiful

Advertisements in The Sporting News during the first decade of the 1900s were varied, if not plentiful. Every week readers could count on learning who was appearing in what shows at the St. Louis theaters as well as the latest excursion rates of the Frisco and Mobile and Ohio Railroads to New Orleans or Texas.

When the Detroit Tigers won the 1907 pennant in the American League, the Coca-Cola Company exulted with a three-column announcement that "Detroit Wins With the Aid of Ty Cobb, Who Always Drinks Coca-Cola."

Cobb, of course, was a major investor in the soft drink company from which he derived the major portion of his wealth.

Other regular advertisers were Budweiser and the Reach and Spalding Sporting Goods Companies. When Gabby Street caught a ball dropped from the top of the Washington Monument, the Reach Company made good use of the accomplishment. A three-column ad reminded the public that:

"A Reach Mitt caught the ball dropped from the Washington Monument, a fall of over 500 feet. This feat was accomplished by Charley Street, catcher with the Washington American League club. This proves that Reach goods are built to wear, consequently."

Charles C. Spink registered a major breakthrough at this time when he obtained a full-page ad from the manufacturers of Fatima Cigarettes. "On receipt of 40 coupons," the ad promised, "we will send you a big photo of your favorite team, any team in the National or American League, enlarged from the original photograph."

Appended were directions on how to obtain the "15 by 21-inch photo mounted and ready for framing and without advertising."

Anheuser-Busch still was a regular advertiser in the early 1900s as railroads and local businesses continued to dominate the back page of each issue.

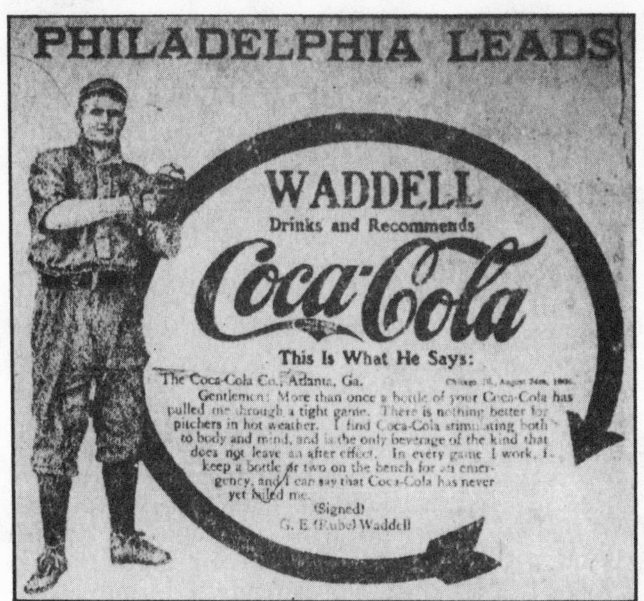

Coca-Cola relied on the endorsements of such baseball stars as Rube Waddell and Ty Cobb to sell its already popular soft drink.

The Reach Company capitalized when catcher Gabby Street used one of its gloves to catch a ball dropped from the Washington Monument in 1908. The Oscar Lear Company showed off the latest in horseless carriages in the same issue.

Spalding sought help from TSN readers the same year while seeking to increase its supply of wagon tongues, which were needed to produce bats. The bats, the ad states near the bottom, sold to baseball clubs for $1 apiece, $10 per dozen.

As the reputation of The Sporting News expanded through the early 1900s, so, too, did the Spink influence. An influential friend of Charles Spink was Charles A. Comiskey (above), owner of the Chicago White Sox.

The Spink Influence

As the reputation of The Sporting News expanded, baseball figures at home and abroad sought the advice and counsel of Publisher Charles C. Spink.

In 1911, a page 1 story revealed that Spink had sailed from New York aboard the Mauretania bound for London "where he will meet with a number of English sportsmen and confer with them as to the possibility of forming a six-club baseball league."

The article explained further that while baseball had been played in the British Isles for some time, the English sportsmen interested in organizing a league sought Spink's advice.

In the fall of 1912, Spink visited Australia. Originally, he had been scheduled to accompany a tour arranged by Cal Ewing, president of the Pacific Coast League. The junket was cancelled when Australian authorities could not guarantee the trip against financial loss, so Spink went at his own expense.

He discovered three leagues operating in Sydney and reported his findings in the January 16, 1913 issue of TSN. His bylined story bore the heading, "Australia a Fertile Field for Base Ball Development / Charles C. Spink Finds Game Flourishing Among Amateurs and Believes Visit of American Teams Would Start a Boom."

At another time, Spink accepted an invitation to go on a Mississippi River cruise as a guest of Charles A. Comiskey, owner of the White Sox. The friendship between the two had ripened in the years since the Old Roman was manager of the St. Louis Browns, four-time champions of the American Association, and Spink was a struggling young publisher in that city.

At a time when personal journalism was in full flower, Spink reported on the cruise in the following week's St. Louis newsletter. His account bore the headline: "Ashore or Afloat / Comiskey in Class by Himself as Host."

AUSTRALIA A FERTILE FIELD FOR BASE BALL DEVELOPMENT

Charles C. Spink Finds the Game Flourishing Among Amateurs and Believes Visit of American Teams Would Start a Boom.

THE ORDINARY Englishman may not care for our bally Yankee game, you known, but this Australian brother does and only awaits an American invasion to surrender all his other sports, cricket and the like, to the Only Game. So says Charles C. Spink, publisher of The Sporting News of St. Louis, who has recently returned from a sojourn in Australia with plenty of evidence secured first hand to convince him that some day the Island Continent is going to be just as enthusiastic over base ball as the United States of America is today. In fact he thinks the enthusiasm with which the "national game" has been accepted in Cuba, Japan, the Philippines or Honolulu will be mild compared to the boom that awaits it among the Australians.

Mr. Spink had gone to Australia prepared to return with a story that would not be encouraging to Charles A. Comiskey or any others who have been considering an Australian invasion. This was in part due to his disappointment in failure to find that the game had made any progress in England when he visited that tight little island of cricket and tea a year ago. He had pictured in his mind that the Australians were only transplanted Englishmen, anyway, and he was not very hopeful of them.

There was also the fact that the much advertised trip planned by J. Cal Ewing of the Pacific Coast League to Australia had been called off at the last minute because the Australians were unable to guarantee Mr. Ewing against financial loss. This failure, argued The Sporting News man, did not indicate that the Australians were keen to see a real exposition of the American game.

Cal Ewing had planned to take two teams to Australia, one made up of Coast League players, the other of players gathered from the major leagues. It fell through, however, because there was not sufficient time for the Australians interested to arrange for funds. Fifteen thousand dollars would have been necessary to guarantee the trip against financial loss, and the venture was suggested on such short notice that the Australians could not meet their part of the arrangement.

Found Australians Alive to Game.

Mr. Spink had agreed to make the trip with the Ewing party, had already arranged for his transportation, with passage engaged via the Oceanic Steamship Company, and he decided he would go anyway, even if alone, and see for himself just how the Australians were getting along with what President Eliot calls a greater civilizer than a shipload of missionaries—base ball. A few days in Sydney, the capital of New South Wales, convinced him that it was not lack of interest in "our" game that prevented carrying out arrangements for Ewing's invasion.

In fact Mr. Spink found Australia much alive base ballically and hungry for more of the game, standing with open arms, so to speak, to welcome Americans who [illegible]

the players on their good conduct. Evidently good conduct is regarded as essential and Mr. Spink got the impression that the Australian umpires, instead of being "robbers" and "crooks" as they are in America, are very highly regarded gentlemen and that the disputing of one of their decisions would be looked upon as an outrageous offense against clean sport.

Having been disappointed in the failure of the American "base ballerz" to visit them during the winter the Sydney fans were discussing during Mr. Spink's visit the arrangement of an "international" base ball tournament, in which the best teams that Sydney could put on the field should be matched against teams from the neighboring island of Tasmania and from Melbourne. Mr. Spink suggested that the proper "international" feature would be a series of games with Comiskey's White Sox or John McGraw's Giants and the Australians assured him that it was not lack of desire on their part that had prevented such a meeting. They were curious to know how he thought their game would compare with that of the Americans and while he could not give them any information, since their season had closed and he saw no games, yet he admits that from some of the husky "base ballers" he happened to meet, he was led to believe that if size is to count they might make Ed Walsh hustle.

Still Remember Anson's Visit.

Mr. Spink met Australians who still have a keen recollection of the visit paid them many years ago—in 1888—by Cap Anson's Chicago White Stockings and the All-American team. In fact base ball in Australia might be said to have its birth from the interest stirred by that visit. Cap Anson's world tourists, on that visit, found the Australians playing cricket. In order to stage a ball game the two visiting teams of Americans had to do the work. Were Old Man Anson to take a team to Australia today he could find plenty of opposition from the team that the Australians would put in the field, and it is likely that he would also find them just as expert in the fine points of the game as were his old-time White Stockings.

The impression Mr. Spink got was that Australia is ripe for base ball, hungry for it, in fact. He believes that the professional game, operated on lines that would not interfere with the amateur organizations, could be made to go big. The test of his opinion may come if Comiskey takes the contemplated trip next winter. That he is not alone of the opinion is indicated by the fact that the Oceanic Steamship Company and A. G. Spalding & Bros. have each subscribed $500 toward defraying expenses of the trip if taken.

Honolulu Already a Hotbed.

The steamship company operates liners which make the trip from San Francisco in 19 days, the distance being 7,500 miles. These boats sail every two weeks, via Honolulu, which, incidentally is already a hotbed of base ball, as a live American colony should be. The season was still in full blast in Honolulu when Mr. Spink [illegible]

The Spink influence was further enhanced in 1912 when Charles visited Australia and reported on baseball's development on foreign soil.

When Charles Spink was invited to go on a Mississippi River cruise as a guest of Charles A. Comiskey, a glowing account (below) of the trip appeared in The Sporting News.

ASHORE OR AFLOAT.

COMISKEY IN CLASS BY HIMSELF AS HOST.

Browns' Center Field Bleachers to Be Rebuilt So as to Provide Over 2,000 More Seats.

NEXT to the addition of an American League pennant and emblem of the World's Championship to the collection which he started while manager of the St. Louis Browns, Charlie Comiskey's chief delight is in the entertainment of his friends in the wilds of Wisconsin or on the waters of the Mississippi. Hughey Fullerton relates that the old Roman once remarked: "Dick Padden is not a good batsman, fast base runner or reliable fielder, but he is a h—— of a ball player." The master of the White Sox is not a sure shot, an expert angler or a foul-weather sailor, but every guest that has accompanied him to the woods or bunked on his boat places his percentage as a host at 1.000. During the recent voyage of the White Sox, Comiskey's last thought at night and first on awakening was the comfort and enjoyment of the kindred spirits he had gathered around him. The party that boarded the White Sox at Helena, Ark., on January 11 consisted of John Agnew and John Higgins, Joe Cantillon, manager of the Washington Club, Herman Schaefer, Detroit's second baseman, who accompanied Comiskey from Chicago, James A. McTague, St. Louis' leading caterer and C. C. Spink, publisher of THE SPORTING NEWS. The latter two left the boat at Robinsville, Miss., on Jan. 20, and on its arrival at Memphis Comiskey and Cantillon took the train for Chicago, the former to complete preparations for the Mexican trip of his World's Champions and the latter on account of the illness of his mother. The others continued the voyage to Cairo where the White Sox will undergo minor repairs.

Good fellowship was in evidence throughout the cruise and except on the eve of the celebration of Schaefer's birthday, there was no formality and then as good cheer asserted itself, host and guests cast off conventionalities and buckled down to making the occasion one that the Tigers' star player will treasure after the close of his professional career.

BASE BALL politics and the game itself are tabooed on a trip of this kind. If a question were put to Comiskey, Cantillon or Schaefer, the information sought would be given, but before a discussion of the merits of players or a comparison of teams could get under way [illegible]

LATE NEWS

TWO PROTESTS A RESULT

ST. LOUIS-CINCINNATI GAME A FARCE

MR. BRUSH SLIGHTLY BETTER BUT END IS NEAR

CHICAGO NATIONALS ESCAPE FINE ON KLING'S ACCOUNT.

Latest Base Ball News From All Points of Compass.

Special to The Sporting News.

CINCINNATI, O., May 4.—Just what action will be taken by President Lynch in regard to the farcical actions of Manager Roger Bresnahan of the Cardinals in the game here on last Monday, is a problem. Two protests have been filed with President Lynch. The first came from Manager Bresnahan, who alleged that Umpire [illegible] was incompetent and that his decisions were unfair and made the game a farce. Directly following this was a protest from President August Herrmann

Late News Can Be Bad News

One of the most popular segments of The Sporting News in the early 1900s was the "Late News" column on page 1. This feature contained stories on almost any subject and was not designed to enhance individual reputations.

When Heinie Peitz was stabbed by a rejected lady friend in Cincinnati, the catcher found his name emblazoned in bold type: "Just Grazed His Heart / Peitz Stabbed by Woman."

Cy Seymour, Cincinnati outfielder, was held up to public censure with this headline: "Seymour's Break / Went on Field the Worse for Drink."

Chances are that Rube Waddell, generally oblivious to public opinion, was undisturbed in May 1910 when a "Late News" story reported out of New Orleans that:

"The latest Mrs. George Edward Waddell is in this city. George Edward is in the East with the Browns. This is the closest Mr. and Mrs. Waddell will be for some time, according to Mrs. Waddell, the former Margaret McGuire. 'Rube is too crazy for me,' was the laconic explanation of Mrs. Waddell. 'I've quit him cold.' "

The couple had been married in St. Louis three weeks earlier and, the story noted, "Rumors of their estrangement became rife two weeks ago."

Nor was John T. Brush reassured in the spring of 1910 when he spotted a headline that told the world: "Brush Slightly Better, But End Is Near." According to the yarn out of San Antonio, the Giants owner was told to prepare for the end in 30 days. Brush lived another 30 months and when he died on a

New York Giants Owner John T. Brush might have been taken aback in 1910 when a TSN headline (left, fourth deck) told him the end was near. Brush lived another 2½ years.

LATE NEWS.

YANKEES CALL ON TEDDY.

GRIFFITH PRESENTED PLAYERS.

RECORD OF WATKINS' STAR PITCHER.

SITUATION AT ERIE IS BECOMING SERIOUS.

Latest Base Ball News From All Points of Compass.

Special to The Sporting News.

WASHINGTON, D. C., May 6.—Manager Clark Griffith introduced the New York American League base ball team to President Roosevelt yesterday. The president talked for some time with the members of the team, mentioning the fact that his son, Quentin, is an enthusiastic base ball player, belonging to the same team with Charlie Taft, a son of Secretary Taft. The president told the visitors that Quentin kept the averages of all the leading ball players. He spoke of the progress of the game and the rugged honesty of players, emphasizing the benefit to base ball of the elimination of gambling.

Watkins' Prize Pitcher.

Special to The Sporting News.

INDIANAPOLIS, Ind., May 6.—Rube Marquard's work in th[illegible]

train en route to California, TSN ran a page 1 story, an editorial and a full, two-column obituary. Part of the page 1 headline read: "For Years a Power in Baseball / Mind and Money Saved National League From Ruin."

In death he received the eulogies that were denied him in life.

On two occasions, United States Presidents were featured in the "Late News" showcase. In May 1908, Theodore Roosevelt qualified with "Yankees Call on Teddy." Clark Griffith, manager of the New York team, introduced his players to Roosevelt at the White House. In another issue, the cover illustration was a photo of the honorary pass to American League games presented to the 26th Chief Executive.

Shortly after his inauguration in 1913, Woodrow Wilson was cited for his endorsement of sports with a headline that reported, "Wilson to Be Real Ball Fan / Will Pay His Way to See Games."

U.S. Presidents have played a significant role in baseball history and The Sporting News has gone out of its way to salute the country's chief executive whenever possible. Theodore Roosevelt was featured in a page 1 headline (above left) in 1908 while Woodrow Wilson's TSN debut (right) occurred shortly after he took office in 1913.

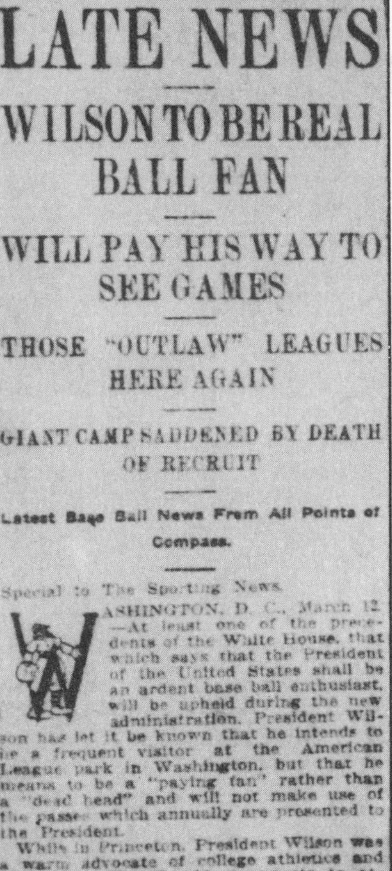

LATE NEWS

WILSON TO BE REAL BALL FAN

WILL PAY HIS WAY TO SEE GAMES

THOSE "OUTLAW" LEAGUES HERE AGAIN

GIANT CAMP SADDENED BY DEATH OF RECRUIT

Latest Base Ball News From All Points of Compass.

Special to The Sporting News.

WASHINGTON, D. C., March 12.—At least one of the precedents of the White House, that which says that the President of the United States shall be an ardent base ball enthusiast, will be upheld during the new administration. President Wilson has let it be known that he intends to be a frequent visitor at the American League park in Washington, but that he means to be a "paying fan" rather than a "dead head" and will not make use of the passes which annually are presented to the President.

While in Princeton, President Wilson was a warm advocate of college athletics and [illegible] The President expects to at-

Dramatic Changes

After 10 years at 810 Olive St., Charles C. Spink moved The Sporting News to more spacious offices at 10th and Olive (right), where it remained for 36 years.

As The Sporting News approached its 24th birthday, changes were occurring in rapid, and sometimes dramatic, fashion.

After nearly 10 years at 810 Olive Street, the firm's offices were moved to more spacious quarters at Tenth and Olive Streets, where they were to remain for 36 years.

Joe Flanner abdicated the editor's chair after an irreconcilable dispute with Charles Spink and accepted a position as secretary to Ban Johnson, president of the American League. Later he moved to Cincinnati, where he served as aide to Garry Herrmann, chairman of the National Commission, Organized Baseball's governing body.

Flanner was succeeded as editor by Joseph M. Cummings, who had been the paper's Baltimore correspondent. Cummings was competent and his personality meshed well with Spink. But a year later, after the death of his wife, Cummings grew homesick and parted company with TSN.

The new editor was Ring Lardner, a young Chicago newspaperman with a fluid writing style and a flair for the amusing. Lardner's name was already well known to readers of The Sporting News through publication of his "Pullman Pastimes," a series of humorous articles portraying life on the road with a major league team.

Lardner's term as editor was even shorter than Cummings'. His name first appeared on the editorial page masthead in the December 28, 1910, issue. Seven issues later—February 15, 1911—it was gone.

Lardner chafed under the yoke of editorial responsibility. He yearned for the less-disciplined life of a daily newspaperman and moved to the East, where his reputation as a humorist soon blossomed.

The fourth editor within a three-year period was Earl Obenshain, who had been TSN's correspondent in Decatur, Ill. Obie was in editorial command during the paper's spectacular growth prior to World War I.

But the most significant change during these years was a new corporate title. It no longer was "The Sporting News Publishing Co." Now it was "Charles C. Spink and Son."

The change was necessitated by the addition to the firm of John George Taylor Spink, the only son of Charles who was approaching his 21st birthday in the fall of 1909.

John George Taylor, named for his maternal grandfather, was born on November 6, 1888, when the paper was in its third year. As a newspaperman, young Taylor was without peer and years later a biographer asserted that "if Taylor Spink had not been born, baseball would have had to invent him."

As a student in the city's public schools, Taylor made average grades, except in algebra, which was his Waterloo. After many importunities, he obtained parental consent to quit the halls of learning and enter the business world. He had hoped to join his father and was crushed when the elder Spink found a job for him as a stock boy with the Rawlings Sporting Goods Company. It was a humbling experience for a youth with elaborate ambitions.

A year later, Taylor was ready

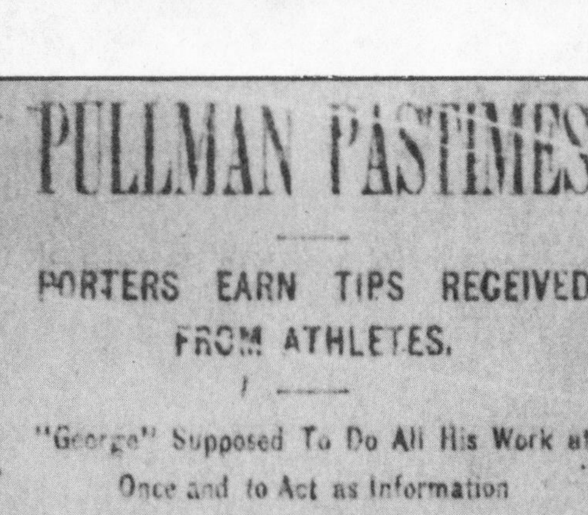

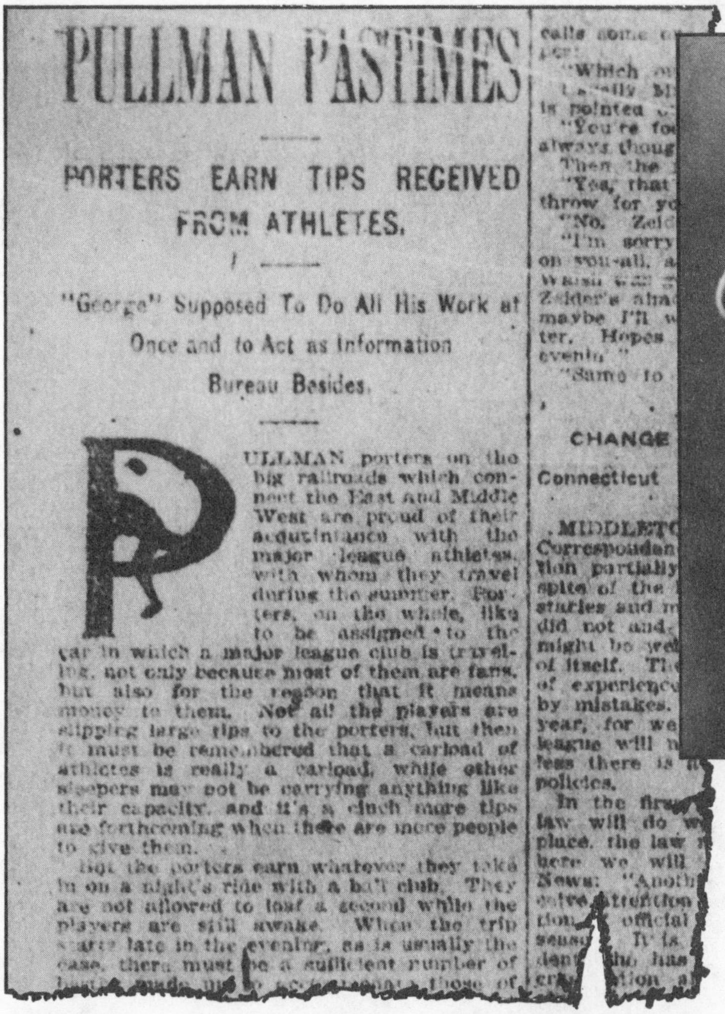

PULLMAN PASTIMES

PORTERS EARN TIPS RECEIVED FROM ATHLETES.

"George" Supposed To Do All His Work at Once and to Act as Information Bureau Besides.

PULLMAN porters on the big railroads which connect the East and Middle West are proud of their acquaintance with the major league athletes, with whom they travel during the summer. Porters, on the whole, like to be assigned to the car in which a major league club is traveling, not only because most of them are fans, but also for the reason that it means money to them. Not all the players are slipping large tips to the porters, but then it must be remembered that a carload of athletes is really a carload, while other sleepers may not be carrying anything like their capacity, and it's a cinch more tips are forthcoming when there are more people to give them.

But the porters earn whatever they take in on a night's ride with a ball club. They are not allowed to loaf a second while the players are still awake. When the trip starts late in the evening, as is usually the case, there must be a sufficient number of

Ring Lardner was young and on his way up in 1910 when he wrote his column 'Pullman Pastimes' for The Sporting News and began his short stint as the publication's editor.

for a step upward. He sought entry to the inner circle of Tenth and Olive streets, but once more he was thwarted. His father obtained employment for him on the sports staff of the Post-Dispatch. Here Taylor served his final year of apprenticeship. At last, Charles decided, the world was ready for his son.

Quickly, baseball sat up and took notice. Although Taylor had never scored a baseball game, he was confident that he could handle such a chore.

There followed a barrage of telegrams to Ban Johnson, requesting the assignment as the American League's representative in the press box for the World Series. Partly in exasperation, and partly because of his closeness to the Spink family, the league president yielded. In conjunction with Francis C. Richter, the National League representative, Taylor Spink scored so capably that he was reappointed to the job seven times. He relinquished the post after his eighth Series.

J.G. Taylor Spink (right) also was young and on his way up in 1910 when he scored his first World Series with Sporting Life Editor Francis C. Richter (left).

Book serializations, such as Frank Chance's 'The Bride and the Pennant' (right), began to appear in The Sporting News after Taylor Spink's arrival.

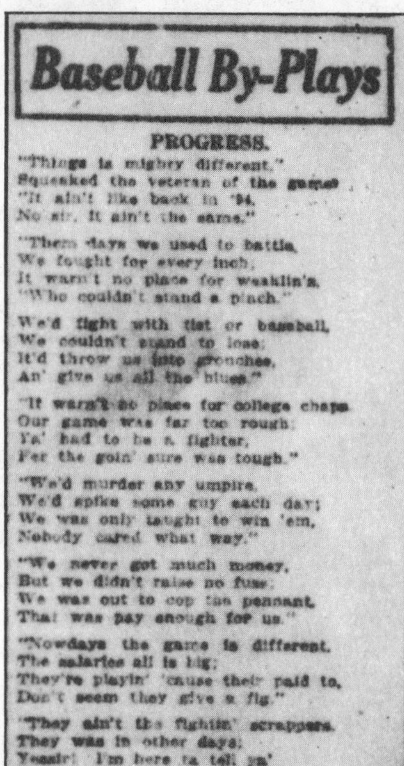

Baseball By-Plays

PROGRESS.

"Things is mighty different,"
Squeaked the veteran of the game.
"It ain't like back in '94,
No sir, it ain't the same."

"Them days we used to battle,
We fought for every inch;
It warn't no place for weaklin's,
Who couldn't stand a pinch."

"We'd fight with fist or baseball,
We couldn't stand to lose;
It'd throw us into grouches,
An' give us all the blues."

"It warn't no place for college chaps,
Our game was far too rough;
Ya' had to be a fighter,
Fer the goin' sure was tough."

"We'd murder any umpire,
We'd spike some guy each day;
We was only taught to win 'em,
Nobody cared what way."

"We never got much money,
But we didn't raise no fuss;
We was out to cop the pennant,
That was pay enough for us."

"Nowdays the game is different,
The salaries all is big;
They're playin' 'cause their paid to,
Don't seem they give a fig."

"They ain't the fightin' scrappers
They was in other days;
Yessir! I'm here ta tell ya'
The game has changed its ways."

L. H. ADDINGTON.

'Baseball By-Plays' (above), a column that generally led off with a poem, and 'Base Ball By Billy Evans,' a major league umpire, were bright additions to the editorial page.

BASE BALL abounds in freak plays. While the rule makers have attempted to make provision for all the peculiar plays that are possible, yet nearly every days during the summer presents some freak stunt that has been pulled on the diamond.

I got a letter the other day from a former International League umpire that related a rather interesting incident, one which, by the way, is liable to happen in most any game. Relative to the play the umpire has the following to say:

"The game was played at Montreal in 1912, the contesting teams being the Buffalo and the Montreal Clubs. Murray of Buffalo was on second base and McCabe on first base. McCabe took too big a lead off first base, and was caught napping by the Montreal pitcher. Naturally he at once headed for second base, while Murray hiked toward third. The play then shifted to third, the Montreal first baseman throwing the ball there to head off Murray. The next moment both Murray and McCabe were sliding back into second. The ball was thrown to the second baseman, and both men touched by the fielder with the ball. I pointed to McCabe, signifying that he was out, but to my great surprise Murray walked off the bag and to the bench.

"Murray's action presented a problem to me that was a bit puzzling. I desired to

ARE YOU READING

"THE BRIDE AND THE PENNANT"

FRANK CHANCE'S

GREAT BASE BALL ROMANCE

Appearing Serially in The Sporting News, at no advance in cost. Starts in this issue, and will be continued indefinitely.

"He turned the corner of the bleachers and there was—Lucile."

This is only one of the many features of this great base ball paper, which will be inaugurated during the off-season. We are going to give you something of interest in every issue. Don't miss any of these good things by subscribing today.

Pictures of the Champion Athletics and Cubs, double the size of the regular supplements, are on the way, and soon will be announced.

Five Cents A Copy--On Sale at All First-class Newsstands

CHARLES C. SPINK & SON, Publishers, ST. LOUIS.

Taylor Fires First Shots

If Taylor Spink was not the embodiment of perpetual motion, he was, at least, a close approximation.

Charles C. Spink had designed a passive role for his son, but that hope soon was shattered by Taylor's counter-punches.

Taylor Spink arrived with all guns blazing—and a bottomless supply of ammunition. His first target was the quality of writing in TSN, which he considered "run-of-the-mill and stodgy." Taylor shook up the corps of correspondents and his father as well, and, when his task was completed, there was a correspondent in every city in Organized Baseball. News no longer was stale when it came off the press. It was fresh and lively.

Graphically, the paper assumed a new appearance, too. Through an arrangement with book publishers, novels bearing the bylines of prominent personalities were serialized from week to week. Among the authors was Christy Mathewson, star pitcher of the New York Giants, who wrote, "Won in the Ninth" and "Pitching in the Pinch."

A question-and-answer department was launched, as well as a column containing letters from readers. Ernest J. Lanigan, now located in New York where he was an official of the International League, helped to brighten the pages with a column and feature articles.

Multi-column headlines began to appear in greater frequency. In 1911, before the Athletics met the

THE SPORTING NEWS.

The Sporting News' Question and Answer Bureau Covering All Base Ball Topics

KNOTTY POINTS SUBMITTED BY PUZZLED FANS.

Interpretation of Playing and Scoring Rules for Those Who Wish To Be Sure They're Right.

IN this column from week to week will be found answers to questions covering practically every department of base ball. On ... things the

11. Certainly. Send $2 and address to this address and paper will be mailed to you for one year.

WACO, Tex.—Was Gene Moore, of Pittsburg, eligible to participate in the distribution of the World's Series money? X. Y. Z.

Yes.

BENTON, Wis.—Can I get a picture of the game played at Chicago on September 5, 1909, between the Cubs and the Pittsburg team? If so, where. LEO M'CARTY.

Write to the art department of the several Chicago dailies.

HONG KONG, China.—What is the pres-

INFORMATION MAKING PLAIN MANY HAZY POINTS.

Players' Records Past and Present Unearthed and Movements Traced Through Base Ball World.

taking for granted, of course, that the illegal batsman is detected and the penalties demanded of the umpire before the batter who follows B has a delivery made to him by the pitcher.

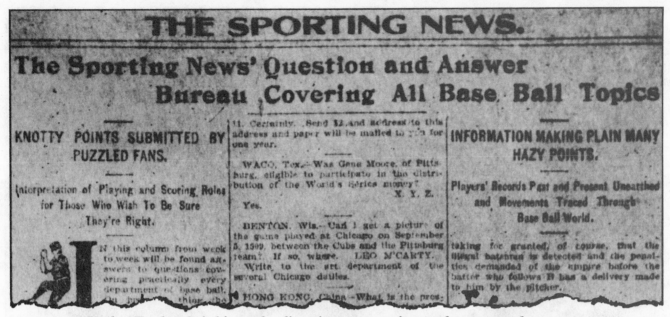

Under Taylor Spink's early direction, a question-and-answer column was launched, allowing readers to submit their 'knotty problems' to TSN editors.

Giants in the World Series, pages 2 and 3 were devoted to a symposium of writers' predictions on the outcome of the event.

The most revolutionary change occurred on the editorial page. Long a gray hodge-podge of editorials and baseball miscellany, the page was transformed into a bright and readable segment of the paper.

Billy Evans, American League umpire, wrote an off-season column. Bill Phelon, witty Cincinnati scribe, contributed "Phelon's Pickups" and Taylor Spink, for a short while, added a "Current Comment" column. The cause for the brevity of Taylor's handiwork might reasonably be attributed to disciplinary action by Charles against his over-eager heir or the restless young man's quest for new summits to scale.

For an extended period, the brightest editorial-page column was "Baseball By-Plays," a collection of anecdotes and sidelights. Generally, the column was headed by a piece of poetry submitted by one of several writers, but none so clever as Grantland Rice, then on his way to becoming the foremost sports scribe in the nation.

A typical Rice poem was published in 1912 after he saw a photo of National League club owners that included one lady magnate, Helene Hathaway Britton of the Cardinals. It read:

They've had the hobble on business for many a weary day,
They've hung their skirts on politics and hung 'em there to stay;
They've ruled the drama and the home and, having put that through,
They're going after baseball and some day they'll get that, too.
Some day we'll read where Pearl or Grace stepped out to take their turn,
Where Lizzie Walsh, the spitball kid, had speed and curves to burn;
Where Bessie Wagner led the league or Lucy Cobb, the queen,
Got four hits off of Jennie Gregg, the pitching nectarine.
We'll read where Nannie Marquard, who was there with all the dander,
Won out in the eleventh from young Katie Alexander;
And where in some hard battle or an old-time slugging bee,
The umpire took a rap at scrappy Bess Magee.
They've gone out after baseball and they stand the one best bet,
But as full of conversation and as fancy as they get;
When they start the old hair-pulling and hatpin stabs some mogul,
They'll have no bloomin' edge upon C. Ebbets, Murphy or Fogel.

Charles Ebbets of Brooklyn, Charles Webb Murphy of Chicago and Horace Fogel of Philadelphia were abrasive personalities in the National League. Another Grantland Rice offering was:

Sing of your Four Hundred hitters,
Chant of your league-leading file,
Up with your glasses—hey, laddies and lasses,
To those who can hit 'em a mile.

I'm one with the raging and roaring,
When bludgeon and leather collide;
But facing the call, here's the king of them all,
The bloke who can hit in a pinch.

His record may stick on two-twenty,
And dull be the gleam in his eye;
But here in the roaring of smashing and scoring,
His pals need a run for a tie.

They know him—and wait for the echo,
They've lamped him before at the clinch;
No Hans on the job—or a second Ty Cobb,
Just a bloke who is there in the pinch.

Hans was the early nickname for Honus Wagner, superstar shortstop of Pittsburgh.

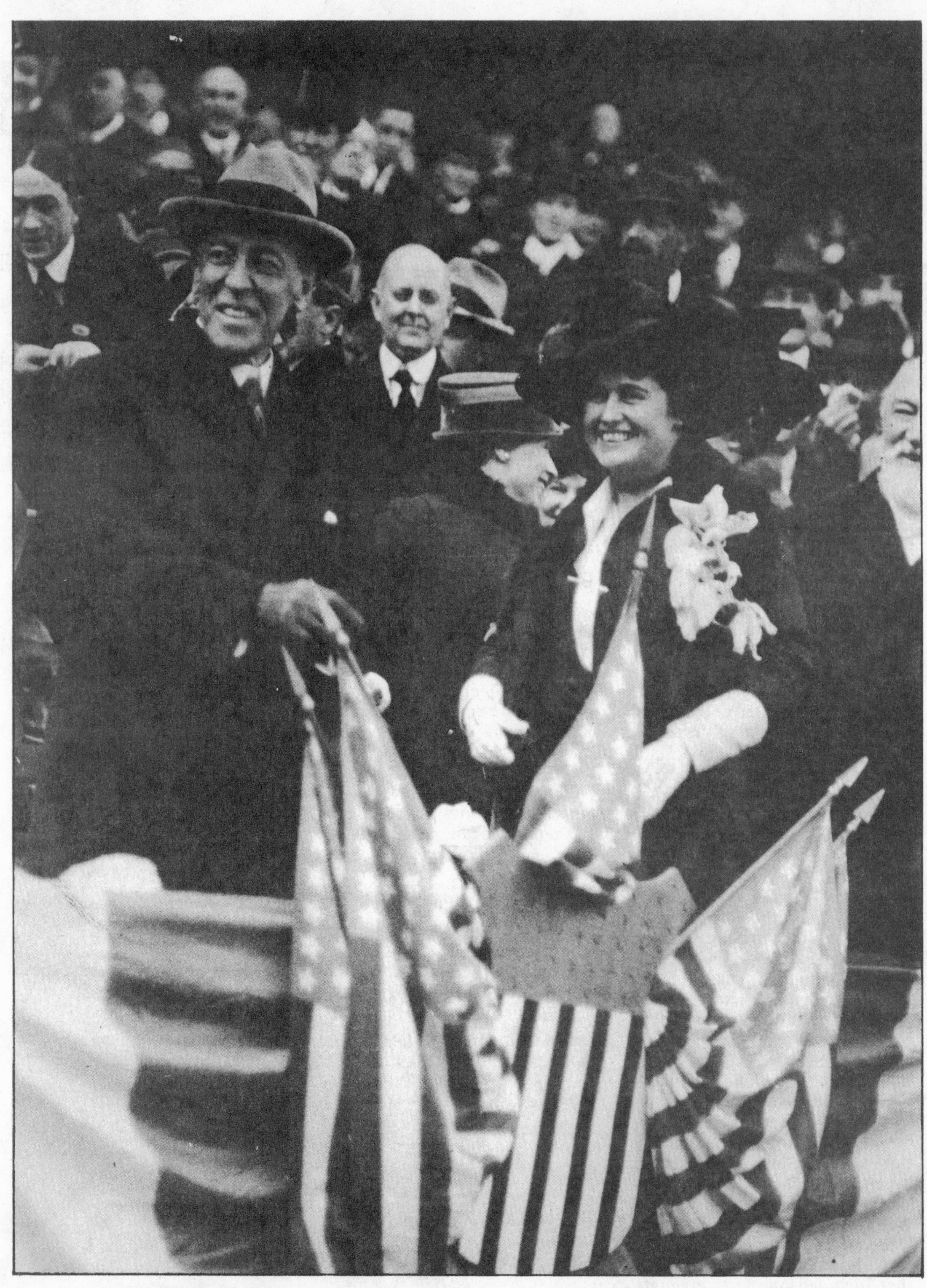

President Woodrow Wilson presided over several baseball openers before the United States entered World War I.

1914-1920:

WAR AND SCANDAL

For months there had been ominous rumblings, warning of a new circuit that called itself the Federal League and was about to challenge the American and National Leagues as a third major.

The World Series of 1913 had not yet started when an early October headline in The Sporting News suggested: "Federal Wiggles Like a Live One / Much Happens—Provided Coin Is Forthcoming / Promoters of the Outlaw Admit Their Only Chance Is to Make Noise Like a Major League."

In January another headline announced: "Tinker and Miner Brown Jump to Federal League / They Sign Contracts as Managers / Salaries Will Be Deposited / Johnson (Ban) and Herrmann (Garry) Both Doubt Reports That Former Stars Have Deserted Organized Ball."

The doubts of the American League president and the National Commission chairman may have been genuine, but so were the actions of Joe Tinker and Mordecai (Three Finger) Brown, who took over the managerial posts of Federal League clubs in Chicago and St. Louis, respectively.

Other established major league players followed suit. The lure of higher salaries proved irresistible as the trail of defectors led also to Brooklyn, Baltimore, Kansas City, Pittsburgh, Buffalo and Indianapolis.

James A. Gilmore, a wealthy Chicago coal merchant, was president of the new circuit. A persuasive individual, he enlisted affluent sportsmen in key cities, including Charles Weeghman, owner of a restaurant chain, in Chicago; Otto Stifel, a brewer, and Phil Ball, manufacturer of ice machinery, in St. Louis; Robert Ward of the well-known baking family, in Brooklyn, and Harry Sinclair, famous oil baron, who took over the Newark franchise in 1915.

Tinker, a member of the Cubs' famed double play combination of Tinker-to-Evers-to-Chance, was shortstop for the Cincinnati Reds in 1913. When he was sold to Brooklyn for $15,000, Tinker demanded a slice of the sales price. The request was denied and Tinker signed to manage the Chicago Whales.

Indianapolis won the Federal League pennant in 1914, edging Chicago by 1½ games. In 1915, the Whales won by one percentage point over St. Louis and a half-game over Pittsburgh.

When Sinclair announced plans to move his club to New York in 1916, the National League appointed a three-man commission to negotiate peace terms with the outlaw circuit. Among the conditions of the pact, Weeghman was allowed to buy the Chicago Cubs and Ball to purchase the St. Louis Browns. The Ward family received $400,000, paid over a 20-year period, while other club owners received lesser amounts. Federal League players were placed in a pool and major league clubs permitted to buy those who had originally jumped their contracts.

Only the Baltimore Feds refused to accept the terms of surrender. The Terrapins sued the major leagues under the Sherman Antitrust Act. When a lower court ruled in favor of the Feds, the National and American Leagues appealed to the United States District Court of Northern Illinois. A page 1 headline in The Sporting News dated February 10, 1916, disclosed the outcome: "Outlaw Anti-Trust Suit Is Dismissed by Judge Landis / Ban Johnson Forces the Feds to Keep Their Agreement / Disgruntled Baltimore Is Brought Into Line and Agrees With the Rest, But Says It Is Because Herrmann Has Made Promises."

A two-column photo of the judge was captioned, "He's the Game's Good Friend."

Damage wrought by the Federal League strife was incalculable, but nowhere was it more devastating than in Baltimore where Jack Dunn of the International League Orioles struggled against the outlaw Terrapins.

By midseason of 1914 Dunn was engulfed in red ink. Daily, he slipped deeper into debt until only one course remained. He would sell his choice players to a major league club in an effort to regain solvency.

Dunn packaged his three best players and offered them to his good friend, Connie Mack. But the Philadelphia A's manager, at war himself against Federal League assaults, declined the offer. Mack explained that he was unable to pay dollar value and suggested that Dunn seek another market.

Jack found a buyer in Boston. For an estimated $25,000, the Red Sox acquired a catcher, a righthanded pitcher and a 19-year-old lefthanded pitcher.

The catcher, Ben Egan, was traded almost immediately to Cleveland. The righthanded hurler, Ernie

Shore, starred for the Boston pennant-winners of 1915-16. The southpaw attained recognition not only as a superb pitcher, but also as the game's most illustrious slugger.

George Herman Ruth was the son of a Baltimore saloonkeeper. By the time he was 7, he was an accomplished incorrigible. He was committed to St. Mary's Industrial School where he learned discipline as well as the rudiments of pitching a baseball.

Ruth was recommended to Dunn and made his first training trip with the Orioles in 1914. Because of his youth, Ruth was nicknamed "Babe," a sobriquet that was applicable to his age, but not to his advanced pitching talents. In spring exhibitions, he defeated the defending-champion Athletics, the Dodgers and the Phillies. When the International League season opened, Babe was in the Birds' starting rotation.

Dunn started to dismantle his club in July. After a month with the Red Sox, for whom he compiled a 2-1 record, Ruth was assigned to Providence. Like Baltimore, Providence was in the International League. At season's end, Babe had a combined International League record of 22-9.

Ruth won 18 of 26 decisions for Boston in 1915 and clouted four homers. One of his blasts cleared the right-field pavilion roof at Sportsman's Park in St. Louis and shattered the show window of a car agency across the street.

But Babe was a pitcher first, and a great one at that. He was the league's earned-run champion in 1916 with an average of 1.75. He won three World Series games (1916 & '18) in which he had an ERA on 0.87 and pitched 29⅔ consecutive scoreless innings.

By 1918, it had become apparent to everyone that Ruth's future was as an outfielder. That season he not only won 13 games, but clubbed 11 home runs to tie for the league lead. In 1919, playing in 130 games (17 as a pitcher), Babe belted 29 homers to set a major league record.

As the fortunes of the Bambino climbed, those of his boss declined sharply. Harry Frazee, a theatrical producer who owned the Red Sox, was burdened heavily with debt in the winter of 1919-20. The Yankees offered him a way out of the financial woods. They would buy Ruth for $125,000. The deal was consummated on January 3, 1920. Babe celebrated his move by socking 54 home runs the following season.

When Babe joined the Boston team in 1914, the bulk of baseball attention was not directed on the second-place Red Sox, but rather on the cross-town Braves who were captivating a nation with their unprecedented spurt up the National League ladder.

In their second season under George Stallings, the Braves occupied eighth place on the morning of July 19. That afternoon, however, they scored three runs in the ninth inning to defeat Cincinnati, 3-2, and escaped the cellar.

After the game, a traveling correspondent wired his paper in Boston: "If nothing else is accomplished, Stallings at least has demonstrated that he knows how to handle a team and knows how to make it fight."

Much of the fight displayed by the Braves was inspired by Johnny Evers, the former Cubs second baseman who teamed with Rabbit Maranville, a pixyish shortstop just three years out of the minors.

The spark that was struck on July 19 kindled a raging inferno. The Braves were sixth after games of July 20 and fourth a day later.

A headline in The Sporting News revealed: "Braves Dazed by Their Own Glory / Fans Bewildered, Too, But Able to Get Out and Root / Most of the Present Day Bugs (Fans) Were in Short Pants and Dresses When Team Last Saw First Division."

By August 10, the Braves had advanced to second place and trailed the Giants by 6½ games.

In its August 20 issue, a TSN headline reported that the Philadelphia A's, who had beaten the New York Giants in the World Series of 1911 and 1913, were watching the N.L. race with uncommon interest. It read, "Macks Would Like Braves as Rivals / This Thing of Beating Giants Is Monotonous / Quaker City, Too, Is Interested in Stallings, Who Is Remembered as Former Leader of Phillies."

The A's got their wish. On September 8 the Braves stormed into first place and never relaxed their grip. As soon as the race was decided, baseball writers started to predict the outcome of the World Series. Almost unanimously, the A's were picked to win their fourth world title in five years. One dissenting vote was cast by Joe Vila, a perceptive New York scribe. A TSN headline over Vila's pre-Series yarn said, "Braves Will Give A's a Plenty / Vila Won't Be Surprised to See Team Win / Mack's Champs Have Little on Stallings' Men Except in the Outfield."

Vila called the turn correctly. In a stunning, four-game sweep, the Miracle Braves humbled the powerful A.L. champs by scores of 7-1, 1-0, 5-4 and 3-1. The Boston Big Three of Dick Rudolph, Bill James and George (Lefty) Tyler outpitched Mack's aging mound stars while Hank Gowdy, a .243-hitting catcher, provided much of the punch with a .545 batting average built on one single, three doubles, a triple and a home run.

From world supremacy, the Braves declined steadily until in 1918 they finished in seventh place. The Red Sox, meanwhile, won world championships in 1915 and 1916 and finished second in 1917.

An air of uncertainty permeated baseball as the 1918 season got underway. The United States was at war and every able-bodied male was expected to abide by the "Work or Fight" order promulgated by Secretary of War Newton Baker and General Enoch Crowder, director of the military draft. The question of whether the major leagues would be permitted to finish their schedule was answered in July when Baker ordered the circuits to close their races by Labor Day. Correspondents of The Sporting News did not view the order kindly. A headline shouted, "Baker's Order a Blow to Nation's Morale / Not Only Civilians But Boys in Service Are Hot." A two-column photo of Baker was captioned, "He's New Czar of Baseball."

When Garry Herrmann sought to extend the season in order to play the World Series, Crowder told the chairman of the National Commission that September 16 was the absolute limit.

Because of wartime travel restrictions, it was agreed that the site of the Series between the Cubs and Red Sox would be shifted only once, from Chicago to Boston after the third game. In anticipation of heavy turnouts, the Cubs arranged to play their home games in Comiskey Park, the White Sox's stadium with a considerably larger capacity than their own North Side park. The strategy was questionable as the games drew crowds of only 19,274, 20,040 and 27,054.

With Ruth and Carl Mays pitching superbly, the Red Sox won two of the first three games. Sunday was a day for travel and as the train carrying the Series troupe rattled eastward, the players started to grumble among themselves. Why, they wondered, did the National Commission pass up a lucrative Sabbath date in Chicago? Why had it not set Monday aside for travel?

Two other factors intensified their discontent. For the first time members of all first-division teams were to share in the Series pool and the Series players had voted to donate 10 percent of their swag to war charities. The player payoff promised to be small.

The issue came to a head on Tuesday, September 10. Fans arriving early at Fenway Park were puzzled to see the field devoid of players.

The athletes, it developed, were in conference. With Harry Hooper representing the Red Sox players and Leslie Mann speaking for the Cubs, the players were pouring out their grievances to Herrmann, chairman of the National Commission, and John Heydler, president of the National League. Missing from the parley was Ban Johnson, president of the American League and the most dominant figure in the game.

Five minutes before the scheduled start of the game, Johnson arrived. He had been tippling at a local bar and was aghast at what his blurry vision beheld. He demanded an explanation. He was informed that it was impossible to accede to the players' demands because the club owners themselves had voted on the distribution of the money. Herrmann and Heydler, Johnson was told, also had rejected flatly Hooper's suggestion that, if $1,500 could not be guaranteed to each winner and $1,000 to each loser, then "Let nobody get anything; let's give all the receipts to the Red Cross."

Struggling to maintain his equilibrium, Johnson threw a heavy, if unsteady arm around Hooper and boomed, "Harry, do you realize you are a member of one of the greatest organizations in the world, the American League? And do you realize what you will do to its good name if you do not play? Go out there, Harry, the crowd is waiting for you."

Recognizing the futility of dialogue with an inebriate, Hooper and Mann shrugged helplessly. The teams took the field nearly an hour late. The Sox lost the game but clinched the Series a day later when Mays hurled a three-hitter.

The players' shares were minuscule. After deductions for war charities, each winner received $890 and each loser earned $535.

The player revolt of 1918 was but an abrasion compared to the permanent scar left by the unconscionable conduct of eight players in 1919. Once more money was the root of the shabbiest chapter of baseball's first century.

By most calculations, the Chicago White Sox were vastly superior to the Cincinnati Reds, their Series opponents. The Pale Hose attack was led by Joe Jackson, with an average of .351. Edd Roush, a .321 hitter, was the best of the Reds.

The Chicago mound staff featured Eddie Cicotte (29-7) and Claude (Lefty) Williams (23-11). Cincinnati pitchers were paced by Slim Sallee (21-7) and Dutch Ruether (19-6).

As the favored Sox and underdog Reds prepared for the Series opener in Cincinnati, reports circulated that the previous evening a man had stood on a chair in the lobby of a downtown hotel and waved sheafs of large denomination bills in the faces of incredulous folks, offering to wager any amount of money on the Reds.

Incredulity turned to strong suspicion the next afternoon when the Reds bombed Cicotte for five runs in the fourth inning and won handily, 9-1. Another Cincinnati victory the next day sent reverberations through the baseball establishment. Heads shook in disbelief—and fear mounted that the worst might be true.

The White Sox won three games, two by Dickie Kerr, but the Reds captured the championship, five games to three.

In the months that followed, rumors persisted that the Series had been fixed. A headline in a December issue of The Sporting News read: "Revival of Series Scandal Emphasizes Need of Inquiry / Charges Have Been Bandied About So Freely That Fans Are Entitled to Some Declaration From Baseball."

Inquiries already were underway. Charles A. Comiskey, owner of the White Sox, offered $10,000 for evidence of crookedness. Ban Johnson, furnished numerous valuable leads by Publisher J.G. Taylor Spink of The Sporting News, conducted his own investigation.

In the summer of 1920, a grand jury was convened in Cook County, Ill., and indictments were returned against Cicotte, Williams, Jackson, Chick Gandil, Swede Risberg, Buck Weaver, Hap Felsch and Fred McMullin. Cicotte confessed that he had found $10,000 under his pillow in his hotel room on the eve of the Series. Jackson testified that he had received $5,000. Felsch and Williams also confessed. Gandil had not reported to the Sox that year which, in the eyes of many, was tantamount to guilt. Weaver, Risberg and McMullin protested their innocence and posted $10,000 bonds.

Delays and legal maneuverings postponed the trials of the eight players, now known as the "Black Sox," until July of 1921.

At that time it was discovered that the players' signed confessions were missing from the district attorney's office. It was never proved nor disproved, but there were strong suspicions that Arnold Rothstein, alleged architect of the fix, had paid to have the documents destroyed.

Without evidence of conspiracy to fix the Series, the jury returned a verdict of not guilty. From the courtroom the players and jurors adjourned to a nearby bistro where they celebrated far into the night.

With the reputation of baseball on the gallows in 1920, the sport's government had undergone a significant change. The National Commission, long the ruling body, was abolished and replaced on November 12 by the first commissioner, Judge Kenesaw Mountain Landis, who had ruled in the Federal League case.

With the United States' involvement in World War I, basebal

As baseball's first czar, with dictatorial powers, Landis ruled with a mailed fist. There was nothing to cushion his blows, as the Black Sox discovered when Landis banished them to outer darkness.

"Regardless of the verdicts of juries," the Judge's announcement began, "no player who throws a game, no player who entertains proposals or promises to throw a game, no player who sits in a conference with a bunch of crooked players and gamblers where the ways and means of throwing games are discussed and does not promptly tell the club about it will ever play professional baseball.

"Of course, I do not know if any of these men will apply for reinstatement, but if they do the above are at least a few of the rules that will be enforced. Just keep in mind that regardless of the verdicts of juries, baseball is entirely competent to protect itself against crooks, both inside and outside the game."

Not surprisingly, there were applications for reinstatement. Buck Weaver, for one, pleaded to have his name cleared on the grounds that he was not a party to the plot, even though he had knowledge of it. Neither the great third baseman nor any of the other seven ever played a game of professional baseball again.

While baseball attempted to shake off the Black Sox stigma in 1920, the Cleveland Indians experienced a season of tragedy and triumph.

In a game at the Polo Grounds on August 16, the Indians led the Yankees, 3-0, when shortstop Ray Chapman batted against Carl Mays in the fifth inning. Mays, a submarine righthander, delivered his pitches from his shoetops. The ball rose as it approached the plate, frequently sending the batter sprawling and earning for Mays the reputation of a "head hunter."

As Chapman crouched, with his head over the plate, as was his style, Mays fired a blazing fastball that crashed into the left side of the batter's skull. Chapman took a few faltering steps toward first base, then collapsed.

training sometimes took a backseat to different kinds of drills.

For a fleeting moment there was a general impression that the ball had struck Chapman's bat. After the ball was fielded and thrown to first base, Yankee players thought they had retired Chapman before noticing the horrified expression on Mays' face that told them the terrible truth.

Chapman was rushed to a hospital where two operations were performed in an effort to save his life. He died the next morning, the only major league player to die as the result of injuries in a game.

Three weeks later, the Indians promoted Joe Sewell from New Orleans to fill the vacancy at shortstop. The move was made after the September 1 deadline for World Series eligibility so, as a result, when the Indians won the pennant, it was necessary to obtain permission for Sewell to play in the World Series.

Few fall classics can compare with the 1920 Series for remarkable events. For the first time a pitcher hit a home run. He was Jim Bagby, Cleveland's 31-game winner who connected against Burleigh Grimes in the fifth game.

The fourth-inning blast was the second yielded by Grimes in the game. In the first inning, the Brooklyn spitballer grooved a pitch that Elmer Smith clouted over the wall of Cleveland's League Park for the first Series grand-slam homer.

But the most notable achievement occurred in the fifth inning, with Pete Kilduff running at second base and Otto Miller at first for the Dodgers. Clarence Mitchell's line drive to the right of second base was speared by Bill Wambsganss, who stepped on second base to retire Kilduff and then tagged the slow-footed Miller to complete an unassisted triple play. The feat has never been duplicated in Series play.

Later Mitchell hit into a double play, giving the pitcher the unique distinction of accounting for five outs in two trips to the plate.

The Dodgers found little solace in the fact that they outhit the Indians, 13 to 12. They lost the game, 8-1, and the Series, five games to two.

Toys and Novelties was a publication Spink started in 1909 to go along with another member of his library, The Toy Buyer's Guide.

Another Era Comes To an End

Charles C. Spink was a 51-year-old millionaire when he died at 2 a.m. on April 22, 1914.

In the 28 years after abandoning his homestead project in South Dakota, he had become a prominent member of the St. Louis business community. He had married Marie Taylor, whose father, John George Taylor, operated the Richardson-Taylor Medicine Company, and sired one son, John George Taylor, and two daughters, Freddie and Frances.

Several times he was urged to enter the political arena but declined, explaining that his time and energies were needed by the publications that had carried him to success. They included The Sporting News, The Sporting Goods Dealer, The Sporting Goods Trade Directory, Toys and Novelties, a trade magazine, The Toy Buyer's Guide and The Sporting News Baseball Record Book.

Outwardly, the 6-foot-2 Spink was in the prime of health as the 1914 baseball season approached. In mid-April he attended his son's marriage to Blanche Keene and bid the honeymooners a fond farewell as they boarded a midnight train to Chicago. But the next morning, the most punctual of men was an hour late arriving at the office. "I have the perfect alibi," he quipped, "my son's wedding."

The same day marked the opening of the Federal League season. Although The Sporting News' motto was: "Devoted to Organized Baseball," Spink accepted an invitation to accompany some friends to the outlaw circuit's inaugural. "I go in the hands of good friends," he told curious associates, "and they are paying for the box."

During the game, Charles engaged in lighthearted banter with those about him and commented on the progress of the contest. Afterward, he complimented the club owners on their new park and said that his only disappointment was the loss by the home team.

He then returned to his home on "Millionaires Row" across from Forest Park. That night he was stricken by an intestinal disorder from which he had suffered attacks in the past. He was confined to his home for several days, during which time he received a visit from his brother Alfred. The two, who were so close in the early days of The Sporting News, had been estranged for a number of years, allegedly because of a dispute over stock in the firm. But they were reunited in a tearful reconciliation as Charles struggled for life.

On the night of April 21, doctors recommended surgery. The patient was moved to St. Luke's Hospital where he underwent an operation. He died several hours later without regaining consciousness.

After Episcopal services and full Masonic rites, Charles Spink was buried the next day in Bellefontaine Cemetery. Among the pallbearers were Byron Bancroft Johnson, president of the American League, and Charles A. Comiskey, owner of the Chicago White Sox, old cronies from numerous hunting expeditions in the pine woods of Wisconsin.

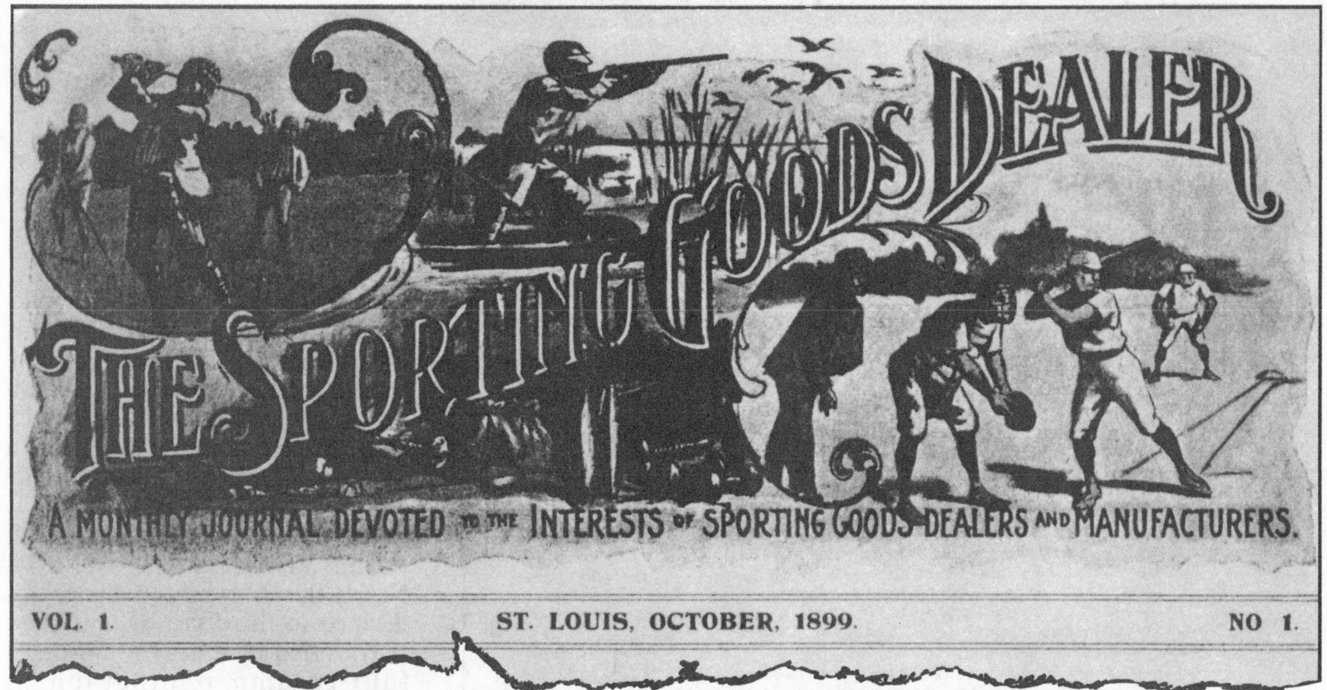

THE SPORTING GOODS DEALER
A MONTHLY JOURNAL DEVOTED TO THE INTERESTS OF SPORTING GOODS DEALERS AND MANUFACTURERS.
VOL. 1.
ST. LOUIS, OCTOBER, 1899.
NO 1.

In 1914, the Charles C. Spink legacy neared completion. The Sporting Goods Dealer (above), Spink's brainchild in 1899, was alive and well, as was The Sporting Goods Trade Directory (below left), a Dealer offspring. Spink had been publishing The Sporting News Record Book (below right) since 1909.

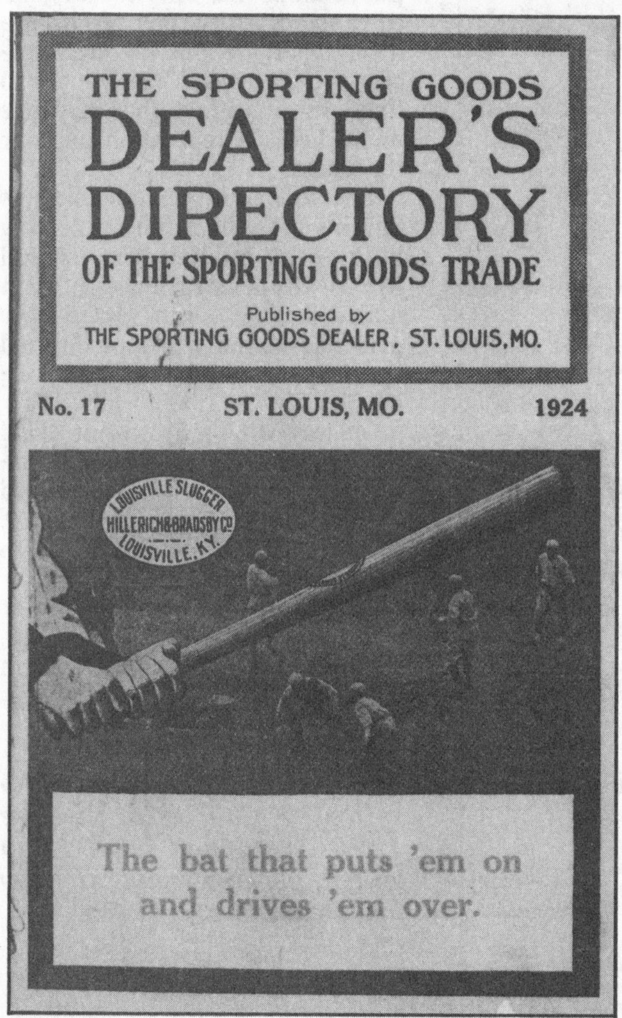

THE SPORTING GOODS
DEALER'S
DIRECTORY
OF THE SPORTING GOODS TRADE
Published by
THE SPORTING GOODS DEALER, ST. LOUIS, MO.
No. 17
ST. LOUIS, MO.
1924
LOUISVILLE SLUGGER
HILLERICH & BRADSBY CO.
LOUISVILLE, KY.
The bat that puts 'em on
and drives 'em over.

The
SPORTING NEWS'
RECORD BOOK FOR 1915
CHARLES A. COMISKEY
Published by
CHARLES C. SPINK & SON
... ST. LOUIS, MO. ...
Publishers ... The Sporting News
PRICE FIVE CENTS

April 30

22, 1914

AN ELDER BROTHER'S TRIBUTE

BY AL H. SPINK

READERS of The Sporting News in all parts of the world will read with sincere regret of the passing of Charles Claude Spink, the publisher of this paper. Mr. Spink died in St. Louis on Wednesday morning, April 22, after an operation performed to relieve him of an intestinal trouble.

A week before he had attended the wedding of his only son, John George Taylor Spink, to Blanche Margaret Keene.

At the wedding dinner Mr. Spink told of how he was growing old and of how his children, a son and two daughters, would soon be hoeing their own row, leaving him and his wife at home all alone.

But he did not appear old. Just turned 50, with stalwart form, handsome face, ruddy cheeks and only a gray hair or two to mark the passing of Father Time, he looked good for many years to come. There seemed nothing in the way of his reaching the biblical age of three score years and ten.

But now, a week later, he lies cold in death, a powerful proof of the old saying that death comes strangely and loves a shining mark.

It may sound a bit too broad, but no man has done more to keep St. Louis in the public eye than Charles Claude Spink. He was the owner of three publications—The Sporting News, The Sporting Goods Dealer and Toys and Novelties.

To his immense energy is due the great success they scored. They are all so finely made, in fact, that they give to St. Louis a reputation all over the world of circulating three publications, each and every one at the top of its class, and all a credit to the city they represent.

In each of them the spirit of their owner was so finely engraved that it served to mold a close friendship between publisher and reader, a friendship that has existed since 1886, 30 years in all, the year in which The Sporting News, the first of the Spink publications, was launched and out of which grew the other two great mediums.

These publications going all over the world naturally introduced their publisher to an army greater and broader than any ever before organized.

The Sporting News each week speaks to many thousand of readers and all interested in America's national game, and nearly all having some knowledge of or real personal acquaintance with its owner.

Solely on account of his high and sterling character, his opposition always to offensive and personal journalism, and his staunch friendship for organized base ball, Mr. Spink numbered his friends by the thousands, and players and club owners alike were his boon companions and friends.

When Ban Johnson, president of the American League, and considered by many the biggest and broadest man in base ball, came to St. Louis, he made his lodging in Mr. Spink's spacious home opposite Forest Park. And when Charles Comiskey, owner of the Chicago White Sox, and known as the noblest Roman of the base ball field, visited here the Spink domicile was always his first calling place.

Giving up a tour planned for pleasure and recreation in the piney woods of Wisconsin, Comiskey and Johnson came all the way to St. Louis from Chicago to attend the Spink obsequies. This incident is mentioned merely to show the esteem in which the deceased was held even among the greatest and most powerful men in base ball.

The severance of relations, therefore, between the publisher and readers caused by his death might be likened to the breaking of a tie between father and son or brother and brother.

Mr. Spink was a self-made man in every respect. When he came to St. Louis a boy of 22, nearly 30 years ago, it was to join me in the publication of The Sporting News.

The paper was having a hard row to hoe and made little headway until he took hold of its business management. From that day it prospered. He was the one Ixion of the organization, the one man who always held his place at the wheel regardless of the calls from other directions.

Nothing interested him so much as attending to his own business. He was often invited to take a prominent part in politics or to enter some civic strife. But he only laughed at such invitations, stuck to his own line, and prospered. It was this close application to his own affairs and his refusal to listen to the call of outsiders that led to his building up the most prosperous publishing business in this part of the country.

His death came when he had reached the very pinnacle of his long and arduous endeavors, and fate was cruel to rob him of the reward that was due him in what should have been the happiest ten or 20 years of all his life.

Mr. Spink was the youngest of four Spink brothers. Three of the brothers, William, Alfred and Charles were connected with the building up of base ball.

William and the writer were the first "sporting editors" in St. Louis. Until the former, in 1866, began writing articles dealing with base ball games, such events were not considered of moment enough to get mention in a newspaper. William Spink brought base ball from the prairies into the enclosure as it is known today and was the man who formed definite teams to play the game. Together we established the first local professional team—the St. Louis Browns of 1875. Teams broadened into leagues and in 1881 we placed the American Association in the field.

In 1896 William Spink died. In 1886 Charles Spink joined me and we established The Sporting News. Naturally of a roving disposition, I strayed away from the paper, but my brother Charles in his steady, persistent way, stuck to it and made it the great publication which it is today.

This is about the whole story of his life, except as to his family and home affairs. Soon after coming to St. Louis Charles married Marie, the daughter of John G. Taylor, one of St. Louis' prominent business men. As a result of that union there are a son, John G. Taylor and two daughters, Freddie and Francis Spink. Their home life has been beautiful and ideal and had lasted so long and interestingly that the severance of the ties is heartbreaking.

But while the father and head of the family is gone, his influence at home and in his publications will last as long as time itself, for the latter especially are planted on a rock foundation that neither time nor tide nor death nor calamity can affect.

Changing Of the Guard

J. G. Taylor Spink was 26 years old when he succeeded his late father as publisher of The Sporting News. Although his training for the position had been relatively brief, he tackled the job with the confidence of youth and the zeal of a crusader.

The first issue under Taylor's direction was dated April 30, 1914. Nearly the entire editorial page was devoted to the deceased publisher. It consisted of a heavily bordered four-column photograph of Charles C. Spink, a two-column editorial written by editor Earl Obenshain, a eulogy by Taylor Spink and a tribute by Al Spink.

In referring to the numerous publications that Charles had guided to success, Al wrote: "To his immense energy is due the great success they scored. They are all so finely made, in fact, that they give to St. Louis a reputation all over the world. . . ."

The editorial cited Charles Spink's growth in the publishing business, his intimate personal and professional relationship with major league executives and the principles under which he directed the daily operations of The Sporting News.

"It was Mr. Spink's wont," said the editorial, "when asked for instructions or advice, to remind those who carried out his ideas . . . to be fearless, have opinions, do not be afraid to hit, but be just.

"Mr. Spink was one publisher who backed his editors to the limit. He would 'go to the front' for them

Al Spink, the TSN founder who split with Charles in the late 1890s, returned in 1914 to write a glowing tribute (left) to his late brother.

FATHER BUSINESS ASSOCIATE COMRADE

He succeeded in all things he undertook—not because he sat at the gates of fortune and waited for them to open, but because he pressed ever onward.

It is hard in one's bereavement to record the death of a Father, but when that Father has been the constant companion and business associate of a son, allowing that son an opportunity to know, better than anyone else, his many sterling qualities, the task is even more heart-rending.

Charles Claude Spink, beloved husband of Marie Taylor Spink, and Father of John George Taylor, Freddie and Francis Smith Spink, passed away on the morning of April 22d, as a result of an operation for stomach trouble, from which he had long been a sufferer.

My Father was a self-made man. He fought for everything throughout his life, and with such men, of such brilliant character, seemingly the easiest thing is to die, realizing, like all of us, that our time must come at some time and God's will must be done.

Although his business as publisher of three of the leading publications in the United States brought him in contact with people throughout the land, my Father loved his wife, children and home above all things. During his last hours his thoughts were only for his family.

Charles Claude Spink was born August 2, 1862, on the Isle of Orleans, one of the many islands in the beautiful St. Lawrence River. When a boy, his parents moved to Chicago, and, though his father, who was a member of the House of Parliament in Canada, died early, his elder brother, Fred William Spink, was as much of a father to him. It was greatly due to the esteem and love he had always held for this brother that his struggle at that time was lessened. My Father came to St. Louis in 1886, where he became associated with his brother, Alfred H. Spink, in publishing THE SPORTING NEWS. Through his capable management, THE SPORTING NEWS was soon put on a paying basis.

It was in 1887, Charles Claude Spink married Marie Taylor, daughter of John George Taylor, then a prominent citizen of St. Louis. From this union there have been three children.

With the growth of base ball THE SPORTING NEWS developed also, until it soon became the leading base ball publication in the world, which enviable position it still holds.

It was in 1899 that THE SPORTING GOODS DEALER was launched. Through the same tireless energy that built up THE SPORTING NEWS, my Father made a success of his second venture. It was in the summer of 1906 that I became associated with Father in the business which is now known as CHARLES C. SPINK & [illegible] I shall never forget his guidance and patience with me at all times. It was this same year that Father [illegible] The next year he started THE SPORTING GOODS

Charles Claude Spink.

Charles C. Spink, senior member of the firm of Charles C. Spink & Son, publishers of this paper, died at St. Luke's Hospital in St. Louis at [illegible] o'clock on the morning of Wednesday, April 22. He had been taken to the hospital from his home, 5725 Lindell Boulevard, in St. Louis, three hours before to undergo an operation for acute intestinal trouble. The operation had been decided upon as the one desperate chance to save his life, but he never regained consciousness. He was buried in Bellefontaine Cemetery in St. Louis on the following day, Thursday. The burial rites of the Episcopal Church were observed at the house and at the grave the full services of the Masonic order were conducted by Tuscan Lodge, No. 360, A. F. and A. M. and Ascalon Commandery, No. 16, Knights Templars.

Pall bearers, honorary and active, included Byron Bancroft Johnson, Charles [illegible] Comiskey, Robert Lee Hedges, James [illegible] McTague, Colin Selph, [illegible] Moberly, William Dee Becker, A. N. Kerr, Lorenzo [illegible] Anderson, Ben C. Adkins, John D. Johnson, J. A. Huhl, Stewart Scott, Richard Collins, Walter Whittier and William D'Arcy.

The names in this list of [illegible] performed the last and the most sorrowful [illegible]

The editorial-page tribute after Charles C. Spink's death in 1914 included an editorial (above) written by Editor Earl Obenshain and a eulogy (left) written by son J.G. Taylor Spink.

with a courage that . . . is rare in newspaper publishers. But behind that courage was a tenderness for the feelings and a quickening to the sensibilities of others akin to a mother's love. . . .

". . . The spirit of Charles C. Spink lives. It lives in the lessons he has taught those who knew and understood him best, of charity, justice, integrity, faithfulness. All these virtues he practiced. . . . He praised the good plays men made in the game of life and forgot the errors.

"May we be faithful to that which he cherished, true to the trust he has imposed. Only those of us who were close to him know how high we must aim and how true."

In his eulogy to his father, Taylor Spink wrote, "It is hard in one's bereavement to record the death of a father, but when that father has been a constant companion and business associate of a son, allowing that son an opportunity to know, better than anyone else, his many sterling qualities, the task is even more heart-rending.

"I know that the many readers . . . will find that I am my father's son, and (that) I will lend the same tireless energy, in even greater degree, if possible, to merit the continuance of the esteem in which these publications have always been regarded.

"Those who will direct the business in the future will be guided by the invisible hands of him who has gone. No man who has ever worked under the guiding influence of Charles Claude Spink ever need feel that he is alone. In many ways each day the influence will be felt. It will come as a still voice which will continue to be heard by those who have been associated with him."

Marie Spink took a more active role in the operation of The Sporting News after her husband Charles died in 1914.

Female Influence

After the death of Charles C. Spink, his widow assumed a more active role in the daily affairs of The Sporting News.

Marie T. Spink, a slight-figured lady with boundless energy, exerted a positive influence on the publication for more than 40 years.

In the early days, she counseled her husband against what she considered to be "objectionable advertising" which, if accepted, could have added thousands of dollars to the company's sluggish cash flow. She was a vital factor when TSN was "a scissors and pastepot paper" without correspondents and she was there when it attained stature as the "Baseball Paper of the World."

Initially, she served as bookkeeper and helped collect payments. Those collections frequently consisted of shoes for the children and groceries for the table.

As a new widow prior to World War I, Marie occupied a desk next to that of her son, J.G. Taylor Spink. Without fail, she would arrive first at the office, open the first mail and prepare herself for consultation with her son on business

Marie Spink (pictured below in the 1920s) exerted an energetic influence on her son, J.G. Taylor Spink. Marie (left) enjoyed a visit with Cubs pitcher Lon Warneke in 1933 while vacationing in Hot Springs, Ark.

matters before returning to her home.

"Economy" was her never-failing watchword. If an employee left his desk for more than a moment, he could expect, upon his return, to find the overhead light turned off, courtesy of Mrs. Spink, the vice-president and treasurer who never could forget the impecunious days.

Mrs. Spink was an avid sports fan and attended baseball games and wrestling matches at every opportunity. She also was fiercely independent with ideas befitting one many years her junior.

When, at age 62, she arrived in Hot Springs, Ark., for the start of her annual winter vacation, she sported a gold band around an ankle. Asked about her unconventional and slightly daring affectation, she replied somewhat huffily that it was her ankle, she had paid for the band and, moreover, "it's my business."

Mrs. Spink was a charming hostess who knew most of the baseball dignitaries on a first-name basis.

She fell victim to an attack of influenza in February 1944. The illness weakened her heart and she died on March 1 in her apartment.

Her obituary in The Sporting News contained the assertion that she "had exerted a greater influence on baseball and baseball journalism than any other woman in the history of the game."

The Federal League

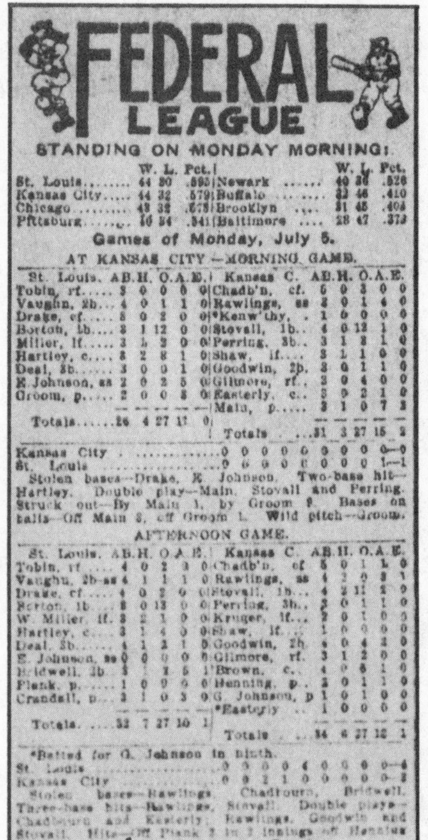
FEDERAL LEAGUE

STANDING ON MONDAY MORNING:

	W.	L.	Pct.		W.	L.	Pct.
St. Louis	44	30	.595	Newark	40	36	.526
Kansas City	44	32	.579	Buffalo	32	46	.410
Chicago	43	32	.575	Brooklyn	31	45	.408
Pittsburg	40	34	.541	Baltimore	28	47	.373

Games of Monday, July 5.

AT KANSAS CITY—MORNING GAME.

St. Louis.	AB.	H.	O.	A.	E.	Kansas C.	AB.	H.	O.	A.	E.
Tobin, rf.	3	0	0	0	0	Chadb'n, cf.	5	0	3	0	0
Vaughn, 2b.	4	0	1	1	0	Rawlings, ss	3	0	1	4	0
Drake, cf.	5	0	2	0	0	*Kenw'thy,	1	0	0	0	0
Borton, 1b.	3	1	12	0	0	Stovall, 1b.	4	0	12	1	0
Miller, lf.	3	1	2	0	0	Perring, 3b.	3	1	3	1	0
Hartley, c.	3	2	8	1	0	Shaw, lf.	3	1	1	0	0
Deal, 3b.	3	0	0	1	0	Goodwin, 2b.	3	0	1	1	0
E. Johnson, ss	2	0	2	5	0	Gilmore, rf.	3	0	4	0	0
Groom, p.	2	0	0	3	0	Easterly, c.	3	0	2	1	0
						Main, p.	3	1	0	7	2
Totals	26	4	27	11	0	Totals	31	3	27	15	2

Kansas City ... 0 0 0 0 0 0 0 0 0—0
St. Louis ... 0 0 0 0 0 0 0 0 1—1

Stolen bases—Drake, E. Johnson. Two-base hit—Hartley. Double play—Main, Stovall and Perring. Struck out—By Main 1, by Groom 8. Bases on balls—Off Main 3, off Groom 1. Wild pitch—Groom.

AFTERNOON GAME.

St. Louis.	AB.	H.	O.	A.	E.	Kansas C.	AB.	H.	O.	A.	E.
Tobin, rf	4	0	2	3	0	Chadb'n, cf	5	0	1	1	0
Vaughn, 2b-ss	4	1	1	1	0	Rawlings, ss	4	2	0	3	1
Drake, cf	4	0	2	0	0	Stovall, 1b.	4	2	11	2	0
Borton, 1b	3	0	13	0	0	Perring, 3b.	3	0	1	1	0
W. Miller, lf.	3	2	1	0	0	Kruger, lf.	2	0	1	0	0
Hartley, c.	3	1	4	0	0	Shaw, lf.	1	0	0	0	0
Deal, 3b.	4	1	2	1	0	Goodwin, 2b	4	0	4	3	0
E. Johnson, ss	0	0	0	0	0	Gilmore, rf.	3	1	2	0	0
Bridwell, 2b	3	1	1	5	1	Brown, c.	4	0	6	1	0
Plank, p.	1	0	0	0	0	Henning, p.	3	0	1	1	0
Crandall, p.	3	1	0	3	0	G. Johnson, p	1	0	1	0	0
						*Easterly	1	0	0	0	0
Totals	32	7	27	10	1	Totals	34	4	27	12	1

*Batted for G. Johnson in ninth.

St. Louis ... 0 0 0 0 4 0 0 0 0—4
Kansas City ... 0 0 2 1 0 0 0 0 0—3

Stolen bases—Rawlings, Chadbourn, Bridwell. Three-base hits—Rawlings, Stovall. Double plays—Chadbourn and Easterly; Rawlings, Goodwin and Stovall. Hits—Off Plank 3 in 3 innings, off Henning

PEACE REIGNS IN GAME AND ORGANIZED BALL IS SUPREME

Agreement Signed in Cincinnati After Federals Surrender Claims They Made in Their Fight for Recognition.

Only Dispute Remaining Concerns Terms of Readjustment of Territory in the International League—Outlaws Shouldered With Their Contracts.

THE PEACE AGREEMENT which ended the war waged by the Federals to establish a third major league was signed in Cincinnati on Wednesday, December 22. By the terms of the Agreement the Federal League discontinues its operations and yields all the points that by its own announcement in the beginning it con-

people with stockholders of a company which went out of existence."

Newark having like Baltimore been abandoned by the Internationals, their return there may be arranged through an agreement to permit partnership of the Newark Fed backers, provided that it is the desire of the Federals.

All these points at issue concerning the Internationals, however, will be settled at the coming conference.

I twas stipulated that in case the International-Federal arrangement provided for abandonment of the Federal parks in International cities then Organized Ball

OUTLAW ANTI-TRUST SUIT IS DISMISSED BY JUDGE LANDIS

BAN JOHNSON FORCES THE FEDS TO KEEP THEIR AGREEMENT

Disgruntled Baltimore Is Brought Into Line and Agrees with the Rest, but Says It Is Because Herrmann Has Made Promises.

BY GEORGE S. ROBBINS

CHICAGO, Ill., Feb. 8.—The famous "trust-busting" law suit of the Federal League against the National Commission and Organized Ball in general in which the promoters of the late outlaw league charged the system of Organized Ball with "monstrous evils" which the Feds themselves later found it necessary to adopt in about every case, is no more. It was dismissed by Judge Kenesaw M. Landis in the United States District Court here yesterday (Monday), all parties to the suit agreeing, including the Baltimore Federals, who had been threatening ever since the Peace Agreement to push the suit because they were angry at not being allowed to either enter one of the major leagues or be given the Baltimore International franchise.

The beginning of the end to the famous case dates from last Saturday, when attorneys for Organized Ball and for the Federals, with the exception of the Baltimore Club, appeared before Judge Landis and made motion for dismissal of the suit that all parties to the suit had consented to the withdrawal.

The withdrawal of the suit was the work of only a few minutes. After entering the order of dismissal, Judge Landis said a careful review of all the evidence and the various arguments of both sides had failed to impugn the honor of baseball or of any individual player.

The motion for withdrawal was presented by Attorney S. L. Schwartz of St. Louis, representing the Federal League, and was concurred in by Attorney Harry P. Webber, representing George W. Miller, counsel for Organized Baseball.

Mr. Webber presented to the court official notices from all the defendants to the suit consenting to the withdrawal.

Fears that objection to the withdrawal would be entered by the Baltimore Club of the Federal League were proved groundless when Attorney Janney, counsel for the Baltimore Federals, entered his appearance in the case, but interposed no objection to the dismissal of the proceedings.

Problems Simple Said Landis.

After directing that the suit be dismissed, Judge Landis said:

"The motion for a preliminary injunction in this suit was presented to this

Though The Sporting News strongly opposed the formation of the Federal League, it still ran standings and box scores (above left) for the outlaw organization. The 1915 headline (above) salutes the collapse of the league and the 1916 headline (left) salutes the dismissal of the league's anti-trust suit.

Like his father, J.G. Taylor Spink believed in having opinions, being fearless and ready to hit while, at the same time, being just. At 5-foot-7, he never hesitated to engage more muscular adversaries if he believed in the cause.

Taylor waged his first major campaign against the Federal League. He was convinced that two major leagues were ideal and that three would be ruinous. While he published the Federal League box scores and reported the league's activities in his columns, he enlisted the aid of his correspondents in fighting the outlaws. As a result of his pugnacious attitude, headlines

BASE BALL
THE YEAR 'ROUND

SINGLE COPIES, 5 CENTS

HE'S THE GAME'S GOOD FRIEND

JUDGE KENESAW MOUNTAIN LANDIS

Judge Landis proved a loyal friend to baseball to the finish and he can be thanked that the professional game is not seriously embarrassed if not altogether disrupted. Knowing the system of Organized Ball, while necessary to the game, still is in many ways unlegal, he held off his decision, his far-seeing wisdom telling him that sooner or later the cause for action—the Federal promotion scheme—must collapse. And that came out as he foresaw. With the anti-trust suit dismissed he has expressed a hope and a belief that the game he has loved as a fan for 30 years will again prosper and be free from the attacks of would-be wreckers for years to come.

When U.S. District Judge Kenesaw Mountain Landis dismissed the Federal League suit in 1916, The Sporting News ran a photograph (left) of the jurist and labeled him a friend of the game. A casualty of the baseball war was TSN competitor Sporting Life (below), which folded in 1917 after supporting the outlaw circuit.

SPORTING LIFE

The Loyal Champion of Clean Sport

THE EYE OF THE SPORT LOVERS WORLD

A Weekly Digest of the World's Progress in Sport

Vol. 69. No. 24 — Philadelphia, August 11, 1917 — Price 5 Cents

1—Rube Marquard, who has "come back" as best pitcher of Brooklyn Club. 2 C. G. Spencer, famous professional trap shot, still going strong. 3 The days of real sport—a sportsman's camp in the lake region. 4—J. E. "Ted" Meredith, world's greatest middle-distance runner, as an United States aviator

in The Sporting News reported:

"Feds Pull Greatest Bone in Their Erratic Career / Nothing to Gain in Law Suit / Only an Admission of Weakness." And, "Desperate Federals Seek Wreck of National Game / Start Suit That If Successful Would Disrupt Organization of Every League and Bring Chaos in Professional Baseball."

In February 1916, after a United States district judge in Chicago ruled in favor of Organized Baseball, The Sporting News printed a two-column photo of the jurist, calling him a friend of the game.

"All hands in the baseball litigation unite in the way Judge (Kenesaw Mountain) Landis conducted the case," TSN said. "The Federal bill of complaint was a mass of allegations concerning this, that and the other thing, but the Judge brought order out of it. Incidentally, the Judge has paid a tribute to baseball by proclaiming from the bench that it is a public institution that no one shall think of harming, thus giving the game an official recognition that is highly complimentary."

The decision by Judge Landis sounded the death knell for the Federal League. It also created an awareness in baseball that, in later years, led to his selection as the game's first commissioner.

The death of the Federal League also started the knockout count for Sporting Life. The Philadelphia publication, which had competed with TSN for many years, supported the outlaw circuit. It was an unwise choice. The eastern weekly folded in 1917 and The Sporting News ruled supreme.

It was not the end of Francis Richter, however. The former Sporting Life editor, who had refused to even mention the birth of The Sporting News in 1886, contributed articles to the St. Louis survivor of the journalistic war in the years that followed.

AN INTERESTING GROUP OF BASEBALL BOOSTERS

The old national game of America is the melting pot that turns them all out in the old mold, inspires them with one thought and makes their hearts beat in time. When Cincinnati sent over a big delegation of fans to St. Louis on the opening day of the National League season in the Mound City to help inaugurate the "Cardinal Idea" of a community-owned ball club, the fans of St. Louis gave the visitors from "Over the Rhine" a royal time, all classes of citizens lending their aid to make the day eventful. One of the features was a visit to one of the St. Louis show places, the Anheuser-Busch plant, the largest brewery in the world, where 6,000 employes stopped work to act as a mammoth reception committee. One of the many photographs taken at the Anheuser-Busch plant to be preserved as mementos was that reproduced here, and its group is typical of how baseball interests men of all nationalities and all walks of life. Take them as they appear in the picture: First, J. G. Taylor Spink, publisher of The Sporting News, who naturally need not explain why baseball interests him. Then Al Jolson, actor, one of the famous funny men of the stage, who got so enthused he bought $1,000 worth of stock in the community-owned Cardinal Club; next, John Heydler, secretary of the National League, who has "risen from the ranks" as a player to become the right bower of National League presidents. Adolphus Busch III, vice-president of the Anheuser-Busch corporation, social dictator and one of the all around big young men of St. Louis, stands on Heydler's left, elbow to elbow with Tom Hickey, whose forefathers never brewed beer, but knew well how to extract good cheer out of a potato. Hickey is president of the American Association, also a man of moment in the insurance field. He is just to the rear of Garry Herrmann himself, who needs no introduction, except to say that baseball is only one of his many activities. His name not only heads the Cincinnati ball club, but it is carried in a prominent place on the list of officers of a score of big concerns and it appears in letters of stone on most of Cincinnati's public buildings. The towering big man is John Kinley Tener, president of the National League, former governor and national legislator, a "big man" in every way. Edward Magnus, a vice-president of the Anheuser-Busch company, who had charge of the brewery's reception arrangements, is arm in arm with Tener. The man on the extreme right is Micheal Mullen, prominent citizen of Cincinnati, who does not hesitate to drop business affars to travel several hundred miles just to boost the game they all love and enthuse over. Some party, representing various lines of endeavor and a wealth of capabilities, but this one day just plain fans.

A Born Newspaperman

Taylor Spink was cast in the same mold as his uncle Al. He was a born newspaperman with a quick grasp of what would appeal to his readers as well as the methods with which to popularize his product.

For example, when the president of the Nashville club of the Southern League wrote a letter to him, Spink quickly capitalized on the correspondence for promotional value.

The letter, published in the next issue of TSN, stated: "If the suggestions outlined by The Sporting News on the editorial page and news columns were followed religiously, I honestly believe that many troublesome questions that have arisen in Organized Baseball would not again arise to bother the club owners, worry ball players or cause dissatisfaction in the ranks of the army of fans who year after year support the game."

Communications such as this convinced Taylor Spink that he was pursuing the proper course, if indeed a doubt ever had existed.

In one of his early moves, Taylor opened advertising offices in Chicago, Kansas City and Detroit. Earlier, a New York office had been opened and later he established outlets in Los Angeles and San Francisco.

Once, he found it necessary to alert his readers to an impostor who was traveling through Nebraska selling subscriptions as an alleged representative of The Sporting News.

At another time, a notice on the editorial page asked readers to refrain from faulting TSN if weekly copies were delivered tardily. Late arrival, the announcement reminded, was due to the railroad switchmen who were on strike.

Semiannually, the paper published a statement of ownership in which the stockholders were listed as J.G. Taylor Spink, Marie T. Spink and her two daughters, Mrs. Freddie Spink Christy and Mrs. Frances Spink Riesmeyer. Later, after the death of Riesmeyer, Frances married Cyrus Merrell.

The statement reported further that "there are no bond holders, mortgagees or other security holders."

A distinguished group (left) graced a page in The Sporting News in 1917. The occasion was the season opener in St. Louis and among the dignitaries with J.G. Taylor Spink (left) were singer Al Jolson (second from left) and Anheuser-Busch Vice-President Adolphus Busch III (fourth from left).

STATEMENT of the ownership, management, etc., of THE SPORTING NEWS, a weekly paper, published at St. Louis, Mo.:

The name of the editor is Earl Obenshain; business manager, J. G. T. Spink; publisher, THE SPORTING NEWS PUBLISHING COMPANY, all of St. Louis.

The publishing company is incorporated and the stockholders are: J. G. TAYLOR SPINK, MRS. MARIE T. SPINK, MRS. FREDDIE SPINK CHRISTY, MRS. FRANCES SPINK RIESMEYER, all of St. Louis.

There are no bond holders, mortgagees or other security holders.

Sworn to by J. G. T. SPINK, business manager, on the 28th day of March, 1917.

THOMAS RIELLEY, Notary Public. My commission expires February 4, 1919.

Play Ball!

The 1917 baseball season is on. The Pacific Coast League and the Texas League, the early birds of baseball, start their seasons this week and within another week the two major leagues will be under way. Coincident with these baseball openings the Congress of the [illegible]ed States meets in special session

The Sporting News published a statement of ownership (above) semiannually during this period, listing stockholders and bragging that 'there are no bond holders, mortgagees or other security holders.'

A 1916 TSN ad offered a combination package (right) that subscribers 'couldn't beat.' For $2.75, a reader could get a year's subscription to TSN and a set of 75 baseball pictures produced by Spalding.

LATEST AND BEST BASE BALL GOSSIP

The Sporting [News]

THE BASE BALL PAPER OF THE W[ORLD]

VOLUME 60, NUMBER 6 — ST. LOUIS, OCTOBER 7, 1915

PHILLIES STAND OR FALL ON ALEX

As Grover Goes, So Goes the World's Series

THUS SAY A MAJORITY OF THE EXPERTS

Concensus of Opinion Seems to Be that Practically All Hope of National League Entry to Beat Red Sox Centers in Moran's One Star Pitcher.

THE SPORTING NEWS in its annual symposiums of opinions from baseball writers of the 11 major league cities as to outcome of World's series has never been able to note that there was anything like a general agreement on the part of the experts. However little a team might appear to have a chance on the best reckonings of form, there always has been a proportion of scribes who would see something to favor the under dog, as in the case of the Boston Braves against the Philadelphia Athletics last year. In this year's assembly of opinions, however, as presented to readers of The Sporting News here, there is something like an agreement—at least the same suggestion running through practically all the hundred or so expressions of opinion. And it is to this effect: **Grover Alexander is the cornerstone of the Phillies' hope. Unless he can master the Red Sox, not in one game or two games, but in three, even perhaps in all four, then the Phillies can be counted out. As Alexander goes, so goes the world's championship.**

This is not the absolute general verdict, it is true; but it is so near it as to be remarkable. Some there are who hold that other pitchers on Moran's staff will prove capable of holding the [Red] Sox, but they are comparatively few, and practically all agree that Moran's star [Alex]ander will be expected to shoulder the burden.

ALMOST A PLEASURE TO LOSE TO MORAN

OF COURSE BOSTON DOES NOT LOOK FOR SUCH A THING.

Should the Unexpected Happen Hub Will Take Off Its Hat to Pat with a Right Good Spirit.

BOSTON, Mass., Oct. 4.—While Boston does not expect to lose, if it should lose this coming World's Series it will feel the sentiment expressed by that famous citizen of Boston who when he stepped for the ring championship of the world, pulled himself together and bravely said: "I am glad an American won, anyway." That expresses Boston's feeling for Pat Moran and when I say Boston I mean all New England. Barring Boston's own ball teams there is no more popular aggregation in the [illegible]

PHILLY ALL READY TO RAISE CURTAIN

KNOWS WELL HOW TO HANDLE A WORLD'S SERIES.

New Actors in the Play, However, Stir an Interest That Sets Even Sleepy Town All Agog.

PHILADELPHIA, Pa., Oct. 4.—The stage is now nearly set and in a few days, after the final rehearsals, the curtain will go up on what should be as good a show as the World's Series Company Limited (very limited) has ever produced. For the sixth successive year the East will have the baseball classic to itself, but so far as the teams are concerned, or the locality of the diamonds on which the games will be played it does not a[ffect th]e interest, which [illegible]

Taylor Moves Quickly

For years, The Sporting News used a one-column format. That style changed quickly with the ascendancy of Taylor Spink.

Before the start of the 1915 World Series, a four-column page 1 headline announced: "Phillies Stand or Fall on Alex / As Grover Goes, So Goes the World Series / Thus Say a Majority of the Experts / Consensus Seems to Be That Practically All Hope of National League Entry to Beat Red Sox Centers in Moran's One Star Pitcher."

The "experts" were correct. After Grover Cleveland Alexander won the opening game for the Phils, Boston swept the next four.

Elsewhere in the paper, other significant changes were in progress. Taylor Spink introduced his staff of major league correspondents with photos and short biographies. The byline of Fred Lieb, baseball writer for the New York Press, appeared for the first time. Lieb specialized in historical articles, comparing present-day players with those of the nineteenth century. Lieb contributed to TSN for 60 years and was a member of the St. Louis staff in the 1940s.

John B. Sheridan, a St. Louis sports editor, authored a weekly column titled "Back of the Home Plate" and during the off-season, when space was more plentiful, readers enjoyed articles by well known writers such as Charles Van Loan and Octavus Roy Cohen.

In 1919, George Wright, star of the game's first professional team, the Cincinnati Red Stockings of 1869, sketched the highlights of baseball for the past half century, reflecting The Sporting News' appreciation of the game's colorful heritage.

In 1917, in a rare departure from TSN philosophy, Taylor Spink trained his editorial artillery on an umpire who had been attacked by a major league manager.

The arbiter was Bill Byron of the National League, the assailant, John J. McGraw of the New York Giants. The unusual defense of McGraw, TSN's longtime adversary, followed a ruckus in Cincinnati and was aired in an editorial that noted:

"The point in mind is this: Sooner or later the struggle against Byronism had to come to a crisis . . . not only for managers and players but the public as well. First regarded as a good deal of a joke, he had developed into a real menace to the game. Tactless, tyrannical, inconsiderate of players or public, something of a notoriety seeker and proud of his record as a storm center, he had, like the fabled toad, apparently come to the point of view that baseball games were staged only for the purpose of permitting Bill Byron to dominate them. . . ."

National League President John K. Tener took a contrary position. John McGraw was suspended for 16 days and fined $500.

With J.G. Taylor Spink calling the shots, TSN abandoned its one-column format, as evidenced by the 1915 World Series heads and stories (above and above right).

Red Sox Win World's Title With Four Games Out of Five

American League Entry Never Hard Pressed, in Spite of the Closeness of Scores, as Proven by Manner in Which It Took the Final Contest.

HE HIGHEST honors of baseball again rest with the American League, and the Boston Red Sox are, for the second time in four years, champions of the world, by virtue of having beaten the Phillies, champions of the National League, four games in five played. Thus does the World's Series of 1915 take its place in baseball history unique for the closeness of the scores and remarkable for the general high class baseball played. In a sense the Series ran true to the predictions, which were that the hope of the Phillies must rest in Grover Alexander. The premier right-hander of the National League found himself pitching in another league and he could not stand against its best attack. Winning his first game by great luck, he lost his second and was humbled so that he did not come back for the third that was expected of him. When Alexander was beaten in the third game of the Series, Philadelphia hopes dropped to a low ebb. The Red Sox were as good as world's champions. Chalmers pitched a noble game, but a one-run lead over him was as good as a million.

The Red Sox were equal to anything called upon. When Foster was hit freely in the fifth game and the Phillies took a lead, Bill Carrigan changed his style of battle immediately and showed that the rival National leaguers could be beaten anyway they wanted to make the fight. Red Sox batters were sent in to hit the ball, and they hit it out of the lot. In fact, the Red Sox were never hard pressed nor called upon for their reserve strength after they had estimated the problem before them in the first meeting of the teams.

The Series produced some great pitching, sensational fielding and finally some wonderful batting, thus furnishing all the elements that the fan delights in, and probably the five games, as a whole, were the best ever played in a World's Series. No particular player stands out as an over-shining star, indicating the fine balance of the two teams. And there were no real "goats" in the Series, though there were players who did not do all that had been expected of them by their admirers.

Financially the Series was a tremendous success and in both games at Boston new records were made for crowds and receipts. The games were well handled from a business standpoint and the best of feeling prevailed consistent with the rivalry bound to exist when so much was at stake. The interest proved that baseball [illegible]

JOE LANNIN'S ABLE LEADER

William Carrigan, Manager of the World's Champion Boston Red Sox

What M

BY WILLIAM CA
Manager of the

THE PHILLIES fought
in them, but cleanly
could not solve the
men, nor was their
the hitting strength we
the Phillies put up a great
er, in fact, than any of
them. Bancroft, Whitted
pecially surprised us by
and ability. The men on
were determined to win.
once we overcame Alexa
be certain. We proved
game. Also, we again pr
of baseball by coming
closing the Series when w
the last game gracefully
question being raised ab
the loss.

belief that by so doing
lucky day. Ignorance
players are happy.

With Bancroft on
matters looked bad fo
the Boston speedball w
Cravath to the mantlepiec
route.

Dick Hoblitzel took a grea
mers' overhand slants and
for three clean ones. Hobb
Chalmers' league and appar
George had.

Rigler made himself a mo
stopping a hard hit foul nea
Hoblitzel's bat in the four
umpire fielded it perfectly a
pitcher with accuracy.

Chalmers apparently was tr
Boston batsmen away from
first few innings. At least
came uncomfortably close to
mers did not look wild.

All the stands with the
two and three dollar seat se
by 11 o'clock and the crowds
during the long wait, with pr
who shouted popular songs
phones, the fans joining in

The scene outside the par
riotous confusion. The cru
that it seemed dangerous
sale of standing room ticket
to this fact that the atta
fell several hundred short o

Whitted made a good
Scott's foul fly in the third i
Cady was on third and Hoop
time he was in position t
third and when Hooper bluf
ond he ran in where he c
man who tried to advance.

Scott came to Shore's res
play which robbed Chalmers
the fourth inning, when the
on second and first

Taylor Spink worked quickly to improve TSN's quality of writing and among his early brainchilds was a column by John B. Sheridan entitled 'Back of the Home Plate' (below) and a story by former player George Wright sketching the highlights of a half century of baseball.

BACK of the HOME PLATE

OBSERVATIONS OF A VETERAN SCRIBE

By JOHN B. SHERIDAN

PARDON me if I write again on the evil as I have seen it in baseball this season of the batters failing to make the pitcher pitch. I'd like to get this violation of the great principle of play to the attention of players and their managers. I have noted that the batters in both major leagues all seem to be hitting the first ball or the second ball pitched, to be hitting with two balls and no strikes or three balls and no strikes, entirely regardless of the conditions of the game or the condition of the pitcher.

From earliest youth to the year 1917, I had heard that the fundamental of good team batting was to "wait him out," to "make him pitch." The more I have seen of baseball the more certain I have been that to draw a pitcher to three and two and then punish him was the very acme of good batting—and as I have seen the game played by every club in both major

JOHN B. SHERIDAN

VETERAN GEORGE WRIGHT SKETCHES GAME'S HIGHLIGHTS

NE of the names that always will be linked with the history and development of baseball is that of George Wright, who was among the pioneers in taking up the game and still lives hale and hearty with a keen memory of the early days. In fact, no one's memory, perhaps, goes back so far. Mr. Wright was a great cricketer before he took up baseball and in the "new" game he became even more famous as player and manager, and from his ideas sprung a number of changes for the better in play.

In response to a request for a story of baseball as he knew it he has written the following brief article, summing up the outstanding features of the history of the game for a period of over 50 years, as they appealed to him. The article will be an interesting addition to the libraries of fans who treasure baseball history.

BY GEORGE WRIGHT.

I REMEMBER the game of ball back in the early days when it was called "town ball," the ball being thrown at the batter when he was running to a stake or post four feet out of the ground, and he was not touched with the ball as it is done at the present time.

It was in the early 40's that the present game of baseball was developed and no doubt taken from the old game of town ball. At that time there were a number of young men who played the game for exercise and recreation on the grounds located at Twentieth street and Fourth avenue, known as Murray Hill, in New York City. From these players the first baseball club was organized, the Knickerbocker. This was in 1845. The following year the club moved to grounds located at Hoboken, N. J., on the banks of the Hudson river, where a very attractive baseball field was laid out. Other clubs were formed and played on the same diamond. Between this date and 1858 many clubs were organized in and about New York city and the game became very popular. It spread to other cities in the East, but being in the formative stage, with each club having its own ideas of play, it took some time [illegible]

HIS MEMORY GOES FAR

George Wright

the underhand to the overhand throwing, the rules being amended to allow these changes, which brought into play a variety of curves to the ball, the drop, rising in-shoot and out-shoot ball. This made the position of catcher an important as well as a dangerous one.

During these years two plays took place that caused a change in the rules. They were as follows: A fly ball hit in the air to shortstop, blocked by him to the pitcher [illegible]

A National Emergency

And the Game Goes On.

We confess without shame to no great understanding of the international differences that have brought Uncle Sam to the edge of the wholesale murder game in Europe, but we do think we know our baseball fan, and we want to say for him that wars and rumors of wars are not going to cause him to turn his back upon the Only Game. Rather, if troubles multiply, he is likely to seek it the more as something that will help him maintain his equilibrium. Therefore, we voice here our protest at the scare heads that tell us "War With Germany Bound to Hurt Baseball."

We have the evidence of the game in Canada, where, even with one in three of every man of military age drafted for duty across seas, the game still survives—Toronto led the International in attendance last season. But in the

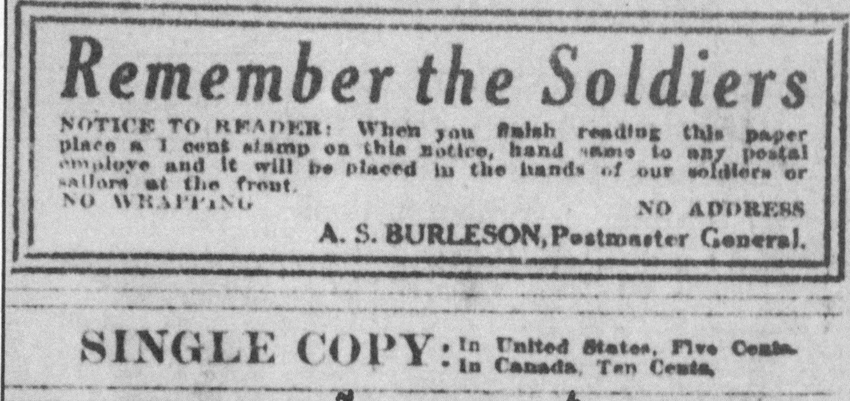

Remember the Soldiers

NOTICE TO READER: When you finish reading this paper place a 1 cent stamp on this notice, hand same to any postal employe and it will be placed in the hands of our soldiers or sailors at the front.
NO WRAPPING — NO ADDRESS

A. S. BURLESON, Postmaster General.

SINGLE COPY: In United States, Five Cents. In Canada, Ten Cents.

As the United States prepared to enter into World War I, The Sporting News campaigned vigorously (above left and below) on behalf of major league baseball. After U.S. involvement began, TSN published a large page 1 notice (above right) urging readers to pass on their copies of TSN to the young men fighting overseas.

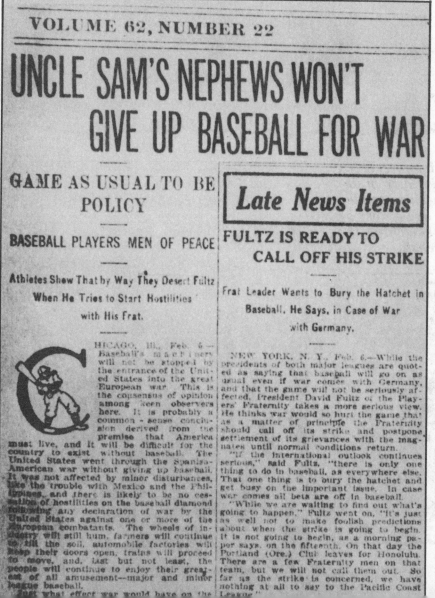

VOLUME 62, NUMBER 22

UNCLE SAM'S NEPHEWS WON'T GIVE UP BASEBALL FOR WAR

GAME AS USUAL TO BE POLICY

BASEBALL PLAYERS MEN OF PEACE

Athletes Show That by Way They Desert Fultz When He Tries to Start Hostilities with His Frat.

CHICAGO, Ill., Feb. 6—Baseball's machinery will not be stopped by the entrance of the United States into the great European war. This is the consensus of opinion among keen observers here. It is probably a common-sense conclusion derived from the premise that America must live, and it will be difficult for the country to exist without baseball. The United States went through the Spanish-American war without giving up baseball. It was not affected by minor disturbances, like the trouble with Mexico and the Philippines, and there is likely to be no cessation of hostilities on the baseball diamond following any declaration of war by the United States against one or more of the European combatants. The wheels of industry will still hum, farmers will continue to till the soil, automobile factories will keep their doors open, trains will proceed to move, and, last but not least, the people will continue to enjoy their greatest of all amusement—major and minor league baseball.

Just what effect war would have on the

Late News Items

FULTZ IS READY TO CALL OFF HIS STRIKE

Frat Leader Wants to Bury the Hatchet in Baseball, He Says, in Case of War with Germany.

NEW YORK, N. Y., Feb. 6.—While the presidents of both major leagues are quoted as saying that baseball will go on as usual even if war comes with Germany, and that the game will not be seriously affected, President David Fultz of the Players' Fraternity takes a more serious view. He thinks war would so hurt the game that as a matter of principle the Fraternity should call off its strike and postpone settlement of its grievances with the magnates until normal conditions return.

"If the international outlook continues serious," said Fultz, "there is only one thing to do in baseball, as everywhere else. That one thing is to bury the hatchet and get busy on the important issue. In case war comes all bets are off in baseball.

"While we are waiting to find out what's going to happen," Fultz went on, "it's just as well not to make foolish predictions about when the strike is going to begin. It is not going to begin, as a morning paper says, on the fifteenth. On that day the Portland (Ore.) Club leaves for Honolulu. There are a few Fraternity men on that team, but we will not call them out. So far as the strike is concerned, we have nothing at all to say to the Pacific Coast League."

The entrance of the United States into World War I gave the prophets of doom opportunity to mount their soap boxes and predict dire consequences for baseball. Taylor Spink did not join that parade.

An editorial sounded a note of optimism. It noted: "People have too long been immured to the thought (of war) that sooner or later the trouble would engulf us; now that it has come it deals no shock to their ordinary habits of life, one of which is going to baseball games. The failure of 'war extras' to sell indicates that and the biggest crowds that we expect to see around the newspaper bulletin boards this summer are those gathered to watch the posting of the scores.

"If this appears to be unpatriotic or too light a view of a thing so regrettable as war, make the most of it. It is a statement of self-evident fact."

Large and enthusiastic crowds at the season's opening games demonstrated that TSN had predicted the national mood correctly.

Throughout the national emergency, while millions of young Americans were attempting to "make the world safe for Democracy," a page 1 notice to readers urged, "When you finish reading this paper place a 1-cent stamp on this notice, hand same to any postal employee and it will be placed in the hands of our soldiers or sailors at the front. No wrapping. No address." The message bore the signa-

THE SPORTING NEWS

ALL LINED UP FOR THEIR OLD UNCLE SAM

CAPTAIN HUSTON AND HIS MILITARY YANKEE PLAYERS ON PARADE

Here's the first impression of that new feature of baseball training, military drill. The picture shows the Yankees at Macon in formation under the sharp ...s of an army drill master, and in addition to the players Captain Til Huston, who is a real captain, by the way, has impressed into service all the newspaper ... and other camp followers, while to show that he believes in universal service and no favorites he is hiking along himself. Some of the boys, it will be ...d, are not in step, but that doesn't matter—the spirit of it's the thing and sooner or later they will learn which is their "hay" foot and which the "straw." ...how, it's hard to make a southpaw keep step with a right-hander. In each American League camp, in some of the National League camps and also in some ...e minor camps this scene is being enacted, and be it said to the credit of the players they are taking the thing seriously and showing real earnestness in their ...rts to get the United States of America out of the China class of nations.

In 1917, a page 3 photo showed co-Owner Tillinghast Huston drilling his Yankees in a very un-baseball-like fashion. In 1917, TSN announced (right) its arrangement with the Y.M.C.A. to provide free copies of TSN to military installations.

FAN IN TRENCH AND CAMP WILL HAVE HIS DEAREST WISH

THE BOYS in the trenches, and those training in camps in the United States and in Canada to enter them, have been unceasing in their calls for the "baseball dope." Even newspapers in London have heard it and have taken to publishing the scores, sometimes by innings, generally the bare results, of the major league games. But that is like offering a teaspoonful of broth to a starving man. What the baseball fan in khaki demands is all the details—and he knows where he can get it, but not always how. He wants The Sporting News. He has said so in a hundred letters to the publishers of this paper.

The "how" of getting it has been the big problem. The Sporting News believes it has found the way. It may interest its readers at peace to know that last week an arrangement was made with the Y. M. C. A. organization that has undertaken to look after the comforts of the boys in France or soon to go there for the sending each week of several hundred copies of The Sporting News to the American Army's training camp behind the trenches in France and to the various cantonments in America as they are formed.

The publishers of The Sporting News will furnish these hundreds of copies free and Secretary Kingman of the Y. M. C. A. has gladly agreed with J. G. Taylor Spink to see that they are placed where they will satisfy the demands of the soldier boys well-nigh famished for the "dope." Uncle Sam will see to it that the weekly consignment gets across the big pond promptly and woe be to the Kaiser if any of his U-boats attempt to deal a blow such as was dealt Clark Griffith's consignment of baseball pharaphernalia. The soldiers might, in a pinch, improvise bats and balls, but they can't find a substitute for The Sporting News.

Hereafter every considerable Army detachment in England or France will have its copies of The Only Baseball Paper on file, with the compliments of the publishers. Later the boys in the training camps at home will be just as well looked after.

But this does not mean the regular subscribers of The Sporting News should neglect their duty. They have been told how they can make the soldier heart glad by mailing their copies after they have finished with them. Doubtless the demand, to be satisfied, will require thousands of copies each week. The publishers ask their regular subscribers to lend a hand in supplying the "dope" to the boys who are just as much interested in Ty Cobb or Grover Alexander as if they had a chance to sit in the grandstand.

ture of A.S. Burleson, postmaster general.

The departure of the nation's youth for military duty put a serious crimp on the circulation of The Sporting News, but absence from home did not diminish their interest in baseball. Taylor Spink took measures to satisfy this hunger for news of the game.

An early August 1917 issue carried this headline: "Fan in the Trench and Camp Will Have His Dearest Wish." In the accompanying article, it was revealed that the publisher had arranged with the national secretary of the Y.M.C.A. to provide weekly 5,000 copies of The Sporting News free of charge to military installations.

"Uncle Sam will see to it," said the story, "that the weekly consignment gets across the big pond promptly and woe be to the Kaiser if any of his U-boats attempt to deal a blow such as was dealt Clark Griffith's consignment of baseball paraphernalia. The soldiers might, in a pinch, improvise bats and balls, but they can't find a substitute for The Sporting News."

(Clark Griffith, president of the Washington Senators, had sponsored a "Bat and Ball Fund" to purchase equipment for troops overseas, the first shipment of which was lost when a German submarine torpedoed the boat carrying it to France.)

The pre-Christmas issue of 1917 contained a full-page "Message of Good Cheer and Remembrance to the Boys Over There From the Boys Over Here." It consisted of good wishes from members of the National Commission, club owners and players.

December 27 THE SPORTING NEWS Page 5

A MESSAGE of GOOD CHEER and REMEMBRANCE

To The Boys "Over There" From The Boys Over Here

CHAS. A. COMISKEY
OWNER OF WORLD'S CHAMPION WHITE SOX

B. B. JOHNSON
PRESIDENT AMERICAN LEAGUE

CLARK C. GRIFFITH
DIRECTOR GENERAL CLARK GRIFFITH BALL AND BAT FUND

AUGUST HERRMANN
CHAIRMAN NATIONAL COMMISSION

CAPT. T. L. HUSTON
OF NEW YORK YANKEES NOW IN SERVICE IN FRANCE

B. B. JOHNSON
Pres. of American League
Chicago, Ill.

FRANK J. NAVIN
Owner of Detroit Club
Detroit, Mich.

FIELDER A. JONES
Manager of Browns
Portland, Ore.

W. T. GASTON
Umpire Western League
Byesville, Ohio

JOE JACKSON
Outfielder of White Sox
Savannah, Ga.

C. B. OWENS
Umpire American League
Kansas City, Mo.

VIC SAIER
Baseman of Pirates
Lansing, Mich.

CHARLEY BARRETT
Scout of Cardinals
St. Louis, Mo.

D. L. DUGDALE
Pres. of Seattle Club
Seattle, Wash.

M. J. O'NEILL
Mgr. of Syracuse Club

CHARLES A. COMISKEY
Pres. Chicago White Sox
Chicago, Ill.

CHARLES H. EBBETS
Pres. of Brooklyn Club
Brooklyn, New York

LEE FOHL
Mgr. of Cleveland Club
Cleveland, Ohio

ST. LOUIS CARDINALS
St. Louis, Mo.

JOHN H. FARRELL
Secretary National Association
Auburn, N. Y.

A. F. SHEAHAN
Pres. of Chicago B. B. League
Chicago Ill.

Victor Sporting Goods Co.
Springfield, Mass.

H. R. HELD
Umpire Pacific Coast League
Los Angeles, Cal.

MEL WOLFGANG
Pitcher for White Sox
Albany, New York

GEO. HILDEBRAND
Umpire American League
San Francisco, Cal.

J. C. CALHOUN
Mgr. of Wilkesbarre Club

COL. JACOB RUPPERT
Pres. of New York Yankees
New York City

BOBBY QUINN
Business Manager Browns
St. Louis, Mo.

MILLER J. HUGGINS
Mgr. N. Y. Yankees
Cincinnati, Ohio

E. G. BARROW
Pres. of International League
New York City

W. J. CLYMER
Mgr. of Louisville Club
Wilkesbarre, Pa.

BERT E. SHOTTON
Outfielder of Washington
Bismarck, Mo.

JAMES C. HAMILTON
Mgr. of Muskegon Club
Chicago, Illinois

CLAUDE P. WILLIAMS
Pitcher of White Sox
Savannah, Ga.

Hillerich & Bradsby Co., Inc.
Mfrs. Louisville Slugger Bats
Louisville, Ky.

P. GOLDSMITH'S SONS
Makers of Sporting Goods
Cincinnati, Ohio

AUGUST HERRMANN
Chairman National Commission
Cincinnati, Ohio

CHAS. H. WEEGHMAN
Pres. Chicago Cubs
Chicago, Ill.

JOHN C. HENDRICKS
Mgr. of Indianapolis Club
Indianapolis, Ind.

HENRY O'DAY
Umpire National League
Chicago, Illinois

GEORGE F. JOHNSON
Pres. of Binghamton Club
Endicott, N. Y.

CHARLES A. DEAL
Third Baseman Chicago Cubs
Chicago, Ill.

FRED McMULLIN
Infielder of White Sox
Los Angeles, Cal.

A. G. SPALDING & BROS.
Makers of Sporting Goods
New York City

ED MONROE
Pitcher N. Y. Yankees
Louisville, Ky.

WM. BYRON
Umpire National League
Detroit, Mich.

CLARK GRIFFITH
Mgr. of Washington Club and Director-General Bat and Ball Fund.
Washington, D. C.

JAMES C. McGILL
Pres. of Indianapolis Club
Indianapolis, Ind.

WILBERT ROBINSON
Mgr. of Brooklyn Dodgers
Baltimore, Md.

LARRY LAJOIE
Manager of Toronto Club
Cleveland, Ohio

FRED TONEY
Pitcher Cincinnati Reds
Nashville, Tenn.

JAKE PITLER
Second Baseman Pirates
Pittsburg, Pa.

FRANK O'LOUGHLIN
Umpire American League
Rochester, N. Y.

JACK SMITH
Outfielder St. Louis Cardinals
Chicago, Illinois

RAY SCHALK
Catcher Chicago White Sox
Litchfield, Illinois

JOHNNY RIGGS

H. N. HEMPSTEAD
Pres. of New York Giants
New York City

HUGO BEZDEK
Manager of Pittsburg Pirates
San Francisco, Cal.

CHARLES TESREAU
Pitcher New York Giants
Ironton, Mo.

IVAN OLSON
Shortstop Brooklyn Dodgers
Los Angeles, Cal.

PETER J. KILDUFF
Infielder of Chicago Cubs
Pittsburg, Kan.

NED EGAN
Mgr. of Waterloo Club
St. Paul, Minn.

JIM VAUGHN
Pitcher of Chicago Cubs
Honey Grove, Texas

ED J. PFEFFER
Pitcher Brooklyn Dodgers
Champaign, Illinois

EDDIE HOOPER
Mgr. of Chambersburg Club
Yorka, Pa.

IVY WINGO
Catcher Cincinnati Reds

LEW McCARTY

PHIL De C. BALL
Pres. of St. Louis Browns
St. Louis, Mo.

JAMES C. DUNN
Pres. of Cleveland Club
Cleveland, Ohio

OTTO F. STIFEL
St. Louis Browns
St. Louis, Mo.

HARRY F. SINCLAIR
New York

JOSEPH B. TINKER
President Columbus Club
Columbus, Ohio

LOUIS COMISKEY
Chicago White Sox
Chicago, Ill.

WM. DINEEN
Umpire American League
Syracuse, N. Y.

CHARLES STIS
Mgr. Ft. Dodge and Regina
St. Louis, Mo.

MIKE GONZALES
Catcher St. Louis Cardinals
Havana, Cuba

A page in the December 27, 1917, issue of The Sporting News was devoted to 'A Message of Good Cheer and Remembrance to the Boys Over There. . . .' Baseball owners, players, managers and umpires joined businessmen with short one-column greetings.

Soldiers Returning to Receive The Sporting News Through the American League

Resolution Unanimously Adopted at Meeting in New York Provides for 150,000 Copies—One for Each 10 of 1,500,000 About to Come Home

Lieut.-Col. Til Huston.

WHEN THE American League had closed its routine business at New York on Thursday, January 16, "Cap" Til Huston, now a lieutenant-colonel of an engineers' regiment awaiting muster out, was called on to tell his fellow magnates some of his impressions, in connection with war and baseball. The New York Yankee magnate thrilled his hearers with his story of the enthusiasm for baseball that the soldiers in France had shown, telling how they clamored for news of the World's Series last fall and how all of them were anxious to return that they might see, first the home folks, and then a real ball game.

Coming over on a transport with several thousand returning soldiers, Huston said, he discovered the boys had little or nothing to read, and the lack of it made the journey wearisome. He suggested that the baseball magnates could do nothing that would be appreciated more than to inaugurate a plan for furnishing returning soldiers with something interesting to read—and the soldier's big idea of something interesting, said Huston, was baseball "dope."

Then and there in the American League meeting a motion was made and passed unanimously that the league provide these dope hungry soldiers with copies of THE SPORTING NEWS without stint. Huston was asked how many copies would be required. He said it was figured a million and a half of soldiers would be returning within the next six months, and that one copy of The Sporting News might last among ten soldiers if they didn't thumb it too hard, "but they read it till it's worn to tissue," he added.

One copy among ten soldiers would mean 150,000 copies of The Sporting News, so that was the order the American League decided to place, and President Johnson was instructed to arrange for forwarding and distributing that number of copies extending over a period of six months. These details of distribution will be arranged at once, so that the dope hungry doughboys will not be long unsatiated. The plan is to send each week to several ports in the East consignments of The Sporting News. These will be taken abroad by transports, carried to French embarkation ports and there distributed among soldiers about to ship for America. Thus they are assured, through the liberality of the American League, "something to read" on the journey home, which otherwise would be long and monotonous.

Enough copies of The Sporting News for a million and a half soldiers means a million and a half fans pouring back from abroad to boost for baseball! We say it will be some boost, and while the American League deserves the credit, all leagues will share in the gain.

Tillinghast Huston, a colonel during World War I and co-owner of the New York Yankees, also was a good friend of The Sporting News, as the headlines and stories (left) attest.

A Good Friend

Tillinghast L'Hommedieu Huston was a captain of engineers in the Spanish-American War, a colonel in World War I and an important friend of The Sporting News.

In 1918, Taylor Spink was in New York to cover a major league meeting when he encountered Col. Huston, a co-owner of the Yankees who had just returned from the battlefields of France.

In the course of their conversation, Col. Huston informed the publisher that the doughboys in the American Expeditionary Forces were famished for baseball news and that the 5,000 copies of The Sporting News distributed weekly by the Y.M.C.A. did not begin to satisfy the voracious appetites of the displaced baseball fans.

The disclosure gave Spink an idea, which he presented to his good friend, Ban Johnson, president of the American League. Taylor proposed that the A.L. purchase copies of TSN at a reduced rate and send them overseas at the league's expense.

Johnson laid the suggestion before his club owners, who adopted it unanimously. Initially, 150,000 copies of the paper were purchased every week, but in time individual clubs made additional purchases. The arrangement supplied a huge boost to the paper's circulation at a critical time and created thousands of new readers in the post-war period.

After the Armistice, Col. Huston again rallied American League support for The Sporting News. At the close of a league meeting in New York, he was summoned to the podium to give his impressions of the war and baseball.

Huston commented at length on the war and remarked about the wearisome boat trip home for "the soldiers who have nothing to read." Asked for his suggestion on the best method to fill the void, Huston recommended that copies of The Sporting News be sent to France and distributed to the war veterans, one to every 10 men, as they embarked for home.

President Ban Johnson was authorized to devise a system of distribution. Weekly for the next six months, copies were sent to Eastern seaports, from where they were shipped to France. As a result of the American League's generosity, approximately 1.5 million servicemen were assured of baseball news to relieve hours of tedium on the long voyage home.

Signs of Encouragement

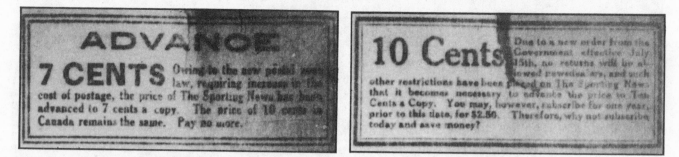

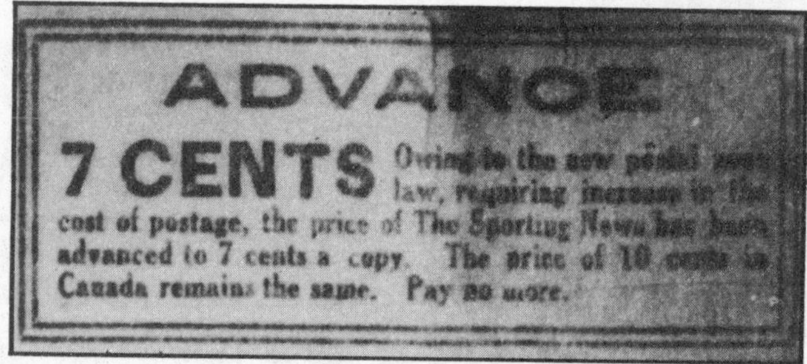

ADVANCE

7 CENTS Owing to the new postal zone law, requiring increase in the cost of postage, the price of The Sporting News has been advanced to 7 cents a copy. The price of 10 cents in Canada remains the same. Pay no more.

10 Cents Due to a new order from the Government effective July 15th, no returns will be allowed newsdealers, and such other restrictions have been placed on The Sporting News that it becomes necessary to advance the price to Ten Cents a Copy. You may, however, subscribe for one year, prior to this date, for $2.50. Therefore, why not subscribe today and save money?

The Sporting News hit readers with a double dose of bad news in 1918. On Page 1 of its July 4 issue, TSN announced that henceforth the price per issue would be 7 cents, marking the first price increase in the publication's history. Two weeks later, the price per issue was jumped to 10 cents.

Advertising revenue during this period of evolution did not permit significant and dramatic changes in The Sporting News. But signs of encouragement were beginning to emerge.

The Reach and Spalding Sporting Goods companies advertised regularly. On occasion, the Wilson Sporting Goods Co. and Hillerich and Bradsby, manufacturer of Louisville Slugger bats, inserted two and three-column ads.

At one point during the war, the four companies shared a full-page advertisement urging readers to "Lend Him a Hand / Buy Third Liberty Loan Bonds / Help Back Up Our Boys." At another time, the same four advertisers told readers "Buy Fourth Liberty Bonds / Don't Let the SON Go Down."

Manufacturers of smoking tobacco and cigarettes promoted their products with greater frequency during the period ending in 1920. Prince Albert and Velvet, "The Friendly Tobacco," scheduled ads regularly, while Camel and Lucky Strike Cigarettes inserted ads almost weekly.

On several occasions Bull Durham ads occupied an entire page while at other times the company promoted its chewing tobacco with two and three-column ads.

The Anheuser-Busch Company advertised Budweiser (before Prohibition) as well as Bevo, its popular soft drink, while the Wrigley Chewing Gum Company told the world that "The Flavor Lasts."

It was during this period that cigarette and tobacco advertisers began appearing in TSN more frequently. Lucky Strike produced both products.

When Jack Dempsey defeated Jess Willard for the world heavyweight boxing championship, he revealed in an ad that he attributed a large part of his success to "Nuxated Iron," an invigorating agent that had been endorsed by Willard, among others, in earlier years.

As he had done successfully in the past, Taylor Spink offered photographs of championship teams and once let readers have a subscription to The Sporting News, plus a copy of A.G. Spalding's "America's National Game," a combined value of $4, for $2.75.

But Spink's most inspired move occurred in 1918. In the July 4 issue, the cost per copy of The Sporting News was increased from five cents, its price for 32 years, to seven cents. Two weeks later, in the issue of July 18, the paper sold for 10 cents a copy and a year's subscription for $5.

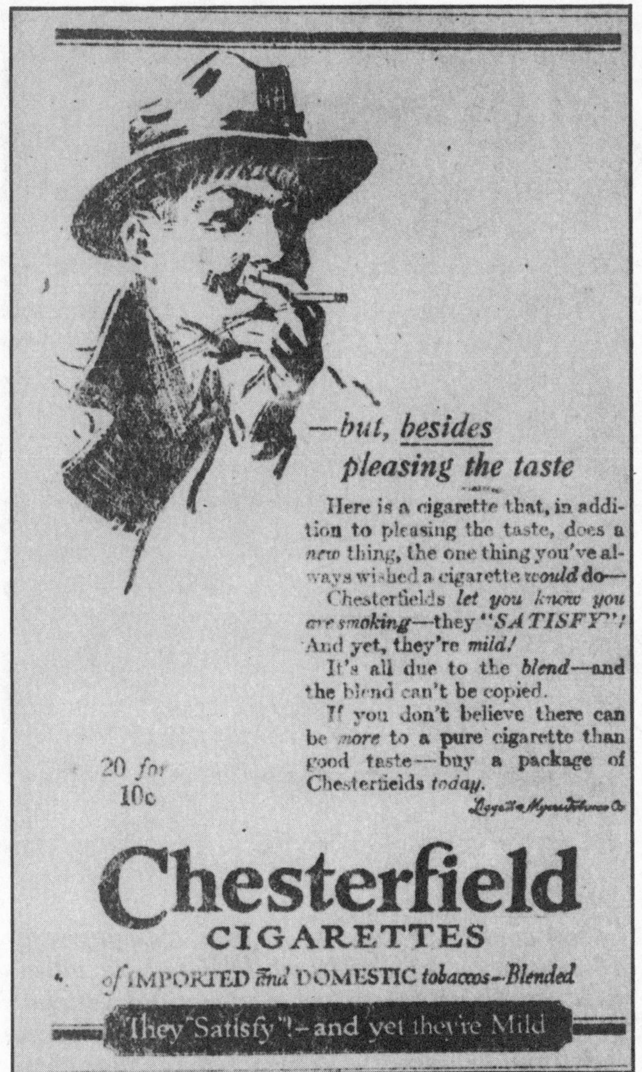

—but, besides
pleasing the taste
Here is a cigarette that, in addition to pleasing the taste, does a *new* thing, the one thing you've always wished a cigarette *would* do—
Chesterfields *let you know you are smoking*—they "*SATISFY*"!
And yet, they're *mild!*
It's all due to the *blend*—and the blend can't be copied.
If you don't believe there can be *more* to a pure cigarette than good taste—buy a package of Chesterfields *today*.
Liggett & Myers Tobacco Co.
20 for 10c
Chesterfield
CIGARETTES
of IMPORTED and DOMESTIC tobaccos—Blended
They "Satisfy"!—and yet they're Mild

A.G. Spalding offered the TSN reader more than baseball equipment. 'We fit your foot to the shoe and then fit the skate to the shoe — no easy task,' read the ad for a $9 pair of ice skates.

Skates and Shoes

The above illustration shows our No. XE Skate with No. 332 Shoe, a very dependable combination. Complete, $9.00
No. XE Skates only, Pr., $4.00
WRITE FOR OUR CATALOGUE

STORES IN ALL LARGE CITIES

Chesterfield cigarettes, which would become synonymous with the back cover of The Sporting News after World War II, could be purchased for 10 cents in 1917 while the R.J. Reynolds Tobacco Co. offered quality and satisfaction every time you light up a Prince Albert.

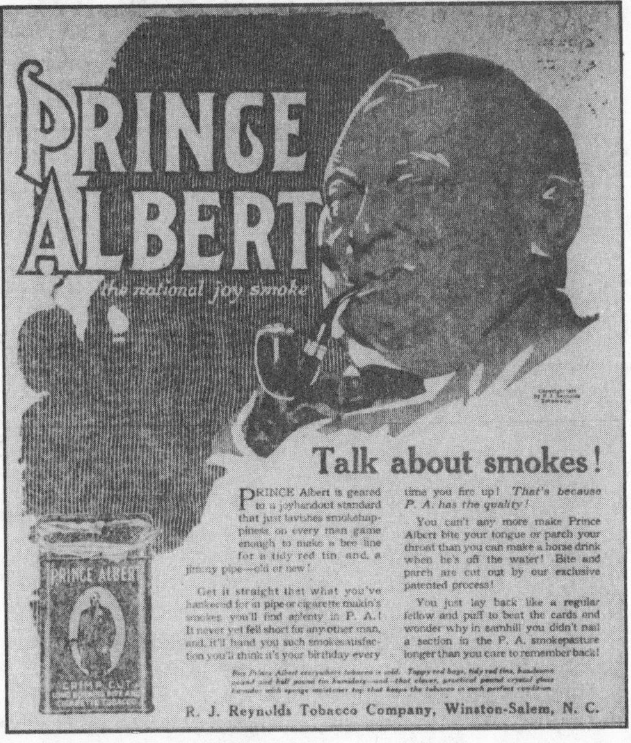

PRINCE ALBERT
the national joy smoke
Talk about smokes!
PRINCE Albert is geared to a joyhandout standard that just lavishes smokehappiness on every man game enough to make a bee line for a tidy red tin, and a jimmy pipe—old or new!
Get it straight that what you've hankered for in pipe or cigarette makin's smokes you'll find aplenty in P. A.! It never yet fell short for any other man, and, it'll hand you such smokesatisfaction you'll think it's your birthday every time you fire up! *That's because P. A. has the quality!*
You can't any more make Prince Albert bite your tongue or parch your throat than you can make a horse drink when he's off the water! Bite and parch are cut out by our exclusive patented process!
You just lay back like a regular fellow and puff to beat the cards and wonder why in samhill you didn't nail a section in the P. A. smokepasture longer than you care to remember back!
R. J. Reynolds Tobacco Company, Winston-Salem, N. C.

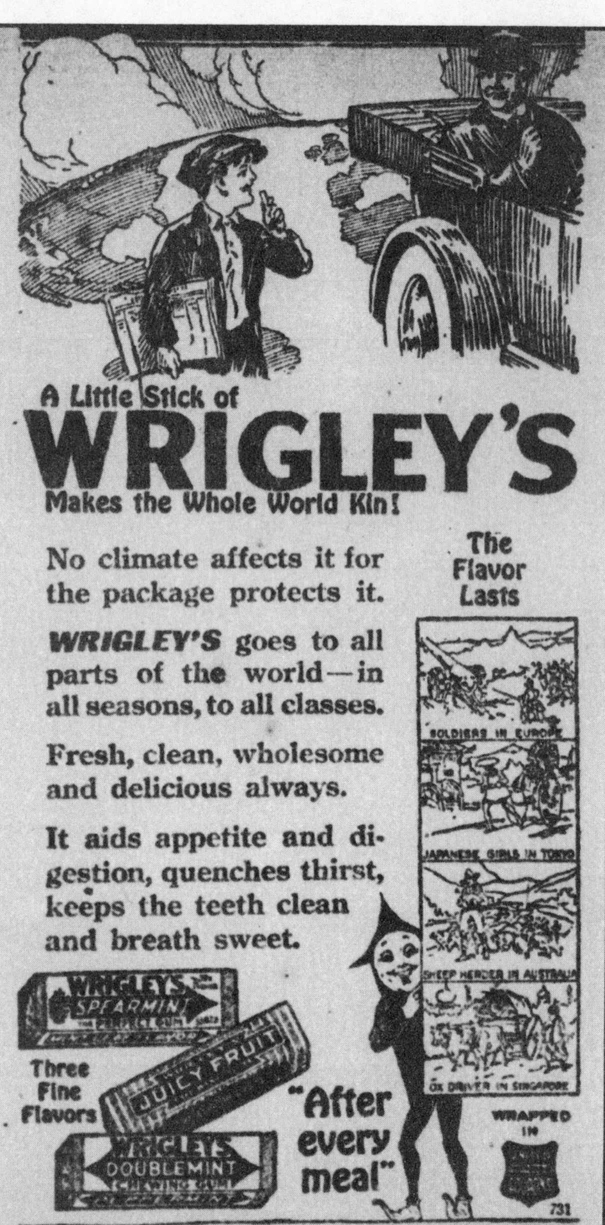

A Little Stick of
WRIGLEY'S
Makes the Whole World Kin!
No climate affects it for the package protects it.
WRIGLEY'S goes to all parts of the world—in all seasons, to all classes.
Fresh, clean, wholesome and delicious always.
It aids appetite and digestion, quenches thirst, keeps the teeth clean and breath sweet.
The Flavor Lasts
SOLDIERS IN EUROPE
JAPANESE GIRLS IN TOKYO
SHEEP HERDER IN AUSTRALIA
OX DRIVER IN SINGAPORE
WRIGLEY'S
SPEARMINT
Three Fine Flavors
JUICY FRUIT
WRIGLEY'S
DOUBLEMINT
CHEWING GUM
"After every meal"
WRAPPED IN
731

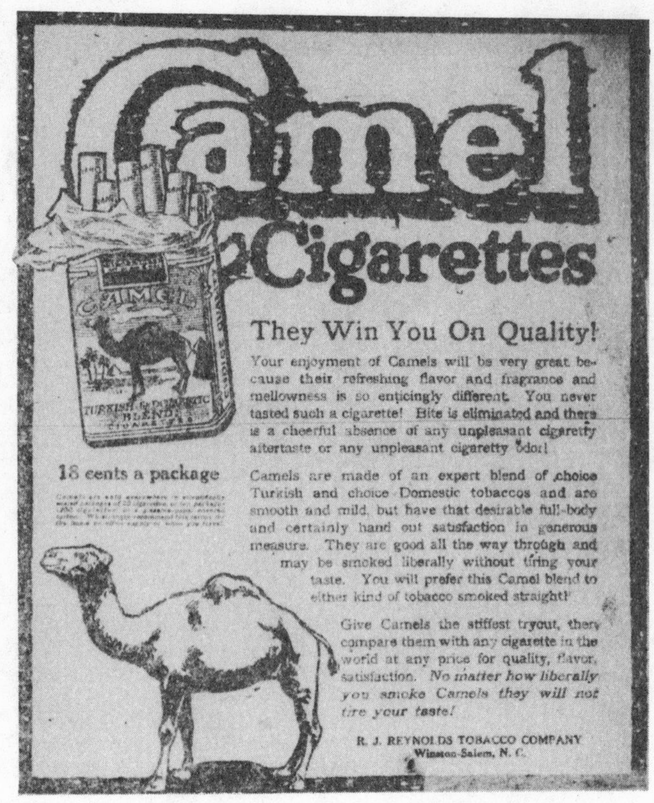

Camel
Cigarettes
They Win You On Quality!
Your enjoyment of Camels will be very great because their refreshing flavor and fragrance and mellowness is so enticingly different. You never tasted such a cigarette! Bite is eliminated and there is a cheerful absence of any unpleasant cigaretty aftertaste or any unpleasant cigaretty odor!
18 cents a package
Camels are made of an expert blend of choice Turkish and choice Domestic tobaccos and are smooth and mild, but have that desirable full-body and certainly hand out satisfaction in generous measure. They are good all the way through and may be smoked liberally without tiring your taste. You will prefer this Camel blend to either kind of tobacco smoked straight!
Give Camels the stiffest tryout, then compare them with any cigarette in the world at any price for quality, flavor, satisfaction. No matter how liberally you smoke Camels they will not tire your taste!
R. J. REYNOLDS TOBACCO COMPANY
Winston-Salem, N. C.

Camel cigarettes were offered on TSN pages for 18 cents a pack in 1919 while Wrigley's advertised its 'Fresh, clean, wholesome and delicious always' chewing gum. Interested in some 'healthful exercise'? A.J. Reach made that possible with its 'perfect shape and swing true' striking bags.

BAG PUNCHING

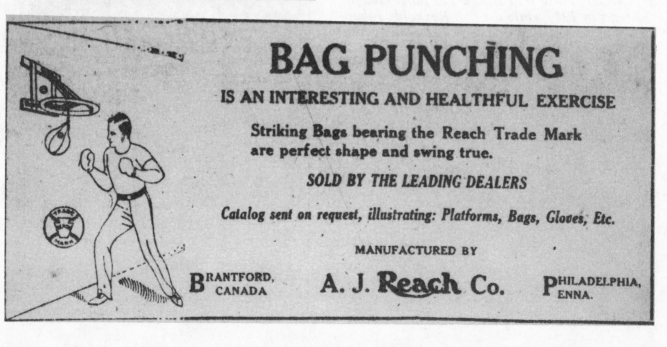

IS AN INTERESTING AND HEALTHFUL EXERCISE

Striking Bags bearing the Reach Trade Mark are perfect shape and swing true.

SOLD BY THE LEADING DEALERS

Catalog sent on request, illustrating: Platforms, Bags, Gloves, Etc.

MANUFACTURED BY

BRANTFORD, CANADA — A. J. Reach Co. — PHILADELPHIA, PENNA.

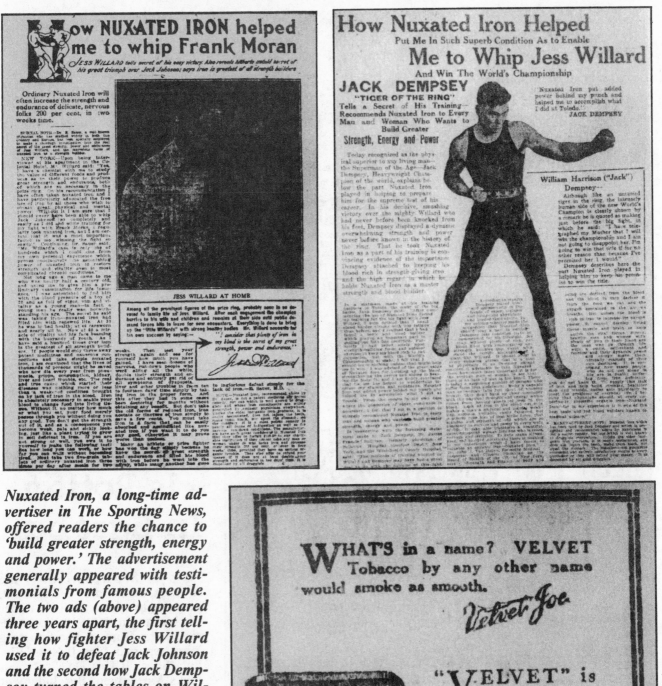

Nuxated Iron, a long-time advertiser in The Sporting News, offered readers the chance to 'build greater strength, energy and power.' The advertisement generally appeared with testimonials from famous people. The two ads (above) appeared three years apart, the first telling how fighter Jess Willard used it to defeat Jack Johnson and the second how Jack Dempsey turned the tables on Willard in 1919. For those pipe smokers who wanted a smooth sensation, the answer was Velvet.

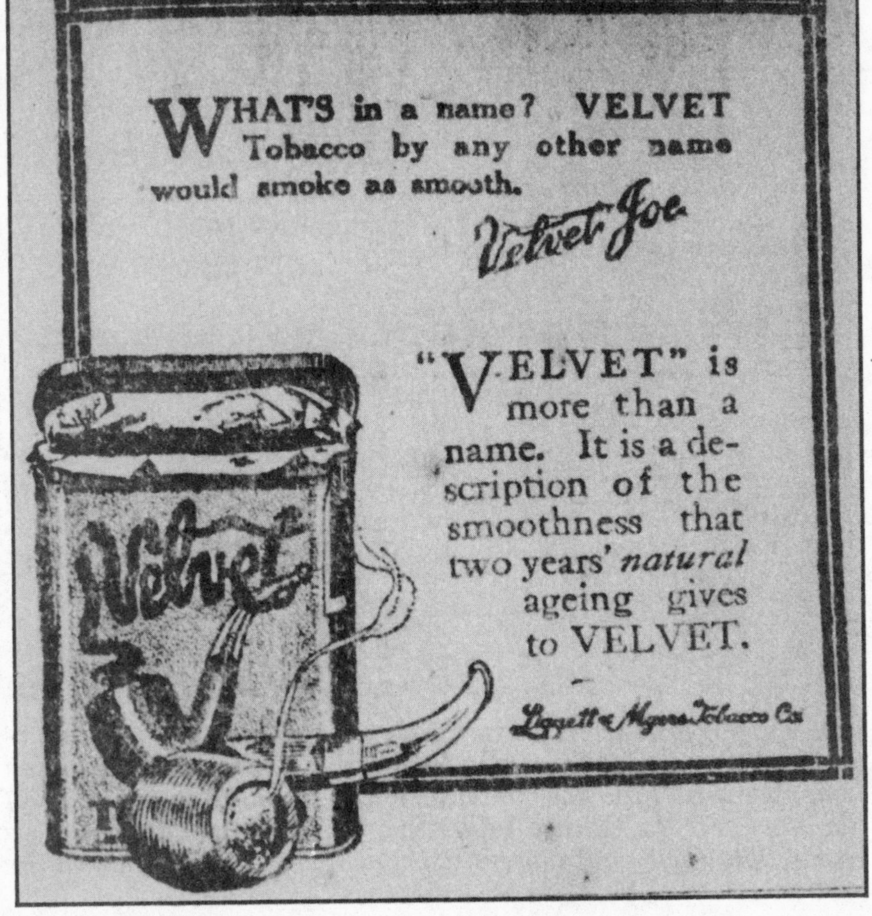

October 2 THE SPORTING NEWS Page 5

JOY IF REDS WIN—BUT A SHOCK IF THEY DO

SENTIMENT WITH MORANMEN BUT JUDGMENT PICKS SOX

Through Opinions of Most Critics Is Noted Thread of Conviction That Gleason Heads Team That Carries a Class Not Possessed by National League Rival.

MEN WHO MAKE HISTORY IN WINNING A FLAG

PAT MORAN AND HIS CHAMPION CINCINNATI REDS

BAN AND GARRY CAN BE PROUD OF ENEMIES

TRITE REMARK BY VETERAN AMONG CRITICS, PAUL EATON.

Agitators Who Have Stirred Trouble Are Apt to Hear Something Drop Before Another Season Opens.

REDS WILL HAVE TO DO BETTER.

SINCE IT'S SETTLED WHY PLAY AT ALL

BY FLOYD BELL

WHITE SOX TO WIN IN SEVEN GAMES

INSANITY OF RED BUGS DOES NOT AFFECT JUDGMENT ON BETS

BY THOMAS S. RICE

KNOWS REDS AND KNOWS THEY'LL WIN

REDS WON FAIR AND SQUARE AND WELL DESERVE HONORS

VILA PAYS TRIBUTE TO THEIR CLASS

POINTS OUT MISTAKE OF GLEASON

White Sox Should Not Have Been Allowed to Ease Up and Burlesque in Final Games of Season.

NEW YORK, N. Y., Oct. 13.—All hats off to Patrick Moran and his new world's champions, the Cincinnati Reds! The details of their victory over the Chicago White Sox have been related by a regiment of war correspondents, but there remain a few things that deserve comment

Late News Items

STILL PAYING OUT BIG SERIES MONEY

Umpires Get a Raise and Cincinnati Club Gives Pat Moran a Bonus of $5,000 for Winning Pennant.

CINCINNATI, O., Oct. 14.—There was no formal session of the National Commission here Monday as expected, to pass upon various matters of detail that have arisen in connection with playing the World's Series. Instead, according to Chairman August Herrmann, the members of the Commission disposed of the business in hand by long distance telephone. Part of that business was to increase the stipend of the four umpires, who officiated in the ... the usual $1,000

The 1919 World Series preview issue (above) featured a team picture of the underdog Cincinnati Reds with a seven-column headline that gave them little hope for victory. But when the Reds pulled off an upset over the Chicago White Sox, TSN correspondent Joe Vila made light (below) of charges that the White Sox had thrown the Series.

Something Is Rotten In Baseball

As the heavily favored White Sox, managed by Kid Gleason, prepared to oppose the Reds, under Pat Moran, in the 1919 World Series, a headline in The Sporting News reported: "Joy If Reds Win, But a Shock If They Do / Sentiment Picks Moranmen, But Judgment Picks Sox / Through Opinions of Most Critics Is Noted Thread of Conviction That Gleason Heads Team That Carries a Class Not Possessed by National League Rival."

After Cincinnati won the world championship, five games to three, there was unfettered jubilation in the Rhineland and mingled shock and suspicion almost everywhere else.

Joe Vila, the usually perceptive New York correspondent who had selected the Reds to win, analyzed the Series under a headline that said: "Reds Won Fair and Square and Well Deserved Honors / Vila Pays Tribute to Their Class, Points

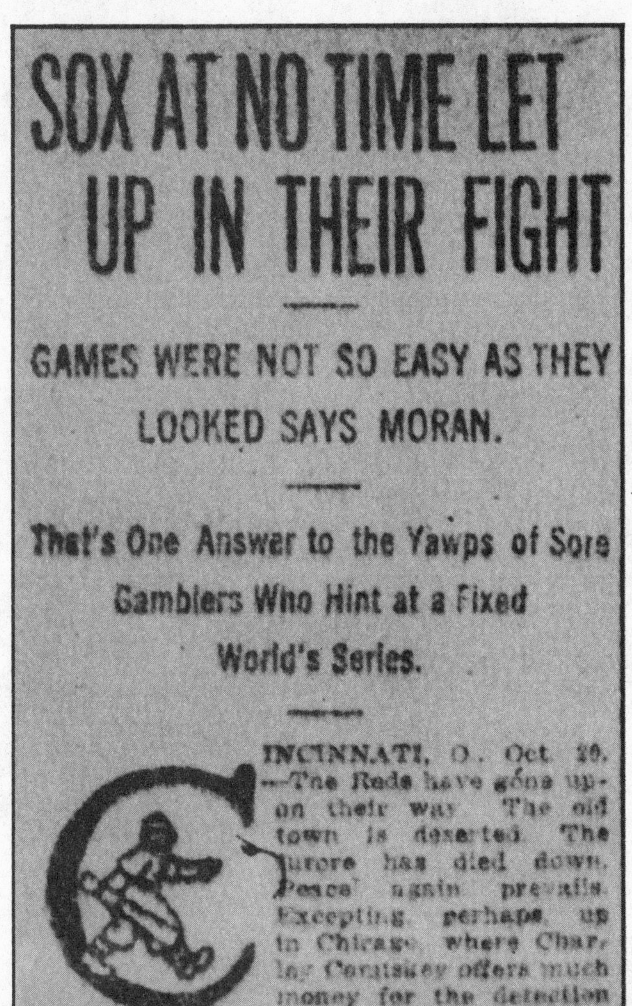

SOX AT NO TIME LET UP IN THEIR FIGHT

GAMES WERE NOT SO EASY AS THEY LOOKED SAYS MORAN.

That's One Answer to the Yawps of Sore Gamblers Who Hint at a Fixed World's Series.

CINCINNATI, O., Oct. 10.—The Reds have gone upon their way. The old town is deserted. The furore has died down. Peace again prevails. Excepting, perhaps, up in Chicago, where Charley Comiskey offers much money for the detection of the miserable skates who have been bellowing about the Series being fixed and the White Sox laying down. This was the cheapest holler on record—a pitiable bawl emitted by a few saps who bet their coin the wrong way—and yet a few "prominent writers" said that the games looked suspicious and that the Series ought to be abolished. Comiskey will soon silence them—not one of them can step out in the open and offer any evidence to substantiate his yowls. If ever a Series was fought on the level, it was this one—there were fifty little

Late News Items

NO EVIDENCE FOUND AGAINST WHITE SOX

Comiskey So States After Investigations Conducted by Himself and Manager Kid Gleason.

CHICAGO, Ill., Dec. 16.—Investigations conducted by President Comiskey and Manager Gleason of charges that certain White Sox players entered into an agreement with gamblers to throw World's Series games resulted in no evidence incriminating any of the players being unearthed. This statement is made following a meeting of Comiskey and Gleason in New York, when they compared notes on their investigations, with the result that both express themselves satisfied the charges had no basis.

Comiskey, who always maintained implicit faith in the innocence of his players, declared the investigation had not ended and that his offer of $10,000 for

As the weeks wore on after the 1919 World Series, stories in The Sporting News continued to report on findings and support the contention that nothing out of line had occurred. Eventually, however, TSN aided American League President Ban Johnson in uncovering the true story.

Out Mistake of Gleason / White Sox Should Not Have Been Allowed to Ease Up and Burlesque in the Final Games of Season."

Another newsletter, datelined Cincinnati, noted: "Sox at No Time Let Up in Their Fight / Games Were Not So Easy as They Looked, Says Moran / That's One Answer to the Yawps of Some Gamblers Who Hint at Fixed World Series."

Reports that some Chicago players had conspired with gamblers to "throw" the Series arose before the last out of the first game, but little credence was expressed by the game's high command due to the lack of concrete evidence. The rumors persisted, however, and a late October headline in TSN revealed: "New Charges May Bring a Statement / Baseball Officials Not Likely to Overlook Accusations Made by Chicago Publication Against White Sox."

In December, another headline read: "No Evidence Found Against White Sox / Comiskey So States After Investigations Conducted by Himself and Kid Gleason."

In the succeeding months, eight Chicago players were acquitted of wrong-doing because their signed confessions of guilt disappeared from the office of the Illinois attorney general. Ban Johnson, however, was not satisfied.

Aided by valuable leads provided by Taylor Spink, the A.L. president obtained evidence to prove the players' complicity. The eight were barred permanently from professional baseball, those who had accepted bribes for their nefarious actions as well as those who, while performing at full efficiency, knew of the conspiracy and remained silent.

3

1921-1929:
BABE TO THE RESCUE

The shade that fell over major league baseball as a result of the 1920 Black Sox scandal began to lift as Babe Ruth and his muscular colleagues started driving baseballs over far distances.

With the dawn of the home run era, a nation of sports fans discovered new idols. Many who sought relief from the oppressive consequence of war found it in the flights of baseballs to faraway places. The arrival of the Ruthian-type blast helped clear away the stench of soiled linen as well as the aftermath of war.

But Ruth and his cohorts would have been powerless to inaugurate the age of power if they had not had accomplices in high places.

Through the years there had been growing concerns about the use of freak pitches. Hurlers had learned that moisture applied to the surface of a baseball caused it to take unpredictable dips and darts as it approached the plate. The spitball achieved what a fastball and curve could not. A cut on the seams or a scuff on the surface of the ball would have the same effect. The pitchers were in total control. It was time to curb the trend.

The death knell for freak pitches was sounded on February 10, 1920, when the joint rules committee of the major leagues outlawed all pitches that resulted from tampering with the ball.

However, this abrupt extermination was not without a strain of mercy. Rather than jeopardize the careers of established spitball pitchers, the committee certified a number of hurlers as legalized spitballers. Seventeen major league spitball pitchers were permitted to throw the moist delivery for the remainder of their careers. They were Yancy (Doc) Ayers and Hubert (Dutch) Leonard, Tigers; Ray Caldwell and Stan Coveleski, Indians; Urban (Red) Faber, White Sox; Jack Quinn, Yankees; Allen Russell, Red Sox; Urban Shocker and Allen Sothoron, Browns; Bill Doak and Marv Goodwin, Cardinals; Phil Douglas, Giants; Dana Fillingim and Dick Rudolph, Braves and Burleigh Grimes and Clarence Mitchell, Dodgers.

As home run totals soared (Babe Ruth cracked 54 in 1920 and 59 in 1921), the game's officials were bombarded with queries about the composition of the baseball. Had the manufacturer changed specifications? Was the yarn wound more tightly? Was the cover more resilient?

A spokesman for the A.J. Reach Company, manufacturer of the official American League ball, declared, "There has been no change in our method of manufacture since the corkball center was adopted in 1910."

President John Heydler of the National League attributed the livelier ball to improved materials and workmanship. Heydler reported that, on a visit to the Spalding plant where N.L. balls were produced, he found "the methods in use precisely the same as heretofore. Only the wool yarn was a better quality and in my opinion more firmly bound.

"During the war, the government commandeered the high-grade wool in the country and private manufacturers were obliged to get along as best they could. Now that it is possible to secure the best workmanship and material, the ball has naturally somewhat improved."

Ban Johnson had another explanation. Writing to a magazine editor, the American League president said: "All I can say on the subject is the fact that Reach and Company are using Australian wool. There was a large shipment into this country during the winter and you possibly know from this quality of wool the best yarn is made. It presents a firmer winding, a harder ball and naturally one that is more elastic."

Johnson's explanation found a willing acceptance in the baseball community. If there were other secrets, they remained well-guarded. But the rapid increase in home run production was no secret. It was common knowledge and endorsed widely. In a four-year period (1918-1921), homer totals skyrocketed from 235 to 447 to 630 to 937.

In the decade known as "The Roaring Twenties," nobody roared louder than the king of clout himself, Ruth. More than any other player in any other decade, the Bambino was dominant with heroic performances on the diamond and a blissful disregard for discipline and training regimens off the field.

Ruth played hard by sunlight and even harder after sunset, when he gave full rein to his gargantuan appetite for fun and frolic. To him, curfews were for adolescents; pleasures of the world were designed for the weakness of his flesh.

In 1921, Babe rode the crest of adulation. His 59

homers, 177 runs, 171 runs batted in and .378 batting average created in his mind a position of power and prestige that made him responsible to nobody.

Several weeks before the end of the season, when it appeared certain that the Yankees would win their first pennant, Babe announed that a team known as the "Babe Ruth All-Stars" would play a postseason series of games in New York and Pennsylvania. The tour violated a regulation, enacted in 1912, that prohibited any World Series player from performing in a postseason exhibition.

When the rule was brought to Babe's attention, he reminded folks that he and some Red Sox teammates had barnstormed in 1916 after their World Series victory over the Dodgers. He conveniently overlooked the fact that the old National Commission, which ruled with an elastic grip, had been replaced by iron-fisted Commissioner Kenesaw Mountain Landis.

The Judge warned Ruth several times that disregard of the rule would lead to serious consequences. Babe listened—but paid no heed. The tour, he insisted, would go on as planned.

The day after the Yankees lost the 1921 World Series to the Giants, Babe and two teammates, outfielder Bob Meusel and pitcher Bill Piercy, departed for Buffalo, where they appeared in a game as advertised. Games in Elmira and Jamestown, N.Y., followed. By the time the troupe reached Scranton, Pa., Ruth had some second thoughts, due primarily to inclement weather and small crowds. Though the remainder of the tour was cancelled, the damage already had been done. Nobody doubted that penalties would be levied. The only question was how severe.

If Ruth expected his bosses to rally to his support, he was sadly disappointed. A headline in The Sporting News reported: "Yankee Owners to Stand by The Judge / Landis Will Take His Time About Fixing Punishment for Ruth and Other Barnstormers."

Thespian that he was, Landis milked the situation for every last nickel's worth of publicity. For nearly two months he let the baseball establishment speculate and the culprits squirm.

Ruth was in Washington, D.C. on a vaudeville tour that allegedly netted him $25,000 when the news arrived in early December. For defiance of authority, the trio was suspended for the first six weeks of the 1922 season and fined $3,362, the loser's share in the World Series.

Overflow crowds hailed Babe on his return to action in 1922, but when he failed to produce in his accustomed style, catcalls cascaded from the stands. The Bambino's frustration exploded in a nasty scene at the Polo Grounds when he leaped into the stands and gave chase to a loud-mouthed heckler, who escaped to safety. For this, Ruth was fined $200, suspended for one day and stripped of his club captaincy, an honor he had enjoyed for all of six games.

Babe's most notable clash with authority occurred in 1925. His adversary was Miller Huggins, the diminutive manager of the Yankees.

The year had started inauspiciously for Ruth. When the Yanks stopped in Asheville, N.C., for a game on their spring junket northward, the big fellow collapsed on the station platform, suffering, it was said, from "a stomach ache heard 'round the world." A few days later in New York he underwent surgery for an intestinal abscess.

Although not fully recovered, Ruth returned to action on June 1. As his strength returned, so did his taste for bright lights, inordinate quantities of food and drink, fast cars and ladies with a similar gait. His deportment took a heavy toll on Huggins' patience until the supply ran out during a late-August series in St. Louis.

Ruth had ruptured the curfew by plenty. After he arrived at the hotel, he explained, he had toured the city with friends in an effort to escape the heat and humidity. Hug knew better. When Babe showed up at the ball park, he informed Ruth that he was under indefinite suspension and fined $5,000.

A string of oaths and obscenities followed, whereupon Huggins declared that Babe would never again wear a Yankee uniform until he apologized for his unseemly language.

Ruth returned to New York via Chicago, where he tried unsuccessfully to obtain a hearing with Judge Landis. Along the way he chatted freely with newsmen. Always the thrust was the same: "Huggins quits or I quit."

When he arrived in New York, Babe was dismayed to learn that Yankee management backed Huggins solidly. The Bambino was backed into a corner. His options were down to one; he would play only on Huggins' terms.

Daily Ruth phoned his manager, seeking amnesty. The answer always was the same: "Not yet, Babe." The suspension was in its 10th day when Hug relented. "Come on in," he said. Ruth apologized to Hug for his untidy remarks before the entire team and was restored to good graces.

A headline in The Sporting News reported the final chapter in the rebellion: " 'The Bambino,' Year's Big Drama, Fizzles Out to Childish Comedy / Ruth Flops From Role of King to Jester / Makes Surrender Complete With Apologies and Admits He Didn't Mean a Word He Said About Huggins."

Ruth played in only 98 games that season with 25 homers and a .290 batting average.

Two months later, another headline confided " 'I've Been the Sappiest of Saps'—Ruth / Home Run King Insists He'll Rise to Greatest Heights in 1926 / When Bambino Wasn't Being Bilked Out of His Money He Was Losing It in Take-a-Chance Ventures / Once Dropped $35,000 on One Horse Race; Suits of Women and Others Who 'Played' Him for a Boob Cost Small Fortune."

True to his promise, the reformed slugger returned in 1926 with 47 homers, 145 RBIs and a .372 batting average.

Babe's good behavior—at least good by his standards—endured through the remainder of the decade. He was the home run king again with a record 60 round-trippers in 1927. That same year he batted .400 in the Yankees' Series sweep over the Pirates and followed that up with a .625 mark against the Cards in 1928. During that Series sweep, Ruth duplicated his 1926 Series feat by hitting three home runs in one game.

After another successful season in 1929, Ruth set his salary sights on $100,000. Yankees Owner Jake Ruppert countered with an offer of $75,000, representing a $5,000 increase. The pair struck an impasse that was not resolved until the day of the first exhibition game in St. Petersburg, Fla., when Babe signed for an unprecedented $80,000 plus a $5,000 gift to repay his fine of 1925.

As Ruth slugged and sinned his way into prominence, the New York Giants also were creating headlines, some favorable, some not.

In 1922, seeking to stem the rising tide of Yankee popularity, the Giants evicted their tenants from the Polo Grounds. The Giants felt that the Yankees, without a park to play in, would fall in public esteem and the Giants would again rule as the city's top team. The National Leaguers' strategy misfired badly. In record time, the evictees built a palatial park across the Harlem River and enjoyed an enlarged public image.

When the Giants won the first of four consecutive flags in 1921, one of their pitching mainstays was Phil Douglas, a huge righthander who won 15 games in the regular season and added two victories in the World Series against the Yankees. Shufflin' Phil also had an unquenchable thirst that led him to take what he called "a vacation" from time to time. In reality, "a vacation" was nothing more than a world-class drinking spree. After one such incident in 1922, Douglas showed up at the Polo Grounds and, in front of his teammates, was blistered unmercifully by John McGraw. "Go home and sleep it off, you big bum," raged the Little Napoleon. "But be here tomorrow or I'll fix you so you'll never pitch again."

When the New York players returned to the clubhouse after their game, Douglas was gone, as was a bottle of lemon extract from the trainer's cabinet.

As the team entrained for Pittsburgh the night of August 15, Douglas was in the party, apparently recovered from his alcoholic bout and in an affable mood. But the next morning the traveling newspapermen were summoned to a press conference in McGraw's suite at the Schenley Hotel. To their surprise, Judge Landis glowered at them from behind an ornate desk. "Gentlemen," the commissioner began, "I have just placed the name of Phil Douglas on the permanently retired list."

Landis displayed a sheet of Giants stationery. "I asked Douglas if he had written this," he explained. "He confessed that he had. There was nothing else for me to do."

In his befogged state and crushed by McGraw's oral onslaught a few days earlier, the Georgian had written to St. Louis outfielder Leslie Mann offering to go fishing for the rest of the season if the Cardinal players "would make it worth my while."

Within hours the pitcher was on the train to oblivion. The transportation was paid for by the Giants; the $100 bill in Douglas' pocket was a gift from McGraw.

In 1924, the Giants were on their way to a fourth straight pennant when a similar incident erupted. The cast of characters included Cozy Dolan, a Giants coach; Jimmy O'Connell, a young and personable outfielder, and Heinie Sand, Phillies shortstop.

The Giants were just one victory short of the pennant when they prepared to meet the Phillies in a late-season game. As the teams were warming up, O'Connell greeted Sand, whom he had known during their days in the Pacific Coast Leaue.

"How do you fellows feel about us?" Jimmy asked Heinie.

"What do you mean?" Sand replied.

"About us winning the pennant," the outfielder said.

"I told him," Sand testified later, "that we didn't care who won, it was all the same to us, and then he said, 'Well, you don't bear down too hard against us this afternoon, it will be worth $500 to you.' "

Sand related the conversation to his manager, Art Fletcher. The account passed through channels to Judge Landis. Separately, O'Connell and Dolan were interrogated by the commissioner. O'Connell said he was encouraged by Dolan to make the offer. He also thought that the bribe was common knowledge among the Giants players, particularly Frankie Frisch, Ross Youngs and George Kelly. The three established stars denied all knowledge of the proposal and were adjudged innocent. When Dolan took the stand, he was stricken with an advanced case of amnesia. To every question, he replied, "I don't remember" or "I don't recall."

That wasn't good enough for Landis. Like O'Connell, Dolan received a lifetime suspension from professional baseball.

The Giants needed no subversive help in winning the 1924 pennant or three of the first five World Series games against the Washington Senators. A 2-1 Nat victory behind Tom Zachary in the sixth game knotted the Series at three wins apiece and reduced the world championship to a one-game playoff.

President and Mrs. Calvin Coolidge were among the more than 31,000 who packed Griffith Stadium on October 10 to watch the minions of crusty old John McGraw do battle with the first-time American League champions under Bucky Harris, the "Boy Manager."

In the first seven innings, the Senators scored only one run and they trailed, 3-1, when they came to bat in the eighth. But a double, single and walk loaded the bases ahead of Harris' two-run single that tied the score.

The teams struggled into the 12th inning. Walter Johnson, in his first Series, had lost two earlier decisions and had blanked the Giants through four innings. How much longer could the 36-year-old righthander go on?

New York pitcher Jack Bentley retired the first Washington batter in the 12th inning and, when Muddy Ruel lifted a pop foul behind the plate it appeared that Bentley would have an easy inning. But Ruel drew a life when catcher Hank Gowdy stepped on his mask, which he had neglected to toss out of his path, and the ball dropped harmlessly.

Given a second chance, Ruel doubled and held second when shortstop Travis Jackson erred on Johnson's grounder. A groan went up from the partisan crowd when Earl McNeely hit a grounder toward third base. A double play was likely, one putout certain. But as Fred Lindstrom braced to field the ball, it struck a pebble and hopped erratically over his head. Ruel raced home and the Nation's Capital celebrated its first and only world championship.

The Sporting News saluted Harris in a page 1 headline that said "The Spirit of Bucky Harris Prevails in 'Greatest Series' / Bucky Given Rank with Ablest Leaders / Every Member of Washington Team Entitled to Equal Share of Credit for Victory."

The 1924 pennant was the 10th and last for McGraw. In 1925 the Giants finished second to the Pirates and the next year they wound up fifth, badly outdistanced by a new power in the National League, the St. Louis Cardinals.

The Redbirds were the product of a new concept in the development of baseball talent. Years earlier, Branch Rickey, general manager and field boss, had grown weary of tail-end finishes. He also was at a disadvantage in building a contender because the Cards suffered from a crippling shortage of funds.

Rickey was an astute appraiser of baseball flesh, but every time he made a modest offer for a minor league prospect, that player's owner would report the bid to a more affluent major league official who, respecting Rickey's superior judgment, would raise the ante and walk away with the prospect.

Rickey's solution came in a stroke of genius. If he could not compete with wealthier clubs, he would raise his own talent. As a starter, the Cardinals acquired a part interest in the Houston club of the Texas League. Later they added Fort Smith of the Western Association and Syracuse of the International League.

By signing raw but promising youngsters in carload lots, Rickey turned spring camps into mob scenes as kids were evaluated, assigned to minor affiliates or released. Some observers were impressed with the revolutionary scheme, others like McGraw were not. "It's the stupidest idea in baseball," grumbled the Little Napoleon.

Cardinals Owner Sam Breadon relieved Rickey of field command in 1925 so that he could confine his boundless energies to front-office duties. His successor was Rogers Hornsby, the club's superb second baseman who had averaged .402 over five years with a high of .424 in 1924.

The move paid off in 1926 when the Cards, stocked with many products of the farm system, won the club's first pennant.

But even better days lay ahead. In the seventh game of the World Series against the Yankees, the Cards led, 3-2, in the seventh inning when the home club loaded the bases with two out. Hornsby went to the bullpen. His craftiest and most reliable pitcher that moment was Grover Cleveland Alexander, who had been acquired in midseason from Chicago. Never mind that Old Pete had pitched the day before and knotted the Series at three games apiece with a 10-2 victory. Never mind that Alex had celebrated far past curfew. Rog summoned the 39-year-old righthander, who fanned Tony Lazzeri and preserved the narrow lead the rest of the way.

But discontent soon clouded the Cardinal Camelot. A rift existed between Breadon and Hornsby, the result of the owner having booked an exhibition game in New Haven, Conn., in the midst of the team's late-season pennant drive. The Rajah blistered Breadon in the clubhouse in front of the players, accusing him of nickel-nursing when the team was trying to concentrate on the championship.

Rumors that the breach was past healing climaxed just before Christmas when Hornsby was traded to the Giants for Frankie Frisch, also a second baseman, and pitcher Jimmy Ring.

A headline in TSN explained Breadon's position: "Hornsby Left No Alternative, Says Breadon, Discussing Trade / Rog Had Just Spurned $50,000 Contract; Manager's Insistence on Three-year Term and Attitude Toward Officials Prompts Action."

The Yankees repeated as A.L. kings in 1927 and '28 before abdicating in favor of the Philadelphia A's, who returned to the top for the first time after their shocking upset by the Braves in 1914.

As the A's warmed up for the opening game of the World Series against the Cubs, Connie Mack prepared a shock of his own for the players and fans. A wave of bewilderment swept through Wrigley Field when Howard Ehmke was announced as Philadelphia's starting pitcher.

The veteran righthander had compiled only a 7-2 record for the season and had not thrown a pitch competitively in two weeks.

But that fortnight had not been wasted. Under instructions from Mack, Ehmke spent the time scouting the Cubs, noting their strengths and weaknesses.

Al Simmons was the most dismayed Philadelphian. "Is he gonna start for us?" the outfielder asked Mack.

"Why, isn't it all right with you?" Mack replied.

"If it's all right with you, it's all right with me," came the sheepish response.

Ehmke had studied the Cubs well. The 35-year-old fanned 13 batters and registered a 3-1 victory.

One such miracle in one Series was about all that Mack could reasonably expect and when the A's fell behind 8-0 in the fourth game, Connie planned silently to lift his regulars if they did not score in the seventh inning.

But Simmons drove a Charlie Root pitch to the roof of the left-field stands to ruin the shutout. "What a way to waste a perfectly good home run," mused Simmons as he circled the bases.

When successive singles by Jimmie Foxx, Bing Miller and Jimmie Dykes produced another run, the 29,921 Shibe Park fans started to take notice. As Joe Boley headed for the plate, Mack called him back. "Root is losing his stuff, swing on the first pitch around the plate," he counseled.

The shortstop did as directed. His single produced a third run. After pinch-hitter George Burns popped out, Max Bishop singled and the score was 8-4.

Now Joe McCarthy took notice, too. The Chicago manager lifted Root in favor of Art Nehf to face Mule Haas, who hit a line drive to center field. Little cause for concern here . . . until Hack Wilson lost the ball in the sun. It rolled to the deepest corner of the park and three runs scored on the home run.

A base on balls to Mickey Cochrane sent Nehf to the showers. It was Sheriff Blake's turn. Simmons greeted the third hurler of the inning with a single and Foxx added another that tied the score. Again McCarthy

Washington celebrated its only World Series title in 1924 when the Senators beat the New York Giants in seven games.

went to the bullpen, bringing in Pat Malone. The change was unavailing. Malone nicked Miller with a pitch and yielded a two-run double to Dykes, completing one of the most productive of all World Series innings.

As the rally developed, Mack ordered his ace pitcher, Lefty Grove, to start warming up in the event he was needed. With a 10-8 lead, Mack took no chances. Grove retired the last six Cubs in order, four on strikeouts.

In the early games of the Series, players on both teams had assailed each other with obscenities and blasphemies. The exchange grew so sulphurous that Commissioner Landis, no prude himself, summoned the managers to his hotel suite and ordered the practice stopped. If it was continued, the Judge threatened, culprits would be fined their Series share, in this case $5,621 for each winner, $3,782 for each loser.

One warning was sufficient. As the players prepared for the final game, the irrepressible Cochrane shouted to the Cubs' bench: "After the game, tea will be served in the clubhouse."

The remark did not escape Landis, seated in the royal box. When he entered the A's clubhouse to congratulate the new champions, he embraced Cochrane and cooed, "Now, shall we have that tea."

Newsdealers supplied direct from this office.

Communications intended for publication should be written on one side of the paper only.

VOL. 82. JANUARY 27, 1927 NO. 2[illegible]

The Lion's Voice Is Stilled.

A Caesar done to his death—and there is a void in baseball that will be felt for long. Other men will carry on, and the game's administration will continue, with no great changes indicated to the man in the street, we may presume. But a personality has been removed from baseball whose departure from the scene leaves the atmosphere drab.

We will hear smug platitudes of how much baseball owes to Ban Johnson, and there will be tears shed, and there will be apologies and regrets expressed, with assertions that certain things had to be done, certain policies had to be carried out, and certain agreements met. And so the death of a Caesar was decreed and encompassed. It had to be, they would have us know.

The voice of the lion is stilled; they say the lion was getting old, that his roar had become but a mumble. It may be so. But never, maybe, will be heard again such a voice—the roar that struck terror to evil doers, in high estate or low, and thrilled to new encouragement those who had ideals and the vision Ban Johnson had. Yes, we speak of Ban Johnson.

From this man, sick unto death, and for whom a fight had to be made by a most loyal few for the mercy due one so stricken, they need not make their apologies; the baseball world does not care for them. It knows as it knows right, and knows wrong, they never can take from Ban Johnson that honor and glory that he has won. The record he has made over more than a quarter of a century—that record is the history of baseball as concerns its being rescued from a condition which

Ban Johnson (above right with J.G. Taylor Spink) was under fire in 1927 when TSN Editor Earl Obenshain wrote his highly acclaimed editorial, 'The Lion's Voice Is Stilled' (left). Johnson, the founder and longtime president of the American League, was being forced to retire by other baseball officials.

A Rapid Turnover Of Editorial Staff

Changes in the editorial structure of The Sporting News occurred frequently during the 1920s.

The procession started in 1924 when Earl Obenshain ended his 12-year career as TSN editor to accept a position in the office of American League President Ban Johnson.

Obie was succeeded by Dick Farrington, the former managing editor of the St. Louis Times who was recognized nationally as a sportswriter and editor.

Farrington served until Obenshain returned for a brief period in 1927-28. During his second term, Obenshain wrote his most widely acclaimed editorial. It was titled "The Lion's Voice Is Stilled" and was a tribute to Ban Johnson, who was virtually forced to resign from the league he had guided for more than a quarter of a century.

The editorial started, "A Caesar done to his death—and there is a void in baseball that will be felt for long . . . .

"The voice of the lion is stilled; they say the lion was getting old, that his roar had become a mumble. It may be so. But never, maybe, will be heard again such a voice—the roar that struck terror to evil doers, in high estate or low, and thrilled to new encouragement those who had ideals and the vision Ban Johnson had . . . ."

After Obenshain departed for the second time, Farrington returned, but only for several months.

The next occupant of the editor's chair was Franklyn J. Adams, a competent writer who, after a short stay, yielded to the call of New York City. For many years, Adams was an integral part of the New York Daily News sports de-

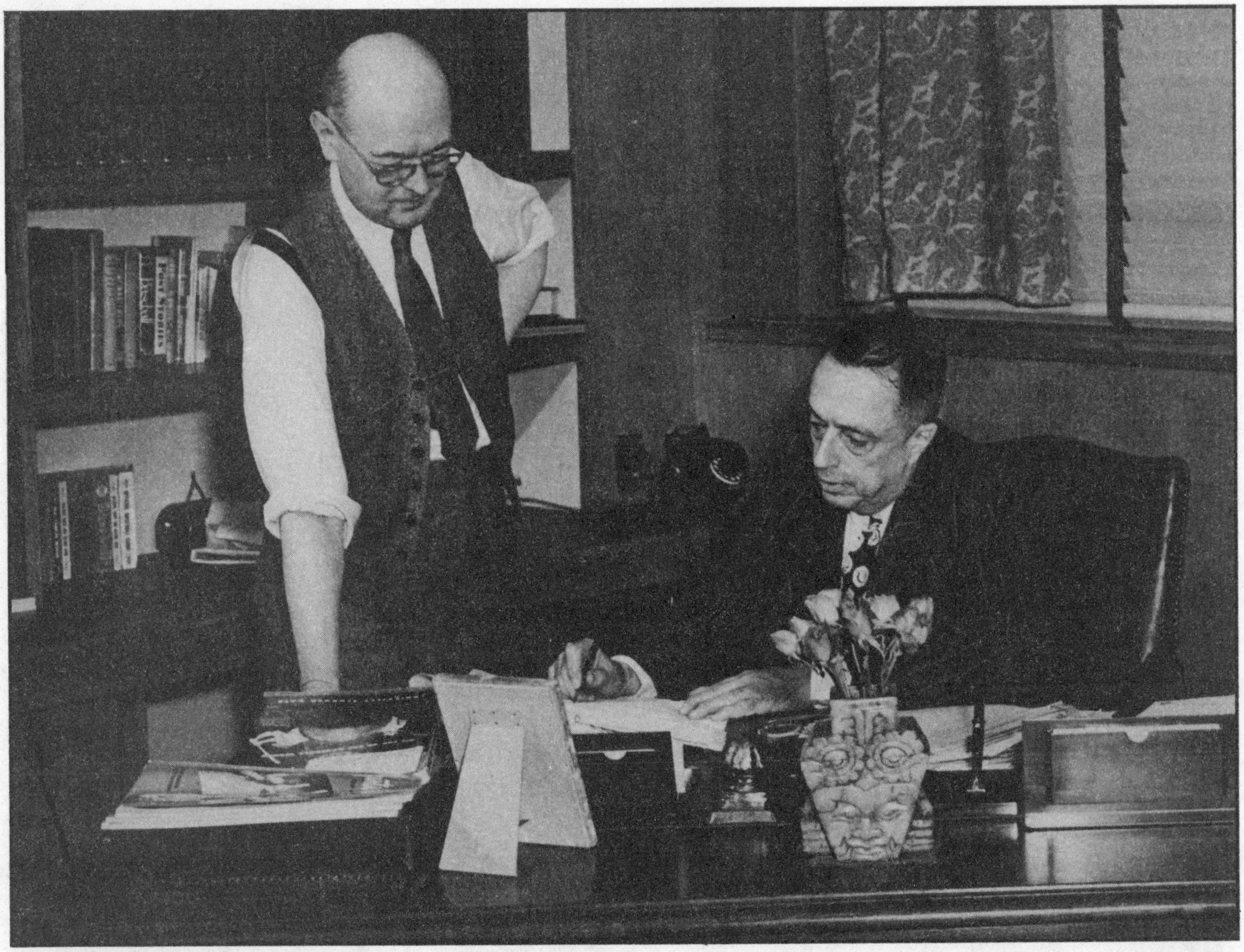

A rapid turnover came to an end in 1930 when Edgar G. Brands (left) took over as editor of The Sporting News. A key figure for many years under J.G. Taylor Spink was Carl Felker (above with Spink), who became known for his catchy headlines and subtle wit.

partment.

Gene Kessler, another extraordinary newspaperman, succeeded Adams. He resigned after a brief tenure and headed for Chicago, where he gained recognition as an editor and columnist.

The rapid turnover ground to a halt with the arrival of Edgar G. Brands in 1930. A graduate of the University of Illinois, Brands was lured from his position as managing editor of the Collyer Publishing Company of Chicago, which published Collyer's Eye and the Baseball World.

Well versed in baseball history and administration, Brands covered every minor league convention and most major league confabs during his 24 years with TSN.

Another key figure in the Spink organization was Carl T. Felker, who joined the firm in 1924. A graduate of the University of Missouri School of Journalism, Felker had served as copy editor for the St. Louis Times and St. Louis Post-Dispatch before he was named editor of The Sporting Goods Dealer, a sister publication of The Sporting News.

Because of his wide experience as a newspaperman, Felker gradually took over the copy-editing duties and headline writing on The Sporting News. His subtle wit and facile pen created catchy headlines that amused readers for the next 30 years.

Eventually, Felker was appointed assistant to the publisher, a role in which he also wrote feature articles and occasional editorials and served as a balance wheel for Publisher J.G. Taylor Spink.

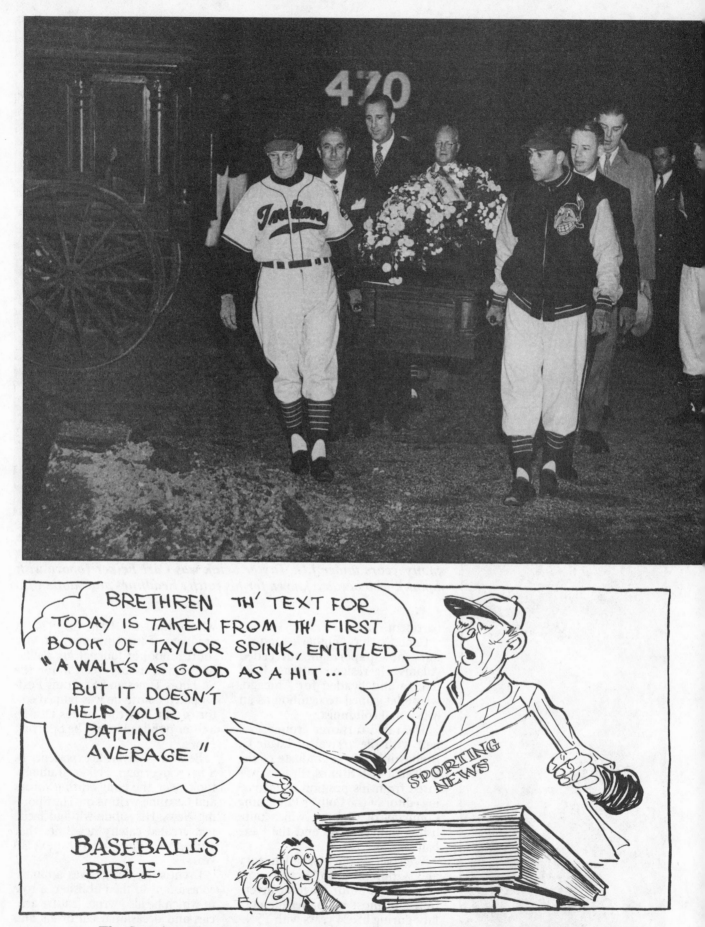

The Sporting News took every opportunity to promote the 'Bible of Baseball' image through word or picture.

When J.G. Taylor Spink first heard The Sporting News called the 'Bible,' he was taken with the idea. So, too, were members of the baseball fraternity and its fans. In 1949, the Cleveland Indians demonstrated how much. After the Indians had dropped from the late-season pennant race, Owner Bill Veeck set up a promotion in which Indians officials and players would bury their pennant hopes at Municipal Stadium. After the funeral procession (above left) had delivered the casket to its appointed site, business manager Rudie Schaffer (above right) read the last rites from The Sporting News, the 'Bible of Baseball.'

'The Bible'

Taylor Spink possessed a keen appreciation of a well turned phrase, a snappy headline or a catchy nickname.

He would laugh uproariously over a punchy headline and was not above telephoning a distant city so that an acquaintance could share in his joy. A chuckle on the other end of the line was assurance that J.G.'s laurels as a publisher were undisturbed.

When he embarked with his wife on a European vacation in the late 1920s, little did he suspect that he would return home with a new synonym for The Sporting News.

The Spinks were in Le Havre, France, waiting to board an ocean liner, when a voice from behind hailed the publisher.

"I had no idea who was calling me from the captain's bridge," Taylor said, "but when I looked up, I recognized Jack Potter and, believe it or not, there was a copy of The Sporting News in his pocket."

Potter, son of a one-time Phillies co-owner, turned to the captain. "There," he said, pointing to Spink, "is the man who wrote the Bible."

"Who is he," asked the captain, "Matthew, Mark, Luke or John?"

"That's Taylor Spink," Potter replied, "and he writes the Baseball Bible."

Spink was smitten by the alliteration and the ring of authority it carried. Through his remaining years, "The Bible" or "Bible" became a handy synonym for The Sporting News. It was discontinued only after TSN became an all-sports publication.

Trouble With Landis

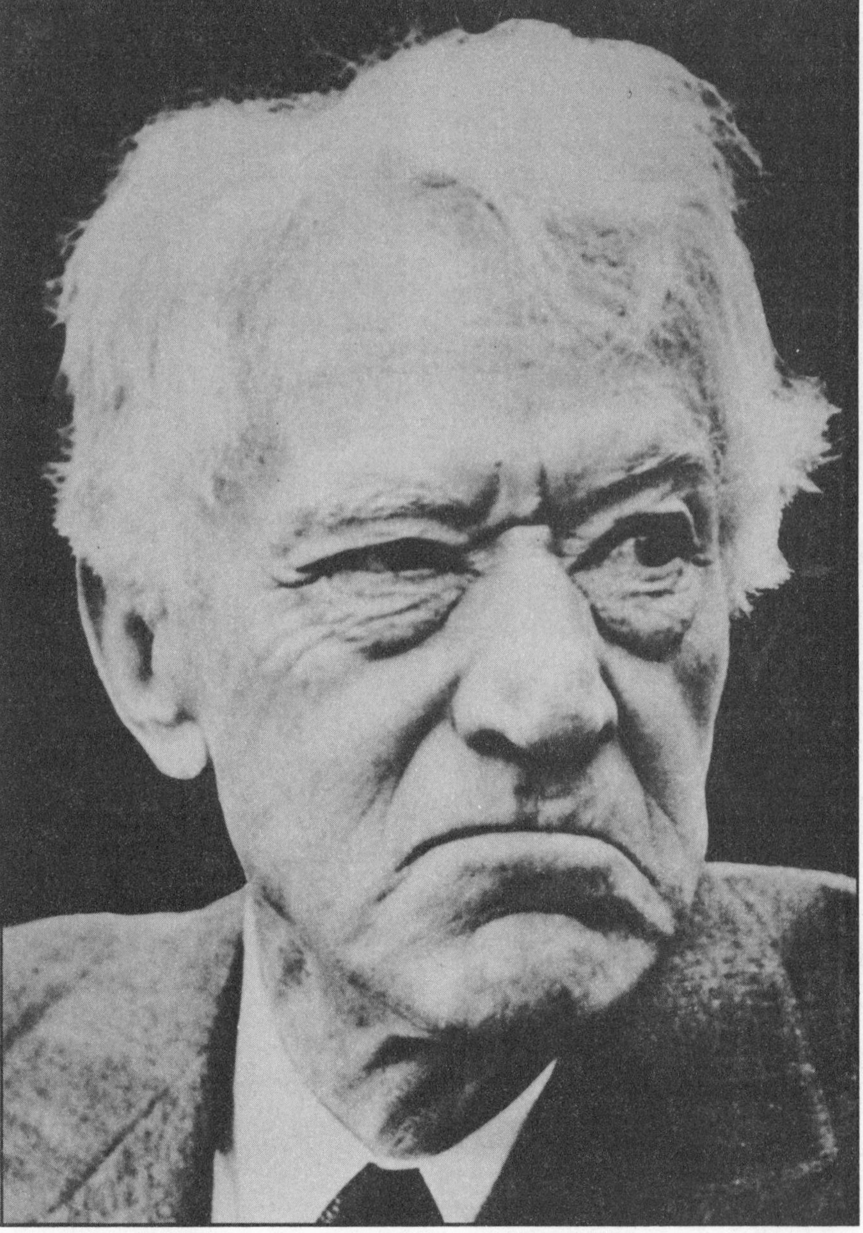

In the early years of Judge Kenesaw M. Landis' reign as Commissioner, The Sporting News applauded his decisions. In time, however, the climate changed.

The first major conflict occurred in October 1922, after umpires called a World Series game in New York because of darkness with the Yankees and Giants locked in a tie. Landis, serving as a one-man court, donated the game receipts to charity.

The Sporting News criticized the former judge in an editorial. "In a World Series game, mere umpires should not have such power as they exercised in calling that game," the editorial said. "The All-Highest Commissioner didn't arise to the occasion as big as he might have arisen or he would have summoned the umpires to him for consultation or instructions.

"Through his conferred powers, he could have taken charge of the situation. The reverence that the baseball public is supposed to have for Commissioner Landis as a personage is not so deep as we were told it would be when he was put in command of baseball."

Other criticisms followed until Landis, his vanity bruised, unleashed a torrent of abuse on TSN at the 1923 winter meetings.

The matter was aired in an editorial, "The Issue With Landis," as follows:

"Commissioner Landis had one of his 'periods' and proceeded to rant and scold against all in baseball who might have the temerity to question his divinity and infallibility and supreme intelligence and honesty."

Landis took occasion, the editorial continued, "to score, among others, The Sporting News, referring to its publisher or editor, or both, as 'swine' and the news and comment printed in its columns as 'swill.'

"To make clear just to whom he referred, he later visited the press room in the Congress Hotel and, with hat in hand, requested that the baseball scribes should get him straight—he didn't refer to them as a class as 'swine'; even though some of them had criticized him, he was only specializing against a few particular critics as he had named them, which seems to bring it up to The Sporting News, and the issue is accepted."

Reminding readers that the motto of The Sporting News was "Devoted to Organized Baseball," the editor declared, "The Sporting News will not endure from any source an attack on the honesty of its motives or question of its position in baseball. It has stood too long for what is right and what is honest and for what is the good of baseball—and sometimes at cost—to permit any mountebank to assail its standing, and it believes a million fans who read it will cry out in protest when Landis or any of his cronies or supporters attempt such tactics.

"But, ah, why grow excited or incensed about it? This Landis, raised up in a moment of hysteria, will pass with his $50,000 contract . . . and even those who elevated him will breathe a sigh of relief as they hand him his old slouch hat, so theatrically worn, and bid him adieu. The game will go on, the men who have kept it alive will get their deserved credit—and The

Baseball Commissioner Kenesaw Mountain Landis (above left) and J.G. Taylor Spink (above) were strong-willed personalities who spent much of the 1920s feuding.

Sporting News, well 'swine' may write 'swill,' but it will continue at the old stand, firm for what it always has been for, even into the third and fourth generations."

Francis C. Richter did little to salve the wounds. Writing in "Casual Comment" on the editorial page, the former editor of Sporting Life observed, "By assuming the illogical position that his temporary office is such a high and sacred one as to place the occupant above human fallibility and to make him immune from all criticism, Mr. Landis shows that he is possessed of vanity and weakness inherent in most autocrats and which will not stand the tests of time and adversity."

'The Issue With Landis' editorial (right) ridiculed the commissioner after he had made derogatory comments about The Sporting News at the 1923 winter meetings.

The Issue With Landis.

Commissioner Landis in that joint meeting of the major leagues in Chicago recently, during which he had one of his "periods" and proceeded to rant and scold against all in baseball who might have the temerity to question his divinity, infallibility and supreme intelligence and honesty, took occasion to score among others The Sporting News, referring to its editor or publisher, or both, as "swine," and the news or comment printed in its columns as "swill."

To make clearer just to whom he referred he later visited the press room in the Congress Hotel and with hat in hand requested that baseball scribes get him right—he didn't refer to them as a class as "swine," even though some of them had criticized him, he was only specializing against a few particular critics, as he had named them, which seems to bring it up to The Sporting News, and the issue is accepted.

It was said the Commissioner broke into the joint meeting of the major leagues with his diatribe hoping for an argument, because he had the answer in the contract or agreement the magnates supinely made with him back in January of 1921. He is said to have offered to tear up that contract, which is to laugh—the magnates presumably prefer to endure him rather than permit him to pose as a martyr, and some of them even have been quoted as say-

The Sporting News—1885 to 1925

IT WAS 40 years ago this year that THE SPORTING NEWS was founded. Down through the long valley of those years it has gone hand-in-hand with Organized Baseball. It has grown bigger and better. Baseball has grown bigger and better. To that end THE SPORTING NEWS can reflect with righteous pride. It can look back over the wide span of years with the sincere and lasting satisfaction of having helped fight baseball's fight to the crowning glory that it is the National Game.

And it can look into the future confidently—baseball is still growing; it will continue to grow.

Beginning the first week in May, THE SPORTING NEWS will increase its size to ten pages. This is done annually as the various leagues begin their campaigns, to enable it to publish box scores of the games in all of the leagues possible. This season this service will be augmented with the addition of the Virginia League, thus making the box scores of 13 leagues to be found weekly in THE SPORTING NEWS. The same leagues carried last year will again be published.

In stepping with the policy of an improved paper, the summary of the major league box scores will also contain the names of the players who scored the runs, and the names of the umpires. Another feature will be the publication of the playing dates of the big league teams for each week, dating from day of publication.

There will be no deviation from the established custom of publishing news letters from all of the cities in Organized Baseball.

THE PUBLISHERS.

Announcement

An Increase in the Size of

The Sporting News

to 10 Pages, Effective with Next Week's Issue

BEGINNING with its next issue (April 20) THE SPORTING NEWS will be increased to ten pages—a move that indicates the faith of the publishers in the future of Organized Baseball and their appreciation of the wonderful support the fans of the nation have given The Only Baseball Paper during the period when the game was in a sense, on trial. THE SPORTING NEWS is not required to make any new announcement of its policy; it stands where it always has stood—for the best interests of the national game, believing those interests are best served through the system of administration and control exercised by a supreme commission, the name of which may change, but the powers and purposes remaining the same. At the head of its editorial column this paper always has carried its acknowledgement of support to this authority, tested through all the years when baseball has been at its best.

The increased size of THE SPORTING NEWS will permit the publication of the box scores of three *additional* leagues affiliated with Organized Baseball, besides relieving the shortage of space that has been an embarrassment in past playing seasons for news letters from the many minor leagues that clamor for recognition and publicity. Added box scores in themselves, we know, will be enough for the fans who dote on the dope, but with provision for more news and gossip as well, fandom will be given such a feast as it never has before enjoyed.

It has been quite a difficult matter to select from the 30-odd leagues ... National Association those whose box scores shall be ... effort has been to not only cover the territory but ... the work of players in leagues where the scouts say ... ll. Box scores of nine minor leagues besides those ... be carried this season. A conscientious effort will ... THE SPORTING NEWS, to keep all interested ... the work of players in all leagues.

... get all that it is possible to give in the new ten- ... NEWS, but you know it is reliable when you get it.

Box Scores Galore

In 1922, The Sporting News discontinued its practice of adding an extra column to its pages in order to accommodate box scores of the minor leagues. It increased the number of pages instead.

An announcement revealed that, starting with the issue of April 20, the paper would be enlarged to 10 pages, "a move that indicates the faith of the publication in the future of Organized Baseball and the appreciation of the wonderful support our fans of the nation have given The Sporting News during the period when the game, in a sense, was on trial.

"The increased size of The Sporting News will permit the publication of box scores of three additional leagues. Adding box scores, in themselves, will be enough for the fans who dote on the dope, but with the provision for more news and gossip as well, fandom will be given a feast as it never before has enjoyed.

"It has been a difficult matter to select from the 30-odd leagues represented in the National Association those whose box scores shall be given publication; the effort has been to not only cover the territory, but to present to fans the work of players in leagues where the scouts say the best prospects dwell. Box scores of nine minor leagues, besides the two majors, will be carried this season. A conscientious effort will be made to keep all interested more fully informed of the work of players in all leagues."

Two Extra Pages of Dope

STARTING with next week's issue, The Sporting News will be increased to ten pages, but there will be no change in the price, which will remain at 10 cents per copy (15 cents in Canada). The increase in number of pages will be made to take care of the box scores of all the larger minor leagues, several of which open during the current week.

Along with these box scores will be the regular reviews from all major league cities and comment from well known writers of the minors. Standings of all leagues in Organized Baseball will be carried, in addition to news notes covering the highlights of play during the week. The Sporting News will offer the same complete service that it has given the fans in past years. Special attention is called to the ten-page issues—starting next week. The entire field covered.

The projection of box scores from nine minor circuits was conservative. Box scores of 10 minor leagues were published, including the American Association and these leagues: International, Pacific Coast, Eastern, Southern, Texas, South Atlantic, Western, Three-I and Michigan-Ontario. Other leagues were covered with weekly standings and notes.

As baseball coverage was expanded, the paper, which reduced to eight pages at the close of the season, enjoyed increased circulation. From 50,986, the low point in the aftermath of the Black Sox Scandal, circulation soared to a record 90,000 in 1924.

In 1922, The Sporting News began the practice of adding two pages every spring to accommodate more box scores. It's interesting to note how the 1922 (above), 1925 (above left) and 1928 (left) announcements were presented.

TEXAS LEAGUE

STANDING ON TUESDAY MORNING.

VIRGINIA LEAGUE

STANDING ON MONDAY MORNING.

MICHIGAN-ONTARIO LEAGUE

STANDING ON SUNDAY MORNING.

SOUTHERN LEAGUE

STANDING ON TUESDAY MORNING.

THREE-I LEAGUE

STANDING ON TUESDAY MORNING.

Games of Sunday, June 7.

WESTERN LEAGUE

STANDING ON TUESDAY MORNING.

EASTERN LEAGUE

STANDING ON SUNDAY MORNING.

INTERNATIONAL LEAGUE

STANDING ON TUESDAY MORNING.

SOUTH ATLANTIC LEAGUE

STANDING ON MONDAY MORNING.

PACIFIC COAST LEAGUE

STANDING ON TUESDAY MORNING.

AMERICAN ASSOCIATION

STANDING ON TUESDAY MORNING.

Games of Sunday, June 7.

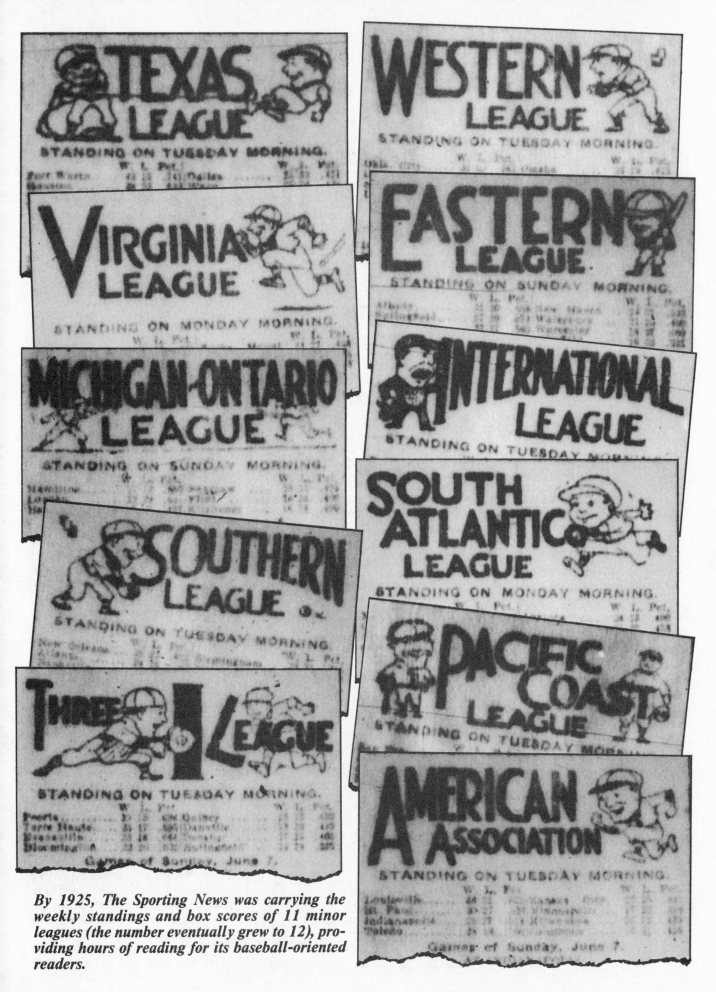

By 1925, The Sporting News was carrying the weekly standings and box scores of 11 minor leagues (the number eventually grew to 12), providing hours of reading for its baseball-oriented readers.

'A Day of Hypocrisy'

YOUNGSTERS INSTILL NEW SPIRIT INTO WAVERING RANKS OF YANKS

GEHRIG'S BAT MAY KEEP PIPP ON BENCH

Wanninger Also Playing Splendidly at Short and Hitting Well; Pitching, However, Continues to Be Wobbly.

MAJOR LEAGUE CLUBS DOWN TO 25 PLAYERS

Time Limit on Intra-league Deals Also Goes Into Effect; Ranks Thinned Early Because of Option Rule.

ST. LOUIS, Mo., June 18.—The 16 major league clubs are now operating

In one of the more prophetic headlines of the decade, The Sporting News suggested in 1925 (above, second deck) that the blazing bat of young Lou Gehrig might keep veteran first baseman Wally Pipp out of the Yankees' lineup. Gehrig, of course, was beginning his iron-man streak of playing in 2,130 straight games.

One of the big issues of 1925 was Sunday baseball and The Sporting News supported and campaigned for such a measure. The poem (right) by Bill Phelon demonstrates TSN's feeling on the subject.

Baseball By-Plays

THE DEACON.

The Deacon wandered forth one day and saw a Sunday game—
Such doing filled the Deacon's soul with agony and shame—
He scowled upon the sinners as they chased and slammed the ball,
And he noticed that the pitcher was a target, that was all!
For the hits were long and frequent, and they crashed and bammed like sin.
And the fans were raising tumult with a loud and awful din—
And the Deacon, as he watched it, felt a sudden wicked thrill—
And he strode right out before them and he seized upon the pill:
(He had pitched a lot of ball games in his youth, the Deacon had,
And the leagues had made him offers that were—well, not half so bad).
So the Deacon started pitching, while the crowd gave ribald jeers,
Which were turned, in just one inning, into rounds of roaring cheers!
For the Deacon fanned six batters in a meek, bewildered row,
Then went up and won that ball game with a stunning home run blow!
Then he realised his errors, and he left the pitching peak,
With a flush of great confusion spreading o'er his weathered cheek—
He had fallen for temptation—but—at least so people say—
He now stands for good, clean ball games, even on the Sabbath day!

—W. A. PHELON.

The Sunday baseball issue was debated hotly for years in states such as Massachusetts and Pennsylvania, which had rich religious heritages. Authorities blinked away amateur sports events on the Sabbath, but thoughts of monetary profits on the Lord's Day horrified many.

Initially, The Sporting News editorialized about the injustice of some citizens imposing their will on six-day-a-week laborers who craved relaxation at the ball park on Sunday afternoon.

Mildly at first, and then with increased vigor, TSN championed the cause of the liberals and in 1925 printed in its editorial columns the sentiments of Burt Whitman, its Boston correspondent:

"Sunday has been a day of hypocrisy, pretense and falsehood. But no longer should it be a day of sorrow and restless idleness. There is no reason why, in the afternoon, the people should live under this black, bitter cloud of restraint.

"I feel that if we are to have recreation we should have the best

Never, at Such a Price.

What's this idea that bobs up in Massachusetts of permitting Sunday ball games in that state, if a certain percentage of the receipts shall go to the churches? Just how the division among the churches shall be made is not stated, though the percentage is fixed. Possibly the church that is most fanatical against Sunday amusements would get the largest sop, which would mean most of it for Methodists and Presbyterians, and mighty little left for Catholics and Episcopalians, a bit for the Congregationalists and nothing at all for the synagogues.

Are we to consider that as a proposal for bribing of bigots? A repugnant idea and one that hardly will prevail; the pastor and his church organization will stomach a lot of sharp business if the gainer in the transaction makes the proper contribution, but business is one thing in the New England mind and sport or amusement something else again.

But repugnant as is the idea of bribing the degenerate and remnant Puritans, even less do we endorse the idea of bribing the political grafters by acceding to a licensing system for ball players, which is part of one Bay State legislator's scheme for greasing through a Sunday baseball bill.

If it is a situation where in order to play Sunday ball games in Massachusetts both politicians and preachers have to be bought off, then it were better to let Massachusetts go without its Sunday baseball games—let them play golf, go motoring or sweat in their tenements, according to their stations in life.

Ye gods, don't we pay licenses enough for the privilege of living in free America without having to pay a fee for swinging a bat or catching a ball? The tax gathering grafters charge you now every time you turn around, and for every lick of honest work you do to make a living. Put a license tag on the ball player and the next step will be to tax you for going to see a ball game—the federal government does that already as a "war" measure.

And beyond all that, as wise old Tom Rice points out, is the entering wedge of supervision by the civil authorities of baseball. License the ball players, then next we will have "commissions" of political grafters to supervise the game, politicians operating baseball clubs as "privileges," putting their henchmen in control of the business end, or mayhap on the field.

The plea that licensing professional ball players, with the idea that their behavior might be improved through fear of losing license to play ball, is a specious one, with which we have small patience. If the time has come that a ball player must be kept straight through fear of arrest or refusal of permission to play, by civil authorities, then indeed is it time that Organized Baseball disband and the national game be made a game of politics entirely.

possible. There have been evasions of the law for amateur sports on Sunday afternoons, evasions which were not worthy of the day. We have been temporizing.

"That Satan finds some evil for idle hands to do is an old saying which holds true in this instance. It is easy for two policemen to control 10,000 gathered to see a game of professional baseball on Sunday afternoon. It takes 10,000 policemen to handle and control 9,000 idle, restless and discontented people scattered around the city.

"Let everybody have their Sunday baseball!"

The editor of TSN concluded the thesis, which was titled, "Let in the Sunshine," with: "The case of the public vs. the long-haired order could not have been more aptly put.

"Let everybody have their Sunday baseball and give the cops a vacation."

Massachusetts was the first to accept Whitman's recommendation, but Pennsylvania held out until the early 1930s.

The editorial (above), 'Never, at Such a Price,' takes strong issue with those who opposed Sunday baseball, suggesting a conspiracy under which the will of a few was being imposed on a helpless majority.

'A Brighter Appearance'

Scribbled by ScribeS

ONCE A PITCHER FOR CLUB HE NOW HEADS

CASUAL COMMENT

BY FRANCIS C. RICHTER

BACK of the HOME PLATE

OBSERVATIONS OF A VETERAN SCRIBE

By JOHN B. SHERIDAN

Editorial pages throughout the 1920s used this basic makeup formula, featuring the columns 'Back of the Home Plate' by John B. Sheridan and 'Casual Comment' by former Sporting Life Editor Francis Richter, a short news item in the center column and 'Scribbled by Scribes,' a notes column featuring different writers from around the country. 'Baseball By-Plays' usually appeared in the outside column under Sheridan's picture with editorials in the two left columns. The 'Questions and Answers' column often appeared at the bottom of the page.

There was little opportunity for the editors of The Sporting News to display imagination or ingenuity during baseball season in the 1920s. With box scores occupying six and one-half pages, sometimes seven, remaining columns were devoted to the editorial page and reports from major league cities.

But the paper assumed a brighter appearance after the close of the minor league campaigns.

During the fall and winter months and through the conclusion of spring training, the publication presented a variety of features ranging from one-column boxes on "Do You Know?" and "A Box Score That Made History" to multi-column articles by nationally known writers.

Some of the features were fiction, such as a January 1921 piece, "The Nut from Pecan University," in which Hugh Fullerton, the author, "Takes a Flight From Fiction to Fancy."

Damon Runyon contributed "On the Road to Hasbeenville," and Herbert Louis McNary appealed to lovers of fiction with "The Twirling Ghost, a Story of Baseball, Love and Intrigue."

Edgar Wolfe, a Philadelphia writer-cartoonist who fancied the byline "Jim Nasium," contributed features regularly, and John B. Sheridan, the St. Louis sage who wrote a weekly column, "Back of the Home Plate," also delved into baseball history, spinning yarns of pioneer players and those who followed.

"Back of the Home Plate" was an editorial-page fixture throughout the 1920s along with "Casual Comment," "Scribbled by Scribes," "Questions and Answers" and "Baseball By-Plays." Other regular TSN columns were "Caught on the Fly," which had survived since the publication's first issue in 1886, and "Stove League Stories."

L.H. Addington's "In the Bull Pen" became a popular feature in the late 1920s and usually opened with a four-line doggerel. Ernest Lanigan became a regular in that same time period with his "Fanning With Lanigan."

American League umpire Billy Evans, who was a sportswriter before taking up the indicator, sized up major league clubs, their strengths and weaknesses, on his annual tour of spring camps, and Bill McGowan, another A.L. arbiter, authored a small feature, "Umpiring Under Difficulties."

Al Demaree, a former player who became a successful sports cartoonist, exhibited his handiwork weekly while Harry Brundidge, a St. Louis newspaperman, profiled prominent major league players.

A promotional blurb in October 1927 alerted readers to the next week's attractions. Among the writers were Ernie Phillips, "a former player who knows the minor league game from every angle and will have some fiction that will make your hair stand; Franklyn Adams, who knows how to put news into features, and Ernest J. Lanigan, whose penchant is figure facts."

The announcement also listed the names of the major league correspondents: Joe Vila, New York; Irving Vaughan, Chicago; Sam Greene, Detroit; Burt Whitman, Boston; James Isaminger, Philadelphia; Tom Rise, Brooklyn; Tom Swope, Cincinnati; Paul Eaton, Washington; Francis Powers, Cleveland, and Ralph Davis, Pittsburgh.

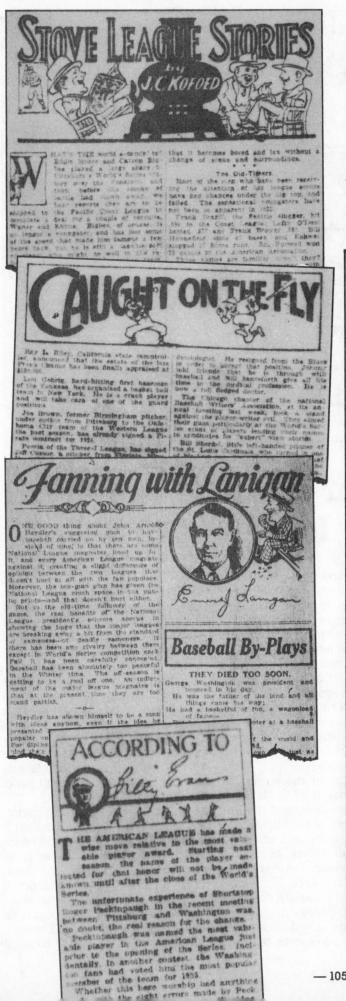

Other TSN regulars during the time period were 'Stove League Stories,' an off-season baseball column; 'Caught on the Fly,' a TSN column dating back to 1886; Ernest J. Lanigan's 'Fanning With Lanigan,' and a column by umpire Billy Evans. Lanigan's column sometimes appeared on the editorial page in place of Sheridan's column and 'According to Billy Evans' sometimes replaced 'Casual Comment.' 'A Box Score That Made History' provided a nostalgic off-season touch for TSN readers.

WHAT'S THE world a-comin' to? Eddie Moore and Carson Bigbee played a large share in Pittsburgh's World's Series victory over the Senators, and then, before the smoke of battle had blown away, we hear reports they are to be shipped to the Pacific Coast League to complete a deal for a couple of recruits, Waner and Rhyne. Bigbee, of course, is no longer a youngster, and has lost some of the speed that made him famous a few years back, but he is still a capable performer, who might do well in the re- [illegible]

that it becomes bored and lax without a change of scene and surroundings.

* * *

The Old-Timers.

Most of the men who have been receiving the attention of big league scouts have had chances under the big top, and failed. The sensational youngsters have not been as apparent in 1925.

Frank Brazill, the Pacific slugger, hit [illegible] in the Coast League, Lefty O'Doul batted [illegible] and Frank Brower [illegible]. Bill Hunnefield stole [illegible] bases, and Schwei[illegible] slugged [illegible] home runs. Bill Burwell won [illegible] games in the American Association.

These names are familiar, aren't they? [illegible]

Ray L. Riley, California state comptroller, announced that the estate of the late Frank Chance has been finally appraised at [illegible].

Lou Gehrig, hard-hitting first baseman of the Yankees, has organized a basket ball team in New York. He is a crack player and will take care of one of the guard positions.

Joe Brown, former Birmingham pitcher, under option from Pittsburg to the Oklahoma City team of the Western League the past season, has already signed a Pirate contract for 1926.

Peoria of the Three-I League has signed Jeff Cusson, a pitcher from Virginia, Min- [illegible]

dentologist. He resigned from the Blues in order to accept that position. Johnny told friends that he is through with baseball and will henceforth give all his time to the medical profession. He is now a full fledged doctor.

The Chicago chapter of the national Baseball Writers' Association, at its annual meeting last week, took a stand against the player-writer evil. They aimed their guns particularly at the World's Series stunt of players lending their names to syndicates for "expert" view stories.

Bill Sherdel, little left-handed pitcher of the St. Louis Cardinals, who turned in one of his [illegible]

Fanning with Lanigan

Ernest J. Lanigan

ONE GOOD thing about John Arnold Heydler's suggested plan to have baseball carried on by ten men, instead of nine, is that there are some National League magnates lined up for it, and every American League magnate against it, creating a slight difference of opinion between the two leagues that doesn't hurt at all with the fan populace. Moreover, the ten-man plan has given the National League much space in the public prints—and that doesn't hurt either.

But to the old-time follower of the game, the real benefits of the National League president's scheme accrue in showing the bugs that the major leagues are breaking away a bit from the standard of sameness—of deadly sameness. If there has been any rivalry between them except in World's Series competition each Fall it has been carefully concealed. Baseball has been absolutely too peaceful in the Winter time. The off-season is getting to be a real off one. An indictment of the major league magnates is that at the present time they are too standpattish.

—o—

Heydler has shown himself to be a man with ideas anyhow, even if the idea he presented [illegible] popular vo[illegible] For diplom[illegible] hind their [illegible]

Baseball By-Plays

THEY DIED TOO SOON.

George Washington was president and honored in his day,
He was the father of the land and all things came his way;
He had a basketful of fun, a wagonload of fame—
But [illegible] rooter at a baseball [illegible]
[illegible] the world and [illegible]nd,
[illegible] cup [illegible] just as

ACCORDING TO Billy Evans

THE AMERICAN LEAGUE has made a wise move relative to the most valuable player award. Starting next season, the name of the player selected for that honor will not be made known until after the close of the World's Series.

The unfortunate experience of Shortstop Roger Peckinpaugh in the recent meeting between Pittsburg and Washington was, no doubt, the real reason for the change.

Peckinpaugh was named the most valuable player in the American League just prior to the opening of the Series. Incidentally, in another contest, the Washington fans had voted him the most popular member of the team for 1925.

Whether this hero worship had anything to do with the eight errors made by Peck [illegible]

A Box Score That —Made History—

AT BOSTON — (American League) July 19, 1918, Boston defeated Detroit, 5 to 0. In this game, John McInnis of Boston, accepted 22 fielding chances, the major league record for chances accepted by a first baseman in a nine inning game.

Following is the score of the game.

Boston.	AB.	R.	H.	PO.	A.	E.
Hooper, right field	4	1	1	2	0	0
Shean, second base	4	0	0	0	6	0
Strunk, center field	4	1	1	0	0	0
Ruth, left field	3	2	2	1	0	0
McInnis, first base	4	1	4	21	1	0
Scott, shortstop	2	0	0	0	3	0
Barbare, shortstop	0	0	0	0	1	0
Schang, catcher	4	0	1	2	0	0
Stansbury, third base	3	0	0	0	4	0
Mays, pitcher	3	0	1	1	4	0
Totals	30	5	10	27	19	0

Detroit.	AB.	R.	H.	PO.	A.	E.
Bush, shortstop	2	0	0	5	2	1
Jones, third base	3	0	1	[illegible]	2	1
Walker, center field	4	0	0	0	0	0
Veach, left field	3	0	0	1	0	0
Stanage, first base	3	0	1	11	0	0
Harper, right field	3	0	0	2	0	0
Coffey, second base	3	0	0	2	0	0
Spencer, catcher	3	0	1	1	2	0
Bailey, pitcher	3	0	0	0	2	0
Totals	28	0	3	24	11	2

Score by innings.

Detroit	0	0	0	0	0	0	0	0	0	—0
Boston	3	0	0	0	0	0	0	2	*	—5

Two-base hits — Jones, Spencer. Three-base hit—Ruth. Stolen base—Strunk. Sacrifices—Bush, Shean, Scott, Barbare. Left on base—Detroit 5, Boston 3. Bases on balls—Off Bailey, 3; off Mays, 1. Struck out—By Bailey 1, by Mays 2. Total bases—Detroit 3, Boston 12.

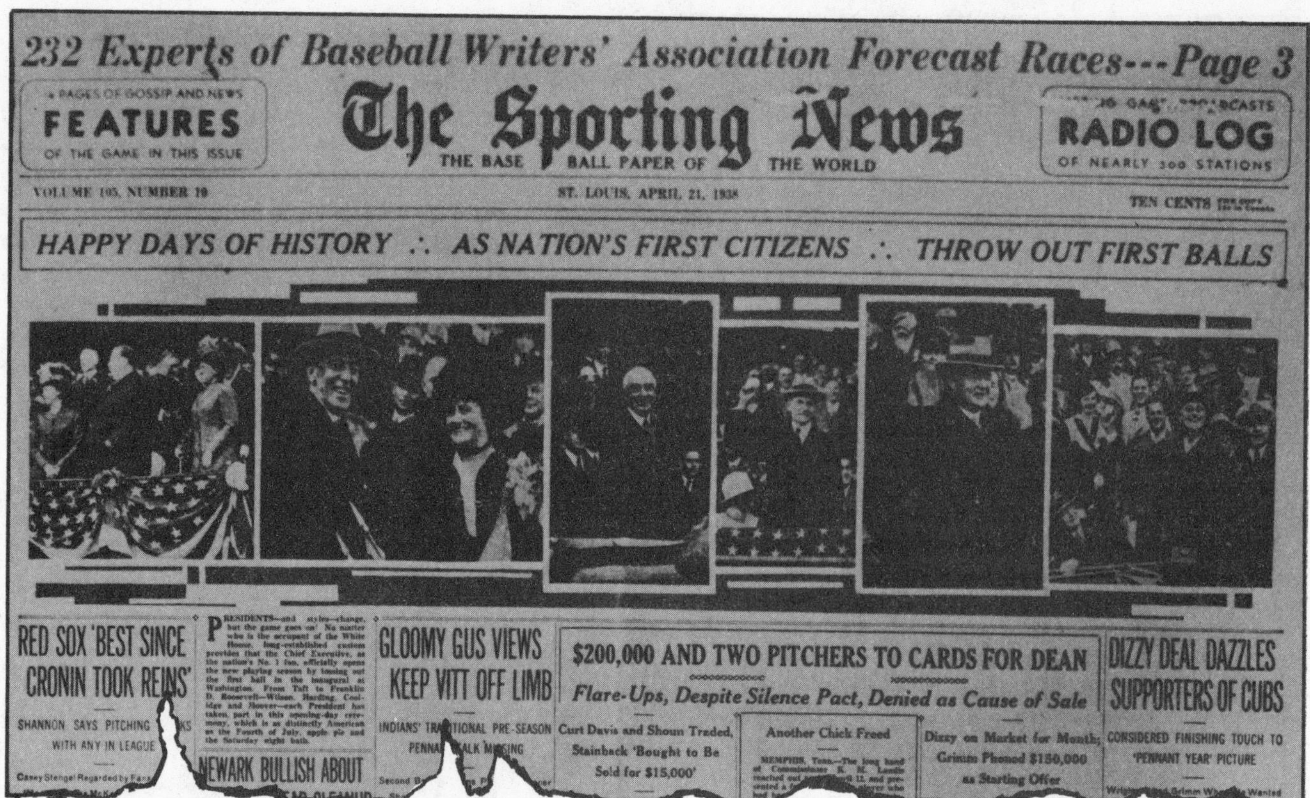

232 Experts of Baseball Writers' Association Forecast Races---Page 3

FEATURES OF THE GAME IN THIS ISSUE

The Sporting News

THE BASE BALL PAPER OF THE WORLD

RADIO LOG OF NEARLY 300 STATIONS

VOLUME 105, NUMBER 10 — ST. LOUIS, APRIL 21, 1938 — TEN CENTS

HAPPY DAYS OF HISTORY ∴ AS NATION'S FIRST CITIZENS ∴ THROW OUT FIRST BALLS

PRESIDENTS—and styles—change, but the game goes on! No matter who is the occupant of the White House, long-established custom provides that the Chief Executive, as the nation's No. 1 fan, officially opens the new playing season by tossing out the first ball in the inaugural at Washington. From Taft to Franklin D. Roosevelt—Wilson, Harding, Coolidge and Hoover—each President has taken part in this opening-day ceremony, which is as distinctly American as the Fourth of July, apple pie and the Saturday night bath.

RED SOX 'BEST SINCE CRONIN TOOK REINS'

SHANNON SAYS PITCHING WITH ANY IN LEAGUE

NEWARK BULLISH ABOUT

GLOOMY GUS VIEWS KEEP VITT OFF LIMB

INDIANS' TRADITIONAL PRE-SEASON PENNANT TALK MISSING

$200,000 AND TWO PITCHERS TO CARDS FOR DEAN

Flare-Ups, Despite Silence Pact, Denied as Cause of Sale

Curt Davis and Shoun Traded, Stainback 'Bought to Be Sold for $15,000'

Another Chick Freed

Dizzy on Market for Month; Grimm Phoned $150,000 as Starting Offer

DIZZY DEAL DAZZLES SUPPORTERS OF CUBS

CONSIDERED FINISHING TOUCH TO 'PENNANT YEAR' PICTURE

Broadcasting of baseball games was a hotly debated issue through the 1920s, but by the late 1930s TSN was carrying a 'Radio Log' for nearly 300 stations.

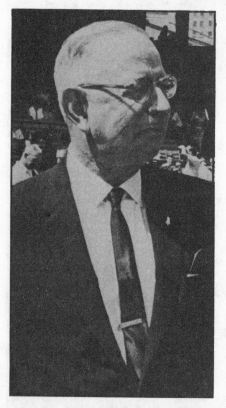

Harold Arlin (pictured in 1965) is credited with handling the first baseball broadcast in 1921, calling a Phillies-Pirates game at Forbes Field.

Major League Baseball Is on the Air

In the early days of radio, newspapermen adopted a rigid, defensive position for fear that the wireless medium would make newspapers obsolete with its rapid dissemination of news.

When members of the Baseball Writers Association of America went on record against "any radio concern given permission to broadcast games play-by-play," The Sporting News tried to allay the apprehensions of its journalistic brethren.

"The argument of the writers," noted an editorial in 1923, "is that if results are thus circulated it will mean curtailment of circulation of newspapers; there will be a lessened demand for 'pink sheets,' as sporting extras are known. Possibly. But we can't exactly agree with the writers that 'it will result in curtailment of baseball publicity.'

"Certainly any broadcasting of baseball should increase the publicity; persons who might never look at a 'pink sheet' to see how the game came out . . . probably would endure the buzzing of the details of play over the wireless as they do of other parts of 'programs' they may not be particularly interested in.

"And thus they might become interested enough in baseball to go to the park some day to see what a game is like."

Two years later, however, TSN applauded Ban Johnson when the president of the American League banned broadcasts from ball parks in the junior circuit.

"Baseball is more an inspiration to the brain through the eye than it is by the ear," proclaimed an editorial. "The greatest value of baseball, next to playing it, is to look upon it. There is nothing about it which appears to appeal to wave lengths. A nation that begins to take its sports by ear will shortly adopt the white flag as its national

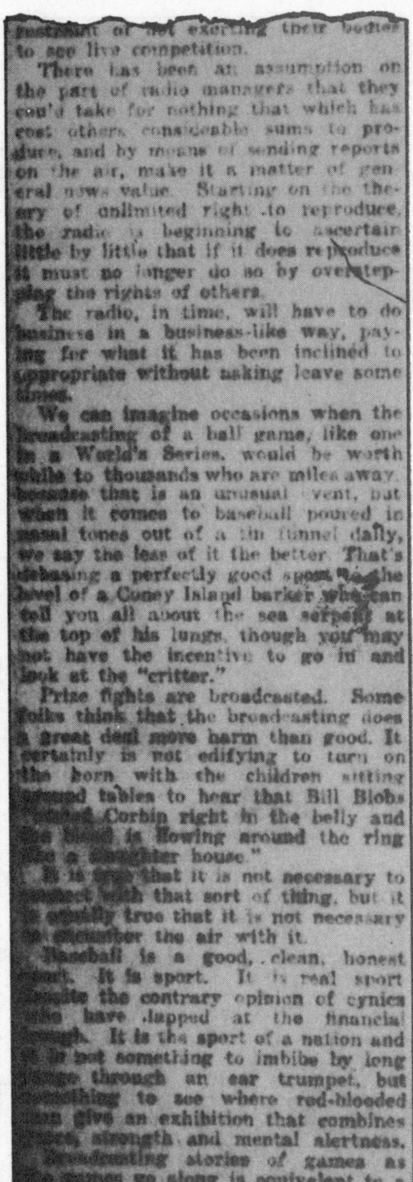

[illegible] of not exerting their bodies to see live competition.

There has been an assumption on the part of radio managers that they could take for nothing that which has cost others considerable sums to produce, and by means of sending reports on the air, make it a matter of general news value. Starting on the theory of unlimited right to reproduce, the radio is beginning to ascertain little by little that if it does reproduce it must no longer do so by overstepping the rights of others.

The radio, in time, will have to do business in a business-like way, paying for what it has been inclined to appropriate without asking leave some times.

We can imagine occasions when the broadcasting of a ball game, like one in a World's Series, would be worth while to thousands who are miles away, because that is an unusual event, but when it comes to baseball poured in nasal tones out of a tin funnel daily, we say the less of it the better. That's debasing a perfectly good sport to the level of a Coney Island barker who can tell you all about the sea serpent at the top of his lungs, though you may not have the incentive to go in and look at the "critter."

Prize fights are broadcasted. Some folks think that the broadcasting does a great deal more harm than good. It certainly is not edifying to turn on the horn with the children sitting around tables to hear that Bill Blobs [illegible] Corbin right in the belly and the blood is flowing around the ring like a slaughter house."

It is true that it is not necessary to [illegible] with that sort of thing, but it is equally true that it is not necessary to encumber the air with it.

Baseball is a good, clean, honest sport. It is sport. It is real sport despite the contrary opinion of cynics who have lapped at the financial trough. It is the sport of a nation and it is not something to imbibe by long [illegible] through an ear trumpet, but something to see where red-blooded men give an exhibition that combines [illegible], strength and mental alertness.

Broadcasting stories of games as the games go along is equivalent to a [illegible] party with neither corn nor [illegible]

A 1925 TSN editorial (above left) expressed reservations about the broadcasting of baseball games. Ball players with journalistic talents often were contributors to the pages of The Sporting News. Joe Munson, a Western League star, produced the above cartoon.

emblem and the dove as its national bird.

"The spectator of a ball game is one who enjoys the skill of athletic effort combined with a display of mental spirit. The skill is vested in the players and the mental effort also. The boy, who desires to be a ball player of conspicuous merit, goes to the game to see how the best play it. The man who has been an old ball player goes because of his intense fondness for a sport of which he knows all the variations. To both of these elements add yet another which goes because it admires all kinds of athletic competition, and still a fourth, which attends because it lives mentally upon the diversities of the pastime pictured to the brain by the eye.

"If all of these elements were to be compelled to take their baseball by radio, we expect most of them would lose interest. . . .

"Broadcasting stories of games as the games go along," concluded the editorial, "is equivalent to a succotash party with neither corn nor beans."

In 1929, after Southern League officials banned microphones from their parks, The Sporting News hailed the action. Commenting on a survey that disclosed a decline in attendance when games were put on the air, the editorial writer chortled: "That, gentlemen of the baseball audience, is the story of the radio and baseball. There can be no doubt that sooner or later broadcasting of the games will be found to be a boomerang. It breeds an indolence which keeps fans away from the park at the slightest provocation and will be found in time to have other drawbacks once started."

Poetry in Motion

IN THE BULL PEN
with
L. H. Addington

FISHERMAN LOU.
Lou Gehrig's quite a fisherman,
With accurate casting eyes;
He uses only first base lines,
And baits his hook with flies.

* * *

RABBIT MARANVILLE, now of the Boston Braves, is a windshield tester. Whatinhell? In order to test the

JOE MUNSON 'DRAWS' A LETTER

Leroy H. Addington (left), known simply as L.H. by his many readers, wrote one of the more popular columns that graced The Sporting News pages through the 1920s. Addington's 'In The Bull Pen' column (above), normally consisting of a number of short baseball-related items, appeared regularly and usually was preceded by a four-line poem that carried a message of its own.

One of the most versatile members of The Sporting News staff during the Roaring Twenties was Leroy H. Addington, who preferred to use his first two initials in bylines.

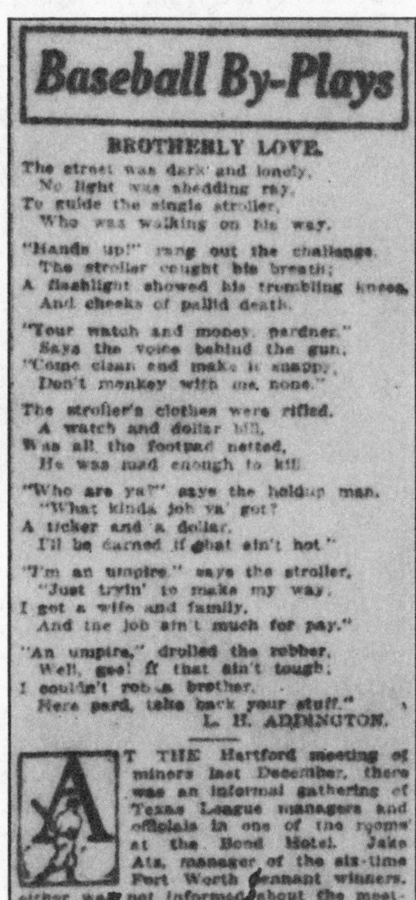

Baseball By-Plays

BROTHERLY LOVE.

The street was dark and lonely,
No light was shedding ray,
To guide the single stroller,
Who was walking on his way.

"Hands up!" rang out the challenge.
The stroller caught his breath;
A flashlight showed his trembling knees,
And cheeks of pallid death.

"Your watch and money, pardner,"
Says the voice behind the gun,
"Come clean and make it snappy,
Don't monkey with me, none."

The stroller's clothes were rifled.
A watch and dollar bill,
Was all the footpad netted,
He was mad enough to kill.

"Who are ya?" says the holdup man,
"What kinda job ya' got?
A ticker and a dollar,
I'll be darned if that ain't hot."

"I'm an umpire," says the stroller,
"Just tryin' to make my way,
I got a wife and family,
And the job ain't much for pay."

"An umpire," drolled the robber,
Well, gee! if that ain't tough;
I couldn't rob a brother,
Here pard, take back your stuff."

L. H. ADDINGTON.

AT THE Hartford meeting of miners last December, there was an informal gathering of Texas League managers and officials in one of the rooms at the Bond Hotel. Jake Atz, manager of the six-time Fort Worth pennant winners, either was not informed about the meet-

Addington, ever the poet, also contributed regularly to 'Baseball By-Plays,' another editorial-page column that appeared regularly in the decade. This column usually led off with a longer piece of poetry and carried the author's byline at the end. The poem 'Brotherly Love' (right) is a fitting example of Addington's work.

A native of St. Louis and a graduate of the University of Missouri, Addington was a newspaperman in Joplin, Mo., and Fort Smith, Ark., before joining The Sporting News. While working for J.G. Taylor Spink, he wrote feature articles, covered major league meetings and authored a weekly column, "In the Bull Pen."

The column was a potpourri of short baseball items, usually in a lighter vein and always preceded by a piece of doggerel that was geared to the season. A sample rhyme, captioned "Hard Words," was:

"Some umpires have a hard old life,"
A baseball wag once said,
"And, yes," replied the Wise Crack Guy,
"Some have a hard old head."

In 1927, Addington's page 1 Christmas message read:

To all the hosts of baseball,
To all its many readers,
To all the men who play the game,
And those who serve as leaders,
And those, by choice, who read these lines,
For any cause or reason,
The Sporting News and staff extend,
The greetings of the season.

After leaving The Sporting News, Addington served as public relations director for the National Association in Durham, N.C., under its president, Judge William G. Bramham.

You Win Some, You Lose Some

The age-old practice of baseball players leaving their gloves on the field while they batted aroused the editorial scorn of The Sporting News prior to the 1925 World Series.

Recalling that a mask had tripped up Hank Gowdy, preventing the Giants' backstop from catching a crucial pop foul in the final game of the 1924 World Series, and that a pebble had deflected a ground ball into a critical base hit in the same game, a TSN editorial noted:

"There should be no obstruction of any kind on the ball field. Under the rules there can be none. Ball players obstruct it all of the time. One of these days an important game will be materially affected because they do so.

"The ball may hit one of those gloves some day and a very hard hit may be noticeably checked because the ball did hit the glove. A fielder may find his feet tangled with a glove—it is plenty big enough. . . . It is still a lazy sort of thing to see a big player take off a glove and throw it carelessly over the field. If it were a hod of coal, we suppose he would do the same thing."

Nearly 30 years passed before, in 1953, baseball officials required that players carry their equipment to the dugout after the third out.

Another campaign by The Sporting News brought results more quickly. Frequently, the paper had urged teams to adopt a system of numbering players' uniforms to facilitate identification by spectators. When the Yankees announced such a plan for the 1929 season, the editors were ecstatic.

"The Sporting News heartily congratulates Colonel Ruppert (owner), Ed Barrow (general manager) and the entire Yankee organization," read an editorial.

Pointing out that football and basketball players wore numbers on their uniforms, the editorial continued: "The thing that stumps us is that the players were not numbered long ago. Some of the more enterprising minors have been doing it for quite a spell and the fans like it.

"Baseball relies on the public to keep it alive and cannot do too much to see that the fans receive full enjoyment. Knowing the players is a big part of the game from a standpoint of common interest. There are many who can tell the players, regulars and substitutes, but there are a lot more who cannot. . . .

"Numbering the players most certainly will appeal to many fans; it will make better fans of the occasional patrons and perhaps a regular out of the newcomer.

"It's high time baseball were taking the initiative in any direction that will attract and hold people to its exhibitions, no matter how trivial or inconsequential the service attempted may occur to the standpatter.

"Let's have more initiative!"

Eventually, but not immediately, all clubs followed the Yankees.

One of the more successful editorial campaigns conducted by The Sporting News in the 1920s involved the use of numbers on the back of major league players' uniforms. When the Yankees met the Pittsburgh Pirates (above) in the 1927 World Series, numberless uniforms still were the norm, making it difficult for the casual fan to identify the game's stars. But in 1929, TSN announced and applauded the Yankees' decision to adopt the numbering system with a page 2 headline (right) and story. That decision, of course, withstood the test of time and the Yankees, more than any other team, have benefited from the association of numbers with great players (below).

YANKS ADOPT NUMBERING SYSTEM

And Tom Rice Gives Three Cheers

Brooklyn Writer, Who Has Hammered Away for Plan to Identify Players for Fans, Thinks Others Will Follow Idea; Argues That Baseball Owes It to Pub'ic

By THOMAS S. RICE.

THREE rousing cheers for Col. Jake Ruppert, or whoever was responsible for the decision to have the New York Yankees wear numbers on their uniforms in 1929. Regular readers of The Sporting News will remember that for several years I harped on that numbering scheme in the interests of the players, the fans, the clubs and the United States Treasury, which collects a tax on baseball tickets. After wearing out my typewriter, patience, nerves and vocabulary, I gave up the task of trying to persuade club owners to display a little business intelligence by making the game more attractive to their patrons.

Now Col. Ruppert comes along and will number his athletes in 1929 as they should have been numbered since 1869. At that, the Colonel's grasping of an idea that has been obvious for 60 years is no small feat in baseball. It generally takes the owners about 70 years to grasp an idea that costs nothing and adds to the attractiveness of their bid for the public coin.

It is not at all certain that I was the first person to suggest numbering baseball players, but I certainly was the first one to advocate the scheme in season and out. Much of the credit should go to The Sporting News and to the Brooklyn Daily Eagle, both of which gave as much space as I asked for my hammering at the subject.

Although the object was not accomplished at the time of my personally conducted, one-man campaign some years ago, the campaign left an impress that will be reflected in other clubs following the example of the Yankees sooner than they would have done otherwise.

Cost Certainly No Barrier.

The strange feature of the passive re-

the gate? In the whole range of human stupidity I know of nothing to equal that of the magnates in booking exhibitions on the strength of high-priced drawing cards and then concealing the identity of the cards.

But, the exhibition fans are by no means the only ones stung. Many fans enjoy the practice before games. Some of them know all of the players, some know the players when they see them in their regular positions, but it is safe to say that on a day when 5,000 fans are at a ball park there will not be 1,000 who can identify all the players who take part in the practice.

Out-of-Town Fans to Consider.

Many a fan from out-of-town strays into a ball park. He is a regular and very important asset in the aggregate. He wants to see and recognize both the home and invading talent. He will see five or six pitchers tossing for each side, he will see half a dozen men in the outfield, and other players batting out flies or tapping bunts. He will want to know who is who, but unless he happens to be sitting by a veteran local fan with good eyesight, the stranger can spot only those men who go to bat when the game begins. He can not go home and make the gossip that makes the game profitable, by telling that Honus Whiffus, who did not take part in the game, was a smaller man than he thought; that Pitcher Pfiggle looked like a good outfielder from the way he shagged flies, that Catcher Mittem was the rottenest fungo hitter he ever did see, and so on.

About 60 per cent of the fans on the major circuits are deprived of about 60 per cent of the enjoyment they should receive from the practice of the home team, and of about 90 per cent of the enjoyment they should receive from the practice and ante-game antics of the visitors.

THE SPORTING NEWS

Big League Writers Select All-Star Team For The Sporting News

Vance, Hornsby Poll Largest Total of Votes For Places; Johnson and Traynor Next

Center Field Berth Goes to Carey By Slight Margin Over Tris Speaker, While Bottomley Beats Out Sisler for First Base.

Baseball Writers' All-Star Teams

WHAT DELIGHT AN OWNER COULD GET OUT OF TEAM LIKE THIS!

Can They Hit? Look 'Em Over

SPARTANBURG COULDN'T THINK OF LOSING KELLY

YOU CAN'T BLAME LANE FOR LOSING HIS SPEECH

ANOTHER SHERIDAN STORY NEXT WEEK

BURCH HAS THREE MEN LIKELY TO GO HIGHER UP

The Sporting News proudly presented its first major league all-star team in 1925 after polling baseball writers from around the country.

'Something Worth While'

All-star teams of one sort or another had been selected from the earliest years of professional baseball, but there was a different tinge to the first such aggregation that The Sporting News presented in 1925.

The selections carried a note of authority that was lacking in previous all-star teams. It was chosen by members of the Baseball Writers Association of America.

The paper was understandably proud of its innovation and remarked on it in an editorial, "Something Worth While."

". . . The method by which this team was produced, the scope on which the players were chosen, makes it somewhat out of the ordinary, especially for authority and standard."

It was further explained that 102 writers had taken part in the poll, "the largest field that has ever participated in a thing of this kind."

The editorial emphasized that "One of the surprising results was the manner in which the writers passed up Roger Peckinpaugh in the balloting on shortstop. Hapless old Rajah was completely forgotten by all but five writers, Glenn Wright of Pittsburgh getting the place with 67 votes. (Peckinpaugh, the American League's Most Valuable Player, had committed eight errors, some at critical junctures, in the Senators' loss to the Pirates in the World Series.)

Concluding his thesis, the editor wrote: "The Sporting News feels justly proud of the team the writers picked for it, and cannot drop the subject without a thought as to how much the 11 men selected would be worth at current market prices."

An editorial (below) in the November 19, 1925, issue of TSN called its newly selected all-star team 'Something Worth While.' It also explained why Roger Peckinpaugh, the American League MVP in 1925, was left off the squad. Peckinpaugh is shown (right) shaking hands with Pittsburgh outfielder Max Carey, an all-star selection.

Something Worth While.

The Sporting News in this issue pub-ishes a major league All-Star team, which it believes it can feel proud to give the baseball public. It is perhaps not a great deal different from other mythical teams that have gone before it. Some of the same names appear on it. That is to be expected. But the method by which this team was produced, the scope on which the players were chosen, makes it somewhat out of the ordinary, especially for authority and standard.

The team was selected by the vote of the major league baseball writers at large. Each member of the National Baseball Writers' Association in the 11 big league cities was given a ballot with open and unrestricted premise to write their nominations as they saw them. These ballots were then recapitulated for a majority vote and there was no shifting about or changing of names to satisfy whim or fancy. James M. Gould, president of the Baseball Writers' organization, supervised the counting of the votes.

In the recapitulation it was found that 102 big league writers took part in the voting. Thus the selection was

In addition to shortstop Wright, the team consisted of pitchers Dazzy Vance, Brooklyn, who received votes from 98 of the 102 scribes; Walter Johnson, Washington, and Ed Rommel, Philadelphia Athletics; catcher Mickey Cochrane, Philadelphia Athletics; first baseman Jim Bottomley and second baseman Rogers Hornsby, both of the St. Louis Cardinals; third baseman Pie Traynor, Pittsburgh, and outfielders Goose Goslin, Washington, and Max Carey and Kiki Cuyler, both of Pittsburgh.

For Turkey Week

READERS of The Sporting News who have come to recognize the high standard of features being carried each week, will find no diminuation of them throughout the Winter season. For Turkey Week there will be an all-star lineup.

Ernest Lanigan will go to bat with another of his interesting reviews, this time dealing with the new players appearing in the National League in 1927. Later will come the American League end of this feature.

Then there will be Franklyn J. Adams, Jim Naslum, the final batch of records from A. H. Bentrup, L. H. Addington's "Bull Pen," MacLean Kennedy's "Greatest Teams of History," Sally League review; final chapter of "Speed Conklin and the Hoodoo," and the regular run of news and official averages.

The 'For Turkey Week' item (left) shows just how baseball-oriented The Sporting News had become by 1927. The highlights for the upcoming Thanksgiving issue featured baseball, baseball and more baseball.

Former Yankee friends and teammates Babe Ruth and Lou Gehrig enjoy a reunion on 'Lou Gehrig Day' in 1939.

1930-1939: DEPRESSING TIMES

Of all the innovations in professional baseball's first century, probably none encountered such formidable opposition nor stirred emotions as much as the introduction of night ball at Cincinnati in 1935.

Artificial lights spelled profits for, and in some cases the salvation of, numerous minor league clubs during the Depression of the early 1930s. Major league officials watched with curiosity as the nocturnal madness took root in Des Moines in 1930 and spread quickly to Buffalo, Omaha, Sacramento, Portland, Ore., Decatur, Ill., Wheeling, W. Va., and Rochester, N.Y. They watched, but they were convinced that the night game was just a novelty, a fancy that would pass with the return of economic prosperity.

Major league executives held their ground despite reports of increased attendance at minor league parks with lights. They were unimpressed by a May 1930 headline in The Sporting News that announced: "Average Night Crowd at Des Moines Is 2,309 / Decatur Opens Before 4,643; Weather Hampers Both Tests."

The most vociferous traditionalist was Clark Griffith, who became owner of the Washington Senators after distinguished careers as a pitcher and then a manager. "Night baseball is just a step above dog racing," the Old Fox thundered.

Griff also declared that "baseball wasn't meant to be played at night; it was meant to be played in the Lord's broad sunshine, just as it has been for the past 100 years. There is no chance of night ball ever becoming popular in the big cities. People there are educated to see the best there is and will stand for only the best. High-class baseball cannot be played at night under artificial lights. Furthermore, the benefits derived from attending are due largely to fresh air and sunshine. Night air and electric lights are a poor substitute."

Five years elapsed between the time that E. Lee Keyser illuminated the first stadium in professional baseball with permanent lights and the day that after-dusk baseball came to the major leagues. It remained for Leland Stanford (Larry) MacPhail, a born iconoclast, to break the resistance and chart a new course toward a baseball bonanza.

The redhead arrived in Cincinnati in the fall of 1933 following a successful season as president of the Columbus (American Association) club. MacPhail's first assignment after entering the National League was to find a civic-minded businessman to buy the Reds from the Central Trust Co., which had held Sidney Weil's controlling stock in the club for three years. He found such an angel in Powel Crosley Jr., a highly respected manufacturer of radios that bore his name.

In one of their first conversations, Powel congratulated Larry on his successful season at Columbus.

"We played under lights," was the modest reply.

"Why not lights in the National League?" Crosley asked.

"They'd never let me," Larry said.

"How do you know, you could try," Crosley suggested.

MacPhail needed no further encouragement. Hat in hand, he appeared before the National League owners at their December meeting and, marshaling all the arguments and statistics, requested permission to play night games in 1935. The magnates reluctantly approved his request by allowing no more than seven games to be played under artificial illumination, but they cautioned Larry that no club could be forced to play at night against its will.

The moment that forever changed the complexion of major league baseball occurred May 24, 1935. In the White House, President Franklin D. Roosevelt pressed a button that transformed Crosley Field into a glittering wonderland. Ford Frick, the newly named successor to John Heydler as president of the National League, was among the 20,422 fans who watched the Reds defeat the Phillies, 2-1. Lou Chiozza, the visitors' second baseman, was the first batter in the historic game, and shortstop Billy Myers of the Reds recorded the first hit, a leadoff double in the first inning.

Despite the arclights' therapeutic effect on arthritic turnstiles, executives were reluctant to endorse unlimited night play. Frick suggested that 10 games were about all that the public would accept. Talk of a "saturation point" was widespread. Even MacPhail, who started it all, accused the owners of greed when they clamored for an unlimited night schedule.

Three seasons passed before a second major league park was wired for nighttime competition. And that interim might have been even greater if MacPhail had not transferred his executive talents to Brooklyn in 1938. MacPhail directed the installation of lights at Ebbets Field, where the first night game was played at a major league stadium other than Crosley Field on June 15, 1938.

That night was made doubly memorable by the performance of Johnny Vander Meer, a Cincinnati lefthander who marked the occasion by throwing his second consecutive no-hit game. Vandy's 6-0 victory over the Dodgers in Brooklyn followed by four days his 3-0 hitless effort against Boston.

Within a month of Vander Meer's remarkable feat, Crosley Field again was the center of the major league stage when the Reds played hosts to the sixth annual All-Star Game. The midsummer extravaganza was initiated in 1933 by Arch Ward, sports editor of the Chicago Tribune, as part of the city's Century of Progress Exposition. As originally conceived, the game was to be a onetime exhibition, but when a capacity crowd turned out at Comiskey Park to see the American Leaguers win, 4-2, behind Babe Ruth's home run, a second game was programmed for the Polo Grounds in New York. When Giants lefthander Carl Hubbell struck out Babe Ruth, Lou Gehrig, Jimmie Foxx, Al Simmons and Joe Cronin in succession in that 1934 contest, the event became even more popular, and the All-Star Game went on to become an annual fixture.

In 1934, Hubbell was in his seventh season with the Giants following a circuitous minor league career that once was interrupted by a spring training trip with the Tigers. Detroit officials were unimpressed with Hubbell, who, against their advice, insisted on throwing a screwball. When he joined the Giants, Hub found no such restrictions on his favorite pitch, and he blossomed as the club's "Meal Ticket."

King Carl threw a no-hitter, won more than 20 games five times, was named the league's Most Valuable Player twice and, on July 2, 1933, pitched an incomparable 18-inning, 1-0 victory over the Cardinals in which he scattered six hits, struck out 12 and walked none. In the second game of the doubleheader, Roy Parmelee outdueled Dizzy Dean, also 1-0, with Parmelee allowing four hits and Dean five.

The garrulous, colorful and often controversial Dean was to St. Louis what Hubbell was to New York. Christened Jay Hanna, Ol' Diz broke in with the Cardinals at the end of the 1930 season. He won his only decision and, without waiting to watch the Cards play in the World Series against Philadelphia, he headed for St. Joseph, Mo., where he willingly submitted to an interview. A headline in The Sporting News reported the gist of the interview. It read: " 'Show Me Another Undefeated Major Pitcher' Dizzy Dean's Greeting on Return to St. Joseph / Predicts He'll be Known as the 'Great Dean' When He Has a Chance to Pitch Regularly for the Birds."

The "Great Dean" did not emerge in 1931. He was in Houston, winning 26 games for the Texas League Buffs while the Cards were capturing their second straight pennant. Nor was he on hand when St. Louis, inspired by Pepper Martin, the free-spirited Wild Horse of the Osage, defeated the defending champion Athletics in a seven-game World Series.

Diz joined the Cardinals to stay in 1932 and peaked as a major league pitcher in 1934 when he won 30 games, a feat no National Leaguer has since matched. The former Arkansas cotton picker also was the ringleader of the unruly troupe known as the Gas House Gang. The Redbird rowdies earned their colorful nickname one afternoon when they swashbuckled onto the field at the Polo Grounds wearing uniforms long overdue at the laundry. Blotched with caked mud, dried blood and sweat stains, the uniforms bore testimony to the Cardinals' untamed style of play. A New York writer took an amused glance at the visitors and declared, "Here comes the Gas House Gang."

Their names were Dean, Medwick, Martin, Durocher and Collins, and under the dynamic leadership of player-manager Frank Frisch, they enjoyed nothing more than a brawl, among themselves or with their opponents. On the mound they were led by Dean, who loved to "fahr" his high, hard one, and his younger brother Paul, a tandem that was immortalized by Diz as "Me 'n' Paul." Joe Medwick, meanwhile, was a terror at the plate.

Indirectly, the Gas House Gang helped create new laurels for Bill Terry as a quote-maker. The previous winter the Giants' manager was asked to evaluate the chances of the Brooklyn Dodgers in the 1934 pennant race. "Is Brooklyn still in the league?" Bill replied in a quaint attempt at humor. His remark was printed in the next day's papers, and the Flatbush Faithful filed it away for future reference.

The opportunity to revive the comment occurred on the final weekend of the 1934 season. The Cardinals were to play two games at home against the Reds, the Giants two games at home against the Dodgers. If the Cards won on Saturday and the Giants lost, St. Louis was assured of at least a tie for the pennant.

On the next to last day, almost 14,000 howling fans defied the wet, muggy weather, and all of them, it seemed, thirsted for Terry's blood. Never was a manager so violently abused in his own ball park. Bad at the start, the situation grew steadily worse for Memphis Bill as Van Lingle Mungo carved up the Giants, 5-1. The Cards also won, so the best that Terry could expect was a tie for the flag.

Sunday brought no relief. The Giants bowed, 8-5, as the Cards won. This time, in more favorable weather, 44,000 leather lungs packed the Polo Grounds and reminded Terry that the Dodgers, although in sixth place, still were members of the National League.

The Dean brothers produced 49 victories for the new champions, 30 by Diz and 19 by Paul. Each also accounted for two wins in the World Series against Detroit. In addition to winning the first and last games, Diz added a curious footnote to Series history when he volunteered his services as a pinch-runner in the fourth game. Trying to break up a double play at second base, Dean neglected to slide soon enough and was struck on the head by the shortstop's throw. The unconscious form of the great pitcher was carried off the field, but he recovered in time to take the mound the next day, when he bowed to Tommy Bridges, 3-1.

Dean won 28 games in 1935, but the Cards failed to repeat as champions. They lost out to the Cubs, who unfurled a 21-game winning streak in September.

Dean dropped to 24 victories in 1936 and started the 1937 All-Star Game at Griffith Stadium in Washington.

In the third inning a line drive off the bat of Earl Averill struck and fractured Dean's toe. Diz returned to action before the injury healed and, using an unnatural delivery, strained his arm. The next April, the damaged merchandise was peddled to the Cubs, for whom Diz won seven games in Chicago's pennant-winning season of 1938. But guile and cunning were poor substitutes for a blazing fastball of other years, and he faded rapidly. He was washed up at 30.

The Cubs lost the 1938 World Series to the Yankees in four games, just as they had in 1932 when Babe Ruth posed the still unanswerable question on whether he had "called" his third-game home run off Charlie Root. The Yankees were under the management of Joe McCarthy, who had been fired by the Cubs in 1930 after failing to duplicate his pennant performance of the year before. McCarthy took over the New York club in 1931 and became the architect of a new Yankee dynasty. The Bronx Bombers took the measure of the Giants in 1936 and '37, and after sweeping the Reds in 1939 they became the first team to win four consecutive world championships.

Babe Ruth had departed the Yankees after the 1934 season to become a vice president-outfielder for the Boston Braves, and Joe DiMaggio quickly became the new idol of the masses. Only Lou Gehrig remained from the powerhouse Yankees of the 1920s, but the Iron Horse was showing the ravages of time. The seemingly indestructible first baseman had more than 2,100 consecutive games to his credit when he reported for spring training in 1939. Outwardly, he looked as healthy as ever, but when he stepped on the field it was evident that his reactions had slowed.

Larrupin' Lou, not yet 36, also was aware of his sluggishness. The Yankees were in Detroit at the start of their first western swing on May 2 when Gehrig removed himself from the lineup after getting only four singles in 28 at-bats. He had played in 2,130 consecutive games since 1925.

A medical examination revealed in June that the Yankee captain was suffering from amyotrophic lateral sclerosis, an insidious form of paralysis that since has come to be known as "Lou Gehrig's Disease." Lou never played another game, but he was tendered an emotional tribute by the Yankees and more than 61,000 admirers on July 4. Between games of a doubleheader and surrounded by his old teammates of the 1927 Yankees, the stricken slugger spoke to a hushed throng at Yankee Stadium. "Today," he said, "I consider myself the luckiest man on the face of the earth."

When the Yankees fell into a slump in the days that followed, The Sporting News' correspondent attempted to explain why in his weekly report. The headline read, "Yank Letdown Due to Emotionalism / That's McCarthy's Word for It; Gehrig Day the Cause."

But the Bronx Bombers recovered and won a fourth flag in a row, beating out the Red Sox by 17 games. As usual, the most prominent figure at the World Series was Judge Kenesaw Mountain Landis, who was close to completing his second decade as commissioner. It had been a memorable 10 years for the former Chicago jurist, with historic decisions and rulings and even a day in court in 1931 as defendant in a suit brought by Phil Ball.

The maverick owner of the St. Louis Browns sought a restraining order after Landis granted free agency to a St. Louis farmhand, Fred Bennett, whom Ball had been shipping around the minors. A federal judge in Chicago ruled that Landis acted wholly within the authority given him by the club owners when he assumed office. Although Ball threatened to take the case to the U.S. Supreme Court, he subsequently yielded to sober counsel and dropped the matter. While the decision upheld the commissioner's authority over Organized Baseball, it also recognized the legality of the farm system by pointing out that major league team owners were free to own minor league properties. It was a split decision for Landis, who despised the growing farm system.

Shortly after the Bennett decision, the ranks of major league executives were riddled by death. Ernest S. Barnard, who had been given a five-year extension on his contract as American League president only a few months earlier, died of a heart attack on March 27, 1931. A day later, American League founder Ban Johnson died, followed by Garry Herrmann, former chairman of the National Commission, four weeks after that. Charles A. Comiskey, owner of the White Sox, died in October and was followed early in 1932 by William Wrigley, owner of the Cubs, and Barney Dreyfuss, owner of the Pirates.

During the 1931 season, Landis severely censured one of Wrigley's foremost employees. The commissioner was distressed when a Chicago newspaper published a photo showing Cubs catcher Gabby Hartnett chatting with mobster Al Capone in a box seat at Wrigley Field. As a result of the picture, which was reproduced nationwide, Landis issued an order forbidding all players from talking to spectators before or during a game, with violators being subject to a fine.

In almost the same breath and as another step in his ongoing fight against gambling, Landis enjoined all club executives from releasing information on the next day's pitchers. The edict was criticized vigorously for its adverse effect on attendance. As an example, critics cited a game at Yankee Stadium in which Lefty Grove, who was on his way to a 16-game winning streak and a 31-4 season, opposed Lefty Gomez, who was en route to a 21-9 season. Properly promoted, the game could have attracted 35,000 fans. Without advance billing, however, it drew fewer than 10,000.

Landis was constantly making decisions that upset somebody. When the pennant-winning Cubs of 1932 excluded Rogers Hornsby from the World Series pool, the former manager—he was replaced by Charlie Grimm in August—appealed to the commissioner. Landis refused to reverse the decision, saying that the money belonged to the players and that it was theirs to divide as they saw fit.

Landis exercised his judicial wisdom in three consecutive World Series, starting with the Giants-Senators matchup of 1933. After umpire Charley Moran ejected Washington outfielder Heinie Manush from a game, Landis announced that in the future only the commissioner would be authorized to banish a World Series player.

The Judge had an opportunity to exercise that right in 1934. In the seventh game of the Cardinals-Tigers Series, St. Louis' Joe Medwick slid hard into third base and engaged in a brief scuffle with Detroit's Marv Owen. When Medwick returned to his left-field position, he was greeted with a shower of overripe fruit and vegetables. Appeals for order were made by the park announcer and the debris was removed from the field. But Medwick's second attempt to take his post brought forth another barrage of produce. For the safety of the player, Landis removed him from the game.

The Cardinals were leading, 9-0, when Medwick was ejected. They went on to win, 11-0, thereby capturing their second world championship in four years. They had defeated the Philadelphia A's, also in seven games, in 1931 as Pepper Martin batted .500 with 12 hits and stole five bases.

In the Tigers-Cubs Series of 1935, Landis ruled that Chicago bench jockeys had exceeded the limits of decency while taunting opposing players and arguing with umpire George Moriarty, who tossed back epithets just as fast as he heard them. The Judge levied $200 fines on Manager Charlie Grimm and substitutes Tuck Stainback and Woody English. He also fined Moriarty, saying that as a representative of his office, the umpire should not have stooped to the level of the cursing players.

Earlier that year, the Judge had been caught in the middle of a controversy that aroused national attention. The situation was created by the Albany Senators' efforts to sign an ex-convict, Edwin C. (Alabama) Pitts, to play in the International League. William G. Bramham, president of the National Association, ruled against the club. When the decision was appealed to Landis, the Judge reversed Bramham and permitted Pitts to join the Senators. The outfielder batted only .233 in 43 games at Albany and drifted into the low minors. He died a few years later from stab wounds suffered in a North Carolina tavern brawl.

A Landis decision that commanded the attention of all levels of baseball was issued on December 10, 1936, and involved a future Hall of Famer, Bob Feller. The young pitcher from Van Meter, Ia., signed with Fargo-Moorhead while still in high school but never joined the Northern League club. His contract was transferred to New Orleans (Southern), again without Feller joining that club, and then to Cleveland, where he remained in relative obscurity until July 6, 1936. On that date, in an exhibition game against the Cardinals, Feller fanned eight of the nine batters he faced. When he struck out 15 St. Louis Browns batters and 17 Philadelphia A's, his name became known nationally. His feats also aroused curiosity in Des Moines. How was it possible, executives of the Western League club wondered, for a player to appear with a major league club without delivering a single pitch in the minors, when the rules strictly prohibited a major club from signing an amateur other than a college player?

Landis pondered the ticklish question for months. Meanwhile, major league clubs eagerly awaited his decision with bankrolls poised to throw at the young righthander if and when he was declared a free agent. But that moment never arrived. Landis validated the Indians' contract partly because Bob and his father had requested it and partly because free agency would have triggered a stampede to the Feller doorstep that could only have been harmful to the teen-ager.

If the Indians won the battle in 1936, they lost in 1937. Because of contract manipulations by the Tribe, Tommy Henrich was granted his free agency. The outfielder-first baseman signed with New York and was known for many years as "Old Reliable" of the Yankees.

Long a foe of the farm system, Landis struck with crushing force against his favorite antagonist, Branch Rickey, the master agriculturist, in 1938. Accusing the Cardinals' general manager of covering up players, Landis emancipated 91 Redbird farmhands, including Pete Reiser, the National League batting champion with Brooklyn in 1941, and Skeeter Webb, shortstop for the world champion Tigers in 1945.

Although Landis' disdain for Rickey was no secret, the commissioner proved that he was not just out to get Rickey by dropping a similar bombshell on the Tigers in 1940. Detecting contract irregularities, the Judge granted 91 Detroit farmhands their free agency. Numbered in the group were second baseman Benny McCoy, who received a $45,000 bonus to sign with the Athletics, and Roy Cullenbine, an outfielder-first baseman who was paid $25,000 to sign with the Dodgers.

The high spot of the 1939 season for the commissioner was a visit to Cooperstown, N.Y., where he presided at ceremonies marking baseball's centennial. The Judge served as grand marshal of a motorcade through the streets of the village, purchased a sheet of first-day centennial stamps from U.S. Postmaster General Jim Farley and presided at the dedication of the Baseball Hall of Fame and Museum. With the Judge were 10 diamond immortals: Connie Mack, Honus Wagner, Grover Cleveland Alexander, Tris Speaker, George Sisler, Napoleon Lajoie, Walter Johnson, Eddie Collins, Babe Ruth and Cy Young. Because of travel difficulties, Ty Cobb did not arrive until after the ceremonies.

Two other events during the decade earned the Judge varying degrees of commendation. In the depths of the Depression, he voluntarily slashed his salary from $65,000 to $40,000. The pay cut was restored five years later. And at the 1934 World Series, the Judge revealed that, after years of trying, he had mastered the technique of spitting tobacco juice through his teeth. Success came, he disclosed, after watching Pepper Martin demonstrate the art. To those who applauded his accomplishment, the 67-year-old Judge flashed a boyish grin.

Lines were long and enthusiasm high when baseball fans lined up outside of Chicago's Comiskey Park to purchase tickets for baseball's first All-Star Game extravaganza in 1933.

Baseball Under Lights

GIANT LIGHTS PROVIDE VISION FOR NIGHT PLAY

BASEBALL fans jammed the Des Moines, Ia., Western League park to see the first real test of night baseball May 2, when the Demons defeated Wichita, 13 to 6. They were pleasantly surprised and were unanimous in pronouncing the experiment a success. The playing field was illuminated by giant floodlights, erected on six galvanized steel towers. In picture No. 1 is shown the field with four towers rising far above the grandstand. The other two were behind the left and right field fences which provided such artificial daylight that fielders had no trouble following the highest hit fly balls.

In picture No. 2 is seen a close-up of one of these artificial daylight towers, showing two workmen adjusting the mammoth lights.

Fans were attracted by the novelty in such numbers they crowded onto the field outside the grandstand. Picture No. 3 shows a section of this overflow crowd. Only one objection was voiced by those present. That was the glare made by the backstop screen wire. In picture No. 3 this glare was reflected in the camera when a ball of light from one of the huge bulbs peered through the upper portions of the picture, somewhat blindingly.

Test at Des Moines Regarded as Success

The critical condition of the national economy in January 1930 dictated innovative measures if baseball's minor leagues were to survive. Many club owners despaired early and suspended operations, believing that a successful business was impossible in depressed times.

Other team executives, however, were not so quick to pull the plug. In the Western League, officials, supposing that any change was worth a try, gave unanimous, if tentative, approval to a revolutionary proposal—baseball played under the lights.

E. Lee Keyser, president of the Des Moines club, requested permission to play night ball. He had been in consultation with electrical engineers for some time, he reported, and offered to stage several experimental games under lights before scheduling a regular league contest.

This radical departure from tradition horrified the conservatives of baseball. Ordinarily, the editors of The Sporting News endorsed change if they regarded it as improvement. But even they were unprepared for such a drastic change.

A 1930 editorial warned: "The night air is not like the day air; The man who goes to baseball after he has eaten a hearty meal is apt to have indigestion if he is nervous and excited; the disturbed and misanthropic fan will not sleep well after a night game. Who wants to go home in the dark when it is twice as pleasant to drive leisurely in the approaching twilight and sniff a good meal cooking on the range when the front door is opened and the aroma of a sputtering steak spreads all through the house?"

When the Des Moines and Wichita clubs drew 10,000 spectators to the first night game in the history of Organized Baseball, other clubs hastened to cash in on the new bonanza. The Sporting News continued to express reservations about the "palpable fad."

Caution was the watchword. In a May editorial, the editor pointed out: "Most of the players asserted that they had no difficulty to locate the ball by artificial light, the fielders being able to recover it after they had fumbled it, and the batters being able to note the break of curved pitching better. The latter statement we take with some salt on the dish. In a first experiment of this kind, there is always a tendency to exaggerate praise. . . . There is one serious fault with (night) baseball. It will tend to help strengthen the alibi of every fielder and batter for lack of success.

"We hope that baseball will not be pushed by the radicals who are seeking to change our notions of sports until it becomes like a thing of the circus, two performances in one day under the big tent. . . .

"If there is any real merit in baseball played under artificial light it will be proved."

When minor league baseball pondered the possibility of night baseball in early 1930, The Sporting News took a conservative stand. An editorial (below) offered reasons why the game shouldn't be played at night and a page 2 spread (above) reported on Organized Baseball's first night game at Des Moines.

Night Baseball.

Every now and then some man who is much interested in baseball and who would see it prosper and entertain even more thousands than it does, suggests baseball at night as a tonic to stir up something that seems not to have been stirred before.

The suggestion is not novel and the experiment has been tried, but with no real success.

Baseball is not to be treated as a novelty. If it were, it might be produced with a promise of some daily outside sensation for the spectacular. The game needs no outside attraction. It creates its own showmanship and always will. It may be doubted whether there is any game that embraces within it such a constant opportunity for the spectacular. The score may be tied in one inning by a home run and may be placed to the advantage of the team behind in the very next inning by another home run. There are sensational feats of pitching and sen-

After the successful Des Moines experiment, other minor league teams began testing baseball under the lights. Seals Stadium (above), opened in 1931, featured a lighting system that probably amazed San Francisco baseball fans. Night baseball also found its way to the Texas League (below) in the 1930s.

TSN Survives the Depression

DIAMOND GLINTS ∴ By Al Demaree
LOU GEHRIG, "IRON HORSE" OF THE NEW YORK YANKEES, MADE FOUR HOME RUNS IN ONE GAME — JUNE 3, 1932 - -IN THE 1ST 4TH 5TH AND 7TH INNINGS -
JIMMY DYKES HANDLED 17 CHANCES WHILE PLAYING FOR THE ATHLETICS IN A 1921 GAME - 9 PUTOUTS AND 8 ASSISTS
ALTHOUGH HE ALLOWED 378 HITS IN 1923, GEORGE UHLE WON 26 GAMES —
CLEVELAND
DID YOU KNOW THAT-
- FORBES FIELD, THE HOME OF THE PITTSBURGH PIRATES, WAS NAMED IN HONOR OF THE BRITISH ARMY GENERAL WHO FOUNDED PITTSBURGH -?
- TWICE DURING THE AMERICAN LEAGUE GAME IN DETROIT BETWEEN THE TIGERS AND THE ST. LOUIS BROWNS ON MAY 1, 1909, UMPIRES KERIN AND O'LOUGHLIN WERE COMPELLED TO CALL TIME BECAUSE OF SNOW - DETROIT FINALLY WON, 5 TO 2 AND TIGER THIRD BASEMAN GEORGE MORIARTY WAS CREDITED WITH HIS SECOND HOME STEAL WITHIN A WEEK —?
AL DEMAREE

Al Demaree was the most popular artist of the 1930s.

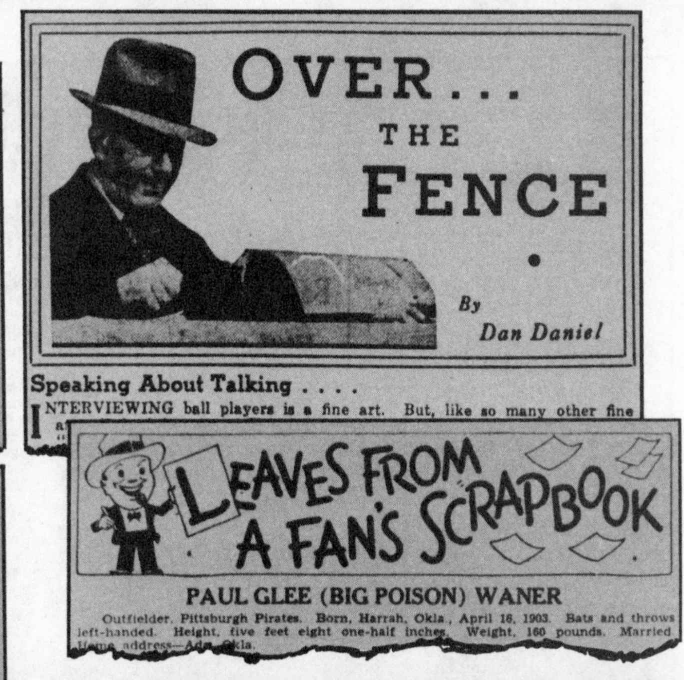

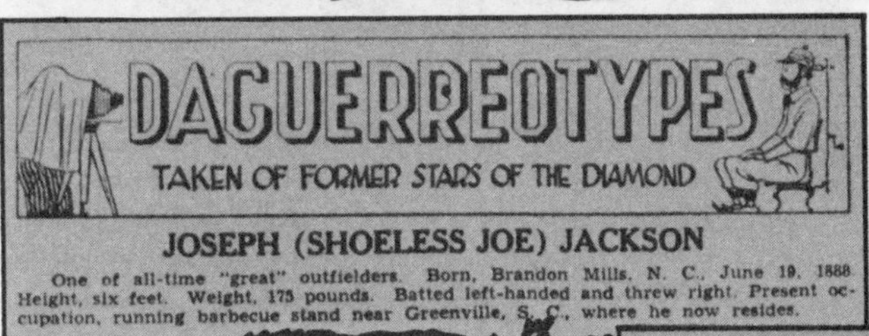

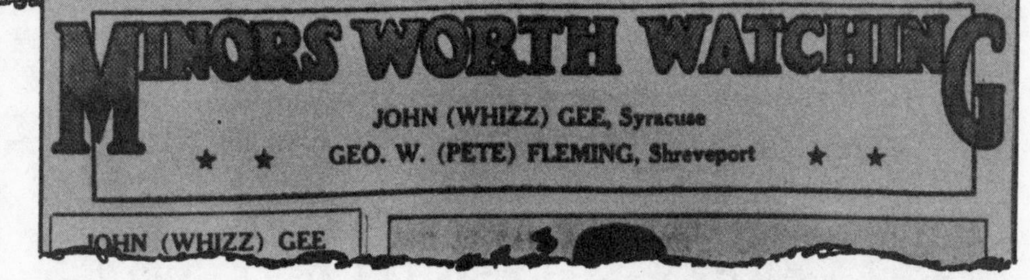

The above logos are but a sampling of the many columns and regular features that entertained readers throughout this decade.

Financial hardship has a way of uncovering both the best and the worst in mankind. In the case of J.G. Taylor Spink, the Great Depression brought forth superior qualities.

"When the stock market crashed," he recalled, "I suddenly realized that I had a daughter and son to educate. I also realized that I had a valuable property in The Sporting News and that if I didn't apply myself to the fullest, I'd lose a lot more than I'd already lost."

From that moment forward, the publisher adopted a seven-day work week and a 15-hour daily schedule. His tireless application to duty showed up in the quality of the publication and enabled Spink to remain solvent.

Half-column photographs, called thumbnails, were used regularly. Multi-photo layouts brightened covers as well as inside features. Cartoons were used to illustrate or convey a message. Al Demaree, a former National League pitcher who became a syndicated cartoonist, was the most popular artist of the decade, while other sketches were supplied by Lank Leonard, a fine portrait artist, and Willard Mullin, who was just beginning a career that would stamp him as baseball's foremost cartoonist.

Writers from all corners of the baseball map helped give The Sporting News greater appeal. Spink himself wrote a weekly column, "Three and One, Looking Them Over With J.G. Taylor Spink." Dick Farrington contributed a notes column that generally contained a "Meet the Missus" segment devoted to the wives of baseball personalities, and Dan Daniel contributed "Over the Fence." Editor Edgar G. Brands authored "Between Innings," while other columns were furnished by H.G. Salsinger (Detroit), Bill Dooly (Philadelphia), Sid Keener (St. Louis) and John B. Foster, the venerable editor of Spalding's "Official Baseball Guide."

Major league newsletters were reduced in length so that reports from minor league teams, three or four paragraphs in length, might be published. This also allowed for small features, such as "In the Press Box" and "On the Air Lines," which reported news from the print and wireless media. "Happy Birthday" noted the anniversaries of prominent figures in the game, "Deals of the Week" listed player transactions, L.H. Addington of the National Association office contributed "In a Minor Key," leading writers produced "I Recall" columns and "Necrology" contained obituaries of those associated with baseball at one time or another.

A column on "Publications," dealing with baseball books and magazine features, was introduced and for those who had a complaint to air, there was the "Beef Box." Active players were profiled in "Leaves from a Fan's Scrapbook" and inactive players in "Daguerreotypes." At times, Ed Burns of Chicago wrote and illustrated a series entitled "Burns-Eye View of Major League Parks," players and managers told of "My Funniest Story" and another series paid tribute to "Champion Fans" in minor league cities. To alert readers to prospective major league players, there was a weekly feature, "Minor Leaguers Worth Watching."

Throughout the depression years, TSN refused to reduce its box score coverage of the minor leagues. In 1932, when 17 minor league circuits operated, the publication carried box scores of 12.

The Sporting News

THE BASE BALL PAPER OF THE WORLD

LATEST and BEST
BASEBALL NEWS—GOSSIP

VOLUME 89, NUMBER 8 | ST. LOUIS, APRIL 17, 1930 | TEN CENTS THE COPY

BABE RUTH, IN LINEUP OF YANKEES, BUT SHOWS TRACES OF LAMENESS

PLAYED SO FANS WOULD NOT BE DISAPPOINTED

McGraw Gets Roettger to Train to Score Center Field Problem of Giants; Mancil is Released

PRES. HOOVER OPENS SEASON IN CAPITAL

TEXAS LEAGUE GETS OFF TO BEST START IN YEARS

Many New Faces, Keen Competition and Team Surprises Indicate Big Season for Lone Star Loop

BROWNS GET PUNCH BACK IN CITY SERIES

WIN ST. LOUIS CHAMPIONSHIP, TAKING TWO GAMES FROM CARDS

Stewart Stands National League Men on Their Heads; Coffman Also Does Well, Gullic Looks Good

Stewart Mesmerizes Cardinals.

BOSTON NO ONE-DAY STAND FOR GRIMES

BRAVES NOT INTERESTED IN TRADES SUGGESTED FOR SPITTER

National Leaguers Defeat Red Sox in Spring Series; Moore and Berger Continue to Play Fine Ball

HEEL STILL REMAINS PAINFUL TO HORNSBY

DOCTORS SAY IT'S O.K., BUT ROGERS LIMPS AS HE PLAYS

Bush Has White Sox Hustling, But Early Showing of Team May Cause Fans to Expect Too Much

Bell Has Trouble With Arm.

MAY BE TIGERS' NEEDED CLAW

SHORTSTOP BILL ROGELL

Win Free Trip to All-Star Game, World's Fair--See Details on Page 3

MAJORS BOX SCORES MINORS

The Sporting News

THE BASE BALL PAPER OF THE WORLD

FROM ALL POINTS OF COMPASS
BASEBALL
NEWS—GOSSIP—COMMENT

VOLUME 95, NUMBER 16 | ST. LOUIS, JUNE 8, 1933 | TEN CENTS THE COPY

BALL DISSATISFIED WITH BROWNS, KILLEFER'S JOB HANGS IN BALANCE

CLUB OWNER DOESN'T LIKE SPIRIT OF TEAM

Hornsby Would Be Welcome as Leader, Report Says; Cardinals Win Seven Straight Before Losing

Browns' Best Team Since 1922.

Repeater on the Coast

Oscar G. Eckhardt

WHITE SOX TWIRLING FAILS TO MEET TEST

FRASIER TRADED FOR WYATT IN HOPE OF STRENGTHENING STAFF

Cubs Live Up to Reputation of Being Able to Win at Home, but Now Face Real Test on Long Road Trip

Both Chaudiers of Texas League.

Flashes as Flag Beacon

Frank Francis Frisch

PAUL DEAN AND BILL LEE

NATIONALS' PITCHING BELOW FORM OF '32

CROWDER ONLY REGULAR HOLDING UP IN EFFECTIVENESS

Hurlers, Aside from General, Allow More Than Four Runs Per Nine Innings; Club Improves at Bat

Batting on Upswing.

OUT OF THE FAMILY ALBUM

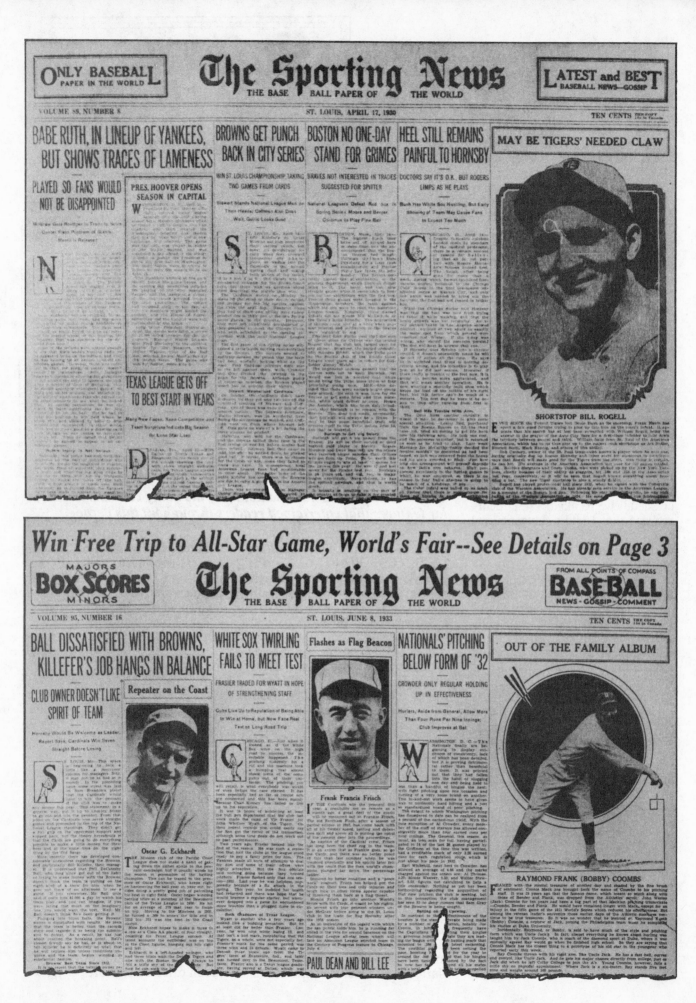

RAYMOND FRANK (BOBBY) COOMBS

The Truce Comes to an End

VOL. 94. JANUARY 5, 1933. No. 20.

Up to the Commissioner.

Commissioner K. M. Landis had an opportunity to show real qualities of leadership at the recent joint meeting of the majors in New York by volunteering to reduce his own large salary as a means of blazing the path to economic normalcy in baseball, but, according to the best information available, he didn't even hint at such a move. Maybe he would have done so, had not the magnates voted unanimously to curtail his power with respect to interfering with transfer of players to and from farms; maybe he will do so yet, when the need for such action is borne home to him.

Whatever his intentions, however, e psychological effect has been lost. ould have been a dramatic gesture he done one of three things—re- ned his position and closed his of- ice, with the statement that he was no longer needed and that the presidents of the two major leagues could carry

The bad relations between The Sporting News and Commissioner Kenesaw Mountain Landis continued in 1933 when a TSN editorial (above) strongly suggested that Landis should have reduced his salary as a sign of leadership in the interest of bringing baseball back to economic normalcy.

As The Sporting News entered the 1930s, it billed itself as 'The Base Ball Paper of the World' and offered the 'Latest and Best Baseball News — Gossip' (above left). By 1933, the logos had changed slightly and TSN was inclined to tout its All-Star Game contest with a headline above the TSN logo (below left).

In the years following Commissioner Kenesaw M. Landis' swine-and-swill charge against The Sporting News, relations between the Judge and Taylor Spink subsided into an armed truce. Landis' name rarely appeared in editorials and then only in innocuous fashion.

In the winter of 1932-33, however, Spink withdrew his stiletto once more. Following the annual major league meeting, an editorial declared: "Commissioner K.M. Landis had an opportunity to show real qualities of leadership . . . by volunteering to reduce his own large salary as a means of blazing the path to economic normalcy in baseball, but he didn't even hint at such a move."

Pointing out the players' reluctance to accept pay cuts while Landis continued to enjoy a princely salary, the editorial continued: "It could have been a dramatic gesture if he had done one of three things—resigned his position and closed his office, with the statement that he was no longer needed and that the presidents of the two major leagues could carry on the little business requiring attention without the heavy overhead of carrying the commissioner's office; or volunteered to serve as a dollar-a-year man for the remainder of his term of office . . . or offered to cut his salary to the figure which Ban Johnson refused to take with him to retirement—$35,000 per annum—even though the founder of the American League had it coming to him according to the terms of his contract."

There is no record of Landis reacting violently to the criticism, but an editorial in a subsequent issue reported that the commissioner had voluntarily slashed his annual pay 40 percent—$20,000 for 1933 and $15,000 retroactive to 1932.

"Everybody is pleased," purred the editorial, "that the commissioner has decided to play ball and keep step with the trend of the times. The announcement should have a stabilizing effect on the game and help in accelerating the return to normalcy."

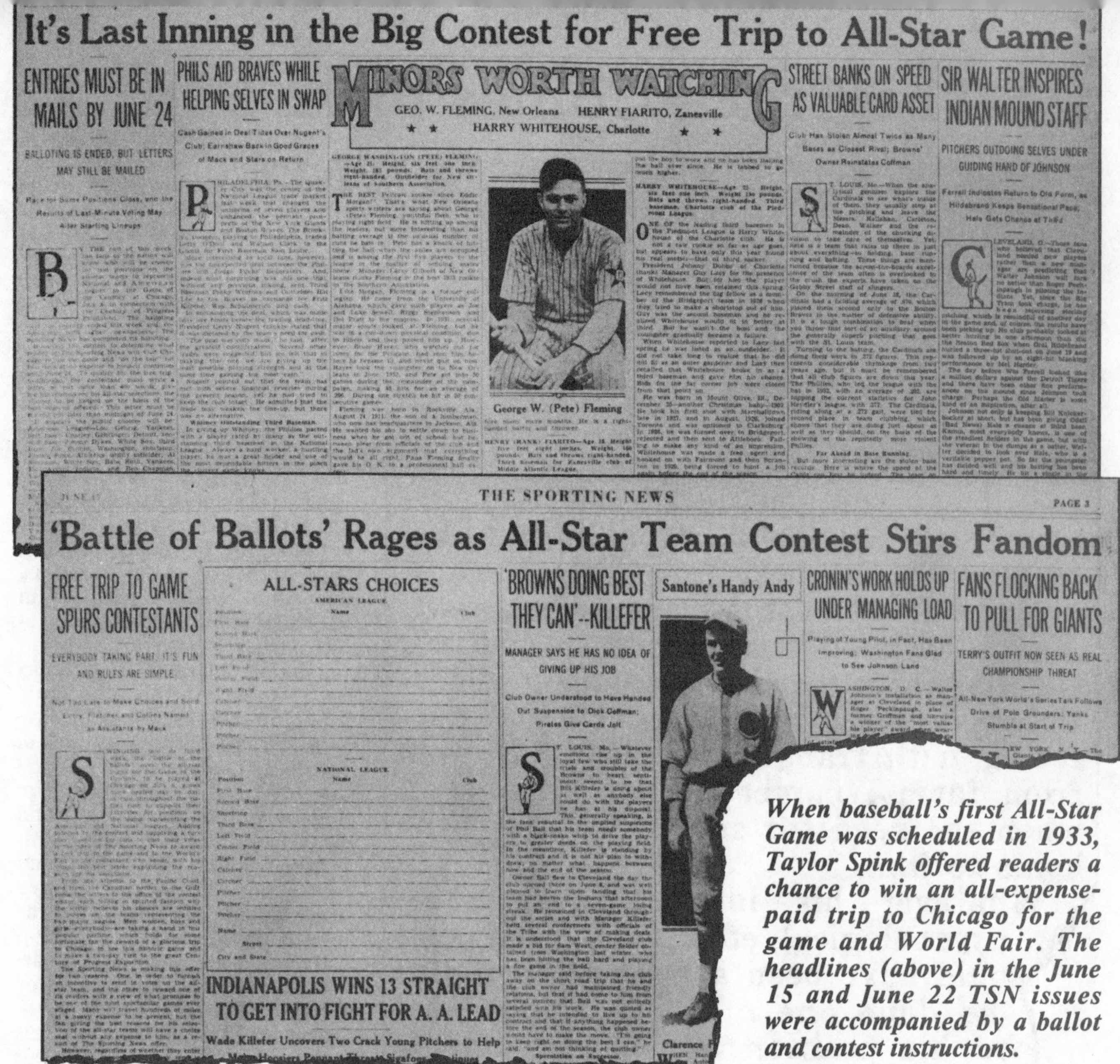

It's Last Inning in the Big Contest for Free Trip to All-Star Game!

ENTRIES MUST BE IN MAILS BY JUNE 24

BALLOTING IS ENDED, BUT LETTERS MAY STILL BE MAILED

PHILS AID BRAVES WHILE HELPING SELVES IN SWAP

MINORS WORTH WATCHING

GEO. W. FLEMING, New Orleans HENRY FIARITO, Zanesville HARRY WHITEHOUSE, Charlotte

George W. (Pete) Fleming

STREET BANKS ON SPEED AS VALUABLE CARD ASSET

SIR WALTER INSPIRES INDIAN MOUND STAFF

PITCHERS OUTDOING SELVES UNDER GUIDING HAND OF JOHNSON

THE SPORTING NEWS

'Battle of Ballots' Rages as All-Star Team Contest Stirs Fandom

FREE TRIP TO GAME SPURS CONTESTANTS

EVERYBODY TAKING PART; IT'S FUN AND RULES ARE SIMPLE

ALL-STARS CHOICES

AMERICAN LEAGUE

NATIONAL LEAGUE

'BROWNS DOING BEST THEY CAN'--KILLEFER

MANAGER SAYS HE HAS NO IDEA OF GIVING UP HIS JOB

Santone's Handy Andy

CRONIN'S WORK HOLDS UP UNDER MANAGING LOAD

FANS FLOCKING BACK TO PULL FOR GIANTS

TERRY'S OUTFIT NOW SEEN AS REAL CHAMPIONSHIP THREAT

INDIANAPOLIS WINS 13 STRAIGHT TO GET INTO FIGHT FOR A. A. LEAD

Wade Killefer Uncovers Two Crack Young Pitchers to Help

When baseball's first All-Star Game was scheduled in 1933, Taylor Spink offered readers a chance to win an all-expense-paid trip to Chicago for the game and World Fair. The headlines (above) in the June 15 and June 22 TSN issues were accompanied by a ballot and contest instructions.

The Game of the Century

As an adjunct of the Century of Progress Exposition in 1933, the Chicago Tribune arranged with the major league club owners to sponsor an All-Star Game between representatives of the American and National leagues.

The newspaper also undertook the selection of the personnel of the two squads and enlisted the help of dozens of the nation's leading publications, including The Sporting News, in collecting and tabulating the votes.

Taylor Spink went a step beyond merely supplying clerical help. He offered an all-expense-paid trip to the game and the World Fair as a prize for the reader who came closest to selecting the consensus All-Star teams and appended a letter that, in the opinion of three judges, offered the most convincing reasons for the choices.

The winner was William J. Hinchman, a 42-year-old motorman from Philadelphia.

A week before the game, The Sporting News envisioned the national appeal that the All-Star Game would engender and urged that the spectacle be made a regular feature of the major league schedule, "with all 11 cities in turn being given a chance to witness one of these games."

The editorial added: "There is no doubt that such an All-Star Game, played in the middle of the season, is a great stimulus for baseball and ought to be encouraged. It creates fresh enthusiasm at a time when interest may begin to lag. Granting it is a radical innovation—something that baseball men occasionally are accused of avoiding—The Sporting News believes that most of them are now awake to the fact that what was good enough for their predecessors is not necessarily good enough for them, and that new

methods must be employed to keep step with new times."

Later, after the two major leagues agreed to schedule another All-Star Game during the 1934 season, The Sporting News applauded the decision, noting: "Probably no single event in the history of the game aroused as much interest and enthusiasm as did the contest last season. It is a development that is good for the sport as a whole, everywhere."

Furthermore, the editorial commented, "The decision indicates a tendency to give the public what it wants, and when that course of action is followed to its logical conclusion there will be no reason for anybody writing a series of articles on 'What's the matter with baseball.'"

The American (above) and National (below) league squads assembled at Chicago's Comiskey Park for the hoopla and picture taking that naturally surrounded what was billed as the game of the century.

The official scorebook for baseball's first All-Star Game pictured White Sox President J. Louis Comiskey and sold for 10 cents.

Cincinnati Lights the Way

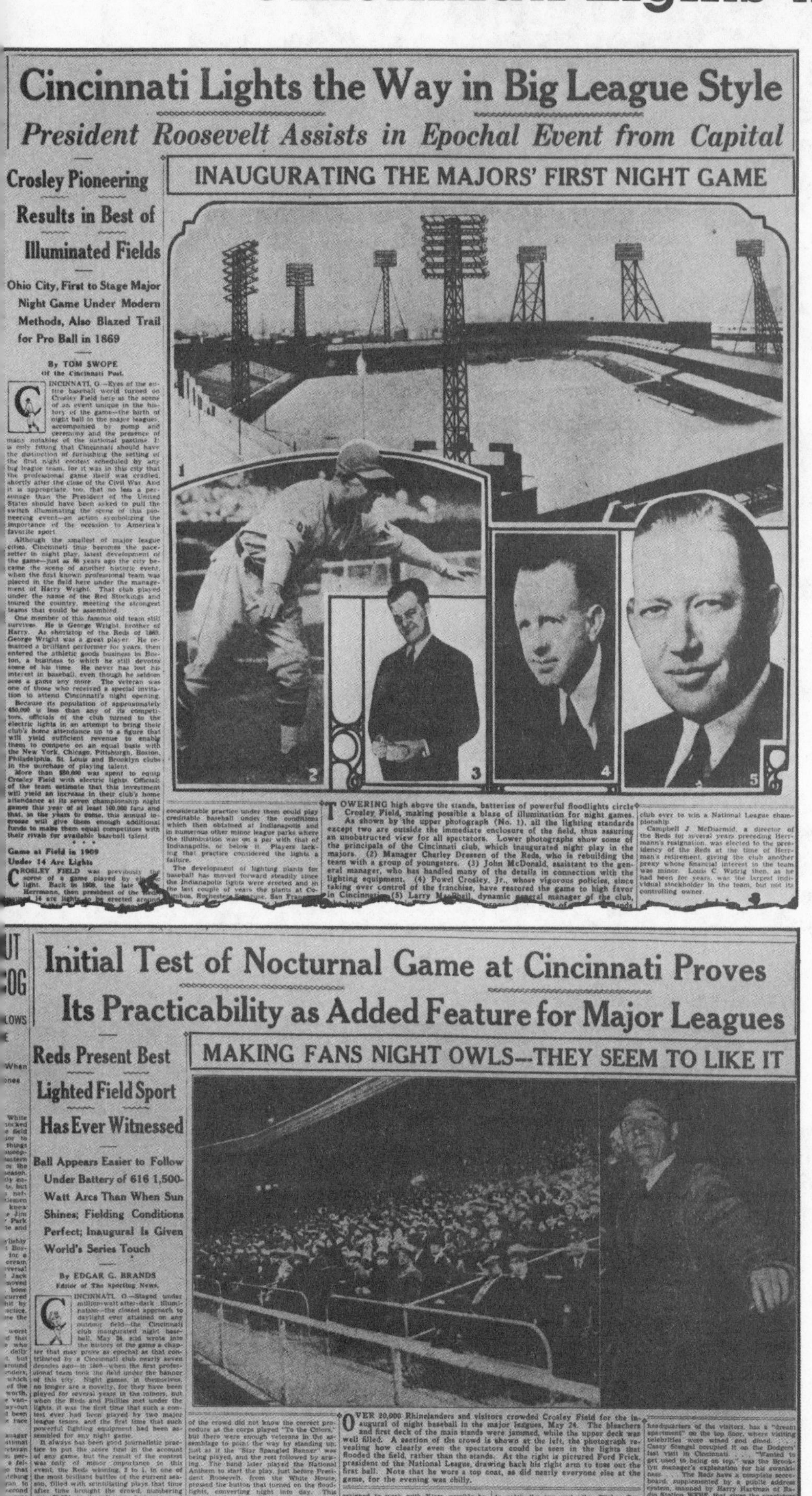

Cincinnati Lights the Way in Big League Style

President Roosevelt Assists in Epochal Event from Capital

Crosley Pioneering Results in Best of Illuminated Fields

Ohio City, First to Stage Major Night Game Under Modern Methods, Also Blazed Trail for Pro Ball in 1869

By TOM SWOPE
Of the Cincinnati Post.

CINCINNATI, O.—Eyes of the entire baseball world turned on Crosley Field here as the scene of an event unique in the history of the game—the birth of night ball in the major leagues, accompanied by pomp and ceremony and the presence of many notables of the national pastime. It is only fitting that Cincinnati should have the distinction of furnishing the setting of the first night contest scheduled by any big league team, for it was in this city that the professional game itself was cradled, shortly after the close of the Civil War. And it is appropriate, too, that no less a personage than the President of the United States should have been asked to pull the switch illuminating the scene of this pioneering event—an action symbolizing the importance of the occasion to America's favorite sport.

Although the smallest of major league cities, Cincinnati thus becomes the pacesetter in night play, latest development of the game—just as 66 years ago the city became the scene of another historic event, when the first known professional team was placed in the field here under the management of Harry Wright. That club played under the name of the Red Stockings and toured the country, meeting the strongest teams that could be assembled.

One member of this famous old team still survives. He is George Wright, brother of Harry. As shortstop of the Reds of 1869, George Wright was a great player. He remained a brilliant performer for years, then entered the athletic goods business in Boston, a business to which he still devotes some of his time. He never has lost his interest in baseball, even though he seldom sees a game any more. The veteran was one of those who received a special invitation to attend Cincinnati's night opening.

Because its population of approximately 450,000 is less than any of its competitors, officials of the club turned to the electric lights in an attempt to bring their club's home attendance up to a figure that will yield sufficient revenue to enable them to compete on an equal basis with the New York, Chicago, Pittsburgh, Boston, Philadelphia, St. Louis and Brooklyn clubs in the purchase of playing talent.

More than $50,000 was spent to equip Crosley Field with electric lights. Officials of the team estimate that this investment will yield an increase in their club's home attendance at its seven championship night games this year of at least 100,000 fans and that, in the years to come, this annual increase will give them enough additional funds to make them equal competitors with their rivals for available baseball talent.

* * *

Game at Field in 1909 Under 14 Arc Lights

CROSLEY FIELD was previously the scene of a game played by electric light. Back in 1909, the late ... Herrmann, then president of the Reds ... 14 arc lights to be erected around ...

INAUGURATING THE MAJORS' FIRST NIGHT GAME

considerable practice under them could play creditable baseball under the conditions which then obtained at Indianapolis and in numerous other minor league parks where the illumination was on a par with that of Indianapolis, or below it. Players lacking that practice considered the lights a failure.

The development of lighting plants for baseball has moved forward steadily since the Indianapolis lights were erected and in the last couple of years the plants at Columbus, Rochester, Syracuse, San Fran...

TOWERING high above the stands, batteries of powerful floodlights circle Crosley Field, making possible a blaze of illumination for night games. As shown by the upper photograph (No. 1), all the lighting standards except two are outside the immediate enclosure of the field, thus assuring an unobstructed view for all spectators. Lower photographs show some of the principals of the Cincinnati club, which inaugurated night play in the majors. (2) Manager Charley Dressen of the Reds, who is rebuilding the team with a group of youngsters. (3) John McDonald, assistant to the general manager, who has handled many of the details in connection with the lighting equipment. (4) Powel Crosley, Jr., whose vigorous policies, since taking over control of the franchise, have restored the game to high favor in Cincinnati. (5) Larry MacPhail, dynamic general manager of the club, ...

club ever to win a National League championship.

Campbell J. McDiarmid, a director of the Reds for several years preceding Herrmann's resignation, was elected to the presidency of the Reds at the time of Herrman's retirement, giving the club another prexy whose financial interest in the team was minor. Louis C. Widrig then, as he had been for years, was the largest individual stockholder in the team, but not its controlling owner.

Initial Test of Nocturnal Game at Cincinnati Proves Its Practicability as Added Feature for Major Leagues

Reds Present Best Lighted Field Sport Has Ever Witnessed

Ball Appears Easier to Follow Under Battery of 616 1,500-Watt Arcs Than When Sun Shines; Fielding Conditions Perfect; Inaugural Is Given World's Series Touch

By EDGAR G. BRANDS
Editor of The Sporting News.

CINCINNATI, O.—Staged under million-watt after-dark illumination—the closest approach to daylight ever attained on any outdoor field—the Cincinnati club inaugurated night baseball, May 24, and wrote into the history of the game a chapter that may prove as epochal as that contributed by a Cincinnati club nearly seven decades ago—in 1869—when the first professional team took the field under the banner of this city. Night games, in themselves, no longer are a novelty, for they have been played for several years in the minors, but when the Reds and Phillies met under the lights, it was the first time that such a contest ever had been played by two major league teams, and the first time that such powerful lighting equipment had been assembled for any night game.

It always has been good journalistic practice to put the score first in the account of any game, but the result of the contest was only of minor importance in this event, the Reds winning, 2 to 1, in one of the most brilliant battles of the current season, filled with scintillating plays that time after time brought the crowd, numbering over 20,000, to its collective feet in a mad frenzy of applause. Apparently, the lights proved no handicap to the fielders. If there was any advantage anywhere, it was with the pitchers, but the same hurlers, in the daytime, may have held the upper hand. Paul Derringer went the chilly route, limiting the Phillies to six hits, and Joe Bowman, together with Jim Bivin, who took the hill in the eighth, yielded only four hits between them. There was only one extra-

MAKING FANS NIGHT OWLS—THEY SEEM TO LIKE IT

of the crowd did not know the correct procedure as the corps played "To the Colors," but there were enough veterans in the assemblage to point the way by standing up, just as if the "Star Spangled Banner" was being played, and the rest followed by arising. The band later played the National Anthem to start the play, just before President Roosevelt, from the White House, pressed the button that turned on the floodlights, converting night into day. This was preceded by a liberal display of fireworks and the explosion of bombs that brought back memories of old Fourth of July days. The pyrotechnics were climaxed by the showing of two brilliantly-lighted sets—one of a huge "C" with "Reds" in the middle, and the other a reproduction of the American flag.

The night was cool—in fact, too cool for comfort, except with a heavy top-coat—and the chill was intensified by an in-

OVER 20,000 Rhinelanders and visitors crowded Crosley Field for the inaugural of night baseball in the major leagues, May 24. The bleachers and first deck of the main stands were jammed, while the upper deck was well filled. A section of the crowd is shown at the left, the photograph revealing how clearly even the spectators could be seen in the lights that flooded the field, rather than the stands. At the right is pictured Ford Frick, president of the National League, drawing back his right arm to toss out the first ball. Note that he wore a top coat, as did nearly everyone else at the game, for the evening was chilly.

assigned to work with Klem, possibly because they had called 'em where lanterns sometimes had been employed. . . . Watty Watkins of the Phillies expressed the opinion that is general among the progressive-minded players: "It's my bread and butter, and while I prefer daylight ball, I'm willing to do my best to help the game." . . . President W. G. Bramham of the National Association; Dan Hill, president of the Piedmont League; J. Alvin Gardner, presi-

to catch the toss and after Pitcher Derringer had made a delivery, Umpire Klem obtained the ball and raced over to the stands, where he handed it to Vice-President Larry MacPhail of the Reds, who turned it over to President Frick for preservation among the archives of the National League, marking the first night game in the majors. . . . An interested spectator was George Cahill, who put in the first lighting plant ever undertaken at Redland ...

headquarters of the visitors, has a "dream apartment" on the top floor, where visiting celebrities were wined and dined. . . . Casey Stengel occupied it on the Dodgers' last visit in Cincinnati. . . . "Wanted to get used to being on top," was the Brooklyn manager's explanation for his swankiness. . . . The Reds have a complete scoreboard, supplemented by a public address system, manned by Harry Hartman of Radio Station WFBE, that gives the spectators all the information they need to follow the game. . . . It was as well lighted as the rest of the field. . . . The ball was easier to follow for the spectators than in the daytime, especially fly balls. . . . The pellet seemed to carry a glow that accentuates its visibility. . . . On one high pop fly, the ball could be followed to the top of its flight, seen to hesitate and then fall, something which could not be observed as closely in ...

No issue in the 1930s received more editorial ink in The Sporting News than the introduction of night baseball to the major leagues.

When Larry MacPhail obtained league approval to install arclights at Crosley Field in Cincinnati and play seven games—one against each National League opponent—in 1935, TSN recommended that the experiment be given a fair test with the best equipment available. Then, an editorial said, "if failure results, it would be established once and for all time that night baseball is not the ready panacea for the majors that has been claimed."

As the historic moment approached, TSN saluted the Cincinnati club management for its vision and added: "Already some of the other club owners are bewailing the slim gates of the early season and wondering whether the receipts for the rest of the year will enable them to break even. None has night games booked, nor has any shown intentions of scheduling such contests. Those clubs may need a wailing wall and a lot of towels, but Cincinnati doesn't need either, for it is making the most of the opportunity presented."

After the Reds played three nocturnal games—and averaged 20,000 fans per contest—TSN conceded that it had been won over by the mazdas, with some reservations. "We might as well look the situation squarely in the face," said an editorial, "and admit that while baseball may be essentially a daytime game, occasional exhibitions at night have their selling points. The Cincinnati experiment has proved beyond any doubt that the night game not only is self-supporting, but can be made the medium for bolstering the financing of the daylight games. From now on there should be less airing of the finan-

When Crosley Field played host to the major leagues' first night game in 1935, The Sporting News reported the 'Epochal Event' (left) and admitted, with reservation, that night baseball was practical.

The Waterford Trophy, an 18-inch glittering hand-cut creation of the renowned Waterford Crystal Ltd. of Ireland, is the award presented annually by The Sporting News to its Man of the Year. Waterford Crystal has placed a value of $15,000 on the piece.

Grid Special--Official NFL Statistics...Pages 46-47

The Sporting News

REG. U. S. PAT. OFF.

Vol. 163, No. 12 APRIL 8, 1967 Price: 35 Cents

FRANK ROBINSON
A Rare Bird ... Page 3

Hustling Dodger
BATTLER BAILEY
Page 5

Bo and Dean
FRIENDS FOREVER
Page 11

NCAA Champs
BRUIN BEAUTS
Page 39

Masters Field
LINKS LORDS
Page 41

BY MALCOLM EMMONS

The April 8, 1967, cover featuring Baltimore Orioles slugger Frank Robinson was the first four-color production in the history of The Sporting News. From that point on, TSN began using process color on a regular basis.

An Insider Presents the Case for Finley... Page 14

The Sporting News

REG. U. S. PAT. OFF.

Vol. 164, No. 9 | SEPTEMBER 16, 1967 | Price: 35 Cents

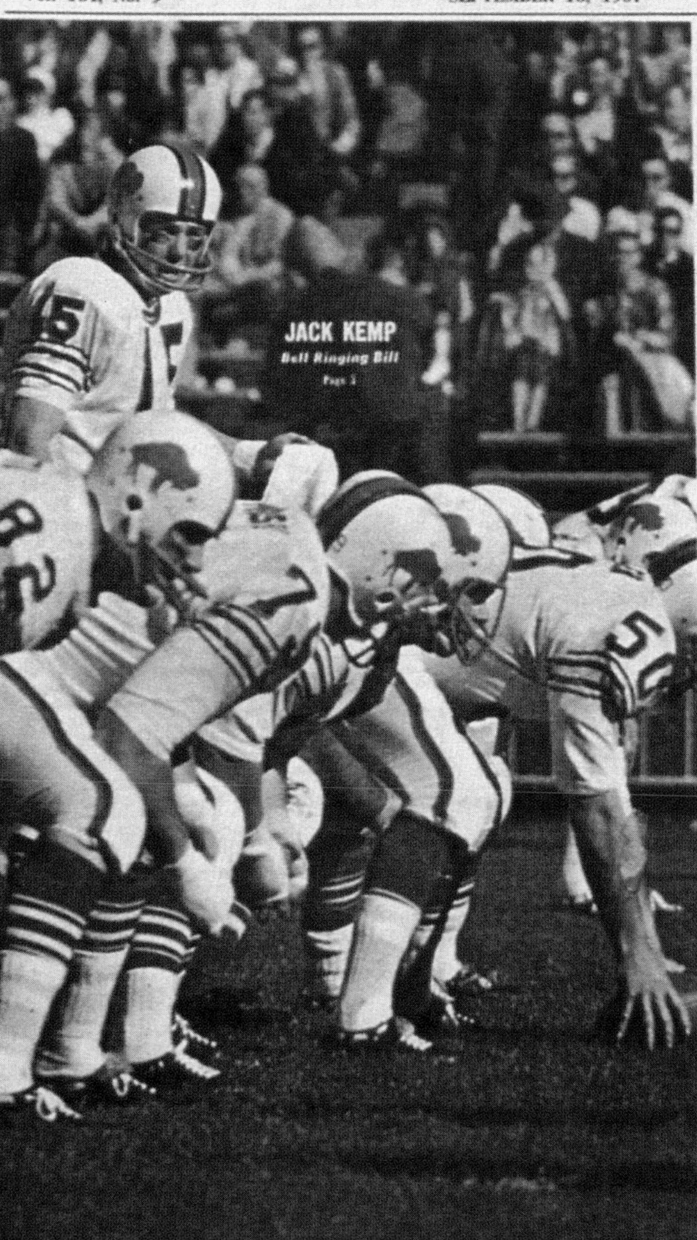

PHOTO BY FRED KAPLAN

Packers and Cowboys

SIZING UP NFL RACE

Page 5

AFL Favorites

RUGGED CHIEFS

Page 7

Harrelson Bonanza

HOW BIG A HAUL?

Page 16

Reliever Ron Kline

TWINS' STOPPER

Page 17

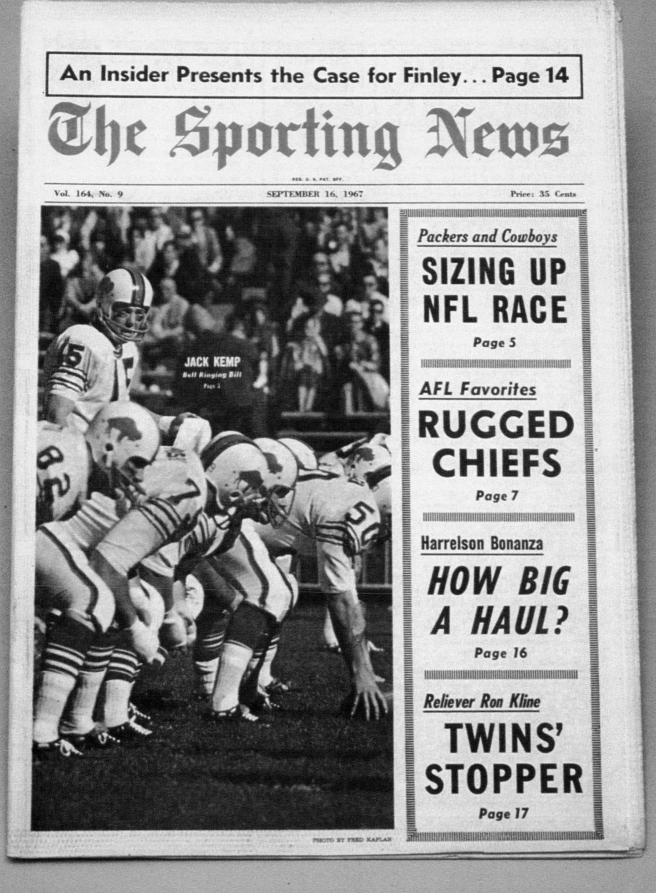

Buffalo Bills quarterback Jack Kemp enjoyed the honor of appearing on TSN's first four-color non-baseball cover on September 16, 1967.

The Man of the Year award, presented annually by The Sporting News to the year's top sports figure, was first given out in 1969, honoring Detroit pitcher Denny McLain (above right) for his 31-victory performance in 1968. The evolution of the award, demonstrated on the next three pages by TSN Man-of-the-Year covers through 1984, shows how The Sporting News has changed from a baseball-oriented tabloid to today's all-sports publication. Non-baseball winners include UCLA basketball Coach John Wooden (above left), golfer Lee Trevino, football star O.J. Simpson, Ohio State football player Archie Griffin, National Basketball Association Commissioner Larry O'Brien, jockey Steve Cauthen, hockey star Wayne Gretzky and Peter V. Ueberroth, the man behind the United States' 1984 Olympic extravaganza. Three Man-of-the-Year winners, Tom Seaver in 1970, Simpson in 1974 and O'Brien in 1977, did not appear on TSN covers.

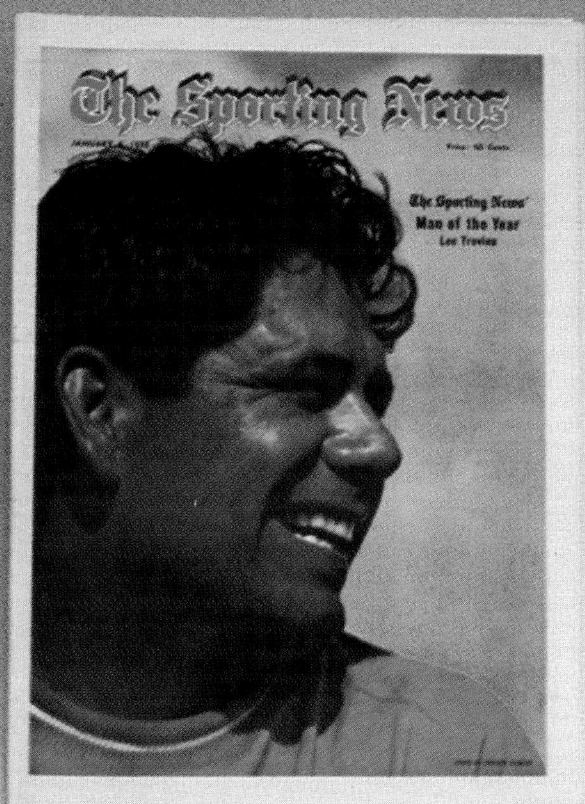
The Sporting News
The Sporting News'
Man of the Year
Lee Trevino

The Sporting News
The Sporting News'
Man of the Year
Charlie O. Finley
Ward scoring
demon of WHA
PAGE 3
Dolphins' Shula
Coach of Year
PAGE 14

Baseball, Football, Basketball, Hockey
The Sporting News
JANUARY 4, 1975
Price: 75 Cents
The Sporting News'
MAN OF THE YEAR
LOU BROCK

The Sporting News
JANUARY 10, 1976
Price: 75 Cents
The Sporting News
MAN OF THE YEAR
GR FFIN

Football, Basketball, Hockey, Baseball
The Sporting News
ONE DOLLAR
The Sporting News
SPORTS MAN OF THE YEAR
Steve Cauthen

The Sporting News
JANUARY 6, 1979
Price: $1.00
Canada $1.25
Ron Guidry
The Sporting News
Man of the Year
Colorado Corrals
Pats' Fairbanks
Jack Patera
NFL Coach of Year
College Basketball's
Hottest Shooter

The Sporting News
Full Reports on NFL Playoff Games
A Fantastic Streak by Philadelphia Flyers
Archibald, Cowens-Has-Beens Heat Up Celtics
MAN OF
THE YEAR
Willie Stargell

The Sporting News
Cowboys and Raiders Roll On as Wild Cards
Great Escape for NHL's Stastny Brothers
1981 Schedules for All 28 NFL Teams
MAN OF
THE YEAR
George Brett

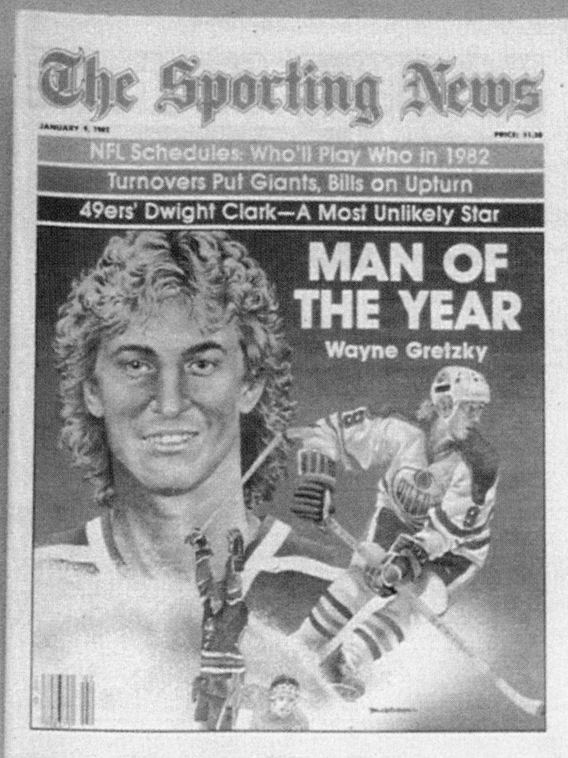
The Sporting News
NFL Schedules: Who'll Play Who in 1982
Turnovers Put Giants, Bills on Upturn
49ers' Dwight Clark—A Most Unlikely Star
MAN OF THE YEAR
Wayne Gretzky

The Sporting News
Rose Bowl Legend of Wrong-Way Riegels
NFL Standings, Statistics, Results
Savard Serves Up Excitement in Chicago
MAN OF THE YEAR
Whitey Herzog Wins Waterford Trophy

The Sporting News
Color John McEnroe Red, White and Blue
The NFL in 1984: Who Faces Whom?
Bernie Nicholls Tries the NHL Fast Lane
MAN OF THE YEAR

The Sporting News
SPECIAL DOUBLE ISSUE
The Year in Sports: A Review of 1984
MAN OF THE YEAR
Peter Ueberroth, Guiding Light Of Golden Olympics

After more than 80 years at a variety of downtown St. Louis locations, The Sporting News offices were moved in 1969 to a modern facility at 1212 N. Lindbergh Blvd., a location west of St. Louis in St. Louis County. The new building (pictured above in 1985), a 1969 story reported, contained 41,000 square feet and was functional in design for efficiency of operation.

Among the interesting attractions that TSN visitors encounter are a two-walled trophy case containing such TSN memorabilia as a replica of the Gold Glove trophy awarded each year to the top fielders in the American and National leagues, racks of autographed bats (above right) on walls adorned by wallpaper reproducing TSN's first issue in 1886, and numerous art exhibits (below right) featuring anything from old baseball cards to paintings.

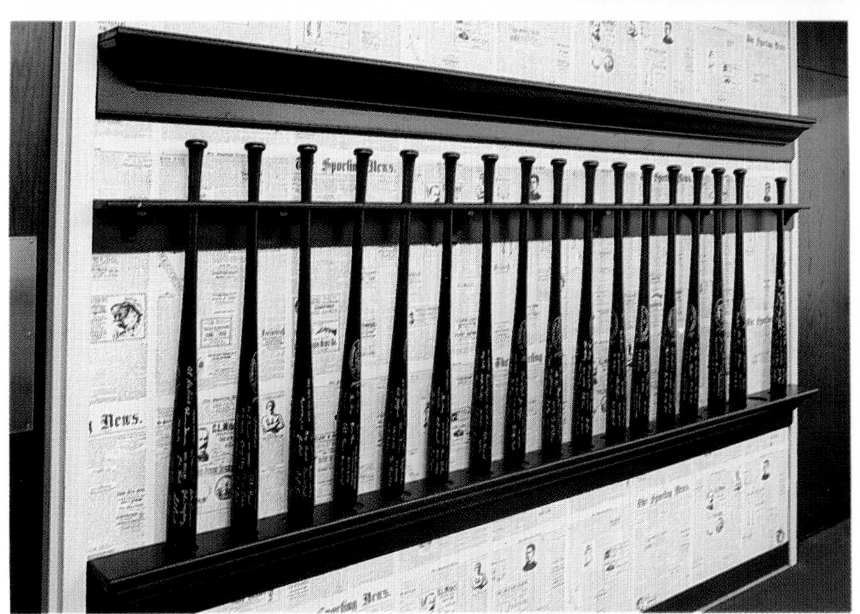

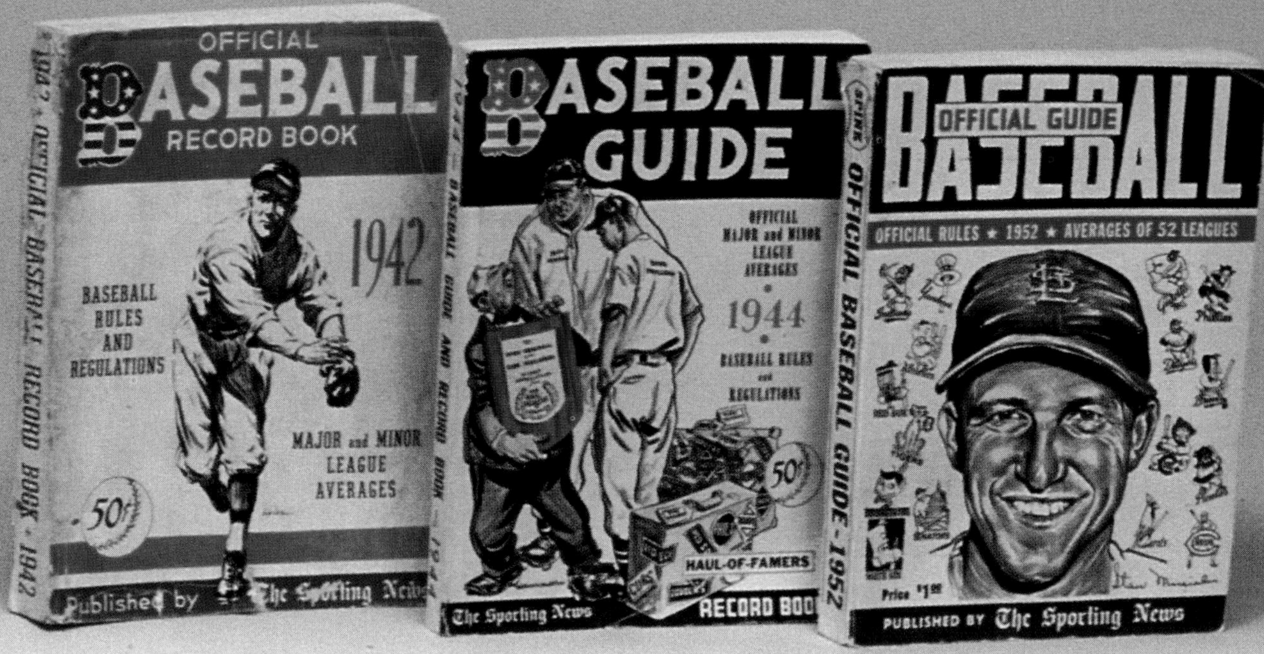

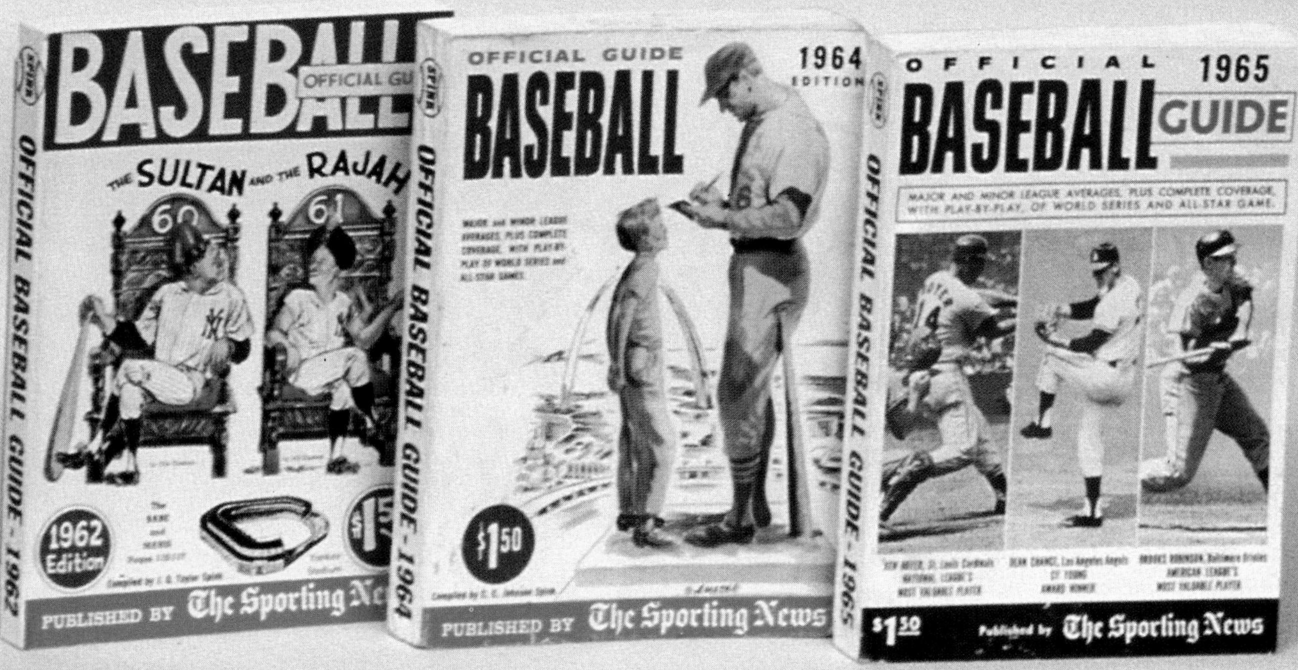

The 'Offical Baseball Guide' has been a major part of The Sporting News Library since 1942 (above left), when J.G. Taylor Spink received permission from baseball Commissioner Kenesaw Mountain Landis to take over 'official' publication of baseball's showcase book. Because of a feud with Landis, TSN published Guides without the 'official' designation for the next four years before the authority was restored by Commissioner Happy Chandler in 1947. TSN has continued publication of the 'Official Baseball Guide' uninterrupted from that point on. The above sampling of Guide covers through the years shows that the only major change, other than cover style and content improvement, occurred in 1982 when the book was published in a larger, easier-to-read format.

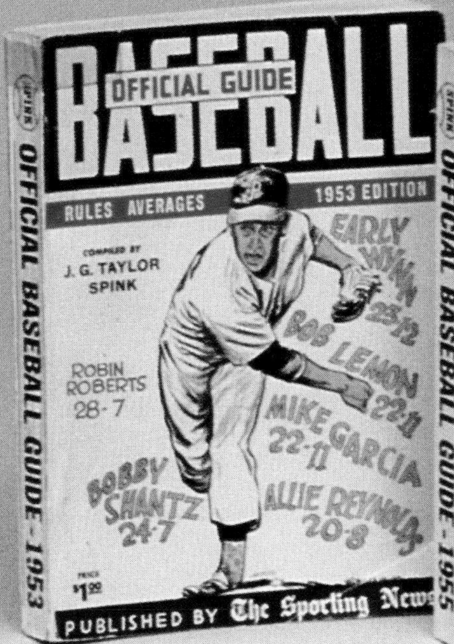
OFFICIAL GUIDE
BASEBALL
RULES AVERAGES
1953 EDITION
COMPILED BY
J. G. TAYLOR SPINK
ROBIN ROBERTS
28-7
BOB LEMON 22-11
MIKE GARCIA 22-11
BOBBY SHANTZ 24-7
PUBLISHED BY The Sporting News
OFFICIAL BASEBALL GUIDE-1953

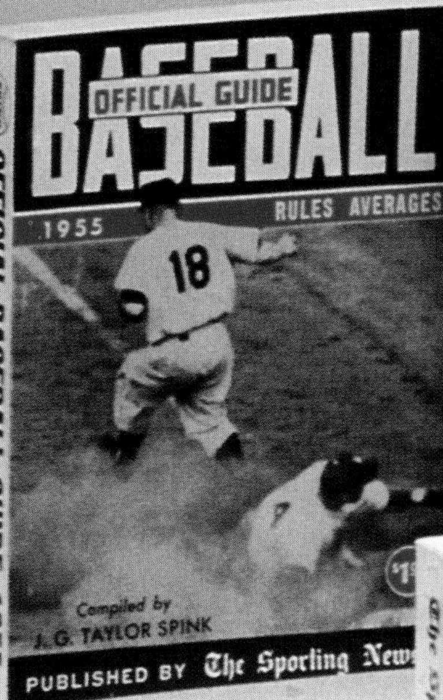
OFFICIAL GUIDE
BASEBALL
1955
RULES AVERAGES
Compiled by
J. G. TAYLOR SPINK
PUBLISHED BY
OFFICIAL BASEBALL GUIDE-1955

BASEBALL
OFFICIAL GUIDE
USEN'T YOUSE T' LIVE IN 'BROOKYN ?
OFFICIAL BASEBALL

OFFICIAL 1969
BASEBALL GUIDE
Published by The Sporting News
OFFICIAL BASEBALL GUIDE-1969

OFFICIAL 1981
OFFICIAL BASEBALL GUIDE-1981

The Sporting News
OFFICIAL
BASEBALL GUIDE
1982
OFFICIAL BASEBALL GUIDE-1982

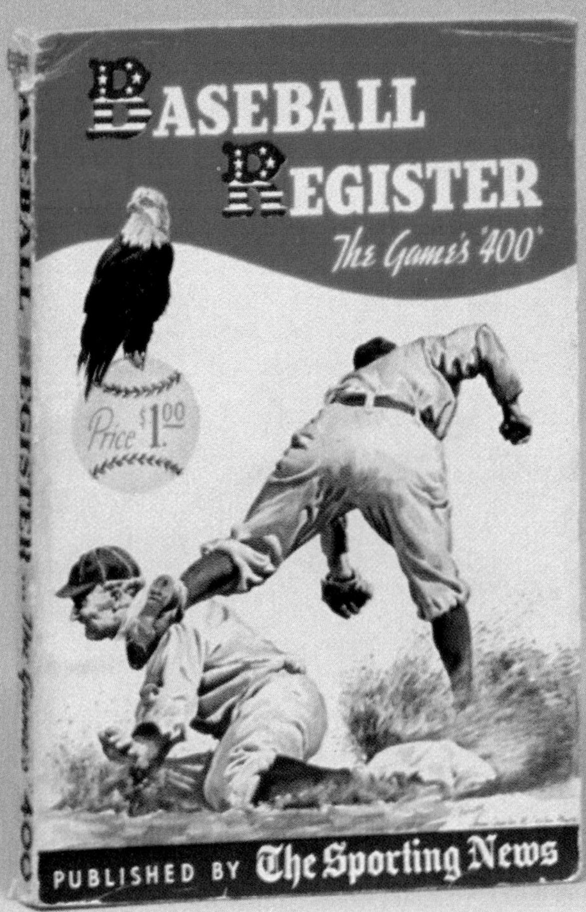

Other early members of The Sporting News baseball library were the 'Baseball Register,' first published in 1940 (above); the 1942 'Dope Book' (below right), which actually was a forerunner to the 1949 'One For the Book' (below center) and today's 'Baseball Record Book'; and the 1948 Dope Book.

No baseball library would have been complete without such TSN offerings as (below, left to right) 'Knotty Problems of Baseball', 'Daguerreotypes' and 'World Series Records,' which was first offered to readers in 1953. The first non-baseball offering came in 1958-59 with TSN's 'Official National Basketball Association Guide' (above left). The first 'Hockey Guide' (above right) was dated 1967-68 and the 'Football Guide' followed shortly thereafter.

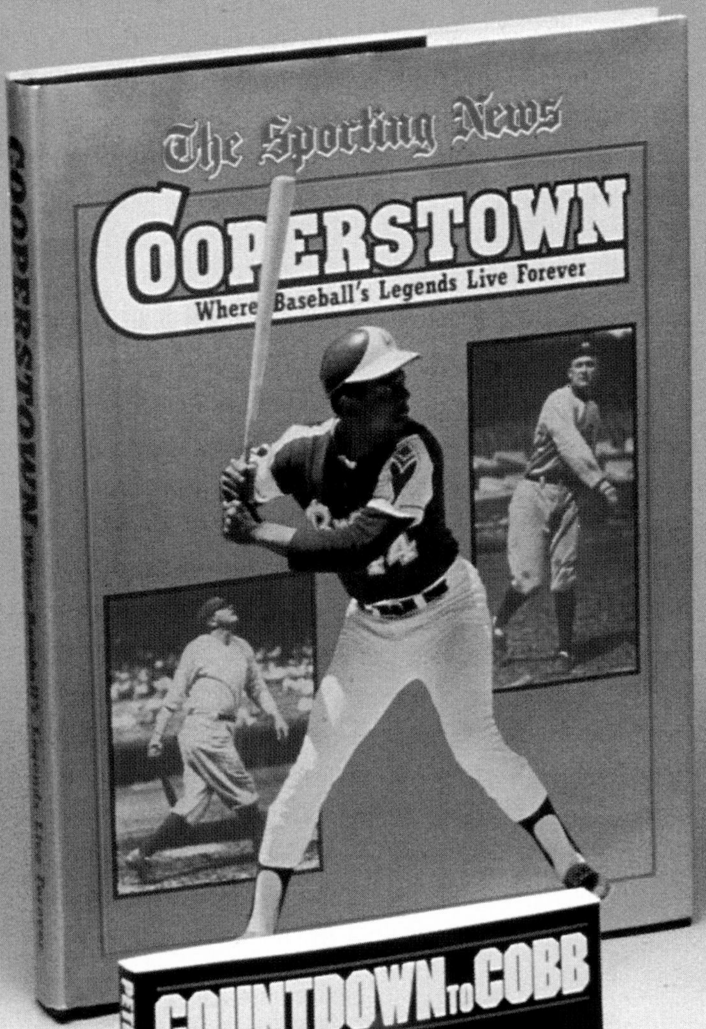

Special books, published infrequently after World War II, became regular TSN offerings in the early 1980s after formation of a book department. 'Cooperstown,' 'Take Me Out to the Ball Park' and 'The Sporting News Baseball Trivia Book' were published in 1983 for those wishing to expand their baseball horizons. For those with an interest in football, 'The Sporting News Football Trivia Book' and 'Heismen, After the Glory' were new 1985 offerings. The latest effort is Pete Rose's diary of his record-breaking 1985 season.

The Sporting News
TAKE ME OUT TO THE BALL PARK
STENGEL'S STREAKS
BABE RUTH
JOLTIN' JOE DiMAGGIO
LOU GEHRIG

The Sporting News
FOOTBALL
Trivia
BOOK
A memorable, unusual, between-the-lines look at the fascinating world of college and professional football.
The Sporting News FOOTBALL TRIVIA BOOK

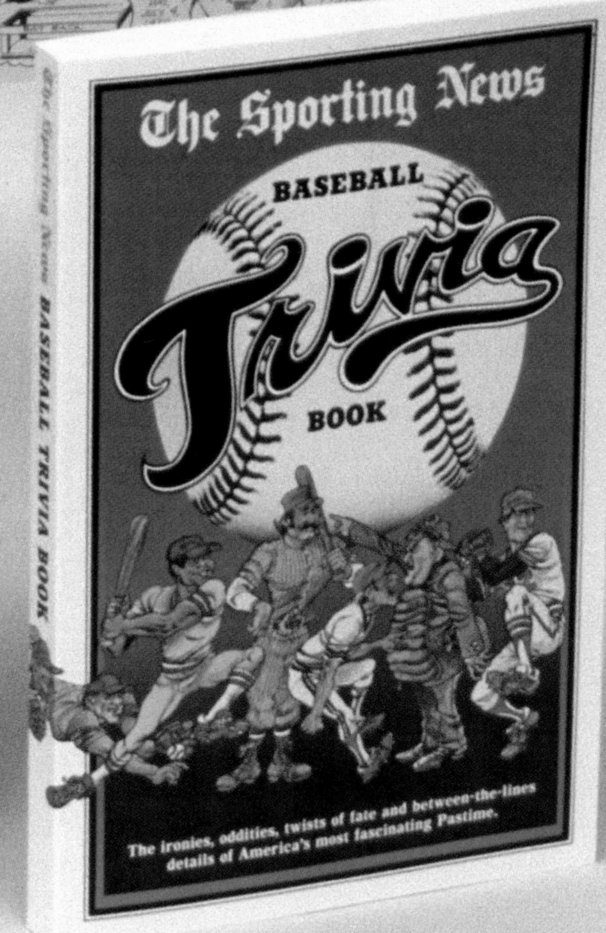
The Sporting News
BASEBALL
Trivia
BOOK
The ironies, oddities, twists of fate and between-the-lines details of America's most fascinating Pastime.
The Sporting News BASEBALL TRIVIA BOOK

The Sporting News expanded its library to include magazines in 1981. A 'Yearbook' series offers readers previews of the baseball, pro football, college football and basketball seasons annually. The Sporting Goods Dealer (above left) has been published monthly since 1899.

cial troubles of various clubs in the daily prints, for the way has been pointed for the easy correction of them. Of course, if the officials do not care to unbend themselves and forget their prejudices and follow the course now paved for them, that is their business, but they cannot expect much sympathy from the public at large, which always goes along with the fellow who helps himself and doesn't cry on every convenient shoulder."

In September 1935, after the Reds had played the last of their allotted seven night games, The Sporting News resumed discussion of the night-ball subject. Among the conclusions to be drawn from the experiment, it noted, "was that a total of 130,337 spectators were attracted—a greater number for seven games than several other clubs in the majors are likely to draw at home all season. Opponents of night games cannot laugh off those figures amassed by a second-division club."

Pointing out that prior objections had disappeared one by one, the editorial continued, "There were some casualties, it is true, but they were of a minor nature, no more than ordinarily occur in the course of a similar period in daylight. The attendance didn't decline, interest didn't lag, players were not maimed and bruised, the pitchers didn't gain any decided edge over the batters except as they might likewise excel in the daylight with superior performances, the dampness of the evening air didn't affect any arms, insects didn't take control and the lights were adequate."

Still, there was this caution: "Unquestionably, a steady diet of night ball would be ruinous to the majors. But one night game a week during the hot period seems to be the most desirable compromise. Thus limited, it does not turn the game into a night hippodrome."

By 1939, all of the paper's fears of a "night hippodrome" had evaporated. Its conversion to the arclights was complete. An editorial titled "Let There Be More Lights" cited the success of after-dark games in Cincinnati, Brooklyn, Philadelphia and Cleveland and added, "Devoted to the best interests of baseball for over half a century, The Sporting News naturally dislikes to see the game become a night pastime instead of continuing as daylight entertainment.

"Until recently, The Sporting News did not believe that more than seven night games a season should be staged by the majors, but realizing that the rules of yesterday do not always apply to activities of today, this publication believes that Clark Griffith's suggestion that the big leagues play at least two continuous months of night games should be adopted and hereby goes on record in favor of that proposal."

The suggestion of the Washington club owner never was adopted formally, but it was patently clear that The Sporting News now embraced arclight baseball without qualifications.

The 1935 editorial cartoon (above) pictured Powel Crosley, owner of the Cincinnati Reds, throwing the switch that brought light to Crosley Field. Curious Reds fans (below) witness the historic event.

MINORS MEET ON ISLAND OF ROMANCE FRINGED BY EMERALD SEA

BEACH SCENES AT GALVESTON, TEX., AS REFLECTED BY THE CAMERA

FOR YEARS there were legends that gold buried by Jean Lafitte, celebrated as a sort of gentleman privateer in the days of 1812, could be found around Galveston, Tex. The island on which the city lies was known as Treasure Island. In later years it has been found that the term was just as applicable to the town itself, and its natural recreational advantages, apart from the buried gold. The city that is entertaining the National Association's thirty-second annual convention this week, has a delightful year-round climate, and 32 miles of beach that see surf bathing, fishing, hunting and world-wide shipping, with 32 piers affording berthing space for 100 ocean-going vessels at a time and ample space for pleasure craft of all kinds. There are some 51 kinds of edible fish caught in the many ...ling spots ...

A 'Special' Event

In the days when railroads provided the fastest and most direct transportation between distant points, large companies frequently furnished "specials" so that passengers with common interests and a common destination could travel in comfort and camaraderie without interference or harassment from other travelers.

Such service was offered by the Missouri Pacific Railroad for those baseball people attending the minor league convention at Galveston, Tex., in 1933. The train, dubbed "The Sporting News Special," was pictured in a large photograph in TSN. The picture's cutline reported that the name added "an official touch to the entourage."

The interiors of the cars were decorated in a baseball motif while elaborately prepared menus greeted the passengers in the dining car.

Among the gentlemen who boarded the train in St. Louis were TSN Publisher J. G. Taylor Spink and Editor Edgar G. Brands and the following representatives of major league clubs: John O. Seys, Charley Grimm, Boots Weber, Clarence (Pants) Rowland, Red Corriden and Bob Lewis, Cubs; Rogers Hornsby and Ray Cahill, Browns; Clarence Lloyd, Bill Walsingham and Charley Barrett, Cardinals; James J. Tierney, Giants;

CELEBRITIES ON THE SPORTING NEWS 'SPECIAL'

THE Missouri Pacific Railroad made up a special train in St. Louis which carried many of the baseball men to the National Association meeting in Galveston, Tex. Baseball features were carried out on the train, including elaborately prepared menus and every comfort and convenience was offered the travelers. The train was called *The Sporting News* Special to add further official touch to the entourage.

Some of those who boarded the special in St. Louis are shown in the accompanying picture. Generally reading, left to right, they are—Ray Cahill, Browns; Charley Grimm, manager of Cubs; Robert C. Lewis, Cubs; Clarence Lloyd, Cardinals; James J. Tierney, Giants; John O. Seys, Cubs; Edgar G. Brands, editor of The Sporting News; Bill Walsingham, Cardinals; Harry Burton, A. G. Spalding & Bros.; J. G. Taylor Spink, publisher of The Sporting News; Rogers Hornsby, manager of Browns; Bob Quinn, Brooklyn Dodgers; Charley Barrett, Cardinals; Red Corriden, Cubs; Max Carey, manager of Dodgers; W. L. Robb, Wilson-Western; Billy Doyle, Detroit Tigers; Clarence Rowland, Cubs; Carl (Boots) Weber, Chicago Cubs; Donie Bush, manager Reds; Jack Hendricks; Joe Cambria, president Albany club; Paul Krichell, Yankees; Bill Friel. Seated in front, Leo Miller, Buffalo; William Manley, secretary International League, and Ray Schalk, manager of Buffalo.

Baseball's winter meetings always have commanded a lot of attention from editors of The Sporting News. Not uncommon was a picture spread (left) and several stories describing the city at which the upcoming convention would be held. In 1933, a train dubbed 'The Sporting News Special' (above) carried a large contingent of baseball men and writers from St. Louis to Galveston, Tex. TSN was not the only publication that devoted time and space to the meetings, however. In 1938, numerous writers waited patiently in cramped quarters (right) for news out of the office where American League officials were gathered.

Bob Quinn and Max Carey, Dodgers; Donie Bush, Reds; Billy Doyle, Tigers, and Paul Krichell, Yankees.

FIFTIETH Anniversary Edition

The Sporting News.

ORIGINAL MASTHEAD IN 1886

Vol. 1 No. 1—Vol. 101 No. 14 MARCH 17, 1886—MAY 21, 1936 TEN CENTS THE COPY—SINGLE COPY 5 CENTS IN 1886

The Sporting News Spans Half a Century With Baseball

Founded March, 1886, by Al and C. C. Spink, Growth Parallels That of Pastime

By ERNEST J. LANIGAN

HERALDED as the "Brightest, the Best and Cheapest Newspaper of Its Kind in America," THE SPORTING NEWS made its appearance on Sunday, March 17, 1886, under the sponsorship of Alfred H. Spink as editor and Charles C. Spink as business manager. Despite its ambitious salutation, THE SPORTING NEWS, at first, was chiefly a local weekly journal devoted to sports and the drama. The subscription price was $1.25 for six months and five cents for single copies, and the distribution was confined mostly to St. Louis and vicinity. In fact, the appearance of THE SPORTING NEWS caused scarcely a ripple nationally in sports or dramatic circles. Its first issue was not commented upon in Sporting Life, published at Philadelphia by Francis C. Richter and then occupying the position that THE SPORTING NEWS holds today, as the "Bible of Baseball." It is true, however, that the St. Louis correspondent of Sporting Life, shortly before, had mentioned incidentally, in one of his news letters, that "Al Spink, a well-known local writer, will issue a new sporting journal. The new sheet will make its appearance next Sunday. It will no doubt be a success."

The next mention of THE SPORTING NEWS by Richter's paper was a brief dispatch from St. Louis some weeks later, announcing that a Western League manager planned to have Editor Spink jailed for stating that he had deserted his ball club. The manager also intended to sue for $25,000.

The founders of THE SPORTING NEWS probably were flattered by that allusion to $25,000, for that represented a mythical sum to the struggling paper of those days, when pay rolls, printing and paper bills were difficult to meet. Nevertheless, the publication date continued to be met each week, and slowly the paper began its climb to national prominence and financial stability.

Al Spink, first editor of THE SPORTING NEWS, was known as one of the most brilliant sports writers of his day. He was particularly interested in baseball, although the drama also claimed a large share of his enthusiasm. It was he who had the vision of a national weekly devoted largely to baseball; it was the business sagacity and perseverance of his younger brother, Charles C. Spink, that overcame early obstacles and started the paper upon the road to success.

Al Spink was born in Quebec, where as a youngster he became an enthusiastic cricketer, along with his brother, William McDonald Spink, who died in 1894. These two brothers soon went to the United States, where they quickly developed an affection for baseball and where both became known as sports authorities.

At the time THE SPORTING NEWS was founded, Al Spink was acting as press agent for Chris von der Ahe, then owner of the St. Louis Browns, and who had been first interested in baseball by Spink.

Charles C. Spink, in 1886, was homesteading in South Dakota, when he received a hurried summons from Al Spink to come to St. Louis as business manager of THE SPORTING NEWS, then in organization, at a salary of $50 a week. Responding to the call, C. C. Spink reached St. Louis with $10 in his pocket, which sum Editor Al Spink promptly borrowed, then invited his younger brother to dinner, using part of the cash to pay for the meal.

* * *

Al Spink Had Started Clubs Before He Launched Baseball Paper

AL SPINK had started ball clubs and leagues before he undertook the task of launching a baseball paper in the West. Charles Spink, at first, had little knowledge of either baseball or newspaper work, but eventually became one of the best-posted men in the game, as well

leave THE SPORTING NEWS in order to devote his time to his theatrical enterprise, Charles C. Spink took over the paper. Though he had been a tireless worker before, keeping the paper going when advertising was hard to get and cash was even scarcer, C. C. Spink now redoubled his efforts. He toiled from early morning to late at night, figuring out new ways of increasing advertising and circulation, and surrounding himself with the ablest men he could find, and could afford to employ.

* * *

Joe Flanner Becomes Editor and Is Followed by Ring Lardner

A. J. (JOE) FLANNER became the brilliant successor to Al Spink as editor in 1895. Under his direction, the paper continued to progress editorially. The editorials became widely read, the staff of correspondents was enlarged and improved, and THE SPORTING NEWS began to shed its sectionalism and to become a national publication. Keeping baseball in the foreground, it gradually dropped all other features, until the paper became, as it is today, exclusively a baseball publication. Flanner had a thorough knowledge of Organized Ball and wielded considerable influence in the game. Among other accomplishments, he is credited with having written the Cincinnati Peace Agreement. He remained with THE SPORTING NEWS until about 1910, when he resigned as a result of a difference on policy. After remaining inactive for a couple of years, Joe became an assistant to Garry Herrmann, chairman of the National Commission.

After Flanner, the editorial chair was occupied by Ring Lardner, who later became one of America's most famous humorists. During his incumbency of about a year, Lardner started on THE SPORTING NEWS his first series of humorous baseball stories, under the title of "Pullman Pastimes." Lardner, on leaving THE SPORTING NEWS, returned to daily newspaper work at Boston.

Following the departure of Ring Lardner, the services of Joseph M. Cummings, a correspondent at Baltimore, were obtained as editor of THE SPORTING NEWS. An able editorial executive, Cummings broadened the scope of the news coverage of the game and gave the paper further strength and prestige. Following the death of his wife, Cummings left THE SPORTING NEWS to return to Baltimore.

In 1912, Earl Obenshain, former Decatur (Ill.) correspondent, became editor of THE SPORTING NEWS, having been recommended for the job by Dick Kinsella, who operated the Springfield club in the Three-I League and later became a scout for the New York Giants. "Obie," as he was known, was a

PLACES AND FACES PROMINENT IN 50 YEARS OF PUBLICATION

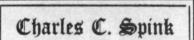

When TSN celebrated its 50th anniversary in 1936, a special section (above) featured the history of the publication, written by Ernest J. Lanigan. Appearing inside was J.G. Taylor Spink's tribute (left) to his father, Charles, after the latter's death in 1914.

Charles C. Spink

Here is the tribute to Charles C. Spink, mentioned above, which appeared in THE SPORTING NEWS the week after his death on April 22, 1914. It was written by his son, J. G. Taylor Spink, present publisher.

IT IS HARD in one's bereavement to record the death of a father, but when that father has been the constant companion and business associate of a son, allowing that son an opportunity to know, better than anyone else, his many sterling qualities, the task is even more heart-rending.

Charles Claude Spink, beloved husband of Marie Taylor Spink, and father of John George Taylor, Freddie and Frances Snaith Spink, passed away on the morning of April 22, 1914, as a result of an operation for stomach trouble, from which he had long been a sufferer.

My father was a self-made man. He fought for everything throughout his life, and with such men, of such brilliant character, seemingly the easiest thing is to die, realizing like all of us, that our time must come at some time and God's will must be done.

Although his business as publisher of three of the leading publica-

TSN Celebrates 50th Anniversary

Franklin Delano Roosevelt occupied the White House when The Sporting News observed its 50th anniversary in the issue of May 21, 1936.

The President offered congratulations to TSN in a letter that was reproduced on the cover of the 44-page issue. It read:

"Please accept hearty congratulations on the occasion of the publication of the Fiftieth Anniversary edition of The Sporting News. Your paper, having passed the half-century mark, should have little difficulty in reaching a hundred. I wish for it continued success in the service of the fans, of which I am one."

Ernest J. Lanigan, a teen-age copyholder in the early days of the paper, wrote a history of the publication as the lead article in the special anniversary section. Publisher J.G. Taylor Spink contributed a two-column series of reminiscences, while other personal recollections were written by Editor Edgar G. Brands, Dick Farrington and Fred Lieb.

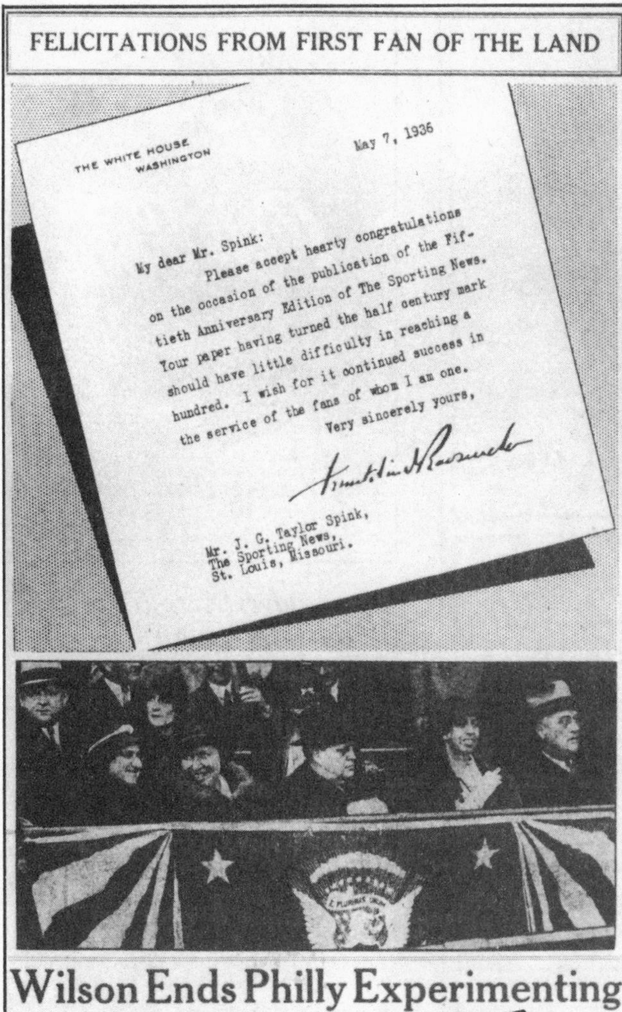

FELICITATIONS FROM FIRST FAN OF THE LAND

THE WHITE HOUSE
WASHINGTON

May 7, 1936

My dear Mr. Spink:

Please accept hearty congratulations on the occasion of the publication of the Fiftieth Anniversary Edition of The Sporting News. Your paper having turned the half century mark should have little difficulty in reaching a hundred. I wish for it continued success in the service of the fans of whom I am one.

Very sincerely yours,

Franklin D. Roosevelt

Mr. J. G. Taylor Spink,
The Sporting News,
St. Louis, Missouri.

Wilson Ends Philly Experimenting

STYLE CHANGES OF HALF-CENTURY IN GAME

MEMORIES

By DICK FARRINGTON

SO. THE first 50 years are the hardest. Oh, yeah. . . Rather a virile youngster, THE SPORTING NEWS, which is putting the figurative finger on half a century of continuous service to the game. . . . The long trail down through the corridors of years has not dimmed its batting eye; there is no limp from a charleyhorse and the arm is as good as ever. . . . Maybe it would be the honest thing to say that the S. N., sitting in on its fiftieth birthday party, has more pep than ever.

And flashing the retrospective mirror back to something like 1906, this writer, then a kid in knee pants, remembers his first copy of baseball's bible. . . . Teddy Roosevelt was president then; farmers were getting 20 cents a bushel for potatoes; automobiles frightened horses; Frank Chance was winning pennants with the Cubs, Fielder Jones with the White Sox; Halley's Comet was already beginning to worry the natives; "23, or skidoo" was a wise crack and the real sports wore stock-ties and smoked

DISCOVERY of Baseball's Bible

By E. G. BRANDS

IT WAS back in the middle 90's when I first came in touch with THE SPORTING NEWS, had impressed on me that it was "the baseball bible" and learned it made oracles of men who read it. That was approximately 16 years before a modest contribution of mine ever appeared in it and 35 years before I became actively associated with the publication. How time does fly!

Born in a small town of some 500 souls, my first contact with the game was through the local team, largely made up of local talent, supplemented by semi-pro and professional players, hired for special occasions. The "sports" of the town and surrounding communities were loyal supporters of the team, so much so that thousands of dollars often rode on the results. This led to the importation of outside talent, even major

REMINISCENCES

By FREDERICK G. LIEB

MY EARLIEST baseball recollection—a little cigar store in Philadelphia, which posted National League scores of the nineties. . . . Seemed as though Baltimore and Brooklyn always were up at the top. . . . The Phillies, with the great Lajoie, Delahanty, Flick, Orth, Bernhard, Thomas and others, always were threatening but never could make the grade. . . . Later, spent good part of quarter of century of baseball writing career campaigning over the baseball trails with two famous members of that old swashbuckling Baltimore crew—the late John J. McGraw and the late Wilbert Robinson.

Coming of Athletics to Philadelphia, with picturesque Waddell-Shreck battery, provided first big thrill. . . . Marched in parade, which celebrated first of Connie Mack's nine Athletic pennants in 1902. . . . Elephant, borrowed from Philadelphia zoo, in a white blanket, led parade, followed by a Rube depicting Waddell, a ghost for Shreckenghost, two crosses marked Lave and Monte for the infield Crosses, a little

Page 1 of TSN's 1936 anniversary issue featured a congratulatory letter (left) from President Franklin D. Roosevelt. Inside features included the above editorial-page sketch and birthday greetings (below) from prominent people.

Other prominent writers from across the nation authored additional articles pertaining to the history of the game.

In a memorial to his father, whose death in 1914 had projected him into the publisher's chair, Spink reprinted the tribute he had written to his progenitor 22 years earlier.

The lead editorial, "An Acknowledgement and Thanks," began, "There comes a time in the lives of individuals and organizations when it is well to pause in the busy succession of daily activities and look back into the past, not only to count what the years have brought, but to discover whether earlier ideals and policies have been faithfully followed.

"Baseball and The Sporting News have traveled a long way during the 50 years they have grown up together, but it was the sterling qualities of their founders that made such a growth possible

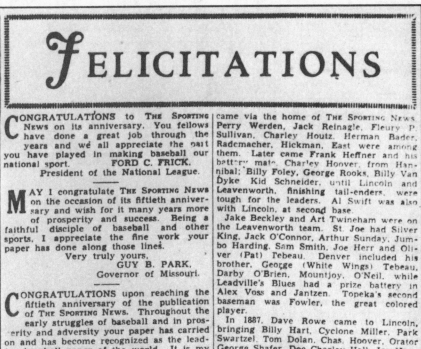

FELICITATIONS

CONGRATULATIONS to THE SPORTING NEWS on its anniversary. You fellows have done a great job through the years and we all appreciate the part you have played in making baseball our national sport. FORD C. FRICK.
President of the National League.

MAY I congratulate THE SPORTING NEWS on the occasion of its fiftieth anniversary and wish for it many years more of prosperity and success. Being a faithful disciple of baseball and other sports, I appreciate the fine work your paper has done along those lines.
Very truly yours,
GUY B. PARK,
Governor of Missouri.

CONGRATULATIONS upon reaching the fiftieth anniversary of the publication of THE SPORTING NEWS. Throughout the early struggles of baseball and in prosperity and adversity your paper has carried on and has become recognized as the leading baseball paper of the world. It is my earnest hope there are many anniversaries for your organization in the years to come and that you and the great sport you represent may continue to grow and enjoy prosperity.
Sincerely yours,
W. G. BRAMHAM,
President, National Association of Professional Baseball Leagues.

came via the home of THE SPORTING NEWS. Perry Werden, Jack Reinagle, Fleury P. Sullivan, Charley Houtz, Herman Bader, Rademacher, Hickman, East were among them. Later came Frank Heffner and his battery mate, Charley Hoover, from Hannibal; Billy Foley, George Rooks, Billy Van Dyke Kid Schneider, until Lincoln and Leavenworth, finishing tail-enders, were tough for the leaders. Al Swift was also with Lincoln, at second base.

Jake Beckley and Art Twineham were on the Leavenworth team. St. Joe had Silver King, Jack O'Connor, Arthur Sunday, Jumbo Harding, Sam Smith, Joe Herr and Oliver (Pat) Tebeau. Denver included his brother, George (White Wings) Tebeau, Darby O'Brien, Mountjoy, O'Neil, while Leadville's Blues had a prize battery in Alex Voss and Jantzen. Topeka's second baseman was Fowler, the great colored player.

In 1887, Dave Rowe came to Lincoln, bringing Billy Hart, Cyclone Miller, Park Swartzel, Tom Dolan, Chas. Hoover, Orator George Shafer, Doc Charley Hall, Joe Herr, Fred Lange, Jake Beckley, Toohey and others. They fought a tough finish with Goldsby's Golden Giants of Topeka, who won the pennant, with Lincoln second. Goldsby had Bugs Holliday, Jack Sheed, Joe Ardner, Maculiar, Johnson, Danny Stearns, Conway, Gunson, Jake Kenyon and others.

Possibly we may have erred in instances, but the majority of the above is correct. Not

When you begin to think about getting into that good physical condition, whether baseball player, golfer, swimmer, jockey, fighter, or wrestler, why not

Come to Hot Springs National Park

The World's Greatest Training Ground. Take a Course of the Famous Thermal Baths, and Sleep Where Life Is Safe — "It's Fire-Proof, Folks"

HOTEL COMO

200 Delightful Rooms

CONTAINING ALL MODERN IMPROVEMENTS KNOWN TO HOTEL CONSTRUCTION. POPULAR PRICES

Headquarters for the Ray L. Doan Base Ball and Umpire School and the Home of Many Celebrities while taking preliminary training, such as,

Rogers Hornsby
George Sisler
Lon Warneke
Dizzie Dean
Paul Dean

Burleigh Grimes
Marvin Owen
Lew Fonseca
Tris Speaker
George Barr

For Further Information, Write

Al. A. Reynolds, Manager, Hotel Como, Hot Springs, Ark.

THE ORIGINAL

Griesedieck Bros. *St. Louis*

LIGHT LAGER BEER

•

On Sale at Ball Park

The pause that refreshes

Many advertisers (left, above) bought space and extended their birthday greetings to TSN on the pages of the special anniversary section. Several of those advertisers, including Coca-Cola, had been buying space in The Sporting News since the publication's early days.

The **"CRACK O' THE BAT" TELLS THE STORY**

Get That Snap in the Game and That Finer Performance

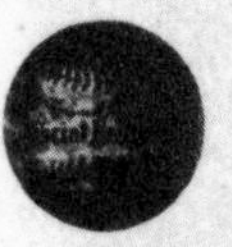

"BRANCH RICKEY"
Official League Baseballs

The Last Word in Baseball Construction —Different in That They Are Better

J. H. Grady Manufacturing Co.

927 TYLER STREET ST. LOUIS, MO.

Heartiest Good Wishes

TO

The Sporting News
Pennsylvania State Association

ELMER M. DAILY, President RUSSELL HOCKENBURY, Secretary

BUTLER—J. J. Dunleavy, Pres. CHARLEROI—S. L. Woodward, Pres. GREENSBURG—M. J. K. Davis, Pres.
JEANNETTE—John H. Harris, Pres. McKEESPORT—Ray Ryan, Pres. MONESSEN—J. C. Gold, Pres.

All good wishes on your
Fiftieth Anniversary
and for your continued success

Bill McKechnie, Manager
BOSTON BEES

We Congratulate

The Sporting News

A record truly great for a truly great publication—fifty years of service in the gathering and dissemination of the most complete and the most interesting news about the nation's great game of baseball.

Congratulations to J. G. Taylor Spink, the publisher, whose friendship we are proud to own—as we were that of his father, Mr. Charles C. Spink, founder of THE SPORTING NEWS.

R. J. LEACOCK, President

Leacock Sporting Goods Company

921 LOCUST ST. ST. LOUIS, MO.

Tribute to the Fiftieth Anniversary
—of—

THE SPORTING NEWS

Albert D. (Dolly) Stark

PHOTOSTAT COPIES

Photostat Copies are LEGAL EVIDENCE

They permit you to retain originals in safe places. Have Photostat copies made of ALL your valuable contracts, documents, etc. We'll reproduce them quickly . . . and confidentially.

- LETTERS
- CHECKS AND NOTES
- WILLS
- PHOTOGRAPHS
- INSURANCE POLICIES
- "ANYTHING"

105 N. Eighth St. St. Louis, Mo.

With Best Wishes for Your Continued Good Work for Baseball.

Bill Bradley
Scout
Cleveland Indians

Rawlings, a close friend of The Sporting News through the years, was present and accounted for, as were both the American and National leagues, which took out full-page congratulatory notices.

PILES HEALED WITHOUT THE KNIFE

Fistula, Fissure and all Rectal Diseases, cured by my Soothing, Gentle Method, Satisfaction Guaranteed or No Pay. No Chloroform. No Danger, No Hospital. No Detention From Business.

FISTULA SUFFERERS DON'T DELAY

Call or write today—IT WILL PAY YOU

176-PAGE BOOK FREE—Valuable to Pile Sufferers

CONSULTATION AND EXAMINATION FREE

Hundreds come, are successfully treated and are grateful. You will be.

DR. C. M. COE, *Rectal Specialist*

861 Pine St. Phone MAin 4181 ST. LOUIS, MO.

Best Wishes and Congratulations to The Sporting News on Its 50th Anniversary

BLAKE HARPER

President, Sportsman's Park Concession and Advertising Company

ST. LOUIS, MO.

With Heartiest Good Wishes on Your Fiftieth Anniversary from a Lifelong Baseball Fan.

James R. Kearney
St. Louis, Mo.

and enabled each to win and to hold the confidence of the public."

A three-column sketch depicting the change in diamond attire during the five decades was featured on the editorial page while elsewhere in the issue more than two columns were devoted to birthday greetings from leading figures in and out of baseball, including Governor Guy Park of Missouri and Mayor Bernard Dickman of St. Louis.

Numerous advertisers, such as Coca-Cola, Rawlings and both the American and National leagues, purchased space to extend happy birthday greetings to TSN.

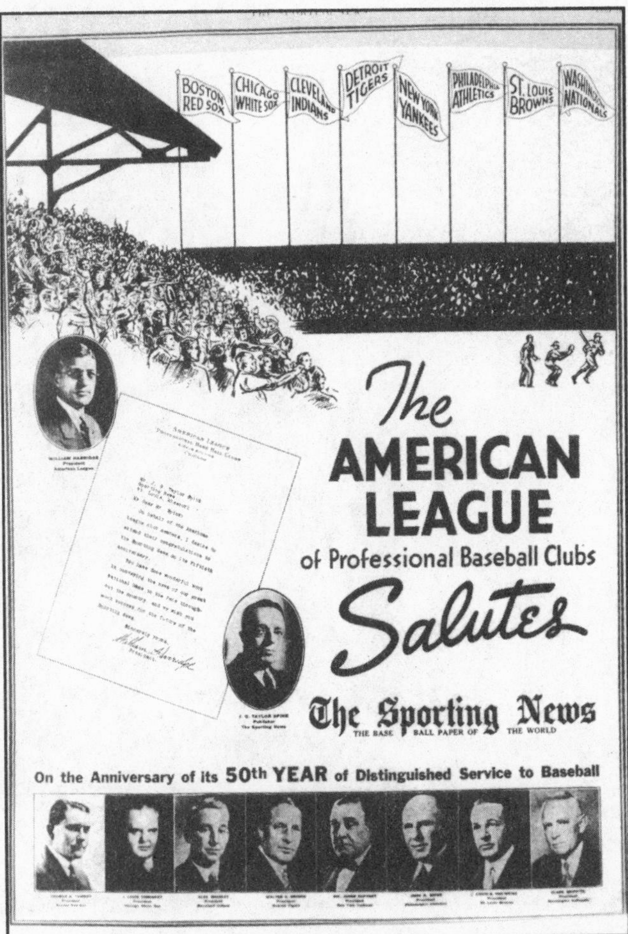

RAWLINGS SALUTES A LEADER!

Congratulations to THE SPORTING NEWS on your 50th Anniversary. It is indeed an outstanding achievement, not only in the publication field but in the invaluable assistance and service you and your editors have contributed to the interests and promotion of baseball . . . May the culmination of your first 50 years be but a stepping stone to future success and achievement.

Just As THE SPORTING NEWS Dominates - - - So Does RAWLINGS in ATHLETIC EQUIPMENT

Originators and Designers of Up-to-the-Minute Equipment

There's True Distinction in RAWLINGS UNIFORMS
Famous for Their

- Perfect Fit, Affording Real Comfort and Ease
- SUPERIOR TAILORING
- FINEST QUALITY FLANNELS
- WEARING QUALITIES
- THE MAJORS DEMAND THEM MINORS CAN AFFORD THEM!
- THE ST. LOUIS CARDINALS Wear Rawlings Uniforms at Home! And on the Road

We have pioneered the following in Baseball Equipment: A large size glove, the celebrated "Bill Doak" which still leads the field - - - oil treated gloves and mitts - - - full leather lined gloves - - - adjustable thumb and little finger loops on catchers' mitts - - - reinforcement tab in crotch between thumb and forefinger on gloves - - - special adjustable ball trap lace - - - shin guard with fibre instep protector - - - fibre umpire body protector - - - detachable base covers and many other improvements too numerous to mention.

Take Your Pick From This All-Star Line-Up

★ The Famous "Bill Doak" Glove
★ "Bosey Berger" Glove
★ "Pepper Martin" Glove
★ "Jim Bottomley" Baseman Mitt
★ "George Sisler" Baseman Mitt
★ "Cy Perkins" Catcher's Mitt
★ "Bob O'Farrell" Catcher's Mitt
★ No. "O" Professional Leg Guards
★ Jimmie Wilson Mask
★ No. "SS" Catcher's Body Protector
★ No. "CRT" Tobin Patented Umpire Body Protector
★ No. "RO" Official Cushioned Cork Center Baseball
★ No. "100" Professional Player Model Bats

Stop in to see your Rawlings Dealer today - - - he will gladly show you and explain the merits of this outstanding equipment - - - There's a Rawlings Glove, Mitt, Mask, Leg Guard, Ball, Uniform, etc., to suit your particular needs and purse, make your selection now!

ST. LOUIS Rawlings MISSOURI
SAN FRANCISCO, CALIF.

TAKE STEWART O-CLUB NEMESIS

Be Satisfied If Southpaw Tigers and Yanks; Halts Slump in New York

Aspirants to Gardner's Job in Lone Star State Will Find Way Well Paved for Them

IF I WERE PRESIDENT OF THE TEXAS LEAGUE

MEMPHIS CHICKS HIGH IN SOUTHER

Fred Hofmann Develops Bro Youngsters to Build Flag Trio of Kid Pitchers C

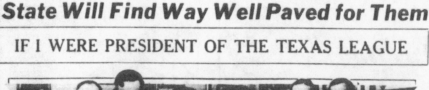

The Head of the Lone Star Loop and the Men Who Run Its Games

From left to right, back row, are Frank Coe, Allyn Davis, Steve Basil, Joe Pate, Steve Colfer and Uley Welsh, Jr.; bottom row, seated, Eddie Palmer, President Gardner, Secretary Milton Price and Lee Ballanfant.

Unusual Play in Big League Game Basis for Seventh Problem in Jig-Saw Contest

Final Installment in Contest for $225 in Prizes Will Appear Next Week

PROBLEM No. 7

A DOUBLE-PLAY is made by the first baseman after a two-base hit and a succeeding grounder to the second baseman on which a perfect play is made, the first baseman getting both putouts, neither batter advancing beyond second and the first baseman never leaving his bag. How is it done?

Contests Attract Readers

As a means of halting the plunge of circulation to below the 50,000 mark during the Depression, Taylor Spink designed a series of contests for readers of The Sporting News.

Scarcely an issue went to press during this period without a contest, an announcement of a forthcoming puzzle or the results of a previous contest.

Annually, there was a crossword

Taylor Spink turned to contests as a means of halting plunging circulation during the depression. The 'If I Were President' contest (above) and the 'Jig-Saw' contest (left) stretched over multiple issues and kept readers in a quandary.

Call the Turn on the Experts and Win $100 in Cash as the First Prize

The Sporting News Presents Its Third Annual All-Star Team Contest--*Put Pictures Together and Name the Players!*

FOR THE third consecutive year, The Sporting News, with the co-operation of members of the Baseball Writers' Association of America, has selected an All-Star team for the year and is giving its readers an opportunity to identify the chosen players before their names are officially announced and, at the same time, to participate in the opportunity to win some valuable prizes. To serve the double purpose of stimulating interest in the selections and to give the fans a chance to profit thereby, another cut-out picture contest has been arranged.

A two-fold task is imposed on the contestants. First, they must identify the players through their photographs, which are cut up in three sections and then re-arranged in a composite picture, no two parts of which are of any one player, from which the original photograph is to be re-assembled. Second, they must prove up their identification by the clues, published with each picture, that have to do with some date, event or characteristic connected with the players.

There will be ten of these composite pictures, the first of which is published this week. The forehead is that of one player, the middle section of the face that of another and the mouth and jaw that of still another. These pictures are to be cut apart and assembled correctly, aided by the clues that will appear with the photographs each week in The Sporting News.

THE FIRST CONTEST PICTURE

This year's team is composed of an unusually large number of newcomers, as compared with last year's, so don't jump to conclusions too quickly. You may not agree with the choices of the experts—193 of them collaborated with The Sporting News in the selection—and that is your privilege. If you do not, write a letter, when you have all the pictures in hand, and send it when you submit all the solutions, giving your own opinion as to who should have been included. If you agree with the Baseball Writers, give your reasons for acquiescing in their choices.

The Sporting News will pay $175 in cash as the capital awards. The first prize is $100, the second $50 and the third $25. In addition, Louisville Slugger bats and Spalding, Reach, Rawlings, Worth and Wilson-Western baseballs will be given to 24 other contestants who may not be successful in winning one of the first three prizes.

There are no restrictions as to entry. Anyone may contest, except employes of The Sporting News and their families, and as many entries may be made as desired, except that in no case will more than one prize be awarded any one contestant. There are no strings attached to this offer—you don't have to solicit subscriptions, or even be a subscriber, although it would be well to assure certain delivery of your paper each week, by subscribing direct, in order not to miss a single installment of the pictures.

Here Are the Rules for Entering the All-Star Team Picture Contest:

These Awards Will Go to the 27 Prize Winners

First Prize $100
Second Prize 50
Third Prize 25

The next 12 winners will receive Louisville Slugger Baseball Bats.

Twelve additional winners will receive Spalding, Reach, Rawlings or Wilson-Western Baseballs.

REMEMBER—Read the rules governing the contest carefully. Some entrants in previous contests have made their solutions ineligible because they did not follow the regulations. The judges will have specific instructions to enforce the

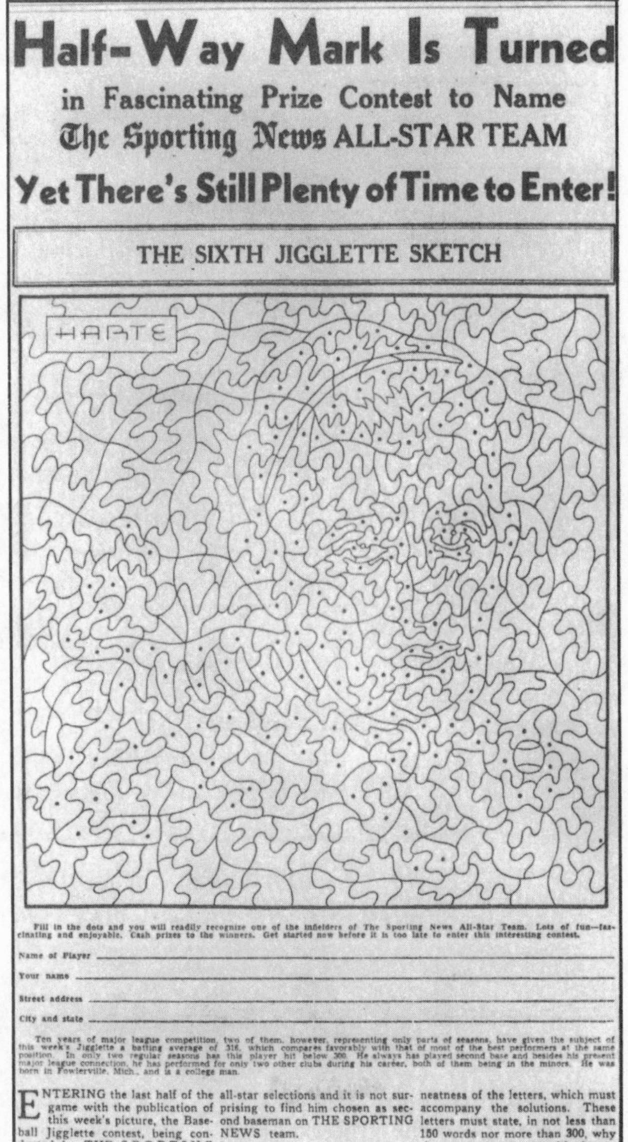

Half-Way Mark Is Turned

in Fascinating Prize Contest to Name The Sporting News ALL-STAR TEAM

Yet There's Still Plenty of Time to Enter!

THE SIXTH JIGGLETTE SKETCH

Fill in the dots and you will readily recognize one of the infielders of The Sporting News All-Star Team. Lots of fun—fascinating and enjoyable. Cash prizes to the winners. Get started now before it is too late to enter this interesting contest.

Name of Player ______

Your name ______

Street address ______

City and state ______

Ten years of major league competition, two of them, however, representing only parts of seasons, have given the subject of this week's Jigglette a batting average of .316, which compares favorably with that of most of the best performers at the same position. In only two regular seasons has this player hit below .300. He always has played second base and besides his present major league connection, he has performed for only two other clubs during his career, both of them being in the minors. He was born in Fowlerville, Mich., and is a college man.

ENTERING the last half of the game with the publication of this week's picture, the Baseball Jigglette contest, being conducted by THE SPORTING all-star selections and it is not surprising to find him chosen as second baseman on THE SPORTING NEWS team.

Contestants will find the comple... neatness of the letters, which must accompany the solutions. These letters must state, in not less than 150 words nor more than 300, why the contestant agrees with the se-

A contest featuring a string of 10 puzzle pictures (above) was held each year in the early 1930s in conjunction with the selection of TSN's major league all-star team. A 1933 contest (right) told readers to fill in the dots and recognize a member of TSN's all-star cast.

puzzle on The Sporting News' All-Star team that was chosen by members of the Baseball Writers' Association of America. A letter of specified length also was required in which the contestant was asked to comment on the players selected.

Generally, a $100 prize was offered to the entrant whose work was adjudged best, while the first two runners-up might receive $50 and $25. Some contests awarded Louisville Slugger bats while others offered baseballs to the also-rans.

For nine weeks early in 1935, photos of league presidents were published in an "If I Were President" contest. Readers were asked to submit suggestions whereby each executive could improve the quality of baseball in his circuit. The winner received an all-expense-paid trip to the All-Star Game in Cleveland.

One year, a two-part contest was presented. First the readers predicted the standings in each major league after games of July 4, and then the standings at the close of the campaign. In addition to monetary prizes for the top three finishers, six-month subscriptions to TSN were presented to the next 10 winners.

In 1931, a contest was conducted for youths under 21. This consisted of a series of baseball questions that a young reader was required to answer and submit with the customary letter. A sample question was: "Is there any time during a game when an outfielder should refuse to catch a fly ball? If so, why?" Among the prizes was a scholarship to the National Baseball School in Los Angeles.

At another time, 10 free scholarships to the All-Star Baseball School of Ray Doan in Hot Springs, Ark., were offered to those who accumulated the most points in selling subscriptions to The Sporting News.

Another popular contest was "Name Your Favorite Baseball Announcer." This contest was divided into several classes, with major league broadcasters in one category, top minor league announcers in another and additional classifications in the lower leagues. Prizes were awarded to contestants on the basis of their answers to specified questions, and the announcer receiving the most votes was given a trophy.

All-Star Team of Majors for 1936, Selected by 211 Experts—Page 3

Chronological History of 1936 in Game
How Detroit Park Is Groomed By NEIL CONWAY
Brands' Gossip of Players' Winter Activities
N. L. PITCHING AND MISCELLANEOUS BATTING FIGURES

The Sporting News
THE BASE BALL PAPER OF THE WORLD

Record Breakers in the Major Leagues
Highlights in the Career of BUDDY HASSETT
Free—Baseball School Scholarships
OFFICIAL AVERAGES OF EVANGELINE LEAGUE

VOLUME 102, NUMBER 20 — ST. LOUIS, DECEMBER 31, 1936 — TEN CENTS THE COPY 15c in Canada

GAME'S NO. 1 MEN OF YEAR ∴ Business, Managing, Playing ∴ IN MAJORS AND MINORS

BRANCH RICKEY — JOE McCARTHY — CARL HUBBELL — EARL MANN — ALLAN SOTHORON — JOHN VANDER MEER

1—Branch Rickey, vice-president and general manager of the St. Louis Cardinals, whose influence on the game was emphasized during the past season by the advancement of three Rickey-trained executives to high positions—George Trautman assuming the presidency of the American Association; Warren Giles becoming vice-president and general manager of the Cincinnati Reds, and Bill DeWitt, vice-president and general manager of the St. Louis Browns—and by his capable administration of the expanding Cardinal chain. 2—Joe McCarthy, who piloted the New York Yankees to the American League pennant by a margin of 19½ games, largest in the history of the majors, and to the world's championship over the New York Giants. 3—Carl Hubbell, pitcher of the New York Giants, who led all major league hurlers in victories, with 26, in winning percentage, .813, and in earned-run average, 2.41, in addition to winning 16 straight games during the season and leading the National League in earned-run average for the second time in three years. 4—Earl Mann, president of the Atlanta Southern Association Crackers, whose efficient administration enabled the club, for the second successive year, to draw more than 300,000 attendance, a record for a minor league club. 5—Allan Sothoron, who piloted the Milwaukee Brewers to the American Association championship and to victory in the Junior World's Series over Buffalo of the International League for the Class AA title. 6—John Vander Meer, 1936 strike-out king of the minors, whose pitching performance of 295 strike-outs, including 20 in one game, 19 victories against six defeats and earned-run average of 2.65 with Durham of the Piedmont League, won him promotion to the Cincinnati Reds.

MORE STING AT BAT CHIEF NEED OF BEES

Rising Stars of A's and Phils Give New Year Hope to Fans

Showing of Chubby Dean, Kelley, Newsome and Finney Brings

MUNGO HELD RIVALS TO .234 MARK AT BAT

Griff Prescribes Same Spring Tonic for Senators He Gave Them Last Year

FIGURES SHOW CUBS HELPED TRAP SELVES

TSN's top major and minor league executives, managers and players were first honored in 1936, their pictures appearing on page 1 of the December 31 issue.

The Award Winners

When the major leagues discontinued the practice of selecting Most Valuable Player winners in the late 1920s, Taylor Spink wasted no time grieving over the decision. He decided to present awards of his own.

Because the American League was the first to abandon the practice, The Sporting News honored Al Simmons of Philadelphia in 1929. The following year, the paper presented its first National League citation to Bill Terry of New York.

When the Baseball Writers' Association of America was designated as the electorate for the official MVP award, Spink continued to honor the players his staff regarded as the most outstanding performers. The practice has continued until the present, although separate trophies were presented to pitchers and regulars in later years.

For a number of years The Sporting News presented trophies to MVPs in the minor leagues as well and also placed in competition a trophy for the winner of the St. Louis City Series.

In 1936, Spink inaugurated annual awards to the leading executive, manager and player in the majors and minors. The first recipients in this 50-year program were:

Major League Executive—Branch Rickey, Cardinals.

Major League Manager—Joe McCarthy, Yankees.

Major League Player—Carl Hubbell, Giants.

Minor League Executive—Earl Mann, Atlanta.

Minor League Manager—Al Sothoron, Milwaukee.

Minor League Player—Johnny Vander Meer, Durham.

When, in 1938, Vander Meer hurled two consecutive no-hitters for the Cincinnati Reds, The Sporting News chortled editorially.

"The staff . . . cannot be blamed for gaining a certain amount of satisfaction from his success," read an editorial, "for this publication, perceiving him to to be a diamond in the rough, named him the No. 1 player in the minors in 1936. Many critics thought we had fumbled one and openly predicted that he would never get back to the majors (having been discarded by the Boston and Brooklyn organizations), or if he did, that he would not stick. For a time last season it seemed as though these critics might be right, for Johnny won only five games and lost 11 for Syracuse of the International League and won three and lost five for the Reds."

Vander Meer was named Major League Player of the Year for 1938, the same year that Warren Giles, general manager of the Reds, was acclaimed as the top executive.

Minor League Player of the Year citations after Vandy's award went to Charlie Keller of Newark (1937) and Fred Hutchinson of Seattle (1938).

Johnny Vander Meer, who holds the distinction of being TSN's first Minor League Player of the Year in 1936, received a citation (right) spelling out his contributions to the Durham club of the Piedmont League. Vander Meer, who joined the Reds in 1937, shows the citation to Reds players Les Scarsella (above left) and Walter Brown (second from right) and Manager Charlie Dressen (right). Vander Meer was named TSN Major League Player of the Year in 1938 after throwing consecutive no-hitters.

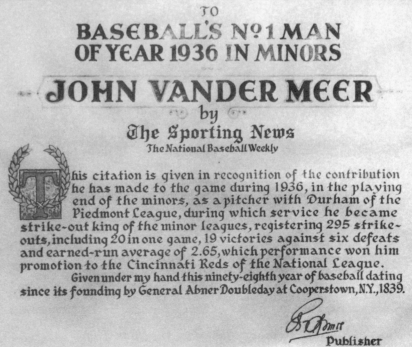

TO

BASEBALL'S No. 1 MAN
OF YEAR 1936 IN MINORS

JOHN VANDER MEER

by

The Sporting News

The National Baseball Weekly

This citation is given in recognition of the contribution he has made to the game during 1936, in the playing end of the minors, as a pitcher with Durham of the Piedmont League, during which service he became strike-out king of the minor leagues, registering 295 strike-outs, including 20 in one game, 19 victories against six defeats and earned-run average of 2.65, which performance won him promotion to the Cincinnati Reds of the National League.

Given under my hand this ninety-eighth year of baseball dating since its founding by General Abner Doubleday at Cooperstown, N.Y., 1839.

Publisher

Boston Red Sox stars Ted Williams (left) and Johnny Pesky hung up spikes and gloves to serve in World War II.

1940-1945:

WAR AND PEACE

By the strictest definition, the major league season of 1941 was a peacetime campaign, but the United States already was feeling the shock waves of global conflict. Armies of the Third Reich were rolling unchecked across Europe, and reports of growing military might in Japan were creating anxieties on Capitol Hill in Washington.

The Selective Service process was nibbling at baseball's manpower, but the exodus into military uniform was nothing more than a trickle. Hugh Mulcahy was the first major league regular to enter the armed forces. The Phillies' pitcher was inducted on March 8, 1941, and he did not return until late in the 1945 season. Hank Greenberg, who had batted .357 in Detroit's World Series loss to Cincinnati in 1940, played 19 games in 1941 before he, too, answered his military summons. When he returned four years later he wore the bars of an Air Force captain.

For remarkable batting accomplishments, the 1941 season belonged to Joe DiMaggio and Ted Williams. Nobody has matched their achievements in the more than four decades that followed.

With the pennant race barely a month old, the Yankee Clipper was batting .306. But he was in a bit of a slump, and he had gone hitless in his last two games, being blanked four times by Bob Feller and three times by Mel Harder, both of Cleveland. When DiMaggio singled off Edgar Smith of the White Sox at Yankee Stadium on May 15, it was little more than the end of a small slump. Nobody envisioned the spectacular hitting feat that lay ahead.

The six-year veteran hit safety in 10 straight games, then 20. As he approached the 30-game mark, newspapers began to take daily note of his progress. Rogers Hornsby's modern National League record of 33 games, set in 1922, was within easy grasp. Beyond that was George Sisler's modern major league record of 41 games, also set in 1922. If DiMaggio cleared those hurdles, he could set his sights on the all-time mark of 44 games, set by Willie Keeler of Baltimore in 1897.

On June 21, the Jolter singled off Detroit righthander Dizzy Trout to eclipse Hornsby's mark. The streak had reached 40 games when the Yankees played a doubleheader at Washington on June 29. A crowd of 31,000 packed Griffith Stadium when Joe doubled off Dutch Leonard in the first game to equal Sisler's record.

When the second game started, DiMag discovered that his favorite bat had been stolen during the intermission. He used a backup bat on his first three trips to the plate and was retired on each occasion. Teammate Tommy Henrich offered his model to the Jolter before his fourth at-bat, and Joe accepted.

On the second pitch from righthander Red Anderson, DiMaggio stroked an off-speed delivery to left field and the modern record was his alone. Keeler's record fell on July 2 when Joe homered off Boston righthander Dick Newsome.

But the streak wasn't over. It stood at 56 games when the Yankees met the Indians at Cleveland on July 17. Municipal Stadium swarmed with 67,468 fans, the largest night crowd ever at that time, and all curious about the Yankee Clipper who, in his last 56 games, had batted .408 with 91 hits in 223 at-bats, 15 home runs and 55 runs batted in.

In the first inning, DiMag pulled a pitch from Al Smith sharply over third base. It had the earmarks of a double until Ken Keltner made a brilliant backhanded grab and threw out the batter.

In the fourth inning, Joltin' Joe walked. In the seventh he drove another torrid smash over third base, and once more Keltner speared the ball and threw him out by a step. The Yankees led, 4-3, when DiMaggio batted in the eighth inning against reliever Jim Bagby Jr. with the bases loaded and one out. He ran the count to one ball and one strike, then rapped a grounder toward left-center field. Shortstop Lou Boudreau glided over behind second base and fielded the ball for the start of a double play via second baseman Ray Mack. Finally, after two months of consistent production, DiMaggio was held hitless—although not for long. In his next game, Joe embarked on a 16-game hitting streak.

DiMaggio's streak had stood at 48 games when he went to Detroit for the ninth annual All-Star Game, and though he slammed a double, scored three runs and drove in another, he was overshadowed by Ted Williams, who was playing in his second midsummer classic.

Not long before, in a bitter denunciation of Boston

fans who were heckling him, the young slugger had fumed, "I'd rather be a fireman." Ted had paid for the thoughtless remark with greater vituperation from the stands. By the summer of 1941, however, animosities generally were forgotten and he was a full-fledged superstar flirting with a .400 batting average.

But the momentum appeared to be with the National League in that summer's All-Star Game. Two two-run homers by Pittsburgh shortstop Arky Vaughan helped stake the senior circuit to a 5-3 lead before the American Leaguers faced their final opportunity to avoid a fourth loss in the series.

One chance was all they needed. Singles by Ken Keltner and Joe Gordon and a walk to Cecil Travis loaded the bases before Joe DiMaggio hit into a force-out, one run scoring. Williams, who had hit a double previously, then brought the 54,674 spectators to their feet by rocketing a pitch from Chicago's Claude Passeau into the right-field seats for a three-run, game-winning homer.

The 23-year-old slugger continued his torrid hitting the remainder of the season and possessed a batting average of .39955 as the Red Sox prepared to bring down the curtain with a doubleheader in Philadelphia. If Williams sat out the two games, his average would go into the records as .400. He would be the first major leaguer to attain that plateau since the Giants' Bill Terry batted .401 in 1930, the first American Leaguer since Harry Heilmann posted a .403 mark in 1923. Manager Joe Cronin gave Williams the choice —sit out the twin bill and be assured of a .400 average, albeit a shaky one, or play the games and risk falling from the cherished plateau.

Ted displayed no reticence. "If I'm going to be a .400 hitter," he said, "I want more than my toenails on the line."

In his first and second at-bats, Williams rapped a single and a homer off Dick Fowler. Then reliever Porter Vaughan surrendered a pair of singles to Williams, who went 4 for 5 in the game. Sitting comfortably at .404, Williams once more was given the option to play or sit out. His reply was the same.

Ted finished the day with a single and a savage double that smashed a public-address horn on the right-center field wall. He was retired on a short fly ball on his last effort in the gathering twilight, but he was a legitimate .400 hitter with an average of .406.

Together, DiMaggio ($37,500) and Williams ($20,000) barely topped the 1941 income of a 20-year-old sophomore at the University of Michigan. Dick Wakefield, experts agreed, resembled a young Williams and could, with proper polish, challenge the Splendid Splinter for top honors among lefthanded hitters.

The chase for the outfielder started early. Bids were submitted by every club that had the funds and was willing to gamble on an untried talent. Once it appeared that Clark Griffith of Washington had won the prize with a bonus offer of $40,000. But Walter O. Briggs, owner of the Tigers, matched the bid, and the pursuit continued until June 21, when Wakefield accepted Detroit's record offer of a reported $52,000 and a custom-built car that was equipped with a horn system that played the Michigan fight song.

After two encouraging seasons in the minors, Wakefield joined the Tigers in 1943 and batted .316. He was in the Navy when the 1944 season started but was discharged in July and rejoined the Tigers, then in seventh place. Instantly, the club came alive. Sparked by Wakefield's consistent hitting, the Tigers leaped into the midst of the pennant race. In 78 games, he batted .355 and was named to The Sporting News Major League All-Star team for the second consecutive year.

But the Tigers lost out to the St. Louis Browns in the pennant drive, and Wakefield never batted .300 again. One mediocre season followed another until he slipped into the minors, leaving many to wonder how great he might have been with a better attitude.

Wakefield's arrival as a professional baseball personality in 1941 coincided with the return to championship class of the Brooklyn Dodgers. Ever since Wilbert Robinson's club won the 1920 pennant, the Flatbush Faithful assured each other that "next year" would find another flag flapping over Ebbets Field. That promise finally materialized in the last season before World War II.

The Dodgers of 1941 were baseball's version of a fishwives' donnybrook. With Larry MacPhail screaming from the front office and Leo Durocher barking just as loudly on the field, "Dem Bums" roared to the pennant. Along the way they picked up legions of new fans, many of them wooed to the Brooklyn banner by the dulcet tones of Red Barber broadcasting the heroics of Pete Reiser and Pee Wee Reese, Dolph Camilli and Joe Medwick, Dixie Walker and Billy Herman, Hugh Casey and Mickey Owen, Whitlow Wyatt and Kirby Higbe.

In the American League, the Yankees captured their fifth pennant in six years, beating out the Red Sox by 17 games after finishing third in 1940. The Yanks and Dodgers split the first two World Series games at Yankee Stadium and were locked in a scoreless tie in the seventh inning of Game 3 when misfortune descended on Ebbets Field. Fred Fitzsimmons had allowed only four hits and was in full command when a line drive off the bat of Marius Russo struck the Brooklyn righthander on the knee. Pee Wee Reese hauled in the carom for the last out of the inning, but the blow forced Fitzsimmons from the game. Rushed to the mound, Hugh Casey surrendered four hits in one-third of an inning and lost the game, 2-1.

But even more sinister events awaited Brooklyn in Game 4 on October 5, which to Dodger fans will always be remembered as "Black Sunday." The Dodgers led, 4-3, with two out in the ninth inning when Casey fired a breaking pitch to Tommy Henrich, who swung and missed for strike three. The game was over, the Series was tied at two victories apiece, and a deafening roar arose from the 33,813 fans at Ebbets Field. But that roar abruptly turned into a gulp. The ball had skipped off Mickey Owen's mitt and rolled toward the stands as Henrich beat the catcher's frantic throw to first base.

The multitudes were stunned, but none more than Casey himself. The heart of the Yankee batting order was coming up, yet nobody thought to call time and restore the reliever's composure. It was a fatal oversight. The righthander surrendered a single to Joe Di-

Maggio, a two-strike double to Charlie Keller, a walk to Bill Dickey and a double to Joe Gordon. The Dodgers could not recover from that four-run uprising in their half of the ninth, and the victory that rightfully belonged to the Dodgers was now the property of the Yankees, who wrapped up the world championship the next day.

Two months later, major league magnates attended their annual meeting in Chicago, where Commissioner Kenesaw M. Landis reported that he had donated $25,000 to a fund to purchase athletic equipment for servicemen and that the proceeds from the 1942 All-Star Game would be donated to the same cause. The date was December 11, four days after the day that, according to President Franklin D. Roosevelt, "will live in infamy" because of the Japanese attack on Pearl Harbor.

For the second time in less than 25 years, the nation was at war. Wonderment pervaded baseball. Would there be another "Work or Fight" order as in 1918, or would the game be permitted to go its untrammelled course while complying with the national war effort?

To clear the air, Landis went to the top by writing a letter to the President. The Judge received his reply in the form of Roosevelt's "Green Light" letter, which read in part: "I honestly feel that it would be best for the country to keep baseball going. There will be fewer people unemployed and everybody will work longer hours and harder than ever before. And that means that they ought to have a chance for recreation and for taking their minds off their work even more than before."

The first wartime season was played with few inconveniences. The Cardinals raced to the 1942 National League pennant by winning 41 of their last 48 games to beat out the Dodgers. St. Louis then defeated the Yankees in a five-game World Series that featured two wins by rookie Johnny Beazley and a decisive home run by rookie third baseman Whitey Kurowski in the 4-2 clinching victory.

At the close of the campaign, Larry MacPhail resigned as chief executive officer of the Dodgers in order to accept a lieutenant colonel's commission in the Army. He was succeeded by Branch Rickey, who ended his tenure with the Cardinals with that stirring World Series upset.

By 1943, the international situation had worsened. Players were leaving for induction stations by the dozens, and the game was asked to reduce travel in conformity with guidelines formulated by the Office of Defense Transportation. In response, Landis ordered all major league clubs to train north of the Potomac and Ohio rivers and east of the Mississippi River, with the exception of the St. Louis clubs. Instead of luxury accommodations in Florida and California, the so-called "Long Underwear League" established training sites in Connecticut, New York, New Jersey, Pennsylvania, Massachusetts, Maryland, Delaware, Indiana, Illinois and Missouri.

The 1943 campaign opened on a hopeful note for the Phillies, who had finished seventh or eighth for 10 consecutive years. In the off-season, the club had been purchased by Bill Cox, a New York lumberman. Cox then hired Bucky Harris, a longtime major league skipper, to manage the new-look Phillies, and for the first time in years, a first-division berth was more than an idle dream.

By midseason, however, the Phils were languishing near the bottom of the league and Harris was fired. But the news that Fred Fitzsimmons was taking over the club was released in Philadelphia before Harris, who was in St. Louis for a series with the Cardinals, had been advised of his ouster. The players, incensed by the shabby treatment of their popular pilot, threatened to strike, but Harris dissuaded them from such rash action. They played that night's game on schedule.

Still, peace did not return to the Phils immediately. Rumors that Cox had run afoul of Landis with alleged bets on his own team circulated widely until November, when the commissioner announced that the betting reports had been confirmed and that Cox was barred from baseball. The Judge said Cox had violated Rule 21 (d) 2, which stipulates: "Any player, umpire, or club or league official or employee who shall bet any sum whatsoever upon any baseball game in connection with which the bettor had a duty to perform shall be declared permanently ineligible." The most damaging testimony against Cox was furnished by Harris, the deposed manager who revealed that he had been in Cox's office when he heard a secretary take wagering odds for her boss over the telephone.

The banishment of Cox represented the last major decision in Landis' 24-year reign. The Judge attended the 1944 All-Star Game at Pittsburgh and presided at the meeting to arrange details for the World Series. But when the all-St. Louis Series between the Cardinals and Browns opened at Sportsman's Park on October 4, Landis was not in his bunting-draped box. He was represented by Leslie O'Connor, his longtime aide, who explained that the Judge was in a Chicago hospital undergoing treatment for a lingering cold. He died there on November 25 at the age of 78 and was named to the Hall of Fame two weeks later.

The Major League Advisory Council governed baseball until a new commissioner could be elected, a task that was accomplished five months later. He was Albert Benjamin (Happy) Chandler, a U.S. senator from Kentucky and the personal candidate of Larry MacPhail, who was back in baseball as a co-owner of the Yankees. MacPhail and two other men had bought the Yanks from the heirs of Col. Jacob Ruppert for $2.8 million.

The wars in Europe and in the Pacific were headed toward victory when the 1945 season commenced, but the player shortage remained acute. Club rosters were dotted with those who were too young, too old or physically unfit for military duty. In fact, the St. Louis Browns had on their roster a one-armed outfielder.

Pete Gray, who lost his right arm a few inches below his shoulder in a childhood accident, played 77 games with the Browns in 1945, batting .218 with six doubles, two triples and 13 runs batted in. Wherever he appeared, Gray was a curiosity and helped spin turnstiles, although his presence on the team was not a publicity stunt. Still, fans were constantly amazed by his ability to catch a ball, flip it into the air, slip his glove under the stub of his right arm, catch the ball again and throw it back to the infield in one fluid motion.

But with the end of international hostilities and the return of major league regulars, Pete's days in the spotlight were numbered. He drifted into the minors and then back to his home in Nanticoke, Pa.

The American League schedule in 1945 was unlike any other in major league history. It permitted the Washington Senators to finish a week earlier than the rest of the league (except for Philadelphia, whose schedule was tailored to fit Washington's) because Clark Griffith, feeling that his eighth-place Nats of 1944 could not possibly compete for the 1945 flag, had rented Griffith Stadium to a football team for the last Sunday in September.

To the surprise of the Old Fox, the Senators made a spirited bid for the pennant. With a pitching staff that featured four knuckleball pitchers—Dutch Leonard, Roger Wolff, Mickey Haefner and Johnny Niggeling—the Nats won 87 games and lost 67. Detroit, heading into St. Louis for two games on the final weekend, had a record of 87-65. Two St. Louis victories therefore would create a tie, making a playoff in Detroit necessary. Anticipating such a possibility—neither the Tigers nor the Senators had been overpowering down the stretch—Griff sent Wolff and three other players to the Motor City ahead of other team members. As the situation developed, Griff could have sent the players home.

Rain prevented the Saturday game in St. Louis, and a heavy mist delayed the start of the Sunday doubleheader by more than an hour. Then, after eight innings in the opener, the Browns led, 3-2. But a single, a bunt on which both runners were safe, a sacrifice and an intentional walk loaded the bases for the Tigers in the ninth, and Hank Greenberg, playing his 78th game following his return from the service, clouted a grand-slam home run to clinch the pennant. It mattered little that the second game was called.

The World Series between the Tigers and the Cubs did little to quicken the national heartbeat. A Chicago writer, asked to predict the outcome of the Series, reflected on the relative ineptitude of the two clubs and replied, "I don't think either team can win."

The observation was made in jest, of course, but the Tigers succeeded in winning in seven games. The pitching highlight was registered by Claude Passeau, the Chicago righthander who had been victimized by Ted Williams' All-Star Game homer four years earlier. In Game 3, Passeau held the Tigers to one hit, a second-inning single by Rudy York, in posting a 3-0 shutout.

Throughout the year there had been reports that a move was afoot to open the major leagues to black players. Brooklyn's Branch Rickey, it was disclosed, had joined with black representatives in an effort to break baseball's color line. A headline in The Sporting News announced: "Negro in O.B. Evolution, Not Revolution—B.R. / Two Insist on Tryouts by Dodgers / Test by Yankees and Giants Also Will be Asked, Says Accompanying Party."

By the end of October, the word was out: A black player would perform in Organized Baseball in 1946.

A new—and more bountiful—era was about to dawn.

Chicago Manager Charley Grimm (second from right) and player Phil Cavarretta listen to the ground rules before a game in the 1945 World Series, the last such appearance for a Cubs team.

The Feud Begins

A decision by the Spalding and Reach Sporting Goods companies to discontinue publication of the annual baseball guides opened the way for Taylor Spink to enter a new field in 1942.

Using his influence with major league club owners, the publisher induced Commissioner K.M. Landis to award him the contract to issue baseball's "official" guide. Although only three months remained before the start of the 1942 season, Spink produced his first guide (which actually bore a title of "Official Baseball Record Book") in about half the normal time required for such a project. The venture cost him about $4,000, but the compendium was well received by the public and Taylor felt well compensated when Landis conceded that the 50-cent guide was "a damn fine book."

In June 1942, the Saturday Evening Post published a feature by Stanley Frank on Spink and The Sporting News in which the publisher was acclaimed the "unofficial conscience, historian and watchdog" of baseball. In the article, titled "Mr. Baseball," the author wrote: "Spink is an energetic, plumpish, bull-voiced man of excellent digestion, and his furious labors in behalf of his favorite sport have earned for him the nickname of Mr. Baseball, a tag he likes so well he will probably have it chiseled on his tombstone."

Landis read the article and seethed. He regarded the nickname Mr. Baseball his alone, acquired through a divine right bestowed by the club owners. Still, he held his tongue.

Spink asked Dan Daniel to write a review of the story for the June 18 issue of The Sporting News. The New York correspondent agreed, with the provision that it appear precisely as he wrote it. Spink accepted the terms.

In his review, Dan hit all of the typewriter keys and hyberbole flowed. This time, Landis read and erupted. Dan had turned the commissioner into a subaltern. It was time for retribution. While he was helpless to erase the printed word, Landis could exercise his authority in another way. He stripped Spink of the right to publish the "*Official* Baseball Guide." That honor was accorded the Judge's office staff.

The "unofficial historian" rolled with the punch. In 1943, Spink produced a "Baseball Guide" before the start of the season. Landis' staff, unfamiliar with the labyrinths of publishing, did not issue its guide until midseason, long after it had lost much of its usefulness.

The commissioner's office did not publish a guide in 1944, but attempted to correct the omission by including the records of two seasons in a 1945 publication. Meanwhile, TSN continued to publish "Baseball Guides" without the "official" designation.

Early in the reign of Commissioner Albert B. Chandler, the "official" imprimatur was restored to The Sporting News, which has published "Official Baseball Guides" without interruption since that time (1947).

A 1942 story in the Saturday Evening Post entitled 'Bible of Baseball' aroused the wrath of Commissioner Kenesaw Mountain Landis by calling Taylor Spink 'Mr. Baseball.' Accompanying the story was a picture of The Sporting News publisher (left), telephone in hand, at his desk in the TSN office.

A St. Louis newsstand (right), possibly with a little nudge from Spink, was quick to jump on the local publication's bandwagon. Promotion was notable in Louisville (below), too.

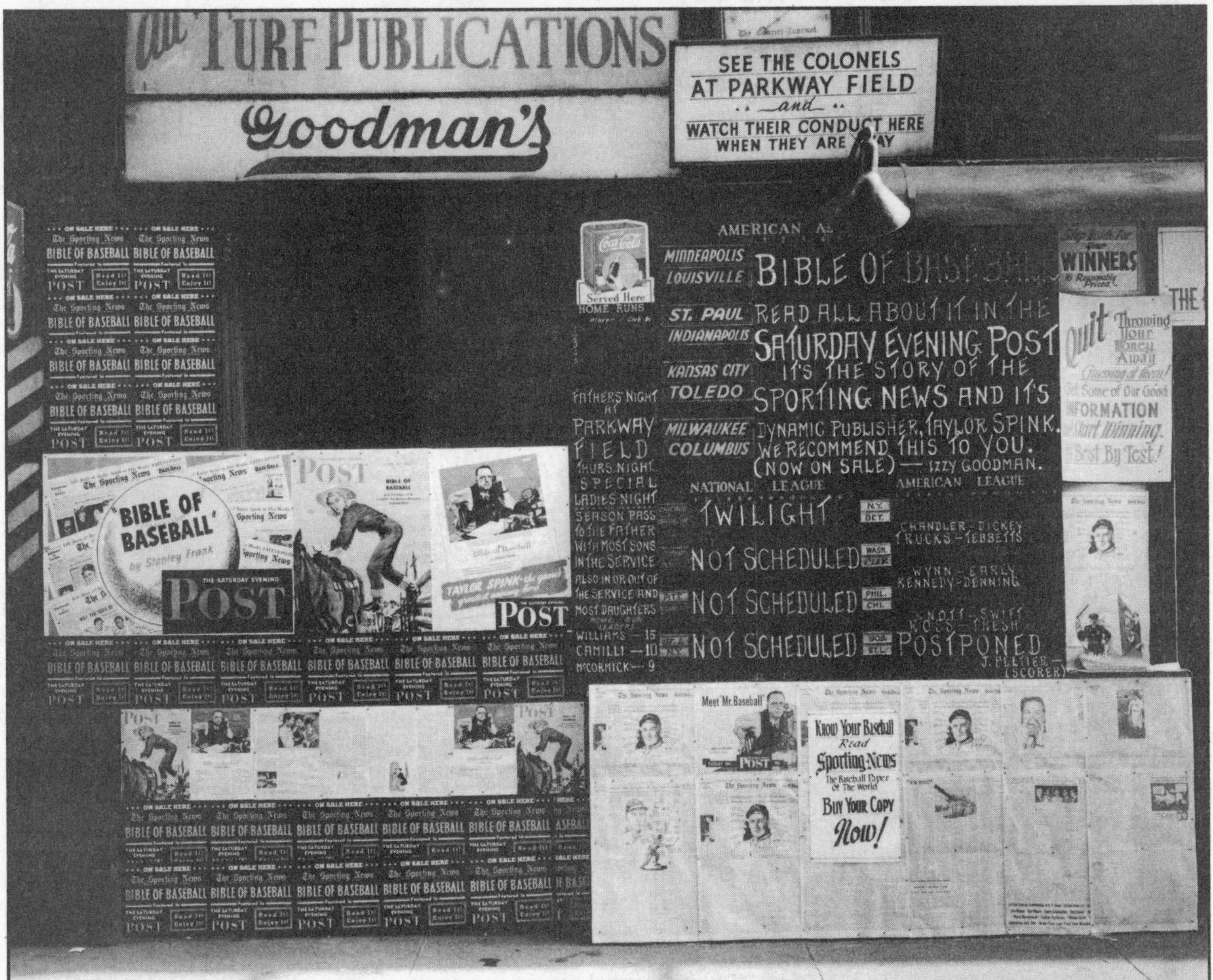

TSN's Library Expands

GIANTS BLOW HEAVY DOUGH FOR BOWMAN

PURCHASE FROM CARDS BUT ONE MOVE IN DRESSING-UP DRIVE

Signing of Hartnett Does Not Mean He'll Eventually Succeed Terry as Pilot, Yankees Sell Jake Powell

CHICAGO, Ill.—Things are beginning to look up for the Giants. They came here determined to continue the good work they started in Atlanta, where they acquired Bob Bowman, righthander, from the liquidating Cardinals for anything from $25,000 to $50,000 in cash, depending on your own optimism and impression of player values. In part payment, the Cards got Hy Vandenberg, righthander, for their Rochester farm. Van may turn up with the Cards, but as a chattel of the Giants he showed quite definitely that the International League was his class.

Having got Bowman, the Giants made a move toward Hank Leiber and Claude Passeau, of the Cubs, for whom they would give Harry Danning. If this deal cooks up here, Billy Herman, definitely on the block, may become involved in some way.

With Bowman and Passeau added to the pitching staff, Herman for second base and Orengo to help out at short if Billy Jurges fails to come through; with Whitey Moore coming from the Reds for Mickey Witek—another deal that was brought here from Atlanta—the New York club would look real fancy, what?

The Yankees sold Jake Powell to San Francisco during the Atlanta session, but other than that they have done nothing. The passing of Powell means that the Yanks have decided to give a job to Tommy Holmes, late of Newark. Or, that they have a deal in the fire for another experienced outfielder. Holmes is a New York boy who has gone right through the farm mill, and while not a long hitter, gets a lot of singles and can do a fine job in the field.

The Giants got Gabby Hartnett in the Atlanta grab-bag. At least the story came out in Atlanta, but the deal was arranged long before that. After the yarn had been printed all over the country, Eddie Brannick said the news was premature. It seems the story was being held for Chicago, and besides, the official papers making Hartnett a free agent had not yet come through. However, the Hartnett yarn was no Atlanta product any more than was the Brooklyn deal for Mickey Owen, which for some reason best known to the strategic MacPhail, kept cooking for three weeks.

More to That Highe Deal

There must have been another deal with the Owen affair. In any event, the dope now is that Brooklyn got Frank Melton along with Kirby Higbe from the Phillies, and that because of the holler in Philadelphia, Gerry Nugent will have to make another trade with MacPhail, and announce the exchange of Melton for Alex Kampouris.

In Atlanta, the Giants got early attention with the signing of Hartnett, who is to be a coach and player. There is some doubt as to whether Travis Jackson will be back for the 1941 season. He has been ill and may sit out next campaign.

Hartnett is to do some catching, especially if Danning is dealt off, and also will coach and pinch hit against lefthanded hurlers.

In some quarters, the acquisition of Hartnett revived the old yarn about Terry's going to the front office.

Some of the dopesters even have it that Stoneham may pay off Terry for 1941 and 1942, and let Gabby run the club.

All this does not scan. We are not familiar with the personal feelings of Stoneham and Terry toward each other. But we do know this—Terry will manage the Giants in 1941 and 1942 and very likely thereafter. Stoneham is not shelling out $80,000 to send Terry on his way. Terry has a civil contract at $42,500 a season.

In short, all that stuff concerning Terry is plain bunk. Hartnett was a flop as a manager in Chicago and he would not be likely ...

SHOP BY AIR MAIL FOR YOUR BASEBALL FRIENDS!

Have The Postman Bring Them These Ideal Baseball Gifts . . . Subscription to THE SPORTING NEWS . . . Plus the Baseball Register or An Ash Tray From Joe DiMaggio's Restaurant

This combination made such a hit last year, it is again being offered. Here is a Baseball Gift that will be prized by your Baseball Friend. Choice of two novel presents. An attractive Christmas card, bearing your name, will announce each gift. Provided we receive your order in time, this card will arrive at Christmas, so please send by Air Mail.

WANT ONE OF THESE GIFTS FOR YOURSELF?

Put a check mark in square below:

[ ]

and check on the "Friend No. 1" order blank the gift you would like to receive. Then leave this page folded open where a gift-baffled wife, sweetheart, relative or friend will be sure to see it. They may take the hint — and welcome such a money-saving opportunity!

Authentic Guide Book to the Game's Stars

Size 6 by 9 inches. A book any fan will be proud to own. Close-up and full-length pictures of outstanding players in the majors. Lifetime playing records in detail, nationalities of stars of today and yesterday, their hobbies, facsimiles of their autographs. Club and individual records. World's Series data, from the inception of the inter-league classic; best performances and other interesting facts. History of Baseball, story of Museum at Cooperstown, etc., etc.

A FRESH GIFT EVERY WEEK OF THE YEAR!

53 GIFTS . . . 53 REMINDERS
For fifty-two weeks, the postman will bring your friend a regular copy of THE SPORTING NEWS, brimming with all the latest, authoritative news of the world of baseball — a weekly reminder of your Christmas good-will. And just as your friend's interest in the new baseball season quickens, he will receive his copy of the new Baseball Register. This new book — a big hit on its introduction last year, size 6 x 9 inches — contains complete data on important players, together with pictures and records brought up to date to include the 1940 season. A handsome Christmas card, bearing your name, will announce this gift, while the book itself will be delivered fresh from the presses on or about February 1. The Register alone is priced at $1.00; a year's subscription to THE SPORTING NEWS costs $5.00 — but our Christmas gift combination offer brings both at the special value of only $4.

ATTRACTIVE GIFT CARD BEARING YOUR NAME SENT TO YOUR BASEBALL FRIENDS

REMEMBER that an attractive Christmas card bearing your name will be sent to your friend, explaining the gift you have selected for him, and telling what is in store for him when receiving THE SPORTING NEWS week after week.

Joe with one of his ash trays

The Ash Tray — It Is in Three Colors

$2.00 BRINGS THE DiMAGGIO ASH TRAY and 26 ISSUES OF THE SPORTING NEWS

An ash tray bearing a picture of Joe DiMaggio in uniform is a prized souvenir of a visit to Joe's famous restaurant on the Wharf at San Francisco. You can have one of these ash trays mailed direct from the City of the Golden Gate to your friend — and send him a twenty-six-week subscription to THE SPORTING NEWS — all for only $2.00! (Regular price of six-month subscription: $2.50.) Because ash tray orders must be forwarded to San Francisco, please order immediately.

RUSH ORDER FORM BY AIR MAIL

THE SPORTING NEWS,
10th and Olive Streets,
St. Louis, Missouri

Please send The Sporting News CHRISTMAS GIFT COMBINATION I have selected for each of the friends' names at right. I enclose check or money order in payment.

MY NAME ....

MY ADDRESS ....

FRIEND No. 1	FRIEND No. 2
NAME	NAME ....
ADDRESS	ADDRESS ....
Send him the gift checked below:	Send him the gift checked below:
[ ] Baseball Register and 52 copies of The Sporting News ($4.00)	[ ] Baseball Register and 52 copies of The Sporting News ($4.00)

On December 12, 1940, readers were offered either a copy of TSN's new 'Baseball Register' or an ash tray from Joe DiMaggio's restaurant with a subscription to The Sporting News.

For more than a quarter of a century, dating back to the early 1900s, The Sporting News published an annual "Record Book," measuring approximately 3 by 5 inches and containing about 100 pages.

The booklet, which sold for 5 cents, was the forerunner of the "Official Baseball Guide" and included a review of the past baseball season, schedules for the upcoming season, statistics and some added features, such as the poem "Casey at the Bat."

In 1940, Taylor Spink expanded his publishing operations. He introduced the "Baseball Register" (which later would carry an "official" designation). The 6-by-9-inch book of more than 200 pages contained, according to an advertisement, "closeup and full-length pictures of outstanding players in the majors, lifetime playing records in detail, source of nicknames, hobbies and other interesting information."

The playing records of more than 200 active major leaguers and more than 30 former stars were included, plus major league coaches and 15 of the 16 managers. The missing managerial record was that of Bill Terry of the New York Giants.

In assembling the material for the book, Spink decided to add an extra frill—the signature of each individual to accompany his record. Terry was slow in replying to Spink's request for his autograph. The publisher went to his favorite instrument, the telephone, and this conversation followed:

Spink: "Where's your autograph?"

Terry: "Do you plan to sell the book?"

Spink: "Why, of course, I do."

Terry: "And do you plan to

The Sporting News library continued to expand during this time period with the addition of the 'Baseball Guide,' the 'Ready Reckoner' and 'How To Score.'

make a profit?"

Spink: "That's a stupid question, why certainly I do."

Terry: "Well, if you plan to make a profit, then my signature should be worth something. What am I offered?"

Spink: "Not a damn cent."

As a result of Terry's intransigence, his signature did not appear in the first Register. His record did appear, however, in the 1941 edition, sans autograph.

At a time when a year's subscription to The Sporting News cost $5, readers were offered the Register—and a 12-month subscription—for $4 in a special Christmas arrangement.

Another publication introduced during this period was "How to Score," a guide to the professional system for tracking the progress of a game.

TSN Becomes Tabloid

Shortly after the United States entered World War II, Taylor Spink demonstrated the same initiative and acumen that he had exhibited in the earlier war.

On a visit to Washington, he persuaded the War Department to authorize The Sporting News to publish an eight-page overseas edition which was flown to foreign countries where American servicemen were stationed. To conserve newsprint, the edition was printed in tabloid form.

Later, Spink arranged with the Liggett & Myers Tobacco Co. to publish a weekly Chesterfield edition that was similar to the overseas edition and was distributed to military installations in the United States as well as military and veterans hospitals.

The reduced size of these wartime editions met with a hearty reception. The convenience in handling was a major factor and Spink reacted quickly. In the last issue of June 1943, there appeared an announcement that bore the caption, "The Sporting News Streamlines."

Readers were informed: "Keeping step with the times and cooperating with the Government in the conservation of paper, The Sporting News, beginning with the next issue, will be streamlined and issued in tabloid form. This is a radical step, for throughout more than half a century of continuous publication, The Sporting News has maintained the conventional newspaper size and it is like parting with a tried and true friend to leave it now, but wartime restrictions and new conditions necessitate a change."

While assuring patrons that TSN would continue "comprehensive coverage of everything worthwhile," the notice added: "The change to a tabloid, in reality, marks another step forward, as it assures . . . brighter, breezier, more sprightly chronicling of the doings of the diamond than was possible

BASEBALL — ALL SPORTS

The Sporting News

THE BASE BALL PAPER OF THE WORLD

VOLUME 115, NUMBER 21 — ST. LOUIS, JULY 1, 1943 — FIFTEEN CENTS

LOOPING THE LOOPS

By J. G. T. SPINK

Pre-Fourth Fire Crackers

'Better Team in L. A.' Shaft Gets Cub Rise

Gallagher Grins, Jabs Back at Needling Lefty O'Doul of San Francisco

By ED BURNS

CHICAGO, Ill.

B. R. Disowns Sunday 2-for-1

Lays Synthetic Bill to Breadon

NEXT — ALL-STAR ISSUE

One of the biggest changes in the history of The Sporting News occurred on July 1, 1943, when the publication produced its first tabloid issue.

with a standard newspaper, while at the same time it enables the editors to meet the requirements of the Government during the emergency, without sacrificing any of the features that have caused the publication to be known as the 'Bible of Baseball.' "

The first tabloid issue of 32 pages was dated July 1, 1943. An editorial observed that in the new format "completeness and accuracy are retained—reader interest is increased."

In an accompanying column, Tom Meany of New York wrote: "The change is as startling as though the players suddenly started running the bases clockwise.

"The Sporting News is to be commended for making this change . . . because it may serve to point the way to changes to other baseball conventions, badly in need of a streamlining in these parlous and swiftly moving times."

Pointing out that writers and players peruse TSN as avidly as financiers follow stock reports, Meany continued: "I've been traveling with ball clubs for 20 years and one of the oddest sights I saw was last year on a train ride from Chicago to St. Louis with the

Announcement of the pending change in size was made June 24, 1943 (right). The change, inspired by wartime restrictions that prompted TSN to send special tabloid issues of its product overseas, was received well by many readers and advertisers (above right). Chesterfield, which advertised on the back cover of TSN for many years, ran a special ad in August 1943 picturing the overseas-bound special edition.

The Sporting News Streamlines

KEEPING step with the times and co-operating with the Government in the conservation of paper, THE SPORTING NEWS, beginning with the next issue, will be streamlined and issued in tabloid form. This is a radical step, for throughout more than half a century of continuous publication, THE SPORTING NEWS has maintained the conventional newspaper size and it is like parting with a tried and true friend to leave it now, but wartime restrictions and new conditions necessitate a change.

Although the dress and format will be different, the comprehensive coverage of everything worthwhile happening in the baseball world will be continued, with box scores, averages, features, news articles, pictures, highlights, personal notes, dope stories as complete as they have been in the past, only presented more concisely and compactly. Throughout 57 years, THE SPORTING NEWS has constantly sought to provide authentic, accurate and complete news coverage, always seeking to improve its service, so as to make it truly representative of the great national pastime and there have been no steps backward.

The change to a tabloid, in reality, marks another step forward, as it assures our readers of brighter, breezier and more sprightly chronicling of the doings on the diamond than was possible with a standard-sized newspaper, while, at the same time, it enables the editors to meet the requirements of the Government during the emergency without sacrificing any of the features that have caused the publication to become known as the "Bible of Baseball." Thus, obligations both to our readers and to the country are being fully met in the adoption of the new policy.

As in the past, nothing will be spared in the way of expense, labor and intelligence to give our readers the best possible coverage and to carry on the tradition of service that has made THE SPORTING NEWS unique not only in the field of sports, but in the weekly publication field, as well.

We hope you will like your new copy of THE SPORTING NEWS—and we believe you will. THE PUBLISHERS.

Dodgers. Coaches Chuck Dressen and Red Corriden were sharing a bedroom. Dressen was reading Red to sleep with items from The Sporting News and I think Charley got all the way down to the standings of the clubs in the West Texas-New Mexico League before Corriden finally dozed off."

'Baseball's Savior'

When, at the start of World War II, Franklin Delano Roosevelt wrote his famous "Green Light" letter to Commissioner Kenesaw M. Landis, the President earned the deep gratitude and undying admiration of The Sporting News.

In the communication, dated January 15, 1942, F.D.R. said: "I honestly feel it would be best for the country to keep baseball going. There will be fewer people unemployed and everybody will work longer hours and harder than ever before.

"And that means that they ought to have a chance for recreation and for taking their minds off their work even more than before.

"Incidentally, I hope that night games can be extended because it gives an opportunity to the day shift to see a game occasionally."

In its issue of January 22, The Sporting News reproduced the letter across three columns on page 1. Underneath, an article by Taylor Spink carried the headline: "Player of the Year / President Bestows a Signal Honor—and Responsibility—on Game."

Through the next several years, TSN frequently hailed the President for his congenial attitude toward professional baseball and in April 1945, following his death, Roosevelt was eulogized in an editorial as "Baseball's Savior."

"But for him," asserted the publication, "the game would have been forced out of business for the duration. So close was his contact with the sport, so tremendously important his friendship and support that, as much as some of the non-playing figures now enshrined in baseball's Hall of Fame, the deceased President deserves a niche at Cooperstown, N.Y."

In May 1945, the paper devoted its editorial columns to "An Open Letter to Hall of Fame Committee" by Taylor Spink. In it, the publisher reminded the electors that prior to their recent meeting, he had sent them telegrams advocating the election of F.D.R. to the Hall of Fame. While 10 old-time figures were chosen, the wartime President was not among them.

After reciting the dire consequences to baseball if Roosevelt had not intervened in 1942, the editorial continued: "You not only enjoy the right and the power, but you have the commission, from baseball itself, from its fans, from its past and its present, from its bright destinies to name Mr. Roosevelt at your next meeting.

"Next meeting? Why not now? You could achieve this by a mail vote. The time is ripe, the occasion is now, the call for action is insistent."

Two issues later, another editorial, urging enshrinement for Roosevelt, was published. But the committee turned a deaf ear and while his picture appeared on war bonds and his likeness on a new dime, the President never was honored by the game he helped to save during World War II.

President Franklin D. Roosevelt helped open the 1935 season at Washington's Griffith Stadium.

Franklin D. Roosevelt had a long association with baseball that earned him the undying admiration of The Sporting News. Roosevelt was Assistant Secretary of the Navy (above) when he marched ahead of Washington players in a 1917 opening-day salute to the war effort. The President, pictured (below) in a Willard Mullin cartoon, wrote his famous 'Green Light' letter (right) in 1942.

PRESIDENT
ROOSEVELT
AT POLO GROUNDS..
PROVES MASCOT AGAIN
FOR AMERICAN LEAGUE
Willard Mullin

THE WHITE HOUSE
WASHINGTON

January 15, 1942.

My dear Judge:-

Thank you for yours of January fourteenth. As you will, of course, realize the final decision about the baseball season must rest with you and the Baseball Club owners -- so what I am going to say is solely a personal and not an official point of view.

I honestly feel that it would be best for the country to keep baseball going. There will be fewer people unemployed and everybody will work longer hours and harder than ever before.

And that means that they ought to have a chance for recreation and for taking their minds off their work even more than before.

Baseball provides a recreation which does not last over two hours or two hours and a half, and which can be got for very little cost. And, incidentally, I hope that night games can be extended because it gives an opportunity to the day shift to see a game occasionally.

As to the players themselves, I know you agree with me that individual players who are of active military or naval age should go, without question, into the services. Even if the actual quality of the teams is lowered by the greater use of older players, this will not dampen the popularity of the sport. Of course, if any individual has some particular aptitude in a trade or profession, he ought to serve the Government. That, however, is a matter which I know you can handle with complete justice.

Here is another way of looking at it -- if 300 teams use 5,000 or 6,000 players, these players are a definite recreational asset to at least 20,000,000 of their fellow citizens -- and that in my judgment is thoroughly worthwhile.

With every best wish,

Very sincerely yours,

Franklin D Roosevelt

Hon. Kenesaw M. Landis,
333 North Michigan Avenue,
Chicago,
Illinois.

Like to See Cooperstown?

AND THEN MAKE A STOPOVER IN N. Y. FOR TWO GAMES OF WORLD'S SERIES!

★ ★ ★

Here's First Crossword Puzzle on Hall of Fame Immortals

★ ★ ★

FREE - - Visit Birthplace of Game and Museum - - FIRST PRIZE

SECOND PRIZE – $50 War Bond; THIRD PRIZE – $25 War Bond
20 Other Prizes – Including Ten One-Year Subscriptions
to THE SPORTING NEWS and Ten Copies of the BASEBALL REGISTER

★ ★ ★

TRY THIS FASCINATING GAME FOR FANS --YOU MAY WIN THE TRIP OF A LIFETIME!

HOW MUCH do you know about the game's immortals? Here is a chance to prove—and improve—your knowledge of these diamond greats, and at the same time win a thrilling vacation trip, or another valuable prize!

For eight weeks, THE SPORTING NEWS will publish crossword puzzles based on the 24 immortals already named to Baseball's Hall of Fame, with three of these men covered in each installment. Missing words relate to their lives, careers and service to the game, or, wherever possible, to some event connected with the sport.

Even if you don't know much about the Hall of Famers, don't let that stop you from entering the contest. It's a chance to learn a lot about these immortals of baseball and at the same time to win a visit to the birthplace of the game, with all expenses paid, or to qualify for 22 other desirable prizes, including a $50 war bond offered as second prize and a $25 war bond as third prize.

• • •

A Glorious Vacation Trip Without Cost

A TRIP to Cooperstown, N. Y., offers a thrilling experience. Located in New York's picturesque lake country, abounding in scenic beauty, Cooperstown is an historic site for both the nation and the game. Here James Fenimore Cooper lived, and here he wrote and laid the scenes of many of his historic "Leather Stocking" novels. But to baseball followers, Cooperstown has even greater significance. It was here that General Abner Doubleday, as a young man, first laid out the modern diamond. It is here that the game's Hall of Fame and Museum are situated. In the Hall of Fame are preserved the names and records of 24 immortals of baseball, while the Museum offers a wealth of souvenirs—uniforms, equipment and other mementoes of the national pastime.

• • •

The Privilege of Naming Your Own Immortals

MANY believe baseball has omitted from the Hall of Fame names of players, umpires, officials and writers who made valuable contributions to the game and should be remembered. Here is your chance to register your choices, the only time and place such an opportunity has been offered. All nominations will be noted and the selections of the fans, as represented by the contestants, will be compiled and ranked, so that those in charge of naming the members will know whom the followers of the game think should be included. It is asked that five who were known in the previous century and five moderns be nominated in the order participants believe they should be ranked.

• • •

Lots of Fun

CROSSWORD PUZZLE NO. 1

Name of Hall of Fame Member ____________

Name of Hall of Fame Member ____________

Name of Hall of Fame Member ____________

YOUR NAME ____________

STREET ____________

CITY ____________ STATE ____________

ACROSS

1. Member of Hall of Fame who organized first baseball club.
10. State in which he was born (abbr.).
12. That which he organized and for which he played was called the Knickerbockers.
13. Month in which he was born.
14. Islands (then called Sandwich) to which he carried baseball in pioneer days (abbr.).
15. His baseball rules were first tried out in game between Knickerbockers and N. Y. Nine, Hoboken, N. J., in 1846.
16. Slang term for home plate.
18. Number of games in which 1 Across participated in 1845.
19. League organized in 1876 (abbr.).
20. Outfielder in Hall of Fame who started [illegible]

DOWN

1. Initials of present owner of Washington club.
2. 30 Across played for Highlanders in this circuit (abbr.).
3. 20 Across holds major league record for most of these in one season—177 (sing.).
4. As batsman, he was credited with 457 for column headed thus (a record) in 1921.
5. Games are sometimes called because of this.
6. As major league pitcher, 20 Across had 1,220 for column headed thus.
7. Nickname for one of minor league clubs for which he played (sing.).
8. 30 Across was successful as place-hitter because he "[illegible] 'em where they ain't."

Spink Turns to Promotions

As the nation's industries functioned at maximum capacity during the emergency of the 1940s, so did Taylor Spink's prowess for increasing circulation and revenue.

One promotion followed another as the publisher devised scheme after scheme to create awareness of his baseball weekly.

Spink organized The Sporting News Fans Club, with Bucky Walters, Cincinnati pitcher, as the national president. For an annual membership of $5, one could receive a one-year subscription to The Sporting News, copies of the "Baseball Register" and the "Record Book" and free answers to 25 questions a year.

After five years of membership, the fan was promised the two books, free answers to 40 questions and a silver membership card for $4 annually.

Ten years of membership entitled a person to the two books, answers to 50 questions without charge and a gold membership card, all for $3 a year.

Crossword puzzles were an annual feature. In 1942, a series of puzzles based on Hall of Fame members offered to the winner an all-expense-paid trip to Cooperstown, N.Y., plus a stopover in New York City for two games of the World Series.

The Sporting News also encouraged reader involvement in issues of the day. Once readers were asked if they thought the game should continue in the face of increased demands for wartime manpower. The response was overwhelmingly affirmative, 6,221 to 172.

Another time, readers were asked if they preferred an increased night-game schedule. Once more the response was convincingly in favor.

When the U.S. government announced a second war loan campaign, Taylor Spink offered a substantial saving on a five-year

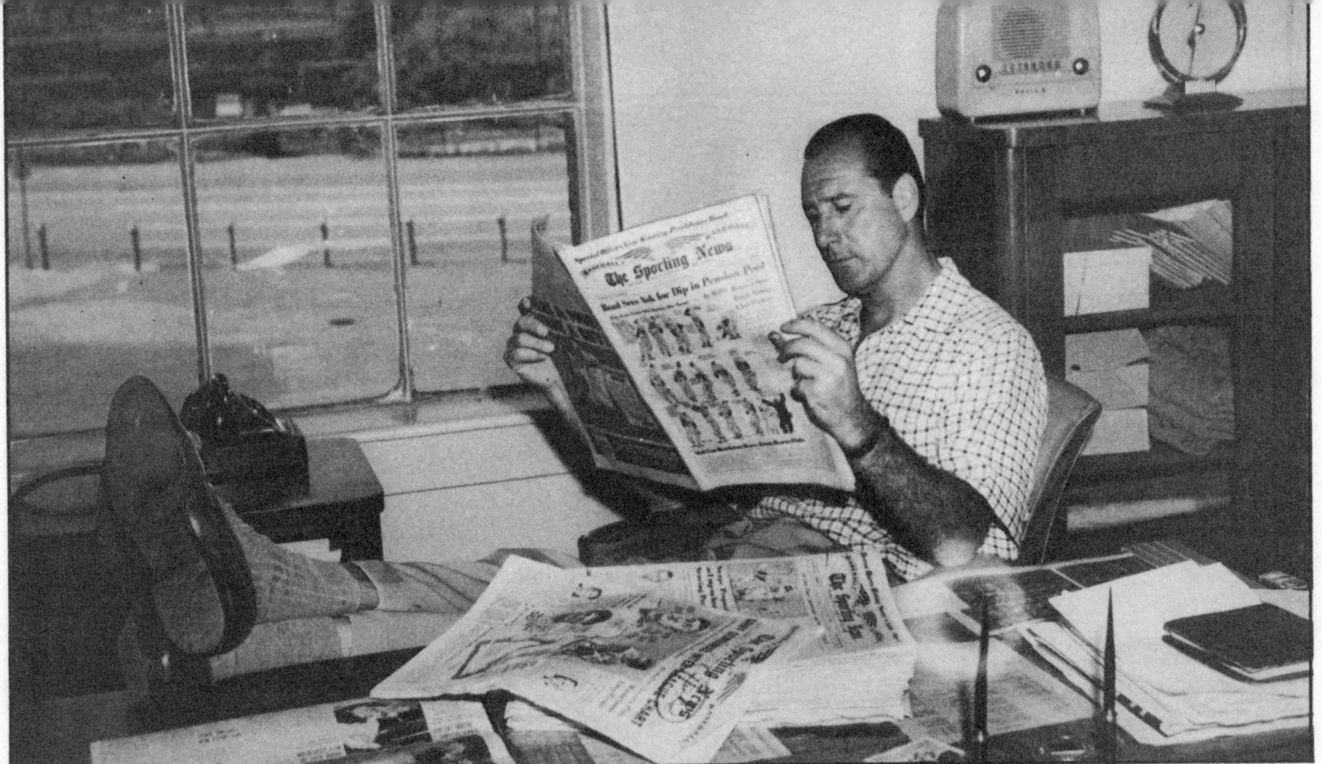

When the U.S. became involved in World War II, J.G. Taylor Spink devised promotional schemes to keep readers interested in The Sporting News. Crossword puzzles (left) appeared annually, cash prizes were offered for the best letters in response to polls (above right) and five-year subscriptions were offered for one $25 U.S. war bond. The best bargain of all, however, came in 1941 when Spink offered a lifetime TSN subscription for $25. Among those who jumped at the offer was Detroit first baseman Hank Greenberg (above).

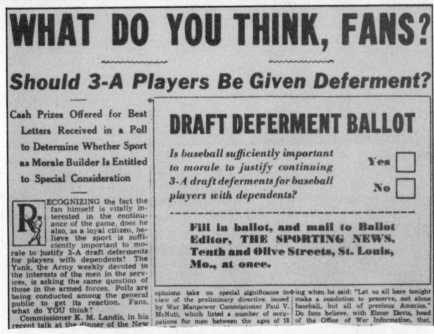

WHAT DO YOU THINK, FANS?

Should 3-A Players Be Given Deferment?

Cash Prizes Offered for Best Letters Received in a Poll to Determine Whether Sport as Morale Builder Is Entitled to Special Consideration

DRAFT DEFERMENT BALLOT

Is baseball sufficiently important to morale to justify continuing 3-A draft deferments for baseball players with dependents?

Yes ☐

No ☐

Fill in ballot, and mail to Ballot Editor, THE SPORTING NEWS, Tenth and Olive Streets, St. Louis, Mo., at once.

RECOGNIZING the fact the fan himself is vitally interested in the continuance of the game, does he also, as a loyal citizen, believe the sport is sufficiently important to morale to justify 3-A draft deferments for players with dependents? The Yank, the Army weekly devoted to the interests of the men in the services, is asking the same question of those in the armed forces. Polls are being conducted among the general public to get its reaction. Fans, what do YOU think?

Commissioner K. M. Landis, in his recent talk at the dinner of the New

opinions take on special significance in view of the preliminary directive, issued by War Manpower Commissioner Paul V. McNutt, which listed a number of occupations for men between the ages of 18

ing when he said: "Let us all here tonight make a resolution to preserve, not alone baseball, but all of precious America." Do fans believe, with Elmer Davis, head of the Office of War Information, that,

subscription to the purchaser of a $25 war bond, with proof of purchase.

No bargain, however, equalled that of 1941 when Spink, in a gesture of incomparable generosity, offered a lifetime subscription to The Sporting News for $25.

One of the first to leap at the bait was Hank Greenberg, slugging first baseman-outfielder of the Detroit Tigers. Then an infantryman at Fort Custer, Mich., the future Hall of Famer took the lifetime offer and received a return of approximately $600 on his investment over the next 45 years.

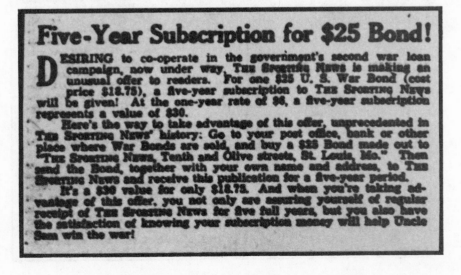

Five-Year Subscription for $25 Bond!

DESIRING to co-operate in the government's second war loan campaign, now under way, THE SPORTING NEWS is making an unusual offer to readers. For one $25 U. S. War Bond (cost price $18.75), a five-year subscription to THE SPORTING NEWS will be given! At the one-year rate of $6, a five-year subscription represents a value of $30.

Here's the way to take advantage of this offer, unprecedented in THE SPORTING NEWS' history: Go to your post office, bank or other place where War Bonds are sold, and buy a $25 Bond made out to "THE SPORTING NEWS, Tenth and Olive streets, St. Louis, Mo." Then send the Bond, together with your own name and address, to THE SPORTING NEWS and receive this publication for a five-year period.

It's a $30 value for only $18.75. And when you're taking advantage of this offer, you not only are assuring yourself of regular receipt of THE SPORTING NEWS for five full years, but you also have the satisfaction of knowing your subscription money will help Uncle Sam win the war!

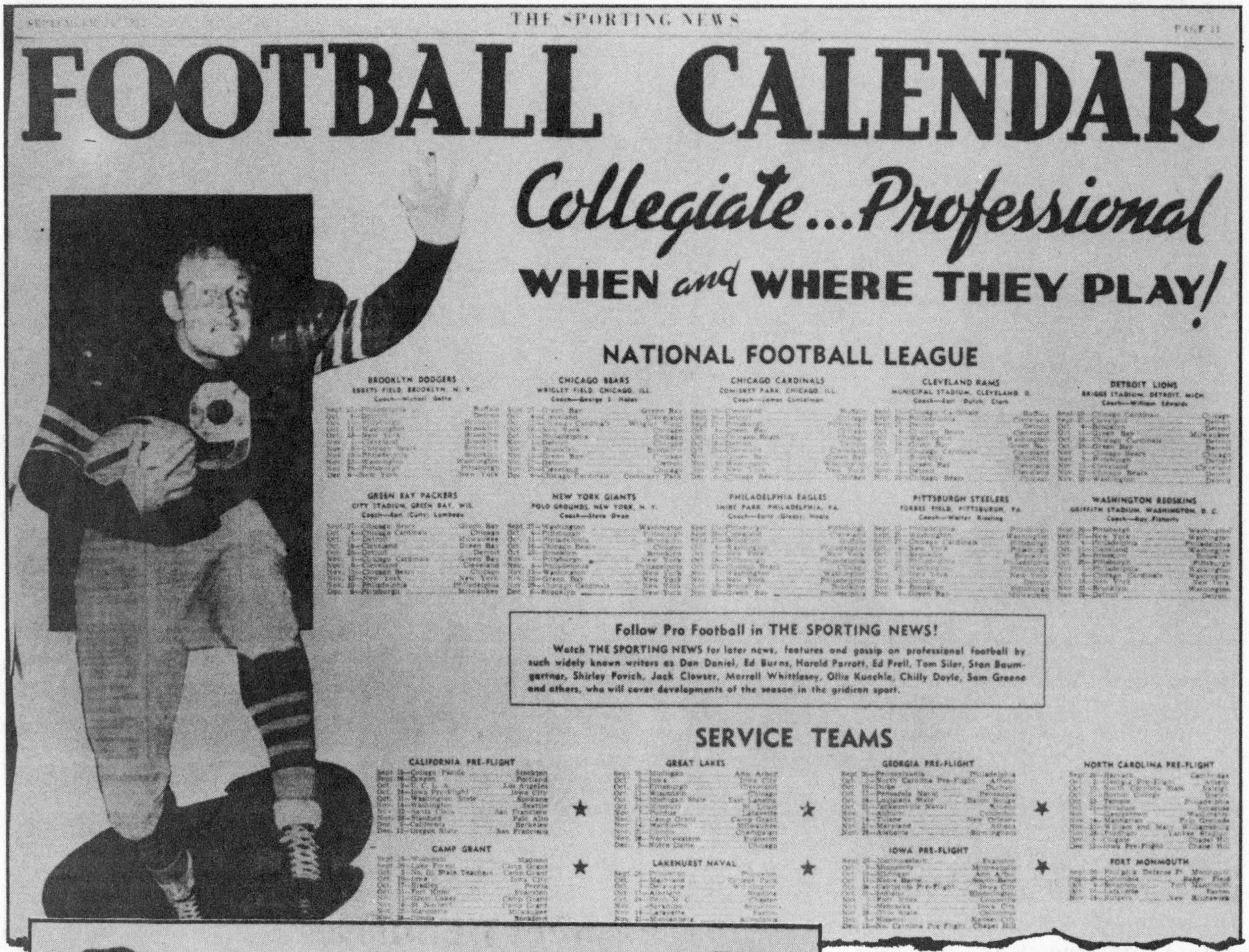

THE SPORTING NEWS

FOOTBALL CALENDAR

Collegiate...Professional

WHEN and WHERE THEY PLAY!

NATIONAL FOOTBALL LEAGUE

BROOKLYN DODGERS — EBBETS FIELD, BROOKLYN, N. Y.

CHICAGO BEARS — WRIGLEY FIELD, CHICAGO, ILL.

CHICAGO CARDINALS — COMISKEY PARK, CHICAGO, ILL.

CLEVELAND RAMS — MUNICIPAL STADIUM, CLEVELAND, O.

DETROIT LIONS — BRIGGS STADIUM, DETROIT, MICH.

GREEN BAY PACKERS — CITY STADIUM, GREEN BAY, WIS.

NEW YORK GIANTS — POLO GROUNDS, NEW YORK, N. Y. — Coach—Steve Owen

PHILADELPHIA EAGLES — SHIBE PARK, PHILADELPHIA, PA.

PITTSBURGH STEELERS — FORBES FIELD, PITTSBURGH, PA. — Coach—Walter Kiesling

WASHINGTON REDSKINS — GRIFFITH STADIUM, WASHINGTON, D. C.

Follow Pro Football in THE SPORTING NEWS!

Watch THE SPORTING NEWS for later news, features and gossip on professional football by such widely known writers as Dan Daniel, Ed Burns, Harold Parrott, Ed Prell, Tom Siler, Stan Baumgartner, Shirley Povich, Jack Clowser, Morrell Whittlesey, Ollie Kuechle, Chilly Doyle, Sam Greene and others, who will cover developments of the season in the gridiron sport.

SERVICE TEAMS

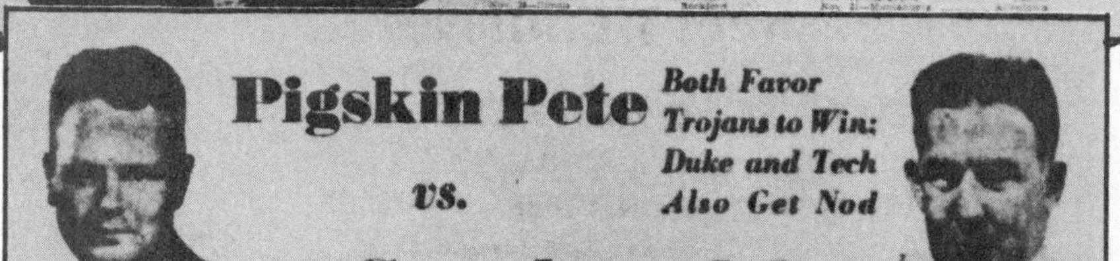

CALIFORNIA PRE-FLIGHT

GREAT LAKES

GEORGIA PRE-FLIGHT

NORTH CAROLINA PRE-FLIGHT

CAMP GRANT

LAKEHURST NAVAL

IOWA PRE-FLIGHT

FORT MONMOUTH

Fred Russell

Pigskin Pete vs. Grandstand Gus

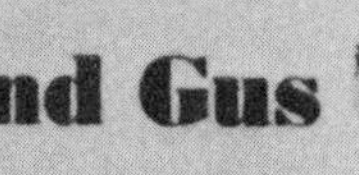

Both Favor Trojans to Win: Duke and Tech Also Get Nod

Rube Samuelson

Described by his paper as the "South's No. 1 sports writer," Fred Russell, sports editor of the Nashville, Tenn., Banner, picks up the ball as Pigskin Pete for the annual bowl game prognostications. A Vanderbilt law school graduate, Russell doffed his legal robes after two years to join the Banner sports staff in 1929. He became sports editor the next year. Fred has covered major football games for 15 years and is southern representative on Grantland Rice's All-America Board. Though Russell also has contributed sports stories to leading national magazines, his greatest thrill was non-sports—an exclusive interview in 1936 with Kidnapper Thomas H. Robinson, No. 1 Public Enemy and fugitive for 19 months. Russell is author of "Fifty Years of Vanderbilt Football," and and also writes a daily column, called "Sideline Sidelights."

Here are Russell's dish-by-dish choices:

Rose Bowl: Southern California 26, Tennessee 13.

The Vols seem to have trouble defending against the T-Formation, but their Buster Stephens breaks loose a few times.

Sugar Bowl: Duke 13, Alabama 7.

The V-12 Blue Devils' power and manpower will overcome the passing of the civilian Tiders.

Orange Bowl: Georgia Tech 21, Tulsa 13.

Two clever, slick ball-handling clubs in action here. It's a question of which way the ball bounces.

Cotton Bowl: Oklahoma A. & M. 27, Texas Christian 7.

Just too much Bob Fenimore, that's all.

Sun Bowl: Southwestern 13, U. of Mexico 6.

Strictly a guess.

Shrine Game: East 14, West 7.

Les Horvath & Company are too versatile offensively for the Pacific Coasters.

In assuming the role of Grandstand Gus for the annual task of selecting the winners of Bowl games, Rube Samuelsen provides a lofty touch, since most of his grandstanding has been done from the high perch of Pacific Coast press boxes. As sports editor of the Pasadena, Calif., Star-News and Pasadena Post, Samuelsen has been covering the Rose Bowl classics since 1928 and major Coast grid clashes during the season. Samuelsen also is well known along the airlanes of the Far West, and has a weekly program for NBC's Pacific Coast network each Saturday at 5 p. m., called "Sports with Rube Samuelsen."

Here are Rube's New Year's Day choices:

Rose Bowl: Southern California 20, Tennessee 6.

Trojans always hot on New Year's Day. Finished season in blaze of glory, beating California and U. C. L. A. under wraps by one-sided scores.

Sugar Bowl: Duke 19, Alabama 6.

Duke, despite four defeats, rates as powerhouse. Record blemished because of drawing several of nation's top teams. 'Bama has good team, but far below prewar par of Tide hey-day elevens.

Orange Bowl: Georgia Tech 28, Tulsa 19.

Two high scoring teams. Both scores could go higher. Outside of lapse in Notre Dame game, Tech's record much better than Tulsa's.

Cotton Bowl: Oklahoma A. & M. 26, Texas Christian 6.

Aggies' class stands out in comparison with Horned Frogs. T. C. U. hit bottom at season's end.

Sun Bowl: Southwestern 19, U. of Mexico 6.

Mexico best in own country, but still not strong enough for also-ran in Southwestern.

Shrine Game: East 19, West 0.

East has much better material from which to choose. West can't match Horvath, Hackett, Kelly, et al.

Among the early football features in TSN were a calendar with pro and college schedules and a predictions column entitled 'Pigskin Pete.'

'Football Next Week'

To those who regarded The Sporting News as the inviolate domain of professional baseball, the announcement in the issue of September 17, 1942, came as a soul-stirring shock.

"FOOTBALL NEXT WEEK" proclaimed an advertisement. Revealing that the paper for many years had received requests to publish news of football on a limited scale, the ad promised: "The Sporting News will start such coverage

1944 GRID RESULTS

ALABAMA
27—L. S. U. 27
63—Howard 7
55—Millsaps 0
0—Tennessee 0
41—Kentucky 0
7—Georgia 14
34—Mississippi 6
19—Miss. State 0
246 54

ARMY
46—North Carolina 0
59—Brown 7
69—Pittsburgh 7
76—Coast Guard 0
27—Duke 7
83—Villanova 0
59—Notre Dame 0
62—Penn 7
23—Navy 7
504 35

AUBURN
32—Howard 0
7—Fort Benning 0
0—Georgia Tech 27

GREAT LAKES
62—Fort Sheridan 0
27—Purdue 18
26—Illinois 26
25—Northwestern 0
38—West. Michigan 0
6—Ohio State 26
40—Wisconsin 12
45—Marquette 7
12—Third Air F'ce 10
32—Marquette 0
28—Fort Warren 7
7—Notre Dame 28
348 134

ILLINOIS
79—Illinois Normal 0
26—Indiana 18
26—Great Lakes 26
19—Purdue 35
40—Iowa 6
39—Pittsburgh 5
7—Notre Dame 13
0—Michigan 14
12—Ohio Stat 26
25—Northwe 6

MISSISSIPPI
7—Kentucky 27
26—Florida 6
7—Tennessee 20
0—Tulsa 47
18—Arkansas 26
0—Jack'ville AAB 10
6—Alabama 34
13—Miss. State 8
77 178

MISS. STATE
42—Jack'ville AAB 0
56—Millsaps 0
49—Ark. A. & M. 20
13—L. S. U. 6
26—Kentucky 0
26—Auburn 21
0—Alabama 19
8—Mississippi 13
265 79

MISSOURI
6—Arkansas 7
0—Ohio State 54
33—Kansas State 0

PENNSYLVANIA
18—Duke 7
20—Dartmouth 6
46—Wm. & Mary 0
0—Navy 26
19—Michigan 41
35—Columbia 7
7—Army 62
20—Cornell 0
165 149

PENN STATE
58—Muhlenberg 13
14—Navy 35
20—Bucknell 6
6—Colgate 0
27—W. Virginia 28
41—Syracuse 0
7—Temple 6
34—Maryland 19
0—Pittsb 14
207 141

TTSBURGH
st Virginia 13

TEXAS
30—S'w'tern (Tex.) 0
6—Randolph Field 42
20—Oklahoma 0
19—Arkansas 0
0—Rice 7
34—S. M. U. 7
6—Okla. A. & M. 13
6—T. C. U. 7
6—Texas Aggies 0
119 76

TEXAS A. & M.
39—Bryan Field 0
27—Texas Tech 14
14—Oklahoma 21
7—L. S. U. 0
7—T. C. U. 13
61—N. Tex. Aggies 0
6—Arkansas 7
39—S. M. U. 6
19—Rice 6
0—Texas 6
70—Miami (Fla.) 14
289 87

TEXAS CHRISTIAN

Football results also appeared regularly in much the same format that they appear today.

beginning next week."

Coverage was minimal at the start, consisting of schedules of professional and college teams, a feature and a column by a nationally recognized football authority.

That same autumn, TSN inaugurated a football prediction contest in which readers were invited to match wits with a professional forecaster known as "Pigskin Pete." To the contestant coming closest to predicting the scores of a dozen college games, the paper awarded $50. The first runner-up received $25, while others received a year's subscription to TSN or a copy of the "National Football League Manual."

At the close of the football season, several pages were devoted weekly to basketball and ice hockey. This, however, was discontinued when major league baseball teams started spring training in late February.

Eventually, the paper published a series of articles on championship boxing matches written by such recognized experts as sports historian Frank G. Menke.

During this period, cover illustrations shifted from photographs to cartoons. The foremost sports artist in the country was Willard Mullin of the New York World-Telegram. Combining a facile brush with a clever and delightful wit, Mullin amused thousands with his caricatures. He used the "Bum" to represent the Brooklyn Dodgers; "St. Louis Swifty," a riverboat gambler, to represent the St. Louis Cardinals, and a "Giant" oaf for the New York Giants, among others.

To Mullin went the distinction of drawing the first non-baseball sketch to grace the cover of The Sporting News. The tradition-shattering cartoon appeared on the issue of November 11, 1943, and depicted in five columns the race for national honors among college football teams. The following week another Mullin sketch appeared on page 1 with the headline: "Hail Irish as All-Time Grid Greats / N.D. Called Better Than Pros' Best."

An early-December issue contained a two-page layout on The Sporting News' first All-America football team.

Other sports also began appearing during this time period. TSN annually presented its college basketball All-America team and followed the National Hockey League weekly with capsule summaries of each game.

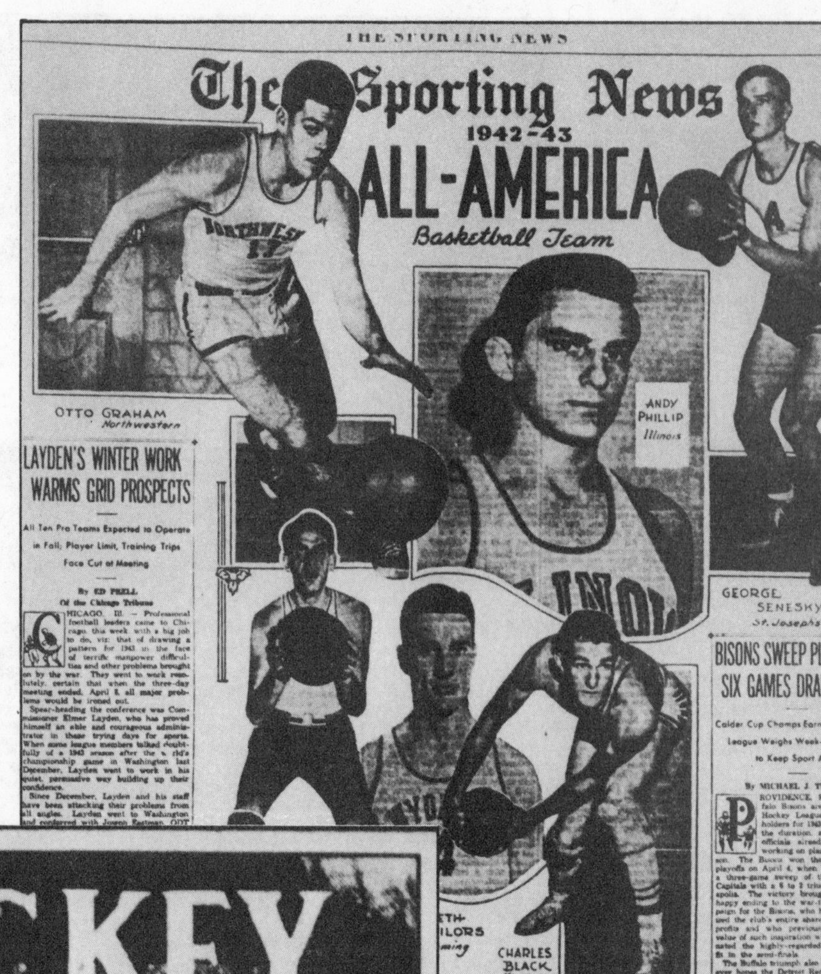

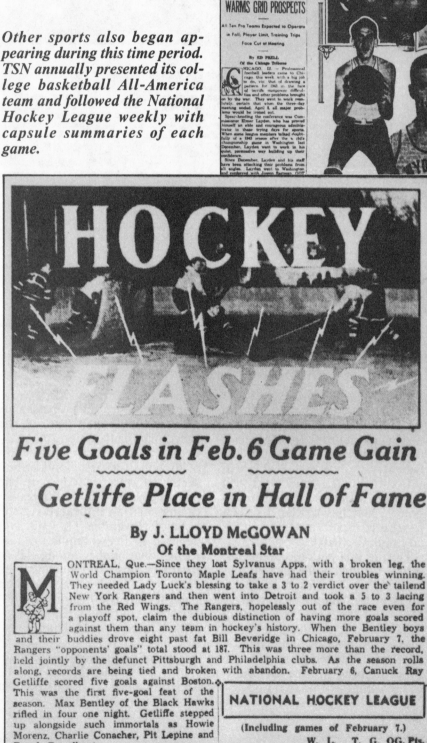

THE SPORTING NEWS

The Sporting News 1942-43 ALL-AMERICA Basketball Team

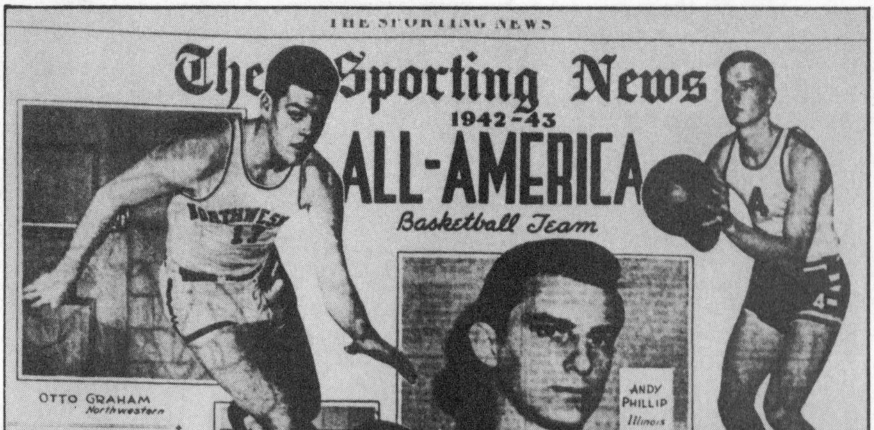

LAYDEN'S WINTER WORK WARMS GRID PROSPECTS

All Ten Pro Teams Expected to Operate in Fall; Player Limit, Training Trips Face Cut at Meeting

By ED PRELL
Of the Chicago Tribune

CHICAGO, Ill. — Professional football leaders came to Chicago this week with a big job to do, viz: that of drawing a pattern for 1943 in the face of terrific manpower difficulties and other problems brought on by the war. They went to work resolutely, certain that when the three-day meeting ended, April 8, all major problems would be ironed out.

Spear-heading the conference was Commissioner Elmer Layden, who has proved himself an able and courageous administrator in these trying days for sports. When some league members talked doubtfully of a 1943 season after the world's championship game in Washington last December, Layden went to work in his quiet, persuasive way building up their confidence.

Since December, Layden and his staff have been attacking their problems from all angles. Layden went to Washington and conferred with Joseph Eastman, ODT

BISONS SWEEP PLAYOFFS; SIX GAMES DRAW 45,000

Calder Cup Champs Earn $1,500 Each; League Weighs Week-End Games to Keep Sport Alive

By MICHAEL J. THOMAS

PROVIDENCE, R. I.—The Buffalo Bisons are the American Hockey League's Calder Cup holders for 1943 and maybe for the duration, although league officials already have begun working on plans for next season. The Bisons won the league's final playoffs on April 4, when they completed a three-game sweep of the Indianapolis Capitals with a 6 to 2 triumph at Indianapolis. The victory brought a decidedly happy ending to the war-threatened campaign for the Bisons, who had been promised the club's entire share of the playoff profits and who previously proved the value of such inspiration when they eliminated the highly-regarded Hershey outfit in the semi-finals.

The Buffalo triumph also killed off whatever hopes the Detroit Red Wings had of scoring a hockey grand-slam. Indianapolis is the Red Wings' farm unit and Manager Jack Adams of the Wings no doubt would have been delighted to place the American League Calder Cup beside the Stanley Cup which Detroit is favored to win in the National League.

The difference between victory and defeat probably meant as much as $1,500 to each of the Bisons and they played classy hockey right down to the clinching game, which was featured by Bill Summerhill's three goals.

Capacity Crowd on Hand

The Bisons outdrew all other clubs in the playoffs by far, approximately 45,000 attending the six games played in Buffalo. A capacity turnout of 10,224 on April 2 watched the second clash of the finals with the Capitals, which the Bisons won, 5 to 2. Buffalo scored three times in the final period after the first two chapters had produced a 2 to 2 deadlock. The Bisons also rallied in the finale to win the inaugural battle, 3 to 1, on March 31, scoring twice to break a one-all tie.

Those two victories and the spirited fashion in which they were tallied ...

...ca Basketball Selections

SECOND TEAM	THIRD TEAM
...WAGE MINOR, Toledo	GENE ROCK, South. Cal.
...HN HARGIS, Texas	GAIL BISHOP, Wash. St.
...N CLOSS, Rice	ED BEISSER, Creighton
...RENSBERGER, N. Dame	JOE WALTHALL, W. Va.
...MULLENS, Fordham	STAN SKAUG, Dartm'th
...N DURDAN, Oregon	BOB FAUGHT, N. Dame

...ney, Western Kentucky; Quinn, Idaho; Dalmar, Stanford; West, ...Duke; Mahnken and Kleus, Georgetown; Murphy, Manhattan; ...ming; Seminoff and Gonzard, USC; Myers, Dartmouth; Mikan and ...Palmer, Princeton; Mates, NYU; Quinlan, Canisius; Evans, Kansas; ...; Crumlo, Penn; Hamilton, West Virginia; Halbert, West Texas; ...ley, Menke, Mathisen and Vance, Illinois; Williams, Indiana; ...

...and Height

Five Goals in Feb. 6 Game Gain Getliffe Place in Hall of Fame

By J. LLOYD McGOWAN
Of the Montreal Star

MONTREAL, Que.—Since they lost Sylvanus Apps, with a broken leg, the World Champion Toronto Maple Leafs have had their troubles winning. They needed Lady Luck's blessing to take a 3 to 2 verdict over the tailend New York Rangers and then went into Detroit and took a 5 to 3 lacing from the Red Wings. The Rangers, hopelessly out of the race even for a playoff spot, claim the dubious distinction of having more goals scored against them than any team in hockey's history. When the Bentley boys and their buddies drove eight past fat Bill Beveridge in Chicago, February 7, the Rangers "opponents' goals" total stood at 187. This was three more than the record, held jointly by the defunct Pittsburgh and Philadelphia clubs. As the season rolls along, records are being tied and broken with abandon. February 6, Canuck Ray Getliffe scored five goals against Boston. This was the first five-goal feat of the season. Max Bentley of the Black Hawks rifled in four one night. Getliffe stepped up alongside such immortals as Howie Morenz, Charlie Conacher, Pit Lepine and Punch Broadbent.

Getliffe's feat brightened the chances of

NATIONAL HOCKEY LEAGUE

(Including games of February 7.)

	W.	L.	T.	G.	OG.	Pts.
Boston	21	13	6	156	138	48
Detroit	17	9	10	121	89	44

Cartoonists Lou Darvas and Willard Mullin were popular figures during this time period. Mullin amused readers for many years with his baseball characters such as the Brooklyn Bum (right, above right) and the hillbilly and hound dog (right, below right) that represented the St. Louis Browns.

BASEBALL — ALL SPORTS

The Sporting News

THE BASE BALL PAPER OF THE WORLD

VOLUME 116, NUMBER 14 — ST. LOUIS, NOVEMBER 11, 1943 — FIFTEEN CENTS

Look Out for Your Hand, Buddy — *These Boys Aren't Fooling*

Sox Get Heads-Up Hal in Head-of-Class Plan

Acquisition of Trosky Expected to Be Followed by Other Moves to Strengthen Club; Several Cubs Likely to Go on Market at Winter Meeting

By ED BURNS

CHICAGO, Ill.

White Sox officials, who gave Chicago a first-division club in 1943, are optimistic about 1944 generally and highly hopeful about giving this city a pennant contender. The purchase of Hal Trosky from the Cleveland Indians, November 6, was only one of several steps already taken and one of several more the Sox expect to make ere the close of the winter meetings in New York several weeks hence.

Hal Trosky

Winning Average of .813 Piled Up by Pigskin Petes

Starting with the opening kick-off, The Sporting News' team of Pigskin Petes has been rolling up an impressive yardage on successful predictions of gridiron results this season.

Including last week-end's games, the combined score for those who have filled the Pigskin Pete role shows the forecasters have called the turn correctly in 109 games, against misses on only 25, for the remarkable percentage of .813.

ON THE INSIDE

Unbeaten Hit Stretch With Irish in Front

By DAN DANIEL

NEW YORK, N. Y.

VOLUME 118, NUMBER 14 — ST. LOUIS, NOVEMBER 9, 1944

Return of Big-Pay Stars to Create

The Bum Ties Himself Up With Some New Finery

LOOPING THE LOOPS

By J. G. T. SPINK

Hal Gets Major Tueboid

For a guy who has only three toes on one foot, Harold Peck can carry the mail, not only on the bases but on the baseball ladder. In fact, a couple of months ago he moved right out of Milwaukee and up to the major leagues when Connie Mack of the

Hal Peck

The Mahatma Digs In

By TOM MEANY

Baseball Editor, PM, New York

It probably would be stretching the truth to say that Branch Rickey is the most popular general manager Brooklyn has had since Larry MacPhail, but...

Burwell Reported Signed as Indianapolis Manager

BOSTON, Mass.—Bill Burwell...

ST. LOUIS, JUNE 17, 1943 — FIFTEEN

Will You Take Army or Navy? .'. Either Could Take a Flag!

TWO UNCLE SAM TEAMS THAT COULD MAKE MAJORS SAY 'UNCLE'

Detroit Twilight Test Shows Tiger Fans Like It Best

VOLUME 118, NUMBER 9 — ST. LOUIS, OCTOBER 5, 1944 — FIFTEEN CENTS

FIGHTING BROWNIES FACE FAVORED CARDINALS

WHOOPEE!

It Is Form vs. Fury for World Title

Statistics Indicate Redbird Victory, but A.L. Champs Point to Their Spirit

By DAN DANIEL

ST. LOUIS, Mo.

For the first time in the 41-year history of the World's Series, St. Louis is the host in both leagues. To the Cardinals came an easy triumph in the National League, which it now has dominated for three successive seasons. To the Browns went the American League pennant in one of the most stirring climax drives in all the annals of the game.

Both Majors' and Minors' Executives in Hospitals

Commissioner K. M. Landis was unable to attend the all-St. Louis World's Series this week, because of illness. His family, in Chicago, reported him in St. Luke's Hospital. A statement from the Commissioner's office said his indisposition was not serious.

At Durham, N. C., William G. Bramham, president of the National Association, was in Watt Hospital. He has been reported suffering from a heart ailment.

Landis is 77 and Bramham 76 years old.

ON THE INSIDE

Facts, Figures and Features About World's Series

'DON'T LET HITLER KILL BASEBALL'--QUENT REYNOLDS

The Sporting News

THE BASE BALL PAPER OF THE WORLD

VOLUME 115, NUMBER 1 — ST. LOUIS, FEBRUARY 11, 1943 — FIFTEEN CENTS

MAJOR LOOPS PLAN ANOTHER MONSTER WAR FUND PROGRAM

LANDIS, FRICK, HARRIDGE GO OVER PRELIMINARY DETAILS

Army Relief Said to Be Ready to Accept Help Again; Heydler Believes N. Y. Dinner May Have Saved Game

By DANIEL M. DANIEL

McNUTT ORDER NO IMMEDIATE THREAT TO GAME

EDICT FOLLOWS LINE LAID DOWN IN 1918 BY GEN. CROWDER

INITIAL DIRECTIVE IS SAME AS GIVEN DURING WORLD WAR I

If Manpower Commission Pursues Like Policies, Season May Be Shortened; All Clubs Plan to Go Ahead

By EDGAR G. BRANDS

MANY NOTABLES MAKE STIRRING TALKS FOR SPORT

'60 MILLION FANS PLEAD OUR CASE,' SAYS COMMISSIONER LANDIS

Willkie, Davis, Rickenbacker, LaGuardia Among Those Heard at Annual Dinner of N. Y. Scribes

By HAROLD PARROTT

CUBS GIVE A HEAVE ∴ To Their No-Sleeve Peeve

BRUINS FULMINATED WHEN COSTUMES CULMINATED IN TIGHTS AT RIGHT

ANKENMAN RESIGNS FROM BUFFS IN HUFF

HOUSTON PRESIDENT FOR 17 YEARS CRITICIZES BREADON

Beefing Cubs Drop Hoot-Suits and Regain That Brawn Look

CLEVELAND TALKING OF INDIAN SUMMER

TRIBE STACKS UP STRONG, DESPITE INROADS BY U. S.

Landis on the Lobby

During the early 1940s, TSN treated the New York Baseball Writers Dinner and other off-season banquets as major events. The 1943 New York Dinner resulted in a banner headline (above) and stories in both the right and left columns.

Changes Occur Rapidly

Devotees of The Sporting News discerned changes almost weekly during the early 1940s as Taylor Spink and his editors tried to keep abreast of rapidly changing scenes and personnel.

To keep readers posted on activities at home and overseas, there were columns titled "In the Service" and "From the Front." Every issue contained at least one photograph of a major league player in Army or Navy uniform far removed from his native habitat. As a reminder of happenings during World War I, there was a column "REMEMBER . . . The Days of World War I in 1918?"

For those who wished to keep a serviceman fully informed of baseball developments at home, a subscription was available for \$3.75, or \$1.25 below the regular rate at the start of the war.

Innovations in TSN's editorial content included "Looping the Loops" by Taylor Spink, dealing with a major league personality; "Bouncing Around With Ed Burns," a Chicago baseball writer, and "From the Ruhl Book," a miscellany of baseball items collected by Oscar Ruhl, who joined the staff as chief of the editorial department in the early 1940s.

Authors of major league newsletters were no longer forced to look at the end of their compositions to find their names. Bylines of all major stories now appeared at the top of the articles.

"Grins," devoted to baseball anecdotes, made its debut during this time period, while in June 1943 TSN saluted its first player for a major achievement under the heading of "Hats Off." He was Mort Cooper, St. Louis Cardinals pitcher. At the start, only one major leaguer was cited weekly, but in time one was selected from each league for every issue.

Because of increased activities in winter sports banquets, TSN introduced a "Tidbits From the Knife and Fork Circuit" column. This contained minor news items. Major events, such as the New York Baseball Writers Dinner, however, were covered in depth, with a large photo of the dining hall, a lengthy story, an alphabetical listing of all the guests and, frequently, the words to all the parodies warbled by the writers-turned-thespians.

Other features in this era included a series on the "Inside of the Game's Famous Deals," "My Greatest Diamond Thrill" and "Famous Streaks."

The change that caught everybody's attention during this period occurred in the issue of April 2, 1942. The cost per copy was increased from 10 to 15 cents.

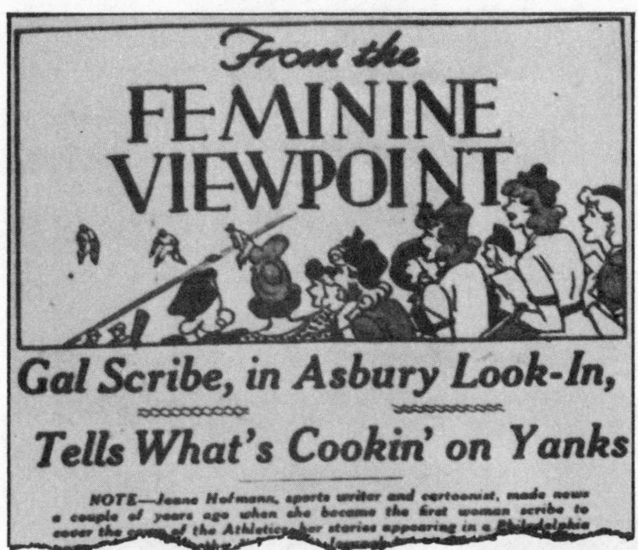

From the
FEMININE
VIEWPOINT

Gal Scribe, in Asbury Look-In,

Tells What's Cookin' on Yanks

NOTE—Jeane Hofmann, sports writer and cartoonist, made news a couple of years ago when she became the first woman scribe to cover the camp of the Athletics, her stories appearing in a Philadelphia

Among the 1940s columns that appeared regularly in TSN were J.G. Taylor Spink's 'Looping the Loops' and a column offering the feminine point of view.

Bouncing Around
With
Ed Burns

Oratory That Made Sports History

THAT must have been quite a party the writers tossed in New York and we are sorry now that we didn't have the owner of a "C" book tow us there and back. We are not a glutton for that part of the New York event which ordinarily wafts from the dais of that always great show of the Gotham scriveners. We are somewhat allergic to the routine brands of squab and filet mignon oratory, so much so that we haven't even enjoyed the sound of our own voice in recent years. But the oratory loosed in the Hotel Commodore ballroom on the night of February 7 has had a very definite aftermath, a gratifying aftermath that our memory can't match in reflection on a million gusts of windjamming at the festive board.

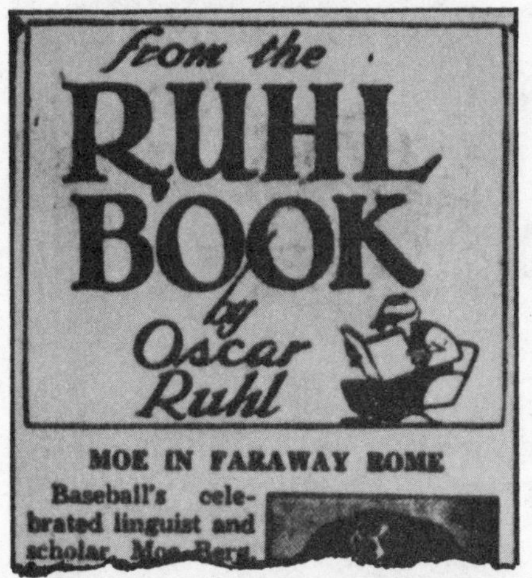

from the
RUHL
BOOK
by
Oscar
Ruhl

MOE IN FARAWAY ROME

Baseball's celebrated linguist and scholar, Moe Berg,

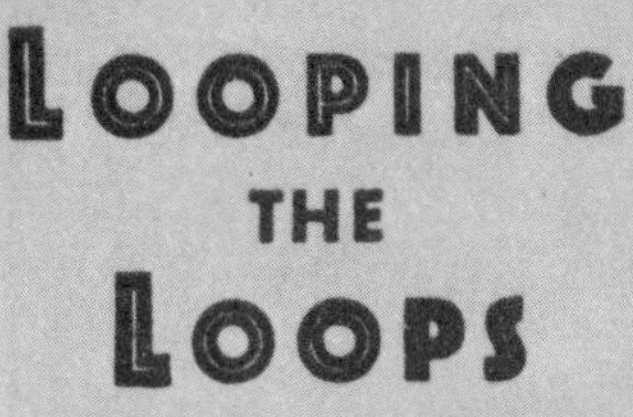

LOOPING
THE
LOOPS

Reg. U. S. Pat. Off.

By J.G.T. SPINK

Fitting Fresco to a Desk

BROOKLYN, N. Y.—It didn't look as strange as we thought it would to see Lafayette Fresco Thompson seated behind a desk. But come to think of it, Tommy was one of those ball players who are just as effective sitting down as they are on the field. That doesn't mean Thompson wasn't a fair sort of infielder in his playing days, but ask any National League umpire who had to undergo Tommy's jockeying from the bench and you'll get an idea of what we mean.

Closing in on 40, Fresco still looks youthful enough and physically fit to go out and play right now if necessary. In fact, it was a standing gag around the Dodger

IN THE SERVICE

NORFOLK CHALKS UP NO. 51

THE Norfolk Naval Training Station team registered its fifty-first victory of the season against 13 defeats, July 25, in coming from behind for the second time in two days to defeat the North Carolina Pre-Flight Cloudbusters, 4 to 3. On their previous meeting the Bluejackets scored twice in the eighth and twice in the ninth on Dom DiMaggio's home run. In the game on July 25 they counted three times in the eighth, aided by a triple from DiMaggio's bat, Charley Wagner, ex-Red Sox, second of three pitchers, getting credit for his twelfth triumph of the year and Joe Coleman, late of the Philadelphia Athletics, being charged with the loss.

The Fort Riley Cavalry Centaurs are the semi-pro champions of Kansas. They won the title, July 26, by defeating Wichita Cessna Aircraft in the final game of the state tournament at Wichita, 10 to 2.

Dale Barron, manager of Jonesboro in the Northeast Arkansas League in 1938 and previously a pitcher with Fort Smith, Muskogee and Hutchinson, is an Army sergeant, last reported in Australia.

Tommy Simone, former Amsterdam and Hornell pitcher who hurled a no-hit no-run game for the Coast Guard in the Galveston, Tex., Service League, against Fort Crockett, June 1, almost duplicated the feat against the same team, July 24. A single by the first batter, Louis Von Oehsen, to face Simone prevented the repetition. The Coast Guard won, 3 to 0.

A Shaughnessy playoff at the end of the season has been ordered for the Army-Navy League in California. The first and third teams and the second and fourth will play in the opening round. A double-header will be staged August 14 and the two winners will meet August 21 and 22 in a two-out-of-three series to decide the winner. If a third game is necessary, it will be played August 29.

TOM CAREY HITTING .363

SEAMAN 2ND CL. TOM CAREY, former Boston Red Sox infielder, is leading the Sampson, N. Y., Naval Training Station team with a batting average of .363. Others in the .300 class include Chief Specialist Rocco English, ex-Elmira Pioneer; Chief Specialist Tony Ravis, from Rochester of the International League, and Chief Specialist Ray Manarel, property of the New York Yankees.

Lieut. John Sanford, former Washington first baseman, is leading the team of the School for Special Service at Lexington, Va., in hitting with a batting average of .488. Bill Hitchcock, shortstop from the Detroit Tigers, is second with .444. Fred Frankhouse, ex-National League pitcher, also is a member of the team. The school trains special service officers. The team is managed by Major Norman Smith, who has just returned from overseas in the Tunisian campaign, and won 15 of its first 17 games.

Sidney Gautreaux, catcher who had trials with Brooklyn in 1937 and 1938 and played with New Orleans, El Dorado, Lake Charles, Jeanerette, Allentown, Elmira and Memphis,

It's Tommy Gun Now Instead of Bat

CARRYING A TOMMY GUN, instead of a bat, Sgt. Ed Freed, who promised to develop into a heavy hitter for the Phillies before he was called into the service, now is a member of the military police, based at Morris Field, N. C. After three seasons with Trenton in the Inter-State League, Freed went to the Phils for a tryout. Ed, an outfielder, batted against Johnny Vander Meer of the Reds in his debut, September 11, 1942. He rapped a triple, a pair of doubles and a single in five times at bat and was prevented from having a perfect day by a shoestring catch by Eric Tipton. The next day, against Elmer Riddle, he made two out of five. Ed spent 20 days with the Phillies, but didn't see much more service, except as a pinch-hitter. However, he wound up with a .303 average in 13 games—and any rookie who can hit that well against big league pitching should do all right swinging a stick as an M. P.

Ruffing Hurls First No-Hit

With the U.S. involvement in World War II, a column called 'In the Service' became a regular feature in TSN.

Milestones That Marked Path ∴ of Sport's Undeviating Leader

JUDGE of FEDERAL COURT in CHICAGO, LANDIS PRESIDED IN LEGAL FIGHT BETWEEN FEDERAL LEAGUE AND MAJORS IN 1915 . . .

LANDIS RULED THE GAME WITH AN IRON FIST

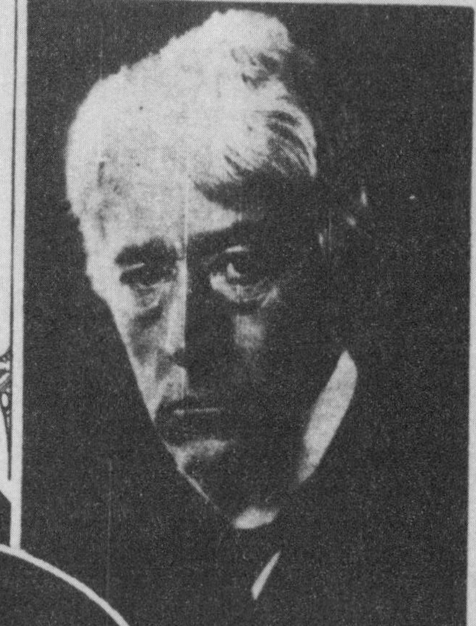

AS LANDIS APPEARED WHEN HE TOOK COMMISSIONERSHIP IN 1921

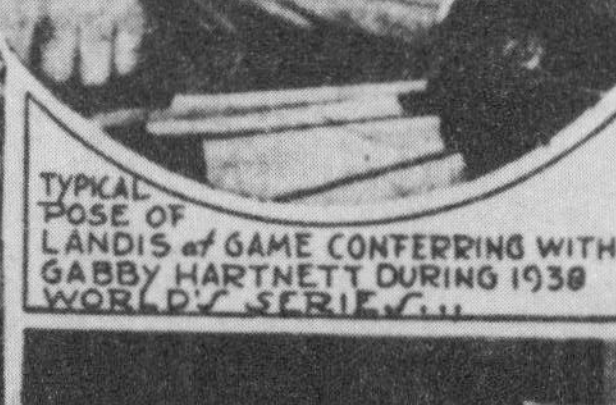

TYPICAL POSE OF LANDIS at GAME CONFERRING WITH GABBY HARTNETT DURING 1938 WORLD'S SERIES . . .

Death Takes Landis, 78, at Top of Power

Game's Iron Man Absolute Ruler 24 Years

Became National Figure By Stern, But Just Reign

Named as Supreme Authority After Exposure of 1919 World's Series, Commissioner Was Re-Elected Three Times by Owners to Whom He Dictated

By EDGAR G. BRANDS

CHICAGO, Ill.

November, which saw his birth, his selection as Commissioner of Baseball and, finally, recommendation of his re-election and the renewal of the expiring pact that created his unique position, also witnessed the passing of Judge Kenesaw Mountain Landis. The end came at 3:35 a. m., November 25, at St. Luke's Hospital in Chicago, five days after he had marked his seventy-eighth birthday anniversary. Cause of death was given as coronary thrombosis.

Landis had entered the hospital October 2 for a rest and a checkup. At that time, he was suffering from a severe cold, contracted while doing some outdoor work at his home in Glencoe, Ill., Chicago suburb. His wife, who had sustained a fractured wrist in a fall on the same day, was undergoing treatment in an adjoining hospital room. She was at his bedside at his death, as were their two children, Col. Reed Graham Landis, a flying ace in the first World War, and Mrs. Suzanne Phillips. He was the sixth of seven children. His five brothers and a sister all preceded him in death.

The czar of the game, by which he came to be known, because of the unlimited powers he held over the national pastime, was selected for the position that paid $65,000 a year, November 12, 1920, and accepted the same day. A joint committee of the majors met in Chicago, November 17, last, and unanimously indorsed him for re-election for seven years from the time his term was due to end January 12, 1946.

No Funeral, No Flowers

CHICAGO, Ill.—In accordance with the expressed wishes of Baseball Commissioner K. M. Landis, there was no funeral and no flowers were sent by friends. Cremation of his body in private followed his own instructions.

President William Harridge of the American League said no memorial would be planned, as that would not be in keeping with Landis' wishes.

27, 1864. An almost spent cannon ball struck the surgeon, shattering his left leg so badly that for a time it was feared the leg would have to be amputated.

Presiding at Last World's Series Meeting

THE LAST MEETING at which Landis presided as commissioner was a conference on August 28 of this year, when plans for the 1944 World's Series were discussed. Left to right, standing: Charles McManus, New York Yankees; Sam Breadon, St. Louis Cardinals; Jack Zeller, Detroit Tigers; William Harridge, American League president, representing the Boston Red Sox; William DeWitt and Donald Barnes, St. Louis Browns, with the commissioner seated in center.

of the Black Sox scandal of 1919, which shook baseball to its foundations in 1920, when it was first aired in a grand jury investigation.

In the words of Will Rogers, "baseball needed a touch of class and dis-

Lawyers' Wrist Watches Riled Landis in Court

Many are the tales that are told of Judge Landis' days on the Fed-

Squire." As a judge, he frequently startled court attaches by interrupting proceedings with bits of humor or pathos. He would supplement a jail sentence with an order to "Take this man up to Mabel's room," or "Take this

A Record of Accomplishment

Time heals all wounds and it finally won out in the breach between J.G. Taylor Spink and Commissioner Kenesaw M. Landis.

Within months after the rupture caused by the Saturday Evening Post feature article on the publisher, The Sporting News, in its September 3, 1942, issue, called for a "Landis Day." TSN said: "Irrespective of the tremendous debt which baseball owes to Judge Landis for the myriad benefices he brought in his many previous years of incalculable service, it has a new and vaster bill to pay to the high commissioner for the things he has done in this wartime season. . . ."

When Landis died in November 1944, the lead editorial in the publication eulogized the first commissioner, emphasizing that he had "left behind a record of accomplishment that it is the privilege of few men to achieve."

Pointing out that Landis had entered baseball at a time of great stress, the editorial continued: "He brought the sport through the most perilous years of its existence and left it so seaworthy that not even three years of war could affect its sound structure." The issue also included an obituary on the Judge that extended to more than three pages, as well as a column by Fred Lieb detailing Landis' significant accomplishments.

For nearly six months thereafter, TSN urged major league club owners to elect a successor quickly. In late April, the selection was made public. He was Albert Benjamin (Happy) Chandler, a U.S. senator from Kentucky.

An editorial acclaimed Chandler as "a perfect choice" and asserted "Baseball is now endowed with a high functionary who will enable it to make the most of the tremendous sports boom which will sweep the country as soon as our fighters become re-established from Portland, Me., to San Diego, Calif., from Key West, Fla., to Portland, Ore."

Describing itself as "highly elated" over the choice, The Sporting News reminded its readers that it had counseled in favor of a commissioner "who would go about the country selling baseball, who would not shut himself up in an ivory tower, who would be highly mobile, thoroughly coherent, absolutely approachable insofar as the press was concerned and young enough to promise baseball a long, progressive administration.

"In selecting Senator Chandler, the major leagues met every one of these essentials."

In early 1947, more than two years after the death of Chandler's predecessor, Taylor Spink published a book, "Judge Landis and 25 Years of Baseball."

When baseball Commissioner Kenesaw Mountain Landis died in November 1944, TSN eulogized its longtime friend and foe through both words and pictures (left).

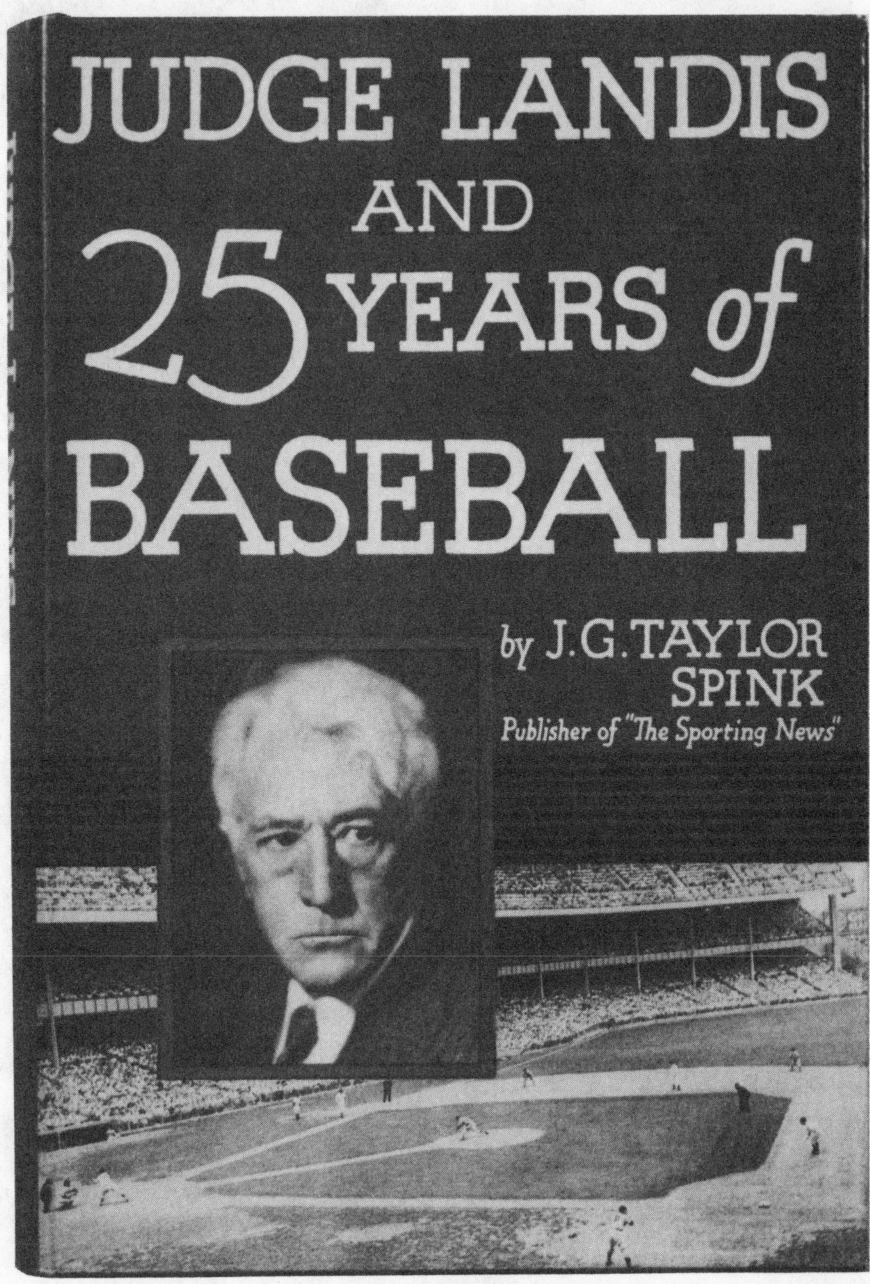

In 1947, more than two years after the death of baseball's first commissioner, The Sporting News further honored Landis with a book chronicling his accomplishments.

New York Giants hero Bobby Thomson makes a curtain call for an appreciative crowd after hitting a dramatic three-run, ninth-inning home run that beat the Brooklyn Dodgers and gave the Giants the 1951 pennant.

1946-1960:

BIG BUSINESS

The guns of World War II fell silent in 1945, but peace did not return immediately to professional baseball.

Player raids reminiscent of the Brotherhood War of 1890 and the Federal League ravages of 1914-15 were threatening the major leagues even before the 1946 season got under way. The despoilers were the fabulously rich Pasquel brothers of Mexico—Jorge, Alfonso, Bernardo, Mario and Gerardo. To major league executives, the most despicable of these was Jorge, president of the outlaw Mexican League.

Major league clubs were in training when the first player of prominence succumbed to the Pasquel blandishments. He was Vernon (Junior) Stephens, who had failed to come to terms with the St. Louis Browns after holding out for $17,500. The shortstop accepted a Pasquel offer that would pay him about $25,000 per year.

Stephens played two games with the Vera Cruz club before deciding that the Mexican brand of major league ball was a poor imitation of American baseball. Aided by friends who drove him to the border, Junior returned to the States and was happy to accept the Browns' contract of about $15,000 per year.

Brooklyn's Mickey Owen, who negotiated with the Pasquels while still in the Navy, signed a five-year pact to manage a Mexican club. Three New York Giants players—Sal Maglie, George Hausmann and Roy Zimmerman—were fired by Owner Horace Stoneham after learning they had negotiated with Mexican agents.

The major league star most earnestly coveted by the Pasquels, however, rejected all their inducements. Stan Musial, the 25-year-old Cardinal outfielder with one batting championship already under his belt, refused a five-year pact for $150,000 to remain with St. Louis for $13,000 a year. Nor could teammates Enos Slaughter, Whitey Kurowski or Terry Moore be wooed to Mexico.

But other Cardinals were more easily swayed. Pitchers Max Lanier and Fred Martin and second baseman Lou Klein fled south in May. Shortly thereafter, club Owner Sam Breadon followed suit, intent on checking out the Pasquels' operation.

On his return to St. Louis, Breadon was summoned to Cincinnati by Commissioner A.B. Chandler to report on his junket. Sam replied that he went to Mexico merely as a club owner and not as vice president of the National League. Breadon ignored the commissioner's summons, for which he was fined $5,000 and denied certain privileges, including attendance at the league meetings in July. Breadon was restored to good standing only after the intervention of National League President Ford Frick and Lou Carroll, league attorney, who described the impasse as the result of a "misunderstanding."

As punishment for their defection to Mexico, the league jumpers were suspended from Organized Ball, a ban that lasted until 1949.

In addition to the Mexican League turbulence, other factors were causing unrest in the major league family in 1946. The American Baseball Guild, organized by Boston attorney Robert Murphy, sought authorization as the players' bargaining agent with management. The issue was resolved, at least temporarily, on August 20 when the Pittsburgh Pirates rejected the Guild by a vote of 15-3, with the other players abstaining.

Although the Guild failed, the seeds of discontent had been planted. The players demanded a pension program, which was obtained through the labors and the persistence of Cardinals shortstop Marty Marion. Player representatives Johnny Murphy and Dixie Walker, and later Allie Reynolds and Ralph Kiner, presented demands to the club owners, who rejected some and granted others, including a minimum salary of $5,000, rather than the $6,500 that was requested.

Many former players warned against a union, and veteran executive Frank Lane cautioned the athletes not to "shoot Santa Claus." But the movement gained momentum. Repeatedly, the players insisted that their organization was a fraternity, not a union. While few were deceived by the semantics, their cause did gain support. The Major League Baseball Players Association, by whatever terminology, was formed in 1954 and has won countless benefits for its members over the years. Union representation thus became a major factor on the professional baseball scene.

As the day of the businessman-athlete dawned in the majors, expansion flowered in the minors. New leagues sprang up across the landscape with names like

Tobacco State, Coastal Plain, Sooner State, K-O-M (for Kansas, Oklahoma and Missouri), Colonial and Longhorn. In the peak season of 1949, nearly 450 franchises formed 59 minor circuits.

Then the decline set in. As rapidly as they blossomed, so quickly they wilted. Patrons of the game no longer were willing to sit on rough planks in unpainted and dimly lighted parks when they could relax in their air-conditioned parlors and marvel at the new electronic device known as television.

Bush league baseball fell into disfavor, if not disrepute. Ultimately, revolutionary suggestions were made that the minors be abandoned altogether and replaced by college programs that would serve the same purpose as proving grounds for big-league talent. The situation never sank to that level, but it was more than a one-man fancy.

The majors, meanwhile, embarked on a new crescendo of popularity. A "Game of the Day" was televised nationwide, acquainting every backwoods community with major league baseball. Restrictions on night ball were relaxed and eventually removed as more and more clubs installed lights. Teams accustomed to crowds in the thousands now reported them in the tens of thousands. From a total of 11 million in 1945, major league attendance zoomed to 18.5 million in 1946 and 20.9 million in 1948.

Simultaneously, dramatic events and colorful personalities created large, glaring headlines for diamond aficionados. The Cardinals, whose string of pennants was snapped at three in 1945, regained championship form in 1946, but only after defeating the Dodgers in the major leagues' first playoff for the pennant. The Cards never stopped, defeating the Red Sox in the World Series. Ted Williams batted only .200 for the losers, while lefthander Harry Brecheen won three games for the victors and Enos Slaughter earned lasting fame for racing from first base to score the title-clinching run on Harry Walker's short double.

Sociologically, the 1946 campaign was a landmark year on baseball's calendar: A black player was poised to break Organized Baseball's color line.

The athlete selected by Branch Rickey to break tradition was Jackie Robinson, a former star athlete at UCLA. The second baseman, who had played with the Kansas City Monarchs, possessed all the attributes, Rickey said, that were essential to such a momentous experiment.

Robinson batted a league-high .349 for Montreal (International) in 1946 and was promptly promoted to the Dodgers in 1947, making him the first black to play in the major leagues in the 20th Century. Jackie incurred immediate abuse from white players and fans. When rumors spread that several members of the Cardinals wanted to strike rather than play the Dodgers on their first eastern trip of the season, Ford Frick took official action.

"I do not care if half the league strikes," the league president announced. "Those who quit will encounter quick retribution. All will be suspended, and I do not care if it wrecks the National League for five years. This is the United States of America, and one citizen has as much right to play as another."

While the statement quashed further talk of a strike, it could not eliminate the indignities hurled from rival dugouts and the stands. Conditions improved in time and eventually became acceptable with the arrival of catcher Roy Campanella and pitcher Don Newcombe on the Brooklyn roster.

Because Eddie Stanky was established at second base, Robinson was shifted to first base as a Dodger rookie. He took the move in stride, batting .297, leading the league in stolen bases and winning The Sporting News' accolade as Rookie of the Year.

Robinson broke into the majors under the gentle leadership of Burt Shotton, who had been called out of retirement by Rickey as a one-year replacement for Leo Durocher. The Lip was suspended by Commissioner Chandler for his off-the-field associations and for a contempt-of-court charge arising from his marriage to actress Laraine Day.

Shotton, who took over for Clyde Sukeforth three days into the season, led the Dodgers to the pennant, but for the fourth time in as many tries, they lost the World Series, bowing to the Yankees, who finished 12 games ahead of the Detroit Tigers. Despite their loss, the Bums furnished the most dramatic moment in the Series. In the fourth game, the Dodgers were held hitless by Bill Bevens for 8⅔ innings, although the righthander's wildness had contributed to a Brooklyn run. The Dodgers trailed, 2-1, as they faced Bevens for the last time, and there appeared little to excite the Flatbush Faithful when, with one down, Carl Furillo drew the ninth walk from Bevens. After Spider Jorgensen fouled out, Al Gionfriddo ran for Furillo and stole second base. Pete Reiser batted for pitcher Hugh Casey and, even though Reiser represented the potential winning run, Yankees Manager Bucky Harris ordered Bevens to walk him intentionally. Eddie Miksis ran for Reiser, who had been kept out of the starting lineup because of a leg injury.

With the Dodger bench now devoid of lefthanded batters, Shotton called on righthanded Cookie Lavagetto to bat for Stanky. The veteran third baseman gave armchair analysts little time to ponder Harris' unorthodox strategy, although they did plenty of that afterward. On the second pitch, he bounced a double off the right-field wall at Ebbets Field to score Gionfriddo and Miksis. With one out to go, Bevens had lost not just his no-hitter, but also the game, 3-2.

The 1947 Series was the first to be televised and also the first to top the $2 million mark in revenue. As the Bombers celebrated the club's 11th world championship the night of October 6, a tearful Larry MacPhail announced his resignation as club president.

The 1948 Yankees won only three fewer games (94) than the '47 team, but they wound up in third place behind Cleveland and Boston, who tied for the flag. The pennant was decided in a one-game playoff at Boston in which Lou Boudreau, the Indians' playing manager, rapped four hits, including two home runs, in Cleveland's 8-3 victory. Boudreau had been appointed manager of the Tribe after the 1941 season at the age of 24 and had become recognized as one of the game's premier shortstops by the time Alva Bradley sold the club for $1.6 million in June 1946.

The new owners were a syndicate headed by a young burr-head, Bill Veeck, who had lost his right leg while serving with the Marines in the South Pacific. Veeck was no stranger to the game. He had spent many of his younger years at Wrigley Field, where his father presided as president of the Cubs. Young Bill, who was noted for his preference for sport shirts and his boundless supply of energy, had left his mark on Milwaukee (American Association) fans as an imaginative and refreshing entrepreneur before World War II. Now he was back, ready to titillate major league audiences with his myriad of promotional schemes.

As a gate attraction, he signed the legendary Satchel Paige for the Indians' bullpen. He also took on a multijointed comedian named Max Patkin to entertain from the coaches' box. There were fireworks, strolling musicians, nylon stockings for guests on Ladies Day and, when Boudreau was ignored as a member of the All-Star team, a night to honor "the greatest shortstop ever left off an All-Star team." Right in the middle of it all was Veeck, shaking hands with customers at the ticket windows, escorting them to their seats and inquiring sweetly if they preferred mustard or relish on their hot dogs.

The personal touch paid off. More games were transferred from cozy League Park to 78,811-seat Municipal Stadium on the lakefront in Veeck's first season, and the move was made permanent a year later. On August 4, 1946, the second-largest paid crowd in major league history (74,529) turned out to watch an Indians-Yankees doubleheader. By season's end, club attendance stood at more than 1 million for the first time ever—and that in a season when Cleveland finished sixth, 36 games behind the Red Sox.

In the pennant-winning season of 1948, the Tribe set a major league record gate of 2,620,627. The team climaxed its remarkable season by winning the six-game World Series from the Boston Braves, who had waited 34 years for a flag, six years longer than the Indians.

Individually, the 1948 season belonged to Stan Musial, a former sore-armed minor league pitcher who peaked as a slugger in his sixth major league season. The Cardinals' outfielder led the National League in batting (.376), slugging percentage (.702), runs scored (135), hits (230), total bases (429), doubles (46), triples (18) and runs batted in (131). His 39 homers were only one shy of the league lead, shared by Ralph Kiner of Pittsburgh and Johnny Mize of New York. The extraordinary season was one of many produced by Stan the Man, who in 1956 was acclaimed as The Sporting News' Player of the Decade.

Musial was at the zenith of his Hall of Fame career when a grizzled but refreshing character made his debut as an American League manager. Renowned as a jester through his earlier years, Casey Stengel had piloted the Dodgers and Braves with scant distinction in the 1930s and '40s. In fact, his most memorable citation may have come from a calloused Boston columnist who, after Casey suffered a broken leg when hit by a motorist, causing him to be shelved for the balance of the season, suggested that the driver be hailed as "the man who had done the most for Boston baseball" that year.

But such jabs failed to snap the Stengel wit or crush his buoyancy. He had managed extensively in the minors, awaiting another knock from opportunity, louder and more forceful than ever before.

In October 1948, the 59-year-old veteran of 38 professional baseball campaigns signed to manage the Yankees, replacing Bucky Harris. The new affiliation worked wonders on Casey. While he still fractured syntax and dangled participles, he was no longer regarded as a clown. Backed by Yankee resources, he was a genius and a winner. Stengel won world championships in his first five years with the Bronx Bombers, thus eclipsing such acknowledged masters as Joe McCarthy, John McGraw and Connie Mack. He held the New York newsmen in the palm of his hand, and they reciprocated by nicknaming him the "Old Perfessor."

Stengel penned the final chapter of his incredible saga in 1960 when he won his 10th pennant in 12 years. The tale ended in much the same manner that it had started back in 1949, when Tommy Henrich hit a ninth-inning home run to provide a 1-0 victory over the Dodgers in Game 1 of Casey's first whirl as a Series skipper. The Yanks proceeded to beat the Dodgers in five games. In 1960, however, the last scene was clouded in disappointment. After beating the Pirates by the scores of 16-3, 10-0 and 12-0, the Yankees led, 7-4, after 7½ innings of the seventh game at Forbes Field. A five-run outburst in the bottom of the eighth enabled the Pirates to take a 9-7 lead, but the Yanks evened the score with a pair of runs in the top of the ninth.

Facing Ralph Terry, the fifth New York pitcher, as leadoff batter in the last of the ninth was Bill Mazeroski. The Pittsburgh second baseman took one pitch for a ball, then hammered the next pitch over the left-field wall to clinch the Pirates' first world title since 1925.

In 1951, major league team owners elected baseball's third commissioner. After serving for 17 years as N.L. president, Ford Frick was named to replace Happy Chandler, who had resigned after the owners refused to extend his contract. Warren Giles, the chief executive of the Cincinnati Reds for many years, moved into Frick's chair.

At about the same time that Frick was changing offices, the Giants were qualifying for the World Series by fashioning a storybook finish not unlike Pittsburgh's nine years later. Under the leadership of Leo Durocher, who had jumped from Ebbets Field to the Polo Grounds in midseason of 1948, the Giants trailed the Dodgers by 13½ games in August, then won 37 of their last 44 games to deadlock for first place on the final day of the season. In the second National League playoff in six seasons, the teams split the first two games and were within three putouts of a Dodger pennant when fortune forsook the Brooks. With a 4-1 lead, Don Newcombe appeared to have matters well in hand when the Giants batted for the last time. But Alvin Dark and Don Mueller tagged the 20-game winner for singles, and after Monte Irvin popped out, Whitey Lockman doubled home a run. Brooklyn Manager Chuck Dressen then lifted Newcombe and brought in Ralph Branca to pitch to Bobby Thomson. Branca made one pitch that the third baseman took for a strike. That was all Thomson took. The second pitch was deposited in the left-field seats to cap "The Little Miracle of Coogan's Bluff."

Thomson's heroics did not carry over to the Series,

however, as the Giants were eliminated by the Yankees in six games. The Bronx Bombers had taken the measure of the Whiz Kid Phillies the year before and then upended the Dodgers the two following years before failing to reach the Series in 1954.

Thomson, an outfielder for most of his career, had been moved to the bench (and later to third base) in May 1951 to make room in center field for a young phenom from the minors. After hitting .477 in 35 games for Minneapolis of the American Association, 20-year-old Willie Mays joined the New York club. Fleet afoot, with a rifle arm and explosive bat, Mays gave the Giants a gate magnet to rival the Brooklyn trio of Robinson, Campanella and Newcombe. Mays went on to clout 660 home runs, including a record-tying four in one game, and to electrify audiences from coast to coast with superlative performances in all departments.

Say Hey Willie made his most unforgettable catch in the 1954 World Series against Cleveland. In the opener, he raced to the farthest sector of the Polo Grounds for an over-the-head grab of a drive by Vic Wertz. The catch—the yardstick by which all of Mays' future defensive plays were measured—preserved a 2-2 tie that the teams carried into the 10th inning, when Dusty Rhodes made his presence known.

Rhodes, christened James Lamar, was a pinch-hitter and outfielder who batted .341 and clouted 15 home runs in 82 games in 1954, but he lingered in the shadows until the Series rolled around. Batting for Monte Irvin with two runners aboard in the bottom of the 10th, Rhodes drove a Bob Lemon pitch 260 feet into the right-field stands for a 5-2 victory. In the second contest, Rhodes singled as a pinch-hitter, remained in the game and smashed a homer off Early Wynn to highlight a 3-1 win. The Giants went on to complete a four-game sweep.

In winning their second flag under Durocher, the Giants beat out the Dodgers and an old rival in a new setting, the Braves. For 50 years, the major leagues had resisted the winds of geographic change, but by the early 1950s, those winds had risen to gale force. The old format of 14 major league clubs east of the Mississippi River and the two St. Louis clubs on the west bank had started to totter, particularly in Boston, where Lou Perini was in financial straits.

Ten years earlier, Perini and partners Guido Rugo and Joseph Maney had purchased the Braves from a syndicate headed by Bob Quinn. The trio, nicknamed the "Three Steam Shovels" because of their many profitable construction projects in World War II, enjoyed quick success as baseball moguls. In the pennant-winning season of 1948, the club drew almost 1.5 million paid admissions, easily a club attendance record, and fans throughout New England expected more winning teams in the years ahead.

That hope faded in 1949, when the Braves tumbled to fourth. The gate went into a steady decline that reached 281,278 in 1952.

Perini, who had bought out his partners, did not intend to sit idly by and watch his team lose another $600,000, as it had done in '52. Greater potential for revenue had to exist somewhere, and Perini thought he knew the spot. He already owned the Milwaukee (American Association) franchise, which the Braves operated as a farm club, so he knew the area was hungry for major league baseball. Moreover, the city had recently constructed a spacious $5 million stadium with plenty of parking facilities. Milwaukee loomed as the place to go.

The Braves already were in training at Bradenton, Fla., in 1953 when the matter came to a head. A headline in The Sporting News on March 13 revealed, "Braves to Milwaukee, Browns to Baltimore," and the baseball establishment took note.

Confronted with the story, Perini at first hedged, but at a March 14 news conference he said: "I have a difficult announcement to make. We are moving the Braves to Milwaukee."

Perini, a Boston native, never had cause for regrets. In the felicious atmosphere of a city and state suddenly gone daft, the Braves prospered as never before. Citizens bombarded their new heroes with every conceivable gift and packed County Stadium with regularity. In their first 13 home dates, the Braves surpassed their gate for all 76 home games at Boston in 1952. Instead of season attendance of less than 300,000, the 1953 Braves attracted 1.8 million fans. Perini had struck an incredibly rich vein.

Emboldened by Perini's success, other club owners cast about for greener pastures. In St. Louis, as The Sporting News headline had reported, Bill Veeck turned his covetous gaze toward Baltimore. Veeck, still sporting open-neck collars, was waging a losing fight against the Cardinals and their new ownership, the Anheuser-Busch brewery. His old promotional schemes, so popular in Cleveland until he sold the Indians in 1949, failed to revitalize the moribund Browns franchise he had purchased in 1951. A move seemed to be the only solution.

Veeck earned lasting fame as a master showman with his most memorable stunt ever in 1951. As part of the American League's 50th birthday celebration, Veeck promised fans at a Sunday doubleheader a party second to none. There would be, he announced, cake and ice cream for the spectators and a special treat of unspecified nature.

The first half of the doubleheader ended, and an air of expectancy pervaded Sportsman's Park. As bands blared and aerial bombs exploded, a huge papier-mache cake was wheeled onto the field. On signal, the top of the cake trembled and from it popped a small figure attired in a Browns uniform and wearing the numeral ⅛.

The fans applauded and settled back. The Detroit Tigers were retired in the first inning, bringing the Browns up to bat. A ripple of laughter passed through the stands, then a roar. The 3-foot-7 midget from the top of the cake was approaching the plate, swinging a miniature bat just like a big leaguer. From the public-address announcer came the words: "Batting for Frank Saucier, Number one-eighth, Eddie Gaedel."

A skeptical Ed Hurley, the home-plate umpire, wanted proof that the newcomer was legally signed to a Browns contract. Hurley summoned Zack Taylor to a conference, and the St. Louis manager, prepared for just such an eventuality, readily produced an American League contract signed by all the principals. Satisfied that everything was legal, Hurley signaled to Bob Cain to pitch to the midget. Four pitches later, Gaedel trotted to first base, where he was replaced by Jim Delsing.

Thousands howled gleefully over Veeck's stunt. In Chicago, Will Harridge howled, too, but in horror. Such an act, intoned the American League president, was an affront to the dignity of the national pastime and must never be repeated. Obediently, Veeck accepted the judgment, but by March 1953 his venturesome spirit was rampant again. He applied for permission to move the Browns to Baltimore and was turned down.

He renewed his application just before the World Series in New York and had reason for hope. In a straw poll the night before, he received only one negative response from the other seven A.L. club owners. There was little doubt, he believed, that he would be given the necessary six votes.

But inimical influences were at work. When the official vote was taken, four clubs opposed the move. In his years as a maverick club owner, Veeck had bruised too many super egos, and he was paying the price with not one, but two pounds of flesh. He learned the horrible truth when a fellow magnate snarled, "We'll keep you in St. Louis until you are bankrupt, then we'll decide where the franchise will go."

The threat was realized only in part. Other moguls might keep Veeck in St. Louis, but bankruptcy was another matter. He sold the Browns to Baltimore interests the day before the Series opener, and the shift was approved.

A year later, the Philadelphia Athletics also were granted permission to move. Connie Mack had retired as manager after the 1950 season—and after 50 years at the helm—and his sons, Roy and Earle, operated the club, which was losing a financial battle with the Phillies. They became the Kansas City A's in 1955.

While other clubs sought fiscal relief in faraway territories, the Yankees continued to mint championships in assembly-line style. Their five-year reign having been snapped by Cleveland in 1954, the Bombers launched another string of pennants in 1955. For the sixth time, their World Series opponents were the Dodgers, who still were searching for their first world title. That prize finally was achieved when Brooklyn prevailed in seven games, with Johnny Podres hurling a 2-0 eight-hitter in the clincher.

The Yankees repeated as pennant winners in 1956—their seventh flag in eight years—and got revenge on the Dodgers, who also defended their league championship. That seven-game World Series produced the most remarkable of all postseason accomplishments, a perfectly pitched game.

Don Larsen, a righthander with vast potential but minimal success, broke into the majors with the Browns, moved to Baltimore (where he posted a 3-21 record in 1954) and then was traded to New York, where he went 9-2 in 1955 and 11-5 the next year. Late in the '56 season he began toying with a no-windup delivery, and in the fifth Series game, played at Yankee Stadium on October 8, the 27-year-old utilized his new method to perfection. He retired 27 batters in order, throwing just 97 pitches. His final delivery was a called strike to pinch-hitter Dale Mitchell, who stood transfixed as he was punched out by umpire Babe Pinelli, who was working his final major league game behind the plate.

Although the Series was not a vintage event for Mickey Mantle, who batted only .250, it capped an extraordinary campaign for the Oklahoman, who led the league in batting (.353), home runs (52) and RBIs (130) to win his first of three Most Valuable Player awards as well as the Triple Crown.

Mantle burst upon the majors in 1951 as a 19-year-old outfielder with all the requisites for stardom—a good glove, a consistent bat, power, speed and a wide smile. Mantle's arrival coincided with Joe DiMaggio's departure, and the youngster ably assumed the Yankee Clipper's role as idol of the masses. Ten times Mantle homered from each side of the plate in one game. Five times he led the league in walks and four times in home runs while building a career total of 536 homers.

Mantle was playing in his sixth World Series, and the Yankees in their 23rd, when the 1957 classic opened at Yankee Stadium. The opposition was furnished by the Milwaukee Braves, who finally rewarded their faithful fans by winning their first flag after two successive years as runners-up. The Braves attracted more than 2 million fans to County Stadium for the fourth straight season, a level the Yankees had not attained since 1950.

Ironically, it was a former New York pitcher who helped hand the Yanks their second Series setback in three years. Lew Burdette, acquired by the Braves in exchange for Johnny Sain and $50,000 six years earlier, defeated the Bombers three times, throwing 24 consecutive scoreless innings. His three complete-game performances were crucial as the Braves triumphed in the seven-game competition.

The Braves and Yankees competed for baseball's highest honor again in 1958, when the Yanks won, but by that time other developments were vying for national headlines. Walter O'Malley, despairing of municipal help in locating a suitable site for a modern stadium to replace cramped Ebbets Field, announced in October 1957 that the Dodgers would move to Los Angeles for the 1958 season. The move was hardly unexpected as Horace Stoneham had revealed in August that the Giants would migrate to San Francisco. Until a new stadium was constructed in Chavez Ravine, O'Malley reported, the team would play in Memorial Coliseum. Pending completion of a new park in San Francisco, the Giants would perform in Seals Stadium.

Californians, after years of clamoring for major league representation, greeted the Easterners with cash-green handclasps. The Giants' home attendance ballooned from 653,923 in their last New York season to 1,272,625 in 1958, while the Dodgers' gate improved from 1,028,258 to 1,845,556.

Before the Dodgers arrived on the West Coast, tragedy removed one of their all-time stars. On January 28, 1958, catcher Roy Campanella, a three-time MVP, was permanently disabled in an automobile accident. In addition, some of the club's best veterans, such as Pee Wee Reese and Gil Hodges, were past their primes, contributing to the Dodgers' seventh-place finish in 1958.

When Dodgers President Branch Rickey signed Jackie Robinson

By 1959, however, the atmosphere brightened considerably. Walter Alston, in his sixth season as Dodgers manager, produced a pennant through a masterful manipulation of talent that included a new double-play combination (shortstop Maury Wills and second baseman Charlie Neal) and only one .300 hitter (Wally Moon). There was no 20-game winner to serve as a stopper, but there was righthander Larry Sherry, a redoubtable reliever who was promoted from the minors at midseason. In the World Series victory over the White Sox, Sherry won two games and saved two others.

But the most spectacular pitching performance of the season belonged to Harvey Haddix, a little left-

to a professional contract, he opened a big door for black America.

hander with the Pittsburgh Pirates. On May 26, Haddix pitched an incredible 12 perfect innings against the Braves at Milwaukee, only to lose, 1-0, on an infielder's throwing error, a sacrifice, a walk and first baseman Joe Adcock's double.

The victory was one of 86 registered by the Braves, but it was not enough. The Dodgers recorded as many and defeated the Braves in a playoff, the third in the National League in 14 seasons.

A league pennant flew over a West Coast city for the first time in history, an event that was indicative of the game's spreading appeal and increasing influence. But the real expansion era in baseball was just around the corner.

When Dodgers first baseman Jackie Robinson was named TSN's Rookie of the Year in 1947, Publisher J.G. Taylor Spink presented a watch to baseball's first modern-day black player.

Jackie Robinson

In the highly emotional days of the mid-1940s, when Branch Rickey signed the first black player for modern Organized Baseball, The Sporting News expressed doubt that Jackie Robinson, at 26, was the ideal athlete for the sociological experiment.

In the issue of November 1, 1945, TSN noted: "Robinson is reported to possess baseball abilities which, were he white, would make him eligible for a trial with, let us say, the Brooklyn Dodgers' Class B farm at Newport News if he were six years younger.

"Here then is the picture which confronts the first Negro:

"(1) He is thrown into the postwar reconstruction of baseball and placed in competition with a vast number of younger, more skilled and more experienced players. (2) He is six years too old for a chance with a club two classifications below the Double-A rating of Montreal. (3) He is confronted with the sweat and tears of toil, with the social rebuffs and the competitive heartaches which are inevitable for a Negro trail blazer in Organized Baseball. (4) He is thrown into the

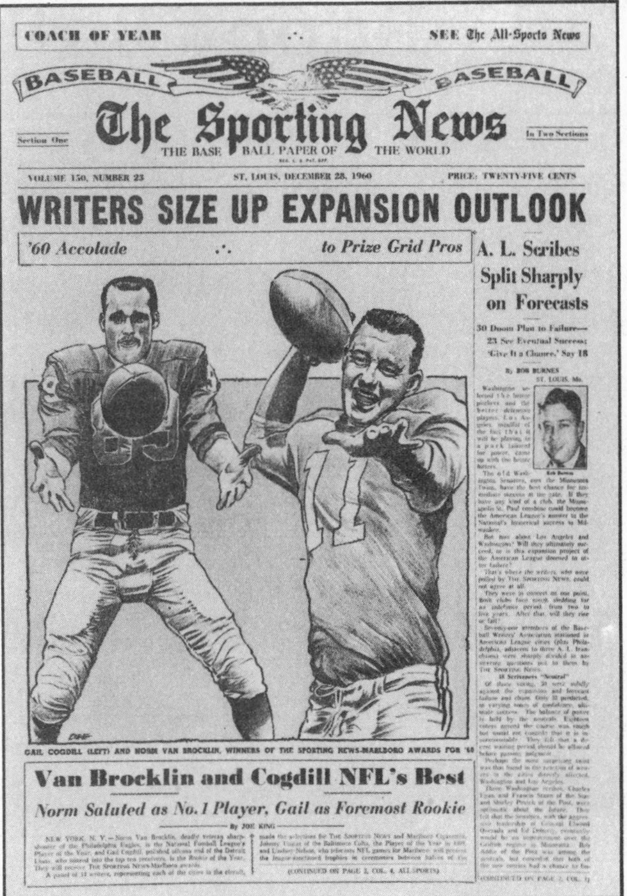

COACH OF YEAR .·. SEE The All-Sports News

BASEBALL BASEBALL

Section One — **The Sporting News** — In Two Sections

THE BASE BALL PAPER OF THE WORLD

VOLUME 150, NUMBER 23 — ST. LOUIS, DECEMBER 28, 1960 — PRICE: TWENTY-FIVE CENTS

WRITERS SIZE UP EXPANSION OUTLOOK

'60 Accolade .·. to Prize Grid Pros

A. L. Scribes Split Sharply on Forecasts

GAIL COGDILL (LEFT) AND NORM VAN BROCKLIN, WINNERS OF THE SPORTING NEWS-MARLBORO AWARDS FOR '60

Van Brocklin and Cogdill NFL's Best

Norm Saluted as No. 1 Player, Gail as Foremost Rookie

Among the features of this time period were trivia puzzles (left) and TSN covers (above) that gradually were branching into sports other than baseball.

spotlight, the one man in his race in any league (who) will be expected to demonstrate skills far beyond those he is reported to possess or to be able to develop.

"Granted that Robinson can 'take it,' insofar as points 2, 3 and 4 are concerned, the first factor alone appears likely to beat him down."

Robinson, the former UCLA star athlete, put all the skeptics to flight. He won the International League batting championship while playing for Montreal in 1946 and earned a promotion to the Dodgers.

In May 1947, following a report that St. Louis Cardinal players threatened to strike rather than face the integrated Dodgers, The Sporting News commented: "A Negro player in the major leagues is an accomplished fact, which no amount of ill-advised strike talk can affect. It remains to judge Jackie Robinson only on his ability as a player. . . The situation calls for tolerance and fair play on the part of players and fans."

Tolerance and fair play were more easily suggested than achieved. Acceptance by white players—teammates and opponents—was slow in developing, much slower than Jackie's skills as a player. Exceeding the expectations of even his mentor, Rickey, Jackie mastered the art of a new position, first base, batted .297, led the league in stolen bases with 39 and sparked the Dodgers to the 1947 National League pennant.

By September, The Sporting News was prepared to announce its choice for Rookie of the Year, an award initiated the previous season with the selection of Phillies outfielder Del Ennis. The headline proclaimed: "Rookie of the Year . . . Jackie Robinson / He's 'Ebony Ty Cobb' on Base Paths / First Baseman Also Rates High on Defensive Play, Hitting, Team Value."

The page-3 story by Publisher J.G. Taylor Spink observed that "in selecting the outstanding rookie. . . The Sporting News sifted and weighed only his baseball values.

"That Jack Roosevelt Robinson might have had more obstacles than his first-year competitors, and that he perhaps had a harder fight to gain even major league recognition, was no concern of this publication. The sociological experiment that Robinson represented, the trail blazing that he did, the barriers he broke down, did not enter into the decision. He was rated and examined only as a freshman player in the big leagues—on the basis of his hitting, his running, his defensive play, his team value.

"Robinson had it all and, compared to other first-year men that were produced, he was spectacularly outstanding."

Before the end of the 1947 campaign, Spink flew to New York to present the award personally to Robinson.

Happy Birthday—Again

Growing With the Game for 60 Years

Early Days of The Sporting News Recalled

Spink Rule Now in 3rd Generation

Facing the Future ... on a Foundation of Progress

The Sporting News

ORIGINAL FORMAT

J.G. TAYLOR SPINK

C.C. SPINK II

Sight Restored, Klein Helps to See Cards Through

The Sporting News

LOOPING THE LOOPS

BASEBALL

GILES CALLS FOR GREATER AGGRESSIVENESS IN GAME

YANK INNER FLANK--Fine First Line Shaped by Bomber Pilot McCarthy Despite War Losses

FRONT PAGE DRESS from 1887 to 1943

BASEBALL — ALL SPORTS

The Sporting News

LOOPING THE LOOPS

B. R. Disowns Sunday 2-for-1

PRESENT TABLOID

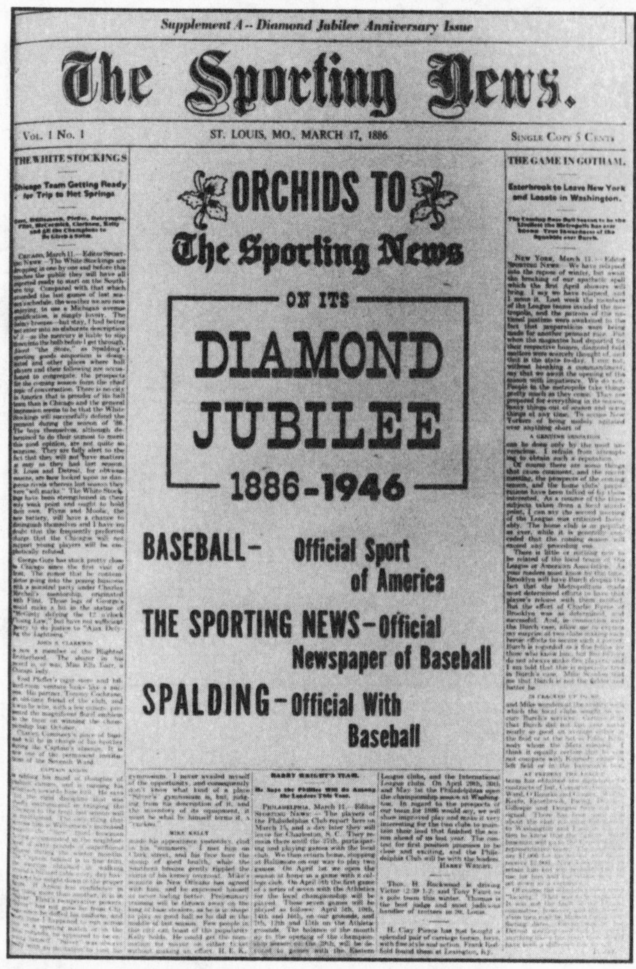

Supplement A -- Diamond Jubilee Anniversary Issue

The Sporting News.

Vol. 1 No. 1 — ST. LOUIS, MO., MARCH 17, 1886 — SINGLE COPY 5 CENTS

THE WHITE STOCKINGS

THE GAME IN GOTHAM.

ORCHIDS TO The Sporting News

ON ITS

DIAMOND JUBILEE

1886-1946

BASEBALL- Official Sport of America

THE SPORTING NEWS- Official Newspaper of Baseball

SPALDING- Official With Baseball

TSN celebrated its 60th anniversary in 1946 by publishing the largest issue in its history — 104 pages. The cover of a special section (left) featured the publication's history and reproductions of past covers while advertisers inside offered birthday congratulations (right).

In October 1946, The Sporting News belatedly observed its 60th anniversary with a 104-page issue, the largest in its history, that required 70 tons of newsprint and two days and two nights to mail.

The headline on the special section read: "Growing With the Game for 60 Years / Early Days of The Sporting News Recalled / Spink Rule Now in Its Third Generation / Brothers Who Established Paper in '86 Overcame Many Difficulties."

As he had in the golden anniversary issue 10 years earlier, Ernest J. Lanigan wrote the lead article that recounted the rise of the sports weekly. The cover illustration contained sketches of J.G. Taylor Spink, the publisher, and his son, C.C. Johnson Spink, the heir apparent. In the background were reproductions of the paper's covers depicting the original conventional size and the modern tabloid.

The section included a lengthy column of reminiscences by Taylor Spink and a year-by-year synopsis on the development of baseball that paralleled the growth of TSN.

Significant changes in the paper's operations occurred earlier in 1946. A page-1 announcement in the May 16 issue notified readers: "Price to Be Advanced to 20 Cents" (from 15 cents). The yearly subscription rate would go to $8.

The increases were necessary, the public was informed, "because of increased costs, and the addition of the Southern and Texas League scores."

However, the announcement continued, "you may subscribe now for only $6." The changes took effect with the issue of July 3.

The price per copy remained at 20 cents until the summer of 1951, when it was boosted to 25 cents because, in the years since the last hike, "the cost of newsprint (has risen) from $62 a ton to $117, an increase of 88.7 percent." The new annual subscription rate was $10, although old subscribers were offered an opportunity to renew at the old rate of $8 until August 1.

In early June 1946, readers were advised that "this issue is dated June 5 instead of May 30. This is due to two reasons:

"(1) The railroad strike which

Price to Be Advanced to 20 Cents

Because of increased costs, and the addition of the Southern and Texas League scores, the price of THE SPORTING NEWS will be advanced to twenty cents a copy or eight dollars a year for a 12-month subscription—soon. You may subscribe now for only $6—see page 30 for coupon you may use in subscribing, without purchasing copy of the new Register.

Price Increase July 4--Your Chance to Subscribe for $8

On July 1, the price of newsprint will be advanced from $107 to $117 a ton. As a result, effective with the issue of July 4, the price of THE SPORTING NEWS will be 25 cents a copy.

Since 1946, when the cost of THE SPORTING NEWS was increased to 20 cents a copy, the price of newsprint has advanced from $62 a ton to $117, an increase of 88.7 per cent. The cost of labor and other expenses have leaped upward almost at the same rate.

Notwithstanding these increases in the cost of production, there was no advance in the price of THE SPORTING NEWS to its readers, although maintaining the quality of the publication.

Because of the increase in the price of newsprint, effective July 1, we find it impossible to continue absorbing this additional cost, as well as other imminent advances in labor and postage, and at the same time maintain the standard of THE SPORTING NEWS.

The subscription price will be advanced to $10 a year, but current subscribers will be given an opportunity to take advantage of the old subscription rate for $8 a year until August 1, and extend their subscription for only one year.

Non-subscribers may receive THE SPORTING NEWS for $8 a year, or $9 in Canada, if they forward the subscription by August 1, 1951. (See blanks on Pages 24, 28 and 33.)

It is with great reluctance that this increase is put into effect, but there is no other choice and we trust that the situation will be understood by our readers.

THE PUBLISHERS.

New Publication Date--Better Paper!

This week's issue of THE SPORTING NEWS bears the date of June 5, instead of May 30. The change is due to two reasons:

(1) The railroad strike, which handicapped the handling of mail.

(2) A permanent change in the publication day of THE SPORTING NEWS, which henceforth will be dated Wednesday of the following week, instead of Thursday of the current week.

The publishers had decided some time ago on changing the publication date of THE SPORTING NEWS, in order to facilitate the handling of news. It had been planned to put the change in effect in July, but the railroad strike and its accompanying effect on mail prompted the decision to carry out the change with this week's issue of the paper.

Under the previous schedule, subscribers would have received five issues during May, as there were five Thursdays in that month. Under the new arrangement, they will get five issues in July, instead of four, as there will be five Wednesdays in that month. Hence, the loss of the fifth issue in May will be compensated by an additional issue in July, and subscribers will get the same number of issues for the year as they would have received under the old publication date.

The change in publication date is primarily designed to make possible an even better paper for readers, with fuller coverage of important developments in baseball, especially important week-end games, and other features.

Three important occurrences during this period were the 1946 price increase to 20 cents (above left), the 1951 increase to 25 cents (center left) and the 1946 announcement (below left) that explained a permanent change in TSN's publication date.

handicapped the handling of mail. (2) A permanent change in the publication day . . . which henceforth will be dated Wednesday of the following week instead of Thursday of the current week.

"The publishers had decided some time ago on changing the publication date in order to facilitate the handling of news. It had been planned to put the change in effect in July, but the railroad strike and its accompanying effect on the mail prompted the decision to carry out the change with this week's issue."

Readers were assured that they would receive as many issues under the new schedule as under the old. "Subscribers would have received five issues during May, as there were five Thursdays," the announcement pointed out. "Under the new arrangement they will get five issues during July instead of four as there will be five Wednesdays during that month."

Within weeks after the 60th anniversary issue in 1946, The Sporting News moved from its longtime headquarters at 10th and Olive streets to a more spacious facility at 2018 Washington Ave., where it occupied the entire seventh floor of the Garrison-Wagner Building.

Shortly after observing its 60th anniversary, The Sporting News moved its headquarters from 10th and Olive to the seventh floor of the Garrison-Wagner Building (below) at 2018 Washington Ave.

BOXING — HOCKEY

The All-Sports News

SECTION OF THE SPORTING NEWS — ST. LOUIS, DECEMBER 17, 1947 — SECTION TWO

BIG FIELD IN RACE TO GRAB LOUIS' CROWN

Case of Mistaken Identity? .·. *By Mullin*

Walcott Is Leader With June Date

Maxim, Tandberg, Others Mentioned as Logical Title Contenders

By LESTER BROMBERG
NEW YORK, N. Y.

The "who won 'it'" controversy over Joe Louis' debated retention of the title, at the expense of Jersey Joe Walcott, is a shot in the arm that restores competitive interest in the heavyweight division for the first time in more than a decade. The might of Louis, which had carried him past 23 previous challenges with mainly token resistance, is being questioned for a change. Also, for the first time, there is an acceptance of Walcott's competence, even by Louis' loyalists.

These two factors mean a reshuffling of the entire deck, as well as a new look on their inevitable second meeting, a view starkly different from that which obtained before their first fight.

In the altered set of heavyweight values, there is a recognition that Louis, at 33, is no longer a top bracket in himself. Not only is Walcott, also 33, elevated to narrow the gap, but others, notably Joe Maxim, must be accepted as capable of giving the champion a fight. ...

Olle Tandberg

'Other' Sports Appear

The ready acceptance of non-baseball news and features in The Sporting News during World War II convinced the publisher that a football publication would find a congenial market. Accordingly, in 1946, he introduced The Quarterback, an eight-page tabloid printed on peach-colored stock and devoted to college and professional football.

In its baptismal season, The Quarterback consisted of a page-1 news story and illustration, two pages of schedules, predictions on leading games, one page of columns reprinted from daily sports pages,

ANNOUNCING ....

RESULTS — FORECASTS

The Quarterback

FOOTBALL - News, Gossip, Schedules, Figures - EXCLUSIVELY

12 Issues Starting October 5--Printed and Mailed on Tuesday Week of Issue

25 Cents a Copy--Subscription $2.50--by Air Mail $4.50

THE SPORTING NEWS, SEPTEMBER 18, 1946

SCHEDULES — FORECASTS

The Quarterback

SECTION OF THE SPORTING NEWS — ST. LOUIS, OCTOBER 1, 1947 — SECTION TWO

NOTRE DAME AND MICHIGAN TOP GRID PARADE

Ten Strong Reasons for Yelling .·. *You Can't Beat the Irish!*

CHARGING DOWN THE FIELD is Notre Dame's forward wall, tops on the gridiron and the main reason why Notre Dame is rated No. 1 by the experts. Left to right, Leon J. Hart, Zygmont Czarboski, Joseph Signaigo, William Walsh, George Strohmeyer, Martin Wendell, William Fischer, George Sullivan, Captain George Connor and James Martin.

N. Carolina Next: Penn East's Best

Iowa and Yale Surprise Teams in First Ten; Army Rated 11th

By L. E. WOLF
KANSAS CITY, Mo.

When the final whistle of the 1947 season is blown early in December, two Midwest teams will be accorded top honors, followed closely by three Southern elevens, a special advance compilation of comparative statistics indicates.

H. O. Fritz Crisler

Notre Dame and Michigan are scheduled to finish one-two in the national rankings, with North Carolina, Louisiana State and Rice completing the first five. Next in line are Pennsylvania, Iowa, Yale, Georgia Tech and Illinois.

PIGSKIN PETE *Picks*

Nation's Top 100

In 1946, convinced that a football publication would receive a warm welcome, J.G. Taylor Spink ran an announcement (above right) that an eight-page tabloid called 'The Quarterback' would begin publication. In 1947, 'The Quarterback' (below right) continued to appear as a separate publication but also ran as a pull-out section in the regular TSN issue. In succeeding years, it was continued as a pull-out section only and when football season ended, the special section was renamed 'The All-Sports News' (above) and continued to appear until the beginning of spring training.

numerous features and a contest that tested readers' ability to predict the outcome of selected college games.

In October 1946, readers were invited to try for "an all-expenses tour to any bowl game." Included in the first prize were tickets for two, all transportation, hotel and meals.

The contest consisted of five crossword puzzles, plus two statements of 100 words or less in which the contestant was required to state his reasons for selecting the greatest current player and the greatest former performer.

The Quarterback sold for 25 cents a copy and 12 issues were published.

The following year, 1947, The Quarterback again appeared as a separate publication, but also was incorporated in the regular issue of The Sporting News as a pull-out section. At the conclusion of the football season, the special section was renamed "The All-Sports News" and was published usually until the major league baseball teams went into spring training (at which time the paper once again became an all-baseball weekly).

Contests were a prominent feature of The Sporting News for many years. In addition to picking winners in football and basketball games, readers could engage in a contest to name an all-star baseball team with a manager and coach. A panel of judges determined the winner "on the neatness of ballots, adequacy of the reasons given for the selection in the letters (also required) and conformity with the all-star team as chosen by the votes of the contenders themselves." First prize was $500 in cash, second $150 and third $75. The next 10 runners-up were given subscriptions to TSN, while copies of the "Official Baseball Register" went to the second group of runners-up and the "Official Baseball Guide" to still another 10.

At another time, contestants competed for an all-expenses-paid trip to the season-opening game between the Yankees and Senators at Washington. In this one, contestants were required to list all the errors they detected in a baseball sketch and submit a letter explaining why they wished to attend the inaugural in the nation's capital.

In August 1949, readers were given a chance to predict the standings in both major leagues on a designated date. First prize was $250—$500 if the winner of the World Series was predicted correctly—while other cash awards were $175, $50, $25 and 10 prizes of $5 each.

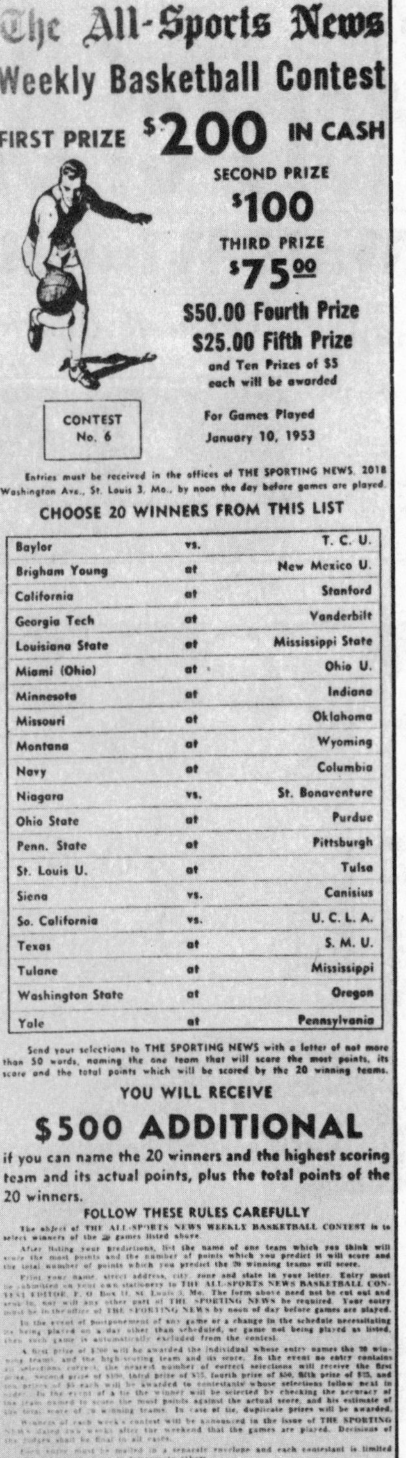

The All-Sports News
Weekly Basketball Contest

FIRST PRIZE $200 IN CASH

SECOND PRIZE
$100

THIRD PRIZE
$75.00

$50.00 Fourth Prize
$25.00 Fifth Prize
and Ten Prizes of $5 each will be awarded

CONTEST No. 6

For Games Played January 10, 1953

Entries must be received in the offices of THE SPORTING NEWS, 2018 Washington Ave., St. Louis 3, Mo., by noon the day before games are played.

CHOOSE 20 WINNERS FROM THIS LIST

Baylor	vs.	T. C. U.
Brigham Young	at	New Mexico U.
California	at	Stanford
Georgia Tech	at	Vanderbilt
Louisiana State	at	Mississippi State
Miami (Ohio)	at	Ohio U.
Minnesota	at	Indiana
Missouri	at	Oklahoma
Montana	at	Wyoming
Navy	at	Columbia
Niagara	vs.	St. Bonaventure
Ohio State	at	Purdue
Penn. State	at	Pittsburgh
St. Louis U.	at	Tulsa
Siena	vs.	Canisius
So. California	vs.	U. C. L. A.
Texas	at	S. M. U.
Tulane	at	Mississippi
Washington State	at	Oregon
Yale	at	Pennsylvania

Send your selections to THE SPORTING NEWS with a letter of not more than 50 words, naming the one team that will score the most points, its score and the total points which will be scored by the 20 winning teams.

YOU WILL RECEIVE

$500 ADDITIONAL

if you can name the 20 winners and the highest scoring team and its actual points, plus the total points of the 20 winners.

FOLLOW THESE RULES CAREFULLY

The object of THE ALL-SPORTS NEWS WEEKLY BASKETBALL CONTEST is to select winners of the 20 games listed above.

After listing your predictions, list the name of one team which you think will score the most points and the number of points which you predict it will score and the total number of points which you predict the 20 winning teams will score.

Print your name, street address, city, zone and state in your letter. Entry must be submitted on your own stationery to THE ALL-SPORTS NEWS BASKETBALL CONTEST EDITOR, P. O. Box 11, St. Louis 3, Mo. The form above need not be cut out and sent in, nor will any other part of THE SPORTING NEWS be required. Your entry must be in the office of THE SPORTING NEWS by noon of day before games are played.

In the event of postponement of any game or a change in the schedule necessitating its being played on a day other than scheduled, or game not being played as listed, then such game is automatically excluded from the contest.

A first prize of $200 will be awarded the individual whose entry names the 20 winning teams and the high-scoring team and its score. In the event no entry contains all selections correct, the nearest number of correct selections will receive the first prize. Second prize of $100, third prize of $75, fourth prize of $50, fifth prize of $25, and ten prizes of $5 each will be awarded to contestants whose selections follow next in order. In the event of a tie the winner will be selected by checking the accuracy of the team named to score the most points against the actual score, and his estimate of the total score of 20 winning teams. In case of tie, duplicate prizes will be awarded.

Winners of each week's contest will be announced in the issue of THE SPORTING NEWS dated two weeks after the weekend that the games are played. Decisions of the judges shall be final in all cases.

[illegible] is limited [illegible]

[illegible] THE SPORT- [illegible]

6 Sect. 2 ★ THE ALL-SPORTS NEWS, DECEMBER 31, 1952 ★

The Sporting News
WEEKLY
Stretch Drive
PENNANT CONTEST

FOR FOUR MORE WEEKS, INCLUDING THIS WEEK'S ISSUE

BIG PRIZES EACH WEEK

CONTEST No. 2

FIRST PRIZE
$250
AND
TWO WORLD'S SERIES TICKETS

$175.00 Second Prize
$50.00 Third Prize
$25.00 Fourth Prize
and Ten Prizes of $5.00 each

EVERY WEEK!

Pick Major League Standings

AS OF DESIGNATED DATE EACH WEEK

Plus Additional $250 Prize
FOR PICKING WORLD'S SERIES WINNER
SPECIAL ADDED AWARD — You can win up to $500.00 plus two World's Series tickets with one winning entry.

I predict the standings on the morning of September 12, with games won and lost for each team, will be as follows:

AMERICAN LEAGUE Team	Won	Lost	NATIONAL LEAGUE Team	Won	Lost

I predict ______ will be leading in the American League and ______ in the National League.
My reasons why, in 50 words or less, are attached.

EXTRA—$250 BONUS PRIZE—EXTRA
IF YOU CAN ALSO PICK WORLD'S SERIES WINNER

I predict ______ will win the World's Series.
My reasons why, in 50 words or less, are attached.

Contests remained a prominent feature in TSN throughout this time period and rewarded readers who could accurately pick basketball winners (left) or the baseball pennant races (above).

Life Story of BABE RUTH

by Fred Lieb

THE SPORTING NEWS, APRIL 23, 1947 ★ 17

Waterfront Waif Who Rose to Fame

Put in Industrial School at 7, Remained 12 Years

Signed Sight Unseen by Jack Dunn of Baltimore Club on Recommendation of Teacher; Proved Immediately Successful as Southpaw Hurler and Slugger

In the middle of that decade known as the Gay Nineties, when

Farewell Appearance in Yankee Uniform

A Man of Many Roles ∴ in His Days Off the Diamond

WHEN HE WENT ON A CANADIAN HUNTING TRIP in 1933...

RUTH AS DODGERS COACH, 1938, with MRS. RUTH and DAUGHTER.

ALWAYS READY FOR A GOOD TURN... RUTH PLAYING SANTA CLAUS with TONY GALENTO, the boxer... 1940

AS A RADIO ANNOUNCER

The BAMBINO BEING MADE UP FOR HIS 1942 ROLE in the LOU GEHRIG PICTURE

AS MILLIONS WILL WANT TO REMEMBER HIM

Babe Ruth Revisited

The baseball spotlight that had beamed brightly on the Sultan of Swat for 20 years found the home run slugger again in April 1947 when professional teams from coast to coast celebrated Babe Ruth Day.

It was overdue recognition for the Bambino, whose might, bat and dramatic flair had lifted the game from the gloom created by the Black Sox scandal.

Babe had only 16 months to live, but much of that time was devoted to a new job as adviser to the Ford Motor Co. in its sponsorship of the American Legion Junior Baseball program.

The Sporting News hailed Babe Ruth Day (April 27) "as a thanksgiving and a celebration for Ruth's

When April 27, 1947, was designated 'Babe Ruth Day,' The Sporting News began work on an April 23 supplement that devoted eight pages to the Bambino's life story (above and below left). An editorial appeared in the same issue (right) praising the man who had lifted baseball out of its doldrums in the 1920s.

recovery from his illness that led him into the valley of the shadow."

In all likelihood, the editorial noted, "it took the gravity of his illness to demonstrate the affection which millions hold for this colorful figure who, with his mighty slugging feats, his boyishness and his ever-ready grin, captured the imagination of the fans."

During this period, The Sporting News started to publish Legion Junior supplements four times annually, from a preview in May until a late-summer wrapup that covered the playoffs and championship series. Generally, the section consisted of four pages of editorial matter plus advertisements of major sporting goods manufacturers.

In the issue following the Babe Ruth Day observance, The Sporting News published an eight-page supplement, "Life Story of Babe Ruth," by Fred Lieb. TSN also published a book, "The Real Babe Ruth," written by Dan Daniel and H.G. Salsinger.

When Ruth died in August 1948, the publication devoted eight pages to his life story and eulogized the Bambino as "the greatest figure the playing side of baseball has produced.

"Ruth was the champion of the turnstiles. He was the human epitome of baseball drama. He was the friend of all, the enemy of none, a man whose sovereign virtue lay in his keen sense of humor, his smiles, his willingness to serve and his high appreciation of the tremendous debt he owed to baseball."

Concluding, the editorial observed: "Baseball well may sit disconsolate amid ashes of its mourning, for there was only one George Herman Ruth. It is quite conceivable that there will not be another."

In Memoriam
Charles C. Spink
Founder of The Sporting News
August 2, 1862--April 22, 1914

GREAT DAY FOR RUTH—AND THE GAME

On Sunday, April 27, all baseball will pay a long-deferred tribute to Babe Ruth, with a heaping measure of honors such as seldom falls to the lot of any man while he still is living.

From coast to coast, and, we hear, even in Mexico and Central and South America, Cuba and Santo Domingo, baseball will wave its cap on Babe Ruth Day and shout its huzzahs for the most dramatic and appealing figure the game yet has known.

From Yankee Stadium, New York, focal point of the widespread ceremonies, will be broadcast a program in which George Herman

GAME MADE RUTH—AND HE REMADE GAME

With bowed heads, with tributes in newspapers and over the radio, with expressions of heart-felt regret by fans, and with eulogies by the leaders of the game, the nation paid its last respects to George Herman Ruth, following the news of his death, August 16.

Ruth was the greatest figure the playing side of baseball yet has produced.

It may be that complete justice is on the side of those who insist that in versatility, in all-round skill, Tyrus Raymond Cobb must be rated the all-time No. 1.

But Ruth was not merely a ball player. He was the idol of the youngsters of America. He will continue on that pedestal, even in death.

Ruth was the champion of the turnstiles. He was the human epitome of baseball drama. He was the friend of all, the enemy of none, a man whose sovereign virtue lay in his keen sense of humor, his smile, his willingness to serve, and his high appreciation of the tremendous debt he owed to baseball.

"What I am, what I have, what I am going to leave behind me—all this I owe to the game of baseball, without which I would have come out of St. Mary's Industrial School in Baltimore a tailor, and a pretty bad one, at that," the Babe said as he watched the making of "The Babe Ruth Story" in Hollywood.

A TSN editorial in August 1948 (above) mourned the passing of Ruth, calling him 'the greatest figure the playing side of baseball yet has produced.' It was partly because of Ruth's involvement with the American Legion Junior Baseball program that TSN began publishing Legion supplements (below) during this period.

Torrid Tourneys for State Crowns Start in Alabama

Championship Meet Will Be Held at Leeds on August 1-3; New York Playoffs Booked August 13-14 at Cooperstown

By OSCAR KAHAN

INDIANAPOLIS, Ind.

Lou Brissie

Opening two tense weeks of playoffs in the American Legion Junior baseball program, Alabama, the first state in alphabetical listing, also will be the first to stage its championship tournament, August 1-3. In rapid order through August 15, other states will pick their title teams to meet in the eight regional eliminations leading up to the national finals at Hastings, Neb., August 28-September 3.

Sites and dates for the state events as reported to Commissioner Brissie's office included the arrangements made by New York, Maine and Vermont in Region 1. Historic Doubleday Field at Cooperstown will be the scene of New York's tournament, August 13-14. Maine's representative will be chosen at Togus, August 5-7, and Vermont's finalists will meet for their state's crown at Rutland, August 6-7.

In Region 2, Connecticut's playoffs will start at Bristol, August 10, and then will be completed on August 13-14. Delaware's tournament will be held at Dover, August 4-6; Maryland's at College Park, August 4-7, and New Jersey's at the home city of the state's northern district winner, August 6-8.

Alabama will stage its August 1-3 tournament at Leeds, with other Region 3 sites and dates including Florida at Melbourne, August 3, and Georgia at Macon, August 4-7.

Oklahoma will determine its state champion at Altus, August 7-10; Tennessee will play at Clarksville, August 2-6, and Arkansas will battle it out at Walnut Ridge, August 2-7, in Region 4.

Region 5, which produced last year's national champion from Detroit, has made the following arrangements: Illinois at Springfield, August 5-8; Indiana at Rockport,

Nebraska Legion Loop 'Pinch-Hits' for O. B. League

Six Towns, Once Members of Class D Circuit, Form New Group of Kid Teams

By DOYLE SMITH

HASTINGS, Neb.

AMERICAN LEGION

JUNIOR BASEBALL PROGRAM

Batter Up--From Tropics to Arctic

IN BALMY WEATHER, John Bateman, .484 hitter with Panama Insurance, at the plate in Panama Canal Zone championship playoff game at Beam Stadium, Albrook Air Force Base, with enlisted men's barracks, framed by palm trees, in the background.

Some New Faces at TSN

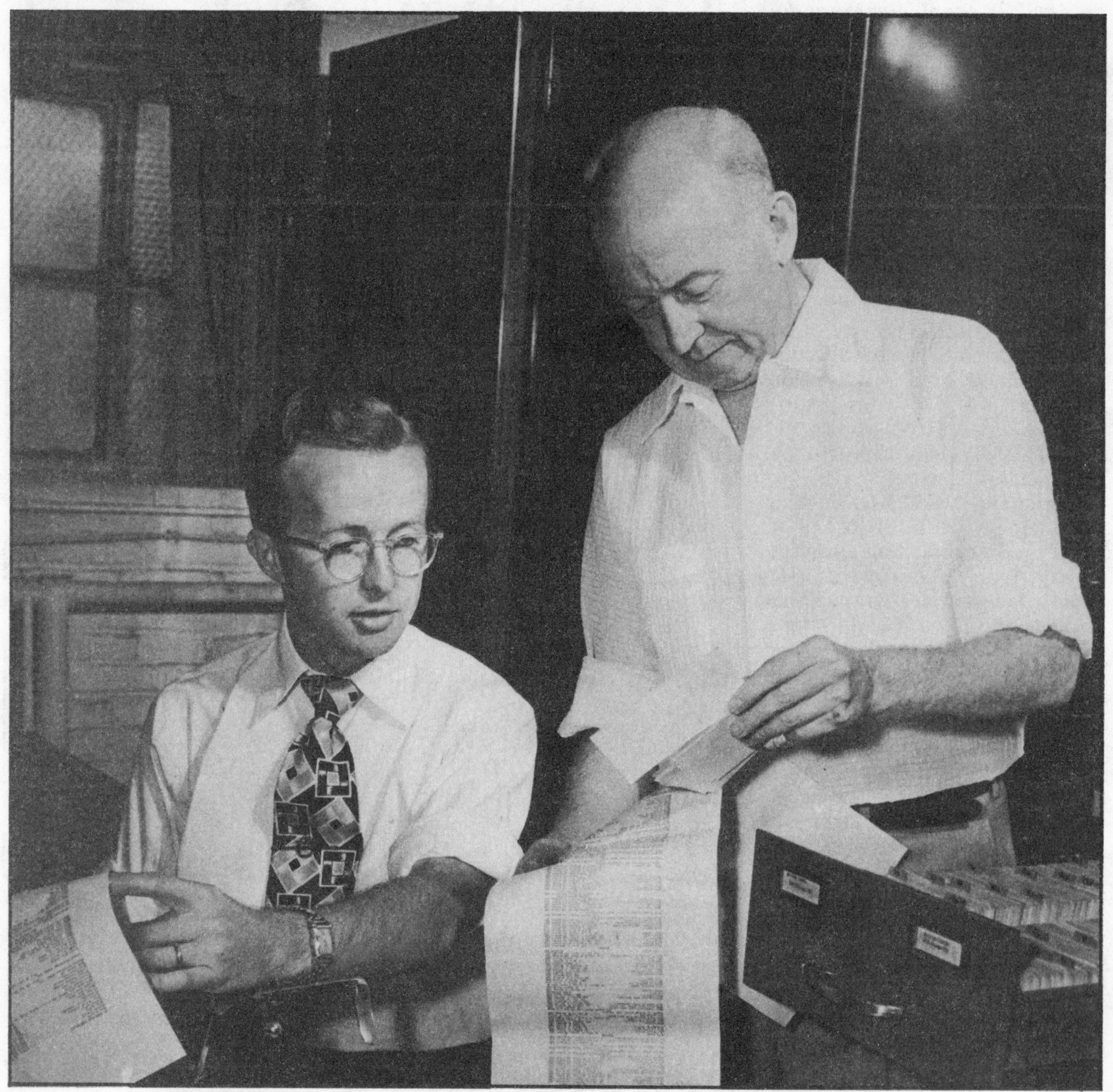

Paul Rickart (right) and Clifford Kachline, members of the editorial staff during this time period, look over proofs for TSN's 'Baseball Record Book.'

As a result of retirements and death, the editorial department of The Sporting News underwent a number of significant changes during the 1950s.

In 1954, Edgar G. Brands retired after serving more than 20 years as editor. Brands, an authority on baseball history and legislation and a man who had a legion of acquaintances in the game, had suffered a heart attack at his desk in 1953. With the departure of the editor, J.G. Taylor Spink assumed that title, to go along with that of publisher.

In August 1958, Oscar K. Ruhl, longtime chief of the editorial department, died of cancer. His passing was noted not only in the obituary column, but in an editorial titled "Oscar K. Ruhl—Big Leaguer."

The editorial, written by Carl T. Felker, commented upon Ruhl's "enthusiasm, energy and friendliness." His special knack for make-up, the tribute added, "made the pages of The Sporting News outstanding in attractiveness and eye-compelling interest. His news judgment enabled him to recognize and develop many stories and features of special interest. He kept in close touch with The Sporting News' network of correspondents throughout the majors and minors who reciprocated his friendliness, his enthusiasm and his constant desire to 'get the story, get it all and get it right.' All regarded him as a personal friend."

Ruhl was succeeded as chief of the department by Lowell Reidenbaugh, who had joined the staff in 1947 after terms with the Lancaster, Pa., Intelligencer-Journal and the Philadelphia Inquirer.

The most noteworthy change of this decade occurred in August 1959 when Felker, the "Old Reliable" of the staff, retired after more than 30 years as first lieutenant under Taylor Spink. He was succeeded as chief copy editor by Ralph Ray, an Illinoisan who had apprenticed in the sports departments of the Chicago Tribune and Buffalo Evening News.

Other key members of the editorial department in these years were Oscar Kahan, a hard-nosed journalist who had been trained by daily journals and the Associated Press; Paul Rickart, the No. 1 proofreader who also doubled as an occasional feature writer and statistician during a career that extended from 1919 to 1965, and Clifford Kachline, a Pennsylvanian whose orderliness and meticulous detail were constantly evident in his writings and his editing of the "Official Baseball Guide" and other Spink publications.

Rickart, a St. Louisan, visited the offices of The Sporting News shortly after returning from overseas duty in World War I. He paid the call to thank Taylor Spink for sending the baseball weekly to servicemen in France. When he walked out the door, he had a job.

Kachline's route to St. Louis was as remarkable. In the early 1940s, an issue contained an advertisement for the "Official Baseball Register." Part of the ad consisted of Frank McCormick's lifetime record as it appeared in the Register.

Gazing over the statistical columns, Kachline spotted an error. McCormick's batting average for one season was not computed correctly. He notified Spink of the inaccuracy. Before long, Kachline received proofs for checking. Cliff's thoroughness impressed the publisher. He joined the staff early in 1943 and remained until 1967.

Oscar Ruhl, longtime chief of the editorial department, is pictured (above) in 1946 delivering anniversary issues of The Sporting News to an airline stewardess.

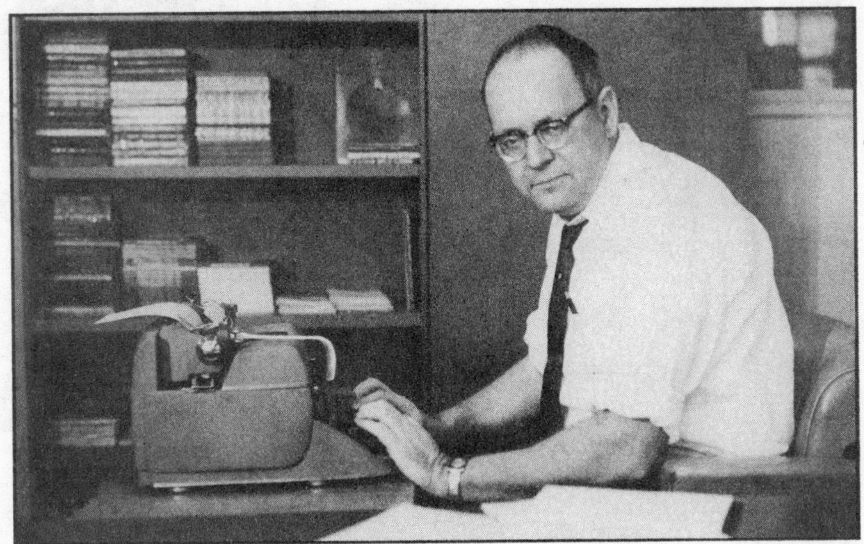

When Oscar Ruhl died of cancer in 1958, he was succeeded as editorial-department chief by Lowell Reidenbaugh (above).

Oscar Kahan remained a key member of The Sporting News' editorial staff until his death in 1980.

Players of the Decade

ALL-STAR ISSUE

23rd ANNUAL GAME

BASEBALL

The Sporting News

THE BASE BALL PAPER OF THE WORLD

ST. LOUIS, JULY 11, 1956

MUSIAL ACCLAIMED PLAYER OF DECADE

Head and Shoulders Above All for Ten Years

He Receives Clock on Eve of Star Tilt

The Man Tops 97 Ballots to DiMag's 83, Ted's 52 in The Sporting News Poll

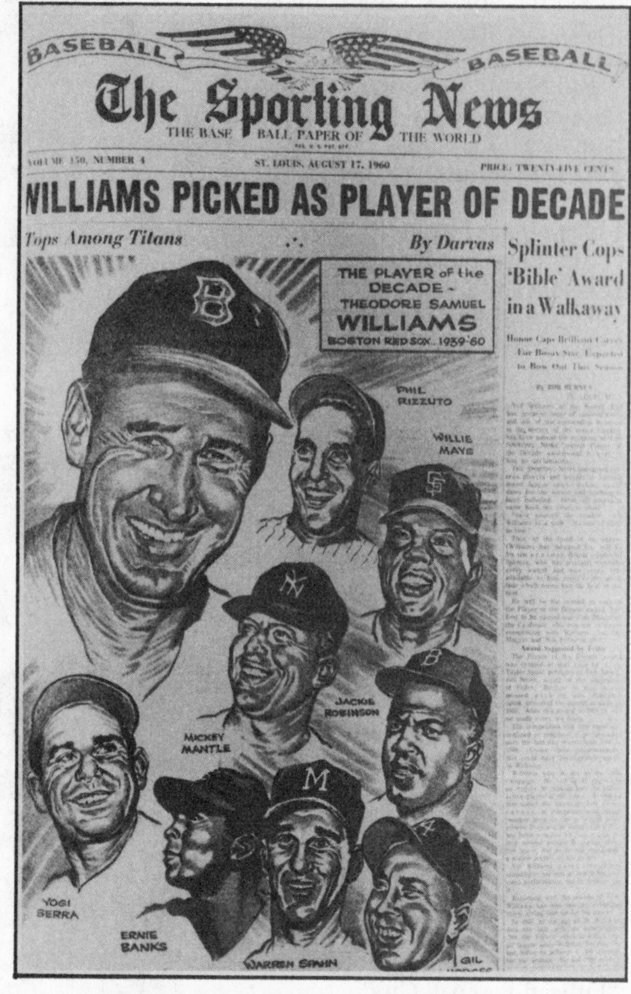

BASEBALL

The Sporting News

THE BASE BALL PAPER OF THE WORLD

ST. LOUIS, AUGUST 17, 1960

WILLIAMS PICKED AS PLAYER OF DECADE

Tops Among Titans

By Darvas

Splinter Cops 'Bible' Award in a Walkaway

Bob Feller was in the final year of his illustrious career when he made a suggestion that caught the ear of Taylor Spink.

Why not, the Cleveland pitcher wondered in 1956, present an award to the "Player of the Decade" from 1946 to 1955?

Why not, indeed, echoed the publisher, who set in motion the machinery to choose the player most deserving of the accolade.

A 260-man panel, consisting of writers, executives and players, delivered its verdict in June 1956. From a field dominated by Stan Musial, Joe DiMaggio, Ted Williams and Feller himself, the selectors picked Stan the Man.

The Cardinals' outfielder-first baseman received 97 first-place votes, the Yankee Clipper 83, the Splendid Splinter 52 and Rapid Robert 14.

On the basis of 14 points for a first-place vote, nine for second, eight for third, seven for fourth, six for fifth and so on, Musial amassed 2,654 points, DiMaggio 2,433 and Williams 2,312.

In an editorial saluting Musial, it was pointed out that the citation went "far beyond one man, however talented."

Musial personified, the editorial continued, "the ambitions, the efforts, the prayers of all the thousands of young men who have aspirations to careers in the game's strongest company." He was "a poor boy . . . bringing to his bid for fame and fortune the only qualification baseball asked—ability to play the game. No one inquired about his nationality, religion or academic excellence. He was given what baseball gives with perfect impartiality to rich and poor, white and colored, farm lads or city youngsters—opportunity."

Musial received his award, a handsome grandfather's clock, during the All-Star Game break in Washington. The presentation was made by Feller, representing Spink, at a luncheon attended by several hundred at the Washington Touchdown Club. All-Star players were among the guests, and Shirley Povich, sports editor of the Washington Post and longtime correspondent for The Sporting News, was master of ceremonies of the affair.

Ted Williams was the next Player of the Decade honoree, winning the award in 1960. Selection of a second recipient so quickly after the naming of the first winner enabled TSN to align its Player of the Decade award into "even" periods, with Willie Mays taking the honor for the decade of the '60s and Pete Rose winning it for the decade of the '70s.

St. Louis first baseman-outfielder Stan Musial was named The Sporting News' first Player of the Decade (above left) in 1956, based on the vote of a 260-man panel that consisted of writers, executives and players. Boston star Ted Williams became TSN's second winner in 1960 when TSN held another vote to align its award with the beginning of each decade. Williams posed with his award (above), a grandfather clock which was pictured (right) originally in the July 4, 1956, issue of TSN.

Award for Winner

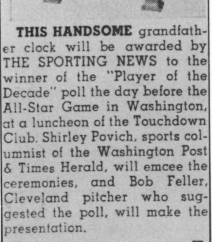

THIS HANDSOME grandfather clock will be awarded by THE SPORTING NEWS to the winner of the "Player of the Decade" poll the day before the All-Star Game in Washington, at a luncheon of the Touchdown Club. Shirley Povich, sports columnist of the Washington Post & Times Herald, will emcee the ceremonies, and Bob Feller, Cleveland pitcher who suggested the poll, will make the presentation.

tinued against Harshman, Zuverink and Johnson.

New York	AB.	H.	O.	A.
McDougald, 2b	4	0	4	6
Kubek, ss....	6	2	1	6
Mantle, cf....	3	3	4	0
Berra, c.....	5	2	2	0
Skowron, 1b..	4	2	8	0
Throneb'ry, 1b	1	0	4	0
Siebern, lf...	2	0	1	0
Howard, rf...	5	3	1	0
Lumpe, 3b....	1	0	0	0
aCarey, 3b....	4	1	2	1
Larsen, p....	3	3	0	0
Maas, p......	1	0	0	1
Totals	39	16	27	14

Baltimore	AB.	H.	O.	A.
Tasby, cf.....	4	2	2	1
Boyd, 1b......	2	0	3	0
Hale, 1b......	3	1	4	2
Woodling, rf..	3	1	3	0
Johnson, p....	1	0	1	2
cGreen	1	1	0	0
Nieman, lf....	5	0	2	0
Triandos, c...	1	0	0	0
Zuverink, p...	0	0	0	2
bPilarcik, rf..	2	1	0	0
Klaus, 3b-ss..	3	2	5	2
Carrasquel, ss.	2	0	3	1
Finigan, 3b...	1	0	0	0
Gardner, 2b..	1	0	1	1
Lockman, 2b..	3	1	0	1
Pappas, p.....	0	0	0	1
Harshman, p..	0	0	0	0
Ginsberg, c...	4	1	3	0
Totals	36	10	27	13

New York .... 4 4 3 1 1 0 0 0 0—13
Baltimore .... 0 0 0 0 1 0 2 0 2— 5

Pitchers	IP.	H.	R.	ER.	BB.	SO
Larsen (Winner 4-0)	7	7	3	3	4	1
Maas	2	3	2	0	0	0
Pappas (Loser 4-2)	⅓	4	4	4	0	0
Harshman	2	6	7	7	3	0
Zuverink	3⅔	4	2	2	3	0
Johnson	3	2	0	0	1	0

aGrounded out for Lumpe in third. bSingled for Zuverink in sixth. cSingled for Johnson in ninth. R—McDougald, Kubek, Mantle 3, Berra 2, Skowron 2, Howard 2, Larsen 2, Tasby 2, Lockman, Ginsberg 2. E—Triandos, Woodling, Carey. RBI—Kubek 2, Mantle 2, Berra, Skowron 3, Howard 2, Larsen 2, Tasby 4, Hale. 2B—Mantle, Howard 2, Kubek, Larsen. HR Skowron, Mantle, Tasby 2. SB—Mantle. SH—McDougald. DP—Tasby and Gardner; Kubek, McDougald and Skowron 2; Hale, Klaus and Hale; Lockman, Klaus and Hale. LOB—New York 7, Baltimore 8. WP—Pappas, Harshman, Zuverink. U—Tabacchi, Paparella, Runge and Hurley. T—2:42. Attendance —15,787.

CHICAGO AT KANSAS CITY (N)—Athletics staged most potent attack of season, rapping out 21 hits to overwhelm White Sox, 16 to 0, behind four-hit pitching of Daley. Until Pinch-hitter Romano singled with two out in sixth, Daley had perfect game going. Landis singled in seventh and Phillips and Aparicio belted one-base blows in ninth to conclude Chisox pop-gun hitting. A's tagged Wynn for three hits and run in second inning, enough to saddle veteran with

GAMES OF SUNDAY, JULY 2

DETROIT AT BALTIMORE (D)—Grand-slam homer by Gentile, third of season for slugging first baseman, and perfect relief pitching of Hoeft enabled Orioles to defeat Tigers, 6 to 3. Loss cut Bengals' lead to one length over Yankees. In third inning, B. Robinson and Snyder singled and Brandt walked to load bases for Gentile's jackpot wallop off Regan. E. Robinson also homered for Orioles in game. Estrada, who gave up round-tripper to Kaline, was chased in seventh when Tigers scored run and had bases loaded with two out. Hoeft, relieving, retired Cash on pop fly and then set down next six Bengal batters in order.

Detroit	ab	r	h	rbi
McAuliffe, ss.	5	0	0	0
Bruton, cf....	4	0	2	0
Kaline, rf....	3	1	2	1
Colavito, lf...	3	1	1	0
Cash, 1b.....	4	0	1	0
Boros, 3b....	3	0	0	1
Wood, 2b.....	4	0	0	0
Roarke, c....	3	1	1	0
Regan, p.....	1	0	0	0
aOsborne ...	1	0	0	0
Woodeshick, p	0	0	0	0
bMorton	1	0	1	0
Aguirre, p...	0	0	0	0
dFernandez .	1	0	0	0
Totals	33	3	8	2

Baltimore	ab	r	h	rbi
B. Robinson, 3b	4	1	3	1
Snyder, lf....	3	1	1	0
cBusby, cf....	1	0	0	0
Brandt, cf-lf.	2	1	0	0
Gentile, 1b...	3	1	1	4
Triandos, c..	4	0	0	0
E. Robinson, rf	4	1	1	1
Hansen, ss...	3	0	1	0
Breeding, 2b..	4	1	1	0
Estrada, p...	2	0	0	0
Hoeft, p......	1	0	0	0
Totals	31	6	8	6

Detroit .... 0 0 0 2 0 0 1 0 0—3
Baltimore .... 0 0 4 1 0 1 0 0 *—6

Pitchers	IP.	H.	R.	ER.	BB.	SO.
Estrada (Winner 6-5)	6⅔	8	3	3	2	2
Hoeft (Save)	2⅓	0	0	0	0	0
Regan (Loser 7-4)	4	6	5	5	2	1
Woodeshick	2	2	1	1	0	2
Aguirre	2	0	0	0	2	2

aCalled out on strikes for Regan in fifth. bSingled for Woodeshick in seventh. cFlied out for Snyder in seventh. dPopped out for Aguirre in ninth. 2B—Colavito, Cash. HR—Gentile, Kaline, E. Robinson. SB—Breeding. SH—Estrada. SF—Boros. E—Roarke. PO-A—Baltimore 27-12, Detroit 24-5. DP—Breeding, Hansen and Gentile. LOB—Detroit 8, Baltimore 6. HP—Estrada (Bruton, Kaline). U—Drummond, Paparella, Runge and Carrigan. T—2:36. Attendance —11,115.

CLEVELAND AT BOSTON (D)—Breaking loose with two out in tenth inning, Indians scored six runs to defeat Red Sox, 12 to 6. Two homers

When the wire services announced in 1958 that they would adopt a new form of box score for nationwide transmission, The Sporting News resisted vigorously (below). TSN continued to convert box scores to the traditional form (above left in 1959) for three seasons before admitting defeat in 1961 (above right).

CRITICISM OF NEW BOX SCORE GROWS

Frank Lane's appeal for the return of individual fielding records to the columns of the box scores deserves the endorsement of everyone in Organized Ball. However well intended the changes adopted by the wire services, whatever the practical typographical advantages gained thereby, the fact remains that the new form has evoked columns of criticism.

If veteran writers consider the dropping of the defensive figures regrettable, it may be assumed that a large fraction of the fans is no less displeased. Lane suggests that Earl Hilligan and Dave Grote, the heads of the major league service bureaus, join Bob Broeg, president of the Baseball Writers' Association of America, in an effort to correct the situation.

The three men named would make a competent and effective committee. All of them are well experienced in observing fan reaction and all of them, of course, have the facilities to round up quickly the opinions of the writers.

If their study shows that objection to the new form is as widespread as we suspect it is, the wire services undoubtedly will be willing to review the matter.

We realize that the change was made effective only after consultation with the appropriate representatives of the client newspapers. But it's one thing to sit in an office and say, "Sure, we can drop the fielding figures; what do they mean, anyway?" and another thing to see the new deal in actual publication and sound out the reactions of the customers.

Perhaps by this time some of the sports editors who approved the new form are ready to reconsider. Perhaps they, too, miss the experience of noting that Joe Outfielder had a busy afternoon or that Bill Third Baseman could have played his position in a rocking chair.

As Lane says, there is no reason to pronounce the change a total failure. The presentation of the pitchers' records in tabular

TSN Loses Box Score Battle

Disciples of baseball tradition received a rude jolt in the spring of 1958 when the Associated Press and the United Press announced that they, after consultation with sports editors of client newspapers, would adopt a new form of box score for nationwide transmission.

Instead of five statistical columns covering at-bats, runs, hits, putouts and assists, there would be only four columns, with figures for at-bats, runs, hits and runs batted in. No longer could a baseball devotee note the number of assists by a shortstop or the putouts by a first baseman. The defensive part of the game was being sacrificed in the interest of fewer apostrophes in players' names (with the reduction in columns, more names could be spelled out).

Cries of protest against the new style were instant and vociferous. An editorial in an April issue of The Sporting News argued that, while four columns made for a neater numerical display, the tidiness was achieved at the cost of a vital segment of the game.

"It is true the new form provides an easy-to-read runs-batted-in column," the editorial said, "but we doubt that anyone ever developed eyestrain while finding the same information (below) in the old summary. The tabular pitching record is a step forward—but nothing new to readers of The Sporting News, which already had used that feature.

"We have no intention of taking the matter to the Supreme Court, but we hope fans everywhere will let the newspapers know how they feel about the new arrangement. If the majority likes it—or doesn't care one way or the other—that's that. But if there's strong sentiment for a return to the old order, we hope the response will be speedy."

Game's Brass Lauds Relief-Hurler Trophies

Frick Cites 'Bible' and Spink for Sponsoring New Awards

BBWAA Head Says Prizes Fill Big Void

'Rescue Aces Were Seldom Seriously Considered for Cy Young Award'—Munzel

By JERRY HOLTZMAN
CHICAGO, Ill.

Presentation of a trophy to the top relief pitcher in each of the major leagues by THE SPORTING NEWS has been hailed by all baseball men, from Commissioner Ford Frick on down. The idea has been called the most forward step in the game's list of prizes since awards first were inaugurated by the Chalmers auto company half a century ago.

"THE SPORTING NEWS and its publisher, J. G. Taylor Spink, are to be congratulated for initiating and sponsoring these awards," said Frick. "It is recognition for players who have been overlooked much too long.

"Concept of the game insofar as pitching is concerned has changed radically in the last three decades. The starting pitchers used to go all the way in the dead-ball era. But after World War I, when the ball

Top Hat in Majors' Fireman Poll

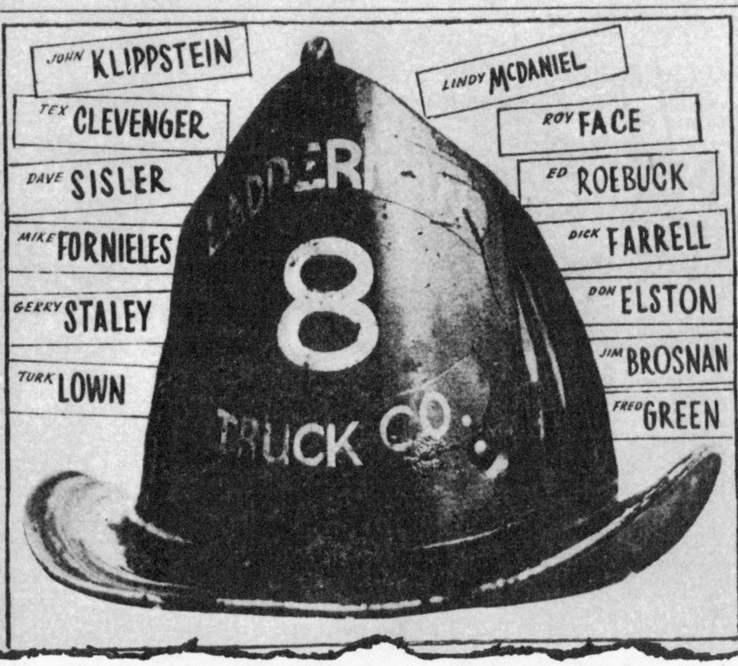
JOHN KLIPPSTEIN
TEX CLEVENGER
DAVE SISLER
MIKE FORNIELES
GERRY STALEY
TURK LOWN
LINDY McDANIEL
ROY FACE
ED ROEBUCK
DICK FARRELL
DON ELSTON
JIM BROSNAN
FRED GREEN
8
TRUCK CO.

Cronin Calls Saves, Wins 'Fairest Way'

Chisox Skipper Lopez Hails Idea—Points Out Value of Own Staley and Lown

or on the bases when the relief hurler enters the game. And only one pitcher can get a save in each game.

Manager Al Lopez of the White Sox, who unquestionably has the finest rescue brigade in the American League with Gerry Staley, Turk Lown and Frank Baumann, vigorously applauded the new awards of THE SPORTING NEWS.

* * *

Credits Relievers for Flag

"I like the idea of the awards and also the method of figuring the saves," said Lopez. "In fact, I like everything about it. Nobody has to tell me how important relief pitching is.

"We won a pennant last year because of relief work. In fact, the pennant-clincher was won when Staley came in against Cleveland and on the first pitch served up a double-play ball that meant the first championship for the White Sox in 40 years.

Within a month, another editorial made a plea to "get back those fielding records. The box score should present, as fully as possible, the story of the game. The new form falls short of that requirement. Baseball is a combination of offense and defense. Its statistical summary should be the same."

The wire services refused to retreat. Taylor Spink did not accept the revised form gracefully. At considerable expense, the publisher arranged for correspondents to furnish fielding statistics which were incorporated into all major league box scores. Minor league box scores adhered to the new style.

For three seasons, TSN published old-style box scores of American and National League games. At the end of that time, Spink acknowledged defeat and acceded to the revised form.

However, for many years thereafter, major league fielding averages were published once monthly during the season so that readers could obtain a line on the relative defensive performances of players in advance of the official averages that were published during the winter months.

In 1960, TSN announced plans to give annual awards to the top relief pitchers in baseball, drawing praise (above and below) from baseball men everywhere. The first Firemen of the Year were Lindy McDaniel of the Cardinals and Boston's Mike Fornieles.

McDaniel and Staley Lead Race for Reliever Award

Redbird Fireman Sets Pace in N. L. With 19 Points—Gerry Tops A. L. With 12

By JERRY HOLTZMAN
CHICAGO, Ill.

Lindy McDaniel of the Cardinals and Gerry Staley of the White Sox are the leading candidates for the 1960 trophies which will be presented by THE SPORTING NEWS to the top relief pitcher in each major league.

According to a survey of THE SPORTING NEWS' correspondents, McDaniel had 19 points and Staley 12 through July 31. One point is awarded for every pitching save and another point is given for every victory, provided it was won in a relief role.

Lindy McDaniel

The 25-year-old McDaniel, a fixture in the Cardinal bull pen for the last two seasons, had 12 saves and seven victories. Staley, who will be 40 this month, had three saves and nine wins.

Runners-up in each league were Ed Roebuck of the Dodgers with 15 points

Salute From Bull-Pen Blazer

SHERATON PALACE

July 30, 1960

Dear Mr. Spink,

Just read your incisive proposal to establish a merit system, with awards, for relief pitchers. It is a refreshing, progressive step worthy of the Sporting News. In the current baseball era pitchers are more often disparaged than not. They're blamed for the length of games, for not completing games they start, and for losing as many games as they win (the indisputable average.) As though pitchers were not just one-ninth of any given club. Relief pitchers, laughingly, have been looked upon with downcast eye, as if they hardly deserved a toe-plate. All of us in the bullpen will greet your proposal in humble, though weary, gratitude.

Sincerely,
Jim Brosnan

REDS' RELIEVER JIM BROSNAN HAILS AWARDS

Elston of the Cubs, 11, and Don McMahon, Braves, ten.

A. L. second division, have the third-ranking reliever in the A. L. in vet-

BASEBALL BASEBALL

The Sporting News

THE BASE BALL PAPER OF THE WORLD

REG. U. S. PAT. OFF.

VOLUME 147, NUMBER 11 ST. LOUIS, APRIL 8, 1959 PRICE: TWENTY-FIVE CENTS

Five-Flight Plan Among Features of '59 Schedules

A. L. Chart Lists Split Trips to Other Section

By HARRY SIMMONS

MONTREAL, Que.

Not since the introduction of the four-trip slate in 1936 have so many new features appeared in major league schedules as will be seen this year.

The important early opening and extra Sunday are only two of several departures.

In the American League, eastern clubs (Boston, New York, Baltimore and Washington) will make five western trips while the western clubs (Cleveland, Detroit, Chicago and Kansas City) make as many the other way.

From 1936 through 1958, four trips were made, except in the war years when only three were permissible.

The first and last of the four-trip jaunts were ten-day affairs (the so-called short trips) while the middle two were two-week sojourns. On each trip, all four clubs in the rival division were

Classy Rookies Flashed in South and West

By JOE KING

NEW YORK, N. Y.—Rookie quality ran high in both the American and National leagues, a tour of training camps in Arizona and Florida revealed, and there is likely to be exciting competition and possibly a surprise or two in the battles for the annual freshman awards.

The leaders, as the opening of the season approached, are, of course, the newcomers who walked into jobs waiting for them, and who have only themselves to beat. In this select group are Johnny Callison, White Sox outfielder, George (Sparky) Anderson, Phillies' second baseman, and Willie Tasby, Orioles' outfielder.

Others who improved as training progressed have offered strong challenges for positions not at first earmarked for them. In this group are

and since there is room on any staff for a hurler of demonstrated quality, some should stick. However, judgment of new pitchers is sometimes difficult and, until the chuckers get a baptism under fire, must be withheld until the 25-man limit goes in effect.

Even so, there was booming enthusiasm in the West and the East for an elite selection of stars from the minors. Foremost are Ernie Broglio of the Cards, Bennie Daniels of the Pirates, Jerry Casale of the Red Sox, Orlando Pena of the Reds, Bob Hartman of the Braves, John Buzhardt of the Cubs and Rodolfo Arias of the White Sox.

The sensational note in the rookie roundup is the extraordinary number of brilliant young catchers to come up this year. All invade squads boasting established receivers, but they will have the chance to

The Season Preview

American League

Headquarters—520 Boylston Street, Boston 16, Mass.
JOSEPH E. CRONIN, President
WILLIAM HARRIDGE, Chairman of Board
THOMAS A. YAWKEY, Vice-President
JOSEPH W. McKENNEY, Director of Public Relations

BALTIMORE

President—James Keelty, Jr.
Chair'n of Board—Jos. A. W. Iglehart
General Manager—Lee MacPhail
Pub. Rel.-Asst. to G.M.—Jack Dunn III
Business Mgr.—Herbert E. Armstrong
Farm Director—Jas. M. McLaughlin
Traveling Secretary—John Lancaster
Offices—Memorial Stadium
Manager—Paul Richards
Memorial Stadium Capacity—47,778

BOSTON

President—Thomas A. Yawkey
Gen. Mgr.—Stanley (Bucky) Harris
Business Mgr.—Richard O'Connell.

Directory of Leag

GOVERNMENT OF O. B.

MAJOR LEAGUES
COMMISSIONER—Ford C. Frick
SECRETARY-TREASURER—Charles M. Segar
HEADQUARTERS—RCA Bldg., West, 30 Rockefeller Plaza, NEW YORK, N. Y.

EXECUTIVE COUNCIL—Ford C. Frick, Commissioner; Joseph E. Cronin, American League president; Warren C. Giles, National League president, George M. Weiss, A. L. representative (alternates, Charles A. Comiskey and Arnold M. Johnson), and Walter F. O'Malley, N. L. representative (alternates, Robert R. M. Carpenter and Richard A. Meyer).

NATIONAL ASSOCIATION
PRESIDENT-TREASURER—George M. Trautman
ASSISTANT TO PRESIDENT—Phillip Piton
DIRECTOR OF PUBLIC RELATIONS—Carl Lundquist
FIELD REPRESENTATIVE—Eddie Stumpf
HEADQUARTERS—720 E. Broad St., Columbus, O.
EXECUTIVE COMMITTEE—Edward S. Doherty, Jr., president of American Association, chairman; Claude Engberg, president of Pioneer League, and Charles Hurth, president of Southern Association.

TEXAS LEAGUE (AA)

President—Dick Butler, 2016 Alamo National Bldg.

Club	President	Gen. Bus. Mgr.
Amarillo	Jay Taylor	Robert Freitas
Austin	Allen H. Russell	George Schepps
Corpus Christi	E. J. Humphries	Bob Hamric
San Antonio	Marvin Milkes	Bill Currie
Tulsa	Grayle Howlett	Grayle Howlett
Victoria	Tom O'Connor	Derrest Williams

EASTERN LEAGUE (A)

President—Thomas H. Richardson, 412 West Third St.

Club	President	Gen. Bus. Mgr.
Albany	Thos. F. McCaffrey	Thos. F. McCaffrey
Allentown	Joseph J. Buzas	Bob Evie
Binghamton	George M. Weiss	Jerry Toman
Lancaster	H. H. Haverstick, Jr.	Edward Abel
Reading	Frank Lane	Daniel Zerbes
Springfield	Chas. A. Stonehain	Charles O'Malley
Williamsport	B. Clair Jones	J. Roy Clunk
York	George T. Stone	William Jury

SOUTH ATLANTIC LEAGUE (A)

President—Sam C. Smith, Jr., 719 Dusy St.

Club	President	Gen. Bus. Mgr.
Asheville	W. Fleming Talman	Arthur Perkins
Charleston	William Ackerman	J. L. Robertson, Jr.

Spink Predicts Yankee, Pirate Pennants

American League

NEW YORK YANKEES

By DAN DANIEL, New York World-Telegram and Sun

PITCHING—Only likely addition from minors is Gabler, who won 19 for Denver last year. If a big need for another starter arises, the club will make a deal. It has the surplus.

CATCHING—Still the most competent staff in the major leagues, with Berra, Howard and Johnson holding over, and Blanchard up from Denver with impressive record.

INFIELD—Availables of 1958 on the job again—Skowron, McDougald, Richardson, Carey and Kubek.

OUTFIELD—Mantle flanked by Bauer and Siebern.

SUMMATION—No club in the league to beat New York.

CHICAGO WHITE SOX

By EDGAR MUNZEL, Chicago Sun-Times

HotFour-Way Scrap Looms in Giles Loop

Dodgers Could Join as Fifth Flag Contender; Chisox Tabbed A. L. Runners-Up

By J. G. TAYLOR SPINK

ST. LOUIS, Mo.

National League

PITTSBURGH PIRATES

By LES BIEDERMAN, Pittsburgh Press

PITCHING—Could be best all-round in league. Friend, Kline, Law, Haddix and Witt as starters and Face in relief.

CATCHING—Foiles and Burgess give Pirates good balance with Kravitz to back 'em up.

INFIELD—Contending caliber with Mazeroski, Groat and Hoak. Nelson, Stuart or Kluszewski at first.

OUTFIELD—Best in league, Pirates think: Skinner-Virdon-Clemente.

SUMMATION—Better team, stronger pitching, greater bench should make Pirates real dark-horses for pennant.

Danny Murtaugh

SAN FRANCISCO GIANTS

By JACK McDONALD, San Francisco Call-Bulletin

Settings for '59 N. L. Pennant Scrap

MEMORIAL COLISEUM, FIGUEROA AND EXPOSITION, L. A.

Huge arena was completed in 1923 at cost of $800,000. Capacity then 76,000. . . . Additional $1,000,000 was expended to enlarge it for 1932 Olympic Games, . . . 101,000 . . . but Dodgers.

'Frisco's New Home Biggest Park Feature

Could Be Occupied in July But Shift Unlikely in '59 Unless Club Wins Pennant

By CARL FELKER

ST. LOUIS, Mo.

The drawings of major league . . .

BUSCH STADIUM, GRAND BLVD. AND DODIER ST., ST. L.

Site of stadium is oldest of any ball park in majors, first N. L. game been played there on May 5, 1876. . . . Chris Von der Ahe's American . . . tion teams made their home at Sportsman's Park, as it long was known, 1882 to 1891. . . . Park was virtually "dark" next 11 years until Browns . . . American League in 1903. . . .

Throughout this time period, the baseball season preview issue (left in 1959) was always TSN's showcase paper of the year. Among the many features that might appear in this issue were a major league directory (above), pennant-race predictions (center) and stadium diagrams and information (below).

Special issues of The Sporting News rolled off the presses at the rate of about five a year during the 1950s. One heralded the start of spring training, another the advent of the regular season, while still others previewed the All-Star Game, the World Series and the winter baseball conventions.

The largest of these issues was that of early April that signaled the arrival of a new season. This usually contained 60 or 64 pages (later it would expand to 72 pages) and contained features, columns and detailed information about the forthcoming campaign.

Annually, the center fold presented the directory of Organized Baseball, with the names of the clubs in each league, major and minor, and the name of each team's chief executive officer and manager, as well as the minor league clubs' parent teams. There also was information on major league uniform numbers, park capacities and sometimes diagrams of the playing fields, guides to the pronunciation of tricky names, a log of major league play-by-play announcers, the flagship stations for the networks and broadcast schedules for the national networks.

Starting in 1955 and continuing for many seasons, there was another feature that won widespread acclaim from readers. It was an editorial-page essay titled "The Game for All America," by Ernie Harwell, well-known major league broadcaster. The tribute to the game was reprinted numerous times into the 1970s.

It began: "Baseball is the President throwing out the first ball and a pudgy schoolboy playing catch with his dad on a Mississippi farm."

It is also, wrote Harwell, "a tall, thin old man waving a scorecard from his dugout" and "the fat guy with the bulbous nose running out one of his 714 home runs with mincing steps.

"It's America, this baseball. A reissued newsreel of boyhood dreams, dreams lost somewhere between boy and man.

"Nicknames are baseball. Names like Zeke and Pie and Kiki and Home Run and Cracker and Dizzy and Dazzy.

"Arguments, 'Casey at the Bat,' old cigarette cards, photographs, 'Take Me Out to the Ball Game'—all of these are baseball.

"Baseball is cigar smoke, hot roasted peanuts, The Sporting News, winter trades, 'Down in front' and the seventh-inning stretch. Sore arms, broken bats, a no-hitter and the strains of the 'Star-Spangled Banner.'

"Baseball is a highly paid Brooklyn catcher telling the nation's business leaders, 'You have to be a man to be a big leaguer, but you have to have a lot of little boy in you, too.'

"This is a game for America, this baseball!" Harwell concluded.

Beginning in 1955, Ernie Harwell's 'The Game for All America' feature (right) appeared annually on the editorial page of TSN's baseball preview issue.

Founded March 17, 1886

Published by Charles C. Spink & Son, 2012-18 Washington Avenue, St. Louis 3, Mo.

Subscription Price $10 a Year — Six Months $5.50 — Three Months $3.00

ENTERED AS SECOND CLASS MATTER FEBRUARY 13, 1904 AT POST OFFICE, ST. LOUIS, MO., UNDER THE ACT OF MARCH 3, 1879.

Vol 139 — APRIL 13, 1955 — No. 11

Printed in U. S. A.

51

The Game for All America

By ERNIE HARWELL

Baseball is President Eisenhower tossing out the first ball of the season; and a pudgy schoolboy playing catch with his dad on a Mississippi farm.

It's the big league pitcher who sings in night clubs. And the Hollywood singer who pitches to the Giants in spring training.

A tall, thin old man waving a scorecard from his dugout—that's baseball. So is the big, fat guy with a bulbous nose running out one of his 714 home runs with mincing steps.

It's America, this baseball. A re-issued newsreel of boyhood dreams. Dreams lost somewhere between boy and man. It's the Bronx cheer and the Baltimore farewell. The left field screen in Boston, the right field dump at Nashville's Sulphur Dell, the open stands in San Francisco, the dusty, wind-swept diamond at Albuquerque. And a rock home plate and a chicken wire backstop—anywhere.

There's a man in Mobile who remembers a triple he saw Honus Wagner hit in Pittsburgh 46 years ago. That's baseball. So is the scout reporting that a 16-year-old sandlot pitcher in Cheyenne is the new "Walter Johnson."

It's a wizened little man shouting insults from the safety of his bleacher seat. And a big, smiling first baseman playfully tousling the hair of a youngster outside the players' gate.

Baseball is a spirited race of man against man, reflex against reflex. A game of inches. Every skill is measured. Every heroic, every failing is seen and cheered—or booed. And then becomes a statistic.

In baseball, democracy shines its clearest. Here the only race that matters is the race to the bag. The creed is the rule book. Color is something to distinguish one team's uniform from another.

Baseball is Sir Alexander Fleming, discoverer of penicillin, asking his Brooklyn hosts to explain Dodger signals. It's Player Moe Berg speaking seven languages and working crossword puzzles in Sanskrit. It's a scramble in the box seats for a foul—and a $125 suit ruined. A man barking into a hot microphone about a cool beer, that's baseball. So is the sports writer telling a .383 hitter how to stride, and a 20-victory pitcher trying to write his impressions of the World's Series.

Baseball is a ballet without music. Drama without words. A carnival without kewpie dolls.

A housewife in California couldn't tell you the color of her husband's eyes, but she knows that Yogi Berra is hitting .337, has brown eyes and used to love to eat bananas with mustard. That's baseball. So is the bright sanctity of Cooperstown's Hall of Fame. And the former big leaguer, who is playing out the string in a Class B loop.

Baseball is continuity. Pitch to pitch. Inning to inning. Game to game. Series to series. Season to season.

It's rain, rain, rain splattering on a puddled tarpaulin as thousands sit in damp disappointment. And the click of typewriters and telegraph keys in the press box—like so many awakened crickets. Baseball is a cocky batboy. The old-timer whose batting average increases every time he tells it. A lady celebrating a home team rally by mauling her husband with a rolled-up scorecard.

Baseball is the cool, clear eyes of Rogers Hornsby, the flashing spikes of Ty Cobb, an overaged pixie named Rabbit Maranville, and Jackie Robinson testifying before a Congressional hearing.

Baseball? It's just a game—as simple as a ball and a bat. Yet, as complex as the American spirit it symbolizes. It's a sport, business—and sometimes even religion.

Baseball is Tradition in flannel knickerbockers. And Chagrin in being picked off base. It is Dignity in the blue serge of an umpire running the game by rule of thumb. It is Humor, holding its sides when an errant puppy eludes two groundskeepers and the fastest outfielder. And Pathos, dragging itself off the field after being knocked from the box.

Nicknames are baseball. Names like Zeke and Pie and Kiki and Home Run and Cracker and Dizzy and Dazzy.

Baseball is a sweaty, steaming dressing room where hopes and feelings are as naked as the men themselves. It's a dugout with spike-scarred flooring. And shadows across an empty ball park. It's the endless list of names in box scores, abbreviated almost beyond recognition.

The holdout is baseball, too. He wants 55 grand or he won't turn a muscle. But, it's also the youngster who hitch-hikes from South Dakota to Florida just for a tryout.

Arguments, Casey at the Bat, old cigarette cards, photographs, Take Me Out to the Ball Game—all of them are baseball.

Baseball is a rookie—his experience no bigger than the lump in his throat—trying to begin fulfillment of a dream. It's a veteran, too—a tired old man of 35, hoping his aching muscles can drag him through another sweltering August and September.

For nine innings, baseball is the story of David and Goliath, of Samson, Cinderella, Paul Bunyan, Homer's Iliad and the Count of Monte Cristo.

Willie Mays making a brilliant World's Series catch. And then going home to Harlem to play stick-ball in the street with his teen-age pals—that's baseball. So is the husky voice of a doomed Lou Gehrig saying, "I'm the luckiest guy in the world."

Baseball is cigar smoke, hot-roasted peanuts, THE SPORTING NEWS, winter trades, "Down in front," and the Seventh Inning Stretch. Sore arms, broken bats, a no-hitter, and the strains of the Star-Spangled Banner.

Baseball is a highly-paid Brooklyn catcher telling the nation's business leaders: "You have to be a man to be a big leaguer, but you have to have a lot of little boy in you, too."

This is a game for America, this baseball!

A game for boys and for men.

Language Class

Almost 6 Pct. of Player[s] on Clubs' Spring Roste[rs] Were Born Outside U.S.

By ED POLLOCK

Of the Philadelphia Bulletin

PHILADELPHIA, Pa.

Bucky Harris

There are schools for almost everything a player has to know in baseball, but it's about time foreign language classes were opened for managers so they could make themselves understood around the major loops.

Baseball has long been Amer[i]ca's national game, but foreigne[rs] have so infiltrated major squa[ds] that they're giving cause for conce[rn] about when Cuba, Mexico or so[me] South American country is going [to] take the sport away from us.

Fourteen of the 16 big league clubs—New York's Yankees and Boston's R[ed] Sox are the exceptions—had at le[ast] one foreign player on their spring ro[s]ters. They added up to 37, which is al[]most six per cent of the total numb[er] of players who trained in Florida a[nd] Arizona.

As ever, Washington leads in [the] league of nationalities. The Sena[tors] are harboring five foreign-born—fo[ur] Cubans and one Venezuelan. The r[e]port is out that Manager Chuck Dre[s]sen is howling for an interpreter, b[ut] that would be an exaggeration. It m[ay] be that he's only howling.

Bucky Harris got the break of h[is] long career when he landed the ma[n]agerial job with the Detroit Tige[rs] after years of futile efforts in tryi[ng] to make the Washington Cubans under[]stand his English.

The dire need for a school of lan[]guages for managers was pointed u[p] by an incident in the Senators' d[...] in Orlando a few springs a[go].

The Nats were having ba[tting prac]tice and it was Connie Mar[...] rero's turn to swing. Connie wa[s sit]ting idly on the bench, dreaming p[rob]ably of Havana's blue skies.

* * *

Conrado No Comprende

Ordinarily, the hitters woul[d] have gone on without him, bu[t] Connie was due to pitch that da[y] and there was no telling when [a] hit would be needed from his ba[t]. Players at the plate shouted a[t] him. Not understanding, he pai[d] no heed.

Harris spoke to him softly from [a] nearby seat. He was rewarded wi[th a] blank expression. Then he made [the] common mistake of shouting. S[till] no dawn of understanding.

Finally, Bucky resorted to the [in]ternational language of signs and m[o]tion. He picked up a bat from th[e] rack, swung it and motioned toward th[e] plate. Connie took off on the double.

"Hasn't that fellow learned an[y] English yet?" someone inquired.

"No," said Harris, "and that make[s] it even. I haven't learned any Spanish."

With the Detroit club, Bucky doe[sn't] need Spanish. His only foreign play[ers] in training were Reno Bertoia, a fo[rmer] University of Michigan student, [whose] birth-place is Italy, and [...] fielder Fred Fle[...] man from Can[ada].

More than a few of the foreign-bor[n] have made good with a wallop in bas[e]ball. Without them, the White S[ox] probably would have finished in [the] second division last season. Their [...] Cubans, Minnie Minoso and Sa[ndy] Consuegra, made off with a load [of] American League batting and pitchin[g] honors, and Venezuelan Chico Ca[r]rasquel is rated by many as the be[st] shortstop in the game.

Minoso led the league in total bas[es] with 324 and his batting average [of] .320 was second only to the .341 co[m]piled by champion Bobby Avila, Cle[ve]land's Mexican star. Consuegra's rec[ord] of 16 games won and only three l[ost] gave him a percentage of .824, highe[st] in either major league.

The Yankees shed themselves [of a] foreign element by trading Wil[ly] Miranda to the Baltimore Orioles ov[er] whom Paul Richards presides as ma[n]ager. Having managed the White S[ox] last year, Richards is well acquaint[ed] with Cubans, but he knows no Spanis[h].

Outstanding among the Puerto Rican[...]

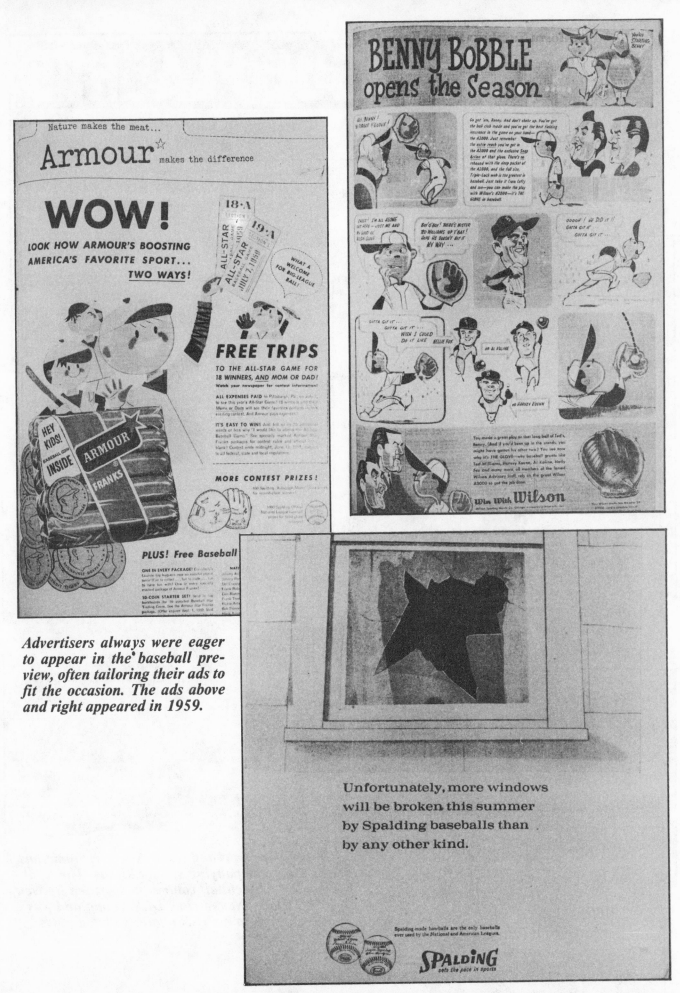

Advertisers always were eager to appear in the baseball preview, often tailoring their ads to fit the occasion. The ads above and right appeared in 1959.

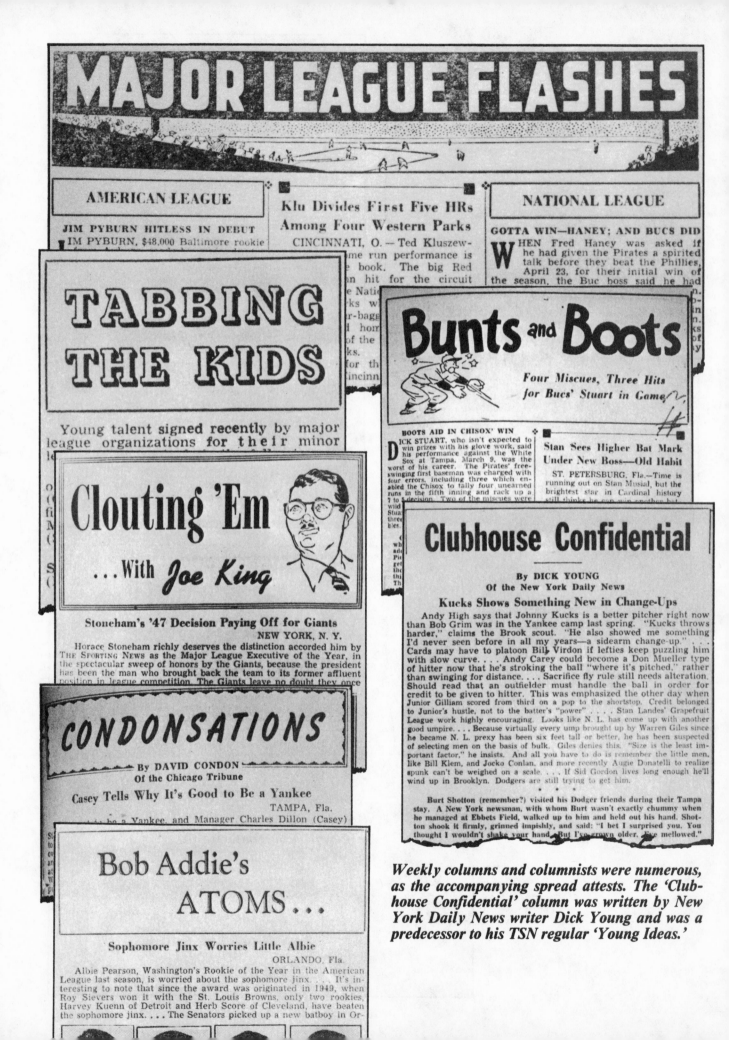

MAJOR LEAGUE FLASHES

AMERICAN LEAGUE

JIM PYBURN HITLESS IN DEBUT

JIM PYBURN, $48,000 Baltimore rookie

Klu Divides First Five HRs Among Four Western Parks

CINCINNATI, O.—Ted Kluszew-

NATIONAL LEAGUE

GOTTA WIN—HANEY; AND BUCS DID

WHEN Fred Haney was asked if he had given the Pirates a spirited talk before they beat the Phillies, April 23, for their initial win of the season, the Buc boss said he had

TABBING THE KIDS

Young talent signed recently by major league organizations for their minor

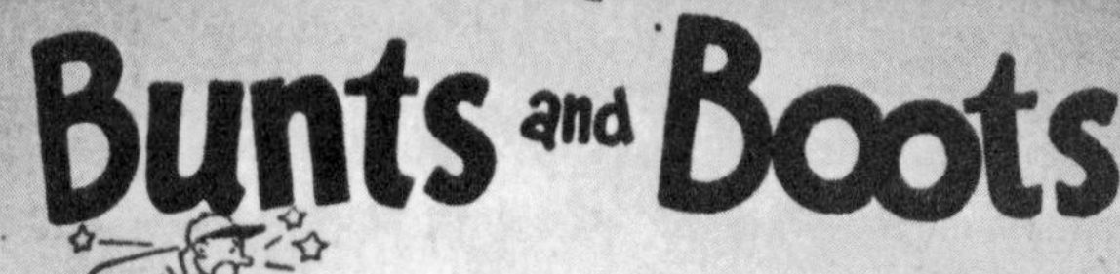

Bunts and Boots

Four Miscues, Three Hits for Bucs' Stuart in Game

BOOTS AID IN CHISOX' WIN

DICK STUART, who isn't expected to win prizes with his glove work, said his performance against the White Sox at Tampa, March 9, was the worst of his career. The Pirates' free-swinging first baseman was charged with four errors, including three which enabled the Chisox to tally four unearned runs in the fifth inning and rack up a 7 to 5 decision. Two of the miscues were

Stan Sees Higher Bat Mark Under New Boss—Old Habit

ST. PETERSBURG, Fla.—Time is running out on Stan Musial, but the brightest star in Cardinal history

Clouting 'Em

...With *Joe King*

Stoneham's '47 Decision Paying Off for Giants

NEW YORK, N. Y.

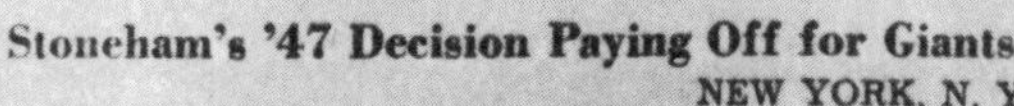

Horace Stoneham richly deserves the distinction accorded him by THE SPORTING NEWS as the Major League Executive of the Year, in the spectacular sweep of honors by the Giants, because the president has been the man who brought back the team to its former affluent position in league competition. The Giants leave no doubt they once

Clubhouse Confidential

By DICK YOUNG
Of the New York Daily News

Kucks Shows Something New in Change-Ups

Andy High says that Johnny Kucks is a better pitcher right now than Bob Grim was in the Yankee camp last spring. "Kucks throws harder," claims the Brook scout. "He also showed me something I'd never seen before in all my years—a sidearm change-up." . . . Cards may have to platoon Bill Virdon if lefties keep puzzling him with slow curve. . . . Andy Carey could become a Don Mueller type of hitter now that he's stroking the ball "where it's pitched," rather than swinging for distance. . . . Sacrifice fly rule still needs alteration. Should read that an outfielder must handle the ball in order for credit to be given to hitter. This was emphasized the other day when Junior Gilliam scored from third on a pop to the shortstop. Credit belonged to Junior's hustle, not to the batter's "power" . . . . Stan Landes' Grapefruit League work highly encouraging. Looks like N. L. has come up with another good umpire. . . . Because virtually every ump brought up by Warren Giles since he became N. L. prexy has been six feet tall or better, he has been suspected of selecting men on the basis of bulk. Giles denies this. "Size is the least important factor," he insists. And all you have to do is remember the little men, like Bill Klem, and Jocko Conlan, and more recently Augie Donatelli to realize spunk can't be weighed on a scale. . . . If Sid Gordon lives long enough he'll wind up in Brooklyn. Dodgers are still trying to get him.

* * *

Burt Shotton (remember?) visited his Dodger friends during their Tampa stay. A New York newsman, with whom Burt wasn't exactly chummy when he managed at Ebbets Field, walked up to him and held out his hand. Shotton shook it firmly, grinned impishly, and said: "I bet I surprised you. You thought I wouldn't shake your hand. But I've grown older. I've mellowed."

CONDONSATIONS

By DAVID CONDON
Of the Chicago Tribune

Casey Tells Why It's Good to Be a Yankee

TAMPA, Fla.

... be a Yankee, and Manager Charles Dillon (Casey)

Bob Addie's ATOMS . . .

Sophomore Jinx Worries Little Albie

ORLANDO, Fla.

Albie Pearson, Washington's Rookie of the Year in the American League last season, is worried about the sophomore jinx. . . . It's interesting to note that since the award was originated in 1949, when Roy Sievers won it with the St. Louis Browns, only two rookies, Harvey Kuenn of Detroit and Herb Score of Cleveland, have beaten the sophomore jinx. . . . The Senators picked up a new batboy in Or-

Weekly columns and columnists were numerous, as the accompanying spread attests. The 'Clubhouse Confidential' column was written by New York Daily News writer Dick Young and was a predecessor to his TSN regular 'Young Ideas.'

Features, Columns Galore In TSN

New features, new columnists and new artists made their debuts in The Sporting News during the 16 years following the close of World War II.

Stan Baumgartner, a former major league pitcher who had graduated into the sportswriting profession, wrote "Stan's Slants" as well as features and news stories out of Philadelphia.

Roger Birtwell of Boston contributed "Between Innings," Dick Young of New York authored "Clubhouse Confidential" (which later was changed to "Young Ideas"), Bob Addie of Washington wrote "Addie's Atoms," Dave Condon of Chicago offered "Condonsations" and Joe King of New York wrote "Clouting 'Em."

King covered baseball and professonal football for the New York World-Telegram and it was not uncommon for his byline to appear atop three or four articles in a single issue.

While Willard Mullin of New York remained the most popular cartoonist, the work of Lou Darvas (Cleveland), Ray Gotto (New York), Vic Johnson (Boston), Amadee Wohlschlaeger (St. Louis) and Karl Hubenthal (Los Angeles) was given frequent exposure.

The life stories of diamond immortals such as Ty Cobb, Eddie Collins and Honus Wagner were serialized during this era and, starting in 1951, the first issue of January featured the foremost sports thrills of the previous year as experienced by more than 75 prominent writers, broadcasters and artists. The section frequently covered 12 pages and was continued as a January feature for 10 years.

Annually, in March and April, TSN published leads and box scores of all major league exhibition games and covered the train-

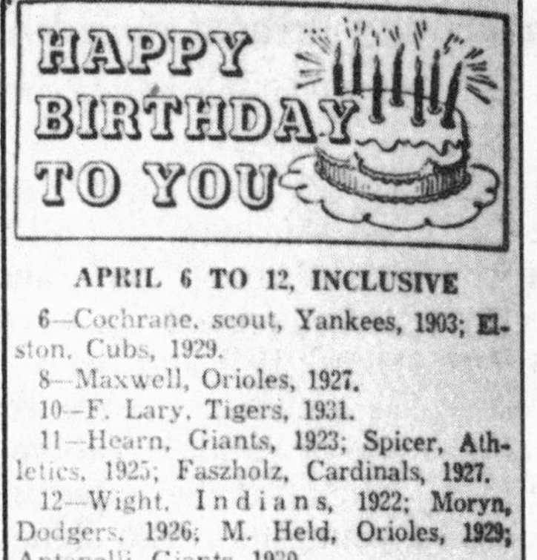

HAPPY BIRTHDAY TO YOU

APRIL 6 TO 12, INCLUSIVE

6—Cochrane, scout, Yankees, 1903; Elston, Cubs, 1929.
8—Maxwell, Orioles, 1927.
10—F. Lary, Tigers, 1931.
11—Hearn, Giants, 1923; Spicer, Athletics, 1925; Faszholz, Cardinals, 1927.
12—Wight, Indians, 1922; Moryn, Dodgers, 1926; M. Held, Orioles, 1929; Antonelli, Giants, 1930.

The Dodgers were Los Angeles-based world champs in 1959 but Willard Mullin's Brooklyn-inspired Bum (above) remained a familiar figure to TSN readers. Also familiar was the 'Happy Birthday To You' feature (left) that had been appearing for years.

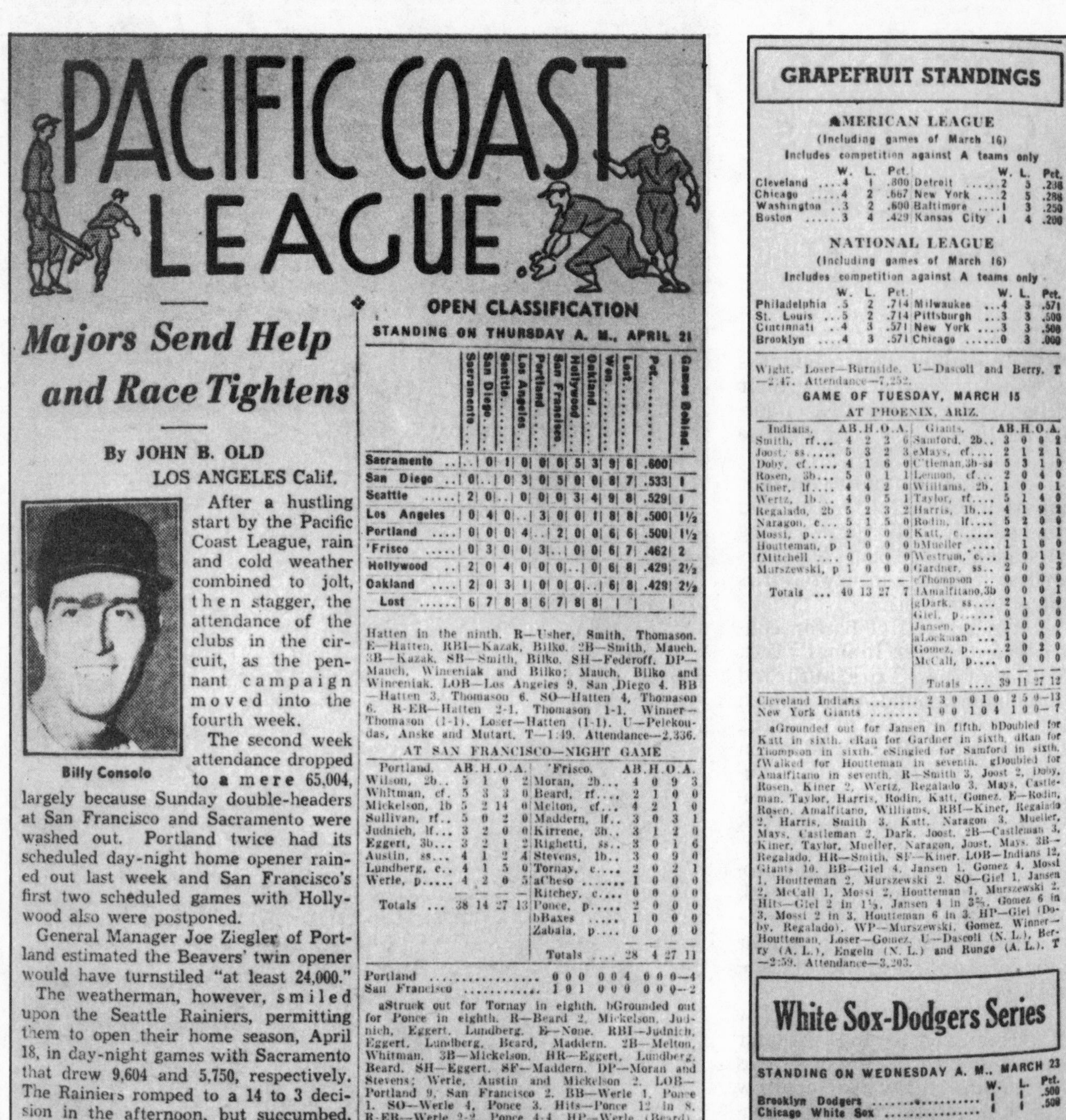

PACIFIC COAST LEAGUE.

Majors Send Help and Race Tightens

By JOHN B. OLD

LOS ANGELES Calif.

Billy Consolo

After a hustling start by the Pacific Coast League, rain and cold weather combined to jolt, then stagger, the attendance of the clubs in the circuit, as the pennant campaign moved into the fourth week.

The second week attendance dropped to a mere 65,004, largely because Sunday double-headers at San Francisco and Sacramento were washed out. Portland twice had its scheduled day-night home opener rained out last week and San Francisco's first two scheduled games with Hollywood also were postponed.

General Manager Joe Ziegler of Portland estimated the Beavers' twin opener would have turnstiled "at least 24,000."

The weatherman, however, smiled upon the Seattle Rainiers, permitting them to open their home season, April 18, in day-night games with Sacramento that drew 9,604 and 5,750, respectively. The Rainiers romped to a 14 to 3 decision in the afternoon, but succumbed, 1 to 0, under the lights as Rookie Johnny Briggs of Sacramento fashioned his

OPEN CLASSIFICATION

STANDING ON THURSDAY A. M., APRIL 21

	Sacramento	San Diego	Seattle	Los Angeles	Portland	San Francisco	Hollywood	Oakland	Won	Lost	Pct.	Games Behind
Sacramento	..	0	1	0	0	0	5	3	9	6	.600	
San Diego	0	..	0	3	0	5	0	0	8	7	.533	1
Seattle	2	0	..	0	0	0	3	4	9	8	.529	1
Los Angeles	0	4	0	..	3	0	0	1	8	8	.500	1½
Portland	0	0	0	4	..	2	0	0	6	6	.500	1½
'Frisco	0	3	0	0	3	..	0	0	6	7	.462	2
Hollywood	2	0	4	0	0	0	..	0	6	8	.429	2½
Oakland	2	0	3	1	0	0	0	..	6	8	.429	2½
Lost	6	7	8	8	6	7	8	8				

Hatten in the ninth. R—Usher, Smith, Thomason. E—Hatten. RBI—Kazak, Bilko. 2B—Smith, Mauch. 3B—Kazak. SB—Smith, Bilko. SH—Federoff. DP—Mauch, Winceniak and Bilko; Mauch, Bilko and Winceniak. LOB—Los Angeles 9, San Diego 4. BB—Hatten 3, Thomason 6. SO—Hatten 4, Thomason 6. R-ER—Hatten 2-1, Thomason 1-1. Winner—Thomason (1-1). Loser—Hatten (1-1). U—Pelekoudas, Anske and Mutart. T—1:49. Attendance—2,336.

AT SAN FRANCISCO—NIGHT GAME

Portland.	AB.	H.	O.	A.
Wilson, 2b...	5	1	0	2
Whitman, cf.	5	3	3	0
Mickelson, 1b	5	2	14	0
Sullivan, rf..	5	0	2	0
Judnich, lf...	3	2	0	0
Eggert, 3b...	3	2	1	2
Austin, ss...	4	1	2	4
Lundberg, c..	4	1	5	0
Werle, p.....	4	2	0	5
Totals ...	38	14	27	13

'Frisco.	AB.	H.	O.	A.
Moran, 2b...	4	0	9	3
Beard, rf....	2	1	0	0
Melton, cf...	4	2	1	0
Maddern, lf..	3	0	3	1
Kirrene, 3b..	3	1	2	0
Righetti, ss..	3	0	1	6
Stevens, 1b..	3	0	9	0
Tornay, c....	2	0	2	1
aCheso	1	0	0	0
Ritchey, c....	0	0	0	0
Ponce, p.....	2	0	0	0
bBaxes	1	0	0	0
Zabala, p....	0	0	0	0
Totals	28	4	27	11

Portland .... 0 0 0 0 0 4 0 0 0—4
San Francisco .... 1 0 1 0 0 0 0 0 0—2

aStruck out for Tornay in eighth. bGrounded out for Ponce in eighth. R—Beard 2, Mickelson, Judnich, Eggert, Lundberg. E—None. RBI—Judnich, Eggert, Lundberg, Beard, Maddern. 2B—Melton, Whitman. 3B—Mickelson. HR—Eggert, Lundberg, Beard. SH—Eggert. SF—Maddern. DP—Moran and Stevens; Werle, Austin and Mickelson 2. LOB—Portland 9, San Francisco 2. BB—Werle 1, Ponce 1. SO—Werle 4, Ponce 3. Hits—Ponce 12 in 8. R-ER—Werle 2-2, Ponce 4-4. HP—Werle (Beard). WP—Ponce. Winner—Werle (1-0). Loser—Ponce (1-1). U—Iacovetti, Valenti and Somers. T—1:54. Attendance—7,007.

GRAPEFRUIT STANDINGS

AMERICAN LEAGUE

(Including games of March 16)

Includes competition against A teams only

	W.	L.	Pct.		W.	L.	Pct.
Cleveland	4	1	.800	Detroit	2	5	.238
Chicago	4	2	.667	New York	2	5	.286
Washington	3	2	.600	Baltimore	1	3	.250
Boston	3	4	.429	Kansas City	1	4	.200

NATIONAL LEAGUE

(Including games of March 16)

Includes competition against A teams only

	W.	L.	Pct.		W.	L.	Pct.
Philadelphia	5	2	.714	Milwaukee	4	3	.571
St. Louis	5	2	.714	Pittsburgh	3	3	.500
Cincinnati	4	3	.571	New York	3	3	.500
Brooklyn	4	3	.571	Chicago	0	3	.000

Wight. Loser—Burnside. U—Dascoll and Berry. T—2:47. Attendance—7,252.

GAME OF TUESDAY, MARCH 15

AT PHOENIX, ARIZ.

Indians.	AB.	H.	O.	A.
Smith, rf...	4	2	3	6
Joost, ss.....	5	3	2	3
Doby, cf.....	4	1	6	0
Rosen, 3b...	5	0	1	1
Kiner, lf....	4	4	2	0
Wertz, 1b...	4	0	5	1
Regalado, 2b	5	2	3	2
Naragon, c...	5	1	5	0
Mossi, p....	2	0	0	0
Houtteman, p	1	0	0	0
fMitchell	0	0	0	0
Murszewski, p	1	0	0	0
Totals ...	40	13	27	7

Giants.	AB.	H.	O.	A.
Samford, 2b..	3	0	0	2
eMays, cf....	2	1	2	1
C'tleman,3b-ss	5	3	1	0
Lennon, cf...	2	0	4	0
Williams, 2b.	1	0	0	1
Taylor, rf....	5	1	4	0
Harris, 1b...	4	1	9	2
Rodin, lf....	5	2	0	0
Katt, c......	2	1	4	1
bMueller	1	1	0	0
Westrum, c...	1	0	1	1
Gardner, ss..	2	0	0	3
cThompson ..	0	0	0	0
dAmalfitano,3b	0	0	0	1
gDark, ss....	2	1	0	0
Giel, p......	0	0	0	0
Jansen, p....	1	0	0	0
aLockman ...	1	0	0	0
Gomez, p.....	2	0	2	0
McCall, p....	0	0	0	0
Totals	39	11	27	12

Cleveland Indians .... 2 3 0 0 1 0 2 5 0—13
New York Giants .... 1 0 0 1 0 4 1 0 0— 7

aGrounded out for Jansen in fifth. bDoubled for Katt in sixth. cRan for Gardner in sixth. dRan for Thompson in sixth. eSingled for Samford in sixth. fWalked for Houtteman in seventh. gDoubled for Amalfitano in seventh. R—Smith 3, Joost 2, Doby, Rosen, Kiner 2, Wertz, Regalado 3, Mays, Castleman, Taylor, Harris, Rodin, Katt, Gomez. E—Rodin, Rosen, Amalfitano, Williams. RBI—Kiner, Regalado 2, Harris, Smith 3, Katt, Naragon 3, Mueller, Mays, Castleman 2, Dark, Joost. 2B—Castleman 3, Kiner, Taylor, Mueller, Naragon, Joost, Mays. 3B—Regalado. HR—Smith. SF—Kiner. LOB—Indians 12, Giants 10. BB—Giel 4, Jansen 1, Gomez 4, Mossi 1, Houtteman 2, Murszewski 2. SO—Giel 1, Jansen 2, McCall 1, Mossi 2, Houtteman 1, Murszewski 2. Hits—Giel 2 in 1⅓, Jansen 4 in 3⅔, Gomez 6 in 3, Mossi 2 in 3, Houtteman 6 in 3. HP—Giel (Doby, Regalado). WP—Murszewski, Gomez. Winner—Houtteman. Loser—Gomez. U—Dascoli (N. L.), Berry (A. L.), Engeln (N. L.) and Runge (A. L.). T—2:59. Attendance—3,203.

White Sox-Dodgers Series

STANDING ON WEDNESDAY A. M., MARCH 23

	W.	L.	Pct.
Brooklyn Dodgers	1	1	.500
Chicago White Sox	1	1	.500

MIAMI, Fla.

Dodgers pounded Bob Keegan for two ... in fifth

Though other sports were making an appearance on TSN pages during this time period, baseball still was king. TSN ran the box scores of all spring training games (above right) and devoted considerable space to the minor leagues (above left).

ing camps of major and high minor league teams with notes and features. During the season, the Triple-A and Double-A leagues were covered with weekly reviews, notes, a feature on an outstanding player, plus standings and averages. News of the lower minors was reported with notes and standings by classifications, plus an occasional feature. Box scores were carried on the Class AAA leagues (a policy that continued through 1967), and box scores accompanied Class AA coverage in 1947, 1948 and 1949.

Managerial changes were recorded in "Parade of Pilots." "Tabbing the Kids" contained the names of free-agent youngsters who signed with major league organizations, while another regular column in the summer months was "Tryout Camps," a table of dates and sites where major league scouts would screen youngsters with aspirations for careers in professional baseball.

For those readers who were inclined to nostalgia, there was "Turning Back the Pages, 5, 10 and 25 Years."

Beginning in 1951, a special January section recapped the top sports thrills of the previous year. Willie Mays' famous World Series catch was featured in TSN's 1955 section (left) while cartoonist Willard Mullin presented his highlights (below) on one page and another page (below left) second-guessed 1954 preseason forecasters.

SECTION OF THE SPORTING NEWS — ST. LOUIS, JANUARY 5, 1955 — SECTION TWO

MAYS' MIRACLE CATCH TOPS '54 THRILLS

THE PRIZE PLAY OF THE YEAR

Willie's Feat Far Ahead in Experts' Poll

Breaking of 4-Minute Mile Barrier by Bannister in Second Place as Tingler

By CARL T. FELKER

WILLIE MAYS' amazing catch of Vic Wertz' powerful drive in the eighth inning of the first game of the World's Series.

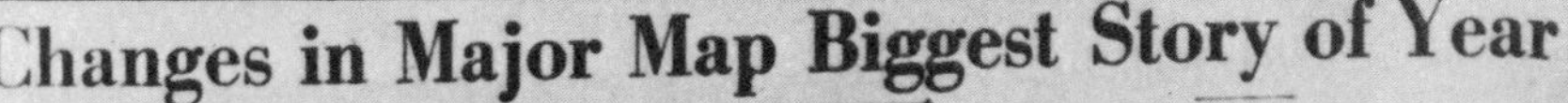

Changes in Major Map Biggest Story of Year

Follies and Feats of '54 ∴ *By Mullin*

Ruins All ∴ By Mullin

Hail the Conquering Hero ∴ By Mullin

Blow, Blow the Man Down ∴ By Mullin

Kaycee's as High as an Elephant's Eye

By Mullin

Yank Dethronement, Giants' Sweep Headline Happenings

Long Reign of Mack Dynasty in Philadelphia Ended; Majors' Attendance Up, But Minors' Continued to Drop

By EDGAR G. BRANDS

ST. LOUIS, Mo.

Mack's Long Reign Ends

Majors' Gate Rises

Gains in 13 Loops

Leading Events

Forecasters Who Flopped on Their Faces

Guessing Games That Produced the Wrong Answers in Sports Last Year

By LARRY MIDDLEMAS
Of the Detroit News

The Voice of Experience

He Wanted to Win 'Em All

JANUARY

FEBRUARY

MARCH

APRIL

AUGUST

SEPTEMBER

OCTOBER

NOVEMBER

DECEMBER

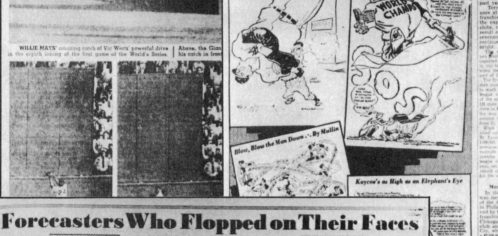

More Books

The publishing empire of Charles C. Spink & Son expanded its borders in the 1940s and '50s with the addition of six new titles, some of which were revised annually, others at longer intervals.

Added to the "Official Baseball Guide," the "Official Baseball Register" and the "Official Baseball Dope Book" in 1948 was the "Ready Reckoner," which, according to an advertisement, "enables one to easily determine a club's won-lost percentage and standings

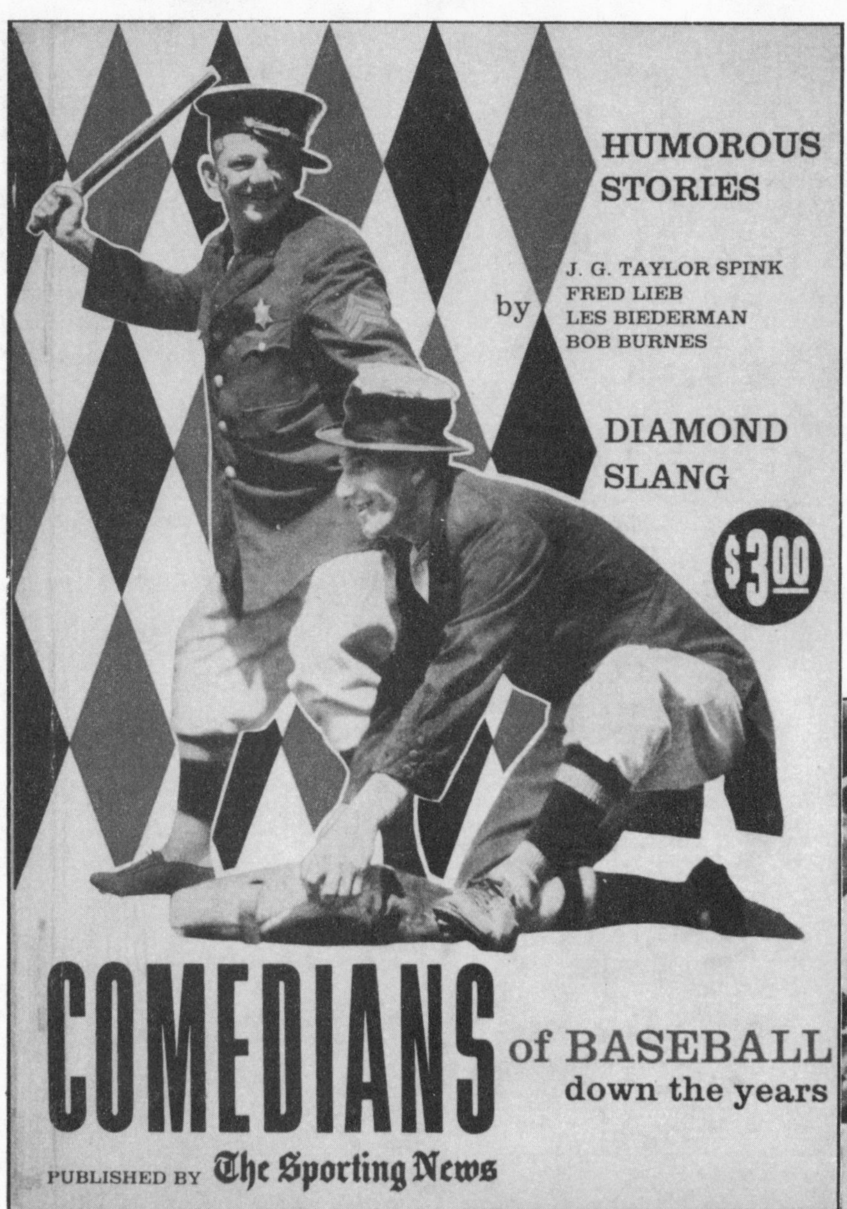

Two new offerings from the Spink library in the 1950s were 'Knotty Problems of Baseball' (right) and 'Comedians of Baseball' (above), which featured some of the comic and colorful personalities of the major leagues.

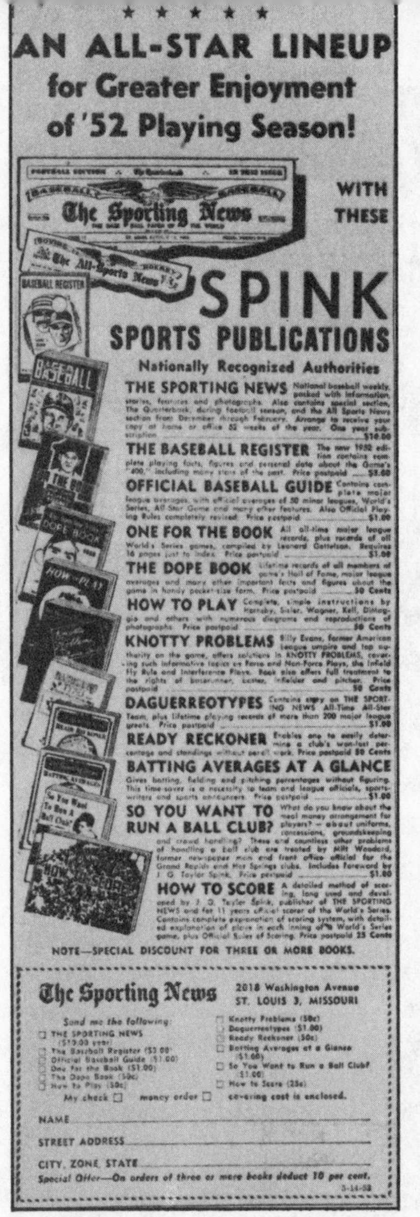

HERE'S A BONUS TOSS..

Basketball with Baseball!

A 12 months—entire year subscription (52 issues)

The Sporting News

will also include FREE this Brand New Book

OFFICIAL NATIONAL BASKETBALL ASSOCIATION GUIDE

1958-1959

$1.00

PUBLISHED BY The Sporting News

HIGH SPOTS IN CONTENTS:

League Directory . . . League Rules . . . Previous Seasons' Records . . . 1957-58 Season Records . . . 1957-58 N.B.A. Records . . . All-Time Scoring Leaders . . . Season Player Records . . . 1957-58 Game Scores . . . Eighth N.B.A. All-Star Game and All-Star Teams . . . Previous All-Star Teams . . . 1957-58 N.B.A. Playoff Statistics . . . Team Won and Lost Records Against Each Other Team . . . All-Time N.B.A. Playoff Records . . . Team Officials . . . Professional Basketball All-Time Records . . . 1947-58 Playoff Records . . . Championship Series Playoff Records . . . N.B.A. Coaches . . . Team Rosters . . . N.B.A. Lifetime Individual Scoring Records . . . 1958-59 Schedules.

MAIL THIS COUPON NOW

To Receive Free Guide!

Ready October 22

The All-Sports News, six to eight pages of professional and collegiate basketball news, appears as part of THE SPORTING NEWS in December, January and February at no increase in price. Feature stories about the nation's top basketball performers, statistics, etc. A special service for baseball fans who enjoy basketball.

The Sporting News 2018 WASHINGTON AVENUE ST. LOUIS 3, MISSOURI

Enter my subscription for fifty-two issues of THE SPORTING NEWS. ☐Check ☐money order for $12 is enclosed. My subscription includes a copy of the 1958-59 National Basketball Association Record Book at no extra cost. Please show if new☐ or renewal☐.

☐Send me a copy of the N.B.A. Guide. Remittance of $1 enclosed.

NAME

ADDRESS

CITY ZONE STATE

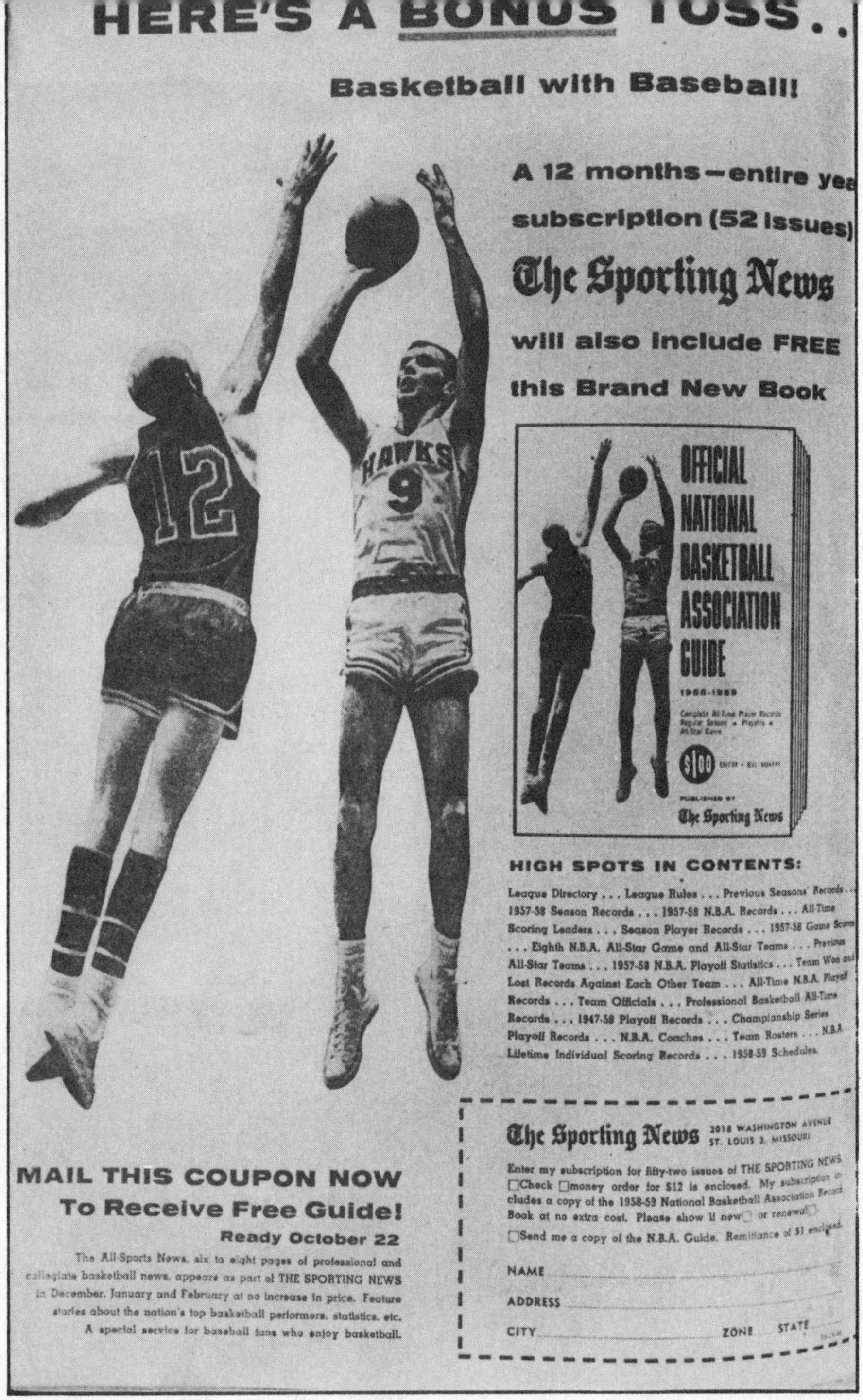

A 1958 advertisement (right) introduced TSN's new 'Official National Basketball Association Guide,' which increased the ever-expanding Spink library (above) of sports books.

without pencil."

The first edition of "One for the Book" was published in 1949. The book, later restyled as the "Official Baseball Record Book," contained 192 pages of all-time major league records compiled by Leonard Gettelson.

"Knotty Problems" joined the Spink library in 1950. This tome consisted of a series of puzzling baseball situations and the official rulings therein, as determined by Billy Evans, an outstanding American League umpire for many years and who at the time was a major league club executive.

"Official World Series Records" was introduced in 1953. This book contained year-by-year accounts of the fall classic, starting in 1903, with box scores, records and related information.

Late in 1958, The Sporting News issued its first "Official National Basketball Association Guide," edited by Bill Mokray of Boston. The 192-page volume, which sold for $1, presented season and all-time scoring records, playoff statistics, All-Star Game records, photos of championship teams, club schedules and a history of the professional circuit.

A second book to reach the market in 1958 was "Comedians and Pranksters of Baseball." This four-section, 112-page book was written by Fred Lieb, Bob Burnes, Taylor Spink and Les Biederman.

Among the comic figures featured in the book were Arlie Latham, Rube Waddell, Ossee Schreckengost, Germany Schaefer, Nick Altrock, Al Schacht, Casey Stengel, Rabbit Maranville, Charley Grimm, Jackie Price, Max Patkin and Bobby Bragan.

Roger Maris (left) and Mickey Mantle formed the Yankees' two-man wrecking crew in 1961. Maris hit a major league-record 61 home runs and Mantle followed suit with 54.

1961-1974:

EXPANDING HORIZON

In the weeks following the departure of the Dodgers and Giants for the golden purlieus of California, the clamor for major league expansion grew into a continuous coast-to-coast roar. Nowhere was the agitation louder than in New York, where millions of fans, accustomed to three teams for half a century, now had only one.

Among those who felt the absence of the National League teams, none grieved more deeply than Mayor Robert Wagner, defender of New York City's pride and a patron of the pastime since early childhood. But Wagner didn't just grieve. He appointed a committee of civic leaders to obtain a National League franchise for the city and named to the chairmanship William A. Shea, a corporate lawyer with inexhaustible energy and a reputation for accomplishing objectives despite almost insurmountable obstacles.

Shea launched his campaign at the top, with Commissioner Ford Frick, and followed with appeals to ranking executives of the league. All endorsed expansion but did nothing. Backed by the mayor's promise that the city would construct a park for a new tenant, Shea then wooed the Reds, Pirates and Phillies, but none was interested in moving. Only one option remained. Since the National League appeared unwilling to let New York in, Shea organized his own league, the Continental, as a third major circuit. To serve as president, he recruited Branch Rickey, the game's elder statesman.

When Shea announced the formation of the Continental League at a press conference, an elderly cynic sniffed and said: "This is the Federal League all over again. It died 40 years ago."

"So what," Shea snapped. "You're the only one in the room old enough to remember."

Gradually, the number of detractors diminished. Shea and Rickey traveled thousands of miles enlisting the support of wealthy sportsmen to back teams in the proposed league. Shea eventually identified the member cities as New York, Buffalo, Atlanta, Toronto, Denver, Houston, Minneapolis-St. Paul and Dallas-Fort Worth.

If Organized Baseball refused to help the Continental loop, Shea and Rickey said, they would operate outside its jurisdiction. The remark got results. Fearful of antitrust reprisals in Washington, major league officials started to talk seriously of expansion. In October 1960, the American League voted to grant two new franchises in 1961. One was awarded to Washington, lately deserted by Senators Owner Calvin Griffith in favor of Minnesota's Twin Cities, and the other to Los Angeles. Earlier that same month, the National League had agreed to expand in 1962, placing franchises in Houston and New York. Having completed their expansion mission, backers of the Continental League silently folded their tents.

With only months remaining before the start of the 1961 campaign, the Senators and the Angels worked feverishly to sew up all the loose ends inherent in newborn teams. In Washington, retired Lt. Gen. Elwood (Pete) Quesada appointed Ed Doherty, a longtime baseball executive, general manager of the new Senators and named Mickey Vernon, a former A.L. batting champion with the Senators, as field manager. On the other side of the continent, Gene Autry, the famous singing movie cowboy, selected a pair of former managers, Fred Haney and Bill Rigney, as general manager and field manager, respectively.

Still unaccounted for were the players. To provide manpower for the new organizations, each club was required to select 28 players, at a cost of $75,000 each, from a pool created from the rosters of existing teams. Some minor league players also were available for $25,000 each. Pitchers Eli Grba (Angels) and Bobby Shantz (Senators) were the first two picks in baseball's original expansion draft.

Despite all the hoopla surrounding the two new franchises, Griffith did better with his transplanted club in 1961 than Autry and Quesada did with their fresh ones. The Twins wound up in seventh place, 38 games out of first, but still attracted 1,256,723 fans to Minnesota's Metropolitan Stadium, an increase of more than 500,000 from the previous season in Washington. Playing at Los Angeles' Wrigley Field, the eighth-place Angels drew 603,510 paid admissions, while the Senators, who tied Kansas City for last place, saw 597,287 fans come through the turnstiles at District of Columbia Stadium (now RFK Stadium).

The cities boasting new National League clubs were a bit more responsive. When the senior circuit displayed its 10-team format in 1962, the Mets, playing at the Polo Grounds, attracted 922,530 fans. Attendance at Houston's Colt Stadium was almost identical (924,456).

The Colt .45s were owned by Judge Roy Hofheinz, who hired Harry Craft as field manager and Paul Richards as general manager. Richards resigned as the Orioles' field boss to take the Houston job after Gabe Paul, Hofheinz's original choice, resigned to accept a similar position in Cleveland. Paul, in turn, was replacing Frank Lane, who had opted for the top post in Kansas City.

The Mets' high command consisted of primary stockholder Joan Whitney Payson, George Weiss in the front office and Casey Stengel on the field. Both Weiss and Stengel had departed the Yankees because of the club's new mandatory retirement age of 65.

Though expansion was a big news item in 1961, the nation's attention was focused on the familiar Yankee pinstripes that year. The Bronx Bombers, now managed by Ralph Houk, captured their 11th flag in 13 years and whipped the Reds for the world championship. But the exciting feature of the pennant race was the assault by Roger Maris on one of baseball's most cherished—and supposedly insurmountable—records: 60 home runs in a single season.

In the years since Babe Ruth set the mark in 1927, some of the game's most illustrious sluggers had assailed the summit and fallen back. Hack Wilson clouted 56 homers in 1930, Jimmie Foxx 58 in 1932 and Hank Greenberg 58 in 1938. If those Hall of Famers failed, who, if anyone, could scale the peak?

That person turned out to be a soft-spoken, 27-year-old outfielder who had never hit more than 39 homers in any previous season. Acquired from Kansas City two years earlier, the lefthanded hitter waged a season-long battle with teammate Mickey Mantle for the home-run leadership. Mantle finished with 54. After 154 games—the number of games in which Ruth hit 60 homers—Maris had 58 round-trippers to his credit. But because a 162-game schedule had been adopted to accommodate the 10-club system, Maris still had eight more games, and he made the most of them. He smacked No. 59 off Milt Pappas at Baltimore on September 20 and the record-tying No. 60 against Jack Fisher of the Orioles at Yankee Stadium on September 26. The record breaker came off Tracy Stallard of the Red Sox at Yankee Stadium on October 1, the last day of the season.

Maris swatted one home run in New York's five-game World Series victory over Cincinnati that fall, another in a seven-game conquest of the Giants in 1962 and a third in 1964, when the Yankees bowed to St. Louis.

The Cardinals were in their first Series since 1946 through the courtesy of the Phillies, who had led the race for most of the season and held a 6½-game lead over the Cards and Reds (seven over the Giants) with only 12 games remaining. After that, however, the Phils lost 10 straight games, and a four-way race for the pennant developed. The fourth-place Giants were not mathematically eliminated until the next to last day of the season, and a three-way tie still was possible on the closing day. But a Cardinals victory over the Mets and a Phillies triumph over the Reds gave St. Louis the pennant.

In the World Series, the Cards defeated the Yankees in seven games. One game was decided by Ken Boyer's grand-slam home run, another by Tim McCarver's three-run blast in the 10th inning. The Bombers' second consecutive Series loss—they had been upset by the Dodgers in four games a year earlier—marked their last appearance in the fall classic until 1976. From 1921 to 1964, the Yanks never had gone more than three consecutive years without winning a pennant.

While the Cardinals celebrated their seventh Series title, the dethroned Dodgers lamented the misfortune that had dropped them from world champions to a sixth-place tie. The plunge was attributed chiefly to injuries that riddled some regulars for an extended period and deprived the team of the services of Sandy Koufax for 11 days early in the season as well as the last seven weeks of the schedule.

In 1963, the lefthander had compiled a record of 25-5 with an earned-run average of 1.88 and 306 strikeouts and had defeated the Yankees twice in the World Series. Despite his idleness in 1964, Koufax won 19 games and lost only five with an ERA of 1.74. The highlight of the season was Sandy's third career no-hitter, pitched on June 4 at Philadelphia.

In 1965, when the Dodgers won another flag and defeated the Minnesota Twins in a seven-game World Series, Koufax tallied an incredible 382 strikeouts, logged a 26-8 mark and hurled his fourth no-hitter, a 1-0 perfect game against the Cubs on September 9. After setting a modern N.L. record for victories by a lefthander (27) and posting a 1.73 ERA to capture his third Cy Young Award in 1966, Koufax made his final appearance in a Los Angeles uniform in the World Series. Facing the Orioles in the second game, he yielded four runs (three unearned) and was tagged for a 6-0 setback. The Dodgers lost the Series in four games. Long troubled by an arthritic elbow, Koufax then retired at the age of 30 rather than risk permanent damage to his arm. He had won 165 games and lost 87 in 12 seasons.

The 1966 World Series was the third to be played in Dodger Stadium, which the team dedicated in 1962, two years after the Giants had quit Seals Stadium for Candlestick Park. The third new stadium of the decade was dedicated in 1964 when the Mets took up residence in their 55,300-seat facility in Flushing Meadow. In tribute to the dynamo who was instrumental in acquiring a National League franchise for the city, the park was named Shea Stadium.

The most extravagant structure of the decade, however, was built in Houston, where a domed stadium, modestly called "the eighth wonder of the world," ushered in a new era for professional sports in 1965. The enclosure was christened the Astrodome and the team renamed the Astros in tribute to the nearby space center. When natural grass refused to grow indoors, the Monsanto Chemical Co. developed an artificial grass called AstroTurf that soon became popular in outdoor as well as indoor arenas.

The Cardinals, Angels and Braves joined the new-stadium movement in 1966. In St. Louis, a multipurpose riverfront bowl was dedicated and, like the Cards' old park, named Busch Stadium. The Angels, after sharing the new stadium in Chavez Ravine with the Dodgers for the previous four years, moved into Anaheim Stadium and henceforth became known as the California Angels. Atlanta, meanwhile, joined the N.L. brotherhood as the new home of the Braves and offered Atlanta-Fulton County Stadium to the roster of new parks. Milwaukee, which had produced record crowds only a few years earlier, disappeared from the major league map.

The Cardinals gave their new park its World Series baptism in 1967 when they engaged the Red Sox, who had captured the A.L. flag under rookie Manager Dick Williams. The Sox extended the Series to seven games before Bob Gibson posted his third victory, a 7-2 decision, on a three-hitter. The Cardinals retained their league title in 1968 as Gibson registered 22 wins and a phenomenal 1.12 ERA. In the opening game of the World Series, Gibby set a record for the classic by striking out 17 Tigers, but Detroit, after trailing three games to one, won the next three contests. Three of the Tiger triumphs were credited to Mickey Lolich and one to Denny McLain.

The Series capped an extraordinary season for McLain. He won 31 games—making him the majors' first 30-game winner since 1934—and was named the league's Most Valuable Player and Cy Young Award winner and was acclaimed by The Sporting News as the Major League Player of the Year.

But Denny's moment of glory was brief. Only 24 at the time of his supreme accomplishment, he won 24 games in 1969 and then fell to 3-5 in a 1970 season that was cut to 14 games by three different suspensions—one for allegedly associating with gamblers, another for drenching two reporters with a bucket of ice water and a third for carrying a gun. McLain never recaptured his artistry. Traded to Washington, he won 10 games in 1971 while losing a league-leading 22, then dropped rapidly into obscurity.

McLain's suspensions were assessed by Bowie Kuhn, who was in his second year as commissioner of baseball. The former Wall Street lawyer and National League attorney succeeded William D. Eckert, a retired Air Force lieutenant general whose reign as successor to Ford Frick was terminated after slightly more than three years of his seven-year contract.

Kuhn's early years in power were sprinkled with frequent altercations with a chronic dissident from the West. Charles Oscar Finley, after years of trying, had been admitted to the American League fraternity in 1960 through his purchase of the Kansas City Athletics from the estate of Arnold Johnson. Founder of an insurance company that bore his name, Finley was a charmer in the drawing room, but a world-class irritant elsewhere.

But Finley had his virtues, too. He had a fertile imagination and never hesitated to shatter tradition. He introduced "Harvey," a mechanical rabbit at Municipal Stadium that leaped from his subterranean hideaway and presented a fresh supply of baseballs to the home-plate umpire. In another innovation designed to relieve umpires of a time-honored chore, Finley installed "Little Blowhard." This device consisted of a hole in the middle of the plate through which compressed air was released to blow away dirt. Finley was the first modern owner to garb his players in white shoes and multicolored uniforms, moves that were ridiculed initially but embraced by other clubs later. He also crusaded for orange baseballs, which he said were more readily visible than white baseballs, but his crusade foundered.

Shortly after taking over the Kansas City club, Finley adopted a Missouri mule as the team mascot. The mule was named "Charlie O.," and some were so calloused as to suggest that it was difficult to distinguish between the obstinate mascot and the magnate.

One of Charlie's first pronouncements after arriving in Missouri was, "I'm here to stay." Unfortunately for the Midwest fans, the owner's staying power was of short duration. He feuded with the press. He tangled with the city government over the stadium lease. He censured the fans for their failure to support his second-division team. And he did little to squelch reports that he was searching for fields of plenty. To inquiries that he was coveting Dallas, Louisville, Atlanta, Oakland or other new environs he muttered the same bland reply: "I am not a man who loves to move his team."

But he delighted in moving employees. In seven years as owner of the Kansas City club he hired seven managers: Joe Gordon, Hank Bauer, Ed Lopat, Mel McGaha, Haywood Sullivan, Alvin Dark and Luke Appling. In one of his less inspired moves, Finley ordered Gordon to manage from the press box, telephoning counsel to an aide on the bench. One game later, Gordon resumed his position in the dugout.

Finley also indulged his fetish for shuffling his office personnel. He lured Frank Lane from Cleveland with a multiyear contract and a Mercedes-Benz as a bonus for becoming his general manager. "He is," Finley declared, "one of the smartest men in baseball."

In the employ of Finley, however, Lane deteriorated quickly. Within months, Lane was gone, dismissed with Charlie's farewell in which he declared, "I know as much about baseball as he does."

Following the breakup, Lane returned to his permanent home in Florida, where he and the Mercedes-Benz were a constant twosome—until the time arrived for him to renew his license. To his annoyance, he discovered that Finley had retained title to the car, and for months the vehicle sat in Lane's garage, a monument to a pair of strong-willed individuals.

Meanwhile, Finley's disenchantment with Kansas City grew. Once when he hassled endlessly with city officials over a new stadium lease, fellow executives delivered an ultimatum—sign within a specified period or face the loss of the franchise. Finley signed and promised domestic tranquility henceforth.

But the peace was superficial. New feuds erupted, and there always was the siren call of Oakland-Alameda County Coliseum wafting eastward. And Kansas City fans, ever cool to teams that only once rose above seventh place (the exception was a sixth-place finish in 1955), kept the rubber bands on their wallets. The breach between the absentee club owner—he continued to function out of his Chicago office—and the disgruntled city fathers widened beyond repair, and in

1967 the American League approved the migration of the A's to the Bay Area, where the Giants had put down roots 10 years earlier.

While the move was applauded in Oakland, it raised some serious doubts elsewhere. The region's population, it was contended, could not support two clubs satisfactorily. Within a year, the skeptics were chortling, "We told you so."

The Giants, who had never failed to draw at least 1.2 million customers in each of their years on the West Coast, attracted only 837,220 in the first year of the A's tenancy in Oakland. Moreover, they scaled the 1 million peak only once in the next nine years. Simultaneously, the A's played to 1 million paid customers—and barely at that—only twice in their first 13 years in the Bay Area. In one of those seasons, the A's were world champions.

One year after Finley moved his green, gold and white-clad minions to Oakland, the major leagues were restructured into East and West divisions, the result of baseball's second wave of expansion. The junior circuit awarded franchises to Kansas City (Royals) and Seattle (Pilots), while the senior loop branched out to San Diego (Padres) and Montreal (Expos). The Pilots didn't fly, though, and after one year the franchise was transferred to Milwaukee, where it became known as the Brewers and provided a new tenant for County Stadium.

With each league split into two sections, a playoff system was devised matching the winners of each division in a League Championship Series to determine the World Series combatants. The best-of-five playoff plan was employed for the first time in 1969, when the Mets defeated the Braves and the Orioles whipped the Twins—both in three-game sweeps.

The Mets, managed by Gil Hodges and featuring the pitching of Tom Seaver and Jerry Koosman, followed up their victory in the playoffs with an even more shocking upset of the Orioles in a five-game World Series. New York had finished no higher than ninth in the seven years before the Miracle Mets of 1969 overcame an opening-game loss at Baltimore to sweep to the world title.

While the Mets slipped to third in their division in 1970, Earl Weaver piloted the Orioles into another World Series. They outdistanced the Yankees by 15 lengths in the division race and then swept the Twins in three straight playoff contests. To climax the season, the Orioles trounced the Reds in a five-game Series that showcased the skills of Brooks Robinson. The third baseman batted .429 and repeatedly quashed Cincinnati threats with his brilliant defense. The Series was the first in which a pitcher, Dave McNally of the Orioles, belted a grand-slam home run, as well as the first to be played on artificial turf. Games 1 and 2 were played at Cincinnati's new Riverfront Stadium, which had replaced Crosley Field as the Reds' home the previous June. Another old ball park, Pittsburgh's Forbes Field, gave way to a new one when the Pirates christened Three Rivers Stadium in July 1970. The Phillies retired Connie Mack Stadium a year later in favor of Veterans Stadium.

The Pirates stifled the Orioles' attempt to retain their world title in 1971. Despite losing the first two Series contests, Pittsburgh rebounded to win in seven games. The Birds boasted four 20-game winners in Jim Palmer, Dave McNally, Mike Cuellar and Pat Dobson, but Steve Blass was pre-eminent among pitchers with two complete-game performances in which he allowed only two total runs. Blass shared headlines with Roberto Clemente, who batted .414 and hit safely in each game. The outfielder collected three of his 12 hits in the fourth game, a 4-3 Pirates victory. It was the first Series game to be played at night and was viewed by an estimated 61 million people on television.

The idea of a night game in the fall classic had been espoused vigorously by Charlie Finley for years. By 1971, Finley was solidly entrenched in Oakland and, not surprisingly, embroiled in new feuds.

Finley tilted with the city's mayor and in retaliation imported the mayor of San Jose, 35 miles distant, to make the ceremonial first pitch at the season opener. He wrangled with a local radio station until, as a last resort, he gave the club's broadcast rights to an outlet in San Jose.

Announcers came and went like clockwork. Each season introduced a new voice to the airwaves—Monte Moore, Red Rush (fired during the Kansas City regime), Harry Caray, Al Helfer, Bob Elson, Jim Woods and countless others. According to one former announcer, failure to mention the owner's name frequently enough on broadcasts often led directly to the guillotine.

Trying to function efficiently in the A's front office was an exercise in frustration. One executive, about to write an urgent letter, found that the supply of office stationery was exhausted. Finley had failed, or had refused, to order a fresh supply. With only one option, the employee communicated his message by telephone, only to be censured later by Finley when he received the long-distance toll bill.

The distance between Oakland and one of the A's league opponents shortened considerably in 1972. Senators Owner Bob Short, citing low attendance in Washington, moved his club to Arlington, Tex., leaving the nation's capital without a major league baseball team after 71 years of uninterrupted play. The team was renamed the Texas Rangers and was managed by Hall of Famer Ted Williams, who was in his fourth year at the helm.

The 1972 campaign was delayed for 13 days because of a players strike—the first in history that involved every major league team. The strike was called by Marvin Miller, executive director of the Major League Baseball Players Association, during the final days of spring training. The teams' player representatives previously had authorized a strike on a 47-0 vote.

At issue were the players' demand for an across-the-board increase in their retirement benefits, plus the demand that the owners absorb the increased premiums of their medical insurance. In essence, the players sought an additional $1.2 million.

The players wound up getting about half of that amount. Settlement of the dispute was announced on April 13, after each club had lost an estimated $175,000 to $200,000 and each player was docked nine days' pay. By mutual consent, the 86 games erased by the strike were not made up.

Off-the-field events made baseball headlines again two months into the season. On June 19, the U.S. Supreme Court, by a 5-3 majority, upheld baseball's exemption from antitrust laws as well as the controversial reserve rule that binds a player to whatever club holds his contract. The decision denied a suit brought by Curt Flood, who had challenged the legality of the reserve clause after he was traded by the Cardinals to the Phillies after the 1969 season. Although Flood, who sat out the 1970 season and played sparingly for the Senators a year later, lost out on his bid for the right to bargain with other teams, the case did make the reserve clause a more visible issue for future negotiations.

On the field, Oakland was playing better than any A's team since the beginning of the Depression. The club had vaulted from sixth place in 1968 to second in the A.L. West in '69 and '70, and it had won the division title in 1971 before losing to Baltimore in the league playoffs. But in 1972, the A's were bound for the World Series. After holding off the White Sox in their division, the A's brushed aside the Tigers in five games in the playoffs, then defeated the Reds in a seven-game World Series. With star slugger Reggie Jackson sidelined with an injury, little-known catcher Gene Tenace emerged as Oakland's top offensive performer, contributing four home runs and nine runs batted in.

Tragedy struck the baseball community on December 31, 1972, when Roberto Clemente was killed along with four other people in a plane crash. Clemente, who had knocked out his 3,000th hit on September 30, was aboard a plane carrying relief supplies to victims of an earthquake in Managua, Nicaragua, when the plane crashed into the water after taking off from San Juan, Puerto Rico.

The "Angry A's"—so named because of the frequent squabbles between Jackson and Finley, Finley and the other players, the other players and other teams, and so on—retained their division crown in 1973. They earned the right to oppose the Mets in the World Series by defeating the Orioles in the playoffs.

Prior to the Series there was widespread doubt about the ability of Oakland pitchers to swing bats with even moderate effectiveness. The anxiety traced to an American League decision the previous winter, and again Charlie Finley had a hand in the innovation.

Since the formalization of playing rules in the 19th Century, a pitcher was an integral part of the batting order. Despite frequent embarrassing results, the pitcher was required to take his regular turn at the plate. But to Finley, the regulation was archaic. If pitchers are not expected to hit, as traditionalists acknowledged, why not replace them in the lineup with players who are? More runs would be scored, he predicted, and ticket-buying fans love to watch high-scoring games.

The notion gained support, and the A.L. club owners revised the league's playing code to include a "designated hitter." The DH would take his turn at the plate and then return to the dugout to await his next at-bat without ever playing in the field. The National League, however, refused to tamper with the rules, preferring that pitchers swing a bat as a vital component of the game's strategy.

By the luck of the A.L. schedule, Ron Blomberg of the Yankees was the first DH in the regular season. Batting in the first inning of the opening game at Boston, Blomberg drew a bases-loaded walk. He finished the day with one hit in three official at-bats.

Designated hitters did, in fact, produce more offense in the American League, but the DH rule also deprived Oakland pitchers of the opportunity to bat during the 162-game schedule and the playoffs. Many fans wondered whether Mets pitchers therefore would have an advantage over their A's counterparts in the World Series.

The concern proved unnecessary. In the third inning of the first game, pitcher Ken Holtzman slapped a double to left field. The hit was one of three yielded by Jon Matlack, but it keyed a two-run outburst that enabled Holtzman and the A's to win, 2-1. Holtzman also cracked a double in the seventh game, and with a single by Rollie Fingers, those three hits represented the total offense by A's pitchers. With only three official at-bats, Holtzman led all Oakland players with an average of .667, and his two hits matched the total of all of New York's pitchers.

The most memorable event of the '73 Series took place after Game 2, when Finley coerced an apparently able-bodied member of his team to sign a statement saying that he was physically handicapped and should be removed from the roster. The player was Mike Andrews, who had batted for Ted Kubiak in the eighth inning of the second game and then stayed in the lineup, playing second base. Andrews' two errors in the 12th inning contributed to a four-run New York rally that produced a 10-7 Mets victory.

Having been rebuffed by the Mets on previous attempts to have rookie Manny Trillo added to Oakland's Series roster, Finley saw Andrews' miscues as an ideal excuse to have the veteran removed from the roster and the rookie added in his place. At Finley's insistence, Andrews submitted to an examination by the club's physician, who determined that the player was suffering from a chronic shoulder injury. Despite Andrews' protests that he suffered no pain and that the condition—"a bicep groove tencosynovitis of the right shoulder," according to the doctor—was not a factor in his performance, the owner persuaded him to sign the statement, allegedly "for the good of the team."

Andrews immediately regretted signing the paper. His teammates, meanwhile, were infuriated by Finley's high-handed tactics and demanded that Andrews be ordered back to the team after a day at his home in Massachusetts. Bowie Kuhn agreed.

"I might add," the commissioner said in a letter to the errant club owner, "that the handling of this matter by the Oakland club has had the unfortunate effect of unfairly embarrassing a player who has given many years of able service to professional baseball."

After the A's defeated the Mets in seven games, Finley received another letter in which he was notified of a $7,000 fine, including $5,000 for the Andrews affair, $1,000 for a public-address announcement at the Series opener in Oakland saying that the Mets were responsible for Trillo's absence from the Oakland roster, and another $1,000 for ordering the lights at the park turned on in the middle of the ninth inning of Game 2 without the commissioner's permission.

"I also determine that you personally shall be placed on probation until further notice," Kuhn wrote, "and warn you that further conduct not in the best interest of baseball may lead to disciplinary action against you as provided in Article I of the Major League Agreement." By terms of that article, an owner can be suspended from Organized Baseball for conduct detrimental to the game.

Andrews made only one more appearance in the '73 Series, as a pinch-hitter in Game 4. When Andrews approached the plate in the eighth inning, the Shea Stadium crowd, apparently sympathetic to Andrews' treatment by his employer, gave him a standing ovation. After grounding out to third, he received another rousing round of applause.

The Andrews incident also was a factor in Dick Williams' decision to resign as manager of the A's after the Series. Finley's previous managers had been chucked after short tenures, but Williams left of his own accord after three years, by far the longest reign of any skipper under Finley. Williams may have been planning to quit before Finley "fired" Andrews, but the incident certainly was the last straw.

When it quickly became apparent that Williams would be named the new manager of the Yankees, Finley struck back. Williams, he insisted, had quit the A's while still under contract, and if he intended to pilot the Yanks, then the A's owner wanted compensation.

New York executives were horrified at the thought. They flatly rejected the suggestion, and the issue was referred to Joe Cronin. When the league president sided with Finley—one of the few times Charlie O. received support from on high—the Yankees signed Bill Virdon as manager and Williams went into temporary retirement. He reappeared in July 1974 as pilot of the Angels.

To replace Williams, Finley turned to Alvin Dark, one of his numerous short-lived skippers in Kansas City. The Sporting News reported the selection in a headline that read, "Finley Finds a Skipper in A's Dark-ened Past."

Finley and the A's and controversy were temporarily forgotten when the national spotlight focused on Atlanta in the spring of 1974. Thirteen years after Roger Maris had broken Babe Ruth's record of 60 home runs in one season, another of the game's supposedly unbreakable records was about to fall before the assaults of a player known as "The Hammer." Henry Aaron, a durable outfielder in his 21st season with the Braves, had finished the previous campaign with a career total of 713 home runs, one shy of Ruth's record.

The Braves opened their season on the road, and Aaron tied Ruth in his first at-bat when he cracked a three-run homer off Jack Billingham on April 4 at Cincinnati. When Aaron went hitless in the next two games and the Braves arrived in Atlanta for their home opener, Hank was under attack from all sides as he patiently tried to handle the deluge of interviews and autograph seekers. And it wasn't just the home folks who were interested. By now an entire nation was caught up in the frenzy. Network television cameras were posted in every corner of Atlanta Stadium when the Braves ushered in their home season on April 8 before a packed house.

Aaron did not keep the spectators waiting long. Facing Al Downing of the Dodgers in the fourth inning, he clouted a drive over the left-field fence, and the long climb was over. The historic homer was hit on Aaron's 11,295th at-bat.

In another historic contest in the '74 season, the Cardinals and Mets played 25 innings at Shea Stadium before Bake McBride, cashing in on a wild pickoff throw, raced home from first base with the run that gave the Cards a 4-3 win. The marathon, which ended at 3:12 a.m. on September 12, prompted a headline in TSN reading, "Oh, Shea, Can You See by Dawn's Early Light."

In the meantime, the A's were romping to another division title, followed by a conquest of Baltimore in the playoffs and a five-game triumph over Los Angeles in the Series, giving the A's three straight world titles. Dark produced a fifth consecutive A.L. West crown for Oakland in 1975, but the A's bowed to the Red Sox in the playoffs. Three days later, Dark again was dismissed by Finley, not for failure to win another world championship, but because he deplored his boss' spiritual life while talking to a church group.

In all probability, Dark would have fared better in 1975 had it not been for Finley's stubbornness in a matter that deprived the team of its foremost pitcher. Years earlier, Finley had traveled to Hertford, N.C., where, for a $75,000 bonus, he signed a high school senior who had pitched five no-hitters (including one perfect game) in prep competition. James Augustus Hunter, who was better known as "Catfish," was assigned to a minor league team in 1964, but he spent that season recovering from surgery to remove shotgun pellets from his foot, which had been blasted when his brother's shotgun accidentally discharged while they were hunting. Without ever pitching in the minors, Hunter arrived in the majors to stay in 1965. From 1972 to 1974, Catfish won 67 games, including 25 in 1974, when he won the Cy Young Award.

Just before the World Series opener, a newspaper disclosed that the righthander was suing Finley for breach of contract because of the owner's refusal to send $50,000, half of his salary, to Hunter's insurance representative, as stipulated in his contract. Catfish contended that Finley's failure to handle his deferred compensation according to the terms of his contract made their agreement void and thus allowed him to become a free agent.

The matter was referred to an arbitration panel, which granted Hunter his free agency. Before the end of the year, he signed a multiyear contract with the Yankees for an estimated $2.85 million.

As they gained a pitcher, though, the Yanks lost a club owner. For making an illegal contribution to a political campaign, George Steinbrenner was handed a two-year suspension by Commissioner Bowie Kuhn. But it wasn't the last the baseball world would hear of Steinbrenner—or free agency.

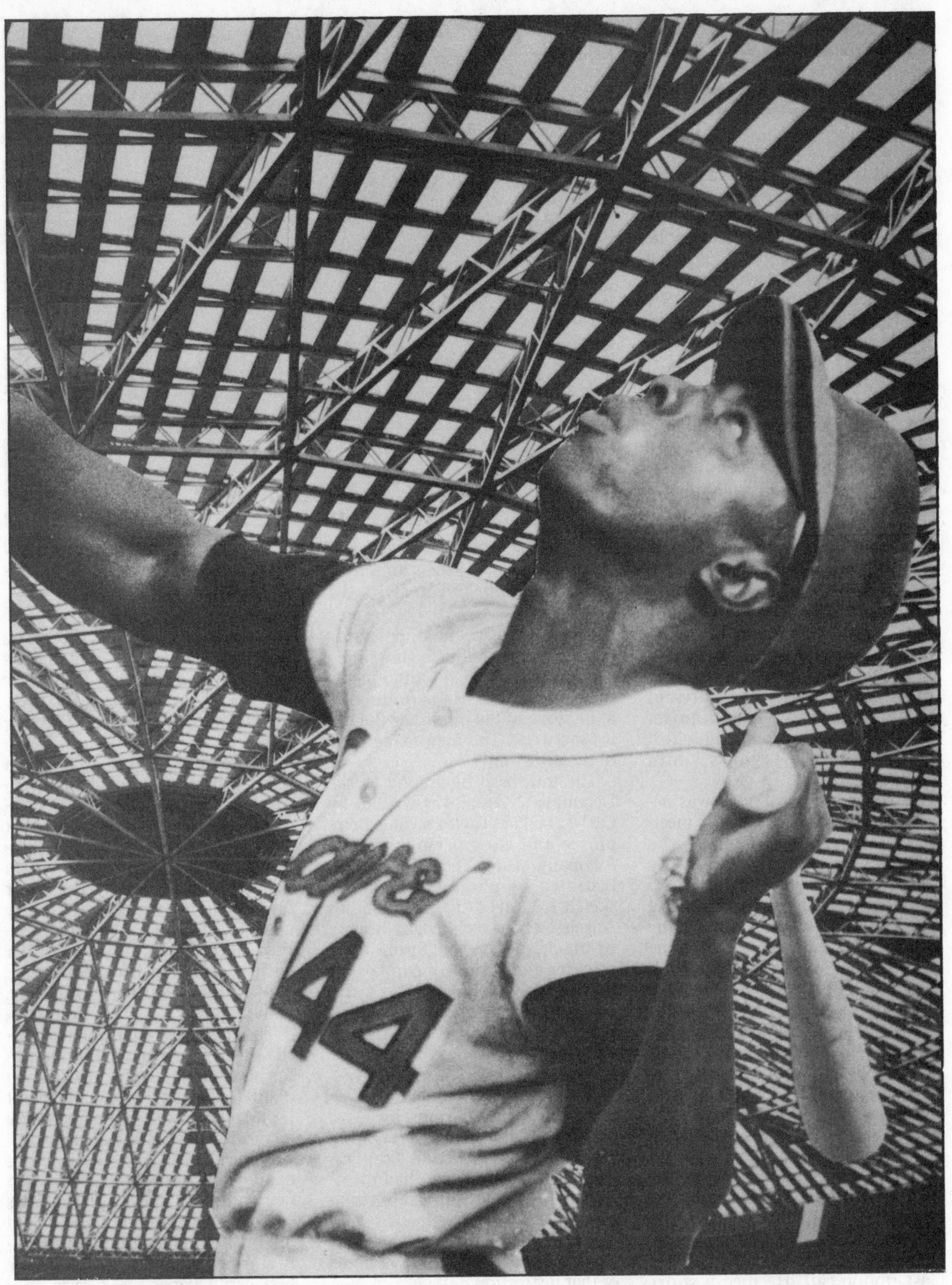

In 1965, baseball moved indoors and Houston's Astrodome was prompting looks of amazement from such stars as Hank Aaron, baseball's future career home run king.

A Legend Passes

Taylor Spink was relaxing in Phoenix, Ariz., seeking relief from the emphysema that had plagued him for years, when he was notified in January 1962 that he had been named winner of the Bill Slocum Memorial Award by the New York chapter of the Baseball Writers' Association of America.

The award, named for one of New York's best-known baseball writers, was presented annually for "long and meritorious service to baseball." Spink was the fifth journalist to receive the citation—and the first from outside New York to be honored.

Because of the publisher's difficulty in traveling, the award was accepted for him by his son, C.C. Johnson Spink.

In May 1962, Charles L. Bacon, national commander of the American Legion, visited the Spink home in suburban St. Louis to present the organization's Americanism Award to Taylor for his "unselfish support" of the Legion's youth baseball program.

A third honor of 1962 was accorded Spink in the annual meeting of the BBWAA during the World Series in San Francisco. By unanimous approval, the group adopted a resolution establishing the J.G. Taylor Spink Award for outstanding baseball writing. The first winner of the award, which was to be displayed at baseball's Hall of Fame at Cooperstown, N.Y., was Spink himself.

In the subsequent months, Spink seldom visited his office. Nevertheless, he remained in constant communication with the editorial staff via telephone and through daily visits from personnel.

It was while at home on December 7, 1962, that Spink telephoned the press room to check on the progress of the December 15 issue of The Sporting News. It was his last phone call. He died a short time later, the victim of a heart attack.

Because the weekly issue was on

Giant of Sports Journalism
JOHN GEORGE TAYLOR SPINK . . . The End of an Era
—PHOTO BY C. C. JOHNSON SPINK

J.G. Taylor Spink, a giant in the publishing world for almost 50 years, died in 1962 and The Sporting News honored him (above and right) appropriately.

the press, there was no opportunity for a make-over, but a short item was inserted on page 1 announcing the death as well as the promise of a life story of the publisher the following week. The item made most of the press run.

The four-page biography in the December 22 issue was written by Carl T. Felker, Taylor's valued employee and close personal friend for many years. The story was illustrated by photographs and a sketch by Karl Hubenthal of Los Angeles. The sketch, edged heavily in black, portrayed Spink's typewriter and a piece of copy paper bearing only the telegrapher's traditional symbol of "30," marking the end. In the background was a grieving figure labeled "All of Baseball."

Accompanying tributes were reproduced from columns by Dave Condon of the Chicago Tribune and Bob Broeg, St. Louis Post-Dispatch sports editor who had introduced the resolution establishing the Spink Award for superior writing two months earlier. Years later, Broeg himself was named winner of that distinction.

The editorial in the same issue began: "J.G. Taylor Spink was such a vital force and dominant personality in baseball and in the sports publishing field for so long that his departure is difficult to realize. He was one of the few men who grew into a tradition during their lifetime.

He seems always to have a part of baseball and of his organization. By any standard of measurement, Taylor Spink was a great personality. In whatever field of action he had been placed, he would have been a leader by the sheer force of his character, his ability and his extraordinary energy. Circumstances made him a publisher with baseball as his chief arena. And in that field he was unique, without a peer."

The full-depth editorial concluded with: "This is a time of sadness for his teammates who have lost an inspiring leader and a steadfast friend. Out of the past come many memories. One of these stands out with particular clarity in the minds of all of (his) associates. When each new issue of The Sporting News was delivered to him . . . he would hold it at arm's length, look proudly at page 1 and exclaim, 'That's the best damn paper we've ever published.'

"He could leave us no finer memory or more inspiring ideal."

Sports Editor of the St. Louis Globe-Democrat

J. G. TAYLOR SPINK—MR. BASEBALL

ST. LOUIS, Mo.

John George Taylor Spink, publisher of THE SPORTING NEWS who d[ied] December 7, was the most remarkable man we've ever known.

There is no particular category into which he fits. You could supply [a] dozen adjectives, some of them pleasant, some of them complimentary [and] some otherwise, and they wouldn't describe all the sides of this man w[ho] built his publication into a remarkably fine sounding board for baseball.

You could say he was gruff and you could say he was pleasant [and] you'd be right. You could ... t and understanding and y[ou] could still ... lent in his likes and disli[kes] ... roach to his business as ...

... e half his age. He wor[ked] ... e shop in the morning ... placed on him to keep h[is] ... He merely conducted b[usiness] ...

... seball. As far as he w[as] ... ent years his publicat[ion] ... he by associates with ...

... as supreme command[er] ... one end of the build[ing] ... ybody jumped.

... With Boss

... name. Many of th[e] ... Such loyalty is ne[ver] ... through college ... hey knew it, but ...

... Johnson, founder ... NEWS helped ma[ke] ... Yet when a team ... baseball histor[y] ... he hardest work[er] ...

... isliked players ... until Cobb's de[ath] ...

... re there was ... ividualists, egot[ists] ... eir opinions ... with a gruff ... at they thou[ght] ...

Happ[y] ... mended fe[w] ... and parte[d] ...

Taylor Spink Dies at 74; 'Bible' Publisher Since '14

ST. LOUIS, Mo.—J. G. Taylor Spink, publisher of THE SPORTING NEWS for 48 years, died at his home in suburban Clayton, December 7. Mr. Spink, 74, had been in failing health for more than a year, but had maintained a close supervision of this paper and its sister publication, The Sporting Goods Dealer, throughout his illness.

The publisher, known internationally for his dynamic campaigns in behalf of baseball, was honored countless times, most recently by the Baseball Writers' Association of America, which established the J. G. Taylor Spink Award to be presented annually to a writer for meritorious service to the game. The award, which will be installed in the Hall of Fame at Cooperstown, N. Y., was presented to Mr. Spink as the first recipient.

Complete details of his career will be carried in next week's issue.

AN INSPIRING LEADER AND STEADFAST FRIEND

J. G. Taylor Spink was such a vital force and dominant personality in baseball and in the sports publishing field for so long that his departure is difficult to realize. He was among those few men who grow into traditions during their lifetime. He seems always to have been a part of the game and of this organization.

By any standard of measurement, Taylor Spink was a great personality. In whatever field of action he had been placed, he would have been a leader by the sheer force of his character, his ability and his extraordinary energy. Circumstances made him a publisher, with baseball as his chief arena. And in that field, he was unique, without a peer.

Taking over the responsibilities of THE SPORTING NEWS as a young man, he developed this publication not only into the "Bible of Baseball" but into an internationally known sports weekly. Under his hand, mind and ceaseless effort, THE SPORTING NEWS came to be regarded as the voice of the game—the spokesman to which officials, players and fans turned for information and guidance. The information was always as complete and accurate as Taylor Spink could make it, and he was never satisfied with anything less than the best. The guidance always was measured by a single test, "What is good for the game?" He crusaded aggressively for progressive policies, cleanliness and honesty; he battled fiercely against unwholesome influences, shoddy practices and the forces of inaction and discouragement. Baseball to him represented the spirit of America. He was jealous of its integrity, zealous in his efforts for its advancement. It is no wonder that he became known as the unofficial conscience of the game.

Baseball owes much to Taylor Spink for its growth during the past half century, its freedom from unsavory influences and its tremendous popular appeal. He campaigned for the spread of the game, both professional and amateur, in this century. He fostered baseball as a good-will force between the United States and the Latin-American countries, as well as other nations. No other individual, over ... did so much for the propagation of the game as T... in B... was ... he r...

Last Story by Game's Greatest Chronicler

Spink Fostered Lardner's Career

Young Taylor Encouraged Ring to Write Humorous Series

ST. LOUIS, Mo.—Taylor Spink was among the first to recognize the ability of Ring Lardner, then a young baseball writer but who later became a famous humorist.

The story was related by Stanley Frank in his article, "Bible of Baseball," carried in the June 20, 1942, issue of the Saturday Evening Post.

"In September, 1910, on Hugh Fullerton's recommendation, Charles C. Spink hired a solemn young baseball writer out of Chicago. The new editor lasted less than a year, but while he was with THE SPORTING NEWS he gave his first evidence of possessing a talent which later was to make an imperishable contribution to American letters.

"The solemn, sometimes morose editor was Ring Lardner. He never was particularly happy working for Charlie Spink; he chafed under the confinement of handling copy and he missed the excitement of the daily baseball beat. Taylor, who was familiar with the editor's work as a traveling correspondent with the Chicago teams, suggested that Lardner do a series of humorous articles dealing with the off-field activities of ball players. Lardner wrote the series under the heading of 'Pullman Pastimes.' This was the genesis of the 'You Know Me, Al' yarns which established Lardner as the master of the short story.

"Strangely, nobody but Taylor Spink and a few baseball writers thought Lardner's stuff was good at the time. There was increasing friction between Charlie Spink and his editor, and Lardner quit to take a job in Boston."

Another Spink Arrives

When Taylor Spink became the father of a son on October 31, 1916, he named the child Charles Claude Johnson Spink, honoring his late father and Ban Johnson, his close friend and founder of the American League.

Young Spink attended Culver Military Academy in Indiana and the University of Missouri before completing his education at Trinity College in Hartford, Conn. Groomed from childhood for the day he would succeed his father, Johnson reported for work in the summer of 1939.

Approaching the boss, he asked, "Waddya want me to do?"

"Clean up the stock room and put things in order," he was told.

"In this Palm Beach suit?" he replied.

"You shoulda asked what to wear before leaving home," was the answer.

His initial assignment completed, Johnson sought out the boss once more. "Waddya want me to do next?" he wondered.

"(Expletive) Must I do the thinking for you, too? Find a desk and sit down."

That was Taylor Spink's style, even with his son.

It was an unforgettable beginning and hardly auspicious. It would never be said that Taylor Spink coddled his son.

Johnson's first desk was located in an out-of-the-way spot. "My grandfather's antique water cabinet was in my father's office," Johnson recalled years later. "When you lifted the lid, there was a mirror on the underside. There also was a bowl into which you could pour water from a nearby pitcher to wash your face and hands before going to lunch. My desk was right behind the water stand."

Unquestionably, cleanliness and humility were the first rungs on the ladder of success in Taylor's Spink's handbook.

C.C. Johnson Spink, young and eager to work his way into the mainstream of The Sporting News operation, labored under the close eye of his boss, father J.G. Taylor Spink (above and below).

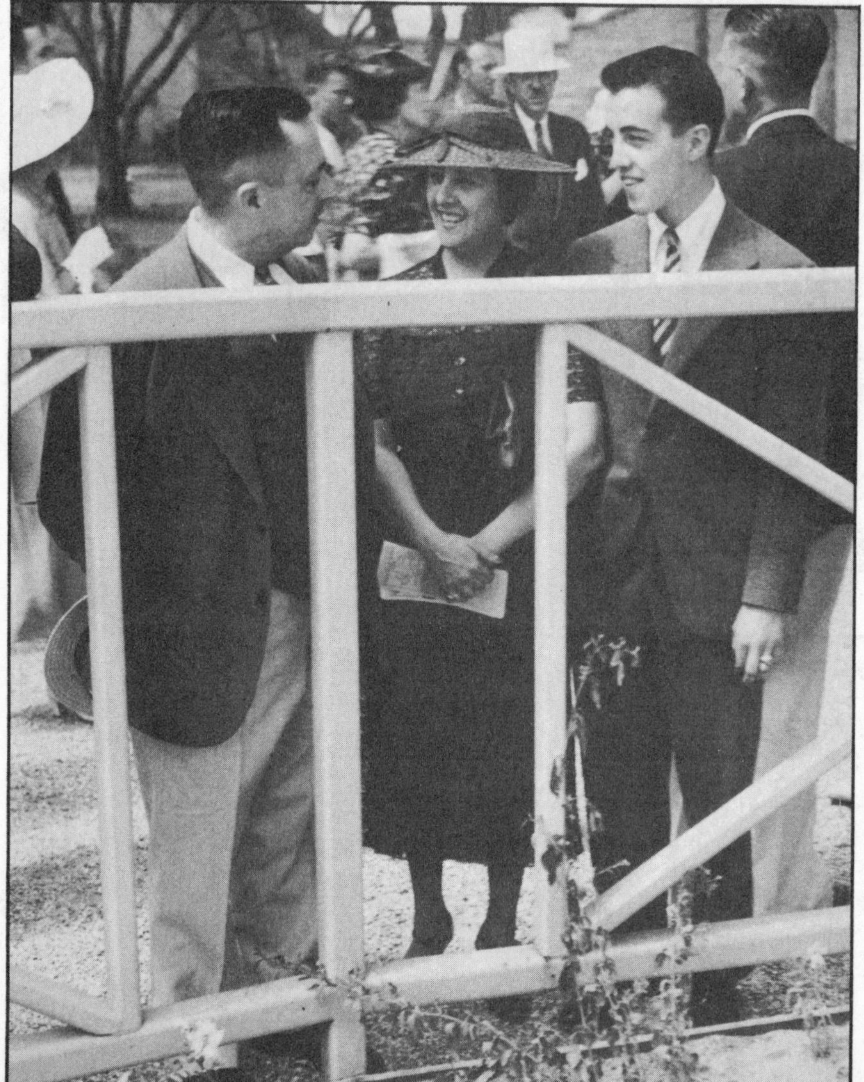

The young Spink had to start at the bottom, get a feel for the daily work routine and prove himself before moving into the upper echelon of TSN's corporate structure.

Initially, Johnson was assigned the task of bringing order out of disarray on The Sporting Goods Directory. Later, he conducted the "Ask the Spinks" column in The Sporting Goods Dealer, which answered questions submitted by readers.

Shortly after the outbreak of World War II, Johnson enlisted in the U.S. Coast Guard and served until 1945, part of the time in the South Pacific as a combat correspondent.

On his return to civilian life, he was placed in charge of advertising for the Dealer and later held a similar position with The Sporting News.

Under his father's demanding work ethic, Johnson labored tirelessly at the office and at home. Reading proofs was standard procedure, and if Johnson could read proofs, so could his wife, the former Edith Swift Jenkin. One of Edith's sessions with proofs of The Sporting Goods Directory led to near calamity.

After Edith had pored over the proofs for more than 100 hours, Johnson gathered up the papers by dawn's early light and strolled to his car. Placing the proofs on the roof of the car, he unlocked the door and proceeded blissfully toward center city. Two blocks later he was struck by a horrifying thought—he left the proofs on the roof.

Screeching to a stop, he opened the door and checked. The roof was as bare as the day the car rolled off the showroom floor. Fortunately, the streets were dry and oncoming motorists viewed sympathetically the young man's plight.

Patiently, Johnson dodged traffic and picked up proofs until he had accounted for the entire set.

Such devotion to duty deserved a reward and Taylor Spink was not oblivious to devotion. He permitted his son to apply for membership in the Baseball Writers' Association of America. A six-year apprenticeship, Taylor ruled, was sufficiently long for membership, a distinction he had bestowed upon himself at a much younger age.

On October 22, 1962, nine days before his 46th birthday, Johnson Spink was named president and treasurer of the firm while his father was elected chairman of the board.

The Changing of the Guard

Following the retirement of Edgar G. Brands as editor in 1954, J.G. Taylor Spink assumed that title, to go along with his 40-year-old office as publisher of The Sporting News.

Other editorial personnel were merely members of the staff without benefit of rank or title.

That situation changed abruptly when Johnson Spink took command. The new editor and publisher assigned titles to every editorial employee.

"We'd Like You to Meet. . ." read a two-column caption on the editorial page of the final issue in 1962. It was followed by: "The 11-man staff boasts more than 150 years of experience with this publication, topped by the 44 years credited to Paul Rickart, the versatile old pro who swapped a doughboy's duds for an editorial pencil when Johnny came marching home in 1919."

Through photos and personal sketches, readers met the paper's first managing editor and his associates. The managing editor was Lowell Reidenbaugh, a veteran of 15 years with TSN. Associate Editors were Clifford Kachline, with 20 years of service; Oscar Kahan, 14 years with the firm, and Ralph Ray, Joe Coppage and Herman Wecke. Rickart and Chris Roewe were reseachers, Paul Mac Farlane served as copy editor and Frank Gritts was the art director.

In subsequent issues, readers were introduced to the business department, headed by William Breitenbach, vice president and chief finanical officer, and to the various columnists, major league correspondents and cartoonists.

From the start of his tenure, Johnson Spink authored a weekly column, "We Believe," in which he expressed opinions on current topics of interest. One of his early columns carried the heading: "Readers Dictate Our Course." In it he assured readers that no dramatic changes were contemplated, but he added that he was not averse to change as long as it represented progress.

To those who feared the inception of radical new policies, Spink offered a word of advice: "Relax."

"Our decision to keep The Sporting News on the same course is dictated by you," he wrote. "In a sampling made less than three months ago, the readers gave the format and the content of The Sporting News a strong vote of confidence.

"For instance, we know that you would like more stories on players rather than legalistic details on waiver rules and bonus transactions.

"The Sporting News is not published for the benefit of the professional athlete, sportswriters or announcers and scouts. It is published for you, the fans. So, tell us what we must know—tell us what you want to know."

The Sporting News library continued to grow under the leadership of C.C. Johnson Spink, as this 1973 advertisement shows.

WE BELIEVE

By C. C. JOHNSON SPINK

Editor and Publisher

Readers Dictate Our Course

ST. LOUIS, Mo.

Contrary to what has been printed elsewhere, there have been four publishers of THE SPORTING NEWS by the name of Spink rather than three. In chronological order they are:

1. Alfred H. Spink .... 1886-1887.
2. Charles C. Spink .... 1887-1914.
3. J. G. Taylor Spink .... 1914-1962.
4. C. C. Johnson Spink .... 1962.

There may still be a very few who can say, "I have been reading THE SPORTING NEWS ever since your Great Uncle Al put out the first issue back in '86."

There are many thousands of readers who grew up with THE SPORTING NEWS as it d e v e l o p e d under my father's skillful hands who may be saying, "I wonder what will happen to THE SPORTING NEWS now that Taylor Spink is gone?"

If you are among those who are wondering, just relax.

No drastic changes are planned. Our decision to keep THE SPORTING NEWS on the same course has been dictated by you, our readers. In a sampling survey made less than three months ago, our readers gave the format and the context of THE SPORTING NEWS a strong vote of confidence.

But don't think for one moment that "no basic changes" means that we will ease our constant efforts to bring you the finest sports paper in the world.

For instance, we know that you would like more stories on players rather than legalistic details on waiver rules and bonus transactions. So be it.

Another example of change that is being considered with you in mind has to do with the paper on which we print. Our mill is experimenting with a paper that is

We'd Like YOU to Meet...

. . . The batting order that produces THE SPORTING NEWS 52 week[s] the year.

The 11-man staff boasts more than 150 years of experience with publication, topped by the 44 years that are credited to Paul Rickart, versatile old pro who swapped a doughboy's duds for an editorial p[ost] shortly after Johnny came marching home in 1919.

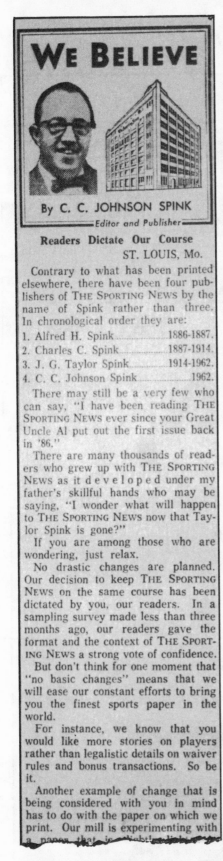

C. C. JOHNSON SPINK, Editor and Publisher—Grandson of C. C. Spink, who gave publication its first boost along road to national prominence in nineteenth century, Johnson succeeds his father, late J. G. Taylor Spink, in No. 1 chair. . . . Named for Ban Johnson, founder of the American League, youngest member of Spink dynasty received thorough grounding in publishing business, serving as his dad's right arm for more than 20 years. . . . Graduate of Culver Military Academy (Culver, Indiana) and attended Trinity (Conn.) College, he served in U. S. Coast Guard during World War II as a combat correspondent. No. 1 hobby is photography.

LOWELL REIDENBAUGH, Managing Editor — F[...] Lititz (Pa.) High School and Elizabethtown (Pa.) Coll[ege] . . . Rounding out 16 years with THE SPORTING N[EWS] following stopovers with Lancaster (Pa.) Intellige[ncer] Journal and the Philadelphia Inquirer, where he pu[t in] three years on the sports desk. . . . Likely to be foun[d on] vacations traipsing over Chancellorsville, Sharpsburg[,] Gettysburg battlefields, communing with spirit of St[one]wall Jackson in Lexington, Va., or trying to prevent [...] from "loading up" on Pennsylvania Dutch antiques. Member of Brentwood (Mo.) Rotary Club. . . . Lowell [and] Ruth are parents of Karen (15) and Kathy (13).

CLIFFORD KACHLINE, Associate Editor—Authority on rules and structure of Organized Baseball. . . . Familiar figure at minor league conventions, having attended all of them since 1945. . . . Co-editor of Official Baseball Guide since 1947 and THE SPORTING NEWS Dope Book since '48. . . . Vice-president of the National Association of Baseball Writers and member of the BBWAA Records Committee. . . . Native of Quakertown, Pa., with experience on North Penn Reporter in Lansdale, Pa., and Bethlehem (Pa.) Globe Times before joining THE SPORTING NEWS in 1943. . . . Forty-one years old, father of two daughters, Jerelyn, 12, and Joyce, 9.

RALPH RAY, Associate Editor—A member of [THE] SPORTING NEWS staff since 1958. . . . In last three y[ears] has written 95 per cent of headlines and edited equal [por]tion of copy. . . . Graduate of Knox College in Galesb[urg,] Ill., with previous experience on Decatur (Ill.) He[rald], Chicago Tribune, four years on sports copy desk, Buffalo Evening News, five years on general copy [desk] and sports copy desk. . . . Saw service in World Wa[r II] and Korean War. . . . Forty-two years old, he's fa[ther] of Barbara, 15; Leonard, 12, and Jennifer, 10. . . . [De]votes considerable amount of spare time to Boy S[cout] work in suburban Kirkwood, Mo.

OSCAR KAHAN, Associate Editor—Diminutive dynamo, 53, he handles major and minor league baseball assignments, other sports and turns out special American Legion baseball sections, among varied duties. . . . Has helped cover major and minor league conventions for past five years. . . . Graduate of University of Missouri, Little O has been staff member since June, 1948. . . . Previously with St. Louis Times, Star-Times and Associated Press in St. Louis, New York and Kansas City. . . . Oscar and Esther are parents of Judith, graduate of Washington University in St. Louis; Laura, Washington U. student, and Jim, student at suburban University City High School.

JOE COPPAGE, Associate Editor—Affiliated with [THE] SPORTING NEWS for ten years. . . . An alumnus of the [St.] Louis Star-Times, Joe started with that daily as copy [boy,] then moved up ladder as news reporter, sports w[riter] and makeup editor, a position he filled for ten years [be]fore paper folded in 1951. . . . Charley Gehringer-t[ype,] he says "hello" in the morning, "good-night" in the [eve]ning and in between he only works, turning out, am[ong] other things, notes that help brighten these pages. . . . Joe, 51, is father of Michael, 15, student at St. L[ouis] Preparatory Seminary; Patricia, 10, and Terence, 9, pu[pils] at Holy Family School.

HERMAN WECKE, Associate Editor—Welcomed aboard in August, 1961, following 50 years of service with St. Louis Times and Post-Dispatch. . . . Started covering game in 1912, when St. Louis Browns trained in St. Petersburg, Fla., first major club to visit Sunshine City. . . . Holds No. 2 card in BBWAA, having joined organization in 1910, dropped out in '11 and returned to fold in '12. . . . Served as official scorer at Cardinal-Yankees World's Series of 1926. . . Son Herman, Jr., outstanding soccer player, having performed for U. S. Olympic team, in Australia, in 1956 Games, and Pan-American team that finished third in 1960 competition.

PAUL MAC FARLANE, Copy Editor — Former [bat]ting practice pitcher for Braves and Red Sox, he's [been] our boo-boo "catcher" since 1948. . . . He's 43, [...] Arlington (Mass.) High School and Marquette Uni[ver]sity (majors in English, Journalism and Philosop[hy]) with way-stop at Harvard for Shakespearean semi[nar] . . . Former member of Massachusetts State Coaches [As]sociation and Catholic Press Association. . . . Rece[ived] tryout with Boston Bruins in '38 and coached Marq[uette] University High School hockey team, 1946-47. . . . W[ife] Dolores, ex-employe of FBI, helps keep Mac the Knif[e] fine, also daughter Karen, 8, and son Paul, 2.

We'd Like YOU to Meet...

. . . Additional members of THE SPORTING NEWS lineup who help m[ake] it the No. 1 team in its league.

The average age of the nine men introduced here is 44, yet t[hey] have contributed a total of 113 years as behind-the-scene particip[ants] in making the task of producing sports news for fans throughout the wor[ld a] smooth and efficient operation. Here they are, from three who have b[een] with us just a year or so, to Joe Unland, a veteran of 39 years:

WILLIAM R. (BILL) BREITENBACH, vice-presid[ent] and secretary of THE SPORTING NEWS and The Sport[ing] Goods Publishing Co.—Perhaps the most popular ge[ntle]man in the organization, Bill keeps the long gr[...] flowing to the battery of correspondents across [the] United States, Canada and Latin America. Bill, [who] also holds the office of treasurer of the Heintz S[...] and Mfg. Co., has been a member of THE SPORTING N[EWS] since 1946, after returning from two years of overseas [ser]vice with the Third Army. . . . Bill and Marie, his spo[use] of 27 years, are parents of Jerol, a junior at Lindenw[ood] College in St. Charles, Mo.

H. G. (HERB) BOLINGER, Circulation Director—Herb, a big man filling a big job, directs distribution of THE SPORTING NEWS and 18 allied sports publications. After spending 15 years with newspapers in Amarillo, Tex.; Sante Fe, N. M.; Orlando, Fla., and Jackson, Miss., he took over the post in August, 1960, upon the retirement of C. R. Baxter. . . . A native of El Reno, Okla., he attended Oklahoma Baptist University. . . . His interests are church, family and job. He's president of Lindenwood Baptist Church Brotherhood and teaches men's Bible class. . . . Herb, who is 38, and his wife, Louise, are parents of Danny, 12; Debbie, 10, and David, 5.

WARREN H. CHURCHILL, Assistant Circulation [Di]rector—A relative newcomer to THE SPORTING NE[WS], Warren had an impressive background in the circula[tion] field when he joined us on March 1, 1961. . . . A na[tive] of New York City, he attended Brooklyn Prep [and] Columbia University. He was with the New York D[aily] News for eight years, spent five years with the [...] Hearst Magazines and one year with the Greensb[oro] (N. C.) Daily News. He and his wife, Doris, had resi[ded] in Des Moines, Minneapolis, Baltimore and New Y[ork] before moving to St. Louis. . . . They have three c[hil]dren—Patricia, 6; David, 4, and Cynthia, 3 months.

WILLIAM G. LINDSEY, Office Manager—After spending three and one-half years in the Navy during World War II, Bill was office manager for the U. S. Chrome Metals Co. and the Christian Children's Fund, Inc., in St. Louis for a total of 12 years before he joined THE SPORTING NEWS a year ago and took over the task of managing the business office, a job he performs in both a friendly and efficient manner. . . . Bill, who is 40, attended high school in St. Louis and took a course in accounting at a St. Louis business college. . . . Married, he is the father of four children—Mary, 16; Susan, 13; Billy, 12, and Karen, 10.

JOE ABRAMOVICH, Manager of Newsstand Sale[s]—Versatile Joe, in addition to circulation duties, has f[lair] for statistics which he applies to other tasks. As [co-]author of Baseball Register, published annually by T[HE] SPORTING NEWS, he collects facts and complete ca[reer] figures on all major league players, managers [and] coaches. During season compiles ledger of team [and] individual feats which is invaluable to staff writers. . . . Managed teams in home town of Madison, Ill. Gave [up] playing, he sadly relates, when own players said [he] could serve team best by managing from bench. . . . Joe, 53, has been with THE SPORTING NEWS since 1[...]

ELDON (MIKE) MEIKAMP, Superintendent of Composing Room—Mike, 40, joined THE SPORTING NEWS 17 years ago after gaining experience on small-town newspapers and was placed in charge of the printing department two years ago. . . . A typographical perfectionist, Mike a p p l i e s his skill mainly to THE SPORTING GOODS DEALER, sister publication of THE SPORTING NEWS. . . . Love of fine printing also embraces photography. Spends vacations taking movies and still travel photos and keeps busy during winter months showing them to school groups. . . . Mike, a World War II veteran is married and a member of Typographical Union No. 8.

JOE UNLAND, Chief Makeup Printer—Joe liter[ally] grew up as a member of THE SPORTING NEWS fam[ily]. He has been with us for 39 of his 55 years. . . . [He] played and loved baseball as a youngster and deci[ded] that the next best thing to being a major leaguer wo[uld] be to work for a baseball publication. Starting as [an] office boy when he was 15, he switched to the compo[sing] room and became a member of Typographical Union N[o.] 8. . . . Meanwhile, he did not lose his batting eye. [He] was an outfielder for the team which represented [St.] Louis in the Typos' national baseball tournament in 1[...] . . . Joe has been the chief makeup man since 1946.

EVERARD J. OPSAL, Linotype Superintendent—Ev can almost make a linotype machine sing, and for good reason. Received bachelor of science degree in printing and journalism from South Dakota State in 1932. Talented linotype keyboard operator sets type for all Spink publications. . . . Formerly published Wilmot (S. D.) Enterprise and served as Quartermaster Group Adjutant during World War II. Now 52 and married, he has been with THE SPORTING NEWS for 12 years. . . . Variety of hobbies include travel, pho[tography ...]

After assigning titles to every editorial employee, C.C. Johnson Spink introduced his staff to readers with a series of 'We'd Like You to Meet' columns on the editorial page. Spink also began writing his own column, 'We Believe,' which appeared through the 1960s and 1970s.

Significant Changes

ARMY-NAVY . . . 29 HOCKEY HERO HULL . . . 40 SPIRIT OF 76ers . . . 41

BASEBALL SINCE 1886

The Sporting News

The Nation's Oldest and Finest Sports Paper

REG. U. S. PAT. OFF.

VOLUME 156, NUMBER 19 ST. LOUIS, NOVEMBER 30, 1963 PRICE: TWENTY-FIVE CENTS

ELGIN TURNS BACK THE CLOCK . . . PAGE 38

The Sporting News

REG. U. S. PAT. OFF.

VOLUME 161, NUMBER 7 ST. LOUIS, MARCH 5, 1966 PRICE: TWENTY-FIVE CENTS

Elbow Ache Gone-- Maloney Deals Out Misery to Batters

By EARL LAWSON

CINCINNATI, O.

Jim Maloney had just shut out the Mets with two hits, retiring the last 22 batters in a row.

"It beats selling used cars, huh?" someone kiddingly remarked to the hard-throwing righthander as he soaked his right elbow in ice after the game.

That was late in March when Seghi, Reds' assistant general manager day Phil Seghi came out to Fresno, I sold three cars and picked up $600."

That was late in March when Seghi, the Reds' assistant general manager, flew to Fresno, Calif., where Maloney's father operates a profitable used-car business. Phil persuaded Jim to end his long holdout siege by dangling a contract calling for a reported $48,000 in front of him.

While holding out, Maloney argued that he felt he was "at least half as good as Sandy Koufax and Don Drysdale of the Dodgers."

Actually, he was just being modest. Drysdale's not in Maloney's class. And Koufax? Well, just give Maloney a little more time.

Maloney wound up his May 17 performance by breezing a side-arm curve past Eddie Bressoud for a called third strike.

"That curve made me flinch even though I was standing in the dugout," cracked the Mets' Dick Stuart.

"Maloney must have had great stuff the way he mowed them down," chimed in Harvey Haddix, the Met pitching coach, "but I was out in the bull pen and really couldn't see."

"Yeah," wisecracked Stuart, "but you surely must have heard him."

Jim Halts Cardinals

Maloney's triumph over the Mets was his third straight without a loss. He picked up his fourth straight, May 21, when he restricted the Cardinals to six hits while registering a 4-1 victory at Crosley Field.

A sixth-inning homer by Orlando Cepeda spoiled Maloney's bid for a second straight shutout and ended a string of scoreless innings at 20.

Maloney's 11 strikeouts in the

1965 Shelling Spurs Ellis To Stop Mets on Four Hits

CINCINNATI, O.—When Sammy Ellis faced the Mets at Shea Stadium, May 18, he remembered his first appearance there in 1965 and vowed he wouldn't give a repeat performance.

"I went into the game last year with a 5-0 record," recalled Sammy, "and really got bombed . . . six earned runs in two-thirds of an inning."

Ellis took the mound, May 18, with a record of one victory and five defeats, the last four coming in a row.

Some two hours later, he had his second victory of the season, a 4-2 triumph. And, in racking up the victory, he limited the Mets to four hits.

"If I get myself straightened out," said Sammy, "we'll have the best pitching staff in baseball."

And the way Red hurlers have been performing, Sammy's remark doesn't leave much room for argument.

10, and beat the Braves, 8-2, in the

MANNY MOTA highballs toward the plate on a successful theft of home against the Braves. Gene Alley is the batter, Joe Torre the catcher and Frank Secory the umpire.

If You Could Buy Stock in Matty And Manny, Price Would Soar

By LES BIEDERMAN

PITTSBURGH, Pa.

Too bad they don't list the batting averages on the stock exchange. Or put the two men who play the same position on the big board as an entry.

If they did, how would you like

Johnson Deals Law His Only Two Losses Since July, '65

PITTSBURGH, Pa. — The pitcher who was the last to beat Vern Law—on July 15, 1965—beat him again on May 19, 1966, to snap Law's ten-game winning

line, scoring Pagan with the run that made it 4-2 against Wade Blasingame. Manny reached third on the throw home.

"I noticed Blasingame was taking his time on the mound and wasn't paying too much attention to me," Mota related. "I made a false start

COAST AVERAGES

(Including Games of May 15)
Compiled by William J. Weiss

BATTING

Player—Club	G.	AB.	H.	HR.	RBI.	Pct.
Barbieri, Spokane	26	89	37	8	17	.416
Werhas, Spokane	19	61	25	2	12	.410
Wm. Williams, Port.	23	77	30	3	13	.390
Schroeder, Phoenix	26	116	44	0	14	.379
F. Torres, Seattle	27	104	37	7	20	.356
Joseph, Vancouver	19	63	22	1	11	.349
Pfeil, Tulsa	22	78	27	0	12	.346
Bond, Denver	23	82	27	4	16	.329
H. Allen, Hawaii	30	122	40	7	23	.328
Reese, Denver	23	67	22	3	9	.328
Spiezio, Tulsa	20	71	23	7	21	.324
Stroud, Indianapolis	24	99	32	1	5	.323
Savage, Tulsa	23	84	27	3	16	.321
Tolan, Tulsa	23	94	30	2	9	.319
G. Williams, Phoenix	26	85	27	1	7	.318
Popovich, Tacoma	23	92	20	0	14	.315
Virgil, Phoenix	26	[illegible]	30	3	[illegible]	.313

♦ American League Averages ♦

Including Games of May 16—Compiled by Chris Roewe

INDIVIDUAL BATTING

Leaders—75 or More At Bats

*Indicates rookie status. †Bats lefthanded. ‡Switch-hitter.

Player—Club	G.	AB.	R.	H.	2B.	3B.	HR.	RBI.	SB.	Pct.
Oliva, Minnesota†	23	87	14	34	7	1	7	20	5	.391
F. Robinson, Baltimore	26	96	23	36	6	2	8	14	4	.375
B. Robinson, Baltimore	26	112	16	39	9	0	4	28	0	.348
*Scott, Boston	28	109	17	36	3	3	11	27	0	.330
Yastrzemski, Boston†	28	111	19	36	9	0	3	20	2	.324
Reichardt, California	29	104	23	33	2	1	9	22	4	.317
Kaline, Detroit	23	83	15	26	5	0	6	14	2	.313
Robinson, Chicago†	24	84	15	26	4	2	2	11	3	.310

BALTIMORE	G.	AB.	R.	H.	2B.	3B.	HR.	RBI.	SB.	Pct.
F. Robinson	26	96	23	36	6	2	8	14	4	.375
B. Robinson	26	112	16	39	9	0	4	28	0	.348
Adair	6	15	2	5	0	0	0	1	0	.333
*Etchebarren	24	84	9	22	5	0	2	4	0	.262
Snyder†	16	24	3	6	1	0	0	1	0	.250
Blair	24	84	5	18	6	0	2	7	4	.214
Aparicio	23	104	12	22	3	1	0	5	2	.212
*D. Johnson	25	101	10	21	0	0	4	7	0	.208
Blefary†	26	92	18	19	2	0	7	15	0	.207
Powell†	25	84	10	17	2	0	5	13	0	.202
R. Johnson	10	18	1	3	0	0	0	3	0	.167
Bowens	5	13	0	1	0	0	0	0	0	.077

BOSTON	G.	AB.	R.	H.	2B.	3B.	HR.	RBI.	SB.	Pct.
*Scott	28	109	17	36	3	3	11	27	0	.330
Yastrzemski†	28	111	19	36	9	0	3	20	2	.324
Tillman	14	44	1	11	3	0	[illegible]	4	0	.250
Petrocelli	[illegible]	[illegible]	[illegible]	[illegible]	[illegible]	[illegible]	[illegible]	[illegible]	[illegible]	[illegible]

INDIVIDUAL PITCHING

Leaders—30 or More Innings

*Indicates rookie status. †Throws lefthanded.

Pitcher—Club	G.	CG.	IP.	H.	BB.	SO.	ShO.	W.	L.	ERA.
McDowell, Cleveland†	7	3	61	27	33	67	2	4	[illegible]	[illegible]
Tiant, Cleveland	5	3	30	21	12	28	3	3	[illegible]	[illegible]
Peters, Chicago†	6	1	46	35	10	26	0	2	[illegible]	[illegible]
Barber, Baltimore†	5	1	32	29	15	15	0	2	[illegible]	[illegible]
Siebert, Cleveland	7	2	41	32	6	25	0	3	[illegible]	[illegible]
Stottlemyre, New York	7	2	54	48	16	25	1	2	[illegible]	[illegible]
McLain, Detroit	6	2	48	25	21	29	2	5	[illegible]	[illegible]
Ford, New York†	6	0	39	34	10	17	0	0	[illegible]	[illegible]

BALTIMORE	G.	CG.	IP.	H.	BB.	SO.	ShO.	W.	L.	ERA.
S. Miller	13	0	23	13	4	15	0	1	[illegible]	[illegible]
Hall	7	0	14	13	2	11	0	2	[illegible]	[illegible]
J. Miller	2	0	14	11	5	10	0	0	[illegible]	[illegible]
*Bertaina†	3	0	13	8	6	12	0	1	[illegible]	[illegible]
Barber†	5	1	32	29	15	15	0	2	[illegible]	[illegible]
*Watt	7	0	17	15	1	15	0	3	[illegible]	[illegible]
McNally†	6	1	46	31	10	26	0	3	[illegible]	[illegible]
Drabowsky	7	0	10	6	6	11	0	0	[illegible]	[illegible]
Palmer	6	2	42	30	21	29	0	3	[illegible]	[illegible]
Bunker	6	2	38	39	12	20	0	2	[illegible]	[illegible]

BOSTON	G.	CG.	IP.	H.	BB.	SO.	ShO.	W.	L.	ERA.
*Brandon	11	0	13	13	7	10	0	0	[illegible]	[illegible]
*Sanders	12	0	32	22	16	21	0	1	[illegible]	[illegible]
Santiago	7	0	33	22	9	25	0	2	[illegible]	[illegible]
Radatz	12	0	15	19	8	13	0	0	[illegible]	[illegible]
Stigman†	6	0	32	32	17	21	[illegible]	[illegible]	[illegible]	[illegible]

Major league averages were expanded and presented in a club-by-club format (right) under Johnson Spink's leadership and batting and pitching statistics of Triple-A leagues (left) also were expanded.

While there were no radical innovations at The Sporting News during Johnson Spink's first decade of rule, there were numerous changes.

The publication dropped the "Base Ball Paper of the World" claim from beneath its page-1 title in November 1963, opting instead for a label of "The Nation's Oldest and Finest Sports Paper"—with "Baseball . . . Since 1886" appearing near the title. By March 1966, a logo-like cover reference to baseball and the drawing of an American eagle that long had accompanied the title became extinct. At that time, The Sporting News' page-1 title was enlarged to full-page width and stood alone; the paper's appellation, now "The International Sports Weekly," was moved inside.

Spot color—red and blue—had brightened covers of the past, but this was possible only in pen sketches that illustrated special issues, such as that which heralded a new baseball season.

Among the more significant changes under Johnson Spink were the removal of 'The Base Ball Paper of the World' motto under the page 1 logo (above left) in 1963, removal of a baseball motto and the American eagle from the page 1 masthead (center left) in 1966 and a brighter inside layout making good use of action photos (below left).

In the spring of 1967 the World Color Printing Co., which had served TSN for scores of years, closed its St. Louis operation. TSN then contracted with the Mid-America Printing Co.—and the tieup proved a boon. Mid-America had a modern facility that engaged in offset printing and was equipped to handle processed color in photographs and advertisements.

The first four-color photo in the paper's 81-year history adorned the cover of the April 8, 1967, issue and featured Frank Robinson, who had starred for the Baltimore Orioles in their four-game sweep of the Los Angeles Dodgers in the 1966 World Series.

Within the next several weeks, page-1 color photos alerted readers to inside features on Roger Maris, the majors' one-season home run king who was starting a new baseball life with the St. Louis Cardinals; Rick Reichardt, California Angels outfielder, and Walter Alston, Los Angeles Dodgers manager.

The interior of the paper also was modernized. Column rules were eliminated, as were the cumbersome decks on headlines. Readers were now able to size up a story by glancing at a brief headline without wading through a maze of type that impeded rapid reading. The net result was a cleaner, more legible product.

Inside illustrations provided a more dramatic appearance as well. Instead of being accompanied by half-column and one-column pictures, features and newsletters were illustrated with action and candid photos provided by the major wire services and a nationwide network of photographers who supplied their products on a regular basis.

Simultaneously, some longtime features of the paper were scrapped. "Happy Birthday," "Press Box" and "Air Lanes" were discarded along with "Hats Off," the two-column salute to an outstanding player that decorated each of the first major league box-score pages. "Hats Off" was replaced by an action photo pertaining to a game reported on the same page.

The weekly batting and pitching records of the major leagues were expanded and presented in a new format that listed the leaders of the league and then the players and pitchers by clubs.

Batting and pitching statistics in the Triple-A leagues also were expanded. But that new look, along with more notes and features, contributed to one major change. Box scores of Class AAA games were discontinued after the 1967 season; as a result, the paper that once printed box scores of 12 minor league circuits and the two big leagues now published box scores of only the two major loops.

The Sporting News Moves On

From 1886 to 1969, offices of The Sporting News were moved six times. All of the locations were in the mid-city area of St. Louis, starting at 11 N. 8th St.

Early success found the headquarters transferred to 907 Market St. in 1888, from where the firm moved to 105-107 N. 6th St. in 1890.

After five years at that site, Charles C. Spink moved his base to Broadway and Olive in 1895 and then to 810 Olive St. in 1900, where it remained until 1910, when it was shifted to 10th and Olive streets. The publication was edited at this address until November 1946 when, requiring more spacious quarters, it was moved to 2018 Washington Ave. Here TSN occupied the entire seventh floor of the Garrison-Wagner Building.

"My father never believed in owning our building," Johnson Spink recalled 35 years later. "But by 1969 we had outgrown two floors and spilled over onto a third. It was an awkward situation and I debated a move for two years or more. The issue was resolved when our landlord raised our rent. I decided it was time to move into our own property, larger and modern in all respects."

Efforts to find a suitable site in downtown St. Louis were futile. An appeal to City Hall for assistance was equally fruitless. Johnson eventually selected a location in an industrial complex at 1212 N. Lindbergh Blvd. in St. Louis County, west of the city.

The publisher knew precisely the type of architecture he wanted for the new structure. During one of his frequent trips abroad, he had spotted a handsome building in Spain situated atop a knoll. With one of the several cameras that always accompanied him on such a junket, Johnson photographed the structure and asked an architect to duplicate the Iberian style as closely as possible.

In the issue of November 22, 1969, readers were informed that "We've Moved." The page-5 notice reported: "The new building, with 41,000 square feet . . . is functional in design for efficiency of operation.

"The editorial office and composing room are located side-by-side to facilitate the flow of copy, with the art department close at hand for the preparation of photographs.

"Despite the tremendous task of moving tons of equipment . . . the transfer was made without interruption to the publication."

We've Moved

THE SPORTING NEWS has moved to its own new building at 1212 North Lindbergh Blvd., St. Louis, Mo. 63132, after occupying leased quarters since the foundation of the paper March 17, 1886.

The new building, with 41,000 square feet, is modern in architecture and functional in design for efficiency of operation.

The editorial department and composing room are located side-by-side to facilitate the flow of copy, with the art department close at hand for the preparation of photographs.

Despite the tremendous task of moving tons of equipment from the paper's former downtown quarters at 2018 Washington Ave., the transfer to the county location was made smoothly without interruption to the publication of THE SPORTING NEWS.

In November 1969, The Sporting News announced to its readers on page 5 that 'We've Moved' (left). The new building (above as envisioned by C.C. Johnson Spink) was the first owned by TSN and afforded more space for the daily operation of the weekly publication. The editorial-page masthead (below) in that same issue carried the new Lindbergh address for the first time.

The Sporting News

THE INTERNATIONAL SPORTS WEEKLY
Trade Mark Registered
Founded March 17, 1886

Published by
The Sporting News, 1212 N. Lindbergh Blvd., St. Louis, Mo. 63166—AC 314 997-7111

Subscription Price $12 a Year | Six Months $6.25 | Three Months $3.25

SECOND CLASS POSTAGE PAID AT ST. LOUIS, MISSOURI

Vol. 168 | NOVEMBER 22, 1969 | No. 19

A LIMIT TO EVERYTHING

Inflation is the curse of our time and the price of pros-

Inflation Forces Price Increases

The sports weekly that sold for a nickel at birth in 1886 and had been available for 25 cents for 15 years yielded to choking inflation in 1966.

An announcement in the April 9 issue reported: "Higher Production Costs Force Increase in Price."

The hike to 35 cents a copy, it was noted, "will be the first increase . . . since July 1, 1951.

"Creeping inflation," the publisher stated in the announcement, "has boosted the cost of production to the point that the increase can no longer be absorbed if the quality of the publication is to be maintained and improved.

"It was with great reluctance that the price increase was ordered, but the publisher trusts that the situation will be understood by our readers. The subscription price will remain the same at $12 a year."

Three years later, in four consecutive issues, readers were informed that another price increase was imminent, this time to 50 cents. While the price per copy advanced, the annual subscription rate of $12 was retained "for the time being."

In justification of the change, an

Higher Publication Costs Force Increase in Price

After 15 years of holding the line, THE SPORTING NEWS has been forced to give way to higher costs of operation and will increase the weekly price per copy to 35 cents, effective with the Opening of the Season issue of April 16.

This will be the first increase in the newsstand price since July 1, 1951.

The "creeping inflation" in the nation's economy has boosted the cost of every phase of THE SPORTING NEWS' production to the point that the increases can no longer be absorbed if the quality of the publication is to be maintained and improved.

It was with great reluctance that the price change was ordered, but the publisher trusts that the situation will be understood by our readers. The subscription price for THE SPORTING NEWS will remain the same at $12 a year.

NEWS for U. S. servicemen in Viet Nam.

We hope our action will spur a similar movement by other American Legion posts throughout the country. RAYMOND BAYSOAR

Finance Officer, Thomas Larkin

The price for sports enjoyment went up quickly during this period, beginning with an April 9, 1966, announcement that baseball's season-opening issue would sell for 35 cents. Three years later, in March 1969, the two announcements pictured here (right) were part of a four-announcement series that explained to readers why the price was increasing to 50 cents.

Centennial Issue First To Carry 50-Cent Price

A 32-page special section in celebration of professional baseball's 100th anniversary will be included in next week's issue of THE SPORTING NEWS, the first to go on sale at the increased newsstand price of 50 cents a copy (the subscription price of $12 a year remains unchanged for the time being).

The features of the section will include:

"The 1869 Red Stockings," by Lee Allen; "Milestones of 100 Years," by Leonard Koppett; "The Great Executives," by Johnson Spink; "The Star Players," by Bob Broeg; "The Mighty Managers," by Neal Russo; "The Game's Umpires," by Lowell Reidenbaugh; "The Sports Writers," by Fred Lieb; "The Century's Chuckles," by Joe Garagiola, and "Next 100 Years?" Koppett's fantasy of the future.

INCREDIBLE OVERSIGHT

I am writing in regard to Bob Fowler's column on the American Basketball Association in your

Box Scores of Exhibitions Part of a Costlier Package

The box scores of all spring training games, starting in this week's issue, are one of the exclusive features of THE SPORTING NEWS. They cannot be found complete in any other publication.

The start of baseball will not mean, however, that THE SPORTING NEWS will cut back on its hockey summaries and basketball box scores. These will appear through the season until the Stanley Cup finals and the NBA and ABA playoffs are over.

Although baseball is moving to the front, THE SPORTING NEWS will continue its feature treatment of other sports in line with the expanded coverage planned by Publisher C. C. Johnson Spink.

What all this adds up to is more human-interest stories, brighter pictures, additional statistical data—and higher costs to carry on the program of constant improvement of THE SPORTING NEWS.

In the belief that our readers will want THE SPORTING NEWS to go forward, we have found it necessary to increase the newsstand price per copy to tasizing on events of the next hundred. Lee Allen has written a superb account of baseball's first professional team, the 1869 Cincinnati Red Stockings. Publisher C. C. Johnson Spink describes baseball's top executives and the roles they played. Fred Lieb covers the giants of the press box, Bill Fleischman tells of the Federal League's bitter struggle to become a third major and Bob Broeg examines the feats and personalities of players who left their mark on baseball . . . and some who didn't.

If you decide after reading the centennial section that baseball has a distinctive past and a bright future, you'll be in accord with those who wrote and assembled the stories.

MOST FOR THE MONEY

The price has gone up. Because we did not want to hand our newsstand customers an unpleasant surprise, a notice of the coming increase appeared in Voice of the Fan the last four weeks. This issue is the first off the press at the new rate of 50 cents. We think THE SPORTING NEWS offers much more than 50 cents in value. If we didn't think so, we wouldn't have raised the price.

Just what does a reader of THE SPORTING NEWS get for his money? For openers, he gets opinion and comment from some of the sharpest observers traversing the sports beat today. Anyone who doubts this has not read Joe Falls, Melvin Durslag, Lee Allen, Dick Young, Bob Addie, Leo Monahan, Phil Elderkin, Bob Fowler, Jim Murray or any of our other regular columnists lately. We are particularly proud of this lineup. THE SPORTING NEWS has carried the by-lines of many talented writers since 1886, but never has it offered as many good ones as it does today. Some are specialists, some range over the entire sports spectrum. All are worth reading.

The reader of THE SPORTING NEWS also gets pictures taken by many of America's finest photographers. He gets weekly reports on the latest developments and outstanding players in every major spectator sport, each in its particular season. He gets the most extensive statistical matter ever published by any sports journal.

Frankly, THE SPORTING NEWS could not afford this array of talent on a full-time basis. We know of no sports publication that could. Many of these men contribute to THE SPORTING NEWS while holding important jobs on daily newspapers all over America. The result: THE SPORTING NEWS presents an unusual concentration of abilities available to readers of no other sports paper. For 50 cents, it's a pretty good package, don't you think?

14 ★ THE SPORTING NEWS, APRIL 5, 1969 ★

Hitting the 50-cent price barrier in 1969 concerned TSN officials who felt compelled to justify the increase on the editorial page (left). That price remained intact for only two years, increasing to 60 cents (below) in 1971.

Price of TSN Up

Many of our readers are aware that THE SPORTING NEWS has absorbed the constantly increasing cost of doing business since 1958 without any increase in the subscription price.

However, after maintaining the same subscription prices for the past 13 years, we finally are forced to announce an increase in both subscription and newsstand prices for THE SPORTING NEWS.

Effective May 1, 1971, the new subscription price to THE SPORTING NEWS will be $15.00 a year and the newsstand price will be 60 cents per copy. Anyone wishing to enter a new subscription to THE SPORTING NEWS at the current price of $12.00 a year may do so until April 30, 1971. Any current subscriber may extend his subscription for a year at the current rate of $12.00 until April 30, 1971.

This price increase will enable us to continue to maintain the quality of the nation's finest sports publication.

C. C. JOHNSON SPINK
Publisher

editorial titled "Most for the Money" asked: "Just what does a reader get for his money?" The answer was: "For openers, he gets opinion and comment from some of the sharpest observers traveling the sports beat today.

"The reader also gets weekly reports on the latest developments and outstanding players in every major spectator sport. He gets the most extensive statistical matter ever published in any sports journal.

"For 50 cents, it's a pretty good package, don't you think?"

In 1971, TSN yielded to the economic crunch once more. An announcement in the issue of April 10 informed readers that, as of May 1, the cost per copy would climb to 60 cents and the annual subscription rate would go from $12 to $15. However, "anyone wishing to enter a new subscription at the current rate of $12 a year may do so until April 30. Any current subscriber may extend his subscripton for a year at the current rate until August 30."

Baseball Shares Spotlight

The Quarterback

by JOE KING

Halftime Histrionics Shunned by Pro Coaches

NEW YORK, N. Y.

In my neighborhood, a quiet backwater in New Jersey, life erupts violently only on Sunday afternoons when the football Giants play. The savage emerges from leaf-raking suburban
imp
tha

the
Es

PUCK POINTS

By LEO MONAHAN

Expansion Steps Up Interest in Junior League

BOSTON, Mass.

The Ontario Hockey Association's Junior

HITTING the HOOP

By JAMES ENRIGHT

Wulk Hops On Texas Western's Wagon

RIMMING The NBA

[By PHIL ELDERKIN]

Big O Drives for Layup . . . West Strives for Jump Shot

BOSTON, Mass.

OFF THE BACKBOARDS—One of the chief differences between Oscar Robertson

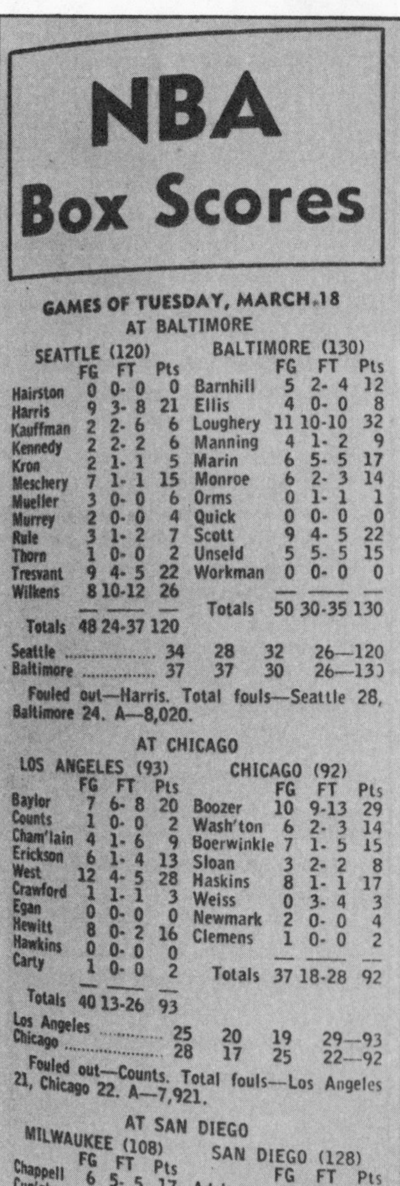

NBA Box Scores

GAMES OF TUESDAY, MARCH 18

AT BALTIMORE

SEATTLE (120)	FG	FT	Pts
Hairston	0	0- 0	0
Harris	9	3- 8	21
Kauffman	2	2- 6	6
Kennedy	2	2- 2	6
Kron	2	1- 1	5
Meschery	7	1- 1	15
Mueller	3	0- 0	6
Murrey	2	0- 0	4
Rule	3	1- 2	7
Thorn	1	0- 0	2
Tresvant	9	4- 5	22
Wilkens	8	10-12	26
Totals	48	24-37	120

BALTIMORE (130)	FG	FT	Pts
Barnhill	5	2- 4	12
Ellis	4	0- 0	8
Loughery	11	10-10	32
Manning	4	1- 2	9
Marin	6	5- 5	17
Monroe	6	2- 3	14
Orms	0	1- 1	1
Quick	0	0- 0	0
Scott	9	4- 5	22
Unseld	5	5- 5	15
Workman	0	0- 0	0
Totals	50	30-35	130

Seattle	34	28	32	26—120
Baltimore	37	37	30	26—13)

Fouled out—Harris. Total fouls—Seattle 28, Baltimore 24. A—8,020.

AT CHICAGO

LOS ANGELES (93)	FG	FT	Pts
Baylor	7	6- 8	20
Counts	1	0- 0	2
Cham'lain	4	1- 6	9
Erickson	6	1- 4	13
West	12	4- 5	28
Crawford	1	1- 1	3
Egan	0	0- 0	0
Hewitt	8	0- 2	16
Hawkins	0	0- 0	0
Carty	1	0- 0	2
Totals	40	13-26	93

CHICAGO (92)	FG	FT	Pts
Boozer	10	9-13	29
Wash'ton	6	2- 3	14
Boerwinkle	7	1- 5	15
Sloan	3	2- 2	8
Haskins	8	1- 1	17
Weiss	0	3- 4	3
Newmark	2	0- 0	4
Clemens	1	0- 0	2
Totals	37	18-28	92

Los Angeles	25	20	19	29—93
Chicago	28	17	25	22—92

Fouled out—Counts. Total fouls—Los Angeles 21, Chicago 22. A—7,921.

AT SAN DIEGO

MILWAUKEE (108)	FG	FT	Pts
Chappell	6	5- 5	17
Cun'gham	3	2- 2	8
Embry	6	0- 0	12
McGl'klin	8	9- 9	25
Niemann	0	0- 0	0

SAN DIEGO (128)	FG	FT	Pts
Adelman	7	3- 3	17
Barnes	0	0- 0	0
Barnett	3	3- 4	9
Block	1	2- 4	4

News, features, columns and statistics on sports other than baseball began appearing regularly in the early 1960s, frequently in the front sections of winter TSN editions. Football, hockey and basketball were the major emphasis of this non-baseball influx.

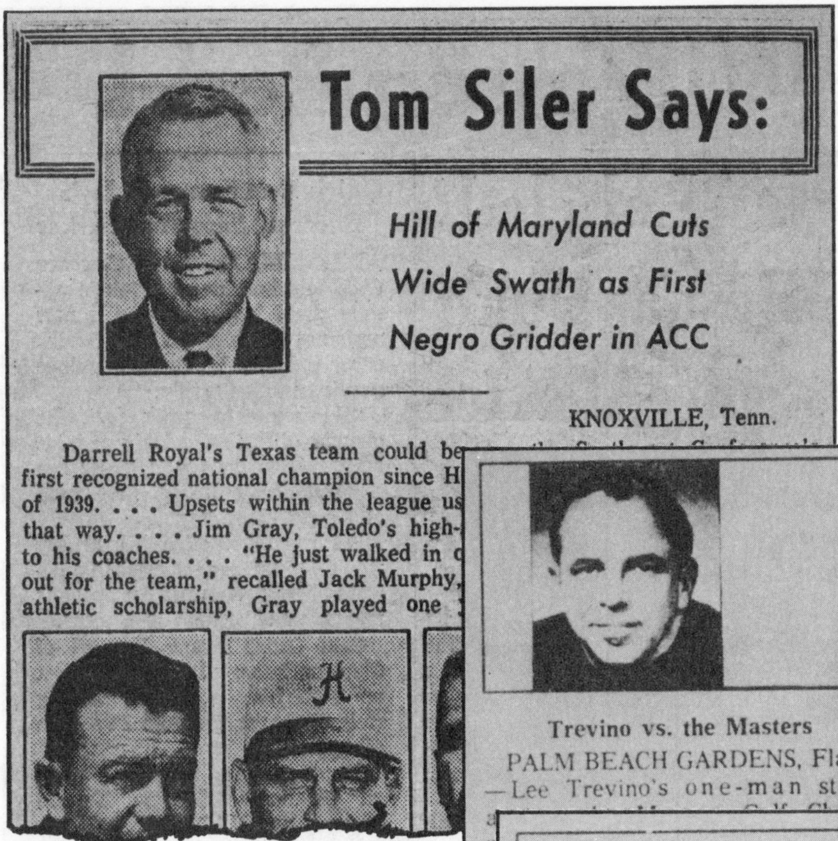

Tom Siler Says:

Hill of Maryland Cuts Wide Swath as First Negro Gridder in ACC

KNOXVILLE, Tenn.

Darrell Royal's Texas team could be ... first recognized national champion since H... of 1939. . . . Upsets within the league us... that way. . . . Jim Gray, Toledo's high-... to his coaches. . . . "He just walked in ... out for the team," recalled Jack Murphy, ... athletic scholarship, Gray played one ...

Among the general columnists appearing during this period were Tom Siler, who concentrated on college football, and Bill Beck, a golf writer. Leonard Koppett, Stan Isle of TSN and Joe Falls contributed general columns.

golf

By BILL BECK

Trevino vs. the Masters

PALM BEACH GARDENS, Fla.—Lee Trevino's one-man stand ...

"Well, almost nothing. I'll bet he'd play, though, if Cliff Roberts (who runs the Masters) would come to him and say, 'Lee, why ...

Leonard Koppett

Ruling that May Upset All Sports

NEW YORK, N. Y.—To understand why Federal Judge Warren J. Ferguson's decision in the Spencer Haywood case has left so many lawyers stunned, one needs a little background in basic antitrust law. But it's worth the effort because the opinion holding the four-year rule in the player draft illegal could upset the applecart in all professional sports ...

sports capsules

By STAN ISLE

BASKETBALL

With rookie **Walt Frazier** leading racehorse attack, New York squared National Basketball Association Eastern Division series by defeating Philadelphia, 128-117, after 76ers ...

selected name Royals from more than 17,000 contest entries. . . . American League umpires, Supervisor **Cal Hubbard** revealed, will wear blue blazers and gray slacks in 1968 season. . . . Watered-down version of controversial spitball ...

Joe Falls

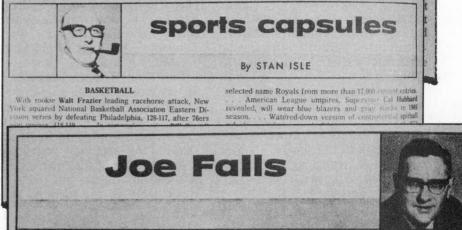

The Most Exciting Moment

DETROIT, Mich. — We have spoken of that feeling of terror, that impending feeling of terror, as those 33 cars drone around the far turn and begin hurtling down the track for the start of the Indianapolis 500. We have spoken of what it's like there at ringside, glaring up into the lights, our hearts pounding away, as everyone clears out of the ring and they sound the bell for the start of round one of the heavyweight title fight. We have spoken of that feeling of anticipation after they've got all the horses into ...

These were the best opening days—w... the fantasies of fandom. Opening day sti... been different working them as a writer ... ing them as a fan but, happily, the mem...

Who could forget that first opener w... 1953? They were opening up against ... Browns in Sportsman's Park in St. Lou...

I had just joined the club, after it c... was really super-charged that night at... writing my first major league baseball ...

The tight grip that baseball held on the pages of The Sporting News ever since infancy was broken in the early 1960s when Publisher Johnson Spink turned the columns over to other sports as they came into prominence.

News, features and statistics of non-baseball activities were printed in the front section of the paper and columnists furnished weekly glimpses of personalities and behind-the-scenes vignettes in their specialized areas.

Tom Siler of Knoxville, Tenn., one of the most literate observers of college football, authored a column on that sport. Bob Oates, Los Angeles; Larry Felser, Buffalo, and Joe King, New York, offered expertise on professional football. At the start of the season, coverage was expanded to include a column by a writer in each division of the NFL and AFL.

Jim Enright, Chicago, and Smith Barrier, Greensboro, N.C., were regular college basketball columnists as well as feature writers, while Phil Elderkin, Boston, reported on the National Basketball Association. In the years of the American Basketball Association, that league was represented by Jim

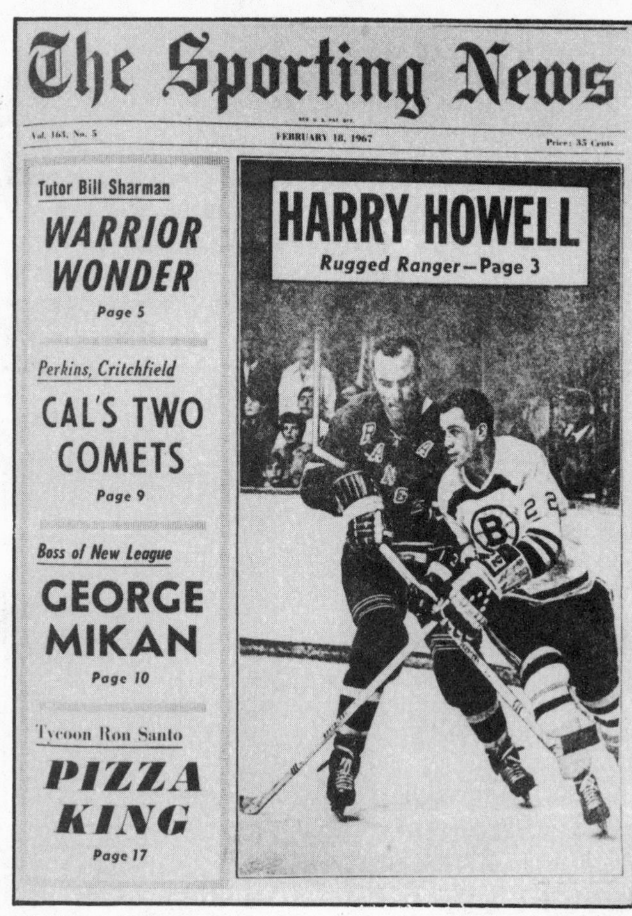

The Sporting News

Vol. 163, No. 5 FEBRUARY 18, 1967 Price: 35 Cents

Tutor Bill Sharman

WARRIOR WONDER

Page 5

Perkins, Critchfield

CAL'S TWO COMETS

Page 9

Boss of New League

GEORGE MIKAN

Page 10

Tycoon Ron Santo

PIZZA KING

Page 17

HARRY HOWELL

Rugged Ranger—Page 3

The Sporting News

MAY 15, 1971 Price: 60 Cents

CANONERO II . . . No.1 at the Wire

O'Brien of New York (and later Pittsburgh).

Ice hockey activities were reported by Leo Monahan of Boston in "Puck Points" and Stan Fischler, New York, in "Speaking Out on Hockey."

Joe Schwendeman of Philadelphia and later Bill Beck of St. Louis covered golf at a time when TSN devoted a page weekly to touraments on the PGA Tour. Ray Marquette of Indianapolis was the auto-racing authority and Chuck Pezzano, Clifton, N.J., was the bowling expert.

Jack Craig of Boston joined the new breed of columnists early with a critique of sports television, while Bob Broeg of St. Louis wrote knowingly of old baseball heroes and Jerome Holtzman of Chicago kept readers apprised of current activities in the major leagues.

As they had for a number of years, Dick Young of New York and Bob Addie of Washington wrote general sports columns on alternate weeks. New additions to the corps of columnists included Joe Falls, Detroit; Leonard Koppett, New York; Furman Bisher, Atlanta, and Wells Twombly, San Francisco.

All the while, cover photographs attested to the diversity of the paper's contents. Football and basketball had broken baseball's page-1 monopoly years earlier, but now ice hockey gained representation. The first National Hockey League player to be featured on the front page of The Sporting News was Harry Howell of the New York Rangers in the issue of February 18, 1967.

In 1971, "The International Sports Weekly" made a serious effort to deserve that sobriquet. The cover of the May 15 issue showed Canonero II winning the Kentucky Derby. Two issues later, page 1 featured a picture of the Indianapolis 500, and in August, golf made its cover debut in the form of Jack Nicklaus.

In 1972, the winter Olympic Games were a page-1 attraction (skier Tyler Palmer was pictured), and Chris Evert scored a cover breakthrough for tennis in March of that year.

The covers (above and right) marked the first-time appearances for the respective sports on the cover of The Sporting News. Hockey appeared for the first time in 1967, with the others making their debuts in 1971 and 1972. The Tyler Palmer skiing cover was a preview for the 1972 winter Olympic Games.

NHL ALL-STAR SELECTIONS
The Sporting News
MAY 29, 1971
Price: 60 Cents
EXCITEMENT AT INDY '500'
Mighty weapon: McCovey's bat
PAGE 3
Bruins, Hawks top All-Stars
PAGE 53
Canonero II's critics shut up
PAGE 57

The Sporting News
AUGUST 28, 1971
Price: 60 Cents
JACK NICKLAUS
Golf's Greatest?

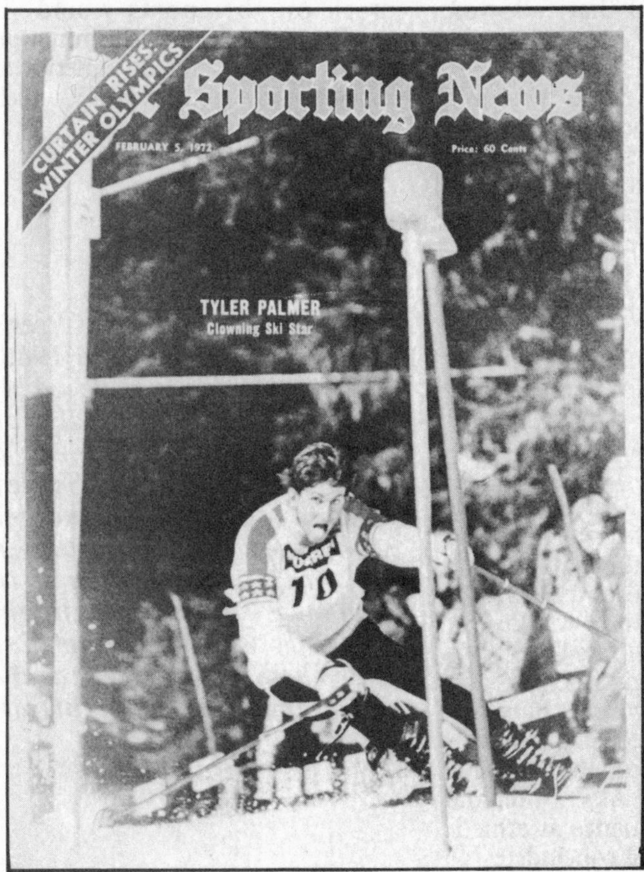
CURTAIN RISES: WINTER OLYMPICS
Sporting News
FEBRUARY 5, 1972
Price: 60 Cents
TYLER PALMER
Clowning Ski Star

The Sporting News
MARCH 11, 1972
OUR NEXT HELEN WILLS MOODY?
Chris Evert
Packers unload versatile Donny
PAGE 19
U. S. pole-vault reign in doubt
PAGE 21
Wise, Carlton: pros and cons
PAGE 29

The Improvement of Baseball

The Sporting News 7-Point Program

Free-agent draft with minimum salary limits in minors sufficiently attractive to lure the best talent.

Tieup between Organized Baseball and colleges that is considered equitable by both parties and includes an expanded, intensified college baseball program or its equivalent.

Orderly expansion of the majors to 12-club leagues of two divisions each—or to three leagues of eight clubs apiece.

Long-range policy for minors by which the majors can assure their source of supply and at the same time stabilize the picture in minor league cities.

Improvement of the product and its presentation in keeping with the times, including better services for the fans, speeding up of games through elimination of dull spots and better plugging of the game's lucrative financial rewards.

Increased co-operation with youth baseball through coaching assistance and instruction.

Establishment of a central headquarters for all of baseball—Commissioner, Major Leagues, National Association, colleges and organized sandlot and youth leagues.

The Sporting News 9-Point Program

Free-agent draft with minimum salary limits in minors sufficiently attractive to lure the best talent.

Tieup between Organized Baseball and colleges that is considered equitable by both parties and includes an expanded, intensified college baseball program or its equivalent.

Orderly expansion of the majors to 12-club leagues of two divisions each—or to three leagues of eight clubs apiece.

Interleague play so that fans in all major league cities will have an opportunity to see each team of rival league at least every other year.

Television policy establishing permissible areas for club coverage and equitable division of fees for national video coverage.

Long-range policy for minors by which the majors can assure their source of supply and at the same time stabilize the picture in minor league cities.

Improvement of the product and its presentation in keeping with the times, including better services for the fans, speeding up of games through elimination of dull spots and better promotion of the game's lucrative financial rewards.

Increased co-operation with youth baseball through coaching assistance and instruction.

Establishment of a central headquarters for all of baseball—Commissioner, Major Leagues, National Association, colleges and organized sandlot and youth leagues.

In the first issue of 1963, TSN presented a seven-point program (above) for the improvement of baseball. By the end of the year, the program had grown (right).

Throughout the past century, editors of The Sporting News have offered frequent suggestions for the improvement of baseball. Some were adopted.

The first issue of 1963 contained a "Seven-Point Program" that called for:

1—Free-agent draft with minimum salary limits in the minors sufficiently attractive to lure the best talent.

2—Tieup between Organized Ball and colleges that is considered equitable by both parties and includes an expanded, intensified college baseball program or its equivalent.

3—Orderly expansion (in the majors) to 12-club leagues of two divisions each—or to three leagues of eight clubs each.

4—Long-range policy for the minors by which the majors can assure their source of supply and at the same time stabilize the picture in minor league cities.

5—Improvement of the product and its presentation in keeping with the times, including better services for the fans, speeding up of games through elimination of dull spots and better promotion of the game's lucrative financial rewards.

6—Increased cooperation with youth baseball through coaching assistance and instruction.

7—Establishment of a central headquarters for all of baseball—Commissioner, Major Leagues, National Association, colleges and organized sandlot and youth leagues.

In the editorial that followed, TSN presented its reasons for each of the seven points.

Before the year ended the publication increased the number of recommendations for improving the game to nine, adding:

1—Interleague play so that fans in all major league cities will have an opportunity to see each team of the rival league at least every other year.

2—Television policy establishing permissible areas for club coverage and equitable division of fees for national video coverage.

The same issue, dated December 7, 1963, published a moving tribute to John F. Kennedy, terming the 35th President of the United States (assassinated on November 22) "the best friend the sports world ever had in the White House."

Reciting Kennedy's activities in numerous sports, his role in resolving the feud between the Amateur Athletic Union and the National Collegiate Athletic Association and his frequent attendance at athletic events, the editorial concluded:

"Mr. Kennedy knew there are no Democrats or Republicans, no rightists or leftists as such on the baseball diamond or football field, that men are judged there by what they do and nothing else.

"Mr. Kennedy left a magnificent mark on the sports world. It should be the quiet determination of all in the world of athletics to carry out the objectives for which he stood."

After the assassination of President John F. Kennedy in 1963, The Sporting News mourned his death with an editorial (far right) that called Kennedy a 'True Friend of Sports.' Shirley Povich suggested in another story that D.C. Stadium in Washington be renamed in Kennedy's honor. President Kennedy was not unfamiliar with The Sporting News, as the 1961 photo (above right) attests.

—Povich—

Rename Stadium for Kennedy, Writer Urges

By SHIRLEY POVICH
In the Washington Post
WASHINGTON, D. C.

Two years ago, Congress brought forth for Washington a magnificent $23,000,000 edifice that has since been given the absurd name of D. C. Stadium. Actually, Congress' intended designation was The District of Columbia Stadium, but this was so formally dull and unimaginative a mouthful that it invited rejection.

Inevitably the wonderful place—envy of almost every other city in the land—has come to be known as D. C. Stadium, merely initialed like an office memo or a shipping clerk's bill of lading. Breathtaking in its architecture and within sight of the nation's Capitol, it begs for something better.

In the Capitol rotunda the other day, President Lyndon Johnson and the majority leaders of the House and Senate, and Chief Justice Earl Warren spoke of the warmth of their feelings, and a bereaved nation's, for the

JOHN F. KENNEDY . . . TRUE FRIEND OF SPORTS

The sports world has lost the best friend it ever had in the White House in the tragic death of President John F. Kennedy.

Most of our Presidents have had some interest, strong or detached, in one sport or another.

The most recent occupants—the yachtsman, Franklin D. Roosevelt; the walker, Harry S. Truman; the golfer, Dwight D. Eisenhower—bear this out.

But President Kennedy was more of a sportsman than any of these. It was not alone that he was proficient in a number of sports—yachting, fishing, golfing and football, to mention a few. Or that he was an avid fan—his enthusiasm at opening-day baseball games and All-Star contests, his eagerness to watch a football game at every opportunity, his postponing of other activities to visit with the late Ernie Davis the day the latter received the Heisman Award.

These in themselves would have stamped Mr. Kennedy as a great friend of sports. These, however, could be called passive or personal interest in athletic activity.

From the outset of his term in office, President Kennedy took an active interest and went to great pains to point up his concern for, and belief in, athletic competition.

One of his first steps after taking office was to announce that former President Eisenhower's national physical fitness program would be continued. The new President voiced his concern over the great number of military rejections for physical reasons and was appalled that such a condition should exist.

He selected Bud Wilkinson, famed football coach at the University of Oklahoma, to head up the physical fitness program. Under Wilkinson's leadership and Mr. Kennedy's strong and continuing endorsement, the physical-fitness program was paying remarkable dividends.

On another occasion, Mr. Kennedy startled his weekly press conference by announcing that he had stepped into the long-standing controversy between the Amateur Athletic Union and the National Collegiate Athletic Association.

He had previously voiced his concern over their interminable power struggle which threatened to weaken our Olympic team. He had urged them to resolve their difficulties in the best interests of the country.

When this failed, the President appointed General Douglas MacArthur as his personal mediator in the row.

The President's intervention, and the calm, incisive mediation of General MacArthur, assisted by Col. Earl Blaik, made consider-

Editorial Writer Supreme

Not since the days of Earl Obenshain 50 years earlier was the quality of The Sporting News' editorials as consistently excellent as during the period when they were written by Ralph Ray.

Starting in 1965, the associate editor wrote well-conceived and handsomely couched essays on the entire spectrum of sports issues.

His prose evoked widespread commendation. A well-read editor in many aspects of sports, Ray researched his subjects thoroughly before airing the views of the publication which generally coincided with his own personal opinions.

The graduate of Knox College in Galesburg, Ill., was particularly fluent on baseball topics. He marshalled facts and figures with consummate skill and was not above injecting a note of sarcasm, as he did when Bob Short moved the Washington Senators club to Texas after the 1971 season.

His editorial in the issue of October 9, 1971, contained these paragraphs:

"There's little doubt that Dallas-Fort Worth deserves major league baseball. Population, per capita income, available capital, TV market, a suitable park . . . they're all there, and the numbers make for fascinating reading. If Short contracts another case of the shorts down there, he should live in sports history as the most inept sports promoter of all time.

"In Washington they're already conceding him that crown and with plenty of evidence to support the charge. One of the most objectionable aspects of Washington's franchise loss is the premium it placed on failure. For acquiring mountainous debts he couldn't pay, for jacking ticket prices to the highest level in baseball, for bungling the self-appointed task of an amateur general manager, for pleading poverty and begging his Washington landlord to bail him out, Short has been miraculously rewarded. His American League lodge brothers have handed him the key to the bank vault."

Ralph Ray (pictured in the mid-1960s) followed in the same spirit as some of his illustrious predecessors, bringing style, excellence and thought-provoking content to TSN editorials for years. Ray's skills remained in evidence in 1985 for The Sporting News.

Although usually congenial toward labor, Ray took issue with major league baseball players when they struck in 1972. Under the headline "Friendless, But Not Hurting," he wrote:

"Maybe the wheel has turned full cycle. Back in 1894 the Pullman Co. was struck by workers who probably were among the most oppressed in the history of American industry. In 1972 major league baseball players have walked out on what most people agree is a positively lucrative setup.

"More and more Americans feel that organized labor has grown fat and too powerful. The baseball strike has done nothing to dispel that notion. If the players are hurting, they have yet to convince millions who follow baseball.

"Some observers lament that baseball no longer is a sport. It must have been a glorious sport 70 or 80 years ago, eh? Well, back in 1889 disgruntled players formed a union, the Brotherhood, and started their own league, which lasted one disastrous season. Then, as now, players found support hard to come by. One newspaper described players attending a meeting of the Brotherhood as 'dressed in fur-lined overcoats, silk hats, patent leather shoes, carrying gold-headed canes, wearing $5,000 brilliants in their neck scarves and smoking 25-cent Rosa Perfectos.'

"It would seem that the players haven't learned much in the last 80 years."

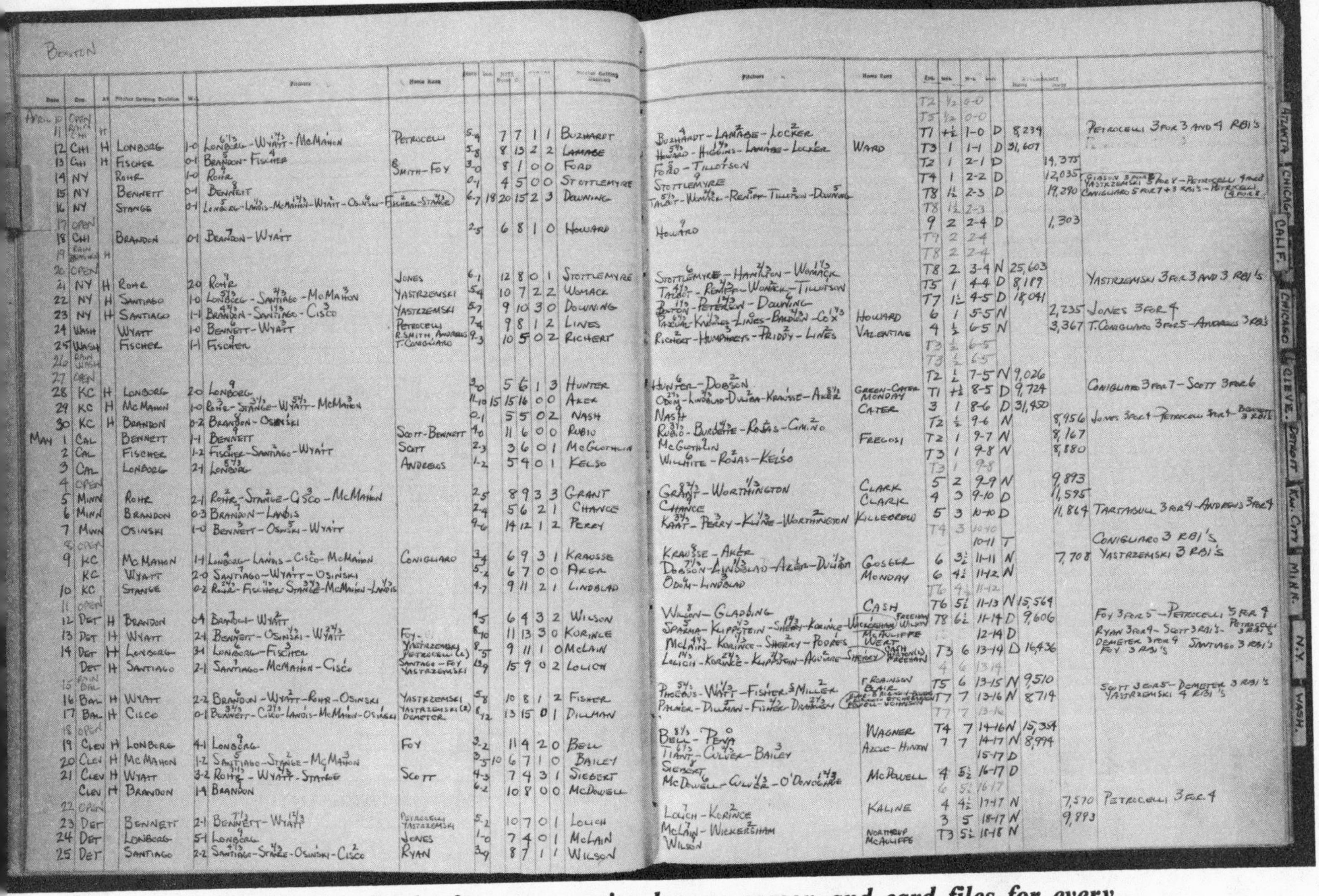

Day-by-day books for every major league season and card files for every player who ever competed at the minor or major league level are among the important research sources at The Sporting News. The day book (above, 1967 Red Sox) records vital information about every game played by each team through a season. The card file (four samples below) records vital statistics and player movement from the beginning to the end of his career.

Name	Position	Bats	Throws
Gooden, Dwight Eugene	P	R	R

Born-Place	Date	Married
Tampa, Florida	November 16, 1964	

Address	Height	Weight
Tampa, Florida	6'3"	185

Teams Played With

FAD New York NL 6/7/82-Kingsport 6/10/82-rel. to Little Falls 8/10/82- RES. FOR '83 rel. to Lynchburg 4/9/83- rel. to Tidewater 9/2/83- RES. FOR '84 rel. to Lynchburg rel. to New York NL 4/1/84- RES. FOR '85

Name	Position	Bats	Throws
(Babe) Ruth, George Herman	P-OF-1B	L	L

Born-Place	Date	Married
Baltimore, Md.	2-6-1895	yes

Address	Height	Weight
173 Riverside Drive New York, N. Y.	6.02	215

Teams Played With

Baltimore 1914-sold with Eagan & Shore to Boston AL 7/14-opt to Providence 7/14-recalled 8/14-15-16-17-18-19-sold to New York AL for $125,000 (See Story) 1/20-21-22-23-24-25-26-27-28-29-Out of game with heart trouble 6/29-res for 30-31-32-33-34-35-rel to Boston NL 4/35-rel 6/35-Coach Brooklyn 7/38-

rel. to Lancaster 9¢26/55-res. for 56-rel.to Abilene 1/5/56-Temp.inactive list 4/12/56-reins. 4/23/56-opt.to Crowley 5/17/56-ret.to Abilene 7/14/56-rel.to COLUmbus,Ohio 7/14/56 opt.to Columbia 7/16/56-rel.to Kansas City 9/8/56-RES. FOR 57- Rel.to Little Rock 3/27/57-Rel.to Kansas City 8/31/57-RES. FOR '58 - Opt.to Buffalo 3/24/58- Opt.trfd.to Little Rock 7/16/58-Rec.by Kansas City 8/22/58-RES. FOR '59 - opt.to Portland 4/28/59- rec.by Kansas City 8/31/59-RES. FOR 60 -Traded for Pitcher Bob Giggie to Milwaukee and rel.to Louisville 5/12/60- rel. to Milwaukee 6/11/60-RES. FOR '61- disabled list 5/5/61- reins.6/4/61- rel. to Vancouver 6/14/61- RES. FOR '62 rel. to Toronto 12/6/62--rel. to Honolulu 4/6/62-rel. to Oklahoma City 5/16/62-

Married Donna June Patterson, Aug.12, 1954- Caren Dawn, 1 wk. (1956)-

rec.by Boston 9/3/69-res. for 70- RES. FOR '71 Military List 5/16/71- Reins. 5/21/71- Traded in deal involving ten players to Milwaukee 10/11/71- RES. FOR '72 -Disabled List 7/16/72-Reins. 8/9/72-Traded in deal involving seven players (see Jim Lonborg card) to Philadelphia 10/31/72- RES. FOR '73 -Traded for second baseman Dave Cash to Pittsburgh 10/18/73 - RES. FOR '74 RES. FOR '75 disabled list 3/25/75-reins. 4/16/75-disabled list 6/5/75-reins. 6/26/75-Res. for 76- Traded with pitcher Dock Ellis and infielder Willie Randolph for pitcher George Medich to New York AL 12/11/75-76- Traded with outfielder Rich Coggins for outfielder Carlos May to Chicago AL 5/18/76- RES. FOR '77 -Traded for pitchers Don Kirkwood and John Verhoeven and infielder John Flannery (latter assigned from Salinas to Iowa) to California Angels 6/15/77-RES. FOR '78 RES. FOR '79

The Designated Hitter

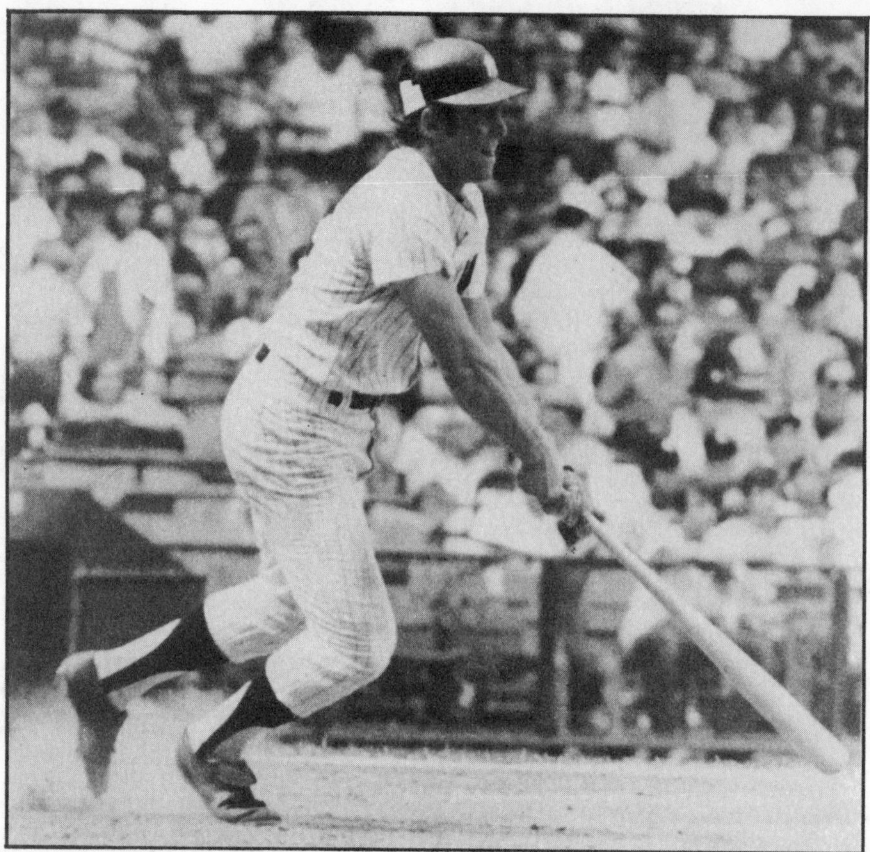

Fans were watching closely in 1973 when Yankee Ron Blomberg (above) became the first designated hitter in baseball history and they were encouraged by TSN (right) to cast a vote for or against the rule halfway through the season. TSN had conducted a preseason poll asking the same question.

Cast Your Vote on the Designated Hitter Rule

Now that the season is half finished, we think this is an appropriate time for the fans to voice their feelings on the Designated Hitter Rule, as used in the American League this season.

Simply mark the following ballot:

I am in favor of the use of the designated hitter .... ( )

I am opposed to the use of the designated hitter .... ( )

Name ....

Address ....

..

City State Zip

Send your ballots to:

DESIGNATED HITTER

The Sporting News

P.O. Box 56, St. Louis, Mo. 63166

Results of the poll will be published and sent on to Commissioner Bowie Kuhn and League Presidents Joe Cronin and Charles Feeney.

When the American League adopted the designated hitter rule on an experimental basis in 1973, The Sporting News gave its hearty endorsement to the innovation.

Although the paper later reversed its stand under different editorial direction, initially it envisioned the designated hitter as a cure for declining offense in the junior league.

In February 1973, before the rule was implemented, TSN conducted a poll of its readers, requesting a pro or con vote as well as the reasons for the fan's views.

The results were not unexpected. Of the first 750 replies, 459 (or 61 percent) opposed the DH and 291 favored it.

Among the reasons for opposing the rule were:

It breaks with baseball tradition; it eliminates the strategy of when and with whom to pinch hit for the pitcher; brings the platoon system to baseball; prevents the pitcher from having a hand offensively in the outcome of the game; gives the pitcher an opportunity to throw beanballs without fear of retaliation; makes all records meaningless under new conditions; reduces bunting.

Reasons for favoring the rule included:

Increases offense and adds excitement; extends careers of aging sluggers; eliminates automatic outs by pitchers; permits pitchers to concentrate on their trade; ends boredom created by parade of pinch-hitters and relief pitchers; makes bunting more of a surprise element than a must; prolongs rallies.

Two months into the season the publication noted editorially:

"The DH is proving a decided plus . . . and is nowhere near the radical departure some opponents had predicted—unless you consider more hitting, more scoring and more action a radical departure."

In two consecutive issues after the All-Star Game, TSN polled its readers a second time, promising to publish the results and also to forward the tabulation to Commissioner Bowie Kuhn and the presidents of the two major leagues.

This poll revealed a change of mind among readers. This time 52 percent embraced the DH and 48 percent rejected it. In American League cities, approval was 57 to 43 percent. In N.L. cities, readers opposed the rule by 52 to 48 percent.

D-H Rule Adds Homers, But Takes Away Game Strategy

ST. LOUIS–With about one-third of the season left, it would appear that the American League's results with the new designated-hitter rule have more than justified the experiment. The DHs, as a whole, were batting only .250–but it was a potent .250.

At the time of the All-Star break, the swingers for the pitchers had 126 homers among their 1,117 hits in 4,470 times at bat and had driven in 574 runs.

In all of 1972, the A. L. pitchers batted only .145 with 664 hits, 21 homers and 226 RBIs. hits, 21 homers and 226 RBIs.

A COMPARISON of the A. L. designated hitters' records and the batting performances of the National League pitchers this season also offered an illuminating contrast. The N. L. pitchers had a plate mark of .150 with 15 homers and 155 RBIs.

Only two A. L. pitchers, Cy Acosta of the White Sox and Rollie Fingers of the Athletics, have had times at bat so far this year. Both struck out.

When Claude Osteen of the Dodgers batted for the N. L. in the All-Star Game at Kansas City, he was the first pitcher ever to come to the plate at new Royals Stadium. Osteen executed a successful sacrifice.

BY HIS APPEARANCE, Osteen pointed up one of the facets of the designated-hitter rule that has bothered the A. L. managers. It takes away some of the strategy of the game. In most situations, where a bunt might be called for, the managers are inclined to let the designated hitter swing away.

The nine DHs who had gone to bat 200 or more times had only five sacrifice hits among them.

Tommy Davis of the Orioles was the leading batter among the designated hitters who were being used regularly. He had been up 303 times and had 95 hits for an average of .314. His hits included four homers and he had driven in 40 runs.

Orlando Cepeda of the Red Sox had the most homers, 14, followed by Frank Robinson of the Angels with 12 and Deron Johnson of the Athletics with 11. Cepeda had the most RBIs, 51, one more than Tony Oliva of the Twins.

ACTUALLY, THE N. L. had one pitcher who was outhitting every designated batter in the A. L. Steve Blass of the Pirates had an average of .455 on 10 hits in 22 trips.

In a collated ranking of A. L. designated hitters and N. L. pitchers, Celerino Sanchez of the Yankees would be next with .400, but the third highest batter would be another N. L. pitcher, Steve Stone of the Mets, with .391. Don Carrithers of the Giants would follow in line with .364.

Ken Brett of the Phillies, who had four homers among his hits, was batting .308 and Reggie Cleveland of the Cardinals had an even .300 average.

THE USE OF the designated-hitter rule is not mandatory, but except for the isolated cases of Acosta and Fingers, the A. L. managers have not chosen to let any of their pitchers come to bat. Nevertheless, there has been enough muttering among the managers about the rule that its extension beyond this season would be in doubt if they had the final word.

There appears to be no sentiment among N. L. managers for adoption of the rule.

Sparky Anderson of the Reds said, "I need a designated hitter more than any other club in the National League–I have the worst hitting staff in baseball–but I am dead against it. It's not baseball as I know it."

The N. L. gave the A. L. permission to experiment with the designated-hitter rule for three years. Whether it will last that long, or what will happen after the three years are up, still is open to question.

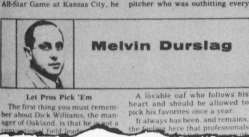

AMERICAN LEAGUE

Designated Hitters

(Including Games of July 22)

Club Totals

Player-Club	AB	H	HR	RBI	Pct.
Baltimore	377	110	4	43	292
Minnesota	396	109	11	55	275
Boston	377	103	15	54	273
Detroit	374	96	11	41	257
Oakland	376	96	15	59	255
Texas	370	93	4	39	251
Cleveland	383	95	14	49	248
Milwaukee	361	86	12	50	238
New York	376	88	11	55	234
Chicago	369	86	6	44	233
California	340	77	15	48	226
Kansas City	371	78	8	37	210
Totals	4470	1117	126	574	250

INDIVIDUAL TOTALS

(Ten or More At-Bats)

Player-Club	AB	H	HR	RBI	Pct.
Sanchez, New York	20	8	1	5	400
McKinney, Oakland	17	6	0	0	353
Davis, Baltimore	303	95	4	40	314
McGraw, California	32	10	1	3	313
Muser, Chicago	43	13	0	4	302
Bando, Oakland	10	3	1	3	300
Oliva, Minnesota	350	102	9	50	291
Cepeda, Boston	347	99	14	51	285
Brown, Milwaukee	209	59	7	24	282
Johnson, Texas	240	67	3	27	279
North, Oakland	26	7	0	0	269
G. Brown, Detroit	224	60	8	27	268
Johnson, Oakland	248	66	11	49	266
Ellis, Cleveland	83	22	4	13	265
Gamble, Cleveland	133	35	7	15	263
Williams, Cleveland	66	17	0	3	258
Howard, Detroit	121	31	3	13	256
Wohlford, Kan. City	59	15	2	4	254
McRae, Kansas City	48	12	1	5	250
Hart, New York	230	57	8	34	248
Andrews, Chicago	110	27	0	9	245
May, Chicago	94	23	3	17	245
Piniella, Kan. City	29	7	2	4	241
Porter, Milwaukee	55	13	2	12	236
Spikes, Cleveland	69	16	2	14	232
Blomberg, New York	65	15	2	10	231
Robinson, California	235	54	12	36	230
Hopkins, Kan. City	87	19	1	6	218
Crowley, Baltimore	53	11	0	2	208
Carty, Texas	113	23	1	11	204
Oliver, California	40	8	1	8	200
Otis, Kansas City	15	3	1	4	200
Johnstone, Oakland	10	2	0	1	200
Bevacqua, Kan. City	36	7	0	5	194
Mangual, Oakland	42	8	2	5	190
Reichardt, Chi.-K.C.	53	10	1	3	189
Henderson, Chicago	87	14	1	10	161
Hovley, Kansas City	42	7	0	3	167
Lahoud, Milwaukee	58	9	2	10	155
Coluccio, Milwaukee	26	4	1	3	154
Walton, Minnesota	29	4	2	5	138
Lolich, Cleveland	22	3	1	4	136
Kirkpatrick, Kan. City	20	2	1	4	100
Freehan, Detroit	10	1	0	0	100
Callison, New York	32	3	0	4	094
Grabarkewitz, Calif.	22	2	1	1	091
Oglivie, Boston	10	[illegible]	0	0	000

Melvin Durslag

Let Pros Pick 'Em

The first thing you must remember about Dick Williams, the manager of Oakland, is that he is not a

A lovable oaf who follows his heart and should be allowed to pick his favorites once a year.

It always has been, and remains, the feeling here that professionals

ndo Cepeda . . . Homer, RBI Leader

Even before the DH experiment had begun, TSN polled its readers and received a strong negative response (below). But with the season nearing an end, TSN ran a story (above) that gave the new rule a vote of confidence.

Readers File a Strong Dissent to New DH Rule

By ART VOELLINGER

ST. LOUIS, Mo.–Even before the first American League designated hitter has stepped into a batter's box, major league baseball fans have voiced a strong "NO" to the new rule.

According to a Voice of the Fan poll in THE SPORTING NEWS, 61 per cent of the readers submitting ballots oppose the designated hitter. As of March 1, a total of 750 replies showed 459 disapproving the DH and 291 favoring the change.

Additional statistics indicate that fans answering the ballot attend approximately 10.6 major league games per season. Those favoring the rule attend approximately 11 games each year and those against it attend approximately 10.7 games. A total of 125 letters other than those included with ballots had 170 readers against and 80 for the DH. A final count showed 1,000 readers participating in the ballot.

ALTHOUGH INFLUENCED by the many opinions already given by baseball executives and players, the fans produced a bagful of reasons for their views.

Fans on both sides of the fence are displeased with the problem the DH creates for the All-Star Game and World Series since the National League has not adopted the rule.

Fans commenting against the DH say it:

1. Breaks too much from baseball's traditional setup.

2. Eliminates the strategy of who and when to pinch-hit for the pitcher.

3. Brings the platoon system to baseball.

4. Prevents pitchers from having a hand offensively in the outcome of a game.

5. Confuses fans since a DH may bat anywhere in the lineup and also may shed the DH designation and play on defense.

6. Keeps pitchers like Babe Ruth and Stan Musial from developing into hitting stars.

7. Gives pitchers an easy opportunity to throw beanballs since they will never have to come to bat.

8. Reduces offense by keeping the starting pitcher in the game.

9. Makes all records meaningless since statistics of hitters and pitchers would be under new conditions.

10. Does not necessarily improve the ninth-place spot in the batting order.

11. Reduces bunting.

12. Slows player development because of the presence of veteran sluggers.

13. Ends the need of a player having to develop his defensive skills as well as his offensive ability.

14. Leads to longer games because of more hitting.

Fans favoring the DH say the rule will:

1. Increase offense and add excitement to the game.

2. Extend the careers of aging sluggers.

3. Eliminate the automatic out of the pitcher at bat.

4. Permit pitchers to concentrate on their trade.

5. Develop more players since a youngster who can hit and not field now has a position.

6. End the boredom created by a parade of pinch-hitters and relief pitchers late in a game.

7. Give weak-hitting pitchers time to relax in the dugout rather than wasting time at the plate.

8. Make bunting more of a surprise element than a must.

9. Give merit to the earned-run average title since a pitcher will face a more potent lineup.

10. Create longer rallies.

Obviously, those favoring the rule think it will boost attendance and improve the image of the American League, which adopted the DH for a three-year trial.

The logic of the arguments for or against the rule may be questioned, but the sincerity of the responses cannot be doubted. Replies came from all parts of the United States, Canada and several foreign countries.

VOTERS RANGED from a grade school student in Brooklyn to a 75-year-old woman in Florida. A California reader even tried to poll fellow office workers.

Ballots were accompanied by varied comments. Some samples:

"Baseball is a beautiful, simple and exciting game with or without a lot of hits. It needs no change." Bob Hall, St. Petersburg, Fla.

"The culture we live in thrives on change. Baseball should change. If it doesn't, then it will stagnate and rot." Clyde Blair, Minneapolis, Minn.

"The designated hitter is the move of gate-conscious American League owners who are running scared. How can the addition of a .220 hitter improve the game?" Loyd E. Poplin, Tahlequah, Okla.

"THOSE WHO are against the DH probably were against pasteurized milk, chlorinated water and the first ballplayers to wear glasses." Jack Michaels, Virginia, Minn.

"Letting the pitcher take his turn at bat is as much a part of baseball as Babe Ruth and hot dogs." Tony Saladino, Brandon, Fla.

"The DH will reincarnate baseball." Randy Murray, Great Neck, N. Y.

"Why clog up the bases with a slow moving DH? Wouldn't it be better to improve hitting instructions?" Paul M. Pelz, LaMirada, Calif.

"Baseball has changed often in the past through the advent of improved equipment, night games, artificial playing surfaces, longer schedules, expanded leagues and playing rules. Each change brought critics, yet baseball will survive." Eric Blumberg, Southfield, Mich.

Some readers also referred to football.

"THE DH WILL specialize baseball like football. A complete ballplayer should be able to play defense as well as offense." Tom Lamont, Mahwah, N. J.

"Baseball doesn't need the DH. It's a publicity gimmick. Gene Tenace, the World Series hero, is more of a household word than Jake Scott, football's Super Bowl star." Ron Muzechuk, Dayton, O.

"The designated hitter should try to find another occupation like

(Continued on Page 38, Column 1)

34 ★ THE SPORTING NEWS, MARCH 10, 1973 ★

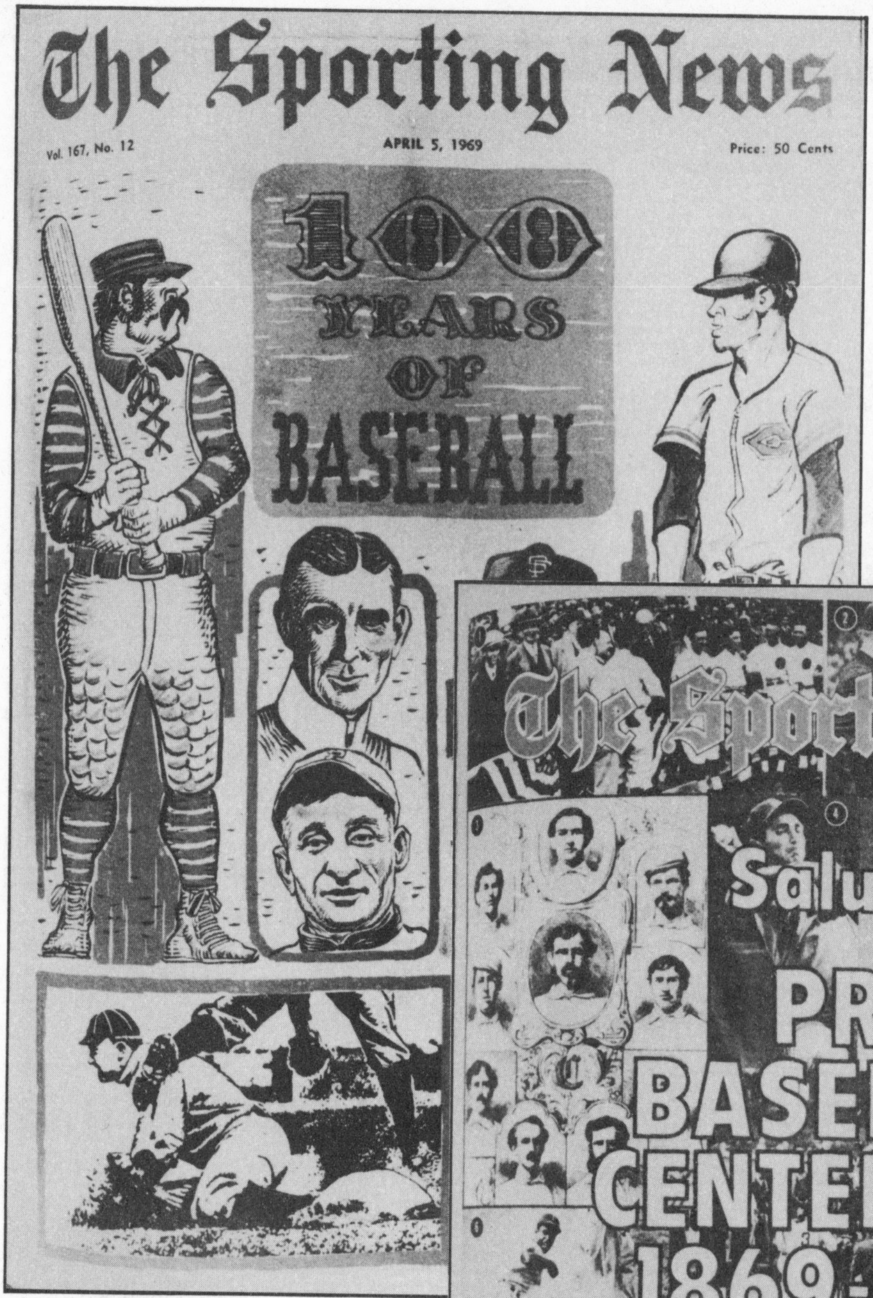

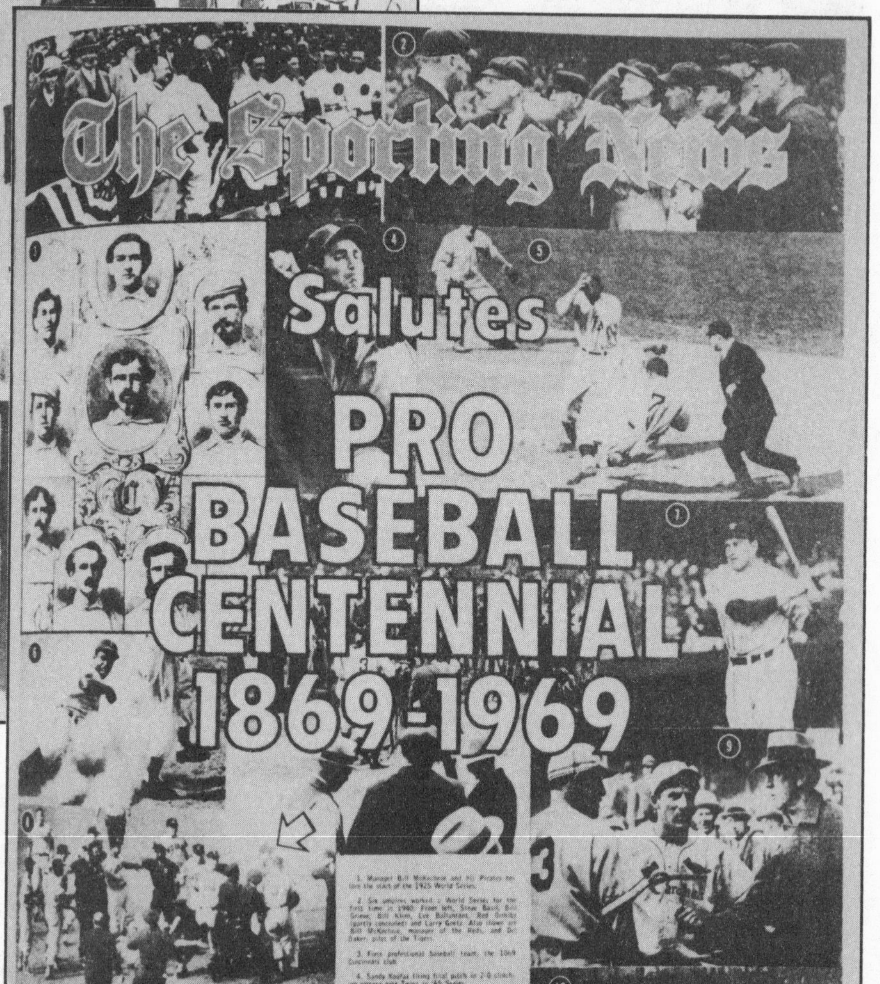

100 Years Of Baseball

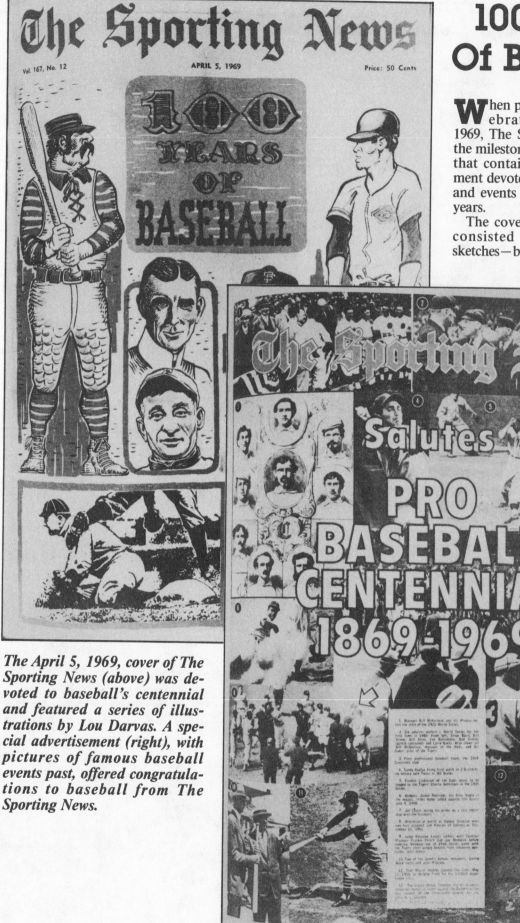

When professional baseball celebrated its centennial in 1969, The Sporting News marked the milestone with an 80-page issue that contained a 40-page supplement devoted to prominent figures and events in the game's first 100 years.

The cover of the April 5 issue consisted of a series of color sketches—by Lou Darvas of Cleve-

The April 5, 1969, cover of The Sporting News (above) was devoted to baseball's centennial and featured a series of illustrations by Lou Darvas. A special advertisement (right), with pictures of famous baseball events past, offered congratulations to baseball from The Sporting News.

land—of the game's leading personalities of the preceding century.

Leading off the special section was a feature on the first professional team. Titled "The Cincinnati Red Stockings," the article was written by Lee Allen, author of a colorful history on the National League franchise and at the time the historian at baseball's Hall of Fame.

Other features were "Roll Call: Anson to Zachary," by Bob Broeg, sports editor of the St. Louis Post-Dispatch; "The Executives," by Publisher C.C. Johnson Spink; "The Great Umpires," by Managing Editor Lowell Reidenbaugh; "Exclusive Company: Big Time Managers," by Neal Russo, also of the Post-Dispatch; "The Writers," by veteran baseball writer Fred Lieb; "The 1880s: Turmoil, Prosperity," by Leonard Koppett of the New York Times; "Gags: Players' Wit in Baseball," by Joe Garagiola, and "Majors Paid Stiff Price to Kayo Outlaw Federal Loop," by Bill Fleischman of The Sporting News staff.

Koppett also engaged in a flight of fantasy with a prediction of conditions when baseball observes its bicentennial. The story was titled: "It's April of 2069 with 3-Platoon Baseball and $50 Ticket."

During the centennial year TSN commenced the publication of lengthy biographies of Hall of Fame immortals, starting with Babe Ruth and Rogers Hornsby. The features were written by Broeg, highly regarded baseball authority for his work as a reporter, editor, columnist, book author and as a member of the Hall of Fame Veterans Committee. The series proved so popular that it was continued for three years, after which the 40 articles were published in "Super Stars of Baseball."

Other additions to the Spink Sports Library from 1962 to 1973 were "Baseball Rules" (1962), "Official American Football League Guide" (1962), "Football Fundamentals for Feminine Fans" (1963), "Football Register" (1966), "Hockey Guide" (1967), "Daguerreotypes" (enlarged and expanded, 1968), "Official American Basketball Association Guide" (1969), "Pro Football Guide" (1970) and "Hockey Register" (1972).

Vol. 167 APRIL 5, 1969 No. 12

THE SPORT THAT WEARS WELL

One hundred years . . . that's a brief period in the history of man, but it's a mighty long time for a professional sport to flourish. Baseball's claim to pre-eminence in American sport has been challenged in recent years. Still, baseball has not gone out of style, nor is there any indication that it will, though there are signs that it must and will make some changes to meet competition. Millions still regard baseball as No. 1. Certainly, it is a formidable contender, and that may be the most that any form of entertainment can boast in modern America. The day is gone when one sport can dominate the American leisure scene as did baseball for many decades.

One distinction baseball retains without dispute: It was the pioneer which has been closely copied by each of its chief competitors—football, basketball and hockey. As one sports historian has put it, "The others imitated baseball's structural pattern in order to compete as commercialized spectacles." As the sport which set the mold, pro baseball has a past worth recalling. That is what this special issue of THE SPORTING NEWS attempts to do.

The issue contains 80 pages, 40 of which make up a section devoted to pro baseball's centennial. This is one of the largest issues THE SPORTING NEWS has ever published, the biggest since October 30, 1946, when a 104-page paper marked THE SPORTING NEWS' 60th-year anniversary. The stories in the centennial section are not a history book. They are, however, of historical interest for the incidents they relate and the men whose deeds are recounted. The writers of these stories have a firm grasp of baseball history, and most fans will find their knowledge of baseball's past considerably broadened after reading them.

Readers of these tales also will encounter more than a few laughs. Especially recommended are a couple in this category. Managing Editor Lowell Reidenbaugh's piece on the great umpires reveals that some were not only great, but hilarious, too. Not to be outdone, Joe Garagiola recalls some of the funniest episodes in his limitless repertoire.

Leonard Koppett, who has contributed some significant stories to THE SPORTING NEWS in recent years, is at his best citing milestones in baseball's first hundred years—and fantasizing on events of the next hundred. Lee Allen has written a superb account of baseball's first professional team, the 1869 Cincinnati Red Stockings. Publisher C. C. Johnson Spink describes baseball's top executives and the roles they played. Fred Lieb covers the giants of the press box, Bill Fleischman tells of the Federal League's bitter struggle to become a third major and Bob Broeg examines the feats and personalities of players who left their mark on baseball . . . and some who didn't.

If you decide after reading the centennial section that baseball has a distinctive past and a bright future, you'll be in accord with those who wrote and assembled the stories.

The lead editorial in TSN's baseball centennial issue praised the game and boasted of the publication's special features and 40-page supplement devoted to memories of baseball events gone by.

The Sporting News

JUNE 27, 1981

PRICE: $1.50

Players Take a Walk

First Midseason Strike Shuts Down Baseball

ON STRIKE
81

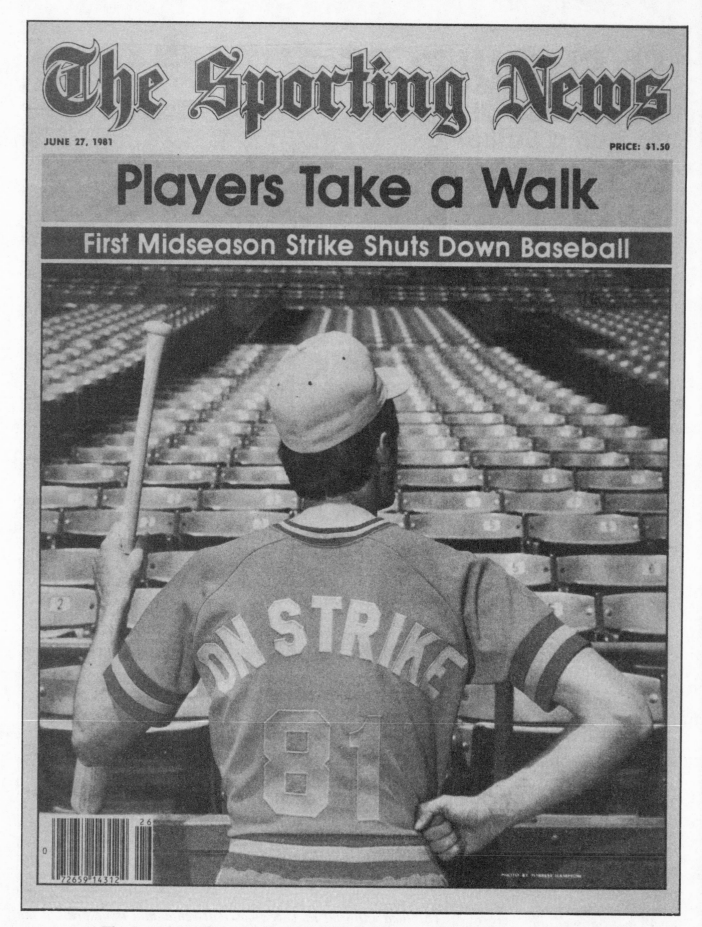

The June 27, 1981, cover of The Sporting News effectively tells the story of baseball's conversion from a game to big business.

1975-1986:
FREE AGENCY

For decades, paragraph 10 (a) of the Uniform Players Contract lay virtually unnoticed among the rules that govern professional baseball. It had been invoked, according to one source, approximately 100 times in the history of the game.

The rule provides that, if a club and player are unable to agree on a contract, the club may renew the pact at the previous year's terms. It remained for John Alexander (Andy) Messersmith to exploit the rule to maximum advantage, gaining untold wealth not only for himself, but also for those who came after him.

In 1974, the righthander posted a 20-6 record and a 2.59 earned-run average for the pennant-winning Dodgers. At 29, he appeared to be on the threshold of many productive years.

Messersmith submitted his salary requests to his bosses in early 1975. In addition to a hefty salary adjustment, he sought a no-trade clause in a multiyear agreement. The Dodgers balked at the no-trade clause, and on that issue negotiations collapsed. Messersmith's contract was renewed at a $25,000 increase over the 1974 terms, and he completed the 1975 season without incident and with a 19-14 record.

On October 7, 1975, the Major League Baseball Players Association, through its attorney, Dick Moss, filed a grievance in which it maintained that Messersmith had fulfilled the terms of his contract and should be declared a free agent. Management dissented vigorously, claiming that Messersmith still was property of the Dodgers according to the reserve clause, and when a series of meetings failed to resolve the impasse, it was referred to a committee consisting of Peter Seitz, an impartial arbitrator; John Gaherin, chairman of the owners' Player Relations Committee, and Marvin Miller, executive director of the Players Association. With Gaherin and Miller voting the party line, the issue rested squarely with Seitz.

The arbitrator agreed with the players. Messersmith, who said he pursued the grievance in order to provide the Players Association with a test case even though the Dodgers by that time had offered him a lucrative three-year contract with a no-trade clause, gained his freedom. So did Seitz, who was fired by the owners.

The decision was appealed to the lower courts without success. Rather than pursue the matter, the owners conceded defeat.

On April 10, 1976, the pitcher signed "a lifetime contract" with Atlanta. The three-year agreement provided a signing bonus of $400,000 and, of course, a no-trade clause. Exultantly, Ted Turner announced his prize catch. "Andy Messersmith will be with the Braves as long as I am," the flamboyant Braves owner chortled. "The contract is forever—until death or old age do us part."

In the case of Messersmith, "forever" meant two years. After winning a combined 16 games and losing 15 in 1976-77, Andy agreed to be sold to the Yankees, for whom he lost all three of his decisions in 1978. He returned to the Dodgers in 1979 and closed out his career with a 2-4 record.

But Messersmith's place in history was secure. The decision in his case ended the era of enslavement in baseball and ushered in an age of instant riches for talented free agents.

As labor celebrated its landmark triumph, management undertook the task of forging a new Basic Agreement to replace the one that expired on December 31, 1975. Nobody expected a quick settlement, and in that, nobody was disappointed.

The imponderable was free agency. Weeks passed without solution, and on February 23, 1976, the owners announced that training camps would not open until a new agreement was reached. A few players worked out as best they could, individually and in groups, and the negotiations continued. Then Bowie Kuhn intervened on March 17.

"Because I think it is now vital that spring training get under way without further delay," the commissioner announced, "I have directed that all camps be opened by the earliest possible time."

The bargaining on a new Basic Agreement continued until July 12, when it was announced that a new pact had been hammered out. Provisions were made for a re-entry draft of eligible free agents, of which there were 24 in 1976. That fall the first re-entry draft sparked lively bidding for proven talent. The first player to cash in on the newly minted opulence was Bill Campbell, a Minnesota reliever who signed a four-year contract with Boston for $1 million, a remarkable boost from his 1976 contract, which returned $23,000.

The most lucrative contract was signed by Reggie Jackson. The outfielder, who played out his option with the Orioles, accepted a five-year Yankee pact that called for $3 million. His former Oakland teammate, Joe Rudi, signed a five-year Angel contract worth $2.09 million, and Don Gullett, a freed Cincinnati pitcher, inked a six-year Yankee pact for $2 million.

Labor squabbles were not the only source of discontent in 1976. Charles O. Finley and Bowie K. Kuhn saw to that.

As the June 15 trading deadline approached, the Oakland club owner announced that he had unloaded three members of his three-time world champions. Outfielder Joe Rudi and pitcher Rollie Fingers were sold to the Red Sox for $1 million each and pitcher Vida Blue to the Yankees for $1.5 million. It was the biggest money deal in baseball history.

"I just refused to let those players drive me into bankruptcy with their astronomical salary demands," Finley explained.

The commissioner took a dim view of the trades. On June 18, Kuhn declared the deals null and void. The ruling was "in the best interests of baseball," he said. "The commissioner is left with the lonely job of determining integrity and confidence. I have to weigh public opinion."

Finley was flabbergasted. Within a week he filed a $10 million damage suit against Kuhn, the American and National leagues, the Executive Council, the Red Sox and the Yankees. Two courts found in favor of Kuhn, supporting the commissioner's view that the "best interests" clause gave him the authority to cancel the deals. Finley traded Blue to San Francisco in 1978, while Rudi and Fingers became free agents after the '76 season.

Finley lost another skirmish in 1977 when he tried to sell the A's to Marvin Davis, a wealthy oilman who planned to move the franchise to Denver. Finley was reminded that 10 years remained on his lease of the Oakland-Alameda County Coliseum. He was informed that the lease might be abrogated, however, if he could persuade the Giants to play 41 (about half) of their home games in Oakland. The Giants, anxious to rid the Bay Area of a competing franchise, reluctantly agreed, but the San Francisco Board of Supervisors, which controlled the Giants' Candlestick Park lease, said that was too many, and on that issue the negotiations for the sale of the club foundered. But there was a benefit of sorts in the aborted deal. On August 23, 1980, Finley sold the A's to Levi Strauss & Co. for $12.7 million, considerably more than the Marvin Davis offer.

As Finley tried to unload his club in 1977, two cities were pleased to gain new major league franchises. Eight years after losing the Pilots to Milwaukee, Seattle welcomed the Mariners to its new enclosed stadium, the Kingdome, and the Toronto Blue Jays became the major leagues' second Canadian team. That expansion gave the American League 14 teams, two more than the senior circuit.

The Yankees captured their second consecutive division title in 1977 and squeezed past Kansas City in the League Championship Series. In their second full season under Billy Martin, the Yanks erased the stigma of their four-straight blowout by the Reds in 1976 by defeating the Dodgers in a six-game World Series.

The deciding game was a personal triumph for Reggie Jackson. Tying a record set by Babe Ruth, Mr. October smacked three home runs in an 8-4 victory. The last clout traveled 450 feet into the center-field bleachers, raising his Series homer total to five (another record) and his batting average to .450.

The 1978 campaign was interrupted by a one-day strike by major league umpires. On August 25, the arbiters took a holiday in protest of their $52 daily allowance, from which they were expected to pay for their hotel, meals and in-town transportation. A federal judge ordered the umpires back to work the next day.

But the most commanding headlines of the year were written by Pete Rose. On April 29 at New York, Rose, in his 16th season at Cincinnati, cracked five hits, including three home runs, to mark the eighth time he had collected at least five safeties in one contest. On May 5, at Riverfront Stadium, Rose singled off Steve Rogers of Montreal for his 3,000th career hit, putting him in the select company of only 12 other players in the history of the game.

Irrepressible Pete's most significant feat lay just ahead, however. When he hit safely twice against Dave Roberts of the Cubs on June 14, Rose launched a batting streak that did not end until August 1, when he was blanked by Larry McWilliams and Gene Garber of Atlanta. During the stretch, Charlie Hustle hit safely in 44 games to equal an N.L. record set by Willie Keeler of Baltimore in 1897.

At season's end, Rose had 3,164 career hits—ninth on the all-time list—and, as a free agent, was casting about for a club that would compensate him as a genuine superstar. In a private jet, Pete crisscrossed the country, offering his services to a free-spending club that would better his Cincinnati paycheck of $375,000. Five clubs coveted the 37-year-old star, but the Phillies won the sweepstakes with an offer of $3.225 million over four years.

An even more lucrative contract was signed by Dave Parker. The slugging Pittsburgh outfielder accepted a five-year pact worth at least $6.725 million, much of that in deferred compensation, thereby becoming baseball's first million-dollar player.

The year also brought another managerial dismissal for the Yankees' Billy Martin. Volatile Billy, who already had been fired by the Twins, Tigers and Rangers in previous seasons, got the ax in July. Martin, who had been feuding with Reggie Jackson all year, committed his fatal mistake when he made a comment about the star outfielder and his boss, Owner George Steinbrenner. "The two of them deserve each other," Martin said. "One's a born liar; the other's convicted." Billy submitted a tearful resignation the next day.

Coach Dick Howser handled the club one night as the Royals beat the Yankees, dropping New York to fourth place, 10½ games out of first. Steinbrenner then hired a new field boss, Bob Lemon, who had been fired 3½ weeks earlier by the White Sox. Under the former pitcher's dispassionate leadership, the Yanks came alive, winning 47 of their last 67 games to tie the Red Sox for the A.L. East crown. A one-game divisional playoff victory and a four-game conquest of the Royals in the league playoffs preceded the Yanks' World Series engagement with the Dodgers.

Tom Lasorda's Dodgers had just become the majors' first club ever to draw 3 million fans in a season, and when they captured the first two Series games at home, their prospects for a world championship looked bright. But the Yanks swept the next four contests, and Lemon became the first manager who, having been fired elsewhere the same season, guided a second team to a world championship.

The umpires' one-day walkout in 1978 was merely a foretaste of the strike that hobbled the majors at the start of the 1979 season. On the advice of their attorney-agent, Richie Phillips, the arbiters refused to sign contracts, and major league games, starting with spring exhibitions, were officiated by local semipros and other umpires recruited from the high minors. The men in blue were idled until May 19, the day after they had ratified a new contract that guaranteed increased pay and summer vacations.

While the umpires tabulated their gains, the Yankees bemoaned their losses. A clubhouse brawl between Goose Gossage and Cliff Johnson resulted in a torn thumb ligament for the ace reliever, who was disabled for more than two months, thus leaving the Yanks without a late-inning stopper. Ron Guidry volunteered to work out of the bullpen for several weeks, but that took a proven 20-game winner out of the rotation. The Yanks fell far off the pace, so George Steinbrenner made another managerial switch on June 19, bringing back—who else—Billy Martin for a second try.

Another reason why the Yankees failed to repeat as champions was the tragic loss of Thurman Munson. Taking advantage of an open date in the schedule, the 32-year-old catcher flew to Canton, O., on August 2 to practice takeoffs and landings in his new twin-engine jet. He crashed 1,000 feet short of the runway at the Akron-Canton Airport. Munson, who had been piloting the plane, was killed, but two passengers survived.

Like the Yankees, the Cardinals meandered through a mediocre '79 season. But there was one exhilarating feature in the speeding form of Lou Brock. The outfielder collected his 3,000th hit on August 13 and closed his career weeks later with a record of 938 stolen bases.

Another ageless veteran, Willie Stargell, clouted three home runs and four doubles to lead the Pirates to a seven-game upset of the Orioles in the World Series. Stargell's 25 total bases tied a Series record.

Although denied World Series prominence in 1979, Billy Martin did not recede from public view. Returning from a hunting trip in South Dakota, Martin visited a bar in Bloomington, Minn., where he kayoed a marshmallow salesman. The punch cost him his Yankee job, but he rebounded quickly as skipper of the Oakland A's in 1980.

That same year, the Phillies captured their first world championship, third baseman George Brett of the A.L. champion Royals flirted with a .400 batting mark—he finished at .390—and another round of labor disputes produced a walkout that threatened an even longer work stoppage in 1981.

The negotiations started early, and when little progress was shown, the players voted to cancel the last 92 spring exhibition games. Marvin Miller of the Players Association also announced that a strike would begin May 23 if there were no new Basic Agreement to replace the one that had expired the previous December.

The chief obstacles to agreement were the owners' proposal for a wage scale and their insistence upon significant compensation for players lost through free agency. With the strike deadline imminent, the magnates accepted a proposal to table the compensation issue and let a special committee hammer out the details of a satisfactory settlement.

The bullet was dodged, but the missile was on a boomerang course. It struck its mark on June 12, 1981, when major league players went out on strike, and again free agency was at the heart of the matter. The strike endured for 50 days and ended only when Miller suggested that a club losing a player via free agency be compensated from a pool of specially designated players set up by all the clubs. The settlement also provided that the season would resume August 9 with the All-Star Game in Cleveland and with the pennant races the next day. No games canceled by the strike were rescheduled, and the '81 season was split into halves, with the teams in the League Championship Series being determined by divisional playoffs that matched the first-half champion against the second-half champion in each division.

When the ticket windows reopened August 10, many fans displayed their annoyance with the strike by staying home. But in Philadelphia, 60,561 fans packed Veterans Stadium hoping to see Pete Rose pass another milestone. They were not disappointed. An eighth-inning single off Bruce Sutter of the Cardinals was the 3,631st of Pete's career, surpassing the N.L. record of Stan Musial.

Before the season ran its course, Nolan Ryan of Houston hurled his fifth no-hitter, a 5-0 masterpiece against Los Angeles, to eclipse the old mark set by Sandy Koufax. Before the strike, Cleveland's Len Barker pitched a 3-0 perfect game against Toronto, while five days earlier, Montreal's Charlie Lea had fashioned a 4-0 no-hitter over the Giants.

But despite these fine performances, attendance was down in the second half. Fans also were upset with the way some of the pennant races were developing. Although Cincinnati's overall record of 66-42 was the best in the majors and the Cardinals' 59-43 mark was supreme in the N.L. East, neither team figured in the playoffs. The split-season format adopted by a vote of the club owners produced half-season titles for the Dodgers and Astros in the West and Montreal and Philadelphia in the East. The Dodgers and Expos captured the preliminary playoffs, then proceeded to the League Championship Series, which Los Angeles won in five games.

The A.L. playoffs produced division crowns for the Yankees, who defeated the Brewers in the East, and the A's, who swept the Royals in the West. New York won the pennant in three games over Oakland but was no match for the Dodgers, who lost the first two games of the World Series but rebounded to win the next four, the first victory coming on a complete-game performance by rookie sensation Fernando Valenzuela. Because of the strike, the Series did not end until October 28, the latest date in history.

Labor strife took a holiday in 1982, but other disruptive influences were at work as baseball ushered in a new season. Snowstorms wiped out opening games in six cities and forced teams to devise emergency measures while awaiting the arrival of more congenial climes. The Brewers, victims of a one-foot snowfall, flew to Houston to work out in the Astrodome, while the Red Sox returned to their Winter Haven, Fla., training base for two days of drills.

The new Hubert H. Humphrey Metrodome, replacing Metropolitan Stadium in Minneapolis, served double duty. While the Twins entertained the Mariners in regular-season games, the Blue Jays and White Sox played two exhibition games in undisturbed comfort. Meanwhile, the Yankees tried to keep in shape at the West Point field house, the Rangers worked out under the stands at Shea Stadium and the Indians used the indoor facilities at Cleveland State University.

The Braves, unhampered by meteorological mischief, won their first 13 games—two more than the A's had registered the previous year—to set a modern major league record. The Braves finally were stopped by the Reds, 2-1, on April 22.

Buoyed by their early success and the far-reaching influence of Owner Ted Turner's WTBS cable network, the Braves captured the attention of the nation and quickly became known as "America's Team." Attendance boomed at Atlanta Stadium, and club officials decided to accommodate more customers by removing Chief Noc-A-Homa's teepee from the left-field bleachers on July 30. The Braves promptly lost 15 of their next 16 games before superstitious fans persuaded the club to reassemble the teepee. The Braves came back to win the division flag on the last day of the season, thanks to a three-run home run by San Francisco's Joe Morgan that prevented a tie with Los Angeles. The Cardinals had clinched the N.L. East championship six days before.

The Angels wrapped up the A.L. West title on October 2, but the race in the East was a nail-biter. Needing just one win in the final four games at Baltimore, the Brewers dropped a doubleheader on Friday and were humiliated, 11-3, on Saturday, leaving them even with the Orioles. They exploded, however, behind Robin Yount's two homers and one triple on Sunday to win the finale, 10-2, thus ruining Baltimore's remarkable effort to come from behind and win another division title for Earl Weaver, who retired after the season.

While the Cardinals disposed of the Braves in three straight games in the N.L. playoffs, the Brewers, after dropping the first two contests, won the next three from the Angels to qualify for their first World Series. No team before had ever rebounded from a 0-2 start to win a League Championship Series.

Paul Molitor's record five hits and Mike Caldwell's three-hit pitching sparked the Brewers to a 10-0 opening victory in the World Series, and after five games, "Harvey's Wallbangers"—so named for the long-ball antics of Harvey Kuenn's team—were within one win of the title. But the Cardinals retaliated with 13-1 and 6-3 victories at home to capture their ninth world championship.

One of the St. Louis pitchers was Jim Kaat, who set a major league mark by hurling in his 24th season. (Kaat made it 25 by playing in 1983 before retiring.) Another graybeard, Gaylord Perry of Seattle, became the 15th pitcher to win 300 games, and Rickey Henderson of Oakland set a modern major league record by stealing 130 bases.

The 1983 campaign was still months away when George Steinbrenner felt the sting of executive wrath. In January, Commissioner Bowie Kuhn plastered the Yankees' owner with a $5,000 fine for his part in a name-calling match with White Sox co-Owners Eddie Einhorn and Jerry Reinsdorf, each of whom was fined $2,500. But that was just for starters.

During a Florida exhibition game, Steinbrenner impugned the integrity of National League umpires and was fined $50,000 by Kuhn. Then in May, Steinbrenner blasted an A.L. umpire for ejecting slugger Dave Winfield from a game. League President Lee MacPhail suspended Steinbrenner for a week, during which time he was forbidden to go to the ball park. And finally, the owner made headlines again two days before Christmas, when he was penalized for "certain public statements" made in connection with the great "pine-tar" incident.

The pine-tar saga began at Yankee Stadium on July 24 when George Brett whacked a two-out, ninth-inning homer to give the Royals a 5-4 lead over the Yankees. But Billy Martin, who had been rehired by Steinbrenner for a third term as manager, had been apprised of an irregularity in Brett's bat a couple of weeks earlier and had a trick up his sleeve. He called the umpires' attention to the fact that Brett had smeared pine tar on the bat handle beyond the legal limit of 18 inches. The arbiters agreed, nullified the home run and called Brett out, ending the game and giving New York a 4-3 victory. Four days later, MacPhail reversed his umpires' decision "in the spirit of the rules," allowing Brett's homer and ordering the game completed from the point of the disputed homer. MacPhail insisted that the rule, as originally written, was intended to guard against doctored bats and needed to be clarified.

Steinbrenner's reaction was instant and explosive. "It sure tests our faith in our leadership," he stormed. "If the Yankees lose the division by one game, I wouldn't want to be Lee MacPhail living in New York. Maybe he should go house-hunting in Kansas City."

The contest took only 12 minutes to complete on August 18, an open date for both clubs. The Royals won, 5-4, but only after the New York State Supreme Court Appellate Division, at 3:34 p.m. that day, had stayed a lower court's ruling that would have barred completion of the game pending the results of two lawsuits from fans who were protesting the $2.50 admission charge.

Because of Steinbrenner's derogatory remarks about MacPhail and the possibility that the owner was involved in the fans' lawsuits, Bowie Kuhn entered the fray and conducted a hearing. The outcome was a

$250,000 fine for the Yankees and an order that the commissioner's office be reimbursed $50,000 for legal fees relating to the litigation "brought by you (Steinbrenner) and the Yankees to enjoin me from conducting the aforesaid hearing."

While not in the Steinbrenner class, a $25,000 fine was slapped by Kuhn on Ted Turner after the Braves acquired pitcher Len Barker from Cleveland for "three players to be named" in August 1983. When outfielder Brett Butler asked Turner about reports that he was one of the players going to Cleveland, the owner said yes. Turner's honesty with his player, however, violated a rule regarding unnamed players in trades. While penalizing Turner, Kuhn allowed Butler to remain with the Braves for the rest of the season "in fairness to the player and his teammates, who remain in the National League West race."

Butler did not accept Kuhn's decision gracefully. "How can a lame-duck commissioner make a judgment on a lame-duck player?" he wondered.

Reference to a "lame-duck commissioner" stemmed from Kuhn's announcement in August that, after months of trying to save his job, he had decided to quit. He agreed, however, to remain until a successor was named, and he eventually stayed until September 30, 1984, the day before Peter V. Ueberroth, the highly successful director of the Summer Olympic Games in Los Angeles, took over as the game's sixth commissioner.

After the 1983 season, which saw the Orioles dominate the Phillies in a five-game World Series, Lee MacPhail ended his 10-year term as A.L. president. MacPhail, the son of former major league executive Larry MacPhail, had announced the previous year that he would resign on December 31, 1983, but rather than leave baseball, he accepted a new position as president of the Player Relations Committee. MacPhail's successor was Dr. Bobby Brown, a former Yankee infielder who had become a distinguished cardiologist in Texas.

The last major controversy faced by Bowie Kuhn during his reign as commissioner involved what was perhaps the ugliest problem to confront Organized Baseball in the history of the game. Drug abuse, a minor concern in previous years, became a matter of public knowledge and a cause of general alarm.

The drug problems of Los Angeles relief pitcher Steve Howe were revealed at a press conference before the '83 season. Howe admitted that he had spent five weeks at a drug rehabilitation center in an effort to conquer his dependence upon alcohol and cocaine. The lefthander had not overcome his drug habit, however, and he was suspended three times during the season by Dodgers President Peter O'Malley. Kuhn decided that three strikes were enough for Howe, and he suspended the pitcher for the entire 1984 season.

The most startling drug disclosure, however, involved four members of the 1983 Kansas City Royals. Outfielders Willie Wilson and Jerry Martin, first baseman Willie Aikens and pitcher Vida Blue were charged in the wake of a federal drug investigation that was not connected with professional sports until FBI wiretaps of a home in suburban Kansas City revealed that the players were attempting to purchase cocaine from the subject of the probe. The players pleaded guilty to misdemeanor drug charges as part of a plea-bargaining arrangement and were each sentenced to serve three months in a federal prison. In addition, Kuhn suspended Wilson, Martin and Aikens for the '84 season but left open the possibility that they could be reinstated pending a May 15 review by the commissioner. Kuhn indicated, however, that Blue, who had been released by the Royals in August 1983, could not return to the game before 1985, and an arbitrator later denied Blue's appeal. The arbitrator previously had ruled that Kuhn must reinstate the other three players on May 15, thus making Wilson eligible to return to the Royals, Martin to play for the Mets (with whom he had signed a free-agent contract) and Aikens to play for the Blue Jays (to whom he had been traded in December).

The Kansas City scandal made the drug problem in baseball a common topic on sports pages. While more and more players' names were mentioned in connection with possible drug use, Wilson returned from his suspension on May 16 to spark a Royals surge that culminated in an 84-78 record, good enough for the A.L. West title but the worst ever for an A.L. division champion. In the East, the Tigers got off to a record 35-5 start and led their division from start to finish. The Padres brought San Diego its first title in franchise history by cruising to the top of the N.L. West, and the Cubs, after a 39-year title hiatus, emerged behind the pitching of Rick Sutcliffe and hitting and fielding of Ryne Sandberg to win the N.L. East.

But umpire discontent reared its head once more at the close of the 1984 pennant races. One day before the start of the playoffs, the major league umpires announced through their agent, Richie Phillips, that they would not officiate the games. Postseason pay and job security were the major grievances. As a result of the walkout, substitute arbiters were on the job when the playoffs began in Kansas City and Chicago.

Replacements officiated the entire A.L. playoffs, which the Tigers won in three games. After four N.L. contests, the major league umpires agreed to submit their issues to the binding arbitration of the commissioner, and four umpires, all living in the San Diego area, handled the fifth game of the series. The Padres won that day to complete a three-game home sweep of the Cubs, who had won the first two games at Wrigley Field. Detroit then went on to highlight its phenomenal season with a five-game World Series triumph over San Diego.

The 1984 campaign produced still more super achievements by Pete Rose, who had signed a one-year, free-agent contract with the Montreal Expos in January. On April 13, the day before his 43rd birthday, Rose whacked a fourth-inning double off Jerry Koosman of the Phillies. It was Pete's 4,000th major league hit. Only Ty Cobb was in the same class.

In August, the longtime Cincinnati favorite returned to his home city as player-manager of the Reds, replacing Vern Rapp. Charlie Hustle amassed 107 hits for the season and entered the record book as the first player to collect at least 100 safeties in 22 consecutive campaigns. The pinch-hitter and part-time first baseman also had surpassed Carl Yastrzemski's lifetime record for games played, Cobb's record for singles and

Pete Rose stole the 1985 spotlight with his drive to the major league career hit record, breaking Ty Cobb's mark by collecting hit No. 4,192 on September 11 against San Diego.

Stan Musial's mark for doubles.

George Steinbrenner and Billy Martin were back in the news as the 1985 season got under way. The campaign was less than a month old and the Yankees were 6-10 when Steinbrenner pulled his 12th managerial switch in 13 years. The victim was Yogi Berra; his successor was, of course, Martin, back for a fourth term.

As Berra pondered his future, new labor problems that had been brewing for months began to disturb the summer's serenity. Again, a new Basic Agreement was the stumbling block. The owners demanded a cap on the amount of salary increase an arbitrator could award a player as well as an increase, from two to three years, in the major league tenure of players who could go to arbitration.

On May 23, player representatives authorized a strike on an undesignated date. On July 15, one day before the All-Star Game in Minnesota, the strike was set for August 6.

The appointed day found major league parks locked, but unlike the 1981 walkout that lasted 50 days, the latest strike endured for only two. On August 7, negotiators reached a settlement. In exchange for management's willingness to withdraw the salary-cap demand, the players agreed to increase arbitration eligibility to three years.

Two days before the strike, two veteran players reached significant milestones. In New York, Tom Seaver of the White Sox posted his 300th major league victory, a 4-1 decision over the Yankees. A short time later, at Anaheim, Rod Carew of the Angels singled off Frank Viola of Minnesota to join 15 others in the 3,000-hit class. Then on the final day of the season, Phil Niekro, the Yankees' ageless knuckleball pitcher, shut out Toronto, 8-0, to register his 300th major league victory and, at 46, become the oldest hurler ever to pitch a shutout.

But the season's most eagerly anticipated event—greater even than the World Series—occurred on September 11 in Cincinnati's Riverfront Stadium. For weeks on end, the baseball community had waited breathlessly as Pete Rose moved ever closer to Ty Cobb's most sacred record: 4,191 career hits. Reports on Pete's progress were transmitted daily coast to coast until, after games of September 6, the 44-year-old player-manager stood within two of tying the record.

Rose drew abreast of Cobb on the afternoon of September 8 at Wrigley Field in Chicago. With more than 28,000 fans whooping in gleeful anticipation, Rose lined a first-inning single to left-center off Reggie Patterson, who was less than a week removed from the minor leagues. Facing Patterson again in the fifth, Rose singled to right to tie Cobb's mark.

Rose did not play in the game of September 9 at Cincinnati and went hitless the next night against San Diego. But he was manning first base when the Reds hosted the Padres on September 11. A crowd of 47,237 gave Pete all the vocal support he needed and he responded heroically. In his 23rd major league season, on his 13,768th at-bat, Rose rapped a first-inning single to left-center off Eric Show. He had scaled the summit. He stood alone. Regardless of what had gone before in an eventful year and what was still to come, the season of 1985 belonged to Peter Edward Rose.

The Spink Era Ends

A GAIN FOR OUR READERS

The change in ownership of THE SPORTING NEWS (as set forth in the story on Page 9 of this issue) will have positive effects for our readers as well as for employes. There will be no personnel switches or changes in the way the paper is presented to our readers. C. C. Johnson Spink continues as editor and publisher and the staff remains as presently constituted.

But readers can look forward to an improved product and better service, particularly on the newsstands, plus stronger marketing and promotion. TSN is proud to join the Times Mirror family, one of the strongest, best managed and most highly diversified organizations in the communications field.

Times Mirror brings important new resources to TSN, including the financial strength to back some exciting new concepts in sports coverage. Among other assets, Times Mirror also has a forest products division which is an important source of newsprint for some of its publications. Thus, the chances of TSN experiencing another acute shortage of newsprint such as occurred a year or so ago are greatly lessened.

We're confident that we'll be serving our readers better as the result of joining the Times Mirror group.

The January 22, 1977, issue of The Sporting News announced to readers (below) that TSN, the property of the Spink family for more than 90 years, was being purchased by Times Mirror. An editorial in the same issue (above) assured everybody that the transaction would have positive effects for both readers and employees.

Times Mirror Purchases TSN, Spink Publications

LOS ANGELES—C. C. Johnson Spink, chairman and president of THE SPORTING NEWS Publishing Company, and Dr. Franklin D. Murphy, chairman of Times Mirror, have announced that Times Mirror has purchased THE SPORTING NEWS and related publications for an undisclosed amount of cash.

The transaction includes all of the outstanding stock of THE SPORTING NEWS Publishing Company and The Sporting Goods Publishing Company, both located in St. Louis. The two companies publish THE SPORTING NEWS, The Sporting Goods DEALER, a monthly trade journal and other related publications. Spink will continue to manage both firms.

Commenting on the sale, Spink said, "We have been a family business for 91 years. Therefore, it was important for us to associate with a solid organization. Times Mirror is one of the nation's leading publishing companies with perhaps the finest management in this field. We are delighted to be associated with them."

Dr. Murphy said, "We are extremely pleased to have Johnson Spink and THE SPORTING NEWS and The Sporting Goods DEALER join Times Mirror. Unquestionably the leaders in their fields, these publications will add new dimensions to our magazine publishing, which already includes Golf, Ski, Outdoor Life and Popular Science."

Times Mirror is a diversified publishing company engaged in newspaper publishing (Los Angeles Times, Newsday, The Dallas Times Herald), book and magazine publishing, directory printing, in addition to information services, television broadcasting, cable communications and the manufacture of newsprint and forest products.

On October 31, 1976, C.C. Johnson Spink was practicing his morning ablutions when he was struck by a sobering thought. The date marked his 60th birthday anniversary. He and his wife were childless. What would become of the firm of Charles C. Spink & Son if he were to be involved in a fatal car accident on the way to the office?

It was time, he concluded, to find a buyer for the company that had been a family property for more than 90 years.

There had been inquiries into the possible purchase of the firm during Taylor Spink's years, but Johnson's father systematically rejected such overtures.

"The decision to sell was mine alone," reported Johnson, a 52 percent stockholder. "I informed the minority shareholders, my cousins, what I planned to do and they approved, if the price was right.

"The company's assets were appraised and I established a price. Several persons said it was excessive, but I determined that if nobody met the figure there would be no sale.

"Five companies expressed an interest, but Times Mirror was my personal choice. Bob Erburu, president of Times Mirror, was a lifelong reader of The Sporting News and was keenly interested in acquiring the firm."

In less than three months after the decision was made to sell, the transaction was completed. Under terms of the sale, Times Mirror would pay $18 million for the company and Johnson Spink would remain as editor and publisher for five years and then serve as consultant for another five years.

An editorial in the issue of January 12, 1977, noted: "The change in ownership . . . will have positive effects for our readers as well as our employees. There will be no personnel switches or changes in the way the paper is presented to our readers.

"But readers can look forward to an improved product and better service, particularly on the newsstands, plus stronger marketing and promotion. TSN is proud to join the Times Mirror family, one of the strongest, best managed and most highly diversified organizations in the communications field.

"Times Mirror brings important new resources to TSN, including financial strength to back some exciting new concepts in sports coverage. Among other assets, Times Mirror also has a forest products division which is an important source of newsprint for some of its publications. Thus the chances of TSN experiencing another acute shortage of newsprint such as occurred a year or so ago are greatly lessened.

"We're confident that we'll be serving our readers better as a result of joining the Times Mirror group."

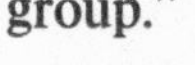

When C.C. Johnson Spink (above) sold The Sporting News in 1977, it marked the end of a glorious era for the first family of sports publishing.

Hierarchy Changes At TSN

In the restructured hierarchy of The Sporting News, following the sale of the firm to Times Mirror Inc., Johnson Spink was named chairman of the board and chief executive officer on December 29, 1978.

His personal selection to fill his vacated offices as president and publisher was J. Michael Hadley.

A native of St. Louis, Hadley was thoroughly acquainted with the publishing business. He was lured from Times Mirror Magazines Inc. of New York, publisher of Outdoor Life, Golf, Ski and Popular Science. Hadley served as chief operations officer for two years before tendering his resignation on January 1, 1981.

Hadley was succeeded in April of 1981 by Richard Waters, a native of Gardner, Mass., and a man well schooled in business and finance.

During World War II, Waters was a Navy radio operator in the Pacific. He earned his bachelor's degree from Hobart College and his master's degree from the Harvard Business School with a major in finance and accounting. After several years with Hunter and Weldon, an auditing firm, Waters joined the Reader's Digest as assistant treasurer in 1955.

By 1972 Waters was the chief financial officer and executive vice president in charge of the company's international operations. By his own estimates, he circled the globe six times in that position.

When the editor-board chairman of the Digest retired in 1977, the opening was filled by a marketing man. Waters, feeling he was entitled to the position, resigned.

After a six-month vacation in which he attempted to plot his next move, Waters accepted an offer as associate dean at the Harvard Business School.

"The dean said that three years on the job was all that I would want," Waters related, "and he was right."

After the sale of The Sporting News in 1977, St. Louisan J. Michael Hadley (below) was selected to fill the president and publisher offices vacated by C.C. Johnson Spink. After Hadley resigned in 1981, Richard Waters (above right with Spink) became TSN's president and chief executive officer.

In 1981, Waters was informed by a New York search firm of the vacancy at The Sporting News. Although "a lifelong sports nut," he turned a deaf ear. "I didn't want to go to St. Louis," he explained. "I was East Coast-oriented. My marketplace was between Boston and Washington, D.C."

Eventually, however, he yielded. A visit to TSN headquarters melted his resistance. He liked what he saw and became the paper's sixth publisher.

Within weeks after taking office, Waters told an interviewer: "We're wondering if we should become more controversial . . . our editorials are somewhat mundane. We may get into the book business . . . we'd like to get into investigative reporting. In short, we're going to make the publication come alive."

Humor in Headlines

In his years as chief copy editor of The Sporting News, Carl Felker amused countless readers with clever headlines. He was a master craftsman and while many attempted to imitate his style, few ever succeeded with any degree of consistency.

But the retirement of Felker in 1959 did not bring an end to TSN's chuckle-provoking headlines. Those who admired and studied the Felker manner produced some grins of their own.

When the Cardinals and Mets played a 25-inning night game at Shea Stadium, the story carried the banner "Cardinals Play Night Owls in Run to Daylight."

A Milwaukee story speculating on the forthcoming season observed "Brewers Bank Heavily on Comeback of Money" (Don Money).

A Los Angeles feature on Jim Brewer noted "Dodgers Drink to Brewer's Stout Relief Work," and a Pittsburgh yarn extolling the excellent play of second-stringers read "Subs Come to Rescue When Pirates Sound SOS."

Any story about the San Diego Padres, particularly pitcher Randy Jones, inspired the best efforts to those who had trained under Felker. These included: "Padre Jones' Sinker Gospel Wins Converts" and "Padre Jones Gets Good Word as Patient of Jobe" (Dr. Frank Jobe, noted orthopedic surgeon). When Alvin Dark was released as manager for failure to communicate with his players, readers chuckled to "Padres Excommunicate Non-Communicator."

Carl Felker was undisputed master of the clever headline.

Dallas Green's tirade to the Phillies after a lackluster performance bore the line "Green Talks Blue Streak Over Colorless Phillies," and the unpopular trade of outfielder Bake McBride was summed up with "Bake Sale Leaves Sour Taste in Philly." A paean to Art Howe of Houston revealed "Astros' New Hymn 'How Great Howe Art.'"

Luis Tiant's rejection of a Boston pay offer announced "Tiant, Refused a Boston Pay Hike, Takes a Walk."

Bowie Kuhn's ban on Charles O. Finley's efforts to sell Vida Blue, Joe Rudi and Rollie Fingers: "Bowie Bombs Finley's Closing Out Sale"; the appointment of Vern Rapp as St. Louis manager: "Rapp, Minor League Magician, Picked to Do Card Tricks," and Lyman Bostock's signing by the California club: "Lyman's Pie in the Sky Proves to Be Angel Food."

But the headline that tickled the most risibilities was perhaps the one over a Dodger newsletter. When Los Angeles executives, having reviewed the pitching staff after losing Tommy John to free agency, agreed that the remaining pitchers were sufficiently strong to produce a third consecutive pennant, the story headline noted "Dodgers Can Feel Flush Even Without John."

A Boston columnist proclaimed it "the headline of the year."

When Felker retired, the humorous headline did not disappear from the pages of The Sporting News. The headlines below are examples of how TSN carried on the Felker tradition.

Angels Ask: Can Big Bra Regain Maiden Form?

By ROSS NEWHAN

ANAHEIM, Calif. — The headline appeared in THE SPORTING NEWS only a few weeks ago. It read: "Can the Big Bra Snap Back?"

The trade was the 25th completed by Walsh since he replaced Fred Haney 2½ years ago. He has dis-

need a man who can come in and throw the ball past a hitter or make him pop it up."

size (6-5 and 220 pounds) is imposing.

in the careers of Brabender and Clyde Wright, the Angels' ace who

Dodgers Embrace Hill Gospel According to John

By ROSS NEWHAN

LOS ANGELES—Tommy John was 7-0 through the first half of the 1968 season. He was the ace of the

Marshall and Jim Brewer in the bullpen, we'd have fewer complete games."

Manager Walter Alston said the

During that time, John never won more than 14 games and in four seasons finished with a sub-.500 record. Often overlooked,

Dodger Stadium, in fact, his name is spelled: "T-t-t-tommy John."

"Generally," he said, "I start to stammer when I'm out of breath of dealing with a subject I'm not fa-

cord three wins. . . . Jimmy Wynn opened sensationally, busting six homers with 17 RBIs in the 12 games. The six homers were more than any L. A. Dodger ever had hit

Quick Bake a Tasty Treat on Cardinal Table

By BOB BROEG

ST. LOUIS—If Bake McBride bats in front of both of the Cardinals' switch-hitters, Reggie Smith and Ted Simmons, the turn-around twins in the 4-5 spot of the Redbirds' batting order just might improve this season on their 1974 RBI totals, 100 and 103.

Well into the Grapefruit League schedule, Manager Red Schoendienst was experimenting with

St. Louis as possible. But Hernandez, who first faced lefthanders when his father threw batting practice to him back home in the San Francisco Bay area, doesn't flinch against lefties.

"He's a good line-drive hitter," said veteran pitching ace Bob Gibson. "He'll do all right."

SO, TOO, hopefully, will be the power men in the middle of the

with Mike Garman pitching, Smith batted righthanded against the righthander, and Schoendienst grunted.

"If a hitter did that to me," one switcher said of another, "I'd stick the ball in his ribs."

Smith overheard Red. "Yeah, skipper, but Mike asked me to bat righthanded."

Garman confirmed that, seeking

hander, Reggie said, "Yeah, in the minors."

And?

"One for two and a walk."

Righthanded against a righthander in the majors?

"Uh-huh, a couple of years or so ago at Milwaukee when my right hand hurt."

And?

"Five for 11," said the versatile

Jim Toomey and Personnel Director Bob Kennedy left camp to join business manager Joe McShane at the funeral of former minor league hitting instructor Joe Medwick, the old Redbird Hall of Famer who died the first day of spring. . . . Club President August A. Busch Jr., wrenching his back, found magic in trainer emeritus Bob Bauman's touch. St. Louis

Restructuring a Staff

Former TSN Editor Dick Kaegel, pictured with Orioles Manager Earl Weaver and Pirates Manager Chuck Tanner in 1980, was a vibrant force in the 1980s restructuring of the editorial staff.

In the middle-1960s, Dick Kaegel was a vibrant force in the editorial department of The Sporting News, writing features, covering conventions and demonstrating a journalistic savvy that augured well for his professional future.

Kaegel left the publication in 1968 to join the sports staff of the St. Louis Post-Dispatch. Moving steadily through the ranks, Dick developed his writing and administrative skills until, in 1979, he was appointed sports editor.

At that time he was invited to return to TSN as managing editor (later changed to editor), succeeding Lowell Reidenbaugh, who was named senior editor.

A graduate of the University of Missouri School of Journalism, Kaegel had worked for newspapers in Columbia, Mo., and Belleville and Edwardsville, Ill., before his first term with TSN. As the new editorial chief, Dick introduced a number of significant changes.

Kaegel's first move, in February 1980, was to lure Bob McCoy from the Post-Dispatch to serve as copy editor. A graduate of the University of Nebraska and a 16-year veteran of the Post-Dispatch, McCoy possessed a facile editing pencil and a retentive memory which, with a whimsical sense of humor, made him a perfect choice to write a weekly column, "Keeping Score," a collection of anecdotes about lesser-known personalities in all strata of sports.

Kaegel later was instrumental in hiring Ron Smith, also of the Post-Dispatch. Smith was named head of the newly created book department.

The most noticeable innovation of Kaegel's regime was the hiring of two national correspondents. The first was Dave Nightingale, highly regarded writer of the Chicago Tribune and a longtime member (17 years) of the staff of the Chicago Daily News (for whom he was a prize-winning columnist).

The hiring of Nightingale, 46, was announced on July 19, 1981, by Kaegel, who said: "This is the first step in building a corps of outstanding reporters who will give

KEEPING SCORE

With
BOB McCOY

A Game for Kids

Trouble in baseball? There doesn't have to be a major league strike to create a hassle; it can happen in a recreation league for kids 10 to 12 years old, as Newsday reported recently on the following incident on Long Island when only one of two assigned umpires showed up:

The middle-aged man coaching one team said, "We're not playing without two umpires."

in the clubhouse, curled up with a good book or a crossword puzzle. Phoenix Gazette writer Doug McConnell found him with the latter, and Rocky confided his greatest ambition.

"It's not to manage in the majors," he said. "I'd like to have my name in the New York Times Sunday crossword puzzle. That would be the pinnacle."

Black and White

Knight & Co. a Powderkeg

PAUL
ATTNER

National Correspondent

LOS ANGELES—The poor Chinese. While the Cultural Revolution was running its course, they had given up basketball for a decade. Then, their tallest player, 7-8 Mu
from international competition and his heir ap
heart attack.

That's not the way to ... ese to play the U...

One of the last talks was delivered by former Kentucky star Alex Groza, who brought along his gold medal. "You hear so much about the medal but, to actually see one, well, it was a thrill for all of us," said assistant coach George Raveling. "We were ready to play after Alex was finished."

Against all this pent-up emotion, the Chinese might as well have come armed with chopsticks. It wasn't pretty, but the overwhelming ease of the Americans' 97-49 victory sent a well-intended calling card to their toughest rivals. This may be a special team playing in a special environment and coached by a special man.

For all his abruptness, Knight is fiercely patriotic. He wants to win the gold very badly, so badly that he said a few days before the opener, "I don't think I have ever gone into anything

Among Kaegel's moves were the hiring of Bob McCoy and a pair of national correspondents, Paul Attner and Dave Nightingale.

our readers exclusive reports on today's most important sports topics."

Nightingale, who was based in Chicago, was joined as a national correspondent in 1984 by Paul Attner. A native of Concord, Mass., the 37-year-old Attner graduated from California State University, Fullerton. He worked for the Washington Post for 17 years, covering professional football and basketball as well as college sports.

Attner, the author of several books and winner of a number of awards for his writing with the Post, drew as his first assignment the '84 summer Olympic Games in Los Angeles, which he covered with Nightingale.

Opening: Almost Perfect

DAVE
NIGHTINGALE

National Correspondent

LOS ANGELES—It was alternately glitzy and tacky.

It was sometimes classic, sometimes Hollywood.

It was part artistic, part commercial.

It was part formal, but more laid back.

It left countless openings for criticism from those who were absent—and criticize they did.

A More Modern Approach

Editorial changes in The Sporting News occurred frequently during its 10th decade, all designed to improve the paper's appearance and attract a wider circle of readers.

Acting on the advice of a graphics consultant, TSN adopted a three-column format except on pages designated for tabular matter (box scores, for example), where the old five-column style was retained.

A single type face for all headlines was adopted, column heads were redesigned and photographs were used with more dramatic effect. The art department, under Bill Perry, also included Valerie Crain, assistant director, and Bill Wilson, a young illustrator whose color sketches frequently brightened the covers of weekly issues.

Occasionally, pages 2 and 3 were devoted to a single feature, or to

DOCTOR K

Is Anyone As Good As Dwight Gooden?

By PAUL ATTNER
National Correspondent

WASHINGTON—The Old Man was standing around, waiting for his turn in the batting cage, when he spotted the Kid.

"You're looking a little tired," the Old Man needled.

The Kid, who was playing catch with a teammate, smiled.

"Why don't you take a couple of weeks off?" the Old Man suggested in his best deadpan manner. "No, just take a week off. That'll get you back after we play you next time. Yeah, a week will be enough."

The Kid, who recognizes a good needle when he hears one, laughed. "Yes sir," he said.

The Old Man returned to the cage, cranking out a few line drives, knowing in another week or so he would have to face the Kid again. Even for Pete Rose, that's not a task to relish, not when Dwight Gooden is on the mound.

Of course, don't call Pete Rose an old man to his face. He's still Charlie Hustle, even at the age of 44, even though his hair is overwhelmed with gray and his face is showing the wear of being a player-manager for the Cincinnati Reds. He may still make headlong slides and race to first on walks, but this is his 23rd major league season, for God's sake. No getting around it, he is the Old Man of baseball.

You tell the Kid that the Old Man was playing in the big leagues before the Kid was born, and there is a brief silence, then a hearty laugh and a look of disbelief. It's just one of many things that Dwight Gooden hasn't quite comprehended about his meteoric rise to the top of baseball's pitching elite.

Of course, don't call Dwight Gooden a kid to his face. No kid could ever pitch this way in the big leagues. Just ask the Old Man, who's been around so long that he faced both Sandy Koufax and Dwight Gooden in the same career. The Kid has earned the Old Man's respect; he doesn't waste time telling average pitchers with all those hittable deliveries to take a vacation.

The Old Man is hustling to the Hall of Fame. Along the way, he's going to run right past Ty Cobb and become baseball's all-time hit leader. The Kid, who says he was "the biggest baseball fan around" when he was, well, a kid, knows all about the quest.

"With him going after the record," said the Kid, "if he gets a hit off of you, your name goes down as the guy who gave up the 20th hit he needed or whatever." The Kid doesn't want his name on that kind of list.

That's why, in the seventh inning the previous night, with the New York Mets cruising to an easy win over the Reds and the Old Man leaning over the plate looking for a pitch he could slap to left, the Kid threw one high and tight. Right under the Old Man's chin. Made'm hop back.

The Kid idolizes the Old Man. Growing up in Tampa, he watched him every year in spring training, where the Reds became his favorite team. But he wasn't about to become charitable to an elder, even with a seven-run lead.

"You can't be intimidated by any hitter or team," said the Kid when asked about the chin scraper. "When you get on the mound, you have to set yourself a game plan and that's what you have to go and do. The main thing with him, he likes to ... the other way with the ball, so I had to pitch him in different spots every time up. You have to keep him loose up there."

"I remember the first time I faced him, last year when he was with Montreal. It was a sensational thrill. Here was a guy I had watched growing up, who had put so much into the game —I had so much going through my mind, I forgot about what pitches I was supposed to throw to get him out."

In this game, the Kid, throwing easily and under control, never forgot his game plan. The Old Man didn't whittle Cobb's lead by even one hit.

"It's a great thrill to be able to face someone like Pete Rose," said the Kid. "I met Hank Aaron earlier this season. To actually hold a conversation with him, you are at a loss for words. You can say you faced this guy, and he's now in the Hall of Fame."

But it works both ways. One day, the Old Man can tell his grandchildren he faced Dwight Gooden.

Okay, so it's a wee bit premature to begin engraving a Hall of Fame plaque for any player who is only 20 years old, who has pitched in the major leagues a mere 1½ years and who still is pinching himself to make sure everything that's happening to him is true.

But in this age of high tech and high speed, rushing to judgment is an all-too-common ailment. We are searching for instant heroes who can match the feats of athletic gods who reigned in a seemingly less complex time. Win a few games, hit some mighty home runs and the forecasts of glory start pouring in, usually to be sadly doused later by a sore arm or

2 THE SPORTING NEWS, JULY 29, 1985

Graphics became an important consideration during this time period as editors tried to present more attractive feature packages. The page 2-3 spread (right) appeared in the July 29, 1985, issue.

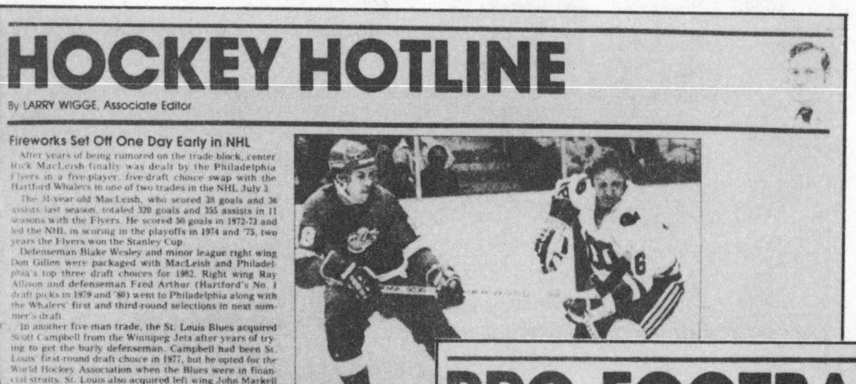

HOCKEY HOTLINE

By LARRY WIGGE, Associate Editor

Fireworks Set Off One Day Early in NHL

After years of being rumored on the trade block, center Rick MacLeish finally was dealt by the Philadelphia Flyers in a five-player, five-draft choice swap with the Hartford Whalers in one of two trades in the NHL July 3.

The 31-year-old MacLeish, who scored 38 goals and 36 assists last season, totaled 320 goals and 355 assists in 11 seasons with the Flyers. He scored 50 goals in 1972-73 and led the NHL in scoring in the playoffs in 1974 and '75, two years the Flyers won the Stanley Cup.

Defenseman Blake Wesley and minor league right wing Don Gillen were packaged with MacLeish and Philadelphia's top three draft choices for 1982. Right wing Ray Allison and defenseman Fred Arthur (Hartford's No. 1 draft picks in 1979 and '80) went to Philadelphia along with the Whalers' first and third-round selections in next summer's draft.

In another five-man trade, the St. Louis Blues acquired Scott Campbell from the Winnipeg Jets after years of trying to get the burly defenseman. Campbell had been St. Louis' first-round draft choice in 1977, but he opted for the World Hockey Association when the Blues were in financial straits. St. Louis also acquired left wing John Markell in exchange for goaltender Ed Staniowski, defenseman Bryan Maxwell and minor league right wing Paul MacLean.

Speaking Out

Comments around the NHL:

"Just because the baseball players are on strike doesn't mean that hockey players, football players or basketball players are going to get the idea that it's time for a strike. It doesn't work that way."—William Wirtz, president of the Chicago Black Hawks.

"I don't think there are very many of us who want what happened in baseball to happen in hockey."—Tony Esposito, Chicago goaltender who is president of the NHL Players

Golden Jet to Try Com...

Bobby Hull's recent comment... back if he were able to play on ... and Ulf Nilsson with the New ... Rangers ...

Aside from its usual strong package of baseball features and reports, TSN began presenting year-round reports on three other sports. Howard Balzer keeps readers up-to-date with his 'Pro Football Focus,' Larry Wigge writes 'Hockey Hotline' and Mike Douchant covers the basketball world with his 'Basketball Bulletin.'

PRO FOOTBALL FOCUS

By HOWARD BALZER, Associate Editor

The Beat Goes On . . . Slowly

With July upon us and training camp openings around the corner, the number of signed first-round draft picks was stuck on eight. And that included the defection of Miami's No. 1 choice, running back David Overstreet, to the Montreal Alouettes. Last year, on the first of July, 16 of the first-round selections had signed contracts.

Ironically, at the time of Overstreet's signing with the CFL, Dolphins Coach Don Shula was in Los Angeles readying himself to testify in the Oakland Raiders' suit against the NFL. Shula revealed that he learned of the signing in the L.A. newspapers. "I do not know the circumstances of Overstreet's signing," Shula said. "That will be my No. 1 priority when I get back."

However, when he was told of reports that Overstreet received a guaranteed contract from the Als, Shula replied, "I would not encourage the Miami management to sign a rookie to a guaranteed contract." Shula recalled

Classy Griese Bows Out

MIAMI—In January of 1973, Miami Dolphins Coach Don Shula was faced with a tough decision. Throughout the spring of 1981, Dolphins quarterback Bob Griese was also faced with a tough decision. How both men handled themselves says a lot about the pair who combined to give Miami some of the best football the NFL has ever seen.

During the 1972 regular season, Griese suffered a fractured ankle in the fifth game of the season and 38-year-old Earl Morrall came on to lead the Dolphins into the AFC title game against Pittsburgh. Morrall started that game but Griese, then recovered, came on late in

Student Gooden works under the watchful eye of Mel Stottlemyre.

...arrassing inability to pound a curve. It almost seems that ...has become a sports era of disappointment, not success. ...of the temptation to encase Gooden with a suit of superla... ...beckons more strongly every time he strides to the ...nd and almost nonchalantly mows down batters with stuff ...y seen in any major league pitcher, much less a youngster

...his time, maybe we have a hero who won't be brought ...n by an Achilles' heel. He surely has qualities to admire: ...esty, an emerging sense of humor, a strong determination ...cceed, mental toughness, a quiet nature and a maturity ...amazes even the closest observers. Besides, at least for the ...nent, he has demonstrated that he is no one-shot fluke. Yes, ...e is hope.

...anything, the accolades that accompanied Gooden's mag... ...ent rookie year of 1984 have mushroomed in 1985. He has ...dded any notion that a sophomore jinx might deflate his ...year accomplishments.

...here may be pitchers as good as Gooden in the majors, but ...e is any better. Remember, this man-child is only months ...oved from his teen-aged years. Yet at the All-Star break, ...e were his National League rankings: 13 wins (second), 1.68 ...(first), 153 strikeouts (first), four shutouts (tied for first), ...⅔ innings (second).

...ven though the Mets averaged only three runs in his vic... ...es, he had won seven straight games and hadn't lost a game ...lmost two months.

...eams have gotten a second, third and fourth look at him, ...nothing has changed. They still can't hit him. He has yield... ...no more than three earned runs in any game this year, and ...was in the season opener against St. Louis. No team has ...e more than nine hits off him, nor does he walk many (a ...of four in one game, twice). That's why he is among the ...in hits per nine innings and strikeouts-to-walks ratio. It's ...er to give away baseball tickets in Pittsburgh than to score ...s off Gooden.

...ip into baseball history and compare him to other hard ...owers. At 20, Walter Johnson also was in his second full ...son, en route to a 14-14 record that would give him 19 wins ...his young career. At 20 Bob Feller was in his fourth season, ...hich he would post a 24-9 record, strike out 246 batters and ...k 142 in 297 innings. (Feller had logged 31 victories in his ...e previous seasons.)

...onus baby Sandy Koufax was a seldom-used wild thrower at ...who would have just four career wins by his 21st birthday. ...Gibson didn't begin his minor league career until he was ...Tom Seaver was still a college pitcher at 20, and both Nolan ...an and Steve Carlton were a year away from starting their ...or league careers.

...t an age when many of those immortals were still strug... ...g to get their fastballs near the plate, Gooden already ...ws where the ball is heading. When he struck out 16 against ...sburgh last year, he never had a three-ball count on a bat... ...He's the stuff legends are made of: a hard-throwing strike... ...artist with control. He's going through none of the expected ...wing pains; indeed, he's already beginning work on his mas... ...s degree in pitching.

...He has the kind of control to throw to spots this year," said ...Stottlemyre, the Mets' talented pitching coach. "Most of ...time he tries to get ahead on the count before he goes to ...s. Guys who throw as hard as him usually are content with ...swing strikes, but he has the ability to go inside and outside, ...and down."

...is most noticeable flaws of last season are gone. The omi... ...s curve now comes at different speeds and consistently for ...kes, which makes the fastball even more dangerous. When ...curve isn't working, he's doing a better job of spotting that ...ming fastball. Runners stole an alarming 47 bases in 50 ...empts off him in 1984. Concentrated work in the winter in... ...ctional league quickened his delivery and now he picks off ...ners regularly.

...He's added a developing change-up, which probably will be... ...e a solid weapon in another year. He's become an excel... ...t finisher. When he senses a win, he grows even stronger at ...me's end.

..."You can rank him anywhere (with the best)," said Philadel... ...'s Mike Schmidt, who has yet to get a hit off Gooden. "He ...es the mound with stuff as good as Gibson's ever was. They ...e different pitchers in that Gibson was more intimidating. He ...ew in your fists, he'd hit eight or 10 men a year and threw a ...ally nasty slider.

..."Gooden works more in the strike zone, high and low and ...t off the plate. ... He has a little better control of his curve ...s year and more confidence to throw it. He'll throw it on a ...nd-1 count or start you off with the breaking ball now as

opposed to last year, when he only seemed confident in throwing it when ahead on the count."

Until August 11 last year, Gooden had done well enough to become the youngest player ever to make the All-Star team (he struck out the side in his one inning). But after that, he was simply dazzling: 8-1 record, 1.07 ERA, 105 strikeouts in 76 innings. Add to that the first half of this season and no wonder he has emerged as one of the game's most important players: 21-4, 1.48 ERA, 258 strikeouts and 56 walks in 231⅔ innings.

Gooden claims he was more a thrower last year, more a pitcher this season. "I realized halfway through last season that I couldn't go out there and say, here comes the curve or here comes the fastball," he said.

"The more you pitch, the more you learn. We go over the scouting reports before we get to the next town. Let's say it says this guy hits a fastball real well, and I'm a fastball pitcher. I still have to go with my best pitch, but it doesn't mean I throw it down the middle. It means I go after locations. I feel more comfortable going after locations this year than I did before."

But what makes Gooden unique as a young pitcher is his knowledge of himself. He knows he can pitch to locations, but you aren't going to see him ignore his fastball and try to pick away at the plate. He has the intelligence and maturity to incorporate his growth as a pitcher into his overall strategy.

Indeed, it is impossible to discuss Gooden with any of the Mets without hearing the word "maturity." This is a 20-year-old going on 30.

"He always seems to be one step ahead of the batters," said Mets second baseman Wally Backman, Gooden's frequent card-playing partner. "Like this year, he realized you don't have to try to blow everyone away to win. Sometimes it's hard to remember he's this young."

Teammates have never seen him lose control of his emotions on the mound, though Gooden swears that "inside I'm hot and swearing and all that stuff." Joe McIlvaine, the Mets' director of player personnel and the man responsible for the drafting of Gooden in 1982, marvels at the degree of Gooden's "confidence, mental toughness and his ability to control his emotions. There are pitchers who throw as hard as he does, but very few that combine those three aspects as well."

Because Gooden is mature beyond his years, it probably should come as no surprise that he quickly learned how to deal with the strains of being a strikeout pitcher. Last year, he carved out his macho space with a rookie record 276 strikeouts. He set one full-blown major league mark by averaging 11.39 strikeouts per nine innings and tied one with 32 strikeouts in two straight games. This year, his strikeouts are down but he's winning even more easily.

"He's really not conscious of strikeouts," said Stottlemyre. "I've tried to make him conscious, from when he started piling up the strikeouts, that you can get a batter out without getting two strikes on him. He's not afraid to let a man hit his pitch.

"At Shea, they'll start clapping when he gets two strikes on someone but we've told him that sometimes you can get wrapped up with strikeouts. Instead of trying to get the hitter out, you are trying for a strikeout and you make a mistake."

So while they count the strikeouts in Shea's K Corner, Gooden considers the wear on his arm. "If you try to strike out everyone," he said, "you wind up throwing a lot of pitches and wearing out your arm. I intend to be around for a long time."

Continued on Page 33, Column 1)

The Gooden Report

A game-by-game performance chart of Dwight Gooden in each of his starts prior to the All-Star break:

Date	Opponent	Result	IP	ER	BB	SO
April 9	Cardinals	ND	6.0	3	2	8
April 14	Reds	W, 4-0	9.0	0	2	10
April 19	Phillies	W, 1-0	8.0	0	1	7
April 24	Cardinals	L, 5-1	7.0	2	3	3
April 30	Astros	W, 4-1	9.0	1	2	8
May 5	Reds	W, 3-2	7.0	2	3	9
May 10	Phillies	W, 5-0	9.0	0	3	13
May 15	Astros	W, 5-3	8.1	3	2	1
May 20	Padres	L, 2-0	8.0	2	0	9
May 25	Dodgers	L, 8-2	7.0	3	1	9
May 30	Giants	W, 2-1	9.0	1	1	14
June 4	Dodgers	W, 4-1	9.0	1	2	12
June 9	Cardinals	W, 6-1	8.0	1	3	4
June 14	Expos	ND	8.0	3	4	11
June 19	Cubs	W, 1-0	9.0	0	2	9
June 25	Cubs	W, 3-2	9.0	2	3	6
June 30	Cardinals	ND	8.0	1	1	3
July 4	Braves	ND	2.1	2	4	3
July 9	Reds	W, 11-2	8.0	2	2	5
July 14	Astros	W, 1-0	9.0	0	2	11

*ND—no decision.

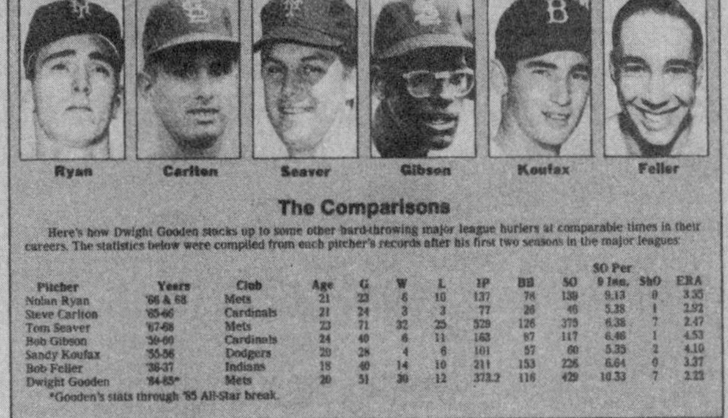

Ryan Carlton Seaver Gibson Koufax Feller

The Comparisons

Here's how Dwight Gooden stacks up to some other hard-throwing major league hurlers at comparable times in their careers. The statistics below were compiled from each pitcher's records after his first two seasons in the major leagues:

Pitcher	Years	Club	Age	G	W	L	IP	BB	SO	SO Per 9 Inn.	ShO	ERA
Nolan Ryan	'66 & 68	Mets	21	23	6	10	137	78	139	9.13	0	3.35
Steve Carlton	'65-66	Cardinals	21	24	3	3	77	26	45	5.26	1	2.92
Tom Seaver	'67-68	Mets	23	71	32	25	529	126	375	6.38	7	2.47
Bob Gibson	'59-60	Cardinals	24	40	6	11	163	87	117	6.46	1	4.53
Sandy Koufax	'55-56	Dodgers	20	28	4	6	101	57	60	5.35	2	4.10
Bob Feller	'36-37	Indians	18	40	14	10	211	153	226	6.64	0	3.27
Dwight Gooden	'84-85*	Mets	20	51	30	12	373.2	116	429	10.33	7	2.22

*Gooden's stats through '85 All-Star break.

THE SPORTING NEWS, JULY 29, 1985 3

This Week's Lineup

FEATURES

COLUMNS

MAJOR LEAGUE REPORT

Vol. 183, No. 3

BASKETBALL BULLETIN

By MIKE DOUCHANT, Associate Editor

PRO

Hoop Scoop

Word was that several NBA teams are for sale and that owners are openly worried that several franchises may fold unless buyers are found. Among the clubs reportedly for sale are the Denver Nuggets, Detroit Pistons, Indiana Pacers and Kansas City Kings. A report by Arthur Andersen, an accounting and consulting firm, said that the collective losses for the league for the 1979-80 season increased in one year from $8 million to $13 million. In the annual report, which is always a season behind, each team submits a financial statement. The report does not cite losses of individual clubs, but rather the total losses in the league. Those problems were discussed at the recent annual meeting of owners at Cambridge, Mass., where, it was learned, the following occurred:

• Commissioner Larry O'Brien formed a committee "to consider what steps may be taken to insure the financial stability of the league." The committee was given 30 days to report its findings.

• The league's law firm was asked to investigate the ... certain teams had undertaken and their ability to ... them. It will recheck whether the other clubs are ... for the debts incurred if a franchise folds.

• Cleveland Cavaliers Owner Ted Stepien was ques... ...about his and the team's finances.

... one embarrasses him, he's finished."

Boise State's Larry McKinney, Indiana's seventh-round selection, missed the Pacers' rookie camp because he was still under contract to a pro team in Brazil. ... The Warriors don't think that their eighth-round choice, ... pound Yasutaka (Chibi) Okayama, is a big joke. Still, Okayama, a 26-year-old sheet metal salesman in Japan, said he doesn't have the confidence to play in the NBA.

COLLEGE

Transfer Talk

Rich DiBenedetto and John Gullickson, Davidson's top two returning scorers, and reserve John Corso said they won't return to the school. All three are being investigated for allegedly turning in term papers they purchased. DiBenedetto probably will enroll at an NAIA school, while Gullickson said he might try to transfer to Duke, Furman or Georgia Tech.

Former Texas A&M center Rudy Woods is considering a transfer to LSU. Woods, who missed most of the Southwest Conference schedule last season while trying to improve his grades at a junior college, set school records as a freshman at A&M for shooting percentage and blocked shots. ... George Bell, the tallest player in college basketball history, has dropped out of the University of California at Riverside. The 7-8 Bell, who redshirted last season after transferring from Morris Brown College in Atlanta, ...

As packaging became more important, so, too, did the need for a detailed index that gave readers a handy guide to points of interest within the publication. A quick look at the 1977 index (above) shows the heavy influx of non-baseball news and features in an off-season issue.

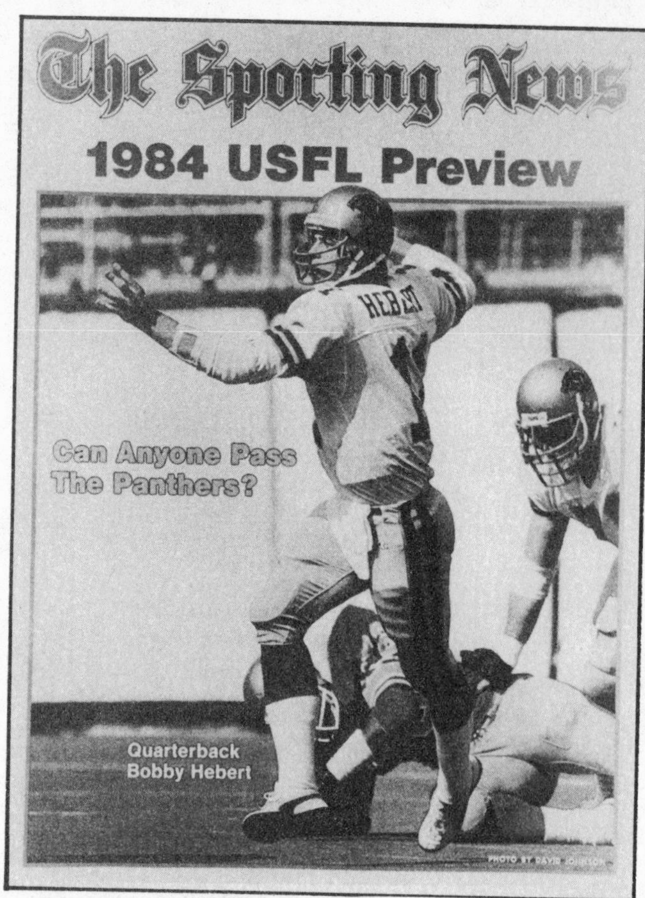

The Sporting News
1984 USFL Preview
Can Anyone Pass
The Panthers?
Quarterback
Bobby Hebert

The Sporting News
PLAY BALL!
N.Y. Fans Are Going
Crazy Over Gooden,
Hernandez and the Mets

The Sporting News turned to supplements in the early 1980s as a means of calling attention to special events. A preview of the United States Football League season, previews of the coming baseball season and Olympic Games are among the special subjects presented in TSN supplements (left, center and right). Two new faces that began appearing regularly in the early '80s were Bill Conlin and Peter Gammons (left). Their 'N.L. Beat' and 'A.L. Beat' columns quickly took their place among the more popular items in TSN.

N.L. BEAT

By BILL CONLIN

CLEARWATER, Fla.—The one constant of the off-season is that every front office man will be sitting on some kind of spot. General managers who wheeled and dealed will have to be justified by on-field deeds, not press conference words. Clubs that sat still had best show enough improvement to justify going with a pat hand. Teams which either paid big money for free agents or chose to ignore the auction will fall under the sharpest kind of scrutiny.

Some spots, of course, will be bigger than others. Here are some:

Bill Virdon inherits an Expos team flat out of excuses for not winning. The kids who contended in 1980 and then took the Dodgers to a fifth game in the '81 League Championship Series are veterans now. They don't have mild-mannered Jim Fanning to kick around any more. They will have a hard time

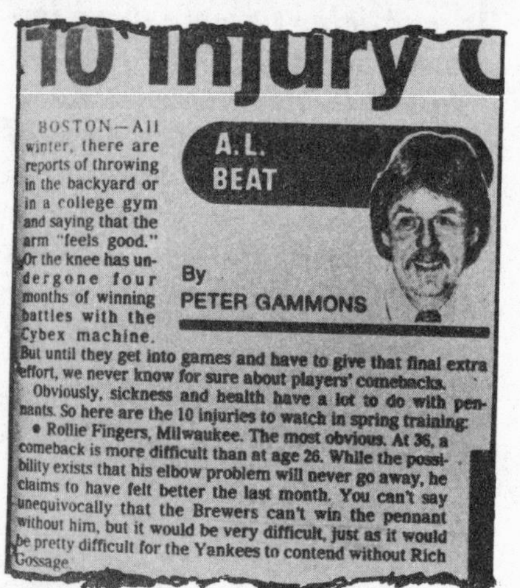

10 Injury

A.L. BEAT

By PETER GAMMONS

BOSTON—All winter, there are reports of throwing in the backyard or in a college gym and saying that the arm "feels good." Or the knee has undergone four months of winning battles with the Cybex machine. But until they get into games and have to give that final extra effort, we never know for sure about players' comebacks.

Obviously, sickness and health have a lot to do with pennants. So here are the 10 injuries to watch in spring training:

• Rollie Fingers, Milwaukee. The most obvious. At 36, a comeback is more difficult than at age 26. While the possibility exists that his elbow problem will never go away, he claims to have felt better the last month. You can't say unequivocally that the Brewers can't win the pennant without him, but it would be very difficult, just as it would be pretty difficult for the Yankees to contend without Rich Gossage.

two related subjects. Another page in the forefront contained a detailed index, together with a roster of the paper's editorial and business personnel.

Hockey and college and professional football and basketball were represented weekly, in and out of season, and new columnists, such as Ray Fitzgerald, contributed additional breadth of opinion.

To enhance major league baseball coverage, Editor Dick Kaegel arranged for Bill Conlin of Philadelphia and Peter Gammons of Boston to write weekly columns on activities in the National and American Leagues, respectively.

As a means of calling attention to special events, an issue would, at times, include a supplement. This insert, smaller in size than the regular paper, included national advertising procured under the supervision of Kent T. Valandra, associate publisher/advertising director, who operated out of New York. Such supplements heralded, for example, the advent of the United States Football League season (32 pages) in the issue of February 28, 1983; baseball's 50th anniversary All-Star Game (24 pages), July 4, 1983; the summer Olympic Games (32 pages), July 23, 1984, and the National Football League season (16 pages), September 3, 1984.

As the editorial contents of TSN gained new stature, the cost per issue advanced accordingly. In May 1977, the cost of the publication that sold originally for a nickel was boosted from 75 cents to $1. In February 1979, the price climbed to $1.25, in July 1980 to $1.50, in January 1984 to $1.75 and in April 1985, when circulation flirted with the 700,000 mark, to $1.95.

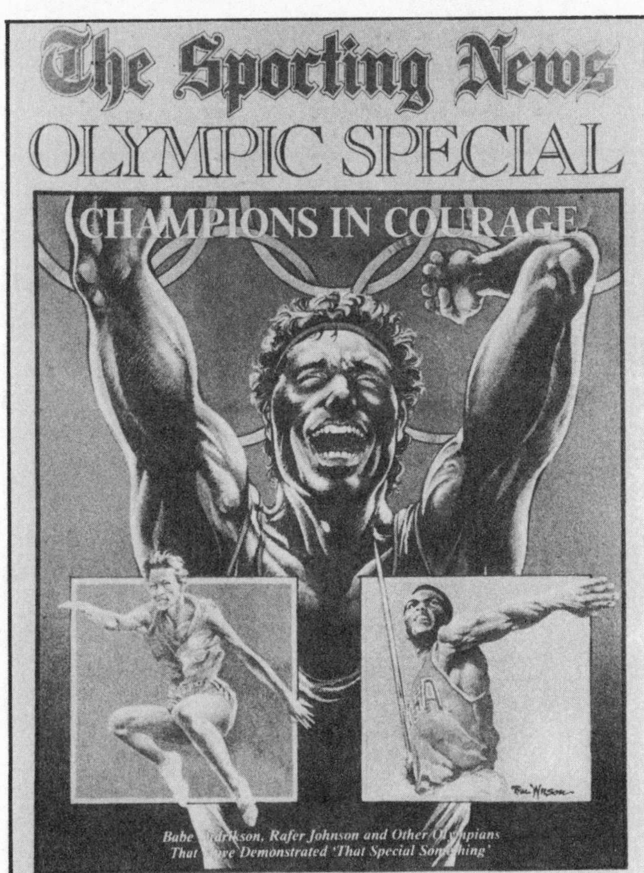

The Sporting News
OLYMPIC SPECIAL
CHAMPIONS IN COURAGE

The Sporting News
SPECIAL ADVERTISING SUPPLEMENT
KOREA
How the host country is preparing for the Games of the 24th Olympiad
REPORTS ON:
The City . Tourism . Facilities . Cuisine

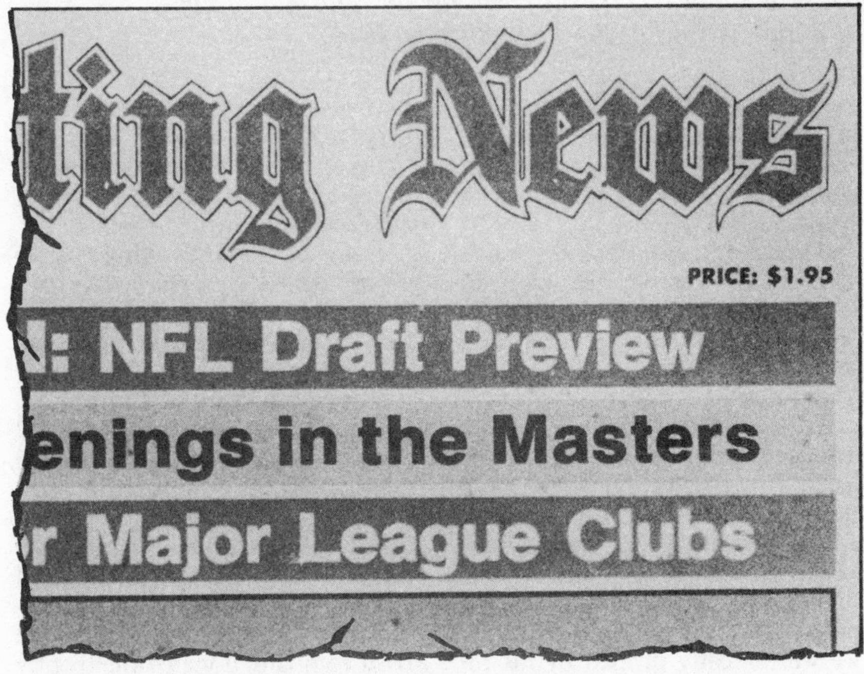

ting News
PRICE: $1.95
N: NFL Draft Preview
enings in the Masters
r Major League Clubs

The price of publishing continued to rise during this period and the cost of The Sporting News rose accordingly. The price per copy reached $1 (right) in 1977 and rose in 1985 (above) to its current mark of $1.95.

PRICE RISE

Beginning with next week's issue, the single-copy price of THE SPORTING NEWS will be one dollar.

This move is taken reluctantly but is necessary in the face of rising operating costs.

The best buy in sports reading—and the surest way to keep abreast of everything important that's happening in all major sports—is a subscription to THE SPORTING NEWS.

A one-year subscription is $18.75 (less than 37¢ per copy) and a two-year subscription is $32.00 (less than 31¢ per copy).

We will continue to expand our coverage of the American sports scene.

Next week's issue will carry an in-depth preview of the Kentucky Derby that will include profiles of all the leading contenders (and some dark horses): Seattle Slew, Clev Er Tell, Run Dusty Run, Habitony and Cormorant.

Besides the Derby preview, we will have all the news from the NBA and hockey playoffs and both major and minor league baseball.

16 Years With Bowie Kuhn

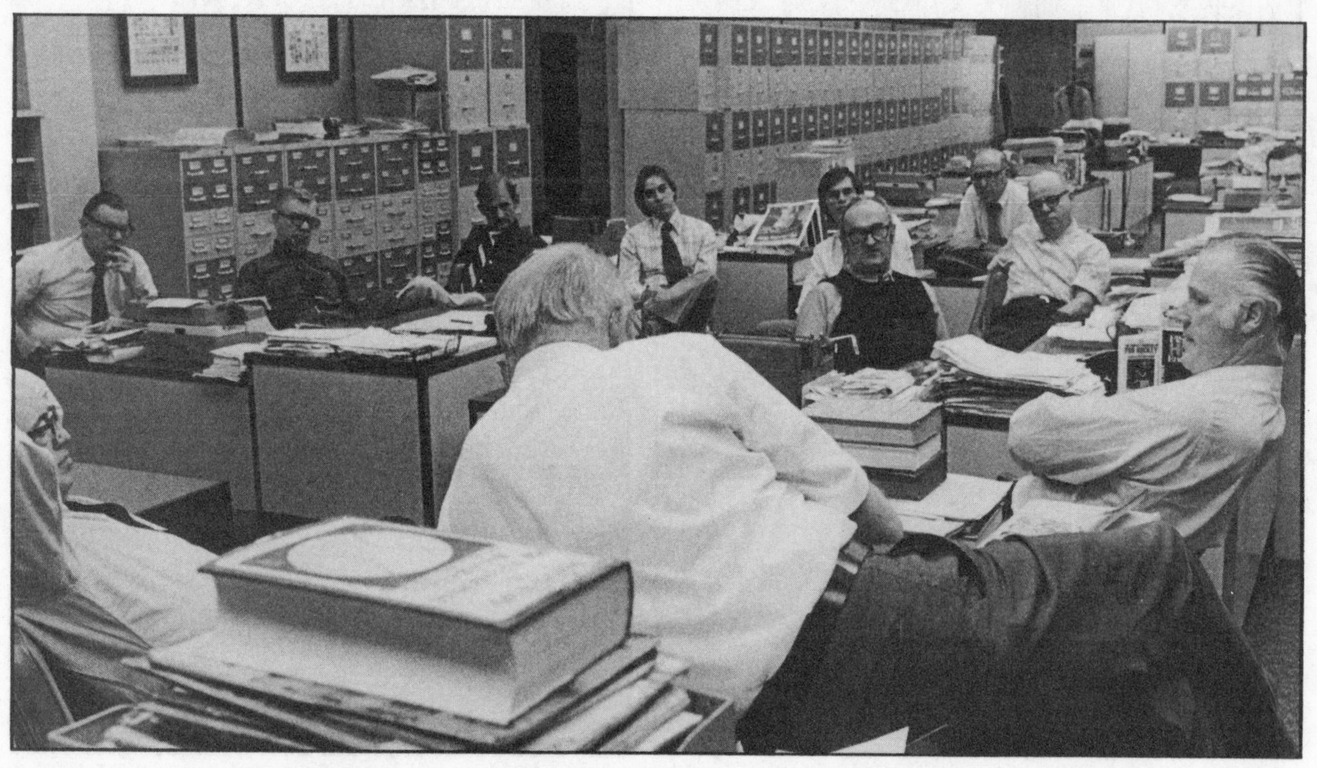

Baseball Commissioner Bowie Kuhn (right) sat down for an informal discussion with members of the editorial staff at the TSN office in 1977.

Throughout his 16 years in office, Bowie Kuhn maintained congenial relations with The Sporting News, but this cordiality did not prevent the publication from criticizing some of the commissioner's decisions that it considered unjust.

Kuhn came under fire when he blocked Charles O. Finley's sale of three superstars in 1976, a decision that cost the Oakland owner megabucks as the result of the free agency that followed. Kuhn's action, declared an editorial, "has plunged baseball into a morass of litigation that can serve only to harm the game."

At other times TSN lambasted Kuhn's failure to insist on uniform expansion by the major leagues, his refusal to resolve the designated hitter differences between the American and National leagues and the adoption of a split season in strike-torn 1981.

In August 1982, an editorial trumpted: "We believe it is time for a fresh face in the commissioner's office." That face, the editorial continued, should be Tal Smith, former Houston Astros executive who had founded a firm that offered executive search services and financial and marketing planning in sports.

Because of past differences, it was all the more remarkable when, in its issue of January 2, 1984, The Sporting News announced it had selected Kuhn as its Man of the Year for 1983.

An editorial commented: "Our differences with Kuhn have been over specific issues. We have praised him as well; for example, applauding his $50,000 fine of Yankee Owner George Steinbrenner for impugning the character of the umpires last spring. And, certainly, we were greatly pleased by his recent rulings penalizing drug users and abusers.

"The main criterion for the Man of the Year is that the winner have a great impact on sport, accomplishing something notable and making special contributions to the game. The commissioner has filled that criterion.

"Baseball has prospered under his leadership and Kuhn's efforts have given the game a new aura of prestige."

Like many others, Kuhn expressed surprise at his selection. "I am deeply touched," he said.

Kuhn was the 16th winner of the award, which was presented initially in 1969 to Denny McLain, who won 31 games for the world champion Detroit Tigers in 1968.

In recognition of his honor, Kuhn was presented the Waterford Trophy, an 18-inch-high crystal creation of the renowned Waterford Crystal Ltd. The presentation to Kuhn in New York marked the second such event for Richard Waters, TSN president, who negotiated the agreement whereby the Irish company donated the trophy that was valued at between $10,000 and $15,000.

Earlier, Waters presented a similar award to Whitey Herzog, manager of the world champion St. Louis Cardinals of 1982, and he repeated the ceremony to Peter Ueberroth, president of the Los Angeles Olympic Organizing Committee in 1984 and Kuhn's successor as commissioner.

Man of the Year

By JOSEPH DURSO

NEW YORK—The Man of the Year in sports for 1983 is Bowie Kuhn, says THE SPORTING NEWS, which often disagreed with him and even called for his replacement as commissioner of baseball.

Kuhn won the designation over a small but accomplished group of athletes that included John Riggins and Joe Theismann of the Washington Redskins in football, Martina Navratilova in tennis and Moses Malone in basketball.

He thereby becomes the 16th winner of the award, which was inaugurated at the close of 1968, when Kuhn was being nominated for commissioner for the first time. And he becomes the second person to receive the Waterford Crystal Trophy, the hand-carved, $10,000 bowl that was given for the first time last year, when Whitey Herzog of the St. Louis Cardinals was chosen Man of the Year.

But Kuhn also becomes the first person named for the award primarily for his career record rather than for one virtuoso season. In fact, after two terms that covered 15 revolutionary years in office, he made the biggest news in the most ironic way: He was denied re-election.

So the award is being given to a man leaving office under pressure, and is being presented by a publication that had expressed its editorial opposition to him on a variety of issues, from the designated hitter, his handling of the players' strike and the split season of 1981 to the irregular expansion of the big leagues and the escalation of salaries.

"Hindsight is terrific," said Richard Waters, president and chief executive officer of THE SPORTING NEWS. "Ten years from now, people will look back and appreciate Bowie Kuhn."

"It's the close of a great era," said Dick Kaegel, editor of THE SPORTING NEWS. "And he's handled it well. He's given the game a lot of dignity and prestige, and he's been an eloquent spokesman for it. He's been the steward of the game in a revolutionary time, and a good one."

Kuhn did not miss the point. He acknowledged that he had been "totally surprised when they told me," and added:

"I said that I was deeply and sincerely touched by this, and I am. There is no other way I can describe it. Particularly considering the fact that we had some differing viewpoints in the past, it's especially gratifying that THE SPORTING NEWS would select me.

"It takes a certain amount of courage, given the differing viewpoints, to make such a selection. And I respect that courage."

For company in the season of honors, Kuhn has a trio of American Leaguers who won the major baseball awards of TSN for 1983: Cal Ripken Jr. of the Baltimore Orioles, the Play-

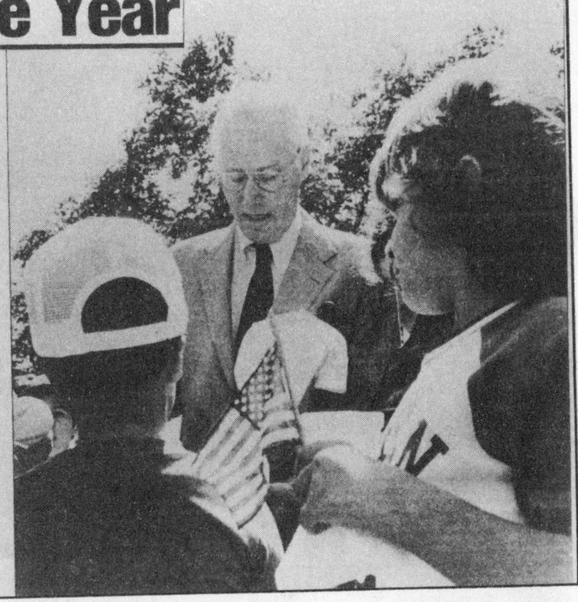

COMMISSIONER'S STRANGE BEHAVIOR

Back in 1919, American League President Ban Johnson refused to give his approval of the sale of pitcher Carl Mays from the Boston Red Sox to the New York Yankees. The Yankees promptly went to court and secured a temporary injunction, later made permanent, which enjoined Johnson "or his agents" from interfering. Mays continued his career with the New York club.

So there is legal precedent for the Oakland A's or any other of the parties concerned going to court to overturn Commissioner Bowie Kuhn's voiding of the sale of players by the A's to the Yankees and Red Sox.

Kuhn's action is, as he admitted, unprecedented and based "in the best interests of baseball."

The sales were perfectly legal and above board and were examples of something that had been done many times in the past. One has only to recall how, for economic reasons, Connie Mack sold off his Philadelphia A's stars in the 1930s, the Red Sox sold Babe Ruth to the Yankees and Washington's Clark Griffith sold star shortstop Joe Cronin to the Red Sox for $250,000 in 1934.

Finley's economic motives appear even more compelling than the cases cited above. For, should Kuhn's decision stand, Finley will lose more than three million dollars. The players involved—outfielder Joe Rudi and pitchers Rollie Fingers and Vida Blue—will become free agents on October 1. Is Kuhn planning to compensate Finley for his losses? If so, how?

Finley was one of two owners to vote against rehiring Kuhn as commissioner last July. There was an open feeling of bitterness between the two men after the meeting that saw Kuhn given a new contract. Kuhn, therefore, leaves himself open to the charge that his decision is a way of getting back at Finley. We believe otherwise and feel that Kuhn's action was above personal recrimination and based on what he considered honest motives.

There is no question that Kuhn has authority to act in what he deems to be the "best interests of baseball." But he doesn't have unlimited authority; he is no absolute czar.

In the case of the sale of the Oakland players, he has grossly overstepped his authority and, rather than acting "in the best interests of baseball," has plunged baseball into a morass of litigation that can serve only to harm the game and which, in the end, could result in Kuhn himself losing his job.

HAPPY BIRTHDAY, U.S.

Throughout the reign of Commissioner Bowie Kuhn, The Sporting News remained flexible on its praise and criticism. TSN sometimes took Kuhn to task with blistering editorials and even went so far as to suggest at one point that baseball would be better off with a new top man. But in January 1984, Kuhn was pictured on the cover and an inside spread introduced him as TSN's Man of the Year (above left).

The Sporting News

OUR OPINION

Man of the Year

Considering all he's been through in 15 turbulent and revolutionary years as commissioner of baseball, it is difficult to shock Bowie K. Kuhn. Yet we managed to do just that during the recent baseball meetings in Nashville, Tenn., by informing Kuhn that he was THE SPORTING NEWS Man of the Year for 1983.

During the past few years of Kuhn's reign, this publication often has been at odds with the commissioner. In fact, on August 30, 1982, shortly after Kuhn dodged an owners' ouster bullet, we declared it was time for the commissioner to be replaced.

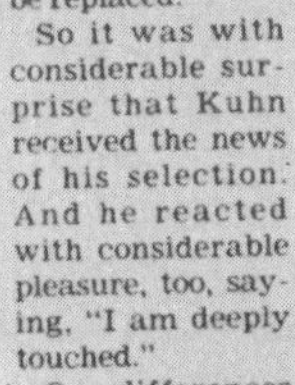

So it was with considerable surprise that Kuhn received the news of his selection. And he reacted with considerable pleasure, too, saying, "I am deeply touched."

Our differences with Kuhn have been over specific issues, such as the designated-hitter rule or the split season in strike-torn 1981. We have praised him as well; for example, applauding his $50,000 fine of Yankee Owner George Steinbrenner for impugning the character of the umpires last spring. And, certainly, we were greatly pleased by his tough action in recent rulings penalizing drug users and abusers.

In a sense, Kuhn's designation as Man of the Year could just as easily be termed Man of 15 Years because we took into consideration his entire term as commissioner. He has presided over the National Pastime, during a time of unprecedented growth and strife, with dignity, honesty and, most of all, an immense love for the game.

When Kuhn took over at the end of this nation's troubled decade of the Sixties, baseball was just scuffling along.

The Sporting News

OUR OPINION

Time for a New Commissioner

Bowie Kuhn was absolutely right when he said baseball needs one man at the top, a "the buck stops here" kind of guy. It's been proven time and again that to be effective, a body—be it business, government or sport—needs one executive at the top to make decisions.

Major league baseball, which is considering plans for restructuring the offices of the commissioner and the leagues, is making noises about incorporating a business leader into the chain of command. This would be an expert charged with making the wisest possible decisions concerning the big bucks currently floating about the game.

Kuhn, after surviving an ouster attempt August 18 in San Diego, said he didn't think it would work to have two men (the commissioner and a chief operating officer) in charge.

Tal Smith

We agree with Bowie Kuhn—baseball should have one guiding hand on the controls and that hand should belong to the commissioner. We do not, however, agree with Kuhn's view that the commissioner's office should continue to be filled by Bowie Kuhn. We believe it is time for a fresh face in the commissioner's office.

The obvious answer to baseball's two-headed dilemma is to appoint a commissioner who has vast knowledge not only about baseball but about financial matters as well. We believe that man is available in the person of Talbot M. Smith.

Tal Smith was in baseball administration for 23 years and became one of the most respected executives in the game. Ironically, after building the Houston Astros into a division winner in 1980, Smith was dismissed as club president by Owner John McMullen—a decision that prompted a palace revolt by McMullen's partners. Smith rebounded immediately, passing up many baseball offers to form Tal Smith Enterprises, a firm that has been a rousing success. Smith's innovative firm operates primarily in the sports arena, offering executive search services and financial and marketing planning. He warmed many an owner's heart last winter with a string of victories on behalf of clubs in

THROUGH THE YEARS WITH BOWIE KUHN

By RALPH RAY
Associate Senior Editor

ST. LOUIS—Bowie Kuhn was elected commissioner of baseball February 4, 1969, on a somewhat tentative basis. Club owners set his term at one year. If Kuhn was merely invited to try out for the job, he soon established himself as action-oriented.

Here in chronological order are Kuhn's significant decisions in a reign second in length only to Judge K.M. Landis' 24 years on the job:

March, 1969—After Montreal traded Donn Clendenon and Jesus Alou to Houston for Rusty Staub, Clendenon refused to report. Instead of voiding the trade, as Astros Owner Judge Roy Hofheinz wished, Kuhn ordered Montreal to furnish suitable talent to replace Clendenon. Hofheinz took legal action and blasted Kuhn publicly, but soon dispatched a written apology after Kuhn indicated a stiff fine was in the works. The deal went through, as Kuhn had ordered.

February, 1970—Suspended Detroit pitcher Denny McLain for three months of the regular season for associating with gamblers.

April, 1972—Kuhn interceded in a contract dispute between Oakland Owner Charlie Finley and pitcher Vida Blue, who had won the Cy Young Award and Most Valuable Player prize in 1971. After a 12-hour session involving Kuhn, Finley and Blue on April 27, Blue agreed to terms. Kuhn fined and reprimanded Finley for criticizing the commissioner's role in the affair.

April 2, 1974—With the season about to start, Kuhn warned Atlanta Braves President Bill Bartholomay not to withhold Henry Aaron from the lineup in the season-opening series in Cincinnati. Bartholomay had suggested Aaron might sit out the Cincinnati series so he could hit the two home runs he needed to pass Babe Ruth's career total before Atlanta fans. The Braves complied with Kuhn's directive. Aaron equaled Ruth's 714 in Cincinnati and passed him before an Atlanta crowd.

November 27, 1974—Suspended New York Yankees Owner George Steinbrenner for two years as the result of his conviction for illegal political campaign contributions. Kuhn lifted the suspension after 16 months.

July 15, 1975—Kuhn survived an effort to unseat him and was re-elected for seven more years to August 12, 1983. Losers in this skirmish were Finley, Baltimore Owner Jerry Hoffberger, Steinbrenner and Texas Owner Brad Corbett.

March 17, 1976—With spring camps closed by the owners' agreement until a new labor contract was signed, Kuhn countermanded the owners' strategy and ordered the camps opened ... new Basic Agreement was approved on July 12.

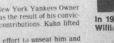

Public Relations

Player of the Year trophies in the four major sports (above) and annual parties, such as the 1985 bash (below) at football's winter meetings in Phoenix, are among the responsibilities of TSN's public relations department.

Among the major innovations effected by Richard Waters in his early years as chief executive officer of The Sporting News was the creation of a public relations department.

To direct the new operation, Waters chose Lou Ann Gorsuch, an associate editor for three years of The Sporting Goods Dealer, sister publication of TSN.

A graduate of the University of Missouri School of Journalism, Gorsuch was a one-person department at the start. But as the complexities of the office grew, she was provided an assistant, Julie Morris, a graduate of Kansas State University who had served as coordinator of the Mental Health Program in Johnson County, Kansas.

In addition to publicizing weekly issues of The Sporting News and the annual publications of the expanded book department, the pair worked closely with national book reviewers and other press departments and greeted visiting dignitaries on their arrival at TSN.

To publicize all phases of the company's activities, the department maintained approximately 25 mailing lists.

Gorsuch and Morris also kept voluminous files, including photos and biographical material on employees in order to answer the many inquiries that arrive regularly.

When not engaged in publicity endeavors, the two supervised the selection process for the nearly 60 annual awards made by TSN. This included the dispersal of ballots, notifying the winner and the media, arranging for trophy engravings and the time and place for the presentations.

Among the awards were those to all-star teams in major league and college baseball, college and professional football and basketball and ice hockey. By sports, the awards were: baseball, 26; football, 13; basketball, 11; hockey, five, and bowling, two.

Much of the public relations department's energies were devoted to social affairs, which increased annually. Starting in 1983, The Sporting News hosted a luncheon a year for front-office personnel and media people of major league baseball clubs. These events were held in St. Louis, Chicago and Kansas City. Gorsuch and Morris determined dates and sites for these affairs, issued invitations and selected menus.

At other times, more lavish parties were held during Super Bowl week, at summer meetings of the National Football League, at the winter baseball conventions and for dignitaries attending the annual Hall of Fame induction ceremonies at Cooperstown, N.Y.

In September 1984, the department was handed another assignment, the publication of an eight-page quarterly in-house paper, TSiNfo, which covered not only news on the home office and its advertising agencies but also of corporate headquarters in Los Angeles.

More Books

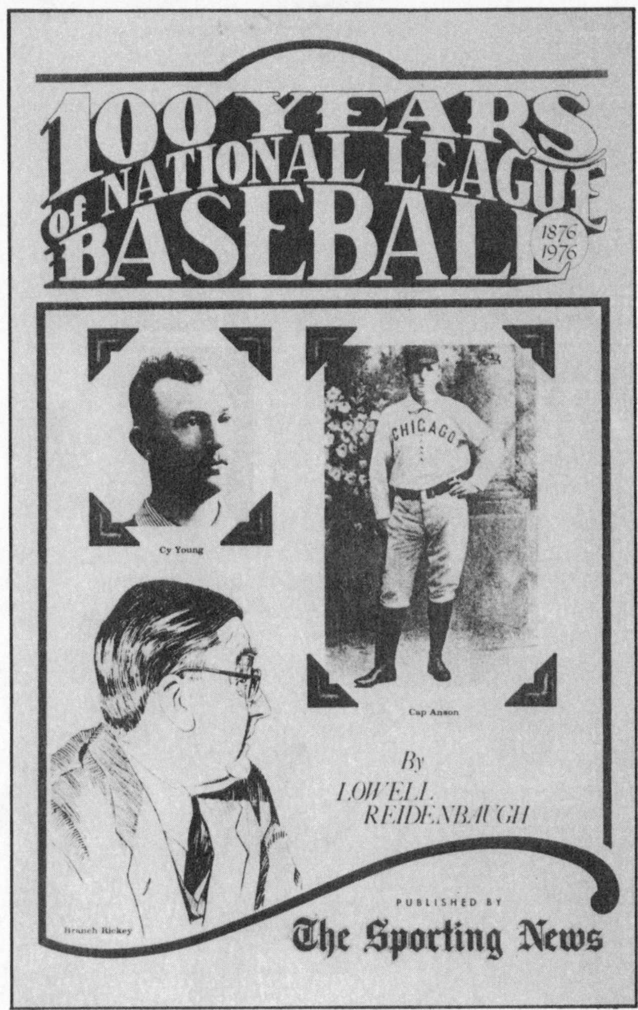

Among the additions to TSN's library during this period were the 'Best Sports Stories' series and '100 Years of National League Baseball.'

The early promise by Richard Waters to expand the book-publishing department of The Sporting News was not long in gaining fulfillment.

One of the first additions to the sports library was "Best Sports Stories." This series had been started in 1944 by Edward Ehre and Irving Marsh and published by E.P. Dutton and Co. The series was discontinued in 1981, then resumed a year later under the imprimatur of The Sporting News through an arrangement with the Dutton company.

The 1985 edition of "Best Sports Stories" contained four prize-winning compositions as well as three photos adjudged best by instructors in the University of Missouri School of Journalism. The panel reviewed nearly 800 entries.

In addition to the prize-winning entries, the 288-page volume included 42 other articles and 11 additional photos.

The book department, under the direction of Ron Smith, included Joe Hoppel, Craig Carter, Barry Siegel, Dave Sloan, Mike Nahrstedt and John Hadley.

At the start of the company's 10th decade, the book inventory included Guides and Registers in major spectator sports, plus several statistical books. In 1976, a centennial history of the National League was added to the list. This was a refinement of four 12-page installments that appeared in The Sporting News in June.

In 1981, an enlarged edition of "Daguerreotypes" was issued along with the "Super Bowl Book." The Super Bowl anthology contained accounts, summaries and photos of all championship games, plus records, as well as leads and statistics of playoff games leading up to the main event.

Also introduced during the 1980s were annual yearbooks previewing seasons of major league baseball, pro football, college football and basketball.

Hall of Fame fact books on baseball and football were published in the same period and, in 1983, a prestigious volume, "Cooperstown, Where Baseball's Legends Live Forever," made its appearance.

At the same time, "Take Me Out to the Ball Park" hit the book stalls. This contained the histories of playing fields, old and new, in major league cities, together with photos and sketches.

The "Cooperstown" and "Ball Park" books were authored by veteran TSN writer Lowell Reidenbaugh.

The "Baseball Trivia Book," co-edited by Hoppel and Carter, appeared in 1983 and the "Football

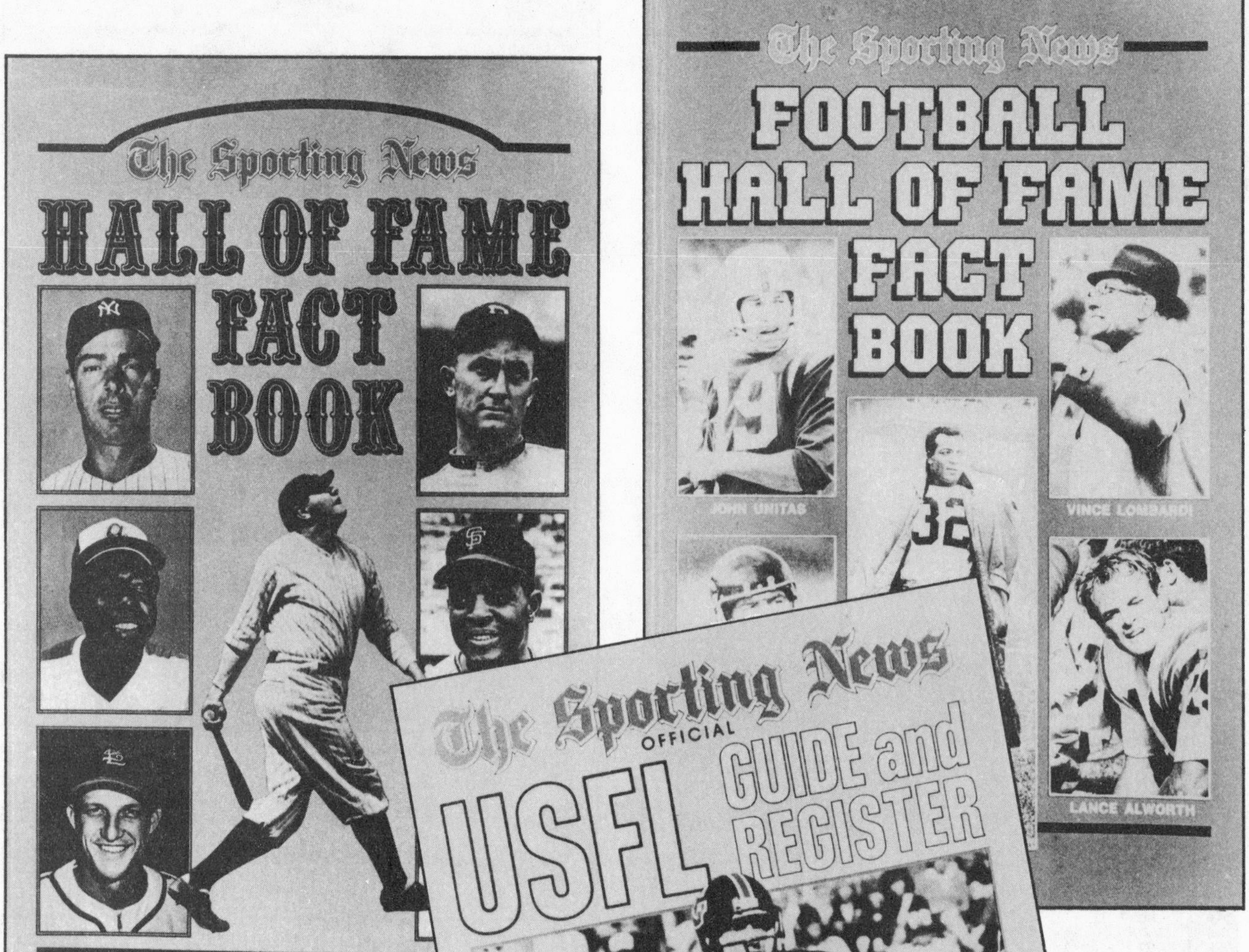

Trivia Book," researched and edited by Hoppel, followed in 1985. The latter production represented a two-year effort and consisted of countless letters to college athletic departments, endless hours in libraries searching through newspaper files and a trip to the Pro Football Hall of Fame in Canton, O.

Another 1985 book was "Heismen, After the Glory." The hardback volume, written by Dave Newhouse, recounted in detail the tales of 17 Heisman Trophy winners, their accomplishments on the gridiron and their post-college careers. Other Heisman winners were covered in shorter pieces.

The most recent addition to The Sporting News' bookshelf was "Countdown to Cobb," a day-by-day diary recorded by Pete Rose and transcribed by Hal Bodley that traced Rose's assault on Ty Cobb's record as the major leagues' all-time hits leader.

Hall of Fame fact books were produced for both baseball and pro football and TSN expanded its football annual line with the 'Official USFL Guide and Register.'

TSN Readers Speak Out on Strike

By JOE MARCIN
Associate Editor

ST. LOUIS—Anger! Sorrow! Disgust! Alarm! Frustration!

Those were some of the emotions expressed by hundreds of fans who wrote THE SPORTING NEWS to express their views on the strike by major league baseball players.

Our request for the fans' opinions is believed to have triggered the largest outpouring of mail ever received by TSN on one subject.

The letters ranged from serious and thoughtful to emotional. Some were comical, others sad. If the strike were a play performed on a stage, the writers had enough heroes and villains to produce a melodrama—Marvin Miller, Ray Grebey, Bowie Kuhn, the players and the owners. Some even invoked the spirit of baseball's past and called for the resurrection of Judge Kenesaw Mountain Landis, the game's most powerful commissioner.

The owners received more support than the players, bu[illegible]

"Send Marvin Miller, Bowie Kuhn, Peter Seitz, Dave McNally, Pete Rose and Reggie Jackson on the next plane to Moscow and let them scream all they want about imperialistic, capitalistic baseball."

Then there were those few who backed the players.

Philip Hastings of Grantham, N.H., said, "The players should be absolute free agents once their contracts have expired because baseball is a business and should be treated like a business."

"The owners," according to Robert G. Schwarz of Philadelphia, "have offered no coherent arguments to support

'A strike against baseball is un-American.'

an incredibly rigid stance. Their true motive appears to be a sad effort to break the union, or an equally sad attempt to [illegible]

budged from square one in those 13 months and I find that incredible. Even the Vietnam peace talks produced some movement in 13 months!"

Richard F. Korts of San Diego, Calif., said, "The uncontrolled greed exhibited by both the owners and the players is hard for most fans to understand."

Resentment was manifested by many fans. Don LoCrasto of Piscataway, N.J., urged that the fans go on strike so they "can get the attention they deserve." Morris Ligansky of Brooklyn, N.Y., was one of those who said, "I am not going to any more games this season."

The probability of a fans' "strike" was questioned by Al Smith of Lawrenceville, N.J. "Despite all the talk of boycotts, the fans get shafted and they still come back for more. Only when they stop their flow of dollars at the box office will baseball get the financial message." He added, "Fans will flock back to the parks in record numbers upon settlement. Ticket prices will rise to pay for the settlement. What it amounts to is that the fans will have to pay for the 'privilege' of being without baseball during the

Should U.S. Boycott Olympic Games?

President Carter has called for a boycott of the 1978 summer Olympics in Moscow, a proposal which has stirred a great deal of hot debate. THE SPORTING NEWS invites readers to give their views on the matter.

Should the United States team withdraw from the Moscow Olympic Games?

Yes____

No____

Should the Moscow Olympics be moved to an alternate site?

Yes____

No____

Mail replies to:

Olympics Poll
The Sporting News
Box 56, St. Louis, Mo. 63166

Reader involvement, an important factor in TSN's success for many years, is solicited when an issue arises that affects the sports world. Such topics as baseball strikes and Olympic boycotts often draw as strong a response as pennant predictions.

Fans' Flag Forecasts Requested

As is our annual custom, THE SPORTING NEWS urges its readers to send in their selections for the major league pennant races. Let us know your choices for the divisional championships, pennants and World Series.

We'll run the results of the survey in our April 12 issue and after the end of the season we'll publish the names of those who submitted correct selections. The deadline for sending in your selections is April 1.

Send your forecast to Pennant Picks, c/o THE SPORTING NEWS, P.O. Box 56, St. Louis, Mo. 63166.

Wanted: Reader Opinions

A large share of the success of The Sporting News over the years has been attributed to reader involvement and the paper frequently has solicited opinions on controversies of the day.

In 1975, following an outburst of public indignation over the fans' selection of starting lineups for the All-Star Game, readers were asked if they favored a continuation of the voting system or if they thought the players would do the job more intelligently.

Of the nearly 1,000 responses, readers favored the players as voters, 72 percent to 28 percent.

Also in 1975, readers were polled on their opinions of the "Rozelle Rule," whereby an NFL team losing a player to free agency is compensated by the team that signs the player, the compensation to be determined by the commissioner. A total of 568 readers (55.1 percent) endorsed the rule, 27.1 percent favored a modification and 17.8 percent voted to abolish the rule.

Is baseball's reserve system good or evil? That was the question presented to readers in 1976 after an arbitrator declared Andy Messersmith and Dave McNally free agents. The returns showed 58.9 percent in favor of the reserve clause, 6.5 percent voting to abolish it and 34.6 percent preferring a modification.

Readers also were asked in 1976 to voice their views on the issue involving Bowie Kuhn and A's Owner Charles O. Finley after the commissioner blocked the sale of three Oakland superstars. The vote favored Finley.

In 1980, opinions were requested on the U.S. boycott of the Olympic Games in Moscow.

At other times readers were invited to voice opinions on the impending strike by the major league baseball players. And when a walkout occurred in 1981, a page-3 article urged readers to contact (by letter or telephone) Kuhn and the negotiators, Marvin Miller and Ray Grebey. Addresses and phone numbers were appended.

For many years readers also were invited to predict the outcome of the major league races. Originally, a free one-year subscription was given to those who forecast correctly.

In later years, however, the only incentive was the possible publication of the names of those who hit the bull's-eye. Still, the predictions arrived in wholesale numbers.

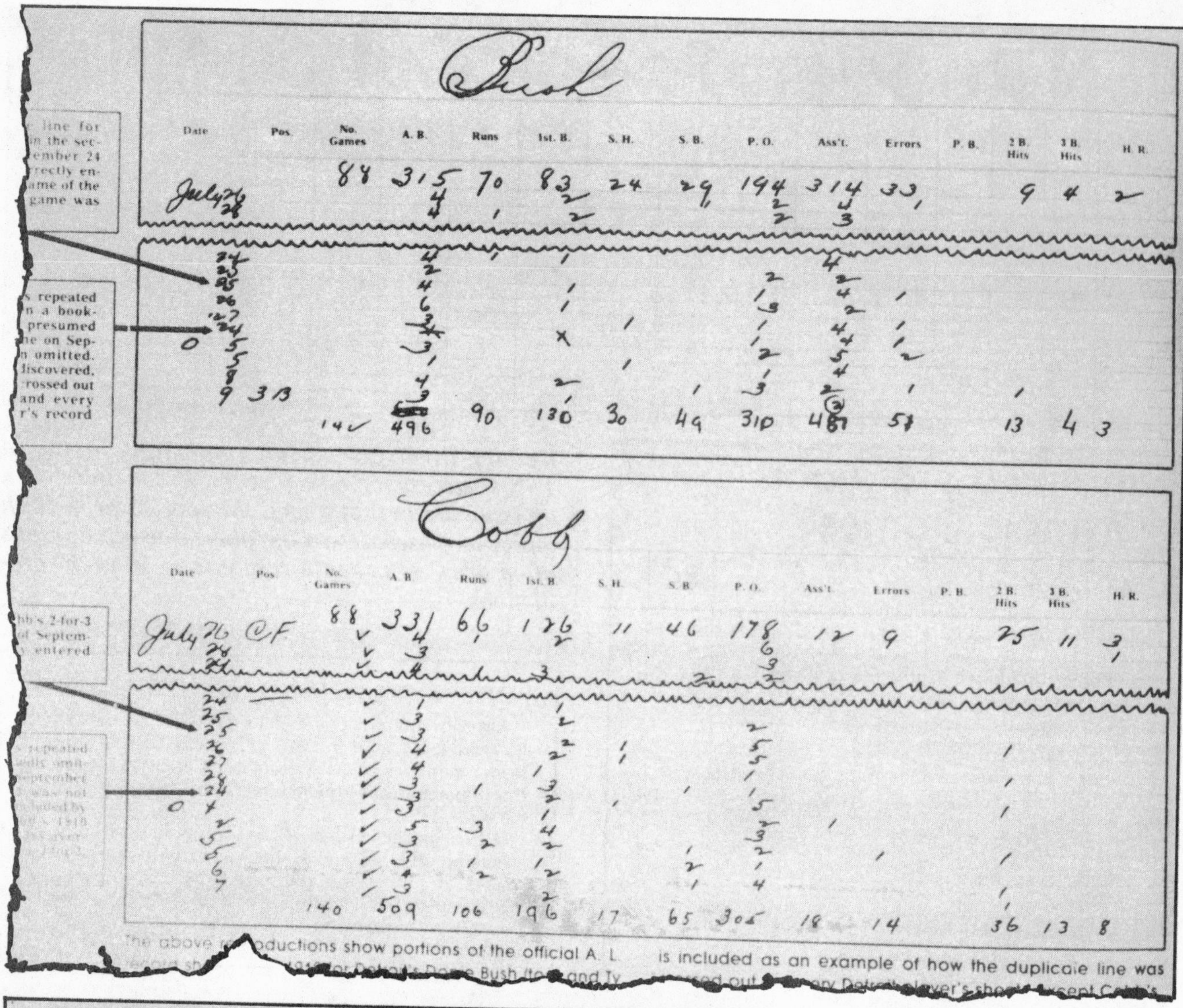

line for
in the sec-
ember 24
rectly en-
ame of the
game was

s repeated
n a book-
presumed
he on Sep-
n omitted.
discovered,
crossed out
and every
r's record

bb's 2-for-3
of Septem-
y entered

Bush

Date	Pos.	No. Games	A. B.	Runs	1st. B.	S. H.	S. B.	P. O.	Ass't.	Errors	P. B.	2 B. Hits	3 B. Hits	H. R.
July 26		88	315	70	83	24	29	194	314	33		9	4	2
		140	496	90	130	30	49	310	487	57		13	4	3

Cobb

Date	Pos.	No. Games	A. B.	Runs	1st. B.	S. H.	S. B.	P. O.	Ass't.	Errors	P. B.	2 B. Hits	3 B. Hits	H. R.
July 26	CF	88	331	66	176	11	46	178	12	9		25	11	3
		140	509	106	196	17	65	305	18	14		36	13	8

The above reproductions show portions of the official A. L. [...] is included as an example of how the duplicaie line was [...]

LAJOIE BEATS OUT COBB

The controversy surrounding the 1910 American League batting championship was so acute that the Chalmers automobile company, which presented a car to the major league batting leader, felt compelled to give a car to both Napoleon Lajoie (left) and Ty Cobb (right). Cobb was declared batting champion but research now reveals that Lajoie was the rightful leader that year.

After 70 Years, Researchers Prove Lajoie Really Did Win

By PAUL Mac FARLANE
Associate Editor

ST. LOUIS—Seventy American league batting races have passed in review since that epic contest between Ty Cobb and Napoleon Lajoie in 1910.

Thirteen Presidents have taken up residence in the White House since that October day when William Howard Taft and the rest of the nation learned that Byron Bancroft (Ban) Johnson, president of the American League, had taken away Lajoie's batting leadership and awarded the leading average to Cobb, thereby ending several days of investigation into questionable circumstances surrounding the last two games of the season.

In the intervening decades, record books have listed a .385 average for Cobb as the league's best in 1910. And that average also won Cobb a Chalmers touring car, presented

[...] only was Cobb credited with an extra 2-for-3 game erroneously entered on his sheet, but two additional hitless at-bats were found—one each on May 26 and August 10.

Thus, addition of the 1-for-8 in 1906 and removal of the phantom 2-for-3 in 1910 drops Cobb's lifetime hits total to 4,190. That means Pete Rose is only 633 hits away from tying Ty, not 634.

And, the corrections involving Cobb's at-bats reduce his career average by one point to .366.

Cobb's corrected average for 1910 is .382 (194-for-508), not the .385 recognized for 70 years. And Lajoie didn't finish at .384 that year, as the record books showed. Research found an extra at-bat for him on May 13 in 1910, and his corrected average that season becomes .383 (227-for-592).

So, Lajoie had the higher average that year, .383 to .382 over Cobb, but does that make him the A.L. leader? Cobb was declared the leader by Johnson, the league president, and the matter was closed [...]

Lajoie, meanwhile, kept his Gallic nose to the grindstone. In the final 17 games, the Cleveland second baseman collected three hits in each of eight contests, two hits in two and four hits in another pair. Those two four-hit games were in a season-ending doubleheader, and therein lay the basis for Johnson's investigation.

Cleveland closed out the campaign October 9 in St. Louis, where the Browns, with nothing at stake, took a lighthearted approach to the contests and shifted players out of their regular positions, as was the closing-day custom of the times.

As a result, rookie shortstop Red Corriden was switched to third base by Manager Jack O'Connor, who cautioned the youngster that it might be in his best interests if he played deep because Lajoie, a powerful righthanded batter, frequently pulled line drives in that direction.

Lajoie, who went into the doubleheader with a .376 average, seven points behind Cobb, resisted the temptation to bunt toward Corriden his first time up. Instead, he rifled a drive past the third baseman that skidded to the left-field fence, good for a stand-up triple.

On subsequent at-bats, Lajoie took advantage of the inviting defense and bunted safely seven times so that, by the end of the second game, he was credited by the official scorer with eight hits in eight at-bats. One of the bunts was pushed toward shortstop Bobby Wallace and the others [...]

The Ty Cobb-Napoleon Lajoie 1910 batting race became a source of controversy in 1981 when TSN Historian Paul Mac Farlane uncovered discrepancies in the players' records. Those discrepancies resulted in an expose that included a story (left), diagrams (above) and an editorial (right) that sought to prove once and for all that Lajoie, not Cobb, should have been credited as the official 1910 American League batting champion. Despite strong evidence supporting the research, the Official Baseball Records Committee declined to take action on the issue.

The Cobb-Lajoie Controversy

Cobb, Lajoie Records in Dispute

The April 18, 1981, issue of The Sporting News carried a story by Associate Editor Paul Mac Farlane detailing record-keeping discrepancies in the playing records of Tyrus Cobb and Napoleon Lajoie. The discrepancies were uncovered during research for the 1981 edition of Daguerreotypes, a book that contains the records of baseball's greatest players.

The Key issue was the 1910 batting championship. At the time, Lajoie was thought to be the winner but, after a review, American League President Ban Johnson ruled that Cobb had won. Therefore, for 70 years, Cobb was listed as the 1910 leader with a .385 average, one point higher than Lajoie's .384. Mac Farlane's findings, corroborated by other researchers, showed that Lajoie actually batted .383 and Cobb .382.

Research revealed that in 1910 Cobb was erroneously credited with an extra 2-for-3 game and was not credited with two additional hitless at-bats. This made Cobb's corrected average for that year .382 (194-for-508). Also, one additional hitless at-bat was discovered in Lajoie's record, making his corrected average .383 (227-for-592).

Furthermore, research showed that in 1906, two games in which Cobb was 1-for-8 were omitted from his record. The 1906 and 1910 corrections dropped Cobb's career hits total by one, to 4,190, and his lifetime average by a point, to .366.

The Sporting News believes the evidence is irrefutable. However, on December 16, 1981, the Official Records Committee met at the commissioner's office in New York and rejected the findings of this research, supporting Commissioner Bowie Kuhn's earlier decision that Ban Johnson's 1910 decision should not be overturned. As a result, the Baseball Record Book lists Cobb as the 1910 batting leader and his career totals as .367 with 4,191 hits and 12 American League batting championships (including nine in succession), but with the appropriate notations that these records are in dispute.

Despite the refusal of baseball's Records Committee to take action on the findings of Historian Paul Mac Farlane (right), TSN's 'Official Baseball Record Book' carried appropriate notations (left) that the 1910 records of Ty Cobb and Napoleon Lajoie were in dispute.

The Sporting News

OUR OPINION

Cobb-Lajoie Appeal Rejected

Baseball Officialdom 1, The Sporting News 0.

That's the current score in the statistical game concerning Tyrus Cobb and Napoleon Lajoie. If you're into baseball lore, you may remember some of the details . . .

The April 18, 1981, issue of The Sporting News carried a story by Associate Editor Paul Mac Farlane detailing record-keeping discrepancies in the playing records of the legendary stars. The discrepancies were uncovered during research for the 1981 edition of Daguerreotypes, a book that contains career records of baseball's greatest players.

Ty Cobb

The key issue was the 1910 batting championship. At that time, Lajoie was thought to be the winner but, after a review, American League President Ban Johnson ruled that Cobb had won. Therefore, for 70 years Cobb was listed as the 1910 leader with a .385 average, one point higher than Lajoie. Mac Farlane's findings, corroborated by other researchers, showed that Lajoie actually batted .383 and Cobb .382.

Research revealed that in 1910 Cobb was erroneously credited with an extra 2-for-3 game and was not charged with two additional hitless at-bats. This made Cobb's corrected average for that year .382 (194-for-508). Also, one additional hitless at-bat was discovered in Lajoie's record, making his corrected average .383 (227-for-592).

Furthermore, research showed that in 1906, two games in which Cobb was 1-for-8 were omitted from his record. The 1906 and 1910 corrections dropped Cobb's career hits total by one, to 4,190, and his lifetime average by a point, to .366.

Despite all the evidence, which we consider irrefutable, the findings were rejected by Commissioner Bowie Kuhn, who felt Ban Johnson's 1910 decision should not be overturned. The Sporting News then filed an appeal to the Official Baseball Records Committee which, over the years, has approved numerous changes in the old records. Changing Babe Ruth's runs-batted-in total or Walter Johnson's earned-run average, though,

While researching statistics for the 1981 edition of "Daguerreotypes," The Sporting News' Paul Mac Farlane discovered discrepancies in the records of Ty Cobb and Napoleon Lajoie.

Among the irregularities was a 2-for-3 entry in Cobb's ledger for 1910. Elimination of the phantom game from Cobb's record and inclusion of two previously unrecorded hitless at-bats dropped the average of the Detroit star from .385 to .382.

Further research revealed that Lajoie had an extra hitless at-bat. With this correction, Nap's average went from .384 to .383, still sufficient to win the American League batting championship.

Research also showed that in 1906, two games in which Cobb went 1 for 8 were omitted from his record. The 1906 and 1910 findings lowered Cobb's career hits total by one, to 4,190, and dropped his lifetime average by a point, to .366.

An expose in the April 18, 1981, issue of The Sporting News reported the details of the mistakes. An official request was submitted to Bowie Kuhn asking that the corrections be made a part of the official records. The commissioner rejected the request, stating he would abide by the opinion of Ban Johnson, the A.L. president who had investigated after suspicions of irregularities first surfaced 70 years earlier.

Subsequently, the issue was referred to the Official Baseball Records Committee, which also declined to take action.

An editorial in the issue of January 2, 1982, presented the case to readers of TSN, noting:

"The committee, over the years, has approved numerous changes. Changing Babe Ruth's runs-batted-in total or Walter Johnson's earned-run average, though, were one thing; changes involving something as 'sacred' as a batting title were quite another.

"The decision came just as our 'Official Baseball Record Book' was about to go to press. As a result of the committee's decision, the 1982 edition of the record book will list Cobb as the 1910 batting leader and with 12 batting titles. But there will be notations that these records are in dispute.

"For now we will honor that decision, however distasteful we find it. We are patient. It took 70 years to uncover the Cobb-Lajoie errors and it may take 70 years more to have them officially accepted. We hope not. After all, opinions and committees and even commissioners change from time to time."

Another New Face

When, in 1982, Bill Jamieson decided that the call of his native Detroit was stronger than his ties to St. Louis and resigned from the staff of The Sporting News, Tom Barnidge was lured away from the St. Louis Post-Dispatch to become managing editor.

The Barnidge byline was not unfamiliar to readers of The Sporting News. He had contributed columns and features frequently, primarily on professional football.

A graduate of the University of Missouri School of Journalism, Barnidge was a 12-year veteran of the Post-Dispatch staff and was sports columnist when he resigned.

In his role with The Sporting News, the St. Louis native wrote a column, enlightening and entertaining, and supervised the editorial department. His journalistic and administrative talents made him the logical choice to take over as editor when Dick Kaegel resigned, effective July 1, 1985.

"One of the greatest strengths of The Sporting News," observed Barnidge in moving up, "has been the breadth and accuracy of the information supplied. Our next step is to improve the way the information is packaged and the clarity with which it is presented. It isn't a matter of fixing something that is broken. It's a matter of improving an already proven product."

The new editor, who also was featured on a daily sports commentary over a local radio station and a weekly television show, "Sports Page," on a St. Louis channel, took charge of a staff that included Corporate Editor Lowell Reidenbaugh, Executive News Editor Bob McCoy, Books and Periodicals Director Ron Smith, Senior Editors Ralph Ray and Stan Isle, National Correspondents Dave Nightingale and Paul Attner, Associate News Editors Larry Wigge and Howard Balzer, Assistant Managing Editor Ben Henkey, Associate Editors Mike Douchant, Richard Sowers, Joe Marcin, Gary Levy, Carl Clark Jr., Mike Nahrstedt, Joe Hoppel, Craig Carter, Barry Siegel, Dave Sloan, John Hadley and Melanie Webb and Historian Paul Mac Farlane.

Tom Barnidge, former sports columnist for the St. Louis Post-Dispatch, contributed a column to the pages of The Sporting News after becoming managing editor in 1982. Barnidge discontinued the column after being named editor in 1985.

Arresting News

Can Athletes Cope After Entering the Real World?

TOM BARNIDGE
Managing Editor

ST. LOUIS—One of the beauties of sport, we have been told so often, is the escape it provides. The escape from pressures. The escape from worries. The escape from reality.

When you walk into a ball park, smell popcorn in the air, hear the crack of the bat and the crowd's roar, your mind is allowed to forget for a moment that you owe $300 on your electric bill. When the quarterback fades back in the pocket and floats a perfect spiral downfield, you momentarily are relieved of the concerns of your still-unfinished 1040 long form.

The stern-faced folks who spend their newspaper lives editing the stories that land on page one often refer to the sports desk as the "toy department." Nothing serious ever happens in sports, you see. Sports is a playground. Sports is silliness. Sports is the escape from the burdens that we all must bear.

For many years, I believed that escape was for the benefit of only the [illegible]. I thought the ticket buyers were the ones who most nee[illegible] troubles beh[illegible]

sion of heroin and cocaine worth $70,000 and a loaded .22-caliber derringer, police said.

The flamboyant, 44-year-old Pepitone, of Brooklyn, was arrested at 10:30 p.m. Monday along with two other men in a 1982 Buick Riviera in the Brownsville section of Brooklyn, said police spokesman Sgt. Raymond O'Donnell.

Officers found in the car one-eighth kilo of cocaine and two bags of heroin packaged in blocks, pills and a loaded .22-caliber derringer, O'Donnell said. Police said records involving drug distribution also were found in the car.

LOS ANGELES—Actor and former football great Jim Brown was formally charged Tuesday with raping, sexually battering and assaulting a school teacher last month at his Hollywood Hills home.

The district attorney's office, which announced Monday it had decided to charge Brown, 49, filed the three-count felony complaint in Municipal Court. Brown is scheduled to be arraigned Thursday.

So much for yesterday's heroes.

Now, no one ever said that athletic excellence translated to excellence as a human being. Just because a man can hit home [illegible] does not mean [illegible]

The Conlon Collection

Charles Martin Conlon was an enterprising young photographer in New York in 1904 when he encountered John B. Foster, a leading sportswriter of the city and future editor of Spalding's "Official Baseball Guide."

Foster had a suggestion for Conlon. In effect, he said, "You can provide a valuable and lasting service to baseball by taking pictures of major league players."

One suggestion was enough for Conlon. For the next 30 years, he prowled dugouts and playing fields, training his unwieldy equipment in the direction of athletes in action and at ease.

Conlon was a master of his trade, working with the eye of an artist. When he retired in 1935, he had accumulated 8,000 glass negatives, which he sold to The Sporting News.

Thereafter a Conlon picture occasionally adorned a feature in TSN, but it remained for the Smithsonian Institution to bring the collection to national attention with an exhibit in the fall of 1984. The show, sponsored in part by The Sporting News and Eastman Kodak Co., was on display at the National Portrait Gallery. Among those who attended the formal opening of the exhibit were Bill Terry, Lefty Gomez and Leo Durocher, all Conlon subjects in the 1920s and '30s.

As a visitors' guide to the 54-picture exhibit, TSN produced a 56-page brochure containing photos and biographies of the players.

After a six-month showing in Washington, the collection was taken on a two-year tour of the United States.

When the Conlon photo collection went on exhibit in 1984 at the Smithsonian Institution, The Sporting News and Eastman Kodak Co. combined efforts to make the formal opening an event worth remembering.

Former baseball greats (left to right) Leo Durocher, Bill Terry and Lefty Gomez posed with a life-size photo of Babe Ruth, which was enlarged from the Conlon collection for display at the opening of the Smithsonian Institution exhibit.

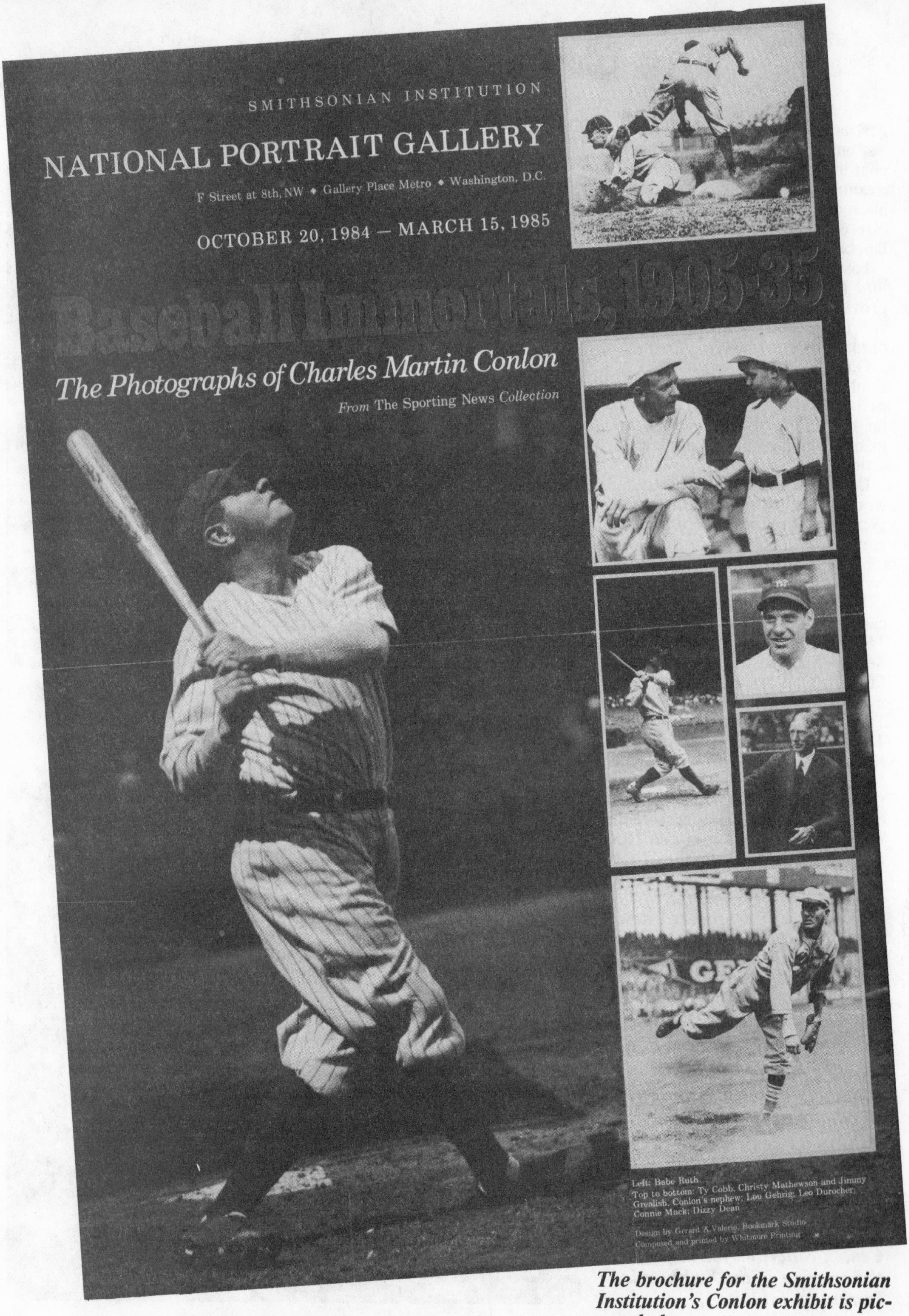

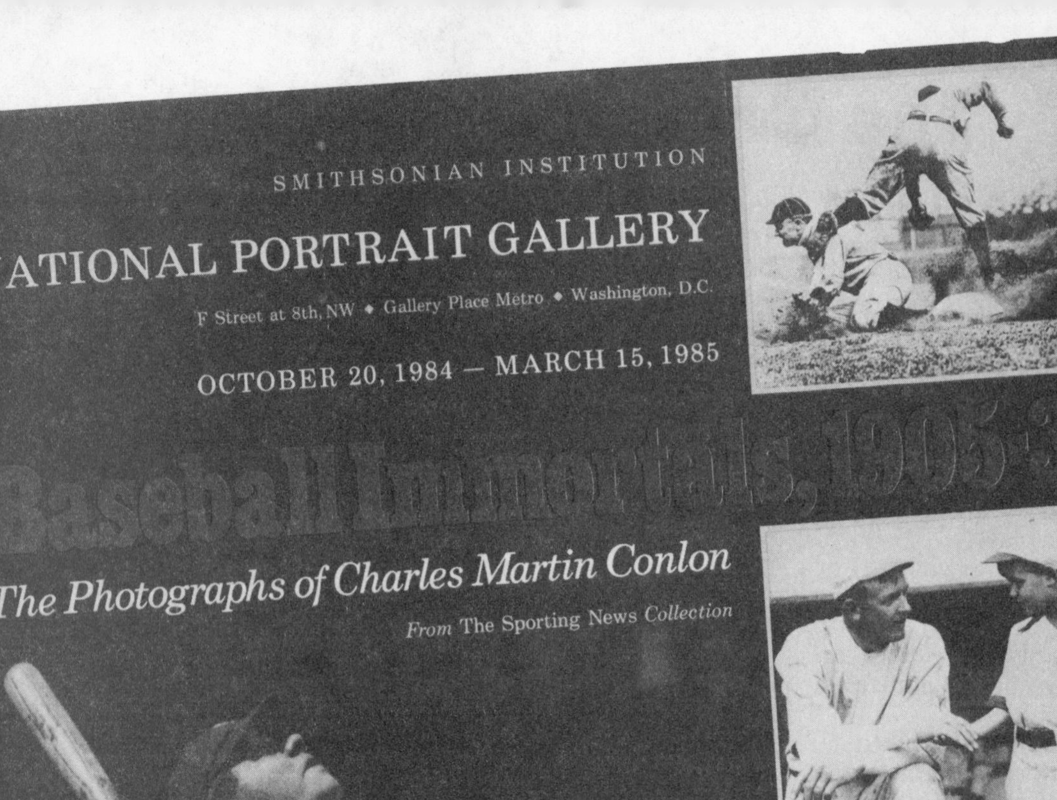
SMITHSONIAN INSTITUTION
NATIONAL PORTRAIT GALLERY
F Street at 8th, NW ◆ Gallery Place Metro ◆ Washington, D.C.
OCTOBER 20, 1984 — MARCH 15, 1985
Baseball Immortals, 1905-35
The Photographs of Charles Martin Conlon
From The Sporting News Collection
Left: Babe Ruth
Top to bottom: Ty Cobb; Christy Mathewson and Jimmy Grealish, Conlon's nephew; Lou Gehrig; Leo Durocher; Connie Mack; Dizzy Dean
Design by Gerard A. Valerio, Bookmark Studio
Composed and printed by Whitmore Printing

The brochure for the Smithsonian Institution's Conlon exhibit is pictured above.